P9-ELI-228

Handbook
of
Organizational
Behavior

PUBLIC ADMINISTRATION AND PUBLIC POLICY

A Comprehensive Publication Program

Executive Editor

JACK RABIN
Professor of Public Administration and Public Policy
Division of Public Affairs
The Capital College
The Pennsylvania State University—Harrisburg
Middletown, Pennsylvania

1. *Public Administration as a Developing Discipline (in two parts),* Robert T. Golembiewski
2. *Comparative National Policies on Health Care,* Milton I. Roemer, M.D.
3. *Exclusionary Injustice: The Problem of Illegally Obtained Evidence,* Steven R. Schlesinger
4. *Personnel Management in Government: Politics and Process,* Jay M. Shafritz, Walter L. Balk, Albert C. Hyde, and David H. Rosenbloom
5. *Organization Development in Public Administration (in two parts),* edited by Robert T. Golembiewski and William B. Eddy
6. *Public Administration: A Comparative Perspective, Second Edition, Revised and Expanded,* Ferrel Heady
7. *Approaches to Planned Change (in two parts),* Robert T. Golembiewski
8. *Program Evaluation at HEW (in three parts),* edited by James G. Abert
9. *The States and the Metropolis,* Patricia S. Florestano and Vincent L. Marando
10. *Personnel Management in Government: Politics and Process, Second Edition, Revised and Expanded,* Jay M. Shafritz, Albert C. Hyde, and David H. Rosenbloom
11. *Changing Bureaucracies: Understanding the Organization Before Selecting the Approach,* William A. Medina
12. *Handbook on Public Budgeting and Financial Management,* edited by Jack Rabin and Thomas D. Lynch
13. *Encyclopedia of Policy Studies,* edited by Stuart S. Nagel
14. *Public Administration and Law: Bench v. Bureau in the United States,* David H. Rosenbloom
15. *Handbook on Public Personnel Administration and Labor Relations,* edited by Jack Rabin, Thomas Vocino, W. Bartley Hildreth, and Gerald J. Miller
16. *Public Budgeting and Finance: Behavioral, Theoretical, and Technical Perspectives,* edited by Robert T. Golembiewski and Jack Rabin
17. *Organizational Behavior and Public Management,* Debra W. Stewart and G. David Garson
18. *The Politics of Terrorism: Second Edition, Revised and Expanded,* edited by Michael Stohl

ANNALS OF PUBLIC ADMINISTRATION

Handbook
of
Organizational
Behavior

edited by
Robert T. Golembiewski
University of Georgia
Athens, Georgia

Marcel Dekker, Inc. **New York•Basel•Hong Kong**

Library of Congress Cataloging-in-Publication Data

Handbook of organizational behavior / edited by Robert T.
    Golembiewski.
        p.   cm. -- (Public administration and public policy; 51)
    Includes bibliographical references and index.
    ISBN 0-8247-9058-8
    1. Organizational behavior.   I. Golembiewski, Robert T.
II. Series.
    HD58.7.H355 1993   93-2237
    302.3'5--dc20   CIP

The publisher offers discounts on this book when ordered in bulk quantities. For more information, write to Special Sales/Professional Marketing at the address below.

This book is printed on acid-free paper.

Copyright © 1993 by MARCEL DEKKER, INC. All Rights Reserved.

Neither this book nor any part may be reproduced or transmitted in any form or by any means, electronic or mechanical, including photocopying, microfilming, and recording, or by any information storage and retrieval system, without permission in writing from the publisher.

MARCEL DEKKER, INC.
270 Madison Avenue, New York, New York 10016

Current printing (last digit):
10 9 8 7 6 5 4 3 2 1

PRINTED IN THE UNITED STATES OF AMERICA

To my "other Mom," Alice Grauer Hughes, who still carries on the good fight and serves as a model for her (and my) Peg, as well as for me.

To my "other Dad," James Thomas Hughes, now enjoying his final reward for these several years, but still in our hearts and minds.

Preface

The *Handbook of Organizational Behavior* finds its place among several competitive and complementary volumes and seeks a distinctive niche. In part, this targeted niche involves an approach to the field of organization behavior (OB) as a market and thus encourages the search for ways and means to fully utilize the available supply of good work and trained OB researchers. A better balance with the supply side will result largely from increasing the demand for standard OB services and insights. However, this volume also emphasizes areas and themes to which OB can give added or even relatively novel attention, with value to OBers as well as to users of their thought and research. The Introduction details this volume's sense of OB as a market and identifies numerous contributions to this volume that seek to increase the demand for what OB can offer.

To a greater extent, however, this *Handbook* will gain its distinctiveness from the covey of authors whose efforts fill these pages. On perhaps too many occasions, I shared with the authors my expectations of their work: "Nothing less than the effort to write the best essay of your lives." This was said in a playful and even joking manner, for I do not believe that anyone has great control over what eventuates in a "career best," or "less than a career average" for that matter. Nonetheless, I believe the authors took my whimsicality in deadly earnest and I am more pleased about that than I can say. The list of contributions contains more than the normal representation of career bests or excellent performances.

Perhaps more than distinctiveness, another D-word—diversity—dominates in this volume. That characterization applies to the selctions of authors—in their training, present organizational affiliations, and public or business sector of primary concern. Diversity also applies to the form and manner of development of these contributions. The targeted areas differ in terms of method and stage of development, as well as their presently perceived relevance to OB as a field. Hence the corresponding range of textures and treatments in this volume.

Paramountly, the *Handbook* seeks diversity in its usefulness. I hope that the volume will be helpful across the full range of settings within which OB has an established presence, perhaps opening up new avenues of thought and knowledge. This range encompasses: business schools and public management; various professions where OB is relevant, such as nursing and education; as well as in the traditional fields in which OB finds a more or less secure home—primarily sociology, industrial and occupational psychology, management, and human resources.

As usual in such editorial efforts, I find myself learning so much from the authors that I know I can never repay them—either in words or in editorial embellishments—for their generous giving of themselves. I find myself unsuccessfully seeking augmented ways to share with the authors the sense of completion and anticipated contributions. Failing that, let me acknowledge my ineluctably symbiotic role in the enterprise—that of vetting the information and insight that the authors will bring to many readers. This vetting also probably had more potential for complicating the lives of the authors than for enhancing their contributions.

Special thanks go to two people, who in different ways facilitated the production of this volume: Sandra Daniel handled the many typing and clerical issues, and Robin Fayman provided useful and appreciated services from the publishing side.

Robert T. Golembiewski

Contents

Contributors

Achilles A. Armenakis Department of Management, College of Business, Auburn University, Auburn, Alabama

Terry C. Blum School of Management, Georgia Institute of Technology, Atlanta, Georgia

Ronald J. Burke Faculty of Administrative Studies, York University, North York, Ontario, Canada

Allan R. Cahoon Faculty of Management, University of Calgary, Calgary, Alberta, Canada

Taylor Cox, Jr. School of Business Administration, Organization Behavior and Human Resource Management, University of Michigan, Ann Arbor, Michigan

Deborah Ann Cutchin Center for Government Services, Rutgers University, New Brunswick, New Jersey

Ronald A. Davidson Faculty of Business Administration, Simon Fraser University, Burnaby, British Columbia, Canada

Elizabeth M. Doherty Department of Managerial Sciences, University of Nevada, Reno, Reno, Nevada

Hubert S. Feild Department of Management, College of Business, Auburn University, Auburn, Alabama

G. David Garson Department of Political Science and Public Administration, College of Humanities and Social Sciences, North Carolina State University, Raleigh, North Carolina

Urs E. Gattiker Centre for Technology Studies, The University of Lethbridge, Lethbridge, Alberta, Canada

Robert T. Golembiewski Department of Political Science and Public Administration, University of Georgia, Athens, Georgia

A. Paul Hare* Department of Behavioral Sciences, Ben-Gurion University of the Negev, Beer Sheva, Israel

---

*Retired

Stevan E. Hobfoll   Applied Psychology Center, Kent State University, Kent, Ohio

Robert G. Isaac   Faculty of Management, University of Calgary, Calgary, Alberta, Canada

Srinika Jayaratne   School of Social Work, University of Michigan, Ann Arbor, Michigan

Karl W. Kuhnert   Department of Psychology, University of Georgia, Athens, Georgia

Paul R. Lawrence*   Graduate School of Business Administration, Harvard University, Boston, Massachusetts

Stella Nkomo   Department of Management, University of North Carolina at Charlotte, Charlotte, North Carolina

Walter R. Nord   Department of Management, College of Business Administration, University of South Florida, Tampa, Florida

Dorothy Olshfski   Department of Public Administration, Rutgers University, Newark, New Jersey

Hal G. Rainey   Department of Political Science, University of Georgia, Athens, Georgia

Astrid M. Richardsen   Department of Psychology, University of Tromso, Tromso, Norway

Paul M. Roman   Department of Sociology , Institute for Behavioral Research, University of Georgia, Athens, Georgia

Julie Rowney   Faculty of Management, University of Calgary, Calgary, Alberta, Canada

Arie Shirom   Department of Labor Studies, Tel Aviv University, Tel Aviv, Israel

William B. Stevenson   Department of Organization Studies, Boston College, Chestnut Hill, Massachusetts

Gordon A. Walter   Faculty of Commerce and Business Administration, The University of British Columbia, Vancouver, British Columbia, Canada

Myron L. Weber   Faculty of Management, University of Calgary, Calgary, Alberta, Canada

Kelvin Willoughby   Department of Management, University of Western Australia, Perth, Western Australia, Australia

---

*Retired

Introduction
A Market Metaphor for Organizational Behavior

Robert T. Golembiewski

University of Georgia, Athens, Georgia

A handbook of even the grandest ambitions cannot encompass "all of it," and so it is with the present example of the genre which deals with organizational behavior, or OB. The implication is direct: selective criteria have to occupy a prominent place in the design of such a volume. Some topics have to receive emphasis; and, perforce, other topics—usually *many* other possible as well as reasonable topics—have to be neglected. This introduction provides two perspectives on this direct implication.

I. OB AS RINGS OF DEVELOPMENT

First, and briefly, this handbook views OB in idealized form as a set of concentric rings. At the heart, as it were, OB's foundations rest on a central core of empirical findings and normative guides. Here, some existing emphases have achieved a substantial stage of development. This not only leaves them already contributing to theoretical networks of some comprehensiveness, but also has generated spin-offs and in addition still gives ample promise of far more to come. These can be called the cutting edges of the discipline, whereas the wheelhorse themes reflect the accepted work going on in the discipline.

Beyond these central areas, two other sets of developmenmtal rings need cultivation; thus, a viable OB also will have a set of leading edges that may become cutting edges in the sense that they already give solid promise of constituting major elements of tomorrow's expanded core. The themes of research and practice here deserve additional emphasis because they promise high rates of return.

Finally, in addition to the core and the leading edges, a robust OB also should direct developmental attention to themes that show great potential; that is, a viable OB concept will encompass emerging themes or areas, concerning which some work has been accumulated but in which far more extensive developments are needed before solid judgments can be made about their contributions to tomorrow's OB foundations. These are strong candidates for leading- and then cutting-edge status, and later possibly may serve as new complements to today's core, or as replacements for parts of the core.

The underlying sense of this first perspective should be clear, then. The handbook's goal is maximum relevance to contemporary students and practitioners in several senses. These dimensions include a thorough grounding in core topics and a growing sense of topics already on OB's expanding periphery, as well as a sampler of topics-on-the-rise. Tables 1 through 3 (also

Table 1 Some Standard or Wheelhorse Themes

1. Paul R. Lawrence, "The Contingency Approach to Organizational Design"
2. Hal G. Rainey, "Work Motivation"
3. Stevan E. Hobfoll and Arie Shirom, "Stress and Burnout in the Workplace: Conservation of Resources"
4. A. Paul Hare, "Small Groups in Organizations"
5. Robert G. Isaac, "Organizational Culture: Some New Perspectives"
6. Srinika Jayaratne, "The Antecedents, Consequences, and Correlates of Job Satisfaction"
7. William B. Stevenson, "Organization Design"
8. Myron L. Weber, "Risk Taking in Organizations"
9. Karl W. Kuhnert, "Leadership Theory in Postmodernist Organizations"

known as Parts I–III in the Contents), respectively, list the contributions in this handbook in those three classes.

II. OB'S MARKET ENVIRONMENT: AN OVERVIEW

Second, to further circumscribe OB, this introduction elaborates a "market" metaphor for OB, and in so doing serves multiple purposes. To varying degrees, three purposes stand out most prominently.

Quite directly, the market metaphor—even if gentle—provides a template for helping choose the topics that get attention below.

In addition, the metaphor as well as the details of its elaboration imply a profile for this handbook that relates both to how the volume distances itself from other efforts of its kind, as well as to how the book is like other similar efforts in some particulars.

Finally, the market metaphor implies conceptual pathways for the future development of OB. This is the most expansive ambition, but also the most problematic because OB's future is at a critical stage in its shaping. Building on those yeasty early days in the 1950s and 1960s when business schools began in a big way to fill a major gap in their faculties by hiring behavioral scientists from various loci—psychology, sociology, education, and political science, in the main—OB has had a curiously self-defeating history. Its subject matter tended to attract far more than its fair share of gifted students; and the methodological and substantive training of individuals with masters' degrees or doctorates tended to cluster in the range from very good to superb; but OB was seldom a seller's market out there in the often-cold and sometimes-cruel worlds of academia, business, and government. In short, the supply of OBers grew in both numbers and quality, but the demand side was usually a bit sluggish—or even constipated, at times.

Let me quickly note two caveats. The paragraph above paints with a deliberately broad brush, hence the characterization does not apply evenly over the last 35 years or so, but it does apply far more rather than less.

Moreover, the description above requires a bit of balancing, or "putting in perspective." Note that the job prospects for OBers are not, and never were, as dismal as those widely

Table 2 Some Themes Requiring Enhanced Emphasis

10. Taylor Cox, Jr. and Stella Nkomo, "Race and Ethnicity"
11. G. David Garson, "Human Factors in Information Systems"
12. Ronald J. Burke and Astrid M. Richardsen, "Psychological Burnout in Organizations"
13. Paul M. Roman and Terry C. Blum, "Work–Family Role Conflict and Employer Responsibility: An Organizational Analysis of Workplace Responses to a Social Problem"
14. Dorothy Olshfski and Deborah Ann Cutchin, "Management Training and Development"
15. Allan R. Cahoon and Julie Rowney, "Valuing Differences: Organization and Gender"

Table 3 Some Themes with Great Potential

16. Gordon A. Walter, "On the Wisdom of Making Values Explicit in Organizational Behavior Research"
17. Ronald A. Davidson, "Behavioral Research in Auditing"
18. Achilles A. Armenakis and Hubert S. Feild, "The Role of Schema in Organizational Change: Change Agent and Change Target Perspectives"
19. Elizabeth M. Doherty and Walter R. Nord, "Compensation: Trends and Expanding Horizons"
20. Urs E. Gattiker and Kelvin Willoughby, "Technological Competence, Ethics, and the Global Village: Cross-National Comparisons for Organization Research"

attributed to those gaining recent doctorates in English, but the imbalance between supply and demand was often felt. Certainly OBers have never experienced the buoyant market that exists for some professionals (e.g., the great shortfall of accountants with doctorates having an interest in teaching jobs in schools of business or in public administration programs).

OBers did not always take this situation with equanimity. At times, in fact, some OBers turned into raiders. For example, OBers—largely trained in business schools—sought to extend their domain into public administration programs. I applauded that effort for several reasons, primary among them being the fact that the raiders were generally superior in training to the retrofitted political scientists who filled most public administration posts having an OB content. OBers also filled many similar posts in other specialized turfs: hospital management, education, social work, hospitality, and so on. And more power to them.

Similarly, but in far greater numbers, OBers have made definite forays into organization development, or OD. To me, this was a very mixed effort. On the one hand, OBers often had superior methodological skills, and this served important purposes in the maturation of OD as a field, especially in terms of research. On the other hand, however, OBers often did not have the values or interventionist skills long associated with OD, and those deficiencies had some very unattractive features. In some cases, in opposition to internalizing those values and to seeking to gain those skills for interventions, OBers sought to redefine the essentials of OD to their own preexisting skills and tastes. Bottom line, this editor concludes, this induced more consternation and conflict than progress.

This thumbnail OB history has a major implication for dealing with a focal issue—on how to minimize its failure in success. Directly, this handbook focuses on how the demand for OB and OBers can be enhanced. In contrast, the dominant style of response to the oversupply of OBers has been to control the supply side of the equation—as by limiting admissions to OB programs, or in a few cases by converting into more or less typical business formats those few generic schools of management in which OB-related approaches played key or even dominant roles. "Typical business formats" cover a wide range, of course, but their dominant specializations are far more likely to emphasize accountancy, economics, and finance than OB.

III. AFFECTING OB ON THE DEMAND SIDE

The present approach to improving OB's performance via emphasis on the demand side of its market has a direct rationale; this handbook seeks to enhance OB's viability as well as to help increase the demand for OBers. The different senses in which this compound point holds will be illustrated by the three classes of OB topics focused on in this handbook:

- Traditional wheelhorse topics or themes
- Recognized topics that merit enhanced attention
- Emerging but neglected topics

Briefly, these three classes of topics relate to the kinds of development distinguished above: a central core; ongoing and already producing additions to the core, or extensions of it; and topics likely to enrich OB's longer-run future.

A. Traditional or Wheelhorse Topics

Table 1 lists the topics and authors in this handbook illustrating the first category, and it suggests that these topics in the core have three distinctive features that all contribute to an increased demand for OD. First, the topics command broad agreement that they are strategic and critical; hence, any degree of success in dealing with them implies a direct payoff of heightened demand for OB talent, time, and perspectives.

Second, all of the topics reflect a mixed bag of results. As the authors of all of the contributions in Table 1 establish in various ways, some central tendencies in results exist, and this contributes positively to OB demand. In addition, however, analyses associated with all of the wheelhorse topics show that attempts to test most (if not all) related associations apply a mixed pattern of results in bivariate analyses. At times, the available evidence supports a direct association between many pairs of variables; then again, other evidence encourages the conclusion that a mixed association exists; and in some research, the variation seems essentially random.

Whatever the pattern of associations, clear possibilities for increasing the demand for OB exist. Thus, any consistently positive findings clearly have that effect. Moreover, unless cynicism sets in, the mixed results also justify increased demand because the required clarifications constitute the critical tests of OB's reach and grasp, and in effect exploit sunk investments. Tests of the mixed associations in effect constitute a key measure of how much more OB can contribute to strategic and critical issues. Finally, if verified, even consistently random associations can demonstrate the power of OB. Clarity about what relationships do not exist constitutes pretty powerful stuff.

Third, the working suspicion about the prime reason for the mixed bag of results also implies a major expansion in the demand for OB and OBers in one central particular. Specifically, treatments of all of the topics in Table 1 suggest that a substantial part of their mixed record in isolating regular empirical associations may well derive from pervasive differences in operational definitions. For example, Srinika Jayaratne draws attention to this central point in his essay on satisfaction and its covariants. It comes as no great surprise that different measures of satisfaction might well account for the typically diverse patterns of associations isolated in numerous tests of any pair of covariants: a positive association in some cases; negative associations in other cases; and no drift one way or the other in still other cases.

Miller and Friesen generalize the point (1984: 14–15) in emphasizing that the common failure to distinguish different "configurations" of organizations in research populations reasonably results in mixed results. They note that theoreticians distinguish various numbers and kinds of configurations; thus Mintzberg (1984) isolates five, Golembiewski (1987) focuses on four, and so on. However, researchers generally fail to distinguish different configurations of organizations in any research population, and this failure has a highly probable effect. As Miller and Friesen conclude (1984: 14–15):

> Now, assuming . . . that at least a good proportion of organizations tended to adapt these or some other configurations of their structural parameters—what would happen if different kinds of organizations were mixed in research samples and then relationships gauged among [various covariants]? We believe that we already have the answer [in the apparently conflicting research findings] cited earlier.

This probable condition suggests a substantial potential for increased demand for OB. Numerous sectors of the OB literature are now at the point at which more focused attention on distinguishing operational definitions might generate major breakthroughs. This is the sense of my earlier call (Golembiewski, 1986: 298–300) for a Manhattan Project in the organization sciences to make the critical choices between numerous alternative operational definitions, with any closure toward preferred definitions being central in clarifying presently mixed evidence concerning many associations in OB (e.g., in the patterns of linkage between cohesiveness and productivity).

Of course, some observers view this "stuckness" of OB as indicating the recalcitrance of behavioral realities, if not their basic unlawfulness. A heightened and focused demand for OB to compare alternative operational definitions will test this possibility, providing perspective on whether *the* problem is in nature, or whether it derives from our tendency to proliferate operational definitions of the same concept while neglecting to differentiate research findings accordingly. This editor definitely inclines toward the latter view.

B. Topics Meriting Enhanced Attention

As Table 2 shows, this handbook also gives illustrative attention to an array of topics or themes that have been recognized but, in effect, still require major pushes to exploit their fuller potential. Any energy invested in such "pushes," of course, will heighten the demand for OB and OBers.

Many reasons explain this shortfall of attention, as several of the contributions in Part II emphasize. Fashions or fads play a role; the difficulties of some specific kinds of research prior to the broad availability of advanced systems for electronic data processing often have played an important role; and human wit and will also have fallen short.

The thematic reviews listed in Table 2 all point to major opportunities for an increased OB demand. The reasons for the existing shortfall of attention to Table 2 themes can vary widely, in short, but attempts to remedy that status will have a direct common effect.

C. Awkwardly Neglected Topics

Finally, Table 3 lists a number of areas in prime contention for enhanced OB attention, along with the authors of reviews of research on those topics. The list is harshly selective, of course, but well represents the far broader range that might have been given attention. In sum, Table 3 focuses on a broad range of themes—from compensation through technology—and includes the key role of values, among several other emphases.

To the degree that new or enhanced attention gets directed at topics such as those in Table 3, of course, so also will the demand for OB inputs increase. Not all of the table's themes will necessarily prove to be winners, but their aggregate potential for enhancing demand for OB and OBers appears substantial.

IV. ADDITIONAL NOTES

Other factors also affected the choice of topics about which critical survey reviews were written for this handbook. For example, OD already receives fulsome attention. In addition to periodic surveys in such sources as the *Annual Review of Psychology*, OD also is the subject of a yearly collection of major essays in a well-received series (e.g., Woodman and Pasmore, 1990, 1992). Hence the decision here to omit OD as a focal topic.

In addition, other useful themes are omitted because it did not prove possible to develop appropriate arrangements with suitable resource persons.

REFERENCES

Golembiewski, R. T. (1986). "Organization Analysis and Praxis: Prominences of Progress and Stuckness," pp. 279–304, in C. L. Cooper and I. Robertson, editors, *Review of Industrial and Organizational Psychology*. London, John Wiley & Sons.

Golembiewski, R. T. (1987). Public-sector organization: How theory and practice should emphasize structure and how to do so. In *A Centennial History of the American Administrative State* (R. C. Chandler, ed.), Free Press, New York, pp. 433–474.

Miller, D., and Friesen, P. H. (1984). *Organizations: A Quantum View*. Prentice-Hall, Englewood Cliffs, N.J.

Mintzberg, H. (1984). A typology of organization structures. In *Organizations* (D. Miller and P. H. Friesen, eds.), Prentice-Hall, Englewood Cliffs, N.J., pp. 68–86.

Pasmore, W. A., and Woodman, R. W. (1990, 1992). *Research in Organization Development and Change*. JAI Press, Greenwich, Conn.

Part I
Some Standard or Wheelhorse Themes

1
The Contingency Approach to Organizational Design

Paul R. Lawrence*

Harvard University, Boston, Massachusetts

It is now an established part of organizational theory that different kinds of organizations are needed to perform different kinds of tasks—that there is no one best way to organize. This was not true some 25 years ago when theory was still searching for the all-purpose organization. The change has been brought about by contingency theory. Many scholars contributed to the origin of the contingency approach to organization design and many more have subsequently developed it.[1] It remains the dominant approach to organizational design.

This chapter will provide an overview of the current state of contingency theory as it bears on the practical topic of organization design. It will review the key concepts utilized by the theory, it will spell out the specific critical contingencies the theory deals with in the design of a business unit, and finally, it will describe how the theory treats design as an organization moves through the life cycle from start-up to large-scale maturity.

I. KEY CONCEPTS

Any organization's design problem must start with the *strategic choice* of its founders: what business will we be in? The answer to this question commits a new organization to cope with a *relevant environment*. It picks the potential customers, the key competitors, the probable suppliers, the regulatory bodies, and the likely technologies. These are the key elements of the *relevant environment*. These environmental elements carry characteristics that can be studied and analyzed. These features point the way to the nature of the *key tasks* which must be performed to deal with this environment—what is to be designed, what is to be made, how, what is to be exchanged, and with whom. So the choice of strategy and environment sets the stage for starting the organizational design process. It allows the designer to analyze the *diversity* and the *uncertainty* in the relevant environment and make an initial assessment of the appropriate internal *differentiation* to create an appropriate division of labor. It permits the designer to assess the *interdependence* between key tasks and therefore the needed *integration* between organizational parts. These are the central concepts that will guide the process of

---

*Retired

[1]The term *contingency theory* was first developed and discussed in organizational terms in Lawrence and Lorsch (1967). Fiedler (1967) first used the same term in respect to leadership.

designing the elements of an organization—its *structure*, its *systems*, and its *staffing*, so that it *fits* its environment and, as a result, will be *effective* in performing its key tasks.

II. SPECIFIC CRITICAL CONTINGENCIES

Research over the years since the start of contingency theory has developed a set of critical contingencies with which organizations need to be designed to cope. The contingency of size and scale has been primarily associated with the Aston research group (e.g., Pugh et al., 1968) and Greiner (1967). The contingency of technology and geography is associated primarily with the work of Woodward (1965), Thompson (1967), Perrow (1967), and Galbraith (1973); the contingency of uncertainty with Burns and Stalker (1961) and Lawrence and Lorsch (1967); the contingency of individual predispositions with Vroom (1960), Turner and Lawrence (1965), and Lorsch and Morse (1974); the contingency of resource dependency with Pfeffer and Salancik (1978) and Davis and Lawrence (1977); the contingency of national differences with Hofstede (1980) and Bartlett and Goshal (1989); and the contingency of scope with Chandler (1962), Lorsch and Allen (1973), Rumelt (1974), and Porter (1980). Other scholars have taken up lesser contingencies, but no others have been shown to have sufficient impact on organizations to warrant inclusion in this essay.

III. DESIGNING THE SINGLE-PRODUCT FIRM

We will start by elaborating on how the critical contingencies bear on the design decisions in creating a freestanding, single-product firm. For purposes of a clear example let us address the design of a shoe company. To be in the shoe business, even in a minimal way, our hypothetical shoe firm must design, manufacture, and sell shoes. These three basic functions are, in some form, the initial units that are differentiated. In order to perform these three tasks in the most effective way, should we organize and operate each department in the same way, or are differences needed? The answers depend on the amount of uncertainty which each department will need to face.

A. Differentiation

Assuming that we are in the fashion end of the shoe business, it would be clear that our design department will need to cope with the considerable uncertainty of the fickle world of rapidly changing tastes. In contrast, our production department will be dealing in the relatively stable world of raw materials and production machinery. The sales department will probably be dealing with the moderately uncertain world of department stores and discount and outlet stores, as well as the traditional specialized shoe store.

   These differences in the uncertainty found in these environments call for different organization forms in order to be effective. To cope with its stable environment it would be appropriate for the production shop to be centralized with formalized procedures, clear-cut shop rules, and a strong chain of command. The rules and procedures can be specified in advance and will be useful for an extended period of time. Only a limited number of decisions need to be made to keep up to date with the slow rate of change in its relevant environment. Managerial costs can be kept relatively low.

   In contrast, the design shop cannot expect to follow predetermined rules. Things change too quickly to keep rules up to date. Here a more flexible organization is called for so that people can communicate in all directions to pick up hot market tips and respond quickly to changing circumstances. More people need to be watching the fashion world and deciding how to respond. The design unit's structure needs to be more of an all-to-all communication network than a hierarchy of command. Joint problem solving is the style rather than giving and executing orders. In addition, it would be expected that the design department will give priority to achieving quality goals even as the production department will give priority to meeting cost objectives. Various terms have been used to describe the contrast between our hypothetical design and production departments: organic versus mechanistic; participatory versus autocratic. These terms define the end points of a continuum of ways of organizing the needed subsystems. The sales department could be expected to function best if it fell in the middle of this continuum between the two contrasting organizational forms of the design and production departments.

The second major contingency that our designer needs to deal with is the people factor; people are not all alike. People with different predispositions find themselves comfortable in one of these work settings and not in the other. The people who would be more comfortable in the manufacturing setting would have a low tolerance for ambiguity, low integrative complexity, and a preference for working in teams and for strong authority relations. The people who would be more comfortable in the design department would have opposite preferences: high tolerance for ambiguity, high integrative complexity, and a preference for individual work, independence, and autonomy. The sales department could expect to attract people who are comfortable in the middle of these ranges.

B.   Integration

Once the three basic departments have been organized with the appropriate characteristics and staffed with people with suitable dispositions, they can be expected to be effective in their functional roles. The problem of integrating the work of the three departments remains, and the very differences that made each department good at its own job will make integration difficult. The differences in style and goals between our shoe departments make it inevitable that they will be in conflict on many issues that need joint resolution. For example, the design and production groups are unlikely to agree on the importance of interrupting the production flow to make an experimental batch of shoes.

Our organizational designer must now set up the mechanisms to secure the needed integration in spite of the necessary differences. Every designer would use the time-honored integrative mechanisms of assigning the three departments to a single shared boss (hierarchy) and setting up some shared procedures (rules). These devices should be adequate if the degree of interdependence is not too much and the differences to be bridged are minimal. In our shoe example these conditions do not, in fact, prevail. Analysis of the tasks indicates that the linkage between shoe design and both production and sales will require some complex joint coordination. Design features can be expected to entail using some complex production methods and some unique selling techniques. Likewise, the shoe designers need to draw on the sales department's knowledge of customer preferences. The designers also need to be educated by the production people about what their proposed styles will require of production in terms of quality and reasonable costs. These *reciprocal interdependencies* require more sophisticated ways to resolve conflict than interdependencies that can be handled *sequentially* or by simply drawing upon common *pooled* resources.

To cope with these reciprocal interdependencies in the face of significant differences, additional integrating mechanisms will need to be employed. Devices such as joint planning teams, special liaison roles, or even a separate integrating department may be required to effectively link the basic units. To do its job properly, the integrating department should be intermediate between the design and production units in terms of its formalization and of its orientation to authority, complexity, individualism, goals, and time.

So far we have been addressing but two of the critical contingencies for our shoe firm—task uncertainty and member dispositions. Based on these contingencies we have been creating an organization that is appropriately differentiated and integrated. With this starting design we can now allow for additional contingencies.

C.   Resource Scarcity

The organization can be expected to adjust to different degrees of resource scarcity or munificence. Under severe shortage of resources (loss of sales, supply blockage, unavailable credit, etc.), the organization can be expected to cut out postponable expenses—for instance, the design of a new line of shoes, image advertising, employee training, materials research, and experimental manufacturing techniques. In times of relative munificence, not only would these long-term expenditures be undertaken, but, for better or worse, expensive member perquisites, institutional advertising, and lobbying are also likely to be included.

D. Technology and Geography

Additional contingencies come up under the heading of technology and geography. An example of technology could be visualized by the production processes for shoe uppers versus soles. The uppers could be expected to be handled in batches of work-in-process that move from machine station to machine station for the performance of the needed operations. In contrast, the soles could be made by a plastic molding process that is continuous. Finally, the finishing and packing steps in the shoe manufacturing could be handled by an assembly line. These three production modes can most effectively be performed by three different kinds of manufacturing organizations. The assembly line would have a wide span of control, few skilled technical and staff roles, and few levels of authority. This is in contrast to the narrow span of control, the larger technical support staff, and the more levels of authority associated with continuous-process technologies. Batch and customized work would generally be intermediate to these two.

We can visualize the geographic contingency arising in connection with the sales department. Let us presume that our shoe firm has decided to set up several factory outlet stores as a way of directly selling its shoes to complement sales through department stores and specialty shoe stores. Now it must face the contingent fact that its customers are widely dispersed geographically. This technical fact leads to the selection of geographically dispersed outlet stores and a corresponding direct sales organization differentiated by territory.

E. Second-Order Differentiation

Both technology and territory have now become the second-order form of differentiation in our production and sales departments that themselves represent a first-order differentiation by function. We can readily think of examples in which these contingencies of technology and territory might be of such overriding importance that they would be the basis of the first-order differentiation. Think of the organization of any railroad—the realities of dispersed operations would indicate a first-order territorial differentiation by regions of the total area served and a second-order differentiation by function (engineering, right-of-way maintenance, train operations, rolling stock maintenance, etc.). Likewise, the differences between the production technologies of steel making from the blast furnace (batch) to the rolling mills (continuous process) dominate other logics of differentiation.

F. Support Units

Once the basic departments of our shoe firm are set up, our organization designer will need to address the design of essential support units. The ones that most readily come to mind are finance and accounting, purchasing, human resources and legal. Most of these units provide linkage to other portions of a firm's relevant environment, including suppliers, banks and money markets, governmental bodies, and labor markets. In addition, our shoe firm might want to add specialists with a longer-term orientation to basic units by adding some researchers to the design group and marketing specialists to the sales group. Again we see the common theme of selecting specialists who can effectively bridge to an important part of the relevant environment with the features of each environmental sector influencing the way its associated functional unit is organized.

G. Power and Influence

Finally, our organization designer might make a further organizational refinement by choosing which major part or parts of the organization should be given differential weight or power in the counsels of the firm. Contingency theory clearly indicates that the rank of "first among equals" should be granted to the department that is positioned to cope with the most critical sector of the environment. If securing sales, for example, is the most serious and difficult survival issue for the firm, it would be appropriate to grant the sales department extra power in interdepartmental conflict resolution. Having said that power and influence is best made contingent on criticality, we should add that under all contingencies it has proved best to use a *problem-solving* approach to conflict resolution rather than a *smoothing* or a *forcing* approach.

IV. CONTINGENCY AND ORGANIZATIONAL DYNAMICS

So far we have discussed design problems in static terms, as if we could freeze environmental conditions and design a full-blown organization from scratch. This unrealistic assumption has been necessary to simplify the design problem and reach some initial solutions. Now we can relax this artificial assumption and approach the design with regard to the full range of challenges organizations face at different stages of their development and at different sizes.

A. Start-Up

Most newly formed firms need to put their organizational emphasis on flexibility to adjust quickly to their environment. This means they need an organic organization form. The original group of founders will be expected to be flexible about their role assignments and stay in all-to-all communication. As the firm goes through its initial growth, the additional personnel will be assigned to more defined roles and their reporting relationship to one of the founders will start creating a hierarchy and a division of labor among the original managers. This will be the start of a functional organization form. The resulting work groups will continue to operate with few formal rules and will maintain lateral communication links to sustain the needed flexibility at this stage.

B. Early Growth

As organizations grow beyond the start-up stage to medium size—100 to 200 employees—they are usually able to routinize some of their operations. This is needed to economize on resources. This process of formalizing the organization involves several aspects. One is developing role assignments for employees with clear expectations and performance feedback mechanisms. The second is creating information systems that record and aggregate key operational variables. Procedures must be established for order processing, work orders, order filling, shipping, invoicing, inventory control, and the like. Third, the chain of command will be defined and one or two additional tiers of managers will be added. This process of formalization will need to be done to achieve economies in all functions, but it should not be carried as far in departments facing environmental uncertainty as in those departments dealing with a more stable environment. In this manner differentiation on the organic-mechanistic continuum will be created so that each department will have an appropriate fit with its special environmental sector.

As this differentiation of form develops, it quickly creates the need for suitable integrating mechanisms that go beyond the hierarchy and shared procedures. Appropriate mechanisms will need to be selected and put in place. The organization that emerges from this process is the effective mature organization, performing as the freestanding single-product business that has been described above. Now we can move on to consider complexities beyond the single business unit.

C. Multistage Firms

As organizations grow beyond the single-product firm, they often move their operations backward to perform earlier steps in the value-adding production chain, or forward to perform functions closer to the ultimate consumer. This process of organizational growth is known as vertical integration. For example, our shoe firm might decide to get into the leather business and develop a tannery to supply its shoe operations with leather. This would be an example of backward integration. Earlier we spoke of our shoe firm deciding to open a chain of its own factory outlet stores—an example of forward integration. What guidelines exist in contingency theory for designing the appropriate organization form for performing these multiple stages of the production supply chain?

As a general response to this question, contingency theory calls for the establishment of separate product divisions for each major step in the supply chain, with each division reporting to corporate headquarters. This kind of differentiation will allow each of these operations to organize so as to fit its own environment and technology. In our example, the tannery and outlet stores will each need its own organization form and style. The performance of each can then be judged by its own results.

However, we must again analyze the nature of the interdependencies between the separate divisions. The tannery will be supplying the shoe factories which, in turn, will be supplying the outlet stores. This represents a sequential interdependency, not as intense as the reciprocal kind discussed above, but still more complicated than a simple shared dependency on central pooled resources. This kind of an interdependency can usually be handled at the home office through a central scheduling office and through a set of ground rules for handling interdivisional pricing and quality control. The upstream divisions can be treated as either cost centers using cost-based transfer prices or as profit centers using market prices. This will depend on the strategic emphasis desired. The downstream divisions will consistently be treated as profit centers. Managers need to be alert to the organizational implications of a shift from one type of divisional interdependency to another. For example, if our shoe division asks the tannery to develop a new type of leather finish, it is initiating a reciprocal interdependency that can best be managed by a direct lateral dialogue between divisions.

D. Multiproduct Firms

The track of growth followed by other firms is the move from single product to a multiproduct operation. In this event, the organization form must reflect the change if it is to be effective. This process is referred to as diversification. In effect, the leadership of the firm is making the strategic decision to expand its environmental domain—to provide additional goods and services to its customers. The degree of diversification among products is the key to the selection and design of the effective organization form.

The different products can be related to one another in several different ways. The products, to state the obvious extreme, may be entirely unrelated—their only connection being their shared financial ownership. In this conglomerate situation, contingency theory calls for a minimal holding company headquarters. The error to be avoided is overstaffing the center and overmanaging the separate businesses. One of the basic principles of contingency theory is that decision-making rights should be placed within the organization where the relevant information is concentrated. In our example, the relevant information about the tannery business would be found in the tannery division, not headquarters. In the case of the totally unrelated conglomerate, the only functions that can best be performed at headquarters are the financial analysis that guides investment decisions, the legal and public relations activity, and the selection and development of general managers.

The choice of the family of products in the multiproduct firm can, however, lead to many kinds of relatedness that will need to be managed from the center. One frequently sees a set of products that are related by sharing a base technology. This condition usually calls for a central research and development department to serve all the separate product divisions. General Motors provides an example. Another interdependence can be caused by the sharing of some key production facility by otherwise separate product divisions. The same can be true if a field sales force is shared by otherwise separate divisions. All of these examples call for the combining of separate product divisions with one or more centralized functional units drawn on for services by all the product divisions. This is often called a hybrid organization—combining the functional and the product forms. This combination also presents an opportunity to adopt the matrix form, a more complex organization that will be discussed below.

E. Multicountry Firms

The growth drive of firms and the need to respond to global competitive challenges often lead firms to move into international markets. This move, of course, represents the strategic choice to expand dramatically the number of customers served by existing products and services. The opportunity of reaching new markets presents the organizational challenge of finding an effective structure to fit these new circumstances.

There are four basic multinational structural choices: worldwide product divisions, geographic divisions, worldwide functional divisions, and a matrix structure that combines two or more of these dimensions. There are, however, several developmental paths to these forms and numerous variations on each one.

Most firms start down the road to becoming multinational by setting up an export sales office. With this modest beginning, the firm looks for distributors and sales representatives in some selected overseas area. Sometimes this results in forming a joint venture with a foreign marketing organization as an alternative to simply setting up an exclusive sales contract. If the business thrives, it can lead not only to seeking sales in more and more countries, but also to starting the process of moving other functions overseas (e.g., warehousing, assembly, and basic manufacturing units). The export sales office is apt to evolve into an international division handling all aspects of overseas operations. This solution, however, is not apt to be satisfactory over the longer term. Handling all products through the one international organization inhibits the needed differentiation of form among the different products. The linkage to the domestic product divisions becomes strained. With overseas growth the scale of activity can justify the choice among the four ultimate options.

Contingency theory specifies that the choice among the basic forms for multinational organization hinges on identifying the most competitively critical variable as between technological leadership, market responsiveness, or production scale economies—or some combination of these. Science and technology are a universal language, and if the critical competitive advantage is to be found in technological leadership, the organization form that fosters it is clearly the worldwide product division. This form allows a focusing of product development efforts even as it provides worldwide distribution. Each worldwide product division can differentiate in ways that fit its environment. General Electric is a leading example of such a firm.

On the other hand, some products need to be linked tightly to the different cultural preferences that exist around the world—think of fashion goods, cosmetics, and the like. When these market conditions are the critical competitive issue, the theory calls for the creation of a complete set of geographic divisions that span the globe, including the home country division as simply another geographic unit to be managed. Coca-Cola is a leading example of such a firm.

Worldwide functional or process divisions are less frequently seen, usually in firms that are vertically integrated. This form is indicated when the technology of each function is highly specialized and permits significant economies by setting up large-scale operations. A clear example is Alcan, which has separate worldwide organizations for, among others, its chemical operations, its smelters, its transport, and its fabricating units.

Finally, there is the matrix option. This form is fairly often used by multinational organizations when the competitive environment makes two dimensions of critical importance. The matrix form permits a dual focus. It creates, for example, both product divisions and geographic divisions, with the managers in any given country responsible to both divisional headquarters in a balanced fashion. Matrix organizations permit a sharing of resources and offer more information-processing capacity, but they also are difficult to manage and necessitate extensive management training to install. Dow is a leading example of a multinational matrix. There are many variations of the matrix form that cannot be spelled out here, but we should also cite the frequent use of the product/functional matrix even in firms operating entirely in the United States. This organization is called for when both product market and technological excellence are required for competitive reasons.

F. Strategic Alliances

In the past decade a new kind of organizational development has emerged that represents a special kind of firm—a network of interorganizational strategic alliances. These linkages between firms go beyond the traditional buyer-seller contractual relationship. They exchange more than goods for money in the spot deal of the classical market relationship. They represent an enriched relationship that extends over time and that is characterized by words such as partnership, joint venture, consortium, and ownership linkage. These linkages represent an exchange of help in many forms. It might be an exchange of product plans and market information that draws a component supplier into the design process. It might be a research joint venture to speed up the development process and to share costs. It might be a way of coordinating a just-in-time supply linkage. It might be a joint venture to enter the newly opening markets in Eastern Europe. It might be a network of small firms that develop into a regional resource in rapidly changing sectors such as microprocessors or sports clothing. These networks seem to be developing where flexible manufacturing methods are allowing for low-cost customized production on a small scale. Such developments also happen where information about markets, costs, and technology is widely available, allowing trustworthy relationships to evolve without expensive legal safeguards. Some of these networks develop around a major firm that serves as the hub coordinator of the supply and information flows. Toyota and Benetton provide examples. Others are strictly small firms networked without a major hub firm. Both forms are showing competitive strength. More research on this newly developing form is needed to specify more clearly what contingencies make the network the appropriate organizational form.

G. Putting Contingency Theory in Context

Contingency theory came into being in the late 1960s at a time in which the search for a universal answer to the organization design question was clearly losing steam. This search had been pushed to its limits by the classical school, with work started early in the century by Weber (1947), Taylor (1911), and Fayol (1925) and carried on later by Urwick (1944), Mooney (1937), Gulick (1937), and Koontz and O'Donnell (1955). The classical school emphasized the formal structure, using the concepts of chain of command, span of control, and line and staff.

The antithesis of classical theory was developed by the human relations school. This school of thought evolved from the late 1920s into the 1960s through the work of such leading scholars as Mayo (1933), Follett (1940), Barnard (1946), Roethlisberger and Dickson (1939), Lewin (1948), Likert (1961), and McGregor (1960). The emphasis was on informal organization, group behavior, participation, and interpersonal relations.

Neither school was able to gain dominance over the other. The beginning of a new approach was signaled by the work of March and Simon (1958). They, in effect, opened up the possibility of a more pluralistic theory without providing much guidance as to what the choice of effective forms was contingent upon. Contingency theory served to provide a synthesis that was timely. It was quickly established as the prevailing paradigm. Over the subsequent quarter century the theory has at various times been challenged by newer formulations, but none has seemed to prevail. The theory does suffer from some signs of aging—younger scholars show evidence of being bored by it. It has, however, been widely taught, and also widely, though rather unevenly, practiced.

So, contingency theory continues to be the strongest, research-based body of knowledge relevant to the practical problems of organizational design. The basic patterns it has identified in organizations continue to be supported by follow-up studies (see Khandwalla, 1977; and Donaldson, 1986). It is an approach that can continue to evolve as it tracks newly developing organizational forms such as the networks of strategic alliances. Perhaps the greatest current challenge to the theory arises from the evidence that the stable environmental conditions that call for a more highly structured, mechanistic organizational form are becoming scarce. This development may appear to some to be falsifying the theory, but in all logic it does not. These developments do, however, call for a more sophisticated application of the theory.

REFERENCES

Barnard, Chester (1946). *Functions of the Executive*. Harvard University Press, Cambridge, Mass.

Bartlett, Christopher, and Goshal, Sumantra (1989). *Managing Across Borders: The Transitional Solution*. Harvard Business School Press, Boston.

Burns, Thomas, and Stalker, G. M. (1961). *The Management of Innovation*. Tavistock, London.

Chandler, Alfred D. Jr. (1962). *Strategy and Structure*. The M.I.T. Press, Cambridge, Mass.

Davis, Stanley, and Lawrence, Paul R. (1977). *Matrix*. Addison-Wesley, Reading, Mass.

Donaldson, Lex (1986). *In Defence of Organization Theory*. Cambridge University Press, Cambridge.

Fayol, Henry (1925). *Industrial and General Administration*. Dunod, Paris.

Fiedler, F. E. (1967). *A Theory of Leadership Effectiveness*. McGraw-Hill, New York.

Follett, Mary Parker (1940). *The Collected Papers of Mary Parker Follett*. Harper Brothers, New York.

Galbraith, Jay R. (1973). *Designing Organizations*. Addison-Wesley, Reading, Mass.

Greiner, Larry E. (May–June 1967). Patterns of organization change. *Harvard Business Review*: 119–30.

Gulick, Luther (1937). Notes on the theory of organizations. In *Papers on the Science of Administration* (Luther Gulick and Lyndall Urwick, eds.), Columbia University, New York.

Hofstede, G. (summer 1980). Motivation, leadership, and organization: Do American management theories apply abroad? *Organizational Dynamics*: pp. 42–63.

Khandwalla, Pradip (1977). *The Design of Organizations*. Harcourt Brace Jovanovich, New York.

Koontz, Harold, and O'Donnell, Cyril, (1955), *Principles of Management*. McGraw-Hill, New York.

Lawrence, Paul R., and Lorsch, Jay W. (1967). *Organization and Environment: Managing Differentiation and Integration*. Division of Research, Harvard Graduate School of Business Administration, Boston.

Lewin, Kurt (1948). *Resolving Social Conflicts*. Harper, New York.

Likert, Ronald (1961). *New Patterns of Management*. McGraw-Hill, New York.

Lorsch, Jay W., and Allen, Stephen A. (1973). *Managing Diversity and Interdependence: An Organizational Study of Multidivisional Firms*. Division of Research, Harvard Graduate School of Business Administration, Boston.

Lorsch, Jay W., and Morse, John J. (1974). *Organizations and Their Members*. Harper and Row, New York.

March, James, and Simon, Herbert (1958). *Organizations*. John Wiley and Sons, New York.

Mayo, Elton (1933). *The Human Problems of an Industrial Civilization*. Division of Research, Harvard Graduate School of Business Administration, Boston.

McGregor, Douglas (1960). *The Human Side of Enterprise*. McGraw-Hill, New York.

Mooney, James (1937). The principles of organization. In *Papers on the Science of Administration* (Luther Gulick and Lyndall Urwick, eds.), Columbia University, New York.

Perrow, Charles (April 1967). A framework for the comparative analysis of organizations. *American Sociological Review*, 32:194–208

Pfeffer, Jeffrey, and Salancik, Gerald R. (1978). *The External Control of Organizations: A Resource Dependence Perspective*. Harper and Row, New York.

Porter, Michael E. (1980). *Competitive Strategy*. Free Press, New York.

Pugh, D. S., Hickson, D. J., Hinings, C. R., and Turner, C. (June 1968). Dimensions of organization structure. *Administrative Science Quarterly*, 13(1):65–105.

Roethlisberger, Fritz, and Dickson, William (1939). *Management and the Worker*. Harvard University Press, Cambridge, Mass.

Rumelt, R. P. (1974). *Strategy, Structure and Economic Performance*. Division of Research, Harvard Graduate School of Business Administration, Boston.

Taylor, Frederick (1911). *Shop Management*. Harper and Brothers, New York.

Thompson, James D. (1967). *Organizations in Action*. McGraw-Hill, New York.

Turner, Arthur, and Lawrence, Paul R. (1965). *Industrial Jobs and the Worker*. Division of Research, Harvard Graduate School of Business Administration, Boston.

Urwick, Lyndall (1944). *The Elements of Administration*. Harper and Brothers, New York.

Vroom, Victor H. (1960). *Some Personality Determinants of the Effect of Participation*. Prentice-Hall, Englewood Cliffs, N.J.

Weber, Max (1947). *The Theory of Social and Economic Organization*. Oxford University Press, New York.

Woodward, Joan (1965). *Industrial Organization: Theory and Practice*. University Press, Oxford.

2
Work Motivation

Hal G. Rainey

University of Georgia, Athens, Georgia

Motivation is one of the central topics in the social sciences, and work motivation plays a similarly central role in organizational behavior (OB). Work motivation has received as much intensive theoretical development as any topic in OB, and as this chapter will do, OB texts typically review a standard series of theories that have competed for acceptance among researchers. As with other major concepts, such as power, leadership, and attitude, scholars have exhaustively debated the proper definition of motivation, and have reported thousands of studies bearing on the topic.

Also as with other major concepts, reviewers of all this work often express disappointment over the weak validation of most of the theories and wonder whether or not we have really learned much (Pinder, 1984). Yet the disappointments are in relation to very high standards that implicitly call for a comprehensive, well-validated theory of motivation. While the research has not yet produced one, each of the well-known theories reviewed here adds valuable insights to our understanding of motivation.

In addition, the dilemmas that scholars face translate into challenges for practitioners in organizations. The problems we have in both precisely defining motivation, and clearly encompassing it in a theory, are reflected in the challenges in measuring and assessing motivation in organizations and in establishing effective incentive systems (Kerr, 1989; Katzell and Thompson, 1990). As illustrated in examples in the sections below, the theories of motivation can aid in the analysis of motivational issues in organizations; therefore scholars and well-informed practitioners need to be aware of the conceptual and theoretical backgrounds that the theory and research on motivation provide.

This chapter summarizes that conceptual and theoretical background, as well as some of the practical implications of the theoretical contributions, and some of the motivational techniques used in organizations. The chapter first reviews efforts to define and measure motivation, pointing out that challenges and controversies have caused motivation to become more of an umbrella concept referring to a set of concepts and issues than a single variable with a precise operational definition. Then the chapter describes the most prominent theories of motivation and the research and debates about their validation and conception. The chapter then summarizes some of the more recent statements about directions for motivation theory. Regardless of whether or not researchers produce well-validated theories, managers and professionals have to try to motivate people in organizations, so the chapter ends with a description of some of the procedures that organizations use to enhance motivation.

I. THE MEANING AND MEASUREMENT OF MOTIVATION

Everyone feels familiar with the concept of motivation, yet scholars struggle with its definition. Reviews have unearthed some 140 distinct definitions (Landy and Becker, 1987; Kleinginna and Kleinginna, 1981). The term derives from the Latin word *motus*, a form of the verb *movere*, to move, from which also derive such words as motor and motif (Steers and Porter, 1987). By motivation, we mean the degree to which a person is moved or aroused to expend effort to achieve some purpose. Work motivation refers to how much a person tries to work hard and well—to the arousal, direction, and persistence of effort in work settings.

Motivation theorists have also sought to clarify distinctions between motivation and other major concepts. For example, they distinguish general work motivation from affective and attitudinal states such as work satisfaction (e.g., Campbell and Pritchard, 1983). They usually define job satisfaction as a matter of affect and attitude, of how one feels about the job and various facets of it, sometimes including behavioral components such as whether or not one intends to quit. Some people express satisfaction, without displaying motivation to perform well. Highly motivated people may express dissatisfaction in certain ways because of their high standards or because they believe they deserve better rewards than they get.

Motivation researchers have also struggled with different ways of measuring motivation, none of which provides an adequately comprehensive measurement. For example, the typical definition of motivation noted above—the willingness and tendency to exert effort toward successful work performance—raises complications about what we actually mean by motivation. Is it an attitude or a behavior, or both? Must we observe a person exerting effort? Does it suffice to have the person tell us that she or he is working hard or trying as hard as possible?

As Table 1 shows, researchers have tried to measure motivation in different ways, which imply different answers to these questions. Some researchers have taken the course of asking people about their behavior and attitudes (entries 1 through 4 in Table 1), while at least one study (entry 5; Guion and Landy, 1972) has tried to develop measures based on observations by a person's co-workers. Interestingly, the literature on organizational behavior and psychology provides very few measures of general work motivation. One of the few available general measures, Patchen's (1965; entry 1 in Table 1), relies on questions about how hard one works and how often one does some extra work. Although researchers have reported successful use of this scale (Cook et al., 1981), one study using this measure found that managers responding to the questions tend to give very high ratings of their own work efforts. The vast majority reported that they work harder than others in their organization. They gave such high self-ratings that there was little difference among them, and so it was difficult to test for the determinants of those differences (Rainey, 1983).

These results underscore the problems of asking people about their motivation, and often reflect the cultural emphasis on hard work and effort that leads some people to report that they work hard whether or not they do. More likely, many people also want to think that they work hard, and feel that they do. Yet what does it mean to work hard and exert effort? By what standard? Compared to what? One of the Patchen items refers to working harder than others in the organization. In the study mentioned above (Rainey, 1983), in reporting very high levels of motivation in this sense, most of the managers in the study were reporting that they worked harder than the others. Consider an organization in which everyone works harder than everyone else. The thought is humorous because it calls to mind Garrison Keillor's fictional town of Lake Wobegone, where all the children are above average.

Researchers also employ scales of job involvement, and intrinsic or internal work motivation, such as the examples in Table 1 (entries 2 and 3; see also Cook et al., 1981). Researchers in organizational behavior define intrinsic work motives or rewards as those that are mediated within the worker, such as psychic rewards deriving directly from the work itself. Extrinsic rewards are externally mediated, and exemplified by salary, promotion, and other rewards that come from the organization or work group. As the examples indicate, the questions on intrinsic motivation ask about an increase in feelings of accomplishment, growth, and self-esteem through work well done. Measures such as these assess important work-related attitudes,

Table 1 Questionnaire Items Used to Measure Work Motivation

1. Job motivation (Patchen, Pelz, and Allen, 1970)
On most days on your job, how often does time seem to drag for you?
Some people are completely involved in their job; they are absorbed in it night and day. For other people their job is simply one of several interests. How involved do you feel in your job?
How often do you do some extra work for your job that isn't really required of you?
Would you say that you work harder, less hard, or about the same as other people doing your type of work at (name of organization)?
2. Job involvement (short form; Lodahl and Kejner, 1965)
The major satisfaction in my life comes from my job.
The most important things that happen to me involve my work.
I'm really a perfectionist about my work.
I live, eat, and breathe my job.
I am very much involved personally in my work.
Most things in life are more important than work.
3. Intrinsic motivation (Lawler and Hall, 1970)
When I do my work well, it gives me a feeling of accomplishment.
When I perform my job well, it contributes to my personal growth and development.
I feel a great sense of personal satisfaction when I do my job well.
Doing my job well increases my feeling of self-esteem.
4. Reward expectancies (Rainey, 1983)
Producing a high quality of work increases my chances for higher pay.
Producing a high quality of work increases my chances for a promotion.
5. Peer evaluations of a person's work motivation (Guion and Landy, 1972; Landy and Guion, 1970)
Dimensions for peer ratings of a fellow employee's work motivation:
  Team attitude
  Task concentration
  Independence/self-starter
  Organizational identification
  Job curiosity
  Persistence
  Professional identification

but they do not ask directly about work effort or direction; rather, they infer that if one feels this way when doing good work, one must be motivated to exert effort.

Similarly, researchers and consultants sometimes use items derived from expectancy theories of work motivation, described in a later section, as proxy measures for motivation. As shown in Table 1, these questions resemble those for intrinsic motivation described above, but often refer to extrinsic rewards such as pay and promotion. Again, these questions do not ask people directly about the level and directions of their work effort, and infer that perceiving such connections between work performance and rewards enhances motivation. Such items have been widely used by consultants in their assessments of organizations, and in huge surveys of federal employees for assessments of the civil service system and its reform (U.S. Office of Personnel Management, 1979; 1980). In this sense, both these procedures and the intrinsic motivation scales also implicitly acknowledge the limitations of asking people to report their levels of motivation and effort.

If one cannot very well ask the people themselves, one can ask others around that person for their observations about that person's motivation, as did Landy and Guion (1970; entry 5 in Table 1). They had peers rate individual managers on the dimensions listed in Table 1. Significantly, their research indicated that peer observers disagree a lot on the same focal case. This method obviously requires considerable time, resources, and organizational access to administer, which probably explains why other researchers have not used this very interesting approach. As indicated earlier, most definitions of motivation mention that it involves direction as well as amplitude of effort. As the Landy and Guion conception shows, however, the issue of direction becomes quite complex, and one can demonstrate motivation along many directions.

As an additional example of the different outcomes or directions on which motivation can concentrate, one of the classic distinctions in the theory of management and organizations concerns the difference between the motivation to join an organization and stay in it on the one hand, and the motivation to work hard and well within it on the other. These two motivations have related, but fairly distinct, determinants. Chester Barnard, and later James March and Herbert Simon, in books widely acknowledged as the most prominent contributions to the field, analyzed this distinction. You might get people to shuffle into work every day, rather than quit, but they can display keen ingenuity at avoiding doing what you ask them to do if they do not want to do it. Currently, management experts widely acknowledge Barnard's prescience in seeking to analyze the ways in which organizational leaders must employ a variety of incentives, including the guiding values of the organization, to induce cooperation and effort (Williamson, 1991; Peters and Waterman, 1982).

A. Rival Influences on Performance

Writers on work motivation also point out that motivation alone does not determine performance. Ability figures importantly in performance, obviously, such that a person may display high motivation but insufficient ability, or have such immense ability that the person performs well with little effort or apparent motivation. The person's understanding of the task influences performance, as do the behaviors of leaders or co-workers that can confuse or clarify, guide or misdirect. These and other factors can also interact with motivation in determining performance, and in intricate ways. A person may gain motivation by feeling greater ability to perform, or lose motivation through the frustrations of lacking the ability to perform well. Alternatively, one may lose motivation for a task that one has mastered completely and that then fails to provide a challenge or sense of growth. As we will see, the major theories try in various ways to capture some of these intricacies.

B. Motivation as an Umbrella Concept

All these complexities have moved the concept of motivation into the status of an umbrella concept that refers to a general topic rather than a precisely defined and measured research variable (Campbell and Pritchard, 1983). Considerable research and theorizing about motivation continue, but usually employing the term as referring to a general concept incorporating many variables and issues (e.g., H. J. Klein, 1989; J. I. Klein, 1990; and Kleinbeck et al., 1990). Locke and Latham (1990b), for example, present a model of work motivation that does not include within it a concept or variable labeled motivation. Motivation currently appears to serve as an implicit theme overarching research on a variety of related topics. These include organization identification and commitment, leadership practices, job involvement and intrinsic work motivation, organizational climate and culture, and characteristics of work goals.

II. THEORIES OF MOTIVATION

No theory explains motivation comprehensively, then, but each contributes an important component of a well-developed conception of motivation and its determinants and outcomes. The theories are diverse, and not easily classified, but one conventional classification distinguishes between content theories and process theories. Content theories are concerned with analyzing the particular needs, motives, or rewards that motivation theories should contain. Process theories concentrate more on the psychological or behavioral processes in motivation, often with no designation of the important rewards and motives. The distinction does not classify perfectly, since most of the theories include some attention to both process and content. Consult more elaborate typologies of motivation theories (Katzell and Thompson, 1990) for more careful distinctions, but this dichotomy serves well enough for introducing the major theories.

A. Content Theories

1. Maslow's Need Hierarchy

Abraham Maslow (1954) proposed a theory of human needs or motives that receives attention in every review of work motivation literature. Interestingly, while researchers on work motivation have shown diminished acceptance of Maslow's approach as an adequate theory of motivation, it continues to influence important intellectual developments (e.g., Burns, 1978).

Maslow argued that human motives or needs follow a hierarchy of prepotency, as he put it, involving the levels listed in Table 2. The lower-order needs, beginning with physiological needs, dominate human motivation and behavior, until they are satisfied. Then needs at the next higher level dominate, and so on up the hierarchy. Once one has satisfied hunger and the need

Table 2 Categories of Needs and Values Employed in Selected Content Theories

Maslow's Need Hierarchy

Physiological needs. Needs for relief from hunger, thirst, and sleepiness, and for defense from the elements.

Safety needs. Needs to be free of the threat of bodily harm.

Social needs. Needs for love, affection, and belonging to social units and groups.

Esteem needs. Needs for sense of achievement, confidence, recognition, and prestige.

Self-actualization needs. The need to become everything one is capable of becoming, to achieve self-fulfillment, especially in some area of endeavor or purpose (such as motherhood, artistic creativity, or a profession).

Herzberg's Two-Factor Theory

Hygiene Factors	Motivators
Company policy and administration	Achievement
Supervision	Recognition
Relations with supervisor	The work itself
Working conditions	Responsibility
Salary	Growth
Relations with peers	Advancement
Personal life	
Relations with subordinates	
Status	
Security	

McClelland: Need for Achievement, Power, and Affiliation[a]

Need for achievement: The need for a sense of mastery over one's environment and successful accomplishment through one's own abilities and efforts, a preference for challenges involving moderate risk, clear feedback about success, and ability to sense personal responsibility for success. Purportedly stimulates and facilitates entrepreneurial behavior.

Need for power: A general need for autonomy and control over oneself and others, which can manifest itself in different ways. When blended with degrees of altruism and inhibition, and low need for affiliation, can facilitate effectiveness at management.

Need for affiliation: The need to establish and maintain positive affective relations or "friendship" with others (McClelland, 1975, p. 160).

Adams: The Need for Equity

The need to maintain a balance between one's contributions to an organization and one's returns and compensations from it, which is equitable or fair, as compared to the balance maintained by others in the organization to whom one compares oneself. The need to feel that one is not overcompensated or undercompensated for one's contributions to the organization.

[a]McClelland and other researchers on these concepts do not provide concise or specific definitions of the need concepts. These definitions summarize the apparent meaning of the concepts.

for sleep, one becomes more concerned with safety and security. Next, needs for social and love relationships dominate. With those needs reasonably satisfied, needs for esteem dominate. The highest-order need, for self-actualization (see Table 2), appeals widely to people searching for a way to express this ultimate human motive for fulfilling one's potential.

In later writings Maslow (1965) further developed his ideas about self-actualization, and its association with work, duty, and group or communal benefits. He sharply rejected conceptions of self-actualization as self-absorbed concern with one's personal emotional salvation or satisfaction, especially through merely shedding inhibitions or social controls. In contrast to some gurus of encounter techniques, Maslow insisted that genuinely self-actualized persons achieve this ultimate mode of satisfaction through hardworking dedication to a duty, form of work, or mission, which serves higher values than one's simple self-satisfaction, and which benefits others or society. Genuine personal contentment and emotional salvation, he argued, come as by-products of such dedication. In this later discussion, Maslow (1965) depicts the levels of need not as separate steps or phases from which one successively departs. Rather, he treats them as cumulative phases of a growth toward self-actualization, a motive that grows out of satisfaction of social and esteem needs and also builds on them.

As described below, Maslow's ideas have had a significant impact on many social scientists, but his model has received little reverence from empirical researchers attempting to validate it. Researchers attempting to devise measures of the needs and to test the theory have not confirmed the existence of a five-step hierarchy. Studies have tended to find a two-step hierarchy, in which lower-level employees show more concern with material and security rewards. Higher-level employees place more emphasis on achievement and challenge (Pinder, 1984). Of course these studies may fail to support the theory simply because of limitations of our ability to operationalize and test the concepts and dynamics of the theory. For example, as implied by the findings mentioned above, the tests often compare lower-level to higher-level employees, and this provides only a static assessment of a process that the theory treats as dynamic. In addition, since the concept of self-actualization is quite complex, questionnaire items in the studies may be too limited or simplified to capture this complexity.

More important, scholars point to theoretical problems with Maslow's model, as did Maslow himself. He said that more than one need may determine behavior, that some needs may disappear, and even that some behavior is not determined by needs. Others offer their generous assistance in pointing out such limitations. Locke and Henne (1986) emphasize ambiguities in the behavioral implications of need deprivation. Need deprivation may induce discomfort, but it does not tell the person what to do about it, and therefore the behavioral implications of the theory remain amorphous. Locke and Henne also criticize the hazy concept of self-actualization as an impediment to developing and testing the theory.

Still, for those less concerned with empirical verification than with face validity, Maslow's theory retains a strong plausibility and attractiveness. Maslow contributed to a growing recognition of the importance of motives for growth, development, and actualization among members of organizations (Golembiewski, 1989: 193–197). The current influences of his ideas have followed some interesting paths. For example, in his analysis of leadership, James MacGregor Burns (1978) drew on Maslow's concepts of a hierarchy of both needs and higher-order needs such as self-actualization. Burns observed that *transformational* leaders—that is, leaders who bring about major transformations in society—do not engage in simple exchanges of benefits with their followers. Rather, they elicit higher-order motives in the population, including forms of self-actualization motives tied to societal ends, with visions of a society transformed in ways that fulfill such motives. As a political scientist, Burns concentrated on political and societal leaders, but writers on organizational leadership have acknowledged his influence on recent writings about transformational leadership in organizations (Bass, 1985; Bennis and Nanus, 1985). In addition, Maslow's (1965) later writings on self-actualization in work settings foreshadow many aspects of the very current discussion of the management of organizational mission and culture, empowerment of workers, and highly participative forms of management (e.g., Block, 1987; Golembiewski, 1985; 1989; and Peters and Waterman, 1982).

2. McGregor: Theory X and Theory Y

Douglas McGregor's (1960) arguments about theories X and Y also reflect the influence of Maslow's views and highlight the general penetration into management thought of an emphasis on higher-order needs. McGregor argued that industrial management in the United States reflected the dominance of a theory of human behavior, theory X, which assumed that workers had fundamental needs for direction and control. Since workers lack the capacity for self-motivation and self-direction, managers must structure organizations and incentive systems to closely control, reward, and punish workers. McGregor called for wider acceptance of theory Y, the theory that workers have strivings akin to those Maslow described as higher-order needs—for growth, development, interesting work, and self-actualization. Theory Y should guide practice, McGregor argued. Managers and organizations must take steps to employ participative management styles, decentralized decision-making, revised performance evaluation procedures that emphasize self-evaluation and objectives set by the employee, and job enlargement to make jobs more interesting and responsible. McGregor's ideas offered only the rudiments of a theory, and researchers do not currently pursue it or treat it as such. Nonetheless his ideas have influenced the thinking of managers seeking change and reform in many organizations (e.g., Warwick, 1975). His general theme served as one of the important influences on very current admonitions about empowering middle managers and employees, as well as on related contemporary directions in organization and management thought.

3. Herzberg: Two-Factor Theory

Frederick Herzberg (1968) proposed one of the best-known analyses of motivational issues in his two-factor theory, which also emphasized the importance of higher-order needs in motivating individuals in organizations. From multiple studies involving about 2000 respondents in numerous occupational categories, he and his colleagues concluded that two major factors influence individual motivation in work settings: "motivators" and "hygiene factors." The absence or insufficiency of hygiene factors can contribute to dissatisfaction with the job, but the presence of hygiene factors does not stimulate high levels of satisfaction. As suggested by the examples in Table 2, hygiene factors are extrinsic both to the work itself and to the individual, involving organizational, group, or supervisory conditions, or externally mediated rewards such as salary. While hygiene factors can only prevent dissatisfaction, motivators produce a heightened level of satisfaction and increased motivation. As Table 2 indicates, motivators are intrinsic to the job and include interest and enjoyment of the work itself, as well as a sense of growth, achievement, and fulfillment of other higher-order needs.

Herzberg concluded that motivators provide the real sources of stimulation and motivation for employees. Hygiene factors can only prevent dissatisfaction; they cannot really stimulate and enhance motivation. Therefore managers must avoid negative techniques of controlling and directing employees, and should arrange job settings to provide for the growth, achievement, recognition, and other needs represented in the motivators. Such procedures as human relations training do not usually solve the problem, he warned. It takes careful job enrichment programs that design jobs to make the work itself interesting, and to give the worker the sense of control, achievement, growth, and recognition that produces high levels of motivation.

Herzberg's work sparked controversy among experts and researchers. He and his colleagues developed their evidence by asking people to describe events on their jobs that led to feelings of extreme satisfaction, and events that led to extreme dissatisfaction. Most of the reports of instances of great satisfaction mentioned the intrinsic and growth factors. Herzberg labeled these motivators in part because the respondents often mentioned their connection to better performance. The reports of dissatisfaction tended to concentrate on the hygiene factors.

Researchers using other methods of generating evidence, however, did not isolate the same two types of factors (Pinder, 1984). Critics argued that when asked to describe an event that made them feel highly motivated, people might hesitate to report great satisfaction over pay or some improvement in physical working conditions. Instead, in what social scientists call a social desirability effect, they might attempt to provide more high-minded answers. On the other hand, when describing an instance leading to dissatisfaction, they might try to attribute bad outcomes to external conditions such as company policies or supervisory behaviors, thereby defending themselves and their self-esteem.

In addition, some researchers raised questions about the conceptual clarity of the two factors and the questions that Herzberg used to assess them. Critics also questioned Herzberg's conclusions about the effects of the two factors on individual behavior. Lawler (1971), for example, cited Herzberg as one of a number of researchers who understated the importance of pay in organizations. Lawler found that numerous surveys highlighted the importance of various rewards. Survey respondents tended to rank pay fairly high—about third overall. Lawler pointed out that pay can serve as an indicator of achievement, recognition, and increased responsibility, and therefore can overlap with intrinsic rewards.

Herzberg and his colleagues responded that many of the attempts to test their theory did not provide accurate and fair tests. Nevertheless, the critiques of the theory, and the inability to reproduce the two factors with alternative methods, appear to be responsible for a decline in interest in the theory. Locke and Henne (1986), for example, find no recent attempts to test the theory, and conclude that theorists no longer take it seriously. Whether or not the particular elements of this theory have been rejected, the idea of restructuring work to make it interesting, and to provide satisfaction of motives for growth and fulfillment, continues to receive serious attention among many practicing managers and organizational researchers.

4.   McClelland: Needs for Achievement, Power, and Affiliation

David McClelland's theory about motivations for achievement, power, and affiliation (the desire for friendly relations with others) has elicited thousands of studies (e.g., McClelland, 1961; Atkinson and Raynor, 1974, and Locke and Henne, 1986). The need for achievement (hereafter, n Ach), the central concept in his theory, refers to a motivation—a "dynamic restlessness" (McClelland, 1961: 301)—to achieve a sense of mastery over one's environment, through success at achieving goals and outcomes through one's own cunning, abilities, and efforts. He originally argued that motivation for achievement in this pattern was characteristic of persons attracted to managerial and entrepreneurial roles, although he later narrowed its application to predicting success in entrepreneurial roles (Pinder, 1984).

McClelland measured n Ach through a variety of procedures, including the thematic apperception test (TAT). The TAT involves showing a standard set of pictures to individuals who then write brief stories about what is happening in each picture. One typical picture shows a boy sitting at a desk in a classroom reading a book. A respondent identified as low in n Ach might write a story depicting the boy as daydreaming, while someone high in n Ach might write a story about how hard the boy was studying to do well on a test, and how anxiously the boy wanted to do well. Similarly, McClelland drew on analyses of the achievement-oriented content of fantasies that people reported, and the stories that people tell to children in different societies. Researchers also measured n Ach through questionnaires asking about such matters as occupational and work role preferences, about the role of luck in outcomes, and about preferences for activities such as stamp collecting or racing another person.

McClelland's (1961) conception of n Ach involved the motivation to achieve in a particular pattern. Persons high in this need, he said, tend to choose reasonably challenging goals and moderate risks in which outcomes are fairly clear and accomplishment reflects success through one's own abilities. Persons successful in certain roles, such as research scientists who have to wait for a long time for success and recognition, would have a motivation to achieve, but not in this particular pattern on which McClelland focused. As one example of the nature of this motive, McClelland (1961) cited the performance of children and students in experiments in which they chose how to behave in games of skill. In a series of experiments, researchers had children and students participate in a ringtoss game. The participants chose how far from the target peg they would stand in trying to throw the ring onto it. The high n Ach participants tended to stand at intermediate distances from the peg, not too close but not too far away.

McClelland interpreted this as a reflection of their desire to achieve on the basis of their own skills. Standing too close made success too easy, and did not satisfy the desire to have a sense of accomplishment and mastery. Standing too far away, however, made success a gamble, a matter of a lucky throw. The high n Ach participants chose a distance that would reflect success through their own skills. McClelland (1961) also offered evidence of other characteristics of persons with high n Ach, such as physical restlessness and particular concern over the rapid passage of time and aversion to wasting time.

Some of McClelland's more ambitious ideas related n Ach to success in business activities and the success of nations in economic development (McClelland, 1961; McClelland and Winter, 1969). He analyzed the achievement orientation in folk tales and children's stories in various nations, and produced some evidence that cultures high in n Ach themes in such stories also showed higher rates of economic development. He has also claimed successes in training managers in business firms in less-developed countries to increase their n Ach and thereby to enhance the performance of their firm (McClelland and Winter, 1969). He suggested more achievement-oriented fantasizing and thinking as a means of improving the economic performance of nations. Others have also used achievement motivation training with apparent success in enhancing the motive and increasing entrepreneurial behaviors (Miner, 1980: 67).

As noted above, McClelland (1975) later concluded that n Ach induced entrepreneurial behaviors, rather than directing a person toward success in managerial roles. He argued, however, that his conceptions of power motivation and need for affiliation did indeed apply to successful management (although there is much less empirical research about these needs to support or refute his claims). McClelland concluded that the most effective managers develop through a set of stages into a stage in which they have high power motivation, but with an altruistic orientation and a concern for group goals. This stage also involves a low need for affiliation, however, since too strong a need for friendship with others can hinder a manager.

Reviewers vary in their assessments of the state of this theory. Some rather positive assessments (Miner, 1980) contrast with others who focus only brief attention on it (Pinder, 1984), or who criticize it harshly (Locke and Henne, 1986). Locke and Henne characterize the body of research as chaotic. They also complain that the domain of the theory has become confused, since McClelland has narrowed the focus of n Ach to entrepreneurial behaviors even though the overwhelming proportion of the numerous empirical studies have not focused on entrepreneurs. Currently, one finds little very recent research on the theory in major management or organizational journals. Regardless of its current prestige among scholars, however, this theory adds another very plausible element to a well-developed perspective on motivation. Individuals do apparently vary in the general level and pattern of the internal motivation for achievement and excellence they bring to work settings.

5. Equity Theory

J. Stacy Adams (1963; 1965) developed a theory about a motive for equity in organizations that has received much attention. He drew on a body of research in psychology about the need for cognitive balance and consistency (our need to feel that our various beliefs and attitudes are consistent with each other and not conflicting). He also drew on research about social comparison processes (our tendency to assess ourselves and our status by comparing ourselves to others whom we accept as referents). He theorized that in their work, people want to feel equitably compensated. People have a need for a sense of equity, and are uncomfortable with indications inconsistent with that need; that is, with evidence that they are inequitably compensated. They compare their own exchanges with the organization to the exchanges between the organization and other employees. If a person senses that he or she receives treatment that is inequitable in relation to the others, he or she will be motivated to reduce the inequity. His other efforts to maintain or restore a sense of equity will have important influences on subsequent behavior.

Although here classified as a content theory because of its emphasis on the equity motive, the theory contains much detail on the processes involved in perceptions of inequity and their effects on behavior. People assess equity by comparing themselves to one or more other persons in the organization. One assesses the balance between one's own "inputs" (contributions such as effort, experience, and credentials; longevity; and successful accomplishments) and one's "outcomes" (returns or compensations from the organization and the work, such as pay, benefits, and enjoyment). One compares this balance to that of the other person, the referent. One experiences inequity if the other person's balance is more favorable or unfavorable. If the other person gets more good outcomes for the same level of inputs, one feels inequity in the sense of undercompensation; the other person is getting more rewards for the same contributions. If the other person gets the same or lower levels of good outcomes, but makes more and better contributions, one feels inequity in the sense of overcompensation; the other person does better but gets less for it.

Adams argued that individuals will be motivated to reduce or avoid inequity in either the form of over- or undercompensation. The person may respond to inequity in various ways: by altering inputs or outcomes, mentally distorting one's inputs and outcomes, acting on the referent person (such as pressuring the person to produce more or less), or leaving through transferring or quitting. Adams's discussions of the theory offer some propositions about choices among these responses; for example, some inputs are costly and require effort, so individuals will be slow to respond by increasing them. Individuals will be less likely to change or distort inputs and outcomes that are very important to their self-esteem. People will quit only at high levels of inequity, and at lower levels of inequity will tend toward more limited responses such as absenteeism.

Adams also proposed and tested some relatively precise hypotheses about responses to inequity under well-specified circumstances, such as piece rate versus hourly rate pay systems. He predicted that a person overcompensated (compared to a referent other) in a piece rate system will try to produce fewer pieces, but of higher quality. A person overcompensated at an hourly rate, however, will strive to produce more outputs. A person undercompensated in a piece rate system will strive to produce more outputs, to bring his or her total compensation up to that of the referent person. A person undercompensated on an hourly basis will slow down and reduce production.

Adams and others have tested hypotheses such as these, but reviews of this research agree that the empirical studies have produced a mixture of supporting and disconfirming studies (Gordon, 1991; Miner, 1980; and Pinder, 1984). The hypotheses about overpayment tend to receive support, but not other hypotheses. The research that successfully supports the hypotheses about overpayment has usually taken place in laboratory settings, in experiments with college students working under clearly defined pay systems for clearly defined tasks. Occasional studies outside the laboratory setting have, for example, examined baseball players' performances after pay changes with inconclusive results (Locke and Henne, 1986).

Critiques of the theory and research typically point out that most of the research consists of laboratory experiments using pay, thus leaving questions about implications for nonlaboratory settings and rewards other than pay. This also reflects the problem that formulations and tests of the theory have not taken into account many factors, such as individual differences and how individuals choose referents. As a result, some of the most recent efforts to extend the theory point out that individuals may vary in sensitivity to inequity and preferences concerning its levels (Huseman, Hatfield, and Miles, 1987). More important, equity theory has trouble overcoming problems cited in a critique by Weick (1966) years ago, which pointed out that the theory leaves a lot of ambiguities in its concepts and predictions. Important issues such as which of the various inputs and outcomes a person will focus on, how a person will respond to inequity, and how a person chooses and maintains referents, have never been well clarified through hypotheses and tests. This explains why Miner (1980) observed that although personnel managers and others have been concerned with equity issues for a long time, Adams's equity theory has apparently led to no applications in industry.

As with previous theories, however, even pending the success of this specific formulation, equity researchers deal with a crucial issue in organizations. Equitable treatment obviously figures significantly in organizations as an influence on many members. As comparable worth and racial and ethnic diversity have become more important issues in organization and management, the issue looms even larger.

B. Process Theories

Another group of theories concentrates more on the psychological and behavioral processes in motivation than on attempting to specify the major needs and values that influence motivation. This dichotomy is somewhat procrustean, in that all the theories to some extent deal with both content and process. What we here call process theories place relative emphasis on how various goals, values, needs, or rewards—often not specified in the theory itself—operate with other factors to determine motivation.

1. Expectancy Theory

For some years the expectancy theory of work motivation in various formulations elicited about as much optimism as any of the theories. Researchers appeared to hope that this departure would provide a fairly well-elaborated theory with predictive capacity. Although such matters are difficult to assess, the theory may well continue to be the most prominent and well-regarded among motivation researchers. Even so, it has taken its full share of criticism. Expectancy theory draws on the classic observation, attributable to various psychologists and philosophers in the past, that humans seek to do what they think is most likely to maximize desirable results and to minimize bad results. Yet those developing the theory sought to refine this point in ways that would aid clarification and analysis of work motivation. Table 3 illustrates an early formulation of this theory in the literature of organizational psychology by Vroom (1964), as well as a more recent version of the theory reflecting revisions caused by criticisms of Vroom's use of mathematical assumptions and symbols.

The mathematical formula provides a shorthand or symbolic expression of some of the intricacies that elaborate the classic observation mentioned above. It posits that an individual will be more strongly motivated to engage in a behavior as he or she perceives stronger probabilities ("expectancies") that the behavior will lead to valued outcomes and avoid bad ones. Vroom used the term *valence* to refer to the values of outcomes. Valences can be positive or negative, as in the case of positively and negatively valent atomic particles. Valence connotes both attraction (when positive) and repulsion (when negative), thus, the outcomes of the behavior are conceived as having positive or negative scores or assessments in the perception of the individual.

In effect, the formula posits that an individual will consider the outcomes that will result from the behavior and assign a probability to each outcome—the expectancy that it will result from the behavior. Then the individual will multiply, or weight, each of these probabilities by its positive or negative valence, and sum up the products of all these multiplications (i.e., the algebraic sum). So, if the person feels that the behavior has a high probability of leading to a very good outcome, this will mean the multiplication of a high expectancy times a high positive valence; the product will be a high positive addition to the sum of all the expectancy-times-valence products. If the person also senses a high probability of another outcome, but a very negatively valent one, this will lead to a very negative product when the two are multipled. This negative product is then subtracted from the high positive product for the outcome described above (i.e., the algebraic sum of the products is taken).

In other words, if a behavior is very likely to lead to some very desirable results (more pay, more interesting work), but also very likely to lead to some undesirable results (more overtime work, more stress), one's motivation to engage in the behavior will depend on just how desirable or undesirable one considers the results, and one's sense of the likelihood of each result. Following the implications of the formula, if the probabilities of the bad outcomes are low, the negative scores in the summation go down. If the probabilities of the good results go up, the positive scores in the summation go up. The theory, then, conceives of motivation as

Table 3 Formulations of Expectancy Theory

A Formulation Similar to Vroom's Early Version:

$$F_i = \Sigma \ (E_{ij} \times V_j)$$

where
  F = the force acting on an individual to perform act i
  E = the expectancy, or perceived probability, that act i will lead to outcome j
  V = the valence of outcome j

and

$$V_j = \Sigma \ (V_k \times I_{jk})$$

where
  V = the valence of outcome
  I = the instrumentality of outcome j for the attainment of outcome k

A Formulation Similar to Various Revised Formulations:

Motivation $= f[E \ I \times E \ II(V)] = f[(E \rightarrow P) \times [(P \rightarrow O)(V)]]$

where
  E I = $(E \rightarrow P)$ = expectancy I, the perceived probability that a given level of work effort will result in a given level of performance
  E II = $(P \rightarrow O)$ = expectancy II, the perceived probability that the level of performance will lead to attainment of outcome j
  V   = the valence of outcome j

involving this joint consideration of outcomes, their probabilities, and their positive or negative values.

The theory appeared to offer an advancement in conceiving and analyzing motivation. One could hope to apply it by asking employees to express their perceptions about the probabilities of outcomes from important work behaviors, express their positive or negative valuations of those outcomes, and develop a score for each employee indicating that person's motivation. In addition, influences on that level of motivation could be examined by looking at the expressed probabilities and valences of various outcomes. There rapidly followed a number of studies applying and testing the theories, reporting some early apparent successes and inducing optimism (Heneman and Schwab, 1972).

Also fairly rapidly, however, problems in applying and validating the theory mounted, along with questions and criticisms. Many contributed to this elaborate discussion, and their numerous points do not summarize easily (Behling, Shriesheim, and Tolliver, 1973; Campbell and Pritchard, 1983; Connolly, 1976; Miner, 1980; and Pinder, 1984).

Researchers found the component constructs hard to clearly define and operationalize. One has trouble identifying and expressing all the relevant "outcomes" sought by the different people in an organization, as well as measuring with questionnaires or other means their perceived probabilities and their positive and negative values. A researcher might try to get employees to rate the expectancy of getting each of a standard set of rewards (such as "a pay raise") on a numerical scale, and then rate the valence of that reward on another scale (say, from +5 to −5), and then multiply the ratings together and sum the products. These proved to be rather cumbersome and imprecise ways of measuring the constructs. Often the summated score would not correlate very highly with other measures of motivation, effort, or work satisfaction. Some studies found one of the components, such as expectancies, to be a stronger predictor than the full model (Behling, Schriescheim, and Tolliver, 1973; Connolly, 1976).

Other theorists pointed to dubious postulates of the theory. The theory posits that people perform extensive and complex mathematics in their heads in a highly rational pattern. Critics pointed out that our minds do not work that way, especially in complex situations involving uncertainty and so many criteria that such calculative faculties would be overloaded (Behling, Schriescheim, and Tolliver, 1973). Defenders of the theory responded that the theory was simply a model generally approximating the mental processes leading to motivation, and did not require strict application of all mathematical postulates to have value. For example, people may do some rough unconscious calculations of this sort for a small set of salient outcomes (Campbell and Pritchard, 1983). Still, critics effectively attacked the mathematical form of the model, pointing out that multiplying E and V together required the assumption that they were independent quantities. Yet we know that our expectations about obtaining rewards can influence the values we attach to those rewards. Prestige products that seek to gain allure from their high prices illustrate this point. So do "sour grapes" responses in which persons say they do not want something because they cannot have it.

All these problems soon deflated any dramatic hopes for the theory, and theorists set about developing revised versions, such as the one in Table 3. The later versions typically removed mathematical procedures such as multiplying E's and V's (Campbell and Pritchard, 1983; and Pinder, 1984). They tend to state the theory as a general conceptual framework without clear postulates as to how the component constructs are supposed to be combined. Newer formulations also distinguish between expectancy I (E I), the probability that effort will lead to performance, and expectancy II (E II), the probability that the level of performance will lead to valent outcomes. The more recent versions also add other variables to the framework, such as task clarity and self-esteem, which can influence E I, and organizational evaluation and compensation procedures, which can influence E II.

For all the discussion of their limitations, expectancy theory constructs have served as a foundation for a prominent theory of leadership—the path-goal theory. Many studies have found that versions of expectancy theory predict self-reported effort fairly well, especially when valences and expectancies are also self-reported (Klein, 1990). Theorists attempting to further develop motivation theories typically employ expectancy theory concepts (Klein, 1989; 1990; and Evans, 1986).

Expectancy models also can be helpful in analyzing motivational issues. For example, in some cases organizations have attempted pay-for-performance schemes for middle managers, only to encounter problems when most of the managers got high evaluations, but there was too little money for raises. Only a very small proportion of the managers got a significant raise (high E I, but low E II). In another case, salesmen complained about an incentive system in a major corporation, because the very high performers got large bonuses, and the vast majority felt that they could never get one (high E II, but low E I). The corporation reformed the system to equalize pay. Analyzing such systems using the more recent versions of expectancy theory, in terms of E I and E II and their determinants, appears to be a useful way to try to foresee such problems (Rainey, 1991: 137).

In addition, researchers on expectancy theory developed questionnaire items about reward expectancies that are frequently used in research and organizational assessments. For example, they have been included in very large surveys of federal employees (U.S. Office of Personnel Management, 1983). These items ask employees or managers for their level of agreement with statements such as these: I will get a pay raise if I do high-quality work. If I perform well, I will increase my chances for a promotion. (See also the intrinsic motivation items in Table 1.) Regardless of controversies over the adequacy of expectancy theory as a general theory of motivation, many researchers and managers consider such perceptions about reward expectancies very important.

While research on expectancy theory has attenuated, it still receives attention in texts as one of the best versions of a motivation theory (e.g., Pinder, 1984; Gordon, 1991). As noted above, recent efforts to advance motivation theory incorporate expectancy theory concepts. The theory clearly covers important dimensions of work motivation.

2.   Operant Conditioning Theory and Behavior Modification

Theorists have also drawn on operant conditioning theory as a basis for analysis of work motivation. Operant theory derives from what psychologists have called the "behaviorist" school in psychology, of which B. F. Skinner served as one of the most prominent members. Behaviorism gained its label because of the emphasis of its proponents on the observation of the overt behaviors of animals and humans, without hypothesizing what goes on inside them. This reflects a classic debate in psychology, in which some of the theorists argued that motivation and learning theories should include hypothetical constructs referring to what goes on within the organism. For example, some of them employed the concept of "incentive" to refer to the internal cognition that corresponds to an external attraction, such as the incentive within a rat to learn to negotiate a maze, in the form of some cognitive vision or depiction of the reward at the end of the maze.

Behaviorists such as Skinner rejected the use of such internal constructs, arguing that one cannot observe them scientifically and that they add only confusing speculation to the analysis of motivation. Skinner argued that one can scientifically analyze only overtly observable behaviors. He and other behaviorists recognized the existence of thought, emotion, and other internal states, but regarded such states as products of the external forces—reinforcements and punishments—that shape behavior. (Actually, behaviorists vary in the degree to which they include references to cognition in their theories. Especially in recent years, psychologists have worked toward a reconciliation of operant behaviorism with cognitive concepts. See Kreitner and Luthans, 1987; and Bandura, 1978.)

Skinner and other researchers developed numerous concepts and observations about how external conditions influence animals in learning and acquiring behaviors. Skinner studied the contingencies of reinforcement, the conditions that cause behaviors to be reinforced. In this terminology, a reinforcement is any condition that increases the probability of occurrence of a behavior. A pigeon pecks a light bulb when it comes on, and we give it a pellet of food, and it shows an increased tendency to peck the light bulb when it comes on. We have reinforced the behavior. The terms and the example are significant. Many of us would use such terms as learning and reward in this instance, but the behaviorists' terminology is cleansed of the cognitive implications of such terms (Skinner, 1953: 64). All we can infer is that the behavior increased, not that the pigeon learned something or experienced some inner sense of reward. Also, this example shows that this body of theory developed out of research on laboratory animals, a detail that feeds later criticisms of the approach as manipulative and applicable mainly to simplified situations unlike those common in complex organizations.

The term *operant conditioning* stems from a revision Skinner and others made in older versions of stimulus-response psychology. Skinner (1953: 65) pointed out that we animals do not develop behaviors simply in response to stimuli. We emit behaviors as well, and our behaviors operate on our environments, generating consequences. We repeat or drop the behaviors depending on the consequences. We acquire behaviors or extinguish them in response to the conditions or contingencies of reinforcement.

Skinner and others carefully studied how contingencies of reinforcement influence acquisition and extinction of behaviors. They pointed out, for example, that one can train a pigeon to turn in a circle when a light comes on, first by reinforcing the behavior of turning slightly when the light comes on. The pigeon will acquire that behavior, and one can then reinforce a larger turn, and so on until the pigeon is turning full circle when the light comes on. This interest in shaping behaviors provided the foundations for later developments in *behavior modification* techniques in therapeutic, educational, and managerial applications.

The operant conditioning theorists developed concepts and principles that influenced later efforts to apply this type of theory in management. They distinguished between types of reinforcement. *Positive reinforcement* applies a stimulus that increases the behavior on which it is made contingent. We receive payment for taking an action, and our tendency to take that action increases. *Negative reinforcement* increases the behavior on which it is made contingent through removal of the stimulus or condition. We find that a bright light in our eyes or a very loud noise is removed when we take an action, so the probability that we will take that action increases when we encounter the stimulus again. Both types of reinforcement increase contingent behaviors. Reinforcing properties of a stimulus can extend or generalize to other stimuli. Primary reinforcers such as food play a role in the development of secondary reinforcers such as pay, which develop their reinforcing properties through association with the primary reinforcers. For example, a very young child shows little more attraction to paper money than to other scraps of paper until its connection to food and other reinforcements is established.

Operant extinction decreases a behavior through removal of a reinforcement that had been contingent on it. We have trained a pigeon to turn in a circle when a light comes on, and we stop feeding it when it does so, and eventually it stops responding to the light. *Punishment* is one means of attempting extinction, and Skinner defined punishment as removal of a positive reinforcer or application of a negative reinforcement (Skinner, 1953: 185). Yet this definition does not distinguish between punishment and negative reinforcement, and Skinner found himself having to refer to the "aversive" nature of the stimuli used in punishment (p. 186). Thus, in spite of his rejection of references to internal states in animals and humans, he came close to having made some assumptions about needs and values within the organism.

Operant theorists also distinguish between various patterns of reinforcement. One can apply reinforcements on a fixed or variable schedule, and a ratio or interval schedule (Skinner, 1953; Pinder, 1984: 193; and Gordon, 1991: 153). A *fixed schedule* applies the reinforcement on a regular basis, after a fixed period of time, or a fixed number of repetitions of the behavior. A *variable schedule* varies the time period or number of repetitions. A *ratio schedule* applies reinforcements according to a designated ratio of reinforcements to responses, such as once for every five repetitions. An *interval schedule* applies reinforcement after a designated time interval. The categories can be combined. A fixed-interval schedule reinforces after a fixed period of time—a weekly paycheck. A variable-interval schedule follows a variable period of time—a bonus every so often. A fixed-ratio schedule reinforces a fixed proportion of responses, as in piece-rate pay scales that pay a certain amount for a certain number of units produced. A variable-ratio schedule reinforces after a varying number of responses, as in praise from a supervisor for a particular behavior, which the supervisor gives after varying numbers of repetitions.

In their research, operant conditioning theorists developed principles concerning reinforcement, some of which help clarify a number of motivational issues and have interesting implications. For example, they typically point out that positive reinforcement provides the most efficient means of influencing behavior. They typically take a very negative view of punishment as less efficient and effective in shaping behavior (Skinner, 1953: 182ff). They point out that a behavior is acquired most rapidly through a low, fixed-ratio reinforcement schedule—a reinforcement after each occurrence of the behavior, for example, or after every other occurrence. Yet a behavior reinforced with that schedule will extinguish more rapidly once reinforcement terminates.

Intermittent schedules, such as a high-variable interval or variable-ratio schedule (reinforcing after long, varying periods or after many responses on a varying ratio) require more time for acquisition of the behavior, but extinction occurs more slowly when the reinforcements cease. This leads some behavior modification proponents (Luthans and Kreitner, 1985; Kreitner and Luthans, 1987) to prescribe such managerial techniques as *not* praising a desired behavior constantly, but on a varying basis after a number of repetitions. They might also prescribe a periodic bonus program to supplement a weekly paycheck, on the argument that the regular check will lose its reinforcing properties over time, while the bonus program will act as a variable-interval reinforcement procedure, thus strengthening the probability of sustained long-term effort. They also have useful suggestions about incremental shaping of behaviors by reinforcing successively larger portions of a desired behavior—as with the circling pigeon described earlier. Operant theorists have described successful correction of various problem behaviors through such procedures as the correction of anorexic behaviors through reinforcement of incremental steps toward eating (Bandura, 1969; Sherman, 1990).

a. Organizational Behavior Modification.   These kinds of prescriptions provide examples of those offered by practitioners of organizational behavior modification (hereafter, OB Mod), which applies versions of operant conditioning theory in organizations. Actually, many people have used the term behavior modification in a variety of ways that often range quite afield from behaviorist psychology and operant conditioning theory. Most motivation theorists, however, regard OB Mod as the effort to apply principles from operant conditioning theory in organizations.

Organizational behavior modification often involves approaches such as these: measuring and recording desirable and undesirable behaviors to establish baselines, determining the antecedents and consequences of the behaviors, determining a strategy for using reinforcements and punishments—such as praise and pay increases—to apply to the behaviors, applying them with some of the considerations of scheduling them mentioned above, and assessing behavioral change. A number of field studies of such projects have reported successes in improving employee performance, attendance, and safety procedures (Pinder, 1984). A highly successful effort by Emery Air Freight, for example, received much attention (Kreitner and Luthans, 1987; Dowling, 1973). That project involved having employees monitor their own performance, setting performance goals, and using feedback and positive reinforcements such as praise and time off.

Yet controversy over explanations of the success of this project reflect more general controversies about OB Mod. Critics have argued that the Emery example, as well as other applications of OB Mod, do not succeed because they apply operant conditioning principles, but because they involve such steps as setting clear performance goals and making rewards contingent upon them (Locke, 1977). These are valuable steps, but they hardly offer any distinctive or original insights deriving from operant conditioning theory. More generally, while one can point to ways in which operant conditioning theory would lead to different hypotheses and prescriptions from expectancy theory, in practice and research they often lead to very similar hypotheses and procedures. Other criticisms of operant theory and OB Mod focus on the questionable ethics of the emphasis on manipulation and control of people, its apparent applicability mainly to relatively simplified conditions amenable to relatively clear measurement, and even then the practical difficulties of all the measuring and reinforcement scheduling required.

For their part, proponents of OB Mod point to the successful applications, of course. Advocates of operant conditioning theory counterattack on the ethical implications of their approach by arguing that they cut through a lot of obfuscating fluff about values and internal states and move right to the issue of correcting bad behaviors and augmenting good ones. Do you want smokers to be able to stop, anorexics to eat, or workers to follow safety precautions, or do you not? Similarly, OB Mod advocates claim that their approach succeeds in developing a focus on desired behaviors (getting Joe to come to work on time), as opposed to attributions about attitudes ("Joe has a bad attitude"), and an emphasis on strategies for positive reinforcement of the desired behaviors (Kreitner and Luthans, 1987).

b. Social Learning Theory Revisions of OB Mod.   Also reflecting the limitations of operant conditioning theory and OB Mod are some recent efforts to revise those theories in light of social learning theory (Bandura, 1978). Social learning theory represents a blending of operant conditioning theory with more recognition of internal cognitive processes. It gives attention to forms of learning and behavioral change that are not tied tightly to some external reinforcement.

For example, individuals obviously learn by modeling their behaviors on those of others and through vicarious experiences. If one sees another person burned by a hot object, one does not need to touch the object to know to avoid it. Humans also engage in anticipation, mental rehearsal and imagery, and self-rewarding behaviors (praising oneself). Applications of such processes to organizational settings have mainly involved the development of frameworks and prescriptions for leadership and self-improvement, with a few studies suggesting that the sorts of techniques mentioned above can improve performance (Luthans and Kreitner, 1985; Manz and Neck, 1991).

While interesting and apparently useful to developing leadership and motivation in organizations, these extensions are unlikely to satisfy the critics of OB Mod (Locke and Henne, 1986). On balance, operant conditioning theory and OB Mod appear to represent a minority position among work motivation theorists, with most theorists not convinced of their value for theory development, but with a fairly impressive number of reports of successful applications in organizations (Pinder, 1984).

3. Goal-Setting Theory

Edwin Locke and his colleagues have advanced a theory of goal setting that reviewers acknowledge as the most successful work motivation theory in gaining validation through well-designed research (Pinder, 1984; Miner, 1980). Relatively simple, the theory (Locke and Latham, 1990a; Locke and Henne, 1986: 17–20) holds that difficult specific goals lead to higher task performance than easy and/or vague goals or no goals (e.g., "do your best"). Difficult goals enhance performance by directing attention and action, mobilizing effort, increasing persistence, and by motivating the search for effective performance strategies. Commitment to the goals, and feedback about performance against the goals, are also necessary for higher performance, but do not in themselves stimulate it without difficult specific goals. Research findings also indicate that participation in goal setting does not enhance commitment to the goal, but commitment increases with the expectancy of success in attaining the goal, as well as in the value of the goal. Also, money may lead to the setting of higher goals and higher goal commitment, and individual differences do show strong relations to the effectiveness of goal setting.

Locke and Latham (1990a) contend that assigning difficult specific goals enhanced performance by way of the goals' influence on an individual's personal goals and his or her self-efficacy. Self-efficacy refers to a person's sense of capability or efficacy in accomplishing outcomes (Bandura, 1989). Assigned goals influence personal goals through a person's acceptance of and commitment to them. They influence self-efficacy by providing a sense of purpose and standards for evaluating performance, and they create opportunities for accomplishing lesser and proximal goals that build a sense of efficacy. Earley and Lituchy (1991) report evidence supporting this explanation.

Many studies support the basic tenets of the theory about the enhancement of task performance through difficult specific goals. Locke and Henne (1986) argue that occasional disconfirmations are all explainable by reference to artifacts of the research designs or other interpretations. Other reviewers mount few criticisms of the theory. One reason for the success of the theory, however, may be its compactness and relatively narrow focus (Pinder, 1984). The theory and research concentrate on task performance, a very important issue, and offer very useful conclusions about enhancing it. The research tends to concentrate on relatively clear and simple task settings, amenable to the setting of specific goals, yet some of the prominent contributions to organization theory in recent decades, such as contingency theory and garbage can models of decision making, have concerned those settings in which clear, explicit goals are quite difficult to specify. The implication of these contributions is that in many of the most important settings, such as high-level strategy development teams, clear, specific goals may be impossible or dysfunctional. For example, might a specific difficult set of goals in a complex task setting drive attention away from important goals not included in the goal set?

Relatedly, important issues surround what might be called *goal validity*. The goals may be specific and difficult, but what if they are not valid indicators of what ought to be accomplished? Some writers on public administration and public policy assert that too often goal clarification in public bureaucracies leads to specification of procedural goals rather than valid impact goals. For example, one might state the goal of having a record of the client intake interview in the file within 1 hour after the interview rather than a goal pertaining to improvement of the client's quality of life. Some of the research on goal setting does focus on relatively complex task settings (Locke and Latham, 1990a), but further clarification of the domain of applicability of the theory would be very valuable. In the meantime, the value of specific difficult goals for work tasks seems well established.

C. Recent Theoretical Forays: Integration and Separation

This issue of domain of applicability, together with the obvious balkanization of motivation theory into the separate theories just reviewed, brings us to the recent considerations of where motivation theory should go from here. Reviewers tend to agree that motivation theory is in a disorderly state (Landy and Becker, 1987), although they disagree in their level of optimism about the amount we have learned about motivation (Katzell and Thompson, 1990; Pinder, 1984: 306). Recent proposals and initiatives for the further development of motivation theory emphasize either the integration of existing theories, or the separateness of theories while recognizing how each theory is useful, or some degree of both.

Those emphasizing separateness call for the development of middle-range theories to apply to different settings or dependent variables. Pinder (1984) argues that the effort to develop and evaluate the existing motivation theories as general, universal theories is fruitless. He proposes the development of a typology of motivational settings (the motivational attributes of a work setting), combined with a typology of motivational types (the motivation-related attributes of individuals in a work group). He suggests development of middle-range theories for application within such setting/type categories. Apparently, he intends that these new theories would draw on existing theories. Somewhat similarly, Landy and Becker (1987) reject the quest for universal theory and contend that the existing theories should be treated as middle-range theories, applicable to different combinations from a set of dependent variables (choice, effort, satisfaction, performance, and withdrawal). They also call for some integration of theories that apply to similar sets of these variables.

Others concentrate more on such integration, with varying levels of comprehensiveness. Katzell and Thompson (1990) report an effort to develop a framework integrating all the existing theories. Both Klein (1989) and Evans (1986) propose models of motivation that integrate elements of expectancy and goal-setting theory, with elements of other psychological theories, such as control and attribution theory. Similarly, there has been a good deal of attention to the integration of goal-setting theory and expectancy theory (Landy and Becker, 1987; Locke and Henne, 1986; and Locke and Latham, 1990a). Klein (1990) proposes a feasibility theory of motivation, which emphasizes the availability of resources for task performance, bringing in need theory and drawing on expectancy theory. These recent integrative models have not yet been subject to empirical testing, and obviously some of them attempt to integrate only parts of the body of motivation theory.

Probably because of the success of goal-setting theory, there appears to be a particularly strong trend toward inclusion and analysis of goal concepts in theories, and to integrate these and other cognitive concepts such as those from the social learning theory approach described earlier (Bandura, 1989; Pervin, 1989; Locke and Latham, 1990 a, b; and Tubbs and Ekeberg, 1991).

These recent attempts to assess the distinct attributes of motivation theories or to partially integrate different theories provide reasonable prospects for progress in the development of fairly distinct middle-range theories. These newer theoretical efforts will require further integration of some of the extant theories into middle-range theories. For the time being, however, motivation theory remains a set of interesting, useful, but partial efforts to apprehend a body of phenomena too complex for any single theory yet too capture.

III. MOTIVATION PRACTICE AND TECHNIQUES

As mentioned at the outset, in spite of the travails of the theorists, organization requires motivated members, and one finds in organizations numerous approaches to the problem. In addition to some of the procedures described in earlier sections, Table 4 provides a description of many of the general techniques, several of which have a large literature devoted to them. As with other dimensions of management and organization, real-world practice often reflects theory only loosely, and places highest priority on pragmatism. Far from making theory and expert knowledge irrelevant, however, the practices of organizations often justify the apparently

Table 4 Methods Commonly Used to Enhance Work Motivation in Organizations

---

- *Improved performance appraisal systems.* Reforms involving the use of group-based appraisals (ratings for a work group rather than an individual), appraisals by a member's peers, and other approaches mentioned below.
- *Merit pay and pay-for-performance systems.* A wide variety of procedures for linking a person's pay to performance (Lawler, 1990).
- *Bonus and award systems.* Offer one-time awards for instances of excellent performance or other achievements.
- *Profit sharing and gain-sharing plans.* Involve sharing profits with members of the organization, usually possible only in business organizations, for obvious reasons. Employee stock ownership plans are roughly similar as a means of rewarding employees when the organization does well.
- *Management by objectives and other performance-targeting procedures.* Organizations of all types have tried MBO programs, which involve evaluating people on the basis of stated work objectives. Superiors work with subordinates on developing objectives for their work, thus enhancing communication. That person's performance appraisal then concentrates on those objectives. This focuses the person's attention on the most important outcomes of work, gives the person more say in what he or she does, and enhances decentralization and autonomy, since agreement on the objectives provides a basis for allowing the person to go ahead and work his or her way, rather than through constant directions by the boss. The most elaborate MBO programs involve mapping broad organizational objectives down through more specific objectives at the different levels of the organization. Organizations also use a wide variety of "performance-targeting" procedures emphasizing productivity or performance targets for groups.
- *Participative management and decision making.* Involve a sustained commitment to engage in more communication and sharing of decisions through teams, committees, task forces, general meetings, open door policies, and one-to-one exchanges.
- *Work enhancement: job redesign, job enlargement, and rotation.* Usage varies, but job redesign usually means changing jobs to enhance control and interest for the people doing the work. Job enlargement, or "horizontal loading," involves giving a person more different tasks and responsibilities at the same skill level. Job restructuring or "vertical loading" involves giving a person more influence over decisions normally made by superiors, such as work scheduling, or more generally to enlarge the employee's sense of responsibility by giving them control of a more complete unit of work output (work teams that build an entire car as a team, or case workers who handle all needs of a client). These approaches may involve job sharing and rotation among workers, and various team-based approaches.
- *Quality of work life (QWL) programs and quality circles (QCs).* Organizations of all types have tried QWL programs, which typically involve efforts to enhance the general working environment of an organization through representative committees, surveys and studies, and other procedures improving the work environment. Quality circles, used successfully in Japanese companies, are teams that focus more directly on improving the quality of work processes and products.
- *Organizational development interventions.* Organizational development (OD), employed widely in the public and private sectors, applies behavioral science techniques to improving communication, conflict resolution, and trust.

---

obvious advice of the theorists and experts, since organizations typically have trouble achieving desirable motivational strategies (Kerr, 1989). For example, surveys find that fewer than one-third of employees in organizations feel that their pay is based on performance (Katzell and Thompson, 1990). For these reasons, just as theorists will go on seeking ways to unravel the complexities of work motivation, members of organizations will go on trying to find ways to enhance it in their work settings.

REFERENCES

Adams, J. S. (1963). Towards an understanding of inequity. *J. of Abnormal and Social Psychology*, 67:422–436.

Adams, J. S. (1965). Inequity in social exchange. In *Advances in Experimental Social Psychology*, vol. 2 (L. Berkowitz, ed.), Academic Press, New York, pp. 267–299.

Atkinson, J. W., and Raynor, J. O. (1974). *Motivation and Achievement.* Winston, Washington, D.C.

Bandura, A. (1969). *Principles of Behavior Modification.* Holt, Rinehart, and Winston, New York.

Bandura, A. (1978). *Social Learning Theory.* Prentice-Hall, Englewood Cliffs, N.J.

Bandura, A. (1989). Self-regulation of motivation and action through internal standards and goal systems. In *Goal Concepts in Personality and Social Psychology* (L. A. Pervin, ed.), Lawrence Erlbaum Associates, Hillsdale, N.J., pp. 19–86.

Bass, B. M. (1985). *Leadership and Performance Beyond Expectations.* Free Press, New York.

Behling, O., Schriesheim, C., and Tolliver, J. (1973). *Present Trends and New Directions in Theories of Work Effort.* Journal Supplement Abstract Service of the American Psychological Association.

Bennis, W., and Nanus, B. (1985). *Leaders: The Strategies for Taking Charge.* Harper and Row, New York.

Block, P. (1987). *The Empowered Manager.* Jossey-Bass, San Francisco.

Burns, J. M. (1978). *Leadership.* Harper and Row, New York.

Campbell, J. P., and Pritchard, R. D. (1983). Motivation theory in industrial and organizational psychology. In *Handbook of Industrial and Organizational Psychology* (M. D. Dunnette, ed.), Wiley, New York.

Connolly, T. (1976). Conceptual and methodological issues in expectancy models of work performance motivation. *Academy of Management Review, 1:*37–47.

Cook, J. D., Hepworth, S. J., Wall, T. D., Warr, P. B. (1981). *The Experience of Work.* Academic Press, London.

Dowling, W. F. (1973). At Emery Air Freight: Positive reinforcement boosts performance. *Organizational Dynamics, 2:*41–50.

Earley, P. C., and Lituchy, T. R. (1991). Delineating goal and efficacy effects: A test of three models. *J. of Applied Psychology, 76:*81–98.

Evans, M. G. (1986). Organizational behavior: The central role of motivation. In *Yearly Review of Management* (J. G. Hunt and J. D. Blair, eds.), *J. of Management, 12:*203–222.

Golembiewski, R. T. (1985). *Humanizing Public Organizations.* Lomond, Mount Airy, Md.

Golembiewski, R. T. (1989). *Men, Management, & Morality.* Transaction, New Brunswick, N.J.

Gordon, J. R. (1991). *Organizational Behavior.* Allyn and Bacon, Boston.

Guion, R. M., and Landy, F. J. (1972). The meaning of work and the motivation to work. *Organizational Behavior and Human Performance,* 7:308–339.

Heneman, H. G., and Schwab, D. P. (1972). Evaluation of research on expectancy theory predictions of employee performance, *Psychological Bulletin,* 78:1–9.

Herzberg, F. (1968). One more time: How do you motivate employees? *Harvard Business Review,* 46:36–44.

Huseman, R. C., Hatfield, J. D., and Miles, E. W. (1987). A new perspective on equity theory: The equity sensitivity construct. *Academy of Management Review, 12:*232–234.

Katzell, R. A., and Thompson, D. E. (1990). Work motivation: Theory and practice. *American Psychologist, 45:*144–153.

Kerr, S. (1989). On the folly of rewarding A, while hoping for B. In *Classic Readings in Organizational Behavior* (J. S. Ott, ed.), Brooks/Cole, Pacific Grove, Calif., pp. 114–126.

Klein, H. J. (1989). An integrated control theory model of work motivation. *Academy of Management Review, 14:*150–172.

Klein, J. I. (1990). Feasibility theory: A resource-munificence model of work motivation and behavior. *Academy of Management Review, 15:*646–665.

Kleinbeck, U., Quast, H. H., Thierry, H., and Hartmut, H., eds. (1990). *Work Motivation.* Lawrence Erlbaum Associates, Hillsdale, N.J.

Kleinginna, P. R., and Kleinginna, A. M. (1981). A categorized list of motivation definitions with a suggestion for a consensual definition. *Motivation and Emotion,* 5:263–292.

Kreitner, R., and Luthans, F. (1987). A social learning approach to behavioral management: Radical behaviorists "mellowing out." In *Organizational Behavior* (J. Gordon, ed.), Allyn and Bacon, Boston, pp. 59–72.

Landy, Frank J., and Becker, Wendy S. (1987). Motivation theory reconsidered. In *Research in Organizational Behavior,* vol. 9 (L. L. Cummings and B. M. Staw, eds.), JAI Press, Greenwich, Conn., pp. 1–38.

Landy, F. J., and Guion, R. M. (1970). Development of scales for the measurement of work motivation. *Organizational Behavior and Human Performance,* 5:93–103.

Lawler, E. E. (1971). *Pay and Organizational Effectiveness.* McGraw-Hill, New York.

Lawler, E. E. (1973). *Motivation in Work Organizations.* Brooks/Cole, Pacific Grove, Calif.

Lawler, E. E. (1990). *Strategic Pay.* Jossey-Bass, San Francisco.

Locke, E. A. (1977). The myth of behavior modification in organizations. *Academy of Management Review,* 2:543–553.

Locke, E. A., and Henne, D. (1986). Work motivation theories. In *International Review of Industrial and Organizational Psychology* (C. L. Cooper and I. Robertson, eds.), John Wiley and Sons, New York, pp. 1–35.

Locke, E. A., and Latham, G. P. (1990a). *A Theory of Goal Setting and Task Performance.* Prentice-Hall, Englewood Cliffs, N.J.

Locke, E. A., and Latham, G. P. (1990b). Work motivation: The high performance cycle. In *Work Motivation* (U. Kleinbeck et al., eds.), Lawrence Erlbaum Associates, Hillsdale, N.J., pp. 3–26.

Luthans, F., and Kreitner, R. (1985). *Organizational Behavior Modification: An Operant and Social Learning Approach.* Scott, Foresman, Glenview, Ill.

Manz, C. C., and Neck, C. P. (1991). Inner leadership: Creating productive thought patterns. *Academy of Management Executive,* V:87–95.

Maslow, A. H. (1954). *Motivation and Personality.* Harper and Row, New York.

Maslow, A. H. (1965). *Eupsychian Management.* Richard D. Irwin, Homewood, Ill.

McClelland, D. C. (1961). *The Achieving Society.* The Free Press, New York.

McClelland, D. C. (1975). *Power: The Inner Experience.* Irvington, New York.

McClelland, D. C., and Winter, D. G. (1969). *Motivating Economic Achievement.* The Free Press, New York.

McGregor, D. (1960). *The Human Side of Enterprise.* McGraw-Hill, New York.

Miner, J. B., (1980). *Theories of Organizational Behavior.* Dryden Press, Hinsdale, Ill.

Patchen, M., Pelz, D., and Allen, C. (1965). *Some Questionnaire Measures of Employee Motivation and Morale.* Institute for Social Research, Ann Arbor, Michigan.

Pervin, L. A., ed. (1989). *Goal Concepts in Personality and Social Psychology.* Lawrence Erlbaum Associates, Hillsdale, N.J.

Peters, T. J., and Waterman, R. H. (1982). *In Search of Excellence.* Harper and Row, New York.

Pinder, C. C. (1984). *Work Motivation.* Scott, Foresman, Glenview, Ill.

Rainey, H. G. (1983). Public agencies and private firms: Incentive structures, goals, and individual roles. *Administration and Society,* 15:207–242.

Rainey, H. G. (1991). *Understanding and Managing Public Organizations.* Jossey-Bass, San Francisco.

Sherman, W. M. (1990). *Behavior Modification.* Harper and Row, New York.

Skinner, B. F. (1953). *Science and Human Behavior.* Macmillan, New York.

Steers, R. M., and Porter, L. M., eds. (1987). *Motivation and Work Behavior.* McGraw-Hill, New York.

Tubbs, M. E., and Ekeberg, S. E. (1991). The role of intentions in work motivation: Implications for goal-setting theory and research. *Academy of Management Review,* 16:180–199.

U.S. Office of Personnel Management (1979). *Federal Employee Attitudes, Phase I.* U.S. Office of Personnel Management, Washington D.C.

U.S. Office of Personnel Management (1980). *Federal Employee Attitudes, Phase II.* U.S. Office of Personnel Management, Washington D.C.

Vroom, V. H. (1964). *Work and Motivation.* Wiley, New York.

Warwick, Donald P. (1975). *A Theory of Public Bureaucracy.* Harvard University Press, Cambridge, Mass.

Weick, K. E. (1966). The concept of equity in the perception of pay. *Administrative Science Quarterly,* 11:414–439.

Williamson, O. E., ed. (1990). *Organization Theory: From Chester Barnard to the Present and Beyond.* Oxford University Press, New York.

3

Stress and Burnout in the Workplace
Conservation of Resources

Stevan E. Hobfoll

Kent State University, Kent, Ohio

Arie Shirom

Tel Aviv University, Tel Aviv, Israel

Stress and the resultant sequelae of stress are critical factors in the workplace. Stress is responsible for billions of dollars of lost income, is a major factor in lost workdays, and affects the quality of performance more profoundly than even these losses can communicate. Kearns (1986) estimates that 60% of absence from work is the result of stress-related disorders. Just replacing men below retirement age who have been incapacitated from coronary heart diseases has been calculated to cost some $700 million dollars annually (Cooper, 1986). Those experiencing the negative sequelae of stress drink more alcohol, take more drugs, have difficulty concentrating on tasks, have more accidents, and are more depressed, angry, irritable, and withdrawn. A staggering estimate of 1.3 billion pounds sterling has been estimated as the cost of alcoholism to industry per annum in Great Britain (Cooper, 1986). Organizations generally try to focus on a simple model of performance based on input and output, but stress is a great moderator of this formula. Challenging work may actually enhance performance and work production, whereas stressful conditions in the workplace or outside work may limit the output of the individual, group, or organization.

This brings up a second point. Businesses and other work settings have distinguished between work and employees' private lives. Employees are expected to leave their personal problems at home, and at least in the past, employees may have seen any attempt by employers to affect their private lives as unwelcome intrusions. This distinction has and will become increasingly weaker because one major source of stress is the interface between work and home demands. Probably the greatest single factor affecting this change is the increased entry of women into the workplace. Women have, of course, always worked, but the recent increases in women from broad social classes and with children of all ages in work settings outside the home have profoundly affected the economy, the family, and organizations. This has resulted in a great increase of stress in the work–family interface for women, especially if they have other family responsibilities, as they typically do. However, it has also resulted in an increase in stress for men. A recent survey of chief executives of the largest European businesses, for example, indicated that even among such heady echelons, factors from work that affect the home have been the principle area of increased work stress since a survey about a decade ago (Cooper, 1991). With over 70% of women in the workplace, men's lives have changed correspondingly. For these reasons this chapter will also concentrate on both work and home stress.

One of the principal consequences of work-related stress is burnout and we will focus especially on the burnout phenomena. Burnout has been defined as a syndrome consisting of the

41

symptoms of emotional exhaustion, depersonalization (referring to a detached and callous response to clients and perhaps co-workers), and reduced personal accomplishment (Maslach, 1982). Pines, Aronson, and Kafry (1981) suggest that burnout also is typified by a sense of helplessness, hopelessness, and entrapment, a marked decrease in enthusiasm about work, and a sense of lowered self-esteem. Cherniss (1980a, b) has found that in the latter stages of burnout individuals behave defensively and hence display cynicism toward clients, withdrawal, and emotional detachment. These attempts at coping have limited effectiveness and often cycle to heighten burnout and problems for both the individuals and the organizations in which they work.

We will present a new theory of stress that helps explain the general phenomena of stress in the workplace and more specifically the process of burnout. Called the conservation of resource (COR) theory, the model delineates both the circumstances that cause stress and the consequences of stress (Hobfoll, 1988; 1989). We will show how the model can facilitate prediction of workplace stress, outcomes of workplace stress, and potential interventions that will limit stress and burnout. We will begin by outlining the theory and its general applications. We will discuss research in which COR theory has been applied or which otherwise supports the principles of COR theory. Then we will turn to the workplace stress and burnout literature and examine how COR theory may be applied to illuminate this area of research. Finally, we will approach the issue of interventions based on COR theory, concluding with a discussion of future directions for research and applications.

I. CONSERVATION OF RESOURCES THEORY

A. Basic COR Theory

Stress has typically been defined as a state that occurs when demands outstrip coping resources (Lazarus and Folkman, 1984), but Hobfoll (1988; 1989) has argued that this is inaccurate and misleading. Most stressful events or circumstances never approach the state at which they outstrip resources. Think about recent stressful conditions in your own life. Only in the case of the most severe stressors, and then usually only temporarily, are people at a state where they experience this extreme level of stress. More typically, coping resources are at work; they may meet demands fully or partially, but they are not overcome. In fact, most psychologists would argue that the state at which coping resources are outstripped is the case of breakdown. Further, stress often occurs when people are coping marvelously.

What then are the conditions during which stress occurs? According to COR theory, *people have a basic motivation to obtain, retain, and protect that which they value*. These things people value can be called resources. COR delineates four basic categories of resources: (1) objects (e.g., car, house); (2) conditions (e.g., good marriage, job stability); (3) personal characteristics (e.g., social aplomb, high self-esteem); and (4) energies (e.g., credit, money, favors). According to COR theory, psychological stress occurs when individuals are (1) threatened with resource loss, (2) lose resources, or (3) fail to gain resources following resource investment.

Earlier stress research suggested that change, transitions, or even positive events can also engender stress. In a comprehensive literature review, Thoits (1983) found that when positive changes occurred no deleterious effects were found. Some event lists used in early studies of stress were ambiguous (e.g., change in work status). Results of these studies seemed to show that change itself was stressful. However, more careful investigation clearly indicated that in these instances, only when the change indicated worsening conditions was it found to be stressful. Indeed, Cohen and Hoberman (1983) found that positive changes buffered effects of other negative changes. In other words, a few positive events had a stress-sheltering effect. There is no research to indicate that transitions are stressful, other than to the extent that the transition includes negative components. Of course, many transitions are therefore stressful and are high-risk periods, but it is the loss events that occur as part of the transition that seem to be the culprit.

The question raised, then, is: "What is a negative event, is it a loss?" In reviews of stressful life event lists and in studies of stressful events, the events that are most stressful are clearly loss events. Across cultures, loss of job, impaired health, loss of loved ones, loss of freedom, and financial loss lead life event lists as the most stressful events (Brown and Harris, 1978; Dohrenwend et al., 1990). Recent work on hassles, which are less clearly loss events, indicates that only when hassles accumulate to more meaningful losses are their effects appreciable (Stephens et al., 1988). We will pursue this point in some depth when discussing job-related stress and burnout, as often the stressors in such circumstances are individually minor, but accumulate to form significant losses in aggregate.

B. Key Corollaries of COR Theory

A number of key corollaries follow from the basic COR tenet and prediction of when stress occurs. The first corollary is that *individuals must invest resources in order to limit loss of resources, protect resources, or gain resources*. Schönpflug (1985) has shown in an interesting series of laboratory studies regarding workplace decisions that coping with stressful challenges was accompanied by attempts to invest other resources at the individual's disposal. For example, in order to raise production, a manager may need to withdraw resources from other efforts, increase staff, or demand that current staff work harder (i.e., invest their resources of time and energy). Similarly, when individuals experience stress in their interpersonal relationships, they may need to increase their investment of time, energy, and trust in those relationships. On a more personal level, a threat to self-esteem often requires investment of social support and calling on one's own sense of self-esteem to combat the threat.

How may individuals invest, say, their sense of mastery, a critical resource? When accepting a difficult assignment, an employee plans investment of her resources, expecting some payoff in terms of future gain. The expectation that she will succeed is based on a sense of mastery, and low-mastery individuals will tend to avoid this investment. If success is obtained, her sense of mastery will actually be strengthened. If, however, she fails, her sense of mastery will be depleted. The low-mastery individual, in contrast, will avoid meeting the challenge, slough off the assignment to another individual, or in some other way avoid investing his sense of mastery.

A second corollary of COR theory is that *those individuals with greater resources are less vulnerable to resource loss and more capable of resource gain*; and contrariwise, *those individuals who lack resources are more vulnerable to resources loss and less capable of resource gain*. This follows because individuals use those resources that they have to offset resource loss, to protect resources, and to gain other resources. The concrete example of insurance as an energy resource is instructive. Those who are insured are less likely to lose their auto following an accident. Further, without insurance, they might leave their car in a garage and not enjoy other gains that come from using the car for transportation. Social support is a more abstract resource, but serves as another good example. People who have a strong network of close others have a safety net that they can fall back on when stress occurs. If stress occurs, they are likely to receive help managing tasks as well as necessary advice and emotional support. Further, if they are challenged with a task, they have others to call upon to meet the challenge and help them gain greater resources. Those who lack social support are likely to be more deeply affected by stressful circumstances; the absence of someone to share the burden means the whole emotional and task burden falls upon them. Moreover, they cannot call on others to help them turn challenges into successes; they must go it alone, and so are at a disadvantage on many tasks.

A third corollary of COR theory emerges when we realize that stress does not really occur as single events. Rather, stressful events are unfolding processes that entail a chain of events when the details are unpacked. The third corollary has two emphases; *that those who lack strong resource pools are more likely to experience cycles of resource loss, and that initial losses beget further losses*. The positive mirror image of this corollary is that *those who possess strong resource pools are more likely to experience cycles of resource gain and that initial resource gain begets further resource gain.* When individuals experience divorce, for example, it is not a single event. There is the loss of the marriage, but this is often accompanied by loss of contact with the children or loss of someone to help with childcare, potential loss of income, loss of companionship, loss of one's home, and loss of friends who were friends of the couple. The initial loss may result in a secondary loss of self-esteem as well. This means that further threats of loss are met by a weakened resource pool. If a job loss follows the divorce, the two events and their consequences may cycle into a forceful spiral of devastating losses, severely damaging self-esteem and individuals' abilities to cope with events. In contrast, following a divorce, establishing a new, loving relationship can result in increased confidence to meet work challenges, can aid with the burden of raising the children, and can increase self-esteem and sense of mastery. This cycle of gains has its own positive energy since the addition of resources means that more resources are available to invest for further gain.

This discussion evokes a fourth corollary of COR theory that has not previously been explicitly discussed. Specifically, *when individuals possess strong resource pools, they are more likely to accept or seek opportunities to risk resources in order to obtain resource gain.* In contrast, *those who lack resources are likely to develop a defensive posture that limits the possibility of further resource loss, but also precludes the opportunities for resource gain.* For example, an employee who feels confident in his boss' approval is likely to suggest new ideas in order to increase productivity or do something in a better way—and not incidentally, to increase his boss' approval. The employee who lacks his boss' approval, in contrast, will act to limit circumstances for suggesting new and different approaches—better to take a low-risk posture and just do what is already accepted.

These principles also generally hold for organizations as a whole; so organizations that are rich in resources are less likely to be devastated by an initial resource loss, are more likely to possess resources that can be invested for future gain, are more likely to experience cycles of resource gains, and are more willing to risk resource loss in hopes of making further gains. The organization that lacks resources will take a more defensive posture, will be more vulnerable to initial losses, and will be more likely to experience cycles of resource losses following initial resource loss.

Overall, COR theory emphasizes aspects of stress that other theories do not. COR theory states that people overweight the effects of loss compared to gain. Even when resources are adequate, loss of resources has impact. COR theory further postulates that loss of resources creates increased vulnerability to future loss. Other stress theories tend to emphasize a more situation-by-situation approach, rather than seeing the stress process as part of people's or organizations' development (see also Vaux, 1988). Similar to efficacy theory, COR theory further suggests that interrupting loss cycles and creating gain cycles is the best course for stress resistance (Bandura, 1982). Bandura does emphasize appraisal (i.e., feeling efficacious), but, as in COR theory, places objective circumstances as the key to such appraisals. COR theory also suggests that when stressful circumstances are not present, people seek to build resource reservoirs. Again, other stress theories tend to focus on how people react in the face of stress and do not make predictions about behavior in the absence of stress. Building on the work of Lazarus and Folkman (1984), COR theory also sees a role for perception and appraisal but sees appraisal as more common among people. Where events are minor and ambiguous, individual appraisals will, of course, be of greater importance.

C. Social Support and COR Theory

Social support is a major potential route to resources that are beyond those possessed directly by individuals. Social support is a metaconstruct that includes those connections we have to either intimate others or others having the potential for providing aid, and the actual receipt of acts that have a supportive intent (Hobfoll and Stokes, 1988; Vaux, 1988). Social support, in the former sense of ties with close others or others who can provide aid, would be viewed as a condition resource. The act of being socially supported, however, could result in access to object, condition, personal characteristics, or energy resources. For example, those with social support may receive the loan of a car or money, help in achieving a new position, and support aimed at bolstering their self-esteem. This distinction is an important one to keep in mind, but for ease of reading we will refer to social support simply as a resource.

Social support has been found to be a critical resource in many stressful situations (Sarason, Sarason, and Pierce, 1990). Not surprisingly, numerous studies have shown that social support is especially important in the face of work-related stress as well as the stress that often occurs in juggling work and private life (Borman, Quarm, and Gideonse, 1984; Morf, 1989). It is puzzling, however, to note that a number of studies have found negative effects of social support (Riley and Eckenrode, 1986; Hobfoll and London, 1986). COR theory helps explain simultaneously why social support is generally beneficial and why support often incurs costs that may, at times, even outweigh support's benefits.

There are two support-related corollaries of COR theory. First, *social support is viewed as the major vehicle by which individuals' resources are widened outside the limited domain of resources that are contained in the self.* Second, *individuals' links with others are part of their identity.* Take, for instance, the fact that individuals often define themselves as husband, father, employee, or supervisor—all labels that describe one's relationship to others. Combined, these two corollaries suggest that people will strive to maintain social support both to meet their needs to preserve other resources and also in order to protect and maintain their identities.

Our identities emerge, in large part, from the process of social ties. Close family ties; a close, stable relationship with parents; good relations with peers in adolescence; and close personal relationships in adulthood at once mold who we are and also provide a supportive base from which to operate.

How we use social support is also a product of our personal resources. Kobasa (1979; Kobasa and Puccetti, 1983) developed a concept that she calls hardiness. Hardy individuals see themselves as having significant control over their environments, see stressful events more as challenges than as threats, and tend to have a strong sense of commitment to important tasks in their lives. Not surprisingly, hardy executives have been found to withstand a shake-up period in their company with better health than less hardy executives (Kobasa, Maddi, and Couvington, 1981). In what may seem paradoxical, the hardy individual is not one who succeeds by operating independently. Rather, hardy individuals have also been found to use social support more effectively than those who are less hardy (Kobasa and Puccetti, 1983).

Similarly, others have found that those who have a greater sense that they have significant control over their lives are helped more by social support than those who lack this sense of control (Lefcourt, Martin, and Selah, 1984; Sandler and Lakey, 1982). Why, however, is sense of control linked to the effective use of social support? It appears that those who have stronger personal coping resources are more attractive to others, and so are more likely to have access to social support (Dunkel-Schetter, Folkman, and Lazarus, 1987). Furthermore, sense of control may be seen as a management resource. Those with high sense of control or mastery tend to use their resources judiciously, relying on themselves when this is most appropriate and calling on others when this is necessary. In a recent study by Hobfoll, Shoham, and Ritter (1991), women who were high in mastery received more support than women low in mastery, but only during high stress conditions. During everyday circumstances, the high-mastery women seemed content to rely on their personal resources and actually received less support under these conditions than the low-mastery women.

Women who were low in self-esteem, another important personal resource, were found in another study to be less satisfied with support, *the greater their social support.* In comparison, high self-esteem women were more satisfied with support when they received more (Hobfoll, Nadler, and Lieberman, 1986). It is possible that the high self-esteem women received "better" social support when they received it than the low self-esteem women. The low self-esteem nurse, for example, may associate with other low self-esteem women. Relationships are likely to be superficial for her and she may react inappropriately by acting overly dependent when any small stress occurs. The high self-esteem nurse is likely to have relationships with others like her and has greater capacity for intimate ties (Hansson, Jones, and Carpenter, 1984). When stress does occur, the quality of the kind of support she has to rely on is better, and therefore more likely to prove beneficial.

Overall, personal and social resources should be reviewed as interrelated. They affect each other and exist as resource pools. Lacking one is often tied with lacking the other, and possessing one makes the likelihood of possessing the other greater. Social support is particularly significant in organizational settings because so many organizational tasks demand team effort. Further, because evaluation is an integral part of organizations, social support is important not only in meeting one's objectives, but also in promoting positive evaluation of the efforts rendered.

D. The Nature of Stress at Work

Organizational stress is most frequently either of the chronic or repeated episodic varieties. Chronic stress occurs when threat or loss conditions continue over long periods of time. Repeated episodic stress is characterized by different stressors emerging at different times, some frequently reoccurring and some idiosyncratic. Of course, since work is foremost a human setting, other kinds of stressors may occur as well. Particular interest has been shown for the major stress of large-scale job layoffs (Kessler, Turner, and House, 1988), which is an acute stressor with many spin-off effects.

For the purposes of our discussion, it is worthwhile to note what COR theory has to say for these stressful circumstances. Chronic stress, for instance, is typified by a significant and ongoing draw on resources. Working for a critical boss or being exposed to a sexually harassing environment places an ongoing toll on resources. This would result in a continued drain on resources, leaving individuals with ever-decreasing resources to combat the chronic stress situation. Also, chronic stress situations will invalidate resources and, in fact, invalidation of resources is a very common chronic stressor. Invalidation of resources relates to the conditions in which resources that should be valued (e.g., competence, social skills) are not valued by the "system." Racism is a classic example of invalidation of resources. For decades, black athletes were not allowed to play major league baseball, and the Negro Baseball League was thought to be inferior. It was not their lack of baseball skills, however, that created these conditions, but the invalidation of the men as blacks. Similarly, assertiveness is often punished in female employees, as unbecoming to a woman (Vianello et al., 1990). Consequently, although assertiveness often is a major resource at work, it is often invalidated. Chronic stressors may also invalidate resources, in and of themselves; as stress continues, individuals try different resource utilization strategies. To the extent the stress continues despite these attempts at coping, resources can become invalidated—individuals lose the belief that their resources are valuable.

Episodic stress is also common at work, and the coping process for individuals and organizations possessing strong resource pools should shine in such circumstances. By investing resources appropriately when stressful demands increase, the individual and organization enter a testing period in which their resources are challenged. Sense of mastery, competence, and social support can go a long way toward successfully managing such circumstances. Many organizations have such periods of peak demand, and often year-end profitability or performance depends on successful coping during such periods. Important also is the point that "episodic stress" implies that there exists a relative relaxation period between stressors. This allows for a regrouping of resources, analysis of what worked and what did not, and a chance to bolster resources for the future. Again, social support is seen as critical during this period since, both for the individual and the organization, social recognition and a sense of community build personal and other social resources. Social support is not only a characteristic of the stress-resistant individual, but also of the competent community (Iscoe, 1974; S. B. Sarason, 1974).

More massive stressors, such as job layoffs, act differently on resources. Here the demand is rapid and intense, especially during the initial period. What were formerly considered to be individuals' major resources can disappear overnight. Self-esteem and sense of mastery typically plummet, income and insurance are lost, and family relations are strained (Pearlin et al., 1981). This initial demand on resources can turn into a chronic stressful condition if the layoffs become long-term or if other work is not found. Nevertheless, both personal and social resources are valuable in such circumstances. Strong senses of self-esteem and mastery are more easily bolstered by social support from family than is a weak self-concept. Those with savings or an employed spouse are less likely to be overcome by financial pressures. Kobasa et al. (1981) have found that hardy individuals can even reconstruct such circumstances into challenges, wherein they see themselves as having new opportunities for success.

The different kinds of stressors and their combinations can thus be seen as making different kinds of demands on resources that are potentially available for the service of the individual or organization. By understanding how these different stressors operate on resources, it is possible to predict what will occur and plan ahead. Likewise, this understanding can provide a clearer picture of current circumstances, which is otherwise often difficult when the organization or individual is in the midst of the storm of stress.

E. Research on COR Theory

It is instructive to take a brief look at research on COR theory. While some of our examples are not focused on organizational settings, they are all instructive for understanding how COR theory can be applied to the workplace. We think that the reader will, in any case, see many parallels to the workplace when we focus on the stress of illness as a chronic stress condition, or on the stress of war as a massive stressor.

In an initial study, we examined the basic tenet of COR theory that loss of resources is more critical than resource gain in the stress experience (Hobfoll, Lilly, and Jackson, 1992). We examined two samples, one student sample and one community sample. We measured individuals' reports of resource losses over the prior year and more recently during the prior few weeks, as well as their gains of resources. Individuals responded to a list of 74 resources that groups of others had determined were key resources. What we found is summarized in Figure 1. Using structural equation modeling, we clearly supported the hypothesis that loss is more consequential than gain. In general, greater loss was related to much greater psychological distress. On the other hand, gain was virtually unrelated to distress.

COR theory also implies, however, that gain is important in the context of loss. Gains help protect us from future losses and can provide comfort. To investigate this more complex model, we examined the effects of loss over and above the effects of gain (Hobfoll and Lilly, in press). If gain were significant in the context of loss, such analysis would show a marked effect of

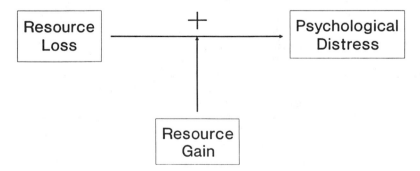

Figure 1   Effects of resource loss and gain on psychological distress.

resource gain—after considering the effect of resource loss. Again, we received strong support for this model. Clearly, neither change nor transition are stressful, if they result only in net gain of resources. However, loss of resources seems clearly related to psychological distress.

COR theory further postulates that resources are depleted in the coping process. One common stressor for women is having a cesarian section during childbirth; postoperative recovery is painful, requiring at least a month of continued discomfort and decreased mobility, and the operation is often viewed by women as a failure on their part. In a study of women who experienced the high stress of cesarian section delivery, versus the relatively lower stress of normal delivery, we found that those with greater mastery received greater support in the month following delivery (Hobfoll, Shoham, and Ritter, 1991). Low-mastery women, in contrast, received more support only in the lower-stress situation. When faced with the more significant stress of cesarian section, their mastery resource appeared depleted and did not result in greater mobilization of aid with childcare. When we looked at a weaker resource—comfort-seeking support (weak because no one is terribly comfortable asking for help)—we found that even those who felt relatively comfortable seeking support were not aided by this resource in the higher-stress conditions, but only in the lower-stress ones. In this instance, we can see that a weak resource is depleted even for those who are relatively well endowed with it.

Under conditions of having an acutely or chronically ill child, we found further evidence for resource depletion. In this instance, social support, intimacy, and comfort-seeking support were valuable resources for mothers of acutely ill children (Hobfoll and Lerman, 1988; 1989). Even though this is an extremely stressful situation, these resources proved valuable. However, mothers of chronically ill children found their resources depleted over a year's period. After a year, those possessing these resources had no apparent advantage over those who had originally lacked them.

COR theory also postulates that resources will spiral. Those who possess strong resources should not only cope better than those who lack resources, but having one resource should increase the benefits of others. Those who lack resources, however, may not have the ability to beneficially utilize other resources. Again studying parents of ill children, we found that women high in mastery not only had less emotional distress than women low in mastery, they also made more effective use of social support (Hobfoll and Lerman, 1988). Women low in mastery actually tended to do worse if they had more social support than if they had less of it; either the way they approached supporters, or the type of supporters they attracted, were decidedly unhelpful. Similarly, in still another study of pregnant women (Hobfoll, Nadler, and Leiberman, 1986), we found that women who were high in self-esteem tended to be more satisfied when they received support. Again, the low self-esteem women actually were less satisfied the greater their support. It would appear that, without a strong personal resource such as mastery or self-esteem, attempts at gaining the benefit of social support are muted or counterproductive.

Before, during, and after the Israel-Lebanon War we had a chance to look at a severe episodic stressor. We interviewed over 11,000 Israelis in order to investigate the kinds of events that resulted in depressive responses (Hobfoll et al., 1989). Not surprisingly, the war itself was responded to with an increase in depression. However, remarkably, a greater peak of depressive mood corresponded with the massacres at the Palestinian refugee camps of Sabra and Shatilla by Christian–Lebanese troops. This was in an area under Israeli control, and many Israelis felt indirectly responsible for the events. Israelis see their nation as founded on the principle of "a light onto other nations," and this event represented to many a significant loss vis-à-vis that dream. Extremely interesting from the point of our discussion here, people's resources seemed to help them through the event fairly quickly. A few months into the conflict, depression levels were already back to normal. More recently we have had a chance to look at Israeli reactions to the Gulf War. As in the previous war, we found an elevated depressive mood that peaked during the period of Scud missile attacks, yet soon after the conflict, people returned to fairly normal levels of mood.

One question arises. Are the same kinds of resources that might help, say, pregnant women, valuable in vastly different stress situations, such as the workplace? Consider our examination of soldiers' reactions to combat stress. We found that a sense of mastery over events, support from family and comrades, and intimacy with a few close others were valuable resources in limiting psychological distress and breakdown in combat (Hobfoll, London, and Orr, 1988; Solomon, Mikulincer, and Hobfoll, 1986). As different as war and pregnancy are, in sum, the same basic constellation of resources seems critical to successful coping.

Finally, before applying COR theory to the organizational literature on stress and burnout, we would like to cite a recent organizational study that directly tested COR theory (Freedy, 1990). In this investigation, nurses received one of two resource-enhancement interventions. At six hospitals nurses received either a five-session intervention that focused on increasing mastery alone, or a five-session intervention that focused on increasing both mastery and social support. It was predicted that the dual resource intervention would be more effective in increasing both mastery and social support because by raising a tandem of resources it was more likely to produce a positive spiral. Further, it was predicted that nurses in the latter group would experience greater alleviation from the negative effects of stress than those in the single resource intervention.

Findings generally supported the COR model. Nurses in the single resource group experienced little benefit from intervention. However, those in the dual resource intervention gained in resources and decreased in emotional exhaustion. From this it would appear that single resources, even if strong, may be insufficient to cope with real-life stressors that people face. Multiple resources ensure resource reserves and increased availability of alternative resources for coping.

II. STRESS, BURNOUT, AND COR THEORY

A. Burnout in Organizations: A COR Theory Perspective

This chapter's focus now moves from stress to burnout, one of the major consequences or concomitants of stress in work organizations. The shift is due to the centrality of loss of personal resources in the process of burnout. The theoretical linkage between the two phenomena will be further elaborated below.

As noted in the introduction, stress is ubiquitous in work organizations. The adverse consequences of it, in terms of employee morale and satisfaction, employee health, and organization-level outcomes such as absenteeism and productivity, are well documented. These consequences were shown to be very significant to the well-being of individual employees and to the viability of organizations. Stress research is also a growth industry (see below), and is characterized by its interdisciplinary nature, involving researchers in such diverse fields as psychology, organizational behavior, physiology, engineering, and medicine. A recent tally of the number of contributions to the periodical literature noted that in 1985 (quite a typical year) about 1150 articles were published in the behavioral sciences and about 700 in the life sciences in the strictly defined area of stress research (Vingerhoets and Marcelissen, 1988). This abundance is indicative of the difficulties of any researcher in keeping abreast of the literature, difficulties exacerbated by the relative paucity of reviews of new knowledge accumulated in this area.

In comparison, burnout researchers publish only about 60 to 80 articles per year (Roberts, 1986). Moreover, the field of burnout has flourished primarily in organizational behavior and psychology. The very term burnout first appeared in print in 1974, when a clinical psychologist, Freudenberger (1974), used it to represent a syndrome he observed in his practice. This syndrome consisted of a certain combination of long-lasting emotional exhaustion, physical fatigue, absence of job involvement, dehumanization of the recipients of one's services, and lowered job accomplishments (Freudenberger, 1980). In subsequent conceptualizations, again based on a distillation of clinical experience, the term's originator redefined it to relate to the process of depletion of physical and emotional resources that may have somewhat different specific symptoms depending on the occupational, organizational, and personal contexts in which it occurs (Freudenberger, 1983; Freudenberger and North, 1985: 9). It might be noted that while the originator of the term moved to a more precise and confined definition of the phenomenon of burnout, popular scales to measure it are still based on his much earlier reasoning (for a review of these scales, see Arthur, 1990). Still, the use of the term burnout, and the scales developed by several researchers to measure it, did not carry over to any of the life sciences (including medicine, with the exception of behavioral medicine) or to engineering. The above major differences between the two areas of research have implication for our presentations of them. We should note, however, that the term burnout has been applied to quite diverse settings in the behavioral sciences, including marital relationships (Pines, 1987; 1988), counseling of college students (Meier and Schmeck, 1985) and domestic work (Tierney, Romito, and Messing, 1990). In this chapter, we shall focus on burnout of employees in work organizations, excluding research that deals exclusively with nonemployment settings, such as in the above examples.

The working definition of burnout adopted here views it as the process of wearing out and wearing down of a person's energy (Freudenberger and North, 1985), or the combination of physical fatigue, emotional exhaustion, and cognitive wearout that develops gradually over time. For an elaboration and support of this definition of burnout, see the review by Shirom (1989). It is commonly regarded as a consequence of one's exposure to job stress, such as overload, and to other stresses in an individual's life spheres (e.g., Farber, 1983; Jackson, Schwab, and Schuler, 1986).

How could COR theory advance researchers' understanding of the phenomenon of burnout? As explained above, according to COR theory, when individuals experience actual loss of resources, they respond by attempting to limit the loss of resources and by maximizing gain of resources. To do this, we must usually employ other resources. Applying these notions to burnout, then it can be argued that individuals experience burnout when they perceive a net loss, which cannot be replenished, of valuable personal resources—specifically physical vigorousness, emotional robustness, and cognitive agility. This net loss is experienced in response to external demands (stressors), and cannot be compensated for by expanding other resources, or by borrowing or in other ways replenishing the original loss. A burned-out person may exacerbate his or her losses by entering an escalating spiral of losses. Then, he or she may reach an advanced stage of burnout, wherein hopelessness, helplessness, and depression become the predominant emotions. We shall next move to describe, under each of the following sections, the ways in which the model of COR can contribute to advancing our understanding of the burnout phenomenon. However, we shall first explain the quite different metatheoretical models used in organizational behavior (OB) to study burnout and in the medical sciences to study a somewhat overlapping phenomenon.

B. The Medical Versus the OB Models of Burnout

The above discussion should not lead one to conclude that this syndrome was overlooked by medical practitioners or researchers. They have been interested in it in its extreme form, when it reached the stage wherein maladaptive behavior or psychiatric disturbance appears in the person as a disease state. Early references to the relevant disease entity often went under the symptomatic categories of asthenia, lassitude, lethargy, or listlessness. The most widely accepted nomenclature for this syndrome, when it appears as a chronic disabling condition, is chronic fatigue syndrome, often abbreviated as CFS (Shafran, 1991). We shall further explore the possible etiological role of burnout in the pathogenesis of CFS in a subsequent section.

In the OB literature, one seldom, if at all, finds reference to any of the above medical terms. This is indicative of the different, almost nonoverlapping, models used in these fields. In the OB literature, the term burnout, when applied to an individual employee, carries with it a minimal stigmatizing burden, substantially lower than those implied by terms such as a depressed or an anxious employee. Again in contrast with the medical model, employees admitting that they are burned out are not necessarily depicted as inept or incompetent. Furthermore, the diagnosis of their complaint is not confined to their personal vulnerabilities, but rather extend to the job, organization, and family contexts, among others (e.g., Bhagat and Allie, 1989; Leiter, 1991; and O'Driscoll and Shubert, 1988). Restricted individual or collective access to economic resources (or objects), social resources (or conditions), and personal energies—resources that can be used to cope effectively with stress and thereby reduce burnout—are factors often viewed as prime causes of burnout, in line with social causation theory (Aneshensel, Rutter, and Lachenbruch, 1991; Mirowsky and Ross, 1989).

The medical model for the study of CFS and the OB model for the study of burnout are qualitatively different. Different questions are posed, and the answers provided by these models are quite incongruent. While psychological pathogenesis has been considered by the CFS research community, it was primarily in the context of the possibility that clinical depression antedate the development of CFS (Shafran, 1991). Stress has rarely, if ever, been considered as a social antecedent of CFS, thus the perspective of the medical model is to explore the immediate antecedents of the disease category under consideration.

The differences between the two models are even more striking when one examines the medical literature on chronic fatigue per se, regardless of whether or not it was diagnosed as CFS. Chronic fatigue is a relatively common complaint presented by patients visiting their primary care physicians (mostly family physicians). Different studies found that between 21% and 24% of patients who visited primary care clinics complained of chronic fatigue (Shafran, 1991). Two epidemiological surveys, which covered sizeable representative samples in the United States and the United Kingdom, found that about 14% to 20% of the male respondents and about 20% to 25% of the female respondents described themselves as always feeling tired or significantly fatigued (Shafran, 1991). Nonetheless, despite the relatively high prevalence of chronic fatigue, we could not find any study in the medical literature that systematically investigated the potential stresses that may have led to this condition.

In contrast, stress research in OB tends to follow a multifactorial type of design; that is, it typically begins with antecedent social and personal variables, attempts to cover relevant stresses in the work environment, and looks at the broad range of potential consequences, including burnout as a salient outcome of stress at work.

C. On Burnout's Construct Validity

The construct validity of burnout, and especially of the two most widely used scales developed thus far to measure it, the Maslach burnout inventory (MBI; Maslach and Jackson, 1981; Maslach, 1982) and the burnout inventory (BI; Pines, Aronson, and Kafry, 1981), have recently been subjected to critical reviews (Handy, 1988; Schonfield, 1990). Lack of construct validity was claimed because these instruments confound stress and its consequences of strain or distress, are vulnerable to attribution error, fail to identify situation-specific or occupation-specific characteristics of burnout, often disregard the social arrangements that antecede burnout, and fail to discriminate between burnout and depressive symptoms. Most of these criticisms of the construct validity of burnout, echo earlier criticisms of the MBI and BI, and were discussed elsewhere (Shirom, 1989). However, it is apparent that the issue of the discriminant validity of the burnout construct, as distinct from depression, needs to be addressed. We emphasize that burnout is conceptualized here in terms of its core meaning (i.e., a combination of physical fatigue, emotional exhaustion, and cognitive weariness).

Nomological validity is a major concern in construct validation (Brinberg and McGrath, 1985; Embertson, 1983). In this context, it refers to the construction and testing of a pattern of relationships between burnout, anxiety, and depression that is expected from theory; that is, the nomological network. One of the developmental models constructed to explain burnout (Shirom, 1989; Ezrahi, 1985) proposed that during its early stages, it is characterized by a continuous process of resources directed toward coping with overly demanding stresses. During this stage, burnout occurs concomitantly with high levels of anxiety, due to direct and active coping behaviors that entail a high level of arousal. When and if these coping behaviors prove ineffective, the individual may give up and engage in the emotional detachment and defensive behaviors associated with depression.

Support for this model was reported in a study of burnout among 700 senior army officers (Ezrahi and Shirom, 1986). Burnout was found to be correlated $r = 0.49$ and $r = 0.46$ with depression and anxiety, respectively (all measures had *alpha* reliabilities of about 0.90). This indicated that the variables under consideration, while moderately correlated, are not interchangeable. The discriminant validity of burnout was supported by a set of findings indicating that each of these strains was predicted by different sets of stresses, and was associated with different coping styles as predicted by the above theory.

Expectedly, burnout would be found to be significantly associated with measures of depressive symptomatology, such as the Beck depression inventory (Beck et al., 1961). These measures often include items whose contents gauge passivity and apparent lack of capacity for purposeful action. This may explain the high correlations between different measures of burnout and the MMPI depression scale reported by Meier (1984). However, as demonstrated by Watson and Clark (1984), depressive symptomatology is affectively complex, and includes lack of pleasurable experience, anger, guilt, apprehension, and physiological symptoms of distress. Cognitive approaches toward depression view it as related primarily to pessimism about the self, capabilities, and the future (Fisher, 1989). Even viewed from this perspective, we claim that the unique core of burnout, as discussed above, is distinctive in content and in its nomological network from either depression or anxiety.

Hobfoll's COR theory (1988; 1989) may provide an insight as to the relationship among the three burnout components and other resources. These three components commonly occur in combinations, but one is not an invariable concomitant of the other. They do not cover the whole gamut of resources in COR theory. Objects and conditions could be considered as the two types of primary resources. They are primary in the sense that they are essential for the survival of human beings. To survive, we need shelter and food; to continue to exist in the future, meaningful relationships, with a spouse and with others, are needed. The loss, depletion, or ineffective replenishment of resources that is reflected by the construct of burnout relates to a secondary type of resources. We refer to them as secondary because they determine a person's competitive position with respect to the ownership and use of the primary resources. Physical power, mental agility, or interpersonal skills relate to the types of resources referred to as personal characteristics and energies in COR theory (Hobfoll, 1988).

An open question is what determines the strength of interrelationships among emotional exhaustion, physical fatigue, and cognitive wearout. There is a piece of evidence that might be interpreted as pointing out that each component is related in a rather unexpected way to a different coping style. Thus Ezrahi (1985) found that problem-focused coping, expressed in investing more time to face external demands, was highly correlated with emotional exhaustion. In a quasi-experimental case-control study of stress, Vingerhoets (1985) found that emotion-focused coping was associated with physical fatigue. However, to our knowledge no study related all three burnout components to coping behaviors or to stress. Emotional exhaustion, as measured by one of the scales of MBI, was found in several studies to be higher for workers who communicate extensively with co-workers on work-oriented matters but have relatively few informal supportive communications with co-workers (Burke, 1988: 95). This finding may give rise to the expectation that one's emotional exhaustion would be closely associated with the type and quality of interaction that one has with others in one's organization.

Burnout has been associated in the literature primarily with employees in people-oriented, caregiving professions, such as teachers, social workers, nurses, counselors, and psychotherapists (Pines, Aronson, and Kafry, 1981; Maslach, 1982). This appears to be an artifact resulting from the fact that the two popular measures of burnout, the MBI and the BI, were designed to measure almost exclusively the emotional exhaustion component of burnout. The extensive research conducted on burnout by Golembiewski and his associates (e.g., Golembiewski, Munzenrider, and Carter, 1983; Golembiewski, Munzenrider, and Stevenson, 1986; and Golembiewski and Munzenrider, 1988) has convincingly demonstrated that burnout exists and is relevant to all or most occupations. It would appear that high priority should be given by burnout researchers to the task of constructing valid measures of all three components of burnout. A theoretical springboard for this task may be provided by COR theory.

D.   Burnout and Individual Characteristics

COR theory allows us to identify certain individual traits that predispose an employee to develop burnout. We focus on individual traits only for the purpose of simplifying the presentation. It should be emphasized that in work organizations, they will always interact with organizational characteristics that tend to produce widespread burnout, such as when a major economic slump requires management to demand that employees invest all their available resources of energy and time to ensure the organization's survival.

Indeed, adverse organizational conditions have been shown to be more significant in the etiology of burnout than personality factors (cf. Cherniss, 1990), thus personality type should always be regarded as it interacts with the characteristics of the workgroup and of the organization in explaining the process of burnout. Therefore, the analytic unit to be considered in explaining burnout is that of the work environment and of the person.

One of the predictions of COR theory is that individuals who lack strong resources are more likely to experience cycles of resource losses. These cycles of resource losses, when not replenished, are likely to result in chronic depletion of energy, namely in progressive burnout.

In a recent paper, Cherniss (1990), who contributed to the burnout literature a developmental model (1980 a, b) that has been supported by several empirical studies (e.g., Burke, 1987; Burke and Greenglass, 1989), advanced a thesis that may have significant theoretical importance. He argued that self-efficacy, a key personal characteristic resource in Hobfoll's COR theory (1988), is a central factor in the etiology of burnout. Employees who lack this resource, namely those who feel inefficacious, may feel so because organizational conditions, such as excessive work loads or lack of support from superiors, constricted and constrained their experiences of competence and success in their work roles. Likewise, lower levels of burnout would be expected in work situations that allow employees to experience success and feel efficacious, namely under job and organizational characteristics that provide opportunities to experience challenge, autonomy, control, feedback of results, and support from supervisor and co-workers (cf. Fisher, 1984).

This view is consistent with our discussion of the interrelations between social and personal resources in this chapter. We advanced the view that both types of resources belong to a pool and that they reinforce each other. Indeed, the observation was offered that social support is important also because it promotes positive evaluation of one's efforts and thus bolsters one's sense of efficacy. In a recent review of the area of social support and stress, Curtona and Russell (1990) summarized a series of four studies that had investigated the effects of social support on burnout. In all four studies (involving public school teachers, hospital nurses, therapists, and critical care nurses) reassurance of self-worth and supervisor support consistently predicted low levels of burnout. The use of the MBI in some of these studies may have caused a possible confounding of a predictor with the criterion, since decreased feelings of accomplishment is one of the three scales in the MBI. Still, the consistency of the results obtained is impressive. An important social resource, namely support from supervisors that reassures individuals of the value of their contribution, was associated with lower levels of burnout across all four studies. This can be interpreted as supportive of the above prediction derived from COR theory. It would appear that supervisors' support interacted with self-efficacy to result in lower levels of burnout.

The role of personality factors in the etiology of burnout is quite complex. In a series of studies, Garden (1991; 1989) concluded that a certain personality type was related to self-selection into specific occupations and that subsequently it interacted with stressful occupational environments to bring about burnout. This conclusion is supported by other studies (e.g., Keinan and Melamed, 1987; McCranie and Brandsman, 1988).

Other possible paths of influence of personality characteristics and burnout may exist. Burnout may exacerbate certain personality traits. Certain personality traits, like neuroticism, may lead people to report higher levels of burnout regardless of the situation (cf. Watson and Clark, 1984). It appears that the complex interactions between personality traits and burnout have yet to be described and understood. The integration of COR theory's predictions and corollaries in future research has the potential of making a significant contribution in that regard.

E. Burnout and Ill Health of Individuals

Researchers in industrial medicine (e.g., Simonson, 1971) have long shown that persistent or relapsing fatigue, or easy fatigability in a person, is a concomitant of physical ill health and accident proneness. The intent here is not to survey all possible disease categories that may potentially be associated with burnout, but to focus on two wherein there is evidence supporting the potential etiological role of burnout.

The plausibility of the proposition that burnout, as conceptualized here in terms of its core meaning, will overlap to some extent with CFS as defined in internal medicine (Shafran, 1991) has yet to be tested. It should be noted that the criteria used by physicians to diagnose CFS are rather strict. To diagnose a case as having CFS, the patient must fulfill two major criteria and several minor ones. The major criteria for CFS include fatigue of at least 6 month's duration that is severe enough to reduce or impaire daily activity below 50% of the patient's premorbid activity, and exclusion of other clinical conditions that may produce similar symptoms (Shafran, 1991). The exclusion is carried out by a systematic evaluation based on history, physical examination, and appropriate laboratory investigations, which require exclusion of these alternative disease categories, among others: autoimmune disease, infections, chronic psychiatric disease, and drug dependency.

In future investigations, individuals who score highest on burnout measures should be followed up for possible development of CFS. Elevated rates of CFS may be an outgrowth of an earlier burnout, or the product of individuals' restricted access to personal energy resources that combat stress and diminish its negative health consequences.

Yet another promising area of research is that viewing burnout as a possible precursor of cardiovascular disease. In the 1960s and 1970s, several studies reported findings that being either tired on awakening or exhausted at the end of the day were antecedents of cardiovascular heart disease. The evidence came from both prospective and case-control studies (for a summary of these early findings, see Kasl, 1978). In a serendipitous finding of the series of prospective studies called the Framingham study, the single questionnaire item "at the end of the day, I am exhausted both mentally and physically" had a high predictive power of subsequent myocardial infarction (Appels, 1988).

The early line of research was recently followed up by a group of researchers in behavioral medicine. These researches conducted several prospective studies of the etiology of cardiovascular disease. They were influenced in the design of their studies by the common clinical observation that more than half of those who suffer a myocardial infarction (or die suddenly because of it) visited a physician in the weeks prior to the coronary event, but their disease went undiagnosed because of the vague symptoms they described to their physician (Salamon, 1969). These symptoms frequently include: (1) discomfort in the chest, and (2) feelings of fatigue and general malaise. Appels and his associates (Appels, 1988; Appels and Mulder, 1988; 1989) developed a questionnaire to measure the symptoms included in the second category—that is, unusual fatigue, feeling of being dejected or defeated, and increased irritability—and called it the Maastricht questionnaire (MQ). In a prospective 4-year study that was conducted among 3877 males, aged 39–65, "exhausted" subjects (i.e., who scored in the upper third of the MQ) were significantly more at risk to develop myocardial infarction (Appels and Mulder, 1988) and angina pectoris (Appels and Mulder, 1989) after controlling for risk factors, including blood pressure, smoking, cholesterol, and age. It is apparent that the MQ is multifactorial and taps several other constructs apart from burnout, including anxiety (irritability), depression, and withdrawal behavior.

Melamed, Kushnir, and Shirom (in press), as a first step in an effort to systematically study the predictive value of burnout for cardiovascular disease, tested the association between burnout and cardiovascular risk factors in a sample of 110 male employees. Indeed, they found that after controlling for the possible confounding effects of 13 known and suspected risk factors, workers scoring high on burnout and tension scales were found to manifest higher levels of cholesterol, triglycerides, and glucose and lower levels of diastolic blood pressure. These results were since substantially replicated in a study involving a much larger sample of 1140 employees, wherein burnout scales were used as predictors and the effects of anxiety and depression controlled for, in addition to obesity and age (Shirom and Melamed, 1991).

The evidence for burnout being a cardiovascular risk factor (after controlling for the effects of age, relative weight, depression, and anxiety) is still sparse, and is based on cross-sectional data that precludes causal assertions. Longitudinal studies of fairly large and occupationally representative samples should be conducted to cross-validate the aforementioned findings. However, the evidence at hand is clearly supportive of the potential etiological role of burnout for the above two categories of disease. Therefore, even for those OB researchers who favor the medical model referred to earlier, the resource theoretical perspective we present may provide insights into the specific processes linking burnout, CFS, and cardiovascular disease.

F. Burnout and Organizational Health

In the concluding section of this chapter, we would like to chart out a possibly promising avenue for future applications of COR theory to theory building on burnout. We submit that an application of a new approach toward burnout, namely reconceptualizing this phenomenon at an organizational level of analysis, would make it possible to integrate disparate streams of thought on resources now coexisting in organization theory. Essentially, we propose that organizations may be burned out as a result of a continuous process of depletion of organizational resources.

As pointed out, there are threads of evidence connecting burnout to various disease states. Heretofore, the literature on burnout has dealt almost exclusively with individual employee burnout. Researchers have by and large overlooked the potentialities of defining and investigating group or organizational burnout. It is plausible that there is a parallelism between individual employee and organizational burnout. The open systems approach, a predominant metatheory in OB (cf. Ashmos and Huber, 1987), postulates dynamic interplay and interconnectedness among elements of any given system, and among subsystems and the more inclusive system. The higher level of analysis, namely the focus on organizational burnout, necessarily means higher system complexity (cf. Staw, Sandelands, and Dutton, 1981).

The study of the phenomenon of organizational burnout, signifying a progressive state of depletion of organizational resources, is regarded as a natural extension of the ecological perspective in the study of job stress developed by Hobfoll (1988, 1989). Organizational burnout may be self-imposed, such as when unrealistic production targets set for employees create overload that eventually impacts on the members' motivation, attitudes, and behavior. It may be externally imposed by stakeholders' excessive demands that continuously deplete the organization's energetic resources.

This line of thinking is offered as having a potential for future theory development. Recently, Kramer (1990; 1991) has summarized the literature on the effects of resource scarcity on both group and intergroup conflict and cooperation. The study of the impact of organizational resources on the birth, growth, and mortality of organizations has been a recurring theme in the organizational ecology literature (Singh and Lumsden, 1990). In recent years, OB has imported from economics the resource-based model of the firm as a major theoretical organizing framework, looking at issues such as resource mobility and heterogeneity as explanatory factors of firms' competitive advantages (Barney, 1991). Yet another theoretical perspective looks at specific structural attributes of organization, like human or physical size, in terms of resource theory (e.g., Siahpush, 1991). We hope that OB researchers would similarly examine the potentialities inherent in COR theory to explain organization-level burnout.

III. CONCLUSIONS

Stress and burnout have often caused attention to be focused on the outcome of stressful conditions. As such, researchers and organizational efforts have focused on the symptoms of stress and burnout and not its causes. As depicted in Figure 2, however, stress effects and burnout are only the endpoints in a process in which resources are depleted without consummate resource restoration. Work, personal, and family stressors interact to deplete resources, while resources at home and work act to limit resource depletion and even to increase resource enhancement. Perhaps because so much organizational research focused on "men at work," the interaction of work and family demands and work and family resources has been left relatively unattended. The increased proportion of women working out of the home must force us to look more carefully at the interface of work and home.

Stress and burnout further contribute, as depicted in Figure 2, to an ongoing loss of resources. As we have discussed, this means that individuals and organizations become decreasingly able to withstand new stressors and increasingly vulnerable to further burnout and other stress-related difficulties. However, just as unsuccessful coping results in further resource loss, successful coping results not only in limiting stress and burnout, but in increasing the systems' capabilities to withstand future stressors. In applying COR theory, it is these cycles that are of greatest interest to both research and intervention efforts. For employees and members of other organizations, we are reminded of the battle cry of the women's unionization movement at the turn of the century: they called for "bread and roses." The meaning of this unusual demand was that increased pay was not enough. Rather, it was women workers' call for better conditions at work, opportunities to care for their children, and the capacity to be both workers and mothers. It seems not to be happenstance that an increased attention to resources in the stress process comes at a time when women have so greatly increased their numbers in all areas of the workforce today. The COR theory provides a template for research and intervention that can contribute to a more holistic understanding of both stress and burnout processes—of bread and roses.

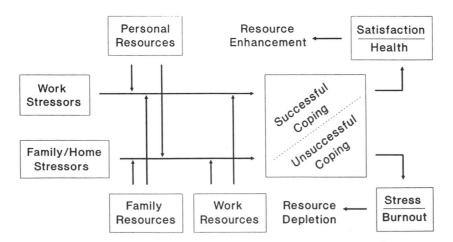

Figure 2 Interplay of family and work stressors on family and work resources.

REFERENCES

Aneshensel, C. S., Rutter, C. M., and Lachenbruch, P. A. (1991). Social structure, stress, and mental health: Competing conceptual and analytic models. *American Sociological Review, 56*:166–178.

Appels, A. (1988). Vital exhaustion as a precursor of myocardial infarction. In *Topics in Health Psychology* (S. Maes, C. D. Spielberger, P. B. Defaves, and I. G. Sarason, eds.), Wiley, New York, pp. 31–35.

Appels, A., and Mulder, P. (1988). Excess fatigue as a precursor of myocardial infarction. *European Heart Journal, 9*:758–764.

Appels, A., and Mulder, P. (1989). Fatigue and heart disease: The association between "vital exhaustion" and past, present and future coronary heart disease. *J. of Psychosomatic Research, 33*:727–738.

Ashmos, D. P., and Huber, G. P. (1987). The system paradigm in organization theory. *Academy of Management Review, 12*:607–621.

Arthur, N. M. (1990). The assessment of burnout: A review of three inventories useful for research and counseling. *J. of Counseling & Development, 69*:186–189.

Bandura, A. (1982). Self-efficacy mechanisms in human agency. *American Psychologist, 37*:122–147.

Barney, J. (1991). Special theory forum on the resource-based model of the firm: origins, implications, and prospects. *J. of Management, 17*:97–98.

Beck, A. T., Ward, C. H., Mendelson, M., Mock, J., and Erbaugh, J. (1961). An inventory for measuring depression. *Archives of General Psychiatry, 4*:561–571.

Bhagat, R. S., and Allie, S. M. (1989). Organizational stress, personal life stress, and symptoms of life strains: An examination of the moderating role of sense of competence. *J. of Vocational Behavior, 35*:231–253.

Borman, K. M., Quarm, D., and Gideonse, S., eds. (1984). *Women in the Workplace: Effects on families.* Ablex, Norwood, N.J.

Brinberg, D., and McGrath, J. (1985). *Validity and the Research Process.* Sage, Beverly Hills, Calif.

Brown, G. W., and Harris, T. (1978). *The Social Origins of Depression: The Study of Psychiatric Disorder in Women.* Free Press, New York.

Burke, R. J. (1987). Burnout in police work: An examination of the Cherniss model. *Group and Organization Studies, 12*:174–188.

Burke, R. J. (1988). Sources of managerial and professional stress in large organizations. In *Causes, Coping and Consequences of Stress at Work* (C. L. Cooper and R. Payne, eds.), Wiley, New York, pp. 77–115.

Burke, R. J., and Greenglass, E. R. (1989). Psychological burnout among men and women in teaching: An examination of the Cherniss model. *Human Relations, 42*:261–273.

Cherniss, C. (1980a). *Professional Burnout in Human Service Organizations.* Praeger, New York.

Cherniss, C. (1980b). *Staff burnout: Job stress in the Human Services.* Sage, Beverly Hills, Calif.

Cherniss, C. (September 1990). The role of professional self-efficacy in the etiology of burnout, paper presented at the First International Research Conference on Professional Burnout, Krakow, Poland.

Cohen, S., and Hoberman, H. M. (1983). Positive events and social supports as buffers of life change stress. *Journal of Applied Social Psychology, 13*:99–125.

Cooper, C. L. (1986). Job distress: Recent research and the emerging role of the clinical occupational psychologist. *Bulletin of the British Psychological Society, 39*:325–331.

Cooper, C. L. (July 1991). Sources of occupational stress, presented at the International Congress of Stress, Anxiety, and Emotional Disorders, Braga, Portugal.

Curtona, C. E., and Russell, D. W. (1990). Type of social support and specific stress: Toward a theory of optimal matching. In *Social Support: An Interactional View* (B. R. Sarason, I. G. Sarason, and G. R. Pierce, eds.), Wiley, New York, pp. 319–361.

Dohrenwend, B. P., Link, B. G., Kern, R., Shrout, P. E., and Markowitz, J. (1990). Measuring life events: The problem of variability within event categories. *Stress Medicine, 6*:179–187.

Dunkel-Schetter, C., Folkman, S., and Lazarus, R. S. (1987). Correlates of social support receipt. *J. of Personality and Social Psychology, 53*:71–80.

Embertson (Whitley), S. (1983). Construct validity: Construct representation vs. nomothetic span. *Psychological Bulletin, 93*:179–197.

Ezrahi, Y. (1985). Burnout in military officers ranks: A construct validation, unpublished doctoral dissertation, Tel Aviv University, Tel Aviv, Israel.

Ezrahi, Y., and Shirom, A. (July 1986). Construct validation of burnout, paper presented at the 21st Congress of the International Association of Applied Psychology, Jerusalem, Israel.

Farber, B. A. (1983). Introduction: A critical perspective on burnout. In *Stress and Burnout in the Human Service Professions* (B. A. Farber, ed.), New York, pp. 1–22.

Fisher, S. (1984). *Stress and the Perception of Control.* Lawrence Erlbaum, London.

Fisher, S. (1989). The vulnerability of the depressed to life efents: Sadder and tougher. *Advances in Behavioral Research and Theory, 11*:271–286.

Freedy, J. (1990). *Stress inoculation for prevention of burnout.* Unpublished doctoral dissertation, Kent State University.

Freudenberger, H. J. (1974). Staff burnout. *J. of Social Issues, 30*:159–164.

Freudenberger, H. J. (1980). *Burnout: The High Costs of High Achievement.* Anchor Press, New York.

Freundenberger, H. J. (1983). Burnout: Contemporary issues, trends, and concerns. In *Stress and Burnout* (B. A. Farber, ed.), Pergamon, New York, pp. 23–28.

Freundenberger, H. J., and North, G. (1985). *Women's Burnout.* Anchor Press/Doubleday, Garden City, N.Y.

Garden, A. M. (1989). Burnout: The effects of psychological types on research findings. *J. of Occupational Psychology, 62*:223–234.

Garden, A. M. (1991). The purpose of burnout: A Jungian interpretation. *J. of Social Behavior and Personality, 6*:73–93.

Golembiewski, R. T., Munzenrider, R., and Carter, D. (1983). Phases of progressive burnout and their work-site covariants. *J. of Applied Behavioral Science, 13*:461–482.

Golembiewski, R. T., Munzenrider, R., and Stevenson, J. (1986). *Stress in Organizations.* Prager, New York.

Golembiewski, R. T., and Munzenrider, R. (1988). *Phases of Burnout.* Praeger, New York.

Handy, J. A. (1988). Theoretical and methodological problems within occupational stress and burnout research. *Human Relations, 41*:351–365.

Hansson, R. O., Jones, W. H., and Carpenter, B. N. (1984). Relationship competence and social support. In P. Shaver (ed.), *Review of Personality and Social Psychology* (Vol. 5, pp. 265–284). Sage, Beverly Hills, CA.

Hobfoll, S. E. (1985). The limitations of social support in the stress process. In *Social Support: Theory, Research and Application* (I. G. Sarason and B. R. Sarason, eds.), Martinus Nijhoff, the Hague, the Netherlands, pp. 319–414.

Hobfoll, S. E. (1988). *The Ecology of Stress.* Hemisphere Publishing Co., Washington, D.C.

Hobfoll, S. E. (1989). Conservation of resources: A new attempt at conceptualizing stress. *American Psychologist, 44*:513–524.

Hobfoll, S. E., and Lerman, M. (1988). Personal relationships, personal attributes, and stress resistance: Mothers' reactions to their child's illness. *American Journal of Community Psychology, 16*:565–589.

Hobfoll, S. E., and Lerman, M. (1989). Predicting receipt of social support: A longitudinal study of parents' reactions to their child's illness. *Health Psychology, 8*:61–77.

Hobfoll, S. E., and Lilly, R. S. (in press). Resource conservation as a strategy for community psychology. *Journal of Community Psychology.*

Hobfoll, S. E., Lilly, R. S., and Jackson, A. P. (1992). Conservation of social resources and the self. In H. O. F. Veiel and U. Baumann (eds.), *The Meaning and Measurement of Social Support* (pp. 125–142). Hemisphere, Washington, DC.

Hobfoll, S. E., Lomranz, J., Eyal, N., Bridges, A., and Tzemach, M. (1989). Pulse of a nation: Depressive mood reactions of Israelis to the Israel-Lebanon War. *J. of Personality and Social Psychology, 56*:1002–1012.

Hobfoll, S. E., and London, P. (1986). The relationship of self-concept and social support to emotional distress among women during war. *Journal of Social and Clinical Psychology, 4*:189–203.

Hobfoll, S. E., London, P., and Orr, E. (1988). Mastery, intimacy and stress resistance during war. *J. of Community Psychology, 16*:317–331.

Hobfoll, S. E., Nadler, A., and Leiberman, J. (1986). Satisfaction with social support during crisis: Intimacy and self-esteem as critical determinants. *Journal of Personality and Social Psychology, 51*:296–304.

Hobfoll, S. E., Shoham, S. B., and Ritter, C. (1991). Women's satisfaction with social support and their receipt of aid. *J. of Personality and Social Psychology, 61*:332–341.

Hobfoll, S. E., and Stokes, J. P. (1988). The process and mechanics of social support. In *Handbook of Social Support: Theory, Research and Interventions* (S. Duck, ed.), John Wiley and Sons, New York, pp. 497–517.

Iscoe, I. (1974). Community psychology and the competent community. *American Psychologist, 29*:607–613.

Iscoe, I., Bloom, B., and Speilberger, C. D. (1977). *Community Psychology in Transition.* Halstead, New York.

Jackson, S. E., Schwab, R. L., and Schuler, R. S. (1986). Toward an understanding of the burnout phenomenon. *J. of Applied Psychology, 71*:630–640.

Kasl, S. V. (1978). Epidemiological contributions to the study of work stress. In *Stress at Work* (C. L. Cooper and R. Payne, eds.), Wiley, New York, pp. 3–51.

Kearns, J. (1986). Stress at work: The challenge of change. BUPA Series, *The management of health: 1. Stress and the city.* BUPA.

Keinan, G., and Melamed, S. (1987). Personality characteristics and proneness to burnout: A study among internists. *Stress Medicine, 3*:307–315.

Kessler, R. D., Turner, J. B., and House, J. S. (1987). Intervening processes in the relationship between unemployment and health. *Psychological Medicine, 17*:949–961.

Kobasa, S. C. (1979). Stressful life events, personality and health: An inquiry into hardiness. *Journal of Personality and Social Psychology, 37*:1–11.

Kobasa, S. C., Maddi, S. R., and Corington, S. (1981). Personality and constitution as mediators in the stress-illness relationship. *Journal of Health and Social Behavior, 22*:368–378.

Kobasa, S. C., and Pucetti, M. C. (1983). Personality and social resources in stress resistance. *Journal of Personality and Social Psychology, 45*:839–850.

Kramer, R. M. (1990). The effects of resource scarcity on group conflict and cooperation. In *Advances in Group Processes*, vol. 7, (E. Lawler, ed.), JAI Press, pp. 151–177.

Kramer, R. M. (1991). Intergroup relations and organizational dilemmas: The role of categorization processes. In *Research in Organization Behavior*, vol. 13 (B. M. Staw and L. L. Cummings, eds.), JAI Press, pp. 191–228.

Lazarus, R. S., and Folkman, S. (1984). *Stress, appraisal, and coping.* Springer, New York.

Lefcourt, H. M., Martin, R. A., and Selah, W. E. (1984). Locus of control and social support: Interactive moderators of stress. *Journal of Personality and Social Psychology, 47*:378–389.

Leiter, M. P. (1991). Coping patterns as predictors of burnout: The function of control and escapist coping patterns. *J. of Organizational Behaviour, 12*:123–144.

Leiter, M. P., and Meachem, K. A. (1986). Role structure and burnout in the field of human services. *J. of Applied Behavioral Science, 22*:47–52.

Maslach, C. (1982). *Burnout: The Cost of Caring.* Prentice Hall, Englewood Cliffs, N.J.

Maslach, D., and Jackson, S. (1981). The measurement of experienced burnout. *J. of Occupational Behavior, 2*:99–115.

McCrainie, E. W., and Brandsman, J. M. (1988). Personality antecedents of burnout among middle-aged physicians. *Behavioral Medicine, 14*:30–36.

Meier, S. T. (1984). The construct validity of burnout. *J. of Occupational Psychology, 57*:211–219.

Meier, S. T., and Schmeck, R. R. (1985). The burned-out college student: A descriptive profile. *J. of College Students Personnel, 26*:63–69.

Melamed, S., Kushnir, T., and Shirom, A. (in press). Burnout and risk factors for cardiovascular disease. *Behavioral Medicine.*

Mirowsky, J., and Ross, C. E. (1989). *Social Causes of Psychological Distress.* Aldine de Gruyter, New York.

Morf, M. (1989). *The Work/Life Dichotomy: Prospects for Reintegrating People and Jobs.* Quorum, New York.

O'Driscoll, M. P., and Schubert, T. (1988). Organizational climate and burnout in a New Zealand social service agency. *Work & Stress, 2*:199–204.

Pearlin, L. I., Leiberman, M. A., Menaghan, E. G., and Mullan, J. T. (1981). The stress process. *Journal of Health and Social Behavior, 19*:2-21.

Pines, A. (1987). Marriage burnout: A new conceptual framework for working with couples. *Psychotherapy in Private Practice, 5*:31–43.

Pines, A. (1988). *Keeping the Spark Alive: Preventing Burnout in Love and Marriage.* St. Martin's Press, New York.

Pines, A., Aronson, E., and Kafry, D. (1981). *Burnout: From Tedium to Personal Growth.* The Free Press, New York.

Riley, D., and Eckenrode, J. (1986). Social ties: Subgroup differences in costs and benefits. *Journal of Personality and Social Psychology, 51*:770–778.

Roberts, C. A. (1986). Burnout: Psychobabble, or a valuable concept? *British J. of Hospital Medicine, 36*:194–197.

Salamon, H. (1969). Prodrama in acute myocardial infarction. *Circulation, 46*:463–471.

Sandler, I. N., and Lakey, B. (1982). Locus of control as a stress moderator: The role of control perceptions and social support. *American Journal of Community Psychology, 10*:65–80.

Sarason, S. B. (1974). *The Psychological Sense of Community: Prospects for a Community Psychology.* Jossey-Bass, San Francisco.

Sarason, S. B. (1977). *The Psychological Sense of Community: Prospects for a Community Psychology.* Jossey-Bass, Washington, D.C.

Sarason, I. G., Sarason, B. R., and Pierce, G. R., eds. (1990). *Social Support: An Interactional View—Issues in Social Support Research.* John Wiley and Sons, New York.

Schonfeld, I. S. (199). Psychological distress in a sample of teachers. *J. of Psychology, 124*:321–338.

Schönpflug, W. (1985). Goal-directed behavior as a source of stress: Psychological origins and the consequences of inefficiency. In M. Frese and J. Sabini (eds.), *The concept of action in psychology* (pp. 172–188). Lawrence Erlbaum, Hinsdale, New Jersey.

Shafran, S. D. (1991). The chronic fatigue syndrome. *American J. of Medicine, 90*:730–739.

Shirom, A. (July 1986). Does stress lead to affective strain, or vice versa? A structural regression tests, paper presented at the Congress of the International Association of Applied Psychology, Jerusalem, Israel.

Shirom, A. (1989). Burnout in work organizations. In *International Review of Industrial and Organizational Psychology, 1989* (C. L. Cooper and I. Robertson, eds.), Wiley, New York, pp. 26–48.

Shirom, A., and Melamed, S. (1991). Burnout as a potential predictor of risk factors of cardiovascular disease, unpublished manuscript.

Siahpush, M. S. (1991). Empowering structures in organizations: Toward a specification of the resource perspective. *Social Science Research, 20*:122–149.

Simonson, E. (1971). *Physiology of Work Capacity and Fatigue.* Charles C. Thomas, Springfield, Ill.

Singh, J. V., and Lumsden, C. J. (1990). Theory and research in organizational ecology. *Annual Review of Sociology, 16*:161–195.

Solomon, Z., Mikulincer, M., and Hobfoll, S. E. (1986). Effects of social support and battle intensity on loneliness and breakdown during combat. *Journal of Personality and Social Psychology, 51*:1269–1276.

Staw, B. M., Sandelands, L. E., and Dutton, J. E. (1981). Threat-rigidity effects in organizational behavior: A multilevel analysis. *Administrative Science Quarterly, 28*:501–524.

Stephens, M. A. P., Norris, V. V., Kinney J. M., Ritchie, S. W., and Grotz, R. C. (1988). Stressful situations in caregiving: Relationship between caregiving, coping, and well-being. *Psychology and Aging, 3*:208–209.

Thoits, P. A. (1983). Dimensions of life events that influence psychological distress: An evaluation and synthesis of the literature. In H. B. Kaplan (ed.), *Psychosocial stress: Trends in theory and research* (pp. 33–103). Academic Press, New York.

Tierney, D., Romito, P., and Messing, K. (September 1990). She ate not the bread of idleness: Exhaustion is related to domestic and salaried working conditions among 539 Quebec hospital workers, paper presented at the First International Research Conference on Professional Burnout, Krakow, Poland.

Vaux, A. (1988). *Social Support: Theory, Research and Intervention.* Praeger, New York.

Vianello, M., Siemienska, R., Damian, N., Lupri, E., Coppi, R., D'Arcangelo, E., and Bolasco, S. (1990). *Gender Inequality: A Comparative Study of Discrimination and Participation.* Sage, Newbury Park, Calif.

Vingerhoets, A. J. J. M. (1985). *Psychosocial Stress: An Experimental Approach.* Swets & Zeitlinger, Lisse.

Vingerhoets, A. J. J. M., and Marcelissen, F. H. G. (1988). Stress research: Its present status and issues for future development. *Social Science & Medicine, 26*:279–291.

Watson, D., and Clark, L. A. (1984). Negative effectivity: The disposition to experience aversive emotional states. *Psychological Bulletin, 96*:465–490.

4

Small Groups in Organizations

A. Paul Hare*

Ben-Gurion University of the Negev, Beer Sheva, Israel

In a handbook that provides detailed information about human behavior in organizations, why include a chapter on small groups? In textbooks on organizational behavior, which are typically introductory psychology texts written for business school students, the small group usually appears in three different chapters. One chapter is on decision making. Since management decisions are often made in small groups, the "group dynamics" can lead either to "creative problem solving," providing "integrative solutions" (Follett, 1924; Pruitt, 1983) or to "groupthink," when group members fail to be critical enough in examining the evidence (Janis, 1982).

A second chapter deals with work groups, often comparing the advantages of having individuals work alone with the advantages of having them work in small groups. Such a chapter cites the positive advantages of providing small "autonomous groups," for example, to assemble automobiles, as in the Volvo experiment (Katz and Kahn, 1978), or to make suggestions for more effective production using the "quality circles" developed in Japanese industry (cf. Kosower, 1987). Or the chapter cites the negative effects of the informal groups in the organization that (1) set limits on production in the form of a "group bogey" (F. W. Taylor, 1903), or (2) form cliques to protect and supply social support for their members (cf. Homans, 1950:70–72), or (3) develop cabals to help their members move up in the system. Homans labels the interaction in informal groups, that is not prescribed by formal work organizational roles, as "elementary social behavior." He observes that "elementary social behavior . . . is not driven out by institutionalization but survives alongside it, acquiring new reason for existence from it" (Homans, 1961:391).

In a third kind of chapter, with a group emphasis, leadership is discussed. Although the focus is often on leadership in a large organization, the examples given of different leadership styles are usually based on data from small experimental groups. Moreover, the effective leader usually deals with a small number of persons, in a face-to-face situation, who are his or her "direct reports." These persons in turn pass the orders on to their direct reports.

In sum, the small group appears in works on organizations because the small group provides a link between the "micro-system" in which the individual is present and the "macro-system" that forms the organization (cf. Golembiewski, 1965:113). As an extension of this idea, Golembiewski, as editor of this handbook, has suggested that this chapter might provide a ground for developing a comprehensive framework for the group-in-organization, and perhaps, for the groups-as-organization, as well as the organization-as-group.

---

*Retired

The presentation of the material to follow is based on two assumptions and draws one conclusion concerning the nature of social interaction in groups and organizations. The assumptions are:

1. All theories of social interaction describe the attempts of one individual to join with others in a social situation to reach some goal.
2. Each theory focuses on a different aspect of the process and thus the choice of theory will depend upon which aspect of the process is judged to be most important.

The conclusion is:

1. For maximum effectiveness in reaching group decisions as the group moves toward a collective goal, consensus has been found to be superior to majority vote or other decision rules.

I. DEFINITIONS OF GROUP AND ORGANIZATION

Continuing the idea of developing a comprehensive theoretical framework, we might ask if small formal groups are simply small formal organizations. The answer turns out to be "yes" since the literature on both groups and organizations provides no definitions that would allow one to distinguish between them. For example, Shaw has written several editions of a popular text on small group dynamics, and he defines the group as: "two or more persons who are interacting with one another in such a manner that each person influences and is influenced by each other person" (Shaw, 1976: 446). Roby, in a text on designing organizations, defines an organization as "a system of roles and a stream of activities designed to accomplish shared purposes" (Roby, 1986: 16).

Some definitions of a group, such as that of Shaw, would seem to apply more to informal groups. However, other definitions, such as that of Cartwright and Zander in their classic text on group dynamics, stress the fact that a "full-fledged" group also has a system of interlocking roles and works toward a common goal (Cartwright and Zander, 1968: 48). Further, although Roby stresses the formal aspects, organizations also have their informal side. Research on organizations tends to focus on the formal side and research on small groups emphasizes informal or "elementary" behavior. However, small groups can also be formally organized, especially if they are part of larger formal organizations, and informal networks of individuals can function as organizations.

The difference between groups and organizations is primarily one of size. Organizations tend to be larger and to contain several small groups with different functions. The common characteristics of both fully functioning small groups and larger organizations, in terms of functional theory, have been presented as a crucial set (Hare, 1982:20):

1. The members are committed to a set of values that define the overall pattern of activity.
2. The members have accumulated or generated the resources necessary for the task at hand.
2. The members have worked out an appropriate form of role differentiation and developed a sufficient level of morale for the task.
4. The members have sufficient control, in the form of leadership, to coordinate the use of resources by the members playing their roles in the interest of the group's (or organization's) values.

An additional reason for viewing small groups as small organizations is that no separate theory or list of variables is needed to understand organizations from that needed to understand small groups. See the appendix for summaries of four of these theories. Finally, much of the research conducted to understand interaction in organizations has actually focused on small groups of persons. Many observers see the small group as a "microcosm" of larger organizations and indeed of whole societies (cf. Slater, 1966). Much of the research cited in all major texts on organizations—e.g., on authoritarian and democratic group atmospheres (White and Lippitt,

1960), on communication networks (Leavitt, 1951), on conformity to norms (Asch, 1955), and on situational leadership (Fiedler, 1967)—was done on small groups.

However, most small groups exist in organizations, which become part of the "external system" that includes the society and the environment, setting boundary conditions on the behavior in the small group (Homans, 1950: 316). The boundary conditions may be set in the form of norms governing behavior in roles, or by physical arrangements of the space available for work (Sundstrom and Altman, 1989). An example of the latter is given by Homans in his description of the "bank wiring observation room" experiment that was part of the study at the Western Electric Company (Roethlisberger and Dickson, 1939). In that experiment, the workers who were placed in the front of the room formed one informal clique and those in the back of the room formed another (Homans, 1950: 70–72). In this connection, Homans notes that informal behavior arising in response to the physical arrangement of the workspace or to other aspects of the task may come to be formalized in norms for the group. These norms, in turn, will change more slowly than the behavior of the group members (Homans, 1950:412).

II. GROUP PROCESS AND STRUCTURE

We want to know something about small groups in large organizations, but what is there to understand? The overall processes and the structures associated with them have been the specific concern of the symbolic interactionist school of social psychology since the turn of the century (Cooley, 1902; Mead, 1950), and are represented in contemporary work in the detailed analyses of social interaction conducted by Bales and his associates (Bales, 1950; 1970; Bales and Cohen, 1979). The basic question for social psychology is: How do individuals in social interaction join together to reach shared goals, either in a given situation that includes an organizational and environmental context or by creating new situations through the social construction of reality? Working answers require an understanding of process, structure, and change.

Process, structure, and change can be divided into task and social-emotional areas. Functional theory helps understand task behavior, dramaturgical theory helps with social-emotional behavior, exchange theory with process in both the task and social-emotional areas, and new field theory (SYMLOG) with structure in the social-emotional area. At present there is no single theory that has the task structure as its major emphasis, although such a theory should at least recognize contributions to the task at different levels of creativity. The theories overlap. A brief summary of the four theories is provided in the appendix as a beginning of the process of developing an integrated theory of social behavior. Many of the main ideas presented in this chapter have been adapted from my book *Groups, Teams, and Social Interaction* (Hare, 1992).

III. RESEARCH IN RELATION TO THEORIES

What is the relationship between the typical findings of research on group dynamics and the four theoretical perspectives noted above? Most of the research on group dynamics deals with the issue of individual conformity to group norms. However, only a few studies report the influence on conformity of more than one variable at a time, and even then the variables are not ranked according to their strength of influence.

The typical handbook or textbook on organizational behavior presents lists of findings without any integrated theory or common set of variables (cf. Organ and Bateman, 1986; Cherrington, 1989). Some of the most frequently cited lists in textbooks are Janis's list of faults that can occur in group problem solving leading to "groupthink" (1982), French and Raven's five sources of power (1959), Kelman's three types of conformity (1958), Benne and Sheats's list of group roles (1948), and Fiedler's (1967) and Blake and Mouton's (Blake, Mouton, and McCanse, 1989) dimensions of leader behavior. Certain processes are also frequently cited—for example, Tuckman's phases in group development based on therapy groups (Tuckman, 1965;

Tuckman and Jensen, 1977). Using the set of common variables and the four theoretical perspectives outlined in the appendix, these and other lists can be brought together as part of an integrated approach for the analysis of behavior in groups and organizations.

Given that all social interaction can be seen as related to an individual's attempts to reach some goal in a given situation, usually in the company of others, we should not be surprised to find that any conceptual (category) scheme for the analysis of social influence is at the same time a scheme for the analysis of social interaction (and vice versa). However, some sets of categories are useful for the analysis of content and others afor the analysis of process. For example, if one only has available the minutes of a series of meetings of a small group with no indication of who was speaking to whom, as I did for the Bicol Development Planning Board in the Philippines (Hare, 1968), the categories that focus on content are easiest to apply. In this case, the functional (AGIL) categories are recommended, and later analysis will elaborate this acronym. On the other hand, if one can observe a group directly, or if one has a fairly complete transcript, including who spoke to whom, then a set of categories with a focus on process can be used in addition to the content categories. Of the sets of process categories, the system developed by Bales (1950; 1970) has been the most widely used in studies of group dynamics. His newer SYMLOG system is the most comprehensive of the current systems (Bales and Cohen, 1979).

Since conformity or nonconformity takes place during social interaction, it is not enough to know what kinds of pressures are being applied, or even how they will be received. We also need to know, following exchange theory, whether or not the person responding to a suggestion was seeking some guidance in the first place. A category system such as that depicted in Figure 1 can provide a framework for sorting out the various findings in the literature. The figure indicates categories for task and social-emotional levels of behavior for a person urging conformity as well as for a person responding to conformity. The figure is a composite of several earlier models (Hare and Naveh, 1986; Hare, 1986).

At the top of Figure 1 are two sets of tables with two columns and five rows. These tables are used to record the behavior of the person urging conformity. There are two similar sets of tables at the bottom of the figure for the person responding to conformity. For each of the two

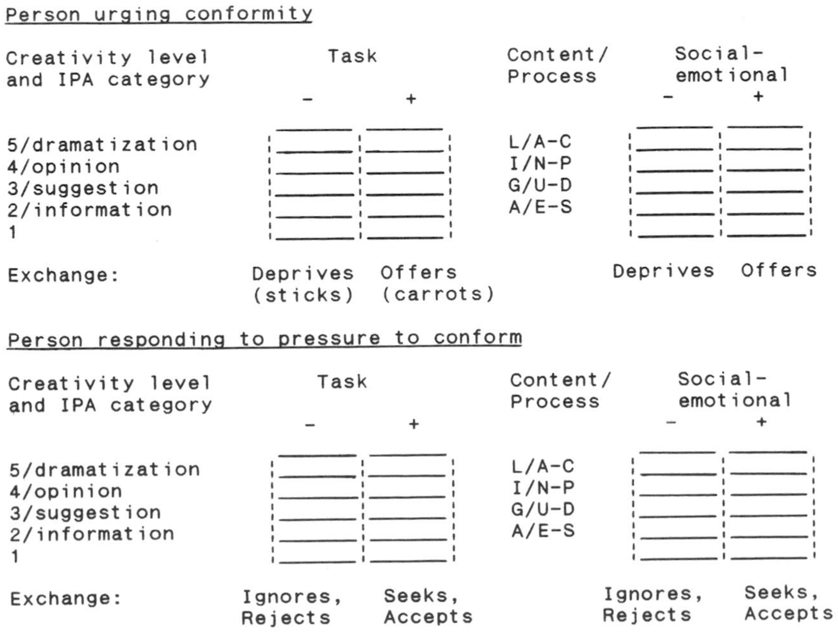

Figure 1 Task and social-emotional levels for person urging conformity and person responding to pressure to conform.

types of persons, one table is for social-emotional behavior and the other for task behavior. In each of the two sets of tables, one column is for behavior that is positive (carrots) and one column is for behavior that is negative (sticks). In the tables, the five rows represent the content and process associated with each level of activity ordered in a cybernetic hierarchy according to their strength of influence—with the highest level containing the most "information" in the cybernetic sense at the top of the table, and the lowest level containing the most "energy" at the bottom. As noted above, depending upon the type of material being coded, the tables in Figure 1 may contain only content data or only process data. If both types of data are being recorded, then two versions of Figure 1 may be needed.

For social-emotional behavior, for both the person urging conformity and the person responding, the content of each of the higher four levels in Figure 1 is represented by one of the functional categories (L, I, G, A), coded as in Table 1 (Hare, 1977:277; Hare, 1982:101; Hare and Naveh, 1986).

The lowest level is left blank, to be filled in by content associated with pressures to conform or to modify behaviors that are not intentional, such as those resulting from the presence of other individuals working on the same task or from the presence of an audience.

In the two social-emotional tables, the process categories that are associated with the content categories at each of the top four levels are the first four dimensions of Couch (1960) and Peabody and Goldberg (1989). (See the appendix for description of process categories and also Hare, Kritzer, and Blumberg, 1979; Hare, 1982:100–108.)

Pattern maintenance (L) plus (+) = conforming (C)
　　　　　　　　　　　minus (–) = anticonforming (A)
Integration (I) plus (+) = positive (P)
　　　　　　　minus (–) = negative (N)
Goal attainment (G) plus (+) = downward (submissive) (D)
　　　　　　　　　minus (–) = upward (dominant) (U)

Table 1　Types of Pressures Toward Conformity in Functional (LIGA) Terms

Pattern maintenance (L)	+ urging conformity on the basis of common values or stressing commitment to an issue; reinforcing values in the other person that will lead to desired behavior – giving negative reactions to values in the other person that will lead to nonconforming behavior
Integration (I)	+ urging conformity for the sake of friendship; citing the desirability of belonging to a group of people who have already conformed – withdrawing or threatening to withdraw friendship or positive regard; indicating that a person may be rejected by other group members if undesired behavior continues
Goal attainment (G)	+ urging conformity for the sake of becoming more powerful in the group; agreeing to follow a person's lead if he or she conforms – attempting to be coercive by blocking path to goal or by citing the opinion of someone who might be expected to have power over the other person
Adaptation (A)	+ urging conformity in exchange for material reward, service, or information – seeking to discourage nonconformity by denying, inhibiting, or preventing the provision of facilities or relevant information

Source: Hare, A. Paul and Naveh, David, "Conformity and Creativity: Camp David, 1978," *Small Group Behavior* 17 (1986). Reprinted by permission of Sage Publications, Inc.

Adaptation (A) plus (+)   = serious (S)
                minus (–)   = expressive (E)

The cybernetic hierarchy for the higher four process categories in the social-emotional table is presumed to work in the following way. The minimum positive reinforcement can be given to persons by taking them seriously, and the minimum negative reaction by being expressive—for example, taking the suggestion as a joke. A more positive reinforcement would be to act submissively and seek directions from the other, and a negative response would be to act in a dominating fashion. An even more effective positive reinforcement would be to be friendly, with a negative response involving unfriendly behavior. At the top of the hierarchy of positive behavioral reinforcement would be to conform to existing norms governing the relationship or to endorse the norms. For a negative response, one would act in an anticonforming way. The lowest row of the process categories is left open to be filled in with unintentional positive or negative effects, possibly including minimal cues from nonverbal behavior.

In the tables for task behavior the rows are for coding the content and the process of contributions. Content is coded in terms of five levels of creativity, as described in the appendix.

In brief, the levels are:

C1 = contributions that are personally need-oriented and unrelated to group work, or ways of avoiding a problem rather than finding a solution

C2 = suggestions for methods of improving communication, providing background facts, or increasing the skills of participants

C3 = suggestions for combinations of the interests of participants in "package deals"

C4 = provision of new perspectives on a problem by extending old concepts to fit a new situation

C5 = provision of a new understanding of both forms and relationships between persons or objects, including ideas that give a new definition of the situation and constitute a "paradigm shift"

Still referring to Figure 1, the two columns in each task table are for positive and negative contributions. If the purpose of the content of the contribution is to provide new material, then the contribution is coded in the positive column. However, if the primary purpose is to contradict or attack an existing idea, then the contribution is coded in the negative column.

For the process categories in the task area, some evidence suggests that level 1 indicates a lack of involvement in the task. Each of the levels 2 through 5 appears to be primarily associated with one of the categories from Bales's revised system for Interaction Process Analysis (IPA) (Bales, 1970; Hare, 1978), as follows:

C2 = positive or negative acts involving the exchange of *information*

C3 = positive or negative acts involving the exchange of *suggestions*

C4 = positive or negative acts involving the exchange of *opinion*

C5 = positive or negative acts involving *dramatization* of images revealing value positions

If one wished to keep track of the exchanges being made during the course of the interaction, then each category in the social-emotional and task table can be given an additional code in terms of one of the modes of exchange identified by Longabaugh (1963). The exchange modalities are listed at the bottom of each table. They differ, depending upon whether one is coding the person urging conformity or the person who is responding to pressure. For the person urging conformity, the modality of positive behavior (either in the social-emotional or task area) is "offers." For negative behavior, the modality is "deprives." For the person responding to the pressure to conform, a positive behavior can be either "seeks" or "accepts." A negative behavior can be either "ignores" or "rejects."

The display of categories in Figure 1 is similar to the "big board" in a stock exchange at the beginning of a day's trading. Each of the commodities has a starting value, represented by its position in the cybernetic hierarchy. However, the values of the commodities change according to supply and demand. The demand varies with the task and the phase of group development, as well as with the characteristics of the group members, the structure of the organization, and the nature of the environment.

IV. RESEARCH ON CONFORMITY AND SOCIAL POWER

Having now provided a fairly detailed paradigm for the analysis of conformity in Figure 1, we can examine some of the classic studies of conformity and the use of social power to see how they fit into the overall scheme for more precise identifications of the types of pressures that the authors describe. One of the earliest studies that identified several different types of pressures was that by Jahoda (1956). She presents a fictitious description of four faculty members on a selection committee who must decide whether or not to appoint a new person to the university staff. The president of the university urges them not to make the appointment because the candidate holds political views that clash with those of a major donor. It is clear that the donor will withdraw support from the university if the candidate is hired. All four faculty members agree to reject the candidate; however, each has a different reason for saying no. The reasons provide four examples of conformity.

One of the types of conformity Jahoda calls *convergence*, because it is based on an assessment of the facts. In Figure 1, this is an example of conformity based on positive task behavior at creativity level 2 that involves the presentation of facts. A second type Jahoda calls *compliance*, which is related to the power of the president over one faculty member who is concerned about his changes for promotion and is not going to disagree at this time. This instance of conformity in response to the inferred power of the president is an example of a negative social-emotional pressure of the goal attainment (G) type. A third type, *conformance*, is related to the sense of friendship toward other members of the committee. This is a positive social-emotional pressure of the integration (I) type. The fourth type, *consentience*, describes the faculty member who is won over by the value argument of the president; that is, this faculty member accepts the president's definition of the situation, a positive task behavior at creativity level 5. Two of Jahoda's types of pressures are thus in the task area and two in the social-emotional area. Three are positive and one is negative. Each is at a different level in the cybernetic hierarchy. Following the cybernetic hierarchy of control, we would expect that conformity pressures at task creativity level 5 to be most persuasive, then social-emotional integration (I) at level 4, then socio-emotional goal attainment (G) at level 3, and least the provision of facts at task creativity at level 2.

Although Jahoda does not discuss these types in connection with the cybernetic hierarchy of control, her further examples suggest reasons why the hierarchy of control might function as it does. Let us consider what it would take to change the minds of the four faculty members after their meeting with the president. Starting at the bottom of the hierarchy, the person who was convinced by the facts should be the easiest to influence. If this person is given a different set of facts, a different decision would be reached. Next would come the person who complied through threat of loss of promotion. After this person is promoted, or if in some other way the threat could be removed, that person would be free to change. More difficult to change would be the person who enjoyed being with a friendly group of faculty members. Even in another situation, this group might remain as a positive reference group and provide an anchorage for that person's opinions. Finally, the most difficult to change would be the person who has actually taken over the beliefs of the president regarding the definition of the situation. This new perspective is now an important part of the person's frame of reference and it becomes a matter of integrity to maintain it.

Kelman (1958) identified only three types of content, which he called compliance (G−), identification (I+), and internalization (L+). He defines the types in terms similar to Jahoda's. However, Jahoda's "consentience" is based more on the acceptance of the president's "good argument," while Kelman's "internalization" is based on accepting the point of view as part of one's personality. Kelman offers some hypotheses concerning the conditions under which each type of response to pressure is performed. His hypotheses follow:

1. When an individual adopts an induced response through compliance, the person tends to perform it only under conditions of surveillance by the influencing agent.
2. When an individual adopts an induced response through identification, the person tends to perform it only under conditions of salience of his relationship to the agent.
3. When an individual adopts an induced response through internalization, the person tends to perform it under conditions of relevance of the issue, regardless of surveillance or salience.

The hypotheses of Kelman add something to our understanding of how the cybernetic hierarchy of control actually works. It is not that ideas (information in the cybernetic sense) are more controlling than energy in some abstract way, but rather that ideas, in the form of values, are carried within the individual while factors that represent energy (facts, in this example) are external. Beginning at the top, the values (L) are the most powerful, since once they are internalized, the individual carries them as part of personality. Next come the norms representing a reciprocal role relationship (I) with another person (or persons). Once adopted through identification, the norms can be called up whenever the other person is present, or whenever the relationship is salient for some other reason. Next in order comes the response to the power of a task supervisor (G), since the power will only be effective when the supervisor is present. Last would be the power of money or another energy source as a means of influence in the adaptive area. Although Kelman does not include this type of influence in his analysis, it should have the least power because money only ensures a response at the moment it is exchanged. Once the deal is closed—the vote is purchased, or whatever form of influence was sought is obtained—the money has no continuing influence. For the next round, more money must be produced if the influence is to be maintained. In a similar way, other sources of high energy tend to be consumed in use.

Unfortunately, few experiments consider more than one variable at a time, so that it is difficult to find evidence to support the hypothesis that the types of influence are ordered according to the task (creativity) or social-emotional (LIGA) hierarchy. Asch's (1955) experiments on judging lengths of lines do provide a good illustration of the hierarchy, although Asch did not discuss his results in terms of a cybernetic hierarchy. In his experiment, Asch would ask a set of university students to judge which of three lines shown on one card was similar to a stimulus line, shown on another card. In each set of students, only one was a "naive" subject. The others had been coached before the experiment to give incorrect responses for most of the trials.

Asch found that an individual could be influenced by a coached majority giving incorrect answers, but that this effect could be countered by having at least one person agree with the individual. Further, the majority would have some influence, no matter how extreme its opinion appeared to be. However, over 60% of the subjects held out against the majority. Many of these subjects said that they typically held out for their own opinions, or that they considered making judgments an individual task. These results illustrate the hypothesis that a variable related to pattern maintenance (L), in this case defining the task as one of individual judgment, was more powerful than an integrative variable (I), in this case having a partner. The integrative variable was in turn more powerful than a goal attainment variable (G), majority pressure. Finally, the adaptive variable (A), modifying the length of the line, was the least powerful.

The results of the Milgram (1963) experiments are similar. There, subjects were asked to give electric shocks of apparently increasing intensity to another person, presumably to help the person learn. Although the negative effect of the shocks was unambiguous (A), the authority of the experimenter (G) was much more powerful as an influence. This power could in turn be modified if one other subject appeared to defy the experimenter (I). Finally, the value the subject placed on not harming another human was the most effective deterrent (L).

Jahoda's and Kelman's analyses of conformity focus on the person who is conforming. For other studies of leadership or social power, the focus is on the person who is trying to persuade or control. However, the basic categories turn out to be the same. French and Raven's (1959) often-cited analysis can be used as an example. They listed five types of power:

1. *Reward power*, which depends on another's ability to administer positive valences and remove negative valences
2. *Coercive power*, which stems from the expectation on the part of a person that he or she will be punished for failure to conform to an influence attempt
3. *Legitimacy*, where conformity is upheld by some internalized norm or value
4. *Referent power*, where a person identifies with another or has a desire for such an identity
5. *Expert power*, which depends on the knowledge or perception that a person attributes to an expert

In relation to the categories given in Figure 1, reward power could refer to any cell in the positive column of the social-emotional categories. However, the example given by French and Raven is that of an increase in pay for more productivity, suggesting that they are thinking primarily of the adaptive (A) cell in the column. Similarly, coercive power could refer to any cell in the negative column of the social-emotional categories. However, from the examples they give—firing a worker or scapegoating—the main cell involved would seem to be goal attainment (G). Legitimacy is similar to Kelman's "internalization" as an example of "L+." Referent power, which is similar to the types defined by Jahoda and Kelman, fits in the I+ social-emotional cell. Finally, expert power, as defined, might refer to any cell in the positive column of the task categories. However, from the examples given—namely, the advice of an attorney or someone providing directions—the emphasis seems to be in providing new facts or creativity at level 2.

Although any one person may urge or respond to actions at all levels of the cybernetic hierarchy, some observers have noted a tendency to specialize. For example, in several studies Bales and his colleagues have distinguished between persons who tend to be task leaders from those who are social-emotional leaders, or who combine a high rank on both activities (Bales, 1958; Bales and Slater, 1955; Borgatta, Couch, and Bales, 1954). Another often-cited example is the list of group roles identified by Benne and Sheats (1948). They list the roles in three sets: group task roles, group-building and maintenance roles, and individual roles. In Table 2, following the name Benne and Sheats give to each role, I have indicated the task or social-emotional category from Figure 1 that seems to provide the best fit.

For the group task roles, the initiator appears to operate at any of the creativity levels from 2 through 5. The other roles are more specialized, with positive contributions centered on one of th creativity levels. An exception is the coordinator, who combines integrating ideas at creativity level 3 with a coordinating function of G+.

In the list of group-building and maintenance roles, two have functions in the goal-attainment area (G). The standard setter evaluates the quality of the progress toward the goal (subrole L of G: G/l). The follower goes along passively with the work (a subrole G of G: G/g). The other five roles can be seen a subroles in the integrative (I) area. The encourager (subrole L of I: I/l) promotes the general idea of cohesiveness. The harmonizer (subrole I of I: I/i) resolves disputes that interfere with cohesiveness, as does the compromiser (also subrole I of I), who, as a participant in the conflict, meets others by coming half way. The gatekeeper (subrole G of I: I/g) coordinates the activity in the interest of cohesiveness. The group observer (subrole A of I: I/a) keeps the records for evaluating the extent to which cohesiveness is maintained.

For the individual roles, the three SYMLOG dimensions provide a good fit since here the attention is more on the manner in which an individual is interacting rather than on the content of the contribution. See also Figure 5. The eight types of roles are generally negative and backward.

Since leaders are distinguished from followers primarily by their success in the use of social power, we should not be surprised if the same categories that apply to conformity also apply to the behavior of leaders. For example, the profiles of the behavior of leaders and followers in the study by Lewin, Lippitt, and White on group atmospheres—in which the leaders were graduate

Table 2 Benne and Sheats's Classification of Group Roles

Role	Table 1 category	Characteristic behavior
Group task roles:		
Initiator	C+	Contributes new ideas about goal
Information seeker	C2+	Seeks factual accuracy
Opinion seeker	C4+	Seeks clarification of values
Information giver	C2+	Offers facts
Opinion giver	C4+	Recommends values
Elaborator	C3+	Spells out suggestions
Coordinator	G+, C3+	Coordinates activities and ideas
Orienter	C5+	Defines group in respect to goal
Evaluator-critic	C5−	Compares work with some standard
Energizer	C4+	Stimulates high-quality activity
Procedural technician	C2+	Performs routine tasks
Recorder	C2+	Writes down decisions
Group-building and maintenance roles:		
Encourager	I/l	Praises; indicates solidarity
Harmonizer	I/i	Mediates differences
Compromiser	I/i	Comes "halfway" in conflict
Gatekeeper, expediter	I/g	Keeps communication open
Standard setter, ideal	G/l	Evaluates quality of progress
Observer, commentator	I/a	Keeps records for evaluation
Follower	G/g	Goes along passively; audience
Individual roles:		
Aggressor	UN	Deflates other's status; attacks
Blocker	NB	Stubbornly resistant
Recognition seeker	UNB	Boasts; acts in unusual ways
Self-confessor	B	Expresses personal feelings
Playboy	UB	Displays lack of involvement
Dominator	UNF	Asserts authority; interrupts
Help seeker	DPB	Calls forth sympathy; insecure
Special interest pleader	N	Cloaks own prejudices, biases

Source: Reprinted by permission of The Society for the Psychological Study of Social Issues, and Kenneth D. Benne.

students and the followers were 11-year-old children (Lippitt and White, 1952)—can be compared in terms of combinations of Bales's 26 types. The authoritarian leader behaves in an upward-negative-forward fashion (giving orders and disruptive commands), drawing a reaction of downward-negative-backward behavior from the followers (leader-dependent actions, critical discontent, and demands for attention). The democratic leader behaves in an upward-positive-forward fashion (giving guiding suggestions, stimulating self-guidance, and being matter-of-fact), drawing a positive-backward reaction from the followers (who are friendly and confiding and who make group-minded suggestions). The laissez-faire leader, who did very little leading, behaved in a forward fashion while the followers were downward-forward. The main follower activity in this case was to ask for information and hold "work-minded conversations" among themselves, turning to the leader when they needed help making papier-mâché masks, or whatever the task was for the group session. The leader's prominent response was "extending knowledge."

Other often-cited studies of leader behavior are those conducted by Fiedler and his colleagues (Fiedler, 1967) that provide a contingency model of leadership. Fiedler states that the most effective leadership style is dependent on the nature of the situation. He identifies two styles: one style is task oriented—controlling, active, structuring leadership, or upward-negative-forward (UNF) in SYMLOG terms—the other style is relationship-oriented—permissive, passive, considerate leadership, or positive-backward (PB) in SYMLOG terms. Fiedler identifies persons with these two styles of leadership by having them complete the "least-preferred co-worker scale." The scale consists of 18 pairs of items representing the ends of eight-point scales, in which a score of 1 is low and 8 is high. At the high end of the scales are such terms as pleasant, friendly, accepting, and warm; and at the low end are such terms as unpleasant, unfriendly, rejecting, and cold.

All but two of Fiedler's scales would be found on the SYMLOG positive-negative dimension, sometimes with a hint that the person is also dominant or submissive, or forward or backward. The two exceptions are the pairs of traits "boring-interesting" and "guarded-open" that have more to do with the forward-backward dimension. Fiedler asks leaders to rate their "least-preferred co-worker" on the 18 scales. If the leader thinks that the person who is least preferred for the particular task is nevertheless a nice person to have around, the leader will have a high LPC score, and will be judged to be "relationship oriented." Leaders who emphasize good interpersonal relationships are presumed to be more considerate, derive their major satisfaction from relationships with others, and not to be influenced in their judgment of co-workers by success or task accomplishment. If on the other hand the leader feels that the person who is least preferred as a co-worker is difficult to get along with, the leader will have a low LPC score, and will be judged to be "task-oriented." The task-oriented leader is presumed to emphasize completing tasks successfully, even at the expense of interpersonal relationships, to gain self-esteem through task completion, and to value job performance.

What Fiedler has to say about the two leader styles is probably true, since similar distinctions between authoritarian and democratic leaders are being continually made in the literature. However, why focus on the "least-preferred co-worker?" Fiedler actually began his research project using a measure of the difference between the rating of the most-preferred and least-preferred co-worker. However, he found that there was very little variance in the ratings of the most-preferred co-worker, so only the score for the least-preferred co-worker came to be used as a measure of the range of the ratings.

Evidence from SYMLOG field diagrams suggests that some people, including leaders, tend not to make distinctions between their co-workers. These people not only see all their co-workers as equally friendly, but also as equally active (upward) and equally task-oriented (forward) as well. Since there is a good chance that the co-workers really do have different degrees of skill and different interpersonal styles, this type of leader would be friendly but not very effective in assigning co-workers to tasks on the basis of skill and the ability to get along with others. On the other hand, some people, including leaders, tend to be able to make distinctions between people, not only on their degree of friendliness (which is what Fiedler mainly measures), but also on the degree of upward-downward and forward-backward behavior as well. It appears that by asking a leader only to rate the least-preferred co-worker, Fiedler has taken a shortcut to obtaining data on how much the leader discriminates in rating all the co-workers on all three dimensions. Since the LPC scale seems to work, this is probably enough.

Fiedler's work is cited as an example of "contingency theory" because he asserts that the task-oriented leader will be more effective in some situations and the relationship-oriented leader in others. He describes the different situations in terms of three dimensions that he treats as dichotomies. The three dimensions can be seen to be related to the three SYMLOG dimensions as follows:

1. Leader-member relations—the extent to which the group trusts and respects the leader and will follow the leader's directions (primarily positive-negative in SYMLOG terms)
2. Task structure—the degree to which the task is clearly specified and defined (primarily forward-backward in SYMLOG terms)
3. Position power—the extent to which the leader has official power, or the potential or actual ability to influence others in a desired direction (primarily upward-downward in SYMLOG terms)

By typing situations according to these three dichotomous variables, on the basis of questionnaire data Fiedler derives eight types of situations—ranging from type I of good leader-member relations plus structured task structure plus strong power position, to type VIII of poor leader-member relations plus unstructured task structure plus weak power position.

For the first three types, in which leader-member relations are good and either the task is structured or the leader is in a strong position, Fiedler suggests task-oriented leadership is most effective because it allows the leader to take charge. In the most difficult situations—types VII and VIII, with poor leader-member relations and unstructured tasks—the task-oriented leader may also be more effective. Actually, neither of these two types of leaders may be able to do very well in these situations, but we cannot know this since Fiedler only presents data showing the *relative* effectiveness of the two leader styles in the different situations. For the middle types of situations (IV, V, and VI), in which only moderate control seems to be necessary, Fiedler recommends the relationship-oriented leader because he says the situations challenge the leader to focus on the cooperation of subordinates.

By way of tying in Fiedler's results with a more general theory of interpersonal behavior, Bales (1986) notes that when each of Fiedler's eight situations are plotted on a SYMLOG field diagram, type I would be found in the forward, slightly positive position, with the leader in an upward position. Types II through IV would form an arc, moving out in the positive direction. Types V and VI are less positive and move in the backward direction, with types VII and VIII being backward and negative. Thus, as has been suggested earlier in this chapter, the same dimensions that are used to describe individual behavior can also be used to describe the situations in which the individuals find themselves.

In addition to the fact that different leader styles may be required in different situations, different leader styles may also be required at different phases in a group's life. When there is a crisis or a deadline to meet, a more authoritarian style may be more effective. However, when there is enough time to involve all members in group decisions, then a more democratic style may be best. Bales (1983) has divided the 26 types of behavior (and values, see Figure 5) into three sets. Some behavior is always helpful if the group is to be effective (13 types, generally positive and forward), some is necessary sometimes but dangerous (6 types, generally negative and forward), and some almost always interfere with group process (7 types, generally downward, negative, and backward).

V. A MODEL GROUP

What is a good model for an effective group? In texts on organizational behavior, one often finds the effective group described as a "team" and instructions are given for "team building" (Patten, 1988:15; Francis and Young, 1979:6–7). In everyday and in scientific usage, *group* is the most general term. However, group is also used to refer to a set of individuals who have some common characteristic without actually meeting each other. This is the sense in which *nominal group* is used in social-psychology. In dictionaries the designations *team* and *crew* refer to particular types of groups (cf. Simpson and Weiner, 1989). The term *team* usually refers to sports groups, and *crew* typically refers to a group of persons managing some form of technology, especially forms of transportation such as boats, aircraft, or spacecraft.

Using the functional (LIGA) cybernetic hierarchy, it is possible to make some distinctions between the different types of groups. Crews of boats, planes, or spaceships can be placed at the bottom of the cybernetic hierarchy (A level) since their function is bound to a particular type of equipment or technology. (See Figure 2.) Change the technology and you change the nature of the team. Aircrews are an example, were a large amount of information about the conditions of the plane and the weather must be processed in a short period of time (Foushee, 1984).

Moving up, at the G level are work teams in business, manufacturing, health, and education. These teams are bound to a product, an object, or the care or education of a person. Change the nature of the product or the service provided and the team must be reorganized. At the I level would be sports teams that are rule-driven. They produce nothing. However, the

LEVEL	CHARACTERISTIC	TEAM TYPE
L	New discovery	Scientific research
I	Rule driven	Sports teams
G	Product driven	Business, manufacturing, health, and education teams
A	Equipment or technology driven	Crews of boats, planes, or spaceships

Figure 2 Teams classified according to the functional (LIGA) cybernetic hierarchy. (Reprinted by permission of Greenwood Publishing Group, Inc., Westport, CT, from *Groups, Teams, and Social Interaction*, by A. Paul Hare. Copyright 1992 by A. Paul Hare and published in 1992 by Praeger Publishers.)

playing field is usually swarming with referees to ensure that the game is played within the rules. Change the rules and you have a new game (Kew, 1987).

At the top of the hierarchy, the L level, are scientific research and development teams. They are not bound by existing equipment, product, or rules. Their task is to develop new concepts and to discover new relationships between old or new concepts. Wolpert and Richards (1988:9) writing about "a passion for science" suggest that "perhaps it is, above all, the thrill of ideas that binds scientists together, it is the passion that drives them and enables them to survive."

In addition to sorting crews and teams by functional specialty (LIGA), they can be classified according to the amount of integration and role differentiation required. Although some merge the two continua (cf. Dyer, 1987), they can be kept separate to form at least a two-by-two table of types of teams that are either high or low on each characteristic. Olmsted made this type of distinction for types of group leadership in his analysis of group activity (Olmsted, 1959; see also Olmsted and Hare, 1978:14). Sundstrom and Altman (1989:185) have also used this double dichotomy in their typology of work teams.

Sports teams provide the easiest example of this type of classification. (See Figure 3.) Golf teams are low on both integration and role differentiation. Synchronized swimming teams are high on integration but low on differentiation. Track teams are low on integration but high on differentiation. Football teams are high on both the need for integration and differentiation. Each type of team requires a different leader style, a different mix of task and social-emotional functions, and thus different solutions to the four functional problems. For some teams, the main function of the members is to support the activity of the central person, such as the surgeon in a surgical team or the pilot of an airplane.

Unfortunately, persons who wish to gain insight concerning the characteristics of effective groups by consulting the social-psychological literature will find that most of the research is based on studies of ad hoc laboratory groups of university students. These groups, that often meet for only 30 minutes or less, have to deal with only a few of the problems of work groups in an organizational setting.

In the laboratory, the functional problem that groups face in the first phase of their development is taken care of by the experimenter who defines the situation (L), sometimes through individual communications when the members are recruited. (See functional analysis of group development in the appendix.) For the second phase, the information for the puzzle or human relations problem to be discussed by the group (A) is also given by the experimenter. Thus the group members have nothing to do in the first and second phases of group development. For the third phase (I), they are usually left as a "leaderless group" to establish their own informal set of roles and rules for discussion. A "task leader" and a "social-emotional" leader

Integration

LOW   HIGH

	LOW	Golf	Synchronized swimming

Role
Differentiation

| | HIGH | Track | Football |

Figure 3 Sports teams classified according to required integration and role differentiation. (Reprinted by permission of Greenwood Publishing Group, Inc., Westport, CT, from *Groups, Teams, and Social Interaction*, by A. Paul Hare. Copyright 1992 by A. Paul Hare and published in 1992 by Praeger Publishers.)

may emerge, but if the group is small enough and meets for a short time, no obvious leadership functions may be required. In the fourth phase (G), usually some simple method of averaging opinions or a majority vote is used. Once the problem is solved, the group is disbanded, so no final phase (L) is required. Often the first two phases take place before the group members enter the laboratory or before the observer, who may also be the experimenter, begins to observe. Thus, most of the activity reported will be in the fourth phase. For example, Bales and Strodtbeck (1951) record that their laboratory groups began by exchanging information (which had already been given by the experimenter), evaluating the information, and reaching a decision (about a problem the experimenter had posed).

VI. GROUP PROBLEM SOLVING

The most effective method of problem solving is the scientific method when the problem involves objects—for example, in developing a new product or deciding on a new method of production. For these types of problems, one clever individual with all the facts at hand can reach a decision as well as a group, provided that the facts and the solution are unambiguous. Most of the advantages of groups for this type of decision are those of having a larger sample of judgments to average if the facts are ambiguous or if having a larger capacity to remember the facts is useful (Hare, 1992). If the individual problem solver is not inclined to be self-critical, then having someone else to test the solution may be an advantage. However, groups can also fail to be critical enough of proposed solutions, leading to the process identified by Janis (1982) as groupthink. Janis suggests that this phenomenon can be avoided if measures are taken to ensure that all negative information is thoroughly considered, and if group members are given a second chance to express doubts. As a safeguard, more than one set of members and experts may be asked to reach a decision and the results compared. Despite the potential hazards of groupthink, the scientific method, or some variation of it, is usually recommended by organizational consultants for group decisions involving objects or processes (Dyer, 1987:53, 79; Francis and Young, 1979:88–89, 216–217; Patten, 1981:162–163).

Over the years, the major proponents of the "human relations" approach to management have recommended consensus as a superior form of group problem solving when the commitment of the group members to the decision is important, especially since no dissatisfied minority is left to disrupt the application of the decision. Mary Parker Follett (1924), Harold Leavitt (1964), and Douglas McGregor (1960:232–235) each went to some length to outline the steps in the process of reaching decisions by consensus, since consensus does not simply refer to the final outcome of the decision but also to the process by which the decision is reached.

For example, Leavitt's *Managerial Psychology* (1964:262–265) urged managers in industry to consider the advantages of the consensus method in reaching group decisions. He noted that most businessmen at that time favored the method of limited discussion as well as the acceptance of majority vote in the parliamentary fashion. When the decision is forced quickly, the minority might psychologically reject the decision and may feel challenged to prove that the majority is wrong. When the time comes for action, they may act in ways to "prove" that the decision cannot be made to work. Leavitt emphasized that "if the group's problems require every member to carry out of the group a desire to act positively on the group's decision, then it is imperative that everyone accept, both consciously and unconsciously, the decisions reached by the group" (1964:264). He also noted that if total agreement could not be reached, an acceptable form of consensus is that everyone agree that there is a need for some kind of decision. "Then, at least, the minority has expressed its position, has announced that it is not ready to change that position, has had a chance to express its own feelings about the position, and has agreed that some decision short of unanimity is necessary" (1964:265).

A brief set of guidelines for arriving at group decisions by consensus is given in Table 3

Table 3 Guidelines for Group Decisions by Consensus in Terms of Functional Analysis

---

Pattern maintenance (L)

Do: Secure agreement to follow the decision rules for consensus; that is, create a decision that incorporates all points of view or one that all members agree is best for the group at this time.

Avoid: A zero-sum solution or using majority vote, averaging, or trading as conflict reduction devices.

Adaptation (A)

Do: Give your own opinions on the issue. Seek out differences of opinion to obtain more facts, especially from low status members.

Avoid: Arguing for your own opinions.

Integration (I)

Do: Address remarks to the group as a whole. Show concern for each individual opinion.

Avoid: Confrontation and criticism.

Goal attainment (G)

Do: Although the main function of the group *coordinator* is to help the group formulate a consensus on each issue and the main function of the group *recorder* is to record each decision as it is reached, all members should help formulate statements about solutions to which all can agree. Even if there appears to be initial agreement, explore the basis of agreement to make sure there is agreement at a fundamental level.

Avoid: Changing your mind only to reach agreement.

Terminal phase (L)

Do: If consensus is reached, make it clear that each group member is responsible to apply the principle in new situations.

Avoid: Pressing for a solution because the time for the meeting is over. If consensus is not reached, postpone the decision until another meeting and do more homework on the problem.

Source: Hare, A. Paul, "Consensus versus Majority Vote: A Laboratory Experiment," *Small Group Behavior* 11 (1980). Reprinted by permission of Sage Publications, Inc.

(see Hare, 1982: Ch. 9, 10). The guidelines are listed in the order that they would appear as phases in group development in terms of functional theory. The process of gathering opinions in a group to reach consensus begins with a recognition of the basic concerns of each individual. Note that in the first phase (L), the outcome of the consensus process can take two forms. The first choice is a decision that each member can identify with, and thus there is unanimity of opinion. A second choice is a decision that seems to be the best possible at the time, even though some members might wish for a different version of the solution if it were possible. With this form, members are able to unite, and will be committed to carry out the decision. In terms of functional theory, the first phase (L) involves a commitment to the process, the second phase (A) the gathering of facts, the third phase (I) the relations between members, and the fourth phase (G) reaching a decision. The fifth phase (terminal L) refers to the implications of the new decision.

A decision rule that calls for majority agreement and one that requires unanimity (all members have, or at least agree to, the same opinion) usually result in the same decision. However, a decision made by consensus has been viewed as superior to majority rule in terms of (1) decision quality, (2) the way in which it values all members, and (3) conflict resolution, although such a decision may take longer to reach (Hare, 1982:142–154).

When the cost is high of bringing group members together in one place to reach a decision, several systems have been suggested to take advantage of the problem-solving abilities of a number of individuals without having them participate in group discussion. In these "nominal groups," individual judgments are combined by some system of averaging (Rohrbaugh, 1981; Ulschak, Nathanson, and Gillian, 1981:85–96).

Unfortunately, many of the procedures recommended for use with nominal groups only provide for a group agreement on the rank order of given items. There is no possibility to combine items into a new idea (creativity level 3), much less to look for an overarching solution that combines all points of view into a new perspective (creativity level 5). Further, contributions of individuals who "own" ideas that do not receive a high rank are left out of the process. Thus, there is little evidence to suggest that nominal groups would be useful for reaching decisions at the higher levels of creativity.

The same problem occurs when tasks, such as the NASA moon walk problem, are used as part of team building to introduce group members to methods of effective problem solving. For the moon walk, group members are asked to agree on a rank order of items of equipment needed for survival on the moon. There is no provision for the introduction of new ideas and therefore no possibility of reaching consensus on a higher level of creativity.

A comparable problem occurs with tasks that purport to demonstrate the advantages of brainstorming. Individuals or groups are given a solution and asked to look for a problem—for example, "What are the uses of a brick?" In actual creative problem solving, the problem usually must first be identified and then a solution sought (Mumford and Gustafson, 1988:32).

Tasks that are suggested for workshops to demonstrate group decision making are often in the form of "eureka" tasks, where once group members have shared the information on their slips of paper, only one individual is needed to find the solution. Then all will agree (Steiner, 1972:23). Practice with more complicated and realistic training tasks would be required for a team with maximum role differentiation and a high degree of integration.

VII. SUMMARY

Since most of the decisions and many of the activities of persons in formal organizations take place in small formal or informal groups, the analysis of small group dynamics has a major place in the study of the larger social entity. In addition, relatively small groups can also have active subgroups within their borders. The same or similar dimensions of behavior or theories of social interaction appear to explain the dynamics of the subgroups, the small groups, and the larger organizations, as well as their relations both with each other and with the society and environment within which they are imbedded.

The review of research in this chapter was based on two assumptions: (1) that all theories of social interaction describe the attempts of one individual to join with others in a social situation to reach some goal, and (2) that each theory focuses on a different aspect of the process, and thus the choice of theory will depend upon which aspect of the process is judged to be most important. There is one major conclusion: that for maximum effectiveness in reaching group decisions as the group moves toward a collective goal, consensus has been found to be superior to majority vote or other decision rules.

A comparison of various definitions of groups and organizations indicates that in order to survive they must solve four basic problems. In terms of functional theory these problems have been identified as (L) agreeing on a common definition of the situation, (A) accumulating resources and skills, (I) developing appropriate role relationships and a sufficient level of morale, and (G) providing sufficient control, in the form of leadership, to coordinate the use of resources and the role to accomplish specific group tasks within the framework of the group's and organization's values.

The four functions form a cybernetic hierarchy with resources (A) at the bottom and values (L) at the top, in the order A-G-I-L. These four levels of activity can be used as sources of social-emotional pressure toward conformity in groups. The four process dimensions of serious-expressive, downward (submissive)-upward (dominant), positive-negative, and conforming-anticonforming also form a hierarchy and have a similar effect. Pressure toward conformity may also be exerted through arguments or counterarguments with regard to task activity. In content, the arguments may range from providing facts, at the bottom of a four-step hierarchy, to providing new theories at the top. The form of the task behavior may be giving information, suggestions, or opinions, or dramatizing images that reflect value positions. For both social-emotional and task behavior, a fifth and lowest level of persuasion is provided as an open category for conformity resulting from the presence of other persons where no conscious attempt at persuasion was intended. Each type of behavior can also be coded according to one of six modes of exchange: offers, deprives, seeks, accepts, ignores, or rejects.

Given this set of categories for coding social interaction, earlier analyses of conformity and social power by Jahoda, Kelman, Asch, Milgram, and French and Raven, of social roles by Benne and Sheats, and of leadership by Lippitt and White and Fiedler, can be seen as combinations of some of the types of content or form.

Although a sports team is often used as a model for the ideal performance of a work group in an organization, the analogy is not apt since a sports team produces nothing; it simply plays by the rules. In terms of the cybernetic hierarchy of functional areas, crews of boats, planes, and other forms of transportation are at the bottom since they are tied closely to their equipment or technology. Work groups in business, manufacturing, health, or education are next. They are product-driven, having to be effective both in producing the product and in maintaining effective intermember relations. As noted, next, the sports team is rule-driven. At the top of the hierarchy are the scientific research and development teams that are new-discovery-driven. They are not bound by existing norms for task or social-emotional behavior. Within each type, groups may be high or low on role differentiation and integration, thus requiring different solutions to the four functional problems.

The most effective method of problem solving is the scientific method when the problem involves objects. However the process of consensus has been found to be superior when the commitment of group members to the decision is important. In functional terms, the process of consensus can be seen as one in which each of the four basic functional problems is effectively solved in turn. Unfortunately, many of the tasks, games, or other methods that are used as models of effective decision making do not allow either a group to reach decisions at the higher levels of creativity or its members to become fully involved in a process of reaching consensus.

VIII. APPENDIX

A. Social Interaction: Seven Variables and Four Theories

Reviewing studies of behavior in small groups, attitudes, personality, and values, Peabody and Goldberg (1989) find seven variables (dimensions) that have accounted for much of the variance in social-psychological research over the years. The first four variables are dimensions of interpersonal behavior or values that can also be used to describe images of groups or organizations as they appear either in real life or in fantasy. As indicators of these dimensions, I rely on the factor analyses of Couch (1960). The dimensions are:

1. Upward (dominant)-downward (submissive)
2. Positive (friendly)-negative (unfriendly)
3. Serious-expressive (joking, laughing)
4. Conforming (to group or organizational norms)-anticonforming

Variable 5 is some measure or measures of variance. One could measure the variation along each of the first four dimensions, or one could use a summary measure such as the extent to which a person or group is "rigid" or "flexible," or one might measure the variance within a set of ratings or the variance between sets of ratings in different situations.

Variable 6 is represented by some measure or measures of intelligence or problem-solving ability. For example, here one can identify five levels of creativity based on the insight of I. A. Taylor (1975:306–308; see list below). His terms are used as labels for each level. For levels 2 through 5 the first part of the definition of the level (art and science) is also Taylor's. He was concerned with identifying levels of creativity in the larger society. Children's drawings were his example for level 1, *expressive*, because they indicated spontaneity, but the originality and quality of the product were not important. As an example of level 2, *technical*, he cited Stradivari's skill in making violins; for level 3, *inventive*, the combinations of materials that were used by Edison for a light bulb and by Bell for a telephone; for level 4, *innovative*, Jung and Adler's elaborations of Freud's theories; and for level 5, *emergentive*, the "paradigm shifts" created by Einstein, Freud, and Picasso.

The second part of the definition of each level of creativity (group discussion) indicates the activity that would be associated with the level in a problem-solving group. These definitions are taken from the category system proposed by Stock and Thelen (1958).

The third part of each definition (negotiation) indicates the activity associated with the process of negotiation and is based on the analysis by Hare and Naveh (1986). It is assumed that negotiations that result in agreements at higher levels of creativity have more lasting effects.

The levels of creativity (from low to high) are as follows:

1. Expressive
    a. *Art and science*: spontaneous contributions that indicate that a person is warming up for the task
    b. *Group discussion*: work that is personally need-oriented and unrelated to group work
    c. *Negotiation*: suggestions that allow a group to bypass a problem without actually solving it
2. Technical
    a. *Art and science*: contributions or solutions that involve skill and a new level of proficiency
    b. *Group discussion*: work that is maintaining or routine in character; provides background facts; provides suggestions for improving interpersonal skills
    c. *Negotiation*: providing a standard "textbook" solution to a problem
3. Inventive
    a. *Art and science*: ingenuity with materials, providing combinations to solve old problems in new ways

    b. *Group discussion*: suggesting alternative ways for solving a problem or clarifying already established plans

    c. *Negotiation*: providing solutions that involve trade-offs, so that each party receives some gain

4. Innovative
    a. *Art and science*: basic principles are understood so that older theories can be extended to cover new areas
    b. *Group discussion*: active problem solving by introducing unusual points of view
    c. *Negotiation*: "extending the margins" of concepts to fit new situations

5. Emergentive
    a. *Art and science*: contributions that involve the most abstract ideational principles or assumptions underlying a body of art or science
    b. *Group discussion*: work that is highly insightful and integrative; often interprets what has been going on in the group, and brings together in a meaningful way a series of experiences
    c. *Negotiation*: suggestions that allow a group to reach consensus through a new definition of the situation

The seventh and last variable identified by Peabody and Goldberg is one of evaluation. Whatever the form of the image of the person, group, or object in terms of the four behavioral (value) dimensions and measures of variance and intelligence, the same image may be evaluated positively by some and negatively by others. Thus, with regard to an image, the last bit of information we will want is whether the person presenting the image is "pro" or "con" the image.

The four theoretical perspectives that I have found useful, in combination, for the analysis of small groups and organizations are functional, dramaturgical, exchange, and new field theory (SYMLOG). They are summarized below.

B. Functional Theory

Functional theory was developed primarily by Parsons to apply to large social systems (Parsons, 1961). However, it can also be used for the analysis of behavior in small groups (Hare, 1983). Functional theory describes four basic functions that must be fulfilled for any social system or small group to survive. There must be a set of *values* that defines the overall meaning and general pattern to be followed in the group's activity. Parsons labeled this area "latent pattern maintenance and tension management," or "L" for short. The group must have sufficient *resources* to meet its goal. Parsons's label for this area is "adaptation," or "A." The *roles* of the group members must be clear and the members must have a sufficient level of *morale* to work together. Parsons's label is "integration," or "I." Finally, there must be adequate coordination in the form of *leadership* for the use of the resources by the persons playing the roles to attain specific group goals. Parsons's label is "goal attainment," or "G."

A set of categories was constructed by Andrew Effrat to identify positive and negative contributions to each functional area as they appear in small group interaction. The categories are given in Table 4.

When the fulfillment of each of these functions is considered as a separate task, then the typical group tends to develop through four phases:

1. (L) Commitment to the basic values and overall purpose of the group
2. (A) Acquisition or development of resources
3. (I) Defining roles and developing a sufficient level of morale
4. (G) Carrying out specific group activities, coordinated by leadership

Table 4 Functional Categories for Small Group Analysis

L phase	+	Seeks or provides basic categories or ultimate values
		Asks for or seeks to define:
		basic purpose or identity of group
		fundamental meaning of "all this"
		general orientation
		basic obligations
	–	Seeks to deny, take away, or inhibit the development and recognition of values.
I phase	+	Seeks or provides solidarity or norms (as primary mechanism of conflict management)
		Asks for or seeks to define:
		how the group can get along better, promote harmony, or decrease conflict
		what the specific norms governing relations should be
	–	Seeks to deny, inhibit, or prevent the formation of norms and movement toward group solidarity
G phase	+	Seeks or provides relatively specific direction, goal-definition, or problem solutions relevant to the group's goals.
		Asks for or seeks to define:
		relatively specific group goals (be careful to distinguish from values and norms)
		decisions which in effect are attainment of group's goals
	–	Seeks to prevent or inhibit movement toward the group's goals
A phase	+	Seeks or provides facilities for goal attainment
		Asks for or seeks to define:
		how to get or increase (especially to generalize) resources, relevant information, or facts
	–	Seeks to deny, inhibit, or prevent the provision of facilities and relevant information

Source: Hare, A. Paul, "Group Decision by Consensus," *Sociological Inquiry* 43 (1973). Reprinted by permission of *Sociological Inquiry*.

Eventually, groups pass through a final termination phase that is similar to the initial phase (L again). The overall meaning of the group activity is once more assessed as the group members prepare to go their separate ways. Thus in functional terms, groups can be seen to develop through five phases in the order L-A-I-G . . . L. Many theories of group development also identify five phases, although the content may differ, depending upon the type of group (problem solving, therapy, negotiation) that was used as a basis for the analysis (Hare, 1976:88–112).

Tuckman's description of a five-phase progression of group development based primarily on data from therapy group is an often-cited example (Tuckman, 1965; Tuckman and Jensen, 1977). However, the type of activity that he identifies in each phase is related directly to the unstructured group therapy situation in which members eventually learn to feel comfortable as they "expose" themselves and again insight into their own problems. This type of content would not be appropriate for a board meeting of a large organization, although the function of each phase would remain the same.

Each of the phases of group development can be further divided into four subphases with similar functions. For example, to develop a resource such as a machine, there must first be a plan (subphase L of A: A/1). Next, tools and raw material will need to be acquired (subphase A of A: A/a). Then persons will need to be trained to work together with the tools (subphase I of A: A/i). In the fourth subphase, the new machine is constructed under the leadership of a supervisor (subphase G of A: A/g).

As part of the functional theory, Parsons suggests that the four functional areas can be ordered in a cybernetic hierarchy. The function providing the most information is at the top, and the function providing the most energy is at the bottom. In this case, the *values* (L) determine more of the variance in the group's activity than the *roles* and level of *morale* (I). Roles and morale are, in turn, more important than coordination through *leadership* (G). The least important are the *resources* (A). Thus the cybernetic hierarchy takes the form L-I-G-A.

C. Dramaturgical Theory

Dramaturgical theory reflects the contributions of many persons from social psychology, anthropology, and the theater (Hare and Blumberg, 1988). One name that is often associated with this perspective is that of Goffman, who contributed many insights into the process involved in the "presentation of self in everyday life," especially in informal teams (Goffman, 1959). I have found Moreno's ideas in his descriptions of psychodrama especially useful as a basis for this analysis (Moreno, 1953).

The main concepts used in dramaturgical analysis are represented in Figure 4. In the center of the figure is a rectangle representing the stage or action area. This can be further divided into two parts, backstage and stage. The backstage area is where the actors prepare for their roles and where special effects are produced to influence the audience. This is the area in which those who arrange the setting and provide props, costumes, and makeup do their work. The stage is where the action takes place in full view of the audience. In the social-psychological literature the concept of "territory" refers to the stage and backstage areas that actors may define for themselves or that may be defined for them (Sundstrom and Altman, 1989). The literature on

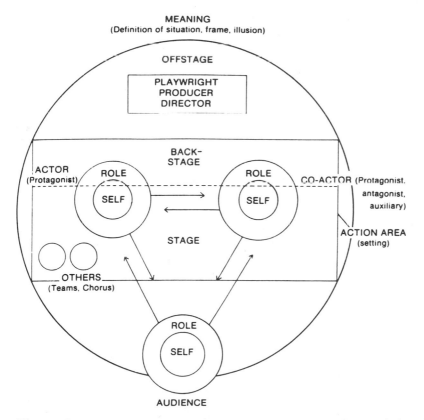

Figure 4 Basic concepts for dramaturgical analysis. (Reprinted by permission of Greenwood Publishing Group, Inc., Westport, CT, from *Dramaturgical Analysis of Social Interaction*, by A. Paul Hare and Herbert H. Blumberg. Copyright 1988 by A. Paul Hare and Herbert H. Blumberg and published in 1988 by Praeger Publishers.)

"interpersonal space" and territory is, in effect, a description of the space that an individual considers optimal for role performance.

For any action area there may also be offstage areas in which persons who have organized the activity (producers), as well as those who have rehearsed the cast and are providing cues for action (directors), remain hidden from the audience. In addition, there may be the person who provided the original idea or script for the performance (playwright). This does not complete the list, as there may also be persons who cater to the audience.

Onstage, in Figure 4, there are two sets of nested circles. One set represents the role played by the principal actor who is central to the definition of the situation at the moment (protagonist). The other set represents some co-actor, who may be a protagonist for another idea, an antagonist of the first idea, or an auxiliary player supporting the protagonist. Inside each of the larger circles representing the roles is a smaller circle to represent the self—the individual characteristics that each person brings to the role. The smaller circles near the protagonist represent additional players who may form a team to support the protagonist or a chorus to echo the mood.

In front of the stage, a set of nested circles represents an audience member. Even if there is no external audience, the actors are themselves an audience for their own and others' actions. Even if no other actor or audience is physically present, all social behavior is performed with some idea of the expectations of one or more reference groups in mind. The large circle, surrounding the stage and other areas, represents the meaning of the event that binds all the participants together. This overall meaning is variously referred to as the definition of the situation, the frame, or the illusion. In Parsonian functional terminology, it is the L area.

The categories of task activity from a dramaturgical perspective parallel those of functional theory. In the order in which a group would typically deal with them, the tasks are:

1. Developing an *actable idea* (functional area L)
2. *Staging* by locating or constructing an action area and providing props, costumes, and other necessary equipment (functional area A)
3. Recruiting the *actors*, if they are not already involved in the development of the actable idea, and training them for their *roles* (functional area I)
4. A period of *enactment* when the "play" is performed under the supervision of the director (functional area G)
5. A final phase when *new meanings* are assessed for the actors and the audience (functional terminal area L)

The actable ideas that form the basis of the social drama may be either very general or very specific in their implications. On one end of the continuum is an actable idea in the form of an *image* that has a program of action packed into it, much as a symbol in a dream may be a merger of waking events. The actable idea may be a more complex *theme*, including a direction of movement and a minimal set of roles to be enacted. The idea may provide the outlines of a *plot*, with a detailed scenario, defined roles, and an indication of the phases the group must go through to reach its goal. At the specific end of the continuum, the idea may be fully developed as a *script* for a play, with parts for each member of the cast and stage directions to guide the performance.

In a group, the actable idea may change from moment to moment, especially if the action is guided by an image. Even with scripts, periods of tragedy may be interspersed with periods of comedy, or a melodrama may turn into a farce, or more than one drama may be enacted simultaneously. In addition to their degree of complexity and specificity, the actable ideas can also be identified by the level of creativity required for their enactment. In a similar way, each action by an actor can be classified according to the level of creativity that is evident. Five levels of creativity that can be used as categories for dramaturgical analysis have been described at the beginning of this appendix. During the course of a group's activity, the behavior of individuals, subgroups, and groups can be plotted along a time line using these five levels of creativity.

D. Exchange Theory

In exchange theory, social interaction is viewed as the exchange of material and nonmaterial goods and services. Major contributors to this theory include Thibaut and Kelley (1959), Homans (1961), Blau (1964), and Emerson (1976), with more recent contributions having been made by Gergen, Greenberg, and Willis (1980) and Cook (1987). For the analysis of interaction in terms of exchange, a category system can be used based on the work of Longabaugh (1963; see also Hare and Mueller, 1979). Longabaugh identified six modalities of exchange: seeking, offering, depriving, accepting, ignoring, and rejecting. In his article reporting his observations of mother-child interaction, he divided the content of the exchanges into four categories: information, control, comfort, and esteem. He later agreed with me that these categories were in effect subsets of the media of exchange associated with functional analysis.

At the social system level, Parsons identified the four media of exchange as money (A), power (G), influence (I), and commitment (L; Effrat, 1968:101). In the small group, in the A area, facts, goods, or services are usually exchanged rather than money. Most of the descriptions of social exchange in the literature do not use any systematic category system, or if they do, they do not tie the categories to any more general theory. For example, Blau (1964) describes six types of rewards in a table with two rows and three columns. The two rows are "spontaneous evaluations" and "calculated actions," and the three columns are "intrinsic," "extrinsic," and "unilateral." However, in functional terms, the columns are a mix of functional types. The two intrinsic rewards are "personal attraction" (I) and "social acceptance" (I), the extrinsic rewards are "social approval" (L) and "instrumental services" (A), while the unilateral rewards are "respect-prestige" (L) and "compliance-power" (G).

E. New Field Theory

New field theory (SYMLOG) has been developed primarily by Bales (1970; 1988; Bales and Cohen, 1979; Polley, Hare, and Stone, 1988; Hare, 1989). The acronym SYMLOG stands for a *s*ystem for the *m*ultiple *l*evel *o*bservation of *g*roups. The system provides for an analysis of the images that guide interpersonal interaction at the level of the individual, group, situation, and society, as well as in fantasy. The system assumes that there are three basic dimensions of interpersonal behavior and values: upward (dominant) versus downard (submissive), positive (friendly) versus negative (unfriendly), and forward (accepting the task-orientation of established authority) versus backward (opposing the task-orientation of established authority).

Bales gives examples of behavior and images as they would be found in all sectors of this three-dimensional space (Bales and Cohen, 1979:355–386). As an indication of the nature of the behavior related to each of the three dimensions, Bales's descriptions of the overt behavior at each end of the dimensions are given in Table 5.

Bales's first two dimensions of interaction are the same as those identified by Peabody and Goldberg (1989). Bales's third dimension is actually a fusion of the third and forth dimensions of Couch (1960), which are similar to those of Peabody and Goldberg. Bales has developed two questionnaires to use in identifying an image of a person, group, or other object in terms of the three dimensions. (See Figure 5.) On the behavior form of the questionnaire, the emphasis in the third dimension is on serious versus expressive behavior. In the value form of the questionnaire, the emphasis in the third dimension is on conforming versus nonconforming values.

By dividing each of the three dimensions into three segments (high, middle, and low), Bales can identify 26 types of individual personalities or group roles. The 27th type is average, or middle, in all directions. Relationships between individuals, roles, or other images can be displayed on a field diagram for the analysis of the extent to which a group is unified or polarized, or contains individuals who are potential scapegoats or mediators. (See Figure 6.)

For the two-dimensional field diagram, the vertical axis goes from forward (at the top of the diagram) to backward (at the bottom). The horizontal axis goes from negative (at the left) to

Table 5   Behavior at Ends of Three Dimensions of SYMLOG Space

Upward (U)	Acts overtly toward others in a way that seems dominant (upward). Examples include taking the initiative in speaking; speaking loudly, firmly, rapidly, or with few pauses for the other to reply; holding the floor with "uh"; or addressing communications to the group as a whole rather than to individuals.
Downward (D)	Acts overtly toward others in a way that seems submissive (downward). Examples include participating only when asked questions, then speaks only to the person who asked the direct question; giving only minimal information in response to a question; or not addressing the group as a whole.
Positive (P)	Acts overtly toward others in a way that seems friendly (positive). Examples include assuming equality between self and others, asking others for opinions, balancing talking with listening, or starting talking and stopping talking flexibly and easily in response to the needs of the other.
Negative (N)	Acts overtly toward others in a way that seems unfriendly (negative). Examples include showing predictable disagreement with others in communication, for example, frequently says "no," "I don't think so," "I disagree," "I can't accept that," "well," or "but," and seeming unfriendly in response to friendly approaches of others; seeming detached, isolated, indifferent, distant, unsocial, secluded, unapproachable, or not a member of the group.
Forward (F)	Acts overtly toward others in a way that seems instrumentally controlled (forward). Examples include working on the task of the group by serious efforts at problem solving; making sincere statements of beliefs, values, or assumptions, but in judicious and controlled way; verbally exploring hypotheses by conjecturing, interpreting, or inferring; or trying to understand, assess, or diagnose the problem by communicating opinions and attitudes.
Backward (B)	Acts overtly toward others in a way that seems emotionally expressive (backward). Examples include changing mood of interaction suddenly; indicating that the content or manner of what is going on is too controlled or constricting; or indicating a desire for a switch from work to play, from reasoning to acting out, or from self-control to expression.

Source: Bales, Robert F., and Cohen, Stephen P., *SYMLOG*, 1979. Reprinted by permission of The Free Press.

positive (at the right). The extent to which an image is dominant (upward) or submissive (downward) is represented by the size of the circle centered on the point representing the location of an image on the forward-backward and positive-negative axes. The larger the circle, the more dominant the image and the smaller the circle, the more submissive.

With the two axes drawn on a square field diagram, the diagram is divided into four quadrants: positive-forward (where ideal behavior and values are found for most task-oriented groups that operate in a democratic mode), negative-forward (representing more authoritarian behavior and values), negative-backward (indicated by uncooperative, pessimistic, and cynical behavior or valuing the rejection of established procedures and conformity), and positive-backward (indicated by likeable, affectionate, and enjoyable behavior or valuing friendship, mutual pleasure, and recreation).

The overlay of lines and large circles on the diagram make it possible to identify probable subgroups as well as scapegoats, mediators, and dominators. Recent additions to SYMLOG theory make it possible to identify several hundred types of individuals and provide, through a computer program, a description of how they would be expected to interact with each other.

		DESCRIPTIVE ITEMS – Behavior Form			**DESCRIPTIVE ITEMS—Individual and Organizational Values**
—	U	1 Dominant, active, talkative	—	U	1 Individual financial success, personal prominence and power
—	UP	2 Outgoing, sociable, extroverted	—	UP	2 Popularity and social success, being liked and admired
—	UPF	3 Persuasive, convincing, shows task leadership	—	UPF	3 Active teamwork toward common goals, organizational unity
—	UF	4 Business-like, decisive, impersonal	—	UF	4 Efficiency, strong impartial management
—	UNF	5 Strict, demanding, controlling	—	UNF	5 Active reinforcement of authority, rules, and regulations
—	UN	6 Tough, competitive, aggressive	—	UN	6 Tough-minded, self-oriented assertiveness
—	UNB	7 Rebellious, unruly, self-centered	—	UNB	7 Rugged, self-oriented individualism, resistance to authority
—	UB	8 Joking, witty, clever	—	UB	8 Having a good time, releasing tension, relaxing control
—	UPB	9 Protects others, sympathetic, nurturant	—	UPB	9 Protecting less able members, providing help when needed
—	P	10 Friendly, democratic, group-oriented	—	P	10 Equality, democratic participation in decision making
—	PF	11 Cooperative, reasonable, constructive	—	PF	11 Responsible idealism, collaborative work
—	F	12 Serious, logical, objective	—	F	12 Conservative, established, "correct" ways of doing things
—	NF	13 Rule-oriented, insistent, inflexible	—	NF	13 Restraining individual desires for organizational goals
—	N	14 Self-protective, unfriendly, negativistic	—	N	14 Self-protection, self-interest first, self-sufficiency
—	NB	15 Uncooperative, pessimistic, cynical	—	NB	15 Rejection of established procedures, rejection of conformity
—	B	16 Expresses emotions, shows feelings	—	B	16 Change to new procedures, different values, creativity
—	PB	17 Likeable, affectionate, enjoyable	—	PB	17 Friendship, mutual pleasure, recreation
—	DP	18 Trustful, accepting, sensitive	—	DP	18 Trust in the goodness of others
—	DPF	19 Modest, respectful, dedicated	—	DPF	19 Dedication, faithfulness, loyalty to the organization
—	DF	20 Cautious, dutiful, obedient	—	DF	20 Obedience to the chain of command, complying with authority
—	DNF	21 Constrained, conforming, self-sacrificing	—	DNF	21 Self-sacrifice if necessary to reach organizational goals
—	DN	22 Depressed, unsociable, resentful	—	DN	22 Passive rejection of popularity, going it alone
—	DNB	23 Alienated, rejects task, withdraws	—	DNB	23 Admission of failure, withdrawal of effort
—	DB	24 Indecisive, anxious, holds back	—	DB	24 Passive non-cooperation with authority
—	DPB	25 Quietly contented, satisfied, unconcerned	—	DPB	25 Quiet contentment, taking it easy
■	D	26 Silent, passive, uninvolved	■	D	26 Giving up personal needs and desires, passivity

```
Note: U = Upward (dominant)
      D = Downward (submissive)
      P = Positive (friendly)
      N = Negative (unfriendly)
      F = Forward (accepting task-orientation)
      B = Backward (opposing task-orientation)
```

Figure 5 SYMLOG questionnaires for general behaviors and individual and organizational values. (Reprinted by permission of SYMLOG Consulting Group.)

Prior to the development of SYMLOG and the more recent summary by Peabody and Goldberg (1989) of the major dimensions of interaction, most theories of interaction, especially those of leadership, only dealt with behavior in the positive, forward, and upward part of the interpersonal space. Little attention was paid to negative or submissive behavior. For example, Golembiewski (1965:89), then author of a comparable chapter in an earlier handbook on organizations and now editor of the present handbook, noted that following Stogdill (1974), three dimensions were often found in previous studies: individual prominence (upward), aiding group attainment (forward), and sociability (positive). Since all leaders were upward by definition, leadership theories usually presented typologies of leaders in terms of the extent to which a leader shows a concern for production (forward) and a concern for people (positive). In these theories the dimensions are measured from zero to forward and zero to positive. There is no description or measurement of either backward or negative behavior.

Blake and Mouton's management grid is an example (Blake, Mouton, and McCanse, 1989). They describe six styles of management behavior based on combinations of two factors,

Values on Accepting Task-Orientation of Established Authority

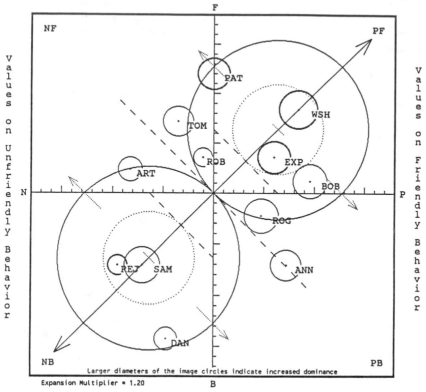

Values on Opposing Task-Orientation of Established Authority

Figure 6   Sample field diagram based on ratings made by PAT. (Reprinted by permission of SYMLOG Consulting Group.)

measured on scales of low (scored 1) to high (scored 9). Four of the styles are represented at the corners of the square grid as combinations of high or low concern for people and concern for production (1,9; 9,1; 1,1; 9,9). A fifth style is represented by a point in the middle of the grid (5,5) where the concerns are balanced. A sixth style is paternalism, a combination of the 1,9 and 9,1 styles.

REFERENCES

Asch, Solomon E. (1955). Opinions and social pressure. *Scientific American, 193*(5):31–35.

Bales, Robert F. (1950). *Interaction Process Analysis: A Method for the Study of Small Groups.* Addison-Wesley, Cambridge, Mass.

Bales, Robert F. (1958). Task roles and social roles in problem solving groups, In *Readings in Social Psychology.* (E. E. Maccoby, T. M. Newcomb, and E. L. Hartley, eds.), Holt, Rinehart, & Winston, New York, pp. 437–447.

Bales, Robert F. (1970). *Personality and Interpersonal Behavior.* Holt, Rinehart, & Winston, New York.

Bales, Robert F. (1983). *How to Read a SYMLOG Bargraph.* SYMLOG Consulting Group, San Diego.

Bales, Robert F. (1986). *SYMLOG and Leadership Theories.* SYMLOG Consulting Group, San Diego.

Bales, Robert F. (1988). A new overview of the SYMLOG system: Measuring and changing behavior in groups. In *The SYMLOG Practitioner* (R. B. Polley, A. P. Hare, and P. J. Stone, eds.), Praeger, New York, pp. 319–344.

Bales, Robert F., and Cohen, Stephen P., with Williamson, Stephen A. (1979). *SYMLOG: A System for the Multiple Level Observation of Groups.* Free Press, New York.

Bales, Robert F., and Slater, Philip E. (1955). Role differentiation. In *The Family, Socialization, and Interaction Process* (T. Parsons, R. F. Bales et al., eds.), Free Press, Glencoe, Ill. pp. 259–306.

Bales, Robert F., and Strodtbeck, Fred L. (1951). Phases in group problem solving. *J. of Abnormal and Social Psychology, 46*:485–495.

Benne, Kenneth, and Sheats, Paul (1948). Functional roles of group members. *J. of Social Issues, 4*(2):41–49.

Blake, Robert F., Mouton, Jane Srygley, and McCanse, Anne Adams (1989). *Change by Design.* Addison-Wesley, Reading, Mass.

Blau, Peter M. (1964). *Exchange of Power in Social Life.* Wiley, New York.

Borgatta, Edgar F., Couch, Arthur S., and Bales, Robert F. (1954). Some findings relevant to the great man theory of leadership. *American Sociological Review, 19*:755–759.

Cartwright, Dorwin, and Zander, Alvin, eds. (1968). *Group Dynamics: Research and Theory.* Harper & Row, New York.

Cherrington, David J. (1989). *Organizational Behavior: The Management of Individual and Organizational Performance.* Allyn & Bacon, Boston.

Cook, Karen S. (1987). *Social Exchange Theory.* Sage, Beverly Hills, Calif.

Cooley, Charles H. (1902). *Human Nature and the Social Order.* Scribner's, New York.

Couch, Arthur S. (1960). Psychological determinants of intepersonal behavior, Ph.D. dissertation, Harvard University.

Dyer, William G. (1987). *Team Building: Issues and Alternatives*, 2nd ed. Addision-Wesley, Reading, Mass.

Effrat, Andrew. (Spring 1968). Editor's introduction [Applications of Parsonian theory.] *Sociological Inquiry, 38*:97–103.

Emerson, Richard M. (1976). Social exchange theory. *Annual Review of Sociology, 2*:335–362.

Fiedler, Fred E. (1967). *A Theory of Leadership Effectiveness.* McGraw-Hill, New York.

Follett, Mary Parker (1924). *Creative Experience.* Longmans, Green, New York.

Foushee, H. Clayton (1984). Dyads and triads at 35,000 feet: Factors affecting group process and aircrew performance. *American Psychologist, 39*:885–893.

Francis, Dave, and Young, Don (1979). *Improving Work Groups: A Practical Manual for Team Building.* University Associates, San Diego.

French, John R. P. Jr., and Raven, Bertram (1959). The bases of social power. In *Studies in Social Power*, (D. Cartwright, ed.), University of Michigan, Ann Arbor, pp. 150–167.

Gergen, Kenneth J., Greenberg, Martin S., and Willis, Richard H., eds. (1980). *Social Exchange: Advances in Theory and Research.* Plenum, New York.

Goffman, Erving (1959). *The Presentation of Self in Everyday Life.* Doubleday, Garden City, N.Y.

Golembiewski, Robert T. (1965). Small groups and large organizations. In *Handbook of Organizations* (J. G. March, ed.), Rand McNally, Chicago, pp. 87–141.

Hare, A. Paul (1968). Phases in the development of the Bicol Development Board. In *Studies in Regional Development* (S. Wells and A. P. Hare, eds.), Bicol Development Planning Board, Philippines, pp. 29–64.

Hare, A. Paul (1976). *Handbook of Small Group Research*, 2nd ed. Free Press, New York.

Hare, A. Paul (1977). Applying the third party approach. In *Liberation Without Violence: A Third-Party Approach*, (A. P. Hare & H. H. Blumberg, eds.), Rowman and Littlefield, Totowa, N. J., pp. 265–287.

Hare, A. Paul (1978). A comparison of Bales' IPA and Parsons' AGIL category systems. *J. of Social Psychology, 105*:309–410.

Hare, A. Paul (1982). *Creativity in Small Groups.* Sage, Beverly Hills, Calif.

Hare, A. Paul (1983). A functional interpretation of interaction. In *Small Groups and Social Interaction*, vol. 2 (H. H. Blumberg et al., eds.), Wiley, Chichester, pp. 429–447.

Hare, A. Paul (1986). Conformity and creativity in negotiations: Israeli-Egyptian examples. *Israel Social Science Research, 4*(2):21–33

Hare, A. Paul (1989). New field theory: SYMLOG research 1960–1988. *Advances in Group Processes, 6*:229–257.

Hare, A. Paul (1992). *Groups, Teams, and Social Interaction: Theories and Applications.* Praeger, New York.

Hare, A. Paul, Blumberg, Herbert H., et al. (1988). *Dramaturgical Analysis of Social Interaction.* Praeger, New York.

Hare, A. Paul, Kritzer, Herbert M., and Blumberg, Herbert H. (1979). Functional analysis of persuasive interaction in a role-playing experiment. *J. of Social Psychology, 107*:77–88.

Hare, A. Paul, and Mueller, John (1979). Categories for exchange analysis in small groups: With an illustration from group psychotherapy. *Sociological Inquiry, 49*(1):57–64.

Hare, A. Paul, and Naveh, David (1986). Conformity and creativity: Camp David, 1978. *Small Group Behavior, 17*(3):243–268.

Homans, George C. (1950). *The Human Group*. Harcourt, Brace, New York.

Homans, George C. (1961). *Social Behavior: Its Elementary Forms*. Harcourt Brace Jovanovich, New York.

Jahoda, Marie (1956). Psychological issues in civil liberties. *American Psychologist, 11*:234–240.

Janis, Irving L. (1982). *Groupthink: Psychological Studies of Policy Decisions and Fiascos*. Houghton Mifflin, Boston.

Katz, Daniel, and Kahn, Robert L. (1978). *The Social Psychology of Organizations*, 2nd ed. Wiley, New York.

Kelman, Herbert C. (1958). Compliance, identification, and internalization: Three processes of attitude change. *J. of Conflict Resolution, 2*:51–60.

Kew, Francis (1987). Contested rules: An explanation of how games change. *International Review of the Sociology of Sport, 22*(2):125–135.

Kosower, Evie (1987). The Shokuba development program: Japan's step beyond quality circles. *Organization Development Journal, 5*(3):18–21.

Leavitt, Harold J. (1951). Some effects of certain communication patterns on group performance. *J. of Abnormal and Social Psychology, 46*:38–50.

Leavitt, Harold J. (1964). *Managerial Psychology*, rev. ed. University of Chicago Press, Chicago.

Lippitt, Ronald, and White, Ralph K. (1952). An experimental study of leadership and group life. In *Readings in Social Psychology* (G. E. Swanson, T. M. Newcomb, and E. L. Hartley, eds.), Holt, New York, pp. 340–355.

Longabaugh, Richard (1963). A category system for coding interpersonal behavior as social exchange. *Sociometry, 26*(3):319–344.

McGregor, Douglas (1960). *The Human Side of Enterprise*. McGraw-Hill, New York.

Mead, George H. (1950). *Mind, Self and Society*. University of Chicago Press, Chicago.

Milgram, Stanley (1963). Behavioral study of obedience. *J. of Abnormal and Social Psychology, 67*(4):371–378.

Moreno, Jacob L. (1953). *Who Shall Survive: Foundations of Sociometry, Group Psychotherapy, and Sociodrama*, rev. ed. Beacon House, Beacon, N.Y.

Mumford, Michael D., and Gustafson, Sigrid B. (1988). Creativity syndrome: Integration, application, and innovation. *Psychological Bulletin, 103*(1):27–43.

Olmsted, Michael S. (1959). *The Small Group*. Random House, New York.

Olmsted, Michael S., and Hare, A. Paul (1978). *The Small Group*, 2nd ed. Random House, New York.

Organ, Dennis W., and Bateman, Thomas (1986). *Organizational Behavior: An Applied Psychological Approach*, 3rd ed. Business Publications, Plano, Tex.

Parsons, Talcott (1961). An outline of the social system. In *Theories of Society* (T. Parsons et al., eds.), Free Press, New York, pp. 30–79.

Patten, Thomas H. Jr. (1981). *Organizational Development Through Teambuilding*. Wiley, New York.

Patten, Thomas H. Jr. (1988). Team building, Part I: Designing the intervention. In *Team building*, (W. B. Reddy with K. Jamison, eds.), NTL Institute for Applied Behavioral Science, Alexandria, Va. University Associates, San Diego, pp. 15–24.

Peabody, Dean, and Goldberg, Lewis R. (1989). Some determinants of factor structures from personality-trait descriptors. *J. of Personality and Social Psychology, 57*(3):552–567.

Polley, Richard B., Hare, A. Paul, and Stone, Philip J. (1988). *The SYMLOG Practitioner*. Praeger, New York.

Pruitt, Dean G. (1983). Achieving integrative agreements. In *Negotiating in Organizations* (M. H. Bazerman and R. J. Lewicki, eds.), Sage, Beverly Hills, Calif., pp. 35–50.

Roby, Daniel (1986). *Designing Organizations*. Irwin, Homewood, Ill.

Roethlisberger, Fritz J., and Dickson, William J. (1939). *Management and the Worker*. Harvard University Press, Cambridge, Mass.

Rohrbaugh, John (1981). Improving the quality of group judgment: Social judgment analysis and the nominal group technique. *Organizational Behavior and Human Performance, 28*:272–288.

Shaw, Marvin E. (1976). *Group Dyanmics*, 2nd ed. McGraw-Hill, New York.

Simpson, J. C., and Weiner, E. S. C. (1989). *The Oxford English Dictionary*, 2nd ed. Carendon Press, Oxford.

Slater, Philip E. (1966). *Microcosm: Structural, Psychological and Religious Evolution in Groups*. Wiley, New York.

Steiner, Ivan D. (1972). *Group Process and Productivity*. Academic Press, New York.

Stock, Dorothy, and Thelen, Herbert A. (1958). *Emotional Dynamics and Group Culture: Experimental Studies of Individual and Group Behavior*. New York University Press, New York.

Stogdill, Ralph M. (1974). *Handbook of Leadership: A Survey of Theory and Research*. Free Press, New York.

Sundstrom, Eric, and Altman, Irwin (1989). Physical environments and work-group effectiveness. *Research in Organizational Behavior, 11*:175–209.

Taylor, Fredrick W. (1903). Group management. *Transactions of the American Society of Mechanical Engineers, 24*:1337–1480.

Taylor, Irving A. (1975). An emerging view of creative actions. In *Perspectives in Creativity* (I. A. Taylor and J. W. Getzels, eds.), Aldine, Chicago, pp. 297–325.

Thibaut, John W., and Kelley, Harold H. (1959). *The Social Psychology of Groups*. Wiley, New York.

Tuckman, Bruce W. (1965). Developmental sequence in small groups. *Psychological Bulletin, 63*(6):384–399.

Tuckman, Bruce W. and Jensen, Mary A. (1977). Stages of small-group development revisited. *Group and Organization Studies, 2*(4):419–427.

Ulschak, Francis L., Nathanson, Leslie, and Gillian, Peter G. (1981). *Small Group Problem Solving: An Aid to Organizational Effectiveness*. Addison-Wesley, Reading, Mass.

White, Ralph K., and Lippitt, Ronald (1960). *Autocracy and Democracy*. Harper, New York.

Wolpert, Lewis, and Richards, Alison. (1988). *A Passion for Science*. Oxford University Press, Oxford.

5
Organizational Culture
Some New Perspectives

Robert G. Isaac

University of Calgary, Calgary, Alberta, Canada

I. INTRODUCTION

The resurrection of the organizational culture concept began in the early years of the last decade, primarily through the notable works *In Search of Excellence* by Peters and Waterman (1982) and *Corporate Cultures: The Rites and Rituals of Corporate Life* by Deal and Kennedy (1982). A great deal of interest continues on this subject, judging from the steady stream of articles appearing in business journals and magazines and the excitement they evoke among "culture vultures."

A. Assumptions About Culture

Organizational culture means an array of things to different people. Consequently, the literature reflects a host of assumptions about the topic brought together in various combinations. While this state of affairs provides variety from the perspective of the reader, it certainly fails to clarify and promote understanding. A partial menu of the premises (and their alternates) from which authors make selections include:

1. Organizations generate culture, as opposed to organizational cultures reflect, on a collective basis, the backgrounds of their members. These constitute the active and passive cases, respectively, of culture formation.
2. Organizations change culture to accommodate operational requirements, contrasted with organizations adjust operations to accommodate or control the effects of their inflexible cultures.
3. Manifestations of culture create and maintain an awareness and an understanding of its many facets among the bearers, in contrast with culture exists as a subtle phenomenon, at a level below conscious awareness, serving to orient the thoughts, feelings, and behaviors of members without their comprehension or permission.
4. Treatment of culture as either an independent or dependent variable, as opposed to a "root metaphor for conceptualizing organization" (Smircich, 1983)—a medium for shared meanings, interpretations, and understanding in the minds of members constituting the organization itself rather than merely one of its possessions.
5. Organizations with strong cultures outperform those possessing weak cultures, contrasted

with culture strength either promotes or impedes organizational performance subject to situational factors (a contingency approach).

The formulation of a consensus on these issues regarding the culture concept does not appear imminent, given the multitude of premises and assumptions, along with a general lack of empirical research on the subject.

B.   The Impact of Culture: An Internal Perspective

Culture receives a great deal of attention as a result of its reported impact on organizations. From an internal perspective, cultural links have been forged to the following organizational outcomes and functions: personal performance and productivity (Akin and Hopelain, 1987; Sherwood, 1988; Fisher, 1989; Welch, 1990); strategic planning and implementation (Arogyaswamy and Byles, 1987; Schein, 1986a; Schwartz and Davis, 1981); recruitment and selection (Gross and Schichman, 1987); self-selection (Soeters and Schreuder, 1988); socialization (Pascale, 1984; Swindle and Phelps, 1984; Schein, 1986a); innovation in new product development (Feldman, 1988); marketing (Arnold, Capella, and Sumrall, 1987); and sales (Tinsley, 1988).

C.   The Impact of Culture: An External Perspective

External to the organization, competitive position associated with a powerful culture remains a dominant theme (Peters and Waterman, 1982; Deal and Kennedy, 1982; Roskin, 1986; Pascale, 1984). Corporate adaptation to changing environmental pressures and conditions also receives attention (Nichols, 1985; Roskin, 1986; Akin and Hopelain, 1986). Finally, the management of cultural effects in relation to acquisitions and mergers continues to evoke interest (Nahavandi and Malekzadeh, 1988; Malekzadeh and Nahavandi, 1990; Siehl et al., 1988; Croft, 1990). In light of such important impacts on organizations, our continuing interest in the topic of culture seems warranted.

The nature of culture receives attention in the next section. Discussion focuses upon definitions of culture and the basic building blocks—cultural components or elements. Most of the literature employs the terms *organizational culture* and *corporate culture* in a synonymous fashion. The former term seems to denote any and all organizations while the latter suggests only commercial ventures. This chapter uses both terms interchangeably, but appreciates the subtle distinction.

II.   THE NATURE AND COMPONENTS OF ORGANIZATIONAL CULTURE

A.   Culture Defined

Insofar as organizational culture serves to reduce ambiguity for members and promotes sanctioned decision-making behavior, it merits credit as the organization's "autonomic nervous system" (Roskin, 1986). Corporate culture, commonly viewed as a phenomenon encouraging uniformity in thinking patterns and behaviors, becomes the "social or normative glue" binding the organization together (Siehl et al., 1988).

While these popular approaches provide a basic sense of understanding the construct, a more complex and complete description of organizational culture is offered by Schein (1984). For him, "culture" refers to the

> pattern of basic assumptions that a given group has invented, discovered, or developed in learning to cope with its problems of external adaptation and internal integration and that have worked well enough to be considered valid, and therefore, to be taught to new members as the correct way to perceive, think, and feel, in relation to those problems (p. 3).

This definition possesses qualities required of societal descriptions of culture. In society, culture involves the sharing of patterns of thought and their passage from generation to generation. In the corporation, this involves the sharing of assumptions and the transmission of these components to new employees. Societal change of culture occurs through experimentation with various alternatives in problem-solving situations (Chibnick, 1981). For the firm, culture change arises as a response to problems requiring internal adjustments to environmental contingencies. Schein's definition of culture in organizations appears to parallel societal versions of this concept.

While assumptions (subconscious values) constitute the fundamental building blocks of culture, other elements also play important roles. All of the components of culture will receive attention during the remainder of this chapter. These components are:

- Values
- Beliefs
- Ideologies
- Attitudes
- Artifacts

B. Values

To most researchers, shared values represent important components of cultures in organizations (Alvesson, 1987), and they often distinguish two types: instrumental and terminal (e.g., Rokeach, 1968). Instrumental values constitute beliefs that guide our behavior and conduct, whereas terminal values represent preferred outcomes enhancing our state of being.

Values exist in a hierarchy in our minds (Ravlin and Meglino, 1987), with each of us ranking them differently. Two individuals, sharing exactly the same sets of terminal and instrumental values, may desire different outcomes and exhibit vastly different behaviors because of variances in their personal hierarchical arrangements.

We become so inured to our values that over the course of time we lose a conscious awareness of their existence (Gagliardi, 1986). These subconsciously held values—better known as assumptions—possess a potency in orienting our behavior equivalent to those values for which a conscious awareness exists (Sathe, 1985). Assumptions and their linkages in various patterns constitute the very essence of culture. It is a fundamental irony that people behave in accordance with the dictates of their culture without, for the most part, recognizing the underpinnings that orient their conduct.

Another perspective on human values distinguishes between "espoused" (Argyris, 1982) and "inferred" (Siehl et al., 1988) values. Our verbal statements contain the values we espouse. Sometimes what people do contradicts what they say. In such cases, we attribute inferred values to people in order to explain their behavior. For example, an executive might state that human resources are the firm's most important asset, and then proceed to lay off workers in large numbers even though other alternatives exist. In such a case, inferences about the real values underlying this individual's attitude toward employees may arise.

The measurement of human values presents a real problem for researchers. The issue does not revolve around how we should measure values, but rather, what values we should measure.

The Rokeach value survey (Rokeach, 1973) measures personal values (18 terminal values and 18 instrumental values) that represent those found in general society. Various studies relating to organizational behavior (Regan, Rokeach, and Grube, 1982) and corporate culture (Swindle and Phelps, 1984) employ this survey. Other researchers tend to use business-oriented value surveys in their studies. The personal values questionnaire (England, 1967), measuring managerial value orientations, and the measures of culture instrument (Hofstede, 1980), assessing work-related values for cross-cultural research purposes, exemplify such surveys.

Inherent in the development of business-oriented value surveys lies an implicit assumption that organizational values differ from societal values and that measurement devices must reflect this distinction. Research efforts directed toward determining the validity of this belief would assist in the investigation of the culture phenomenon.

C. Other Components

Apart from values, beliefs also constitute important cultural elements. Sathe (1985) differentiates values from beliefs by suggesting that the former represent ideals worthy of effort in attaining, while the latter represent our understanding about what really happens within our personal frames of reference. As an example, an individual may value honesty but believe that as a policy, it sometimes requires substantial tailoring for use in the real world.

Ideologies represent shared patterns of beliefs, which unite individuals in a common understanding of how things work in their world (Beyer, 1981). Corporate ideologies orient employee behaviors in interpreting realities at work and variously in other aspects of their lives (Golembiewski, 1979): family relationships, development of political attitudes, and so on.

Attitudes also merit our attention, for they reflect cultural effects upon individuals. Attitudes, which are based upon values and beliefs, express the feelings of employees and predispose their behaviors (Fishbein and Ajzen, 1975).

Other components of culture include cultural artifacts (Schein, 1984), such as the firm's architecture, how people dress, stories often told, and technologies utilized. Arguably, many artifacts no longer possess any substantive significance for their culture. Thrown off at an early stage of cultural development, they once possessed meaning now long lost through transformation processes. Rather than being laden with the overtones of cultural content, these relics stand as empty reminders of the evolutionary nature of culture.

III. CULTURE FORMATION

What is the genesis of cultural elements and what are some major embedding mechanisms associated with culture formation?

Culture formation processes occur through the acceptance of solutions that successfully cope with issues facing the organization (Schein, 1983; Gagliardi, 1986). Problem-solving approaches arise out of educational background, past experiences, personal assumptions, and personality factors of the leader. Through the provision of both explicit and implicit reinforcements, the leader ensures adherences to proposed courses of action.

Given that a solution works, members of the group consciously adopt associated values that indicate "this is the way we do things in this situation." Perceived success determines acceptance and incorporation of these cultural elements. As time passes, group members tend to take these values for granted and they gradually drop out of conscious awareness. These components have now become assumptions, firmly embedded in the subconscious mind.

Gagliardi (1986) suggests that only elements "confirmed by experience" achieve status as components of culture, while Schein (1983) states that "only elements that solve group problems will survive." These two statements imply the existence of a filtering mechanism during the culture formation process that screens out cultural components failing to result in desired group outcomes.

The common wisdom suggesting the deletion of ineffectual cultural components seems doubtful or at least costly. This viewpoint precludes learning among organizational members that "this is the way we don't do things around here" and transmitting this knowledge, through culture, to new members. A knowledge of unsuccessful outcomes appears critical to organizational effectiveness. Embedding cultural components associated with negative outcomes offers corporations a very efficient method of guiding employee behaviors. A culture specifying the unacceptable in the minds of its bearers covers more ground by using fewer assumptions and by freeing participants to take for granted that everything else is sanctioned. The potential existence of error-avoiding cultural components warrants more extensive investigation in relationship to the culture of organizations.

During culture formation, leaders employ a variety of explicit and implicit approaches to embed cultural elements in the minds of employees, with three mechanisms having critical significance (Schein, 1983): what leaders pay attention to; leader reaction to critical events; and role modeling by leaders. Most observers agree (Akin and Hopelain, 1987; Sherwood, 1988; Pratt and Kleiner, 1989). Leadership is singularly important in shaping the "workscape" (Akin and Hopelain, 1987) of the shared images employees possess of their organization.

Numerous other mechanisms directly or indirectly under the control of managers shape the corporate culture. To illustrate only, a reasonable catalogue includes:

- Criteria utilized for making selection and promotion decisions (Schein, 1983)
- Organizational reward systems, criteria for reinforcement and punishment, and their application consistent with organizational priorities (Pascale, 1984)
- Extensiveness of teamwork and the degree of trust and support displayed by members (Akin and Hopelain, 1987)
- Organizational rites relating to status and role changes, personal recognition, loss of power, social facilitation, and other issues (Beyer and Trice, 1987)
- Technology and structure (Pennings and Gresov, 1986)
- Cultural symbols, language, gestures, stories, legends, folk tales, and myths (Beyer and Trice, 1987)
- Organizational structure, systems, and procedures (Schein, 1983)
- The physical design of the work environment (Schein, 1983)

IV. CULTURAL MAINTENANCE

The maintenance of a corporate culture, once firmly established within the organization, has an obvious relevance. Processes within organizations promote congruence and continuance of cultural components. Ironically, membership recognition of mechanisms fostering cultural stewardship seems doubtful given that culture resides at a level below conscious awareness.

Mechanisms include approaches and techniques similar to those employed in the embedding of cultural elements during the genesis of an organization's culture. Cultural symbols, legends, language, rites, and other artifacts, coupled with such factors as organization reward systems, structures, and other mechanisms, all serve to ensure cultural persistence and uniformity.

Again, leader behaviors dominate in reinforcing cultural elements among subordinates. The kinds of activities managers deem critical and monitor closely, the ways they react in various crises, and the day-to-day behaviors they display to employees, among many other factors, significantly promote or detract from cultural maintenance in their groups.

A significant cultural maintenance concern arises from the loss of acculturated employees and their replacement with the culturally naive. While evidence suggests that individuals considering organizational entry often make choices based upon the perceived alignment of their personal values with those of the firm (Soeters and Schreuder, 1988), an organization in maintenance mode still faces two problems with new employees. These "problems" become "opportunities" in organizations seeking change.

A. Problem One: Hiring the New Employee

First, management must ensure some degree of initial cultural congruence between the new employee and the organization. Recruitment and selection processes traditionally receive credit for matching job requirements and candidate's abilities to meet performance expectations, but these same mechanisms also provide screening opportunities for promoting cultural fits between the two parties (Gross and Schichman, 1987). While companies typically worry about hiring candidates with appropriate qualifications and experience, cultural considerations deserve more emphasis than presently given in furthering sanctioned values, practices, and other components.

Others suggest that educational institutions need to play a greater role in assisting organizations to secure better cultural fits with job candidates (Swindle and Phelps, 1984). By paying attention to corporate values, schools stand to minimize cultural incongruence and shock experienced by students upon their subsequent employment to the benefit of all parties.

B. Problem Two: Socialization After Selection

A second issue facing the organization relates to the furtherance of cultural alignment between the employee and the corporation upon completion of the hiring process. Organizations develop socialization mechanisms with processes aimed at ensuring a significant degree of "fit" between the new employee and the organization's structure (Schein, 1986a). Well-developed socialization programs present both the firm and the employee with chances to estimate this level of congruence throughout the process (Gross and Schichman, 1987).

Socialization begins to some extent even before employees enter the corporation. Prior to joining, these individuals commonly develop images of the firm as a result of the organization's interactions with the business community and society. Recruitment and selection processes similarly play a role in the socialization of employees (Pascale, 1984), as do subsequent company orientation programs and mentoring activities (Gross and Shichman, 1987).

Pascale (1984) outlines extensive socialization processes that force new employees to question personal values and assumptions, replacing them with company cultural elements. He suggests that corporations must tie personal rewards to performace in areas critical to the company and promote core cultural elements at every stage in the process. Socialization provides the key in furthering individual and organizational success in developing and maintaining a substantial overlap of interests.

Others view socialization processes in negative terms, as the following four points illustrate. First, socialization processes permit the distortion of communications (Deetz, 1985). For example, some corporate members use such processes to disguise their use of power over others and their pursuit of personal interests, while at the same time avoiding objective criticism of company practices.

Second, Lewicki (1981) equates some company socialization programs to "organizational seduction." Seduction methods include ensuring close cultural and goal alignments between the parties during the selection stage, providing enticing opportunities and stimulating challenges, and extensive reward systems. In sum, a fine line exists between employee socialization and exploitation in corporations, and there may be negative consequences for both parties.

Third, oversocialization can have awkward and even dangerous consequences. Employees exhibiting such qualities as "loyalty," "commitment," and other characteristics (Lewicki, 1981) sometimes receive favorable treatment regarding promotions, whereas important skills and abilities of the less amenable or pliable are ignored. Others suggest that oversocialization leads to a lack of creativity and responsiveness to corporate problems (Schein, 1986a; Lewicki, 1981).

Finally, Kovach (1986) warns that overreinforcement of certain behaviors and personal characteristics early in an employee's career, coupled with a rapid series of promotions involving changing expectations throughout hierarchical levels, may lead to negative outcomes for both the firm and the individual. Qualities developed in early career stages emphasizing personal achievement (such as "arrogance" and a strong sense of "self-determination") require modification at higher levels toward a concern for teamwork and the organization as a whole. Many employees experience difficulty rapidly adjusting behavior, and some become permanently sidetracked, unable to cope (Kovach, 1989).

V. PROBLEMS WITH CULTURE TRANSMISSION

The attribution of positive and negative socialization effects implies salience from both organizational and individual perspectives. Yet the taken-for-granted importance of socialization as a cultural transmission device requires critical examination itself. Here, three points develop this conclusion. They deal with: the problem of transmitting subconsciously held cultural information to others; the degree of employee acceptance and internalization of cultural elements required for effective socialization; and the potential immutability of human values.

A.   Problem One: The Conscious Transfer of Unconscious Awareness

Socialization processes involve the transmitting of cultural elements, and this basic fact implies several concerns. For the most part, culture resides at a level below conscious awareness in the minds of its bearers. Long-held values assume a taken-for-granted status, and over time can slip out of consciousness. Given this situation, one wonders how the transmission of cultural information occurs. Those charged with the responsibility for its transferral to new members may themselves possess severely restricted awareness of its contents. Rather than the blind leading the blind, the culturally unaware teach the culturally naive!

This observation constitutes a major problem, and one possible solution credits new members with the skills of a cultural anthropologist in decoding organizational culture. From this perspective, determining congruent and incongruent realities from espoused cultural elements contained in socialization mechanisms and programs would greatly preoccupy a new employee wishing to share the same patterns of assumptions as everyone else.

This scenario appears highly improbable. More likely, cultural elements presented at an early stage of socialization are taken at face value by new members (whether or not they are internalized), even when the presentation may seem bizarre to newcomers (e.g., Sherif's "autokinetic effect" experiments, 1936). One key factor seems to be the insecurity or threat experienced by new members, which tends to make them uncritical and accepting of cues coming from legitimate authorities (e.g., Milgram's obedience experiment, 1963). Disconfirmations of some of the organization's values, beliefs, and assumptions occur over time when behaviors and conduct of long-standing members do not reflect these espoused cultural elements.

The new member enters a period of what might be termed secondary socialization, a complex set of mental rules governing when to espouse one thing, when to do another, and finally, when to do both at the same time. What initially constitutes a comprehensive socialization process from the organization's perspective degenerates over time into "street smartness" by the employee.

Disconfirmation of espoused cultural elements under this model triggers a partial repudiation of primary socialization (presented by the organization) and initiates secondary socialization, an internal process controlled by the individual, or more likely, by the reference groups of the informal organization to which the person belongs. Consequently, organizations wishing to maximize their return on substantial investments in the development and operation of socialization mechanisms should avoid pulling the trigger as much as possible by ensuring congruence between espoused and experienced cultural elements.

The proposed model demonstrates the potential importance of studying processes relating to the transmission of cultural elements to new organization members. Surprisingly, the development of an understanding of these transmission processes receives low priority in the culture literature, which favors a continuing emphasis on describing the general effects of socialization programs (see previous section). Without a clearer understanding of exactly "what" and "how" the employee is learning during initial stages of organizational membership, it seems premature to speak authoritatively about the benefits and liabilities associated with socialization programs.

B.   Problem Two: The Level at Which Employees Need to Be Socialized

Cultural elements of new members exist for the most part at levels below conscious awareness, assuming an awakened status when situations arise causing them to smash headlong into the elements of an organization's culture that possess a significantly different nature. Collisions of this type probably occur very rarely, with the result that personal and organizational elements generally coexist in relative peace. Even incongruent elements should not pose problems for either party unless the individual experiences sufficient levels of awareness and feelings of dissonance to evoke a negative response.

Should socialization programs therefore attempt to change cultural elements in the backgrounds of new recruits? Does the need exist?

Two authorities hazard responses. Hebden (1986) suggests that socialization represents a process of learning to identify and cope with corporate value systems for the employee rather than one of modifying personal values. Redeker (1990) emphasizes the importance of clearly and understandably communicating a code of conduct that expresses and establishes the organization's culture, without mentioning the modification of personal elements of culture from the employee's perspective.

Neither of these authors sees the cultural metamorphosis of the new member as a prerequisite for success within the organization. Instead, success merely requires a recognition of cultural dictates and an observance of them in behavior and conduct. This approach represents a significant departure from the traditional emphasis in socialization, in which acceptance and internalization of cultural elements by the individual defines a major essence and purpose of the process itself.

An interesting distinction (Golembiewski, 1962) between formal and psychological membership in the identification of groups provides an adaptable and useful method for culturally framing this socialization problem from the organization's perspective. Which of the following does an effective socialization process require?

- Formal membership—a recognition and observance of cultural dictates within the organization
- Psychological (psychocultural) membership—an acceptance and internalization of cultural elements of the organization
- Both of the above by the individual

The degree of importance assigned to the promotion of cultural congruence during member socialization processes deserves urgent attention in the research on this topic.

C. Problem Three: The Immutability of Cultural Elements

Values of an enduring nature become embedded relatively early in life (Sathe, 1985). The effects of family members, friends, neighbors, schools, television, religion, and other factors serve to firmly anchor them in our minds. For this reason, management exerts limited control over employee values (Alvesson, 1987.) For example, Adler and Jelinek (1986) question the degree to which people shed their "ethnicity" each day when entering the workplace. They question the ability of management to change people after selection occurs. In an empirical study of Dutch employees working in American firms, Soeters and Schreuder (1988) report that employee values do not substantially change over time through corporate socialization. Brightman and Sayeed (1990) state "human values are immutable."

Where elements of culture collide between the organization and employee, the ability (let alone the will) of the member to modify personal values to accommodate the former appears questionable. If individuals cannot change, the efficacy of the socialization process in organizations, seeking to promote acceptance and internalization of cultural elements, should decline as the numbers of such collisions increase for each member.

Modifications of cultural elements within the individual constitute an imperative if one wishes to suggest that corporations generate distinctive cultures in the first place. Given immutable personal culture elements, each corporation's culture merely constitutes a collective manifestation of employee value systems. Culture management becomes an exercise in hiring the right people with sanctioned value systems and either managing around them or else getting rid of them when the firm must adjust to environmental contingencies requiring new types of value systems in order to cope. Consequently, research in the area of change as it pertains to personal culture elements is critical, not only to the socialization function, but also in relation to the viability of the corporate culture construct itself.

VI. CHANGING CULTURE: AN ORGANIZATION DEVELOPMENT PERSPECTIVE

In this section, attention focuses upon culture change at the level of the entire organization. Specifically, points of immediate concern relate to processes, tools, and recipes of culture change, as well as issues associated with cultural interventions.

A. Processes of Culture Change in Organizations

Societal change of cultural rules occurs as a result of the exploration of alternative problem resolution approaches (Chibnick, 1981), and culture change in organizations follows this same pattern (Gagliardi, 1986). Organizations explore an array of potential courses of action in order to resolve problems. Constraints of prevailing cultural values and assumptions in the organization limit the range of alternatives checked out by the firm. Successful approaches in resolving problems generate values and beliefs that transform into cultural elements.

Sometimes organizations prefer to perish rather than undergo change processes (Gagliardi, 1986). Companies with powerful cultures find it extremely difficult or impossible to adapt to dynamic environments. Schein (1986b) notes that strong cultures sometimes lead to the derailment of complete industries.

Gagliardi (1986) identifies two types of culture change, apart from cultural suicide. Cultural incrementalism occurs through the incorporation of new values and assumptions that do not challenge the rights of existence for current cultural elements. Cultural revolution, on the other hand, occurs when change requires the abandonment of some cultural elements because they stand in opposition to the new ones that replace them. Actually, "culture change" is a less apt descriptor than "cultural replacement," since it involves the slaying of parts of the culture, frequently along with its bearers, and the creation of a substantially altered one.

Schein (1983) suggests that viable processes of culture change occur through hybridization. A manager adds values and assumptions, acquired through personal experience, to those of the prevailing culture. Where the employees' "zone of indifference" is great enough, or where elements promote positive outcomes to problems, incorporation occurs. As a consequence, the original bearer acquires more authority. Schein views these "hybrid" managers as cultural change agents, capable of observing the old culture, and yet adding new elements as dictated by changing circumstances. The effectiveness of such managers results from their membership in the culture undergoing change and their sensitivity to the relevant issues. They do not face rejection by other members because their ideas and suggestions are perceived as appropriate rather than foreign.

Schein (1984) identifies two separate sets of conditions for the creation of elements within a culture. Circumstances surrounding the generation of cultural elements determine, to a great extent, the degree of subsequent modification or change. First, positive problem-solving elements appear easy to change in an organization's culture. These types of elements arise in situations in which exploration of an array of alternatives occurs until a satisfactory solution emerges. Subsequent utilization of this solution occurs because it works and provides its own positive reinforcement. However, abandonment readily occurs when the solution no longer effectively produces desired outcomes, and this results in an exploration of new approaches.

Schein identifies a relatively enduring second class of elements that relieve members of anxiety. These elements provide satisfactory solutions to problems perceived as threatening. Members continuously practice and observe them, even in the absence of the conditions that originally led to their formation. This occurs because members do not want to take a chance.

Adherence to these cultural components rewards the bearers by reducing their own anxiety. Changing culture under these circumstances involves great effort. Leaders must absorb member anxiety while advocating the exploration of new alternatives and ensuring that experimentation occurs. Another leadership role involves assisting members to readjust their perceptions as the outcomes become known regarding the new approaches.

B. Tools for Intervention in Culture

What tools can leaders employ in changing organizational culture? To begin, see Section III, on culture formation, which emphasizes leadership behavior in terms of role modeling, the kinds of things leaders spend their time on, and how they behave in a crisis.

Powerfully, also, Roskin (1986) highlights the importance of leadership in managing corporate culture by permitting cultural deviance to exist. When carefully managed, such deviance assists managers in avoiding the perpetuation of culturally sanctioned but no-longer-appropriate approaches. Some organizations institutionalize this approach, as in Lockheed's "skunk works" or the multiple religious orders of the Roman Catholic church.

In addition, intrapreneurship provides an important internal process requiring encouragement and management by leaders to promote corporate innovation and to identify and foster the role of change agents where required (Pinchot, 1984). Intrapreneurs question assumptions, values, and other culture components. They work to expand the boundaries of approved behaviors in order to solve problems and raise productivity.

Overall, perhaps, transformational leadership provides a means by which managers articulate their visions and raise subordinate expectations (Bass, 1990). This leadership style calls for a charismatic approach, the establishment of mutual respect between subordinates and the leader, a recognition of subordinate needs, and intellectual stimulation. This type of leadership facilitates the questioning of traditional problem-solving approaches by both managers and subordinates alike. Transformational leaders frequently challenge the organization's culture, changing it in the process. Both transformational leadership and intrapreneurship provide important considerations for organization development practitioners and managers wishing to modify the cultures of corporations.

C. Recipes for Cultural Intervention

The literature provides some guidance for interventions in established organizational cultures, adding credibility to the assumption that culture is under the control of management. As a governable factor generated through corporate life, it provides an important lever for leaders in guiding their organizations (Smircich, 1983; Schwartz and Davis, 1981). Adjustments to the culture of an organization permit alignment with such factors as strategy, the product or service offered by the firm, environmental dynamism, competitive advantage, corporate size, and interdependence between areas necessitated by the nature of the operation (Arogyaswamy and Byles, 1987). Linkage of organizational culture and societal culture as well as technoeconomics and organization structure (Pennings and Gresov, 1986) from vantage points both internal and external to the organization, receives attention relating to the need to make compensatory adjustments.

Many recipes for organizational intervention exist for the shaping of culture. Blueprints for culture change generally include (Edwards and Kleiner, 1988; Kazemek, 1990) such processes as: establishing a strategy, identifying relevant cultural components, setting forth a corporate vision and communicating desired cultural elements, ensuring member involvement, and finally, reinforcing member behavior and conduct. Others (Deal and Kennedy, 1982; Croft, 1990) emphasize the importance of skill and consensus-building processes, enhanced communication, openness and trust, patience and flexibility, and other relevant factors among members experiencing change.

Culture change processes receive attention in relation to many areas warranting corporate concern: productivity (Akin and Hopelain, 1987), marketing (Arnold, Capella, and Sumrall,

1987), competitive advantage (Sherwood, 1988), and sales (Sanfilippo and Romano, 1990). Other considerations, such as how to make a culture more powerful (Gross and Shichman, 1987) or how to adapt culture in the face of mergers, acquisition, downsizing, and other factors (Croft, 1990), reflect continuing and current business issues. Important factors assisting individuals in ensuring the success of their OD interventions also receive attention (Garcia and Haggith, 1989).

D. When Intervention Is Appropriate

Given some clarity about the "how" and "what" of cultural change the issue remains: "When is cultural intervention appropriate?"

An overview of an organization's life cycle helps move toward some working answers. Schein (1984) identifies three stages in the cultural life of an organization. An initial growth stage holds the young group of members together and it is doubtful that required changes could be successfully introduced during this period. During the midlife of an organization, culture may require change in order to permit modification of responses to environmental contingencies. This stage demands sensitivity to internal corporate conditions and the need to limit or encourage cultural diversity. Outsiders, capable of recognizing assumptions and raising awareness, perform a vital function. In the third stage, mature organizations find that the immutability of the culture prevents adaptation to changing environmental requirements. In this case cultural revolution, rather than incrementalism, may be necessary for the replacement of old cultural elements with new ones. Generally, purges permit change, with bearers of the new culture overcoming cultural resistance to change by the survivors.

E. Problems Regarding Culture Change Interventions

Before ending this discussion of culture change, some important issues require consideration. First of all, culture is an extremely subtle phenomenon and does not lend itself to superficial analysis. One must decode patterns of assumptions based upon espoused beliefs, observed behaviors, organizational practices, stories, rites, and other factors. Cooperation between outsiders and insiders working simultaneously facilitates this process (Schein, 1984). Fully understanding a particular organization's culture critically affects the process of change. Roskin (1986) warns that a comprehensive understanding of the culture must exist in the mind of the organization development practitioner before the introduction of change. Schein (1986b) similarly cautions the OD practitioner from simplistically approaching culture change without fully appreciating the ramifications.

Second, confusion relating to the concepts of organizatonal culture and climate occurs frequently. Climate refers to the extent to which employee expectations are being met regarding the workplace at a particular point in time. It measures the degree of alignment between personal and corporate cultural elements (Schwartz and Davis, 1981) and concerns factors such as motivation, morale, and management practices (Nave, 1986). Climate is more observable than culture, dealing with perceptions and feelings of employees.

Third, organization climate appears to be a governable factor (Golembiewski and Carrigan, 1970a,b; Schein, 1986a; Young and Smith, 1988; Cullen, Victor, and Stephens, 1989), highly dependent upon leadership and manager-employee interactions (Kozlowski and Doherty, 1989), with links to organizational effectiveness (Turnispeed, 1988), performance (Sipos, 1988), and behavior (Golembiewski and Carrigan, 1970a,b; Young and Smith, 1988). As a result of its manageable nature, considerations relating to the promotion of an appropriate ethical climate receive substantial attention (Cullen, Victor, and Stephens, 1989; Petrick and Manning, 1990). Concerns also revolve around the suppression of personal values, beliefs, needs, and ideals in favor of those of the company (Golembiewski, 1979). Of interest and concern, managerial and OD interventions relating to cultural, rather than climatic, changes fail to receive similar attention from an ethical perspective in the corporate culture literature.

Finally, Schein (1986a) cautions that organizational climate "can be managed in the traditional sense of management but that it is not at all clear whether the underlying culture can be." Assumptions held by members of an organization have enduring qualities perhaps not subject to manipulation. Others (Kerr and Slocum, 1987) suggest that changes in culture occur over extended periods of time when managers pay attention to the articulation of performance standards and reinforce met expectations.

Resolution of this central issue warrants the attention of researchers. Somewhat ominously, Bibeault (1982) notes that by far the majority of companies managing successful turnarounds replace people in critical positions in the organization. One wonders if a lack of skills in changing the culture of members leads to such outcomes, or if culture change requires basic changes in membership.

VII. CULTURE STRENGTH

Culture strength and change concepts, receiving the bulk of the attention in the organizational culture literature, are often linked because building a strong culture represents a special case of the latter. Culture strength depends upon aligning personal and organizational culture elements. The terms *culture strength* and *powerful culture* frequently appear with reference to such congruence on an organizationwide basis. Reflecting such usage in the literature, these terms are employed throughout the remainder of this chapter.

A. The Nature of Culture Strength

Sathe (1985) defines culture strength in terms of three considerations: the number of significant cultural assumptions found throughout the organization, the extent of sharing of these elements by members in the organization, and finally, the degree to which organizational members similarly prioritize the assumptions. Strong cultures exist when multiple assumptions, widely shared and similarly prioritized, orient member behavior, conduct, performance, and beliefs. Others describe culture strength in relation to consistency of its nature and cohesiveness among the bearers (Arogyaswamy and Byles, 1987).

Organizations possessing strong cultures experience greater difficulty in affecting culture change, because of the ingrained existence of associated assumptions, values, beliefs, and other components in the minds of employees. Such widely held cultural elements guide members' behaviors and conduct as they perform their assigned tasks, whether or not these activities prove detrimental to the firm's survival.

Core values are associated with the overall culture of the firm and represent those shared by most or all of the employees (Arnold, Capella, and Sumrall, 1987; Martin and Siehl, 1983). Members of various subcultures found within the organization hold secondary values. An organization with a strong culture possesses numerous core values, ranked similarly in their order of importance by employees.

B. Culture Strength and Importance to the Organization

Fixing the degree of "culture strength" within the organization appears consequential. Here we sample a few of the arguments for, and several against, promoting robust cultures.

1. Arguments for Promoting Culture Strength

Many authors report the association of a strong culture with superior organizational performance (Deal and Kennedy, 1982; Peters and Waterman, 1982; Roskin, 1986; Schmidt and Posner, 1986; Gross and Shichman, 1987; Bratton, 1989/1990). Denison (1984) suggests beneficial outcomes of strong culture linkage with a participative management approach. Others (Arnold, Capella, and Sumrall, 1987) discuss the positive effects of combining marketing plans with the building of strong cultures in hospitals.

In general, authors stress the importance of aligning cultural components such as values, beliefs, assumptions, and ideologies in the minds of employees. Proponents of powerful cultures suggest they: permit members to view themselves as unique; provide a unity of thought among employees in a purposeful direction, fostering personal commitment and greater individual performance; enhance teamwork and managerial effectiveness; and further organization performance, efficiency, and effectiveness.

2. Contingency Arguments Regarding Culture Strength

Another group of writers on the subject of culture strength suggests that powerful cultures, devoid of elements promoting change, frequently prove detrimental to firms, hampering managerial abilities to adapt successfully to dynamic environmental contingencies (Arogyaswamy and Byles, 1987; Lewicki, 1981; Schein, 1986a). Culture strength, as an internal variable, presents problems (Schein, 1986b) in well-established organizations experiencing marginal or unacceptable corporate performance.

A contingent relationship exists between culture strength and corporate performance, depending upon such factors as size of the organization, environmental characteristics, strategy, dependence between working areas, and the nature of the firm's products or services (Arogyaswamy and Byles, 1987). Internal variables of culture structure and technology (technoeconomics), in relation to their societal or industrial counterparts, require adjustments to account for environmental realities (Pennings and Gresov, 1986).

In conclusion, many authors reject the assumption that powerful cultures always prove beneficial. In some cases, culture strength constitutes an asset and at other times, a liability to the organization.

C. Culture Strength: Reality or Illusion

The debate about cultural strength is, in one sense, muted by the fact that many variables serve to limit the strength of corporate culture. Serious questions arise concerning the degree to which corporations build strong cultures through the use of various embedding mechanisms. A number of subtle factors limit the extent to which managers and employees share values, beliefs, assumptions, and other elements. Six factors receive attention below.

First, the effects of occupational communities (Van Maanen and Barley, 1984) impact culture strength. People engaged in similar lines of work share cultural elements that transcend the corporate boundaries in which they work (Alvesson, 1987). For example, carpenters working for different companies possess common assumptions that may align them culturally more with one another than with any other employees or groups located in their own corporations. The presence of one or more these occupational communities frustrates attempts to strengthen culture within organizations.

Second, functional department membership (Lawrence and Lorsch, 1967) limits the possibility of building a unified and powerful corporate culture (Posner, Randolph, and Schmidt, 1987). Employee values align with those of their department and its functions, whether or not the cultural elements of the department are congruent with the organization. For example, a marketing or a product design group often values innovation among its members while the accounting or auditing group may typically discourage such characteristics. Therefore, the existence of a diverse range of functionally different groups, occurring as a consequence of the fundamental need to organize a firm, serves to detract from the formation of a single powerful culture.

A third consideration relates to differences in values and other cultural components held by employees located in various hierarchical levels within the firm (Posner, Kouzes, and Schmidt, 1985). Kovach (1986) suggests that managerial orientations shift from a narrow focus to a broad perspective as people rise up the corporate promotion ladder. Assumptions and values held by employees therefore vary considerably at different levels because of variances in responsibilities and duties. In this light, it seems unrealistic to imagine a single set of cultural elements, held at all levels by all employees, that create a distinctive and unified culture throughout the organization.

A fourth factor impeding cultural congruence in organizations relates to the existence of subcultures within the corporation (Martin and Siehl, 1983). Some subcultures serve to enhance the dominant corporate culture, while others, of an orthogonal nature, add new cultural elements. Still others, viewed as countercultures, contain values that challenge or subvert those of the dominant culture. The existence of one or more countercultures weakens the prevailing culture of a corporation, for good or ill.

A fifth factor that limits culture strength in an organization concerns the effects of intergroup conflict. Schein (1986a) suggests that conflicts between groups in organizations help each to build and maintain their own cultures. Through conflicts, groups define themselves by contrast with other groups. Intergroup conflict therefore creates numerous subcultures and these subcultures, even if not directly challenging the prevailing corporate culture, each possess distinctive cultural elements. This results over time in a subcultural mosaic forming within the organization. Therefore, the presence of a single culture shared by all groups of an organization does not seem possible under such circumstances.

A sixth factor limiting culture strength relates to the potential immutability of personal values. Incorporation of cultural elements of an enduring nature occurs early in the life of an individual (Sathe, 1985). Attempts to modify or control personal values often prove difficult from management's point of view (Alvesson, 1987). Given such an understanding of personal value systems, the extent of success enjoyed by organizations wishing to increase their culture strength appears questionable. These organizations necessarily seek to interfere with personal cultural elements of members in order to ensure conformity to a sanctioned template.

Given these six factors, the extent to which corporations can build homogeneous cultures appears limited. Perhaps we need to adjust our thinking regarding the concept of culture strength. An alternative viewpoint suggests that employees state openly and carry out activities in line with whatever the organization officially values and this gives the appearance of a powerful culture. They receive rewards for doing so and as long as the values espoused do not collide head on with those really imprinted within each individual, no harm is done from their vantage point. What then passes for a powerful culture within an organization really represents a somewhat superficial collective expression of culturally approved espoused elements. As long as each employee actually believes in the commitment of others to this sanctioned gospel, the espoused culture develops a life of its own, albeit one that cannot withstand environmental realities that challenge personal values.

On a relative basis, some organizations possess very powerful cultures compared to their counterparts. On an absolute basis, from this vantage point, the culture strength concept does not possess the potency often implied. At best, culture strength exists at a modest level in companies successful in inspiring members to believe that they share espoused values with others and therefore must themselves conform. At worst, a distinctive culture does not exist in many firms at all.

D. An Alternative Model of Culture Strength

Perhaps a more robust model of corporate culture strength emphasizes the existence of one or more dominant cliques, in each of which only a select number of managers actually share and similarly prioritize a limited number of cultural elements. Members of a dominant clique typically will represent upper (and a limited number of middle) managers, along with perhaps a few functional specialists. These people possess most of the corporate power, and while their culture represents not the only culture of a firm, it constitutes the only one that matters in the short run. In cases in which two or more dominant cliques exist in an organization, bargaining activity occurs.

Other cliques live in harmony with, or oppose, this (these) dominant clique(s). In either case, associated cultures survive (and perhaps thrive) within the corporate confines as long as the bearers prove useful to members of the dominant clique(s) and its (their) culture(s).

Expulsion, ostracism, or demotion result for members of alternate cultures when they create problems for the dominant culture(s).

Substantial evidence supports a bargaining view of culture. Brightman and Sayeed (1990) report that many authors find "multiple cultures within an organization," and they themselves identify culture gaps between various groups in an empirical study within an electric utility division. Kerr and Slocum (1987) state "subcultures are a natural by-product of the tendency of organizations to differentiate" and discuss the role of multiple reward systems in supporting different subcultures. Many others express the belief that the cultural mosaic exists within organizations of even moderate size. These findings satisfy at least one fundamental assumption underlying the proposed model, that multiple-culture (subculture) organizations exist. Reasonably, it seems safe to conclude that one or more dominant subcultures also exist within each of these organizations (e.g., members of senior management), fulfilling a second necessary condition of the model.

Given this scenario, cultural artifacts of the dominant culture(s) create the work environment and climate for most employees. These many artifacts include corporate mission and philosophy; goals and objectives; policies and procedures; work methods and standards; stories, myths, and rituals; and office/plant decor and layout. They represent the manifest aspects of the dominant culture(s). Nondominant culture employees pay lip service to the values espoused by dominant culture members and perform in accordance with observable features (artifacts) of this (these) culture(s). Apart from culture artifacts, the vast majority of employees may remain largely unaware of the prevailing subconsciously held culture elements of the dominant clique(s), except when someone pays the price for violating such elements.

In this light, culture strength no longer requires concern over such subtle phenomena as the extent to which everyone throughout the organization shares the same assumptions, values, and other elements, and the degree of similarity in which they are prioritized. Under the proposed model, this ubiquitous approach gives way to the following more limited and observable considerations:

1. The nature and number of cultural artifacts thrown off by the relatively small dominant clique or cliques
2. The degree to which members operating outside the sphere of the dominant clique adhere to its cultural artifacts (espoused philosophies, values, goals, procedures, etc.)

Relationships between these points provide many potentially interesting avenues for investigation in terms of their internal and external effects on the organization. Should the efficacy of this model be established, measurement of culture strength (adherence to dominant culture-espoused artifacts) would be enhanced and eased, becoming a two-stage process. Identification of cultural artifacts originating with the dominant culture constitutes the first order of business. This is a relatively easy process because of the manifest nature of artifactual elements. Second, ascertaining the degree of observance of these artifacts by other subcultures and individual members (either or both levels of analysis) determines culture strength.

The need to differentiate between "espousal" and "practice" within the organization—a problem associated with the prevailing gospel on culture strength—fades away under this model because we are no longer dealing with the subtlety of values and assumptions. This distinction between such unobservable elements presents great difficulty because of its complexity (Golembiewski, 1987). The underlying premise of the proposed model ignores a concern about a cultural congruence of elements between the individual and the organization in favor of an observance by the individual of what those in charge deem important—the artifacts of their culture(s). Regarding culture strength, isn't the second outcome what we really want in any case? Furthermore, this proposed method avoids some rather sticky problems regarding the immutability of personal values.

The proposed model of culture strength reduces the concept from what might be termed a broad-range theoretical approach to the level of a "middle-range theory," as first proposed by Robert Merton (Boudon, 1991), the sociologist. Our current understanding of culture strength involves treating it as an overarching (grand) variable, and this approach appears limited. Measurement and manipulation of such a singular, subtle, and complex phenomenon across tens, hundreds, or even thousand of people seems unimaginable!

Reduction of the culture strength construct to represent adherence to dominant culture artifacts by members outside this (these) culture(s) provides benefits typically associated with theories of the middle range. The measurement of culture strength turns away from an analysis of the congruence of personal value systems on an organizationwide basis. Using cultural artifacts of the dominant group as a reference point, measurements of adherence levels by individuals and groups (subcultures) provide a reasonably useful variable for analysis. Identifying subcultures, isolating trouble spots, and planning appropriate interventions from this narrower frame of reference presents more manageable challenges. Finally, dealing with the culture strength construct at the middle range permits federation with other theories of a similar level (organizational climate, group cohesiveness, etc.), thereby promoting a greater degree of integrative conceptualization.

E. Culture Strength: Macro Assumptions and Micro Realities

In this last section on culture strength, problems regarding levels of analysis (macro and micro) and other issues receive attention.

Many authors suggest that building consensus among corporate members, in relation to culture elements, permits the firm to mobilize its workforce in a unified direction in order to respond successfully to environmental problems. This school of thought continuously receives attention not only in the literature but also among culture enthusiasts in the business community. The strong culture–superior corporate performance assumption awaits substantial validation from an empirical stance, although some evidence exists (see Section VII.B.1).

Organizations with cultures in varying strengths and across industries require comparative analysis before we reach conclusions about competitive performance. Unfortunately, this possesses an "easier said than done" quality, requiring the development of standardized methods of measuring culture strength and the establishment of industry-specific standards of culture strength against which to compare measures on a relative basis. Until these activities occur, our beliefs about culture strength and corporate performance depends upon faith rather than empirical findings.

Developing culture strength definitions, measures, and standards presents a formidable challenge. We need to question what we mean by "culture strength." Does it constitute a ubiquitous phenomenon permeating the minds of all employees in the organization, or should adherence by members to the dictates of the dominant culture group determine our beliefs regarding its power (see previous section)? If the former case prevails, how does one identify, inventory, and evaluate the prioritizing of cultural elements of corporate members when, for the most part, they exist at levels below conscious awareness in their minds and in many cases may be espoused but not necessarily practiced? These "what" and "how" questions deserve our attention in the development of culture strength definitions, measures, and standards before we adopt any substantive belief relating culture strength with corporate performance.

Another major area requiring future investigation relates to the need to translate macro culture strength assertions, at the level of the entire firm, into predictive realities at a micro level within the company. A firm possessing an overall powerful culture, according to the current gospel on culture strength, should display substantial congruence in the following cases:

1. Among co-workers within each workgroup
2. Between each workgroup and the workgroup manager
3. Among workgroups within the corporation
4. Among managers at all levels (including those who manage workgroups)

A consensus of culture elements among employees at all levels (the micro perspective) represents a necessary prerequisite condition for an overall strong corporate culture claim (the macro perspective).

Examining the above-mentioned predictions presents real problems apart from those arising due to the subtlety of the culture phenomenon or the presence of multiple cultures. We may find that variables interact in a complex fashion (e.g., on a hierarchical basis). Fortunately, we possess many of the statistical and methodological tools required to unlock these mysteries.

VIII. CONCLUSIONS

A. Current Status

The significance of the culture construct depends upon its ability to offer managers a useful means for enhancing organizational effectiveness. To date, organization culture fails to live up to its potential. A host of questions deserving empirical attention arises from our theoretical perspectives and rationales, and it is time these questions were addressed in order to lay to rest many inconsistencies and uncertainties found within the literature. Until then, ambiguity reigns, along with evangelical persuasions.

B. Points of Concern

Building knowledge of organizational culture requires examination of several central issues about which our thinking appears mired. The points that require attention are included below:

1. *The degree to which personal values and other cultural components are subject to influence and modification by organizations.* Resolution of this issue impacts
   a. The nature of organization culture as reality or apparition. The former case suggests internalization of cultural elements of organizations by individuals. In the latter situation, members fail to internalize elements of culture, and instead enter a conspiracy of espousal.
   b. The degree of culture strength attained by organizations.
   c. The distinctive features exhibited by an organization.
   d. The effectiveness of socialization and other mechanisms promoting cultural congruence between individuals and organizations.
   e. The importance of ethical considerations regarding interventions in personal cultural elements by organizations.
2. *The reality or illusion of simple and sovereign manifestations of culture in organizations.* Are we witnessing cultural unity within organizations with "powerful" cultures or a superficial gestalt—the appearance of cultural alignment among members arising from organizationwide adherence to the cultural artifacts of the dominant subculture(s) despite multiple subcultures? This affects
   a. The meaning we ascribe to culture strength (cultural congruence and observance throughout the organization, or adherence without congruence to dominant cultural dictates)
   b. The methods we employ to measure culture strength (congruence of cultural elements or adherence to dominant culture artifacts)
   c. The methods we employ to change culture (personal cultural elements or dominant culture artifacts)
   d. The measures we develop for culture strength comparisons (standardization across industries/sectors)
3. *The transmission of cultural components to new employees.* Questions include
   a. How do acculturated employees transmit cultural elements, existing for the most part at levels below conscious awareness, to new employers?
   b. Do new employees decode manifestations of culture to extract underlying meaning,

and do they do so with accuracy, or do new employees accept at face value the cultural elements presented?

    c.   Do employees undergo secondary socialization (initiated and controlled by the individual) when cultural elements, transmitted by the organization, prove incongruent with experiences of reality? Is the end result acculturation or merely "street wiseness?"

4. *The degree to which culture strength provides management with a manipulable variable to enhance effectiveness.* Resolution of this issue (assuming organizations build singular and powerful cultures) requires an understanding of

    a.   The degree of congruence of organization culture components required among members and groups at different hierarchical levels as well as within each level.

    b.   Identification of variables contributing to corporate culture strength and the development of an understanding as to how they interact and may be manipulated.

    c.   The benefits and liabilities associated with varying levels of cultural strength in relation to external problems and internal adjustments required.

5. *The extent to which cultural elements suggesting "this is the way we don't do things around here" embed* along with components dictating "the way we do things around here."

REFERENCES

Adler, N. J., and Jelinek, M. (1986). Is "organization culture" culture bound? *Human Resources Management*, *25*(1): 73–90.

Akin, G., and Hopelain, D. (Winter 1987). Finding the culture of productivity. *Organizational Dynamics*: 19–32.

Alvesson, M. (1987). Organizations, culture, and ideology. *International Studies of Management and Organizations*, *17*(3): 4–18.

Argyris, C. (Autumn 1982). The executive mind and double-loop learning. *Organizational Dynamics*: 5–22.

Arnold, D. R., Capella, L. M., and Sumrall, D. A. (1987). Organizational culture and the marketing concept: Diagnostic keys for hospitals. *J. of Health Care Marketing*, *7*(1): 18–28.

Arogyaswamy, B., and Byles, C. M. (1987). Organizational culture: Internal and external fits. *J. of Management*, *13*(4): 647–659.

Bass, B. M. (Winter 1990). From transactional to transformational leadership: Learning to share the vision. *Organizational Dynamics*: 19–31.

Beyer, J. M. (1981). Ideologies, values, and decision making in organizations. In *Handbook of Organizational Design*, vol. 2 (P. C. Nystrom and W. H. Starbuck, eds.), Oxford University, p. 166.

Beyer, J. M., and Trice, H. M. (Spring 1987). How an organization's rites reveal its culture. *Organizational Dynamics*: 5–24.

Bibeault, D. B. (1982). *Corporate Turn Around: How Managers Turn Losers Into Winners*. McGraw-Hill, New York.

Boudon, R. (1991). What middle–range theories are. *Contemporary Sociology*, *20*(4): 519–522.

Bratton, D. A. (1989/1990). Organization challenges of the 1990s: Leadership, service, culture, and morale. *Optimum (Canada)*, *20*(4): 75–78.

Brightman, H. J., and Sayeed, L. (1990). The pervasiveness of senior management's view of the cultural gaps within a division. *Group and Organization Studies*, *15*(3): 266–278.

Chibnick, M. (1981). The evolution of cultural rites. *J. of Anthropological Research*, *37*: 256–268.

Croft, A. C. (1990). The case of the missing corporate culture. *Public Relations Quarterly*, *35*(1): 17–20.

Cullen, J. B., Victor, B., and Stephens, C. (Autumn 1989). An ethical weather report: Assessing the organization's ethical climate. *Organizational Dynamics*: 50–62.

Deal, T. E., and Kennedy, A. A. (1982). *Corporate Cultures: The Rites and Rituals of Corporate Life*. Addison-Wesley, Reading, Mass.

Deetz, S. (1985). Critical cultural research: New sensibilities and old realities. *J. of Management*, 2,(2): 121–136.

Denison, D. R. (Autumn 1984). Bringing corporate culture to the bottom line. *Organizational Dynamics*: 5–22.

Edwards, J. D., and Kleiner, B. H. (1988). Transforming organizational values and culture effectively. *Learning and Organizational Development Journal*, *9*(1): 13–16.

England, G. W. (1967). Personal value systems of American managers. *Academy of Management Journal*, *10*: 53–68.

Feldman, S. P. (Summer 1988). How organizational culture can affect innovation. *Organization Dynamics:* 57–68.

Fishbein, M., and Ajzen, I. (1975). *Belief, Attitude, Intention, and Behavior*. Addison-Wesley, Reading, Mass.

Fisher, K. K. (Winter 1989). Managing in the high-commitment workplace. *Organizational Dynamics*: 31–49.

Gagliardi, P. (1986). The creation and change of organizational cultures: A conceptual framework. *Organization Studies*, *7*(2): 117–134.

Garcia, J. E., and Haggith, C. (1989). OD interventions that work. *Personnel Administrator*, *34*(6): 90–94.

Golembiewski, R. T. (1962). *The Small Group: An Analysis of Research Concepts and Operations*. the University of Chicago Press, Chicago.

Golembiewski, R. T. (1979). *Approaches to Planned Change, Part 1: Orienting Perspectives and Micro-Level Interventions*. Marcel Dekker Inc., New York.

Golembiewski, R. T. (1987). Toward excellence in public management: Constraints on emulating America's best-run companies. In *The Revitalization of the Public Service* (R. B. Denhardt and E. T. Jennings Jr., eds.), Department of Public Administration, University of Missouri at Columbia, 177–198.

Golembiewski, R. T., and Carrigan, S. B. (1970a). Planned change in organizational style based on laboratory approach. *Administrative Science Quarterly*, *15*(March): 79–93.

Golembiewski, R. T., and Carrigan, S. B. (1970b). The persistence of laboratory-induced changes in organizations' styles. *Administrative Science Quarterly*, *15*(September): 330–340.

Gross, W., and Shichman, S. (September 1987). How to grow an organizational culture. *Personnel*: 52–56.

Hebden, J. E. (Summer 1986). Adopting an organization's culture: The socialization of graduate trainees. *Organizational Dynamics*: 54–72.

Hofstede, G. H. (1980). *Culture's Consequences, International Differences in Work-Related Values*. Sage, London.

Kerr, J., and Slocum, J. W. (1987). Managing corporate culture through reward systems. *Academy of Management Executive*, *1*(2): 99–108.

Kovach, B. E. (Autumn 1986). The derailment of fast-track managers. *Organizational Dynamics*: 41–48.

Kovach, B. E. (Autumn 1989). Successful derailment: What fast trackers can learn while they're off track. *Organizational Dynamics*: 33–47.

Kozlowski, S. W. J., and Doherty, M. L. (1989). Integration of climate and leadership: Examination of a neglected issue. *J. of Applied Psychology*, *74*(4): 546–553.

Lawrence, P. R., and Lorsch, J. W. (1967). *Organization and Environment*. Harvard University Press, Cambridge, Mass.

Lewicki, R. J. (Autumn 1981). Organizational seduction: Building commitment to organizations. *Organizational Dynamics*: 5–21.

Malekzadeh, A. R., and Nahavandi, A. (1990). Making mergers work by managing cultures. *J. of Business Strategy*, *11*(3): 55–57.

Martin, J., and Siehl, C. (Autumn 1983). Organizational culture and counterculture: An uneasy symbiosis. *Organizational Dynamics*: 52–64.

Milgram, S. (1963). Behavioral study of obedience. *J. of Abnormal and Social Psychology*, *67*:371–378.

Nahavandi, A., and Malekzadeh, A. R. (1988). Acculturation in mergers and acquisitions. *Academy of Management Review*, *13*(1): 79–90.

Nave, J. L. (June 1986). Gauging organization climate. *Management Solutions*: 14–18.

Nichols, J. R. (1985). An Alloplastic Approach to Corporate Culture. *International Studies of Management and Organizations*, *14*(4): 32–63.

Pascale, R. (May 28, 1984). Fitting new employees into the company culture. *Fortune*: 28–40.

Pennings, J. M., and Gresov, C. G. (1986). Technoeconomic and structural correlates of organizational culture: An integrative framework. *Organization Studies*, *7*(4): 317–334.

Peters, T. J., and Waterman, R. H. Jr. (1982). *In Search of Excellence: Lessons from America's Best-Run Companies*. Harper and Row, New York.

Petrick, J. A., and Manning, G. E. (March 1990). Developing an ethical climate for excellence. *J. for Quality and Participation*: 84–90.

Pinchot, G. III (1984). *Intrapreneuring: Why You Don't Have to Leave the Corporation to Become an Intrapreneur*. Harper and Row, New York.

Posner, B. Z., Kouzes, J. M., and Schmidt, W. H. (1985). Shared values make a difference: An empirical text of corporate culture. *Human Resource Management, 24*: 293–310.

Posner, B. Z., Randolph, W. A., and Schmidt, W. H. (1987). Managerial values across functions: A source of organizational problems. *Group and Organizational Studies, 12*(4): 373–385.

Pratt, K. H., and Kleiner, B. H. (1989). Toward managing a richer set of organizational values. *Leadership and Organization Development Journal (U.K.), 10*(6): 10–16.

Ravlin, E. C., and Meglino, B. M. (1987). Effect of values on perception and decision making: A study of alternative work values measures. *J. of Applied Psychology, 72*(4): 666–673.

Redeker, J. R. (July 1990). Code of conduct as corporate culture. *H.R. Magazine*: 83–87.

Regan, J. F., Rokeach, M., and Grube, J. W. (1982). Personal and corporate values and corporate identification of manager from several levels of an organization. *Academic Psychology Bulletin, 4*: 345–355.

Rokeach, M. (1968). *Beliefs, Attitudes and Values*. Jossey-Bass, Inc., San Francisco.

Rokeach, M. (1973). *The Nature of Human Values*. the Free Press, New York.

Roskin, R. (1986). Corporate culture revolution: The management development imperative. *J. of Managerial Psychology, 1*(2): 3–9.

Sanfilippo, B., and Romano, R. (1990). Cultural evolution: Instilling a sales philosophy throughout the credit union. *Credit Union Management, 13*(2): 6–11.

Sathe, V. (1985). *Culture and Related Corporate Realities*. Richard D. Irwin, Inc., Homewood, Ill.

Schein, E. H. (Summer 1983). The role of the founder in creating organizational culture. *Organization Dynamics*: 13–28.

Schein, E. H. (Winter 1984). Coming to a new awareness of organizational culture. *Sloan Management Review*: 3–16.

Schein, E. H. (1986a). Are you corporate culture? *Personnel Journal, November*: 83–96.

Schein, E. H. (1986b). What you need to know about organizational culture. *Training Development Journal, January*: 30–33.

Schmidt, W. H., and Posner, B. Z. (September/October 1986). Values and expectations of federal service executives. *Public Administration Review*: 446–454.

Schwartz, H., and Davis, S. M. (Summer 1981). Matching corporate culture and business strategy. *Organizational Dynamics*: 30–48.

Sherif, M. (1936). *The Social Psychology of Social Norms*. Harper and Row, New York.

Sherwood, J. J. (Spring 1988) Creating work cultures with competitive advantage. *Organizational Dynamics*: 5–26.

Siehl, C., Ledford, G., Silvermann, R., and Fay, P. (March/April 1988). Preventing culture clashes from blotching a merger. *Mergers and Acquisitions*: 51–57.

Sipos, A. (1988). Organizational climate and employee involvement: Assessing the climate. *J. for Quality Participation, 11*(3): 62–65.

Smircich, L. (1983). Concepts of culture and organizational analysis. *Administrative Science Quarterly, 28*: 339–358.

Soeters, J., and Schreuder, H. (1988). The interaction between national and organization cultures in accounting firms. *Accounting, Organizations and Society, 13*(1): 75–85.

Swindle, B., and Phelps, L. D. (Fall/Winter 1984). Corporate culture: What accounting students are not taught. *Northeast Louisiana Business Review*: 37–44.

Tinsley, D. B. (March 14, 1988). Understanding business customer means learning about its "culture." *Marketing News*: 5–6.

Turnispeed, D. L. (1988). An integrated, interactive model of organizational climate, culture and effectiveness, *Leadership and Organizational Development Journal (U.K.), 9*(5): 17–21.

Van Maanen, J., and Barley, S. R. (1984). Occupational communities: Culture and control in organizations. In *Research in Organizational Behavior*, vol. 6 (L. L. Cummings, and B. M. Staw, eds.), JAI Press, Greenwich, Conn.

Welch, J. F. Jr. (1990). Soft values for a hard decade: A view on winning in the '90s, *Executive Speeches, 4*(10): 1–5.

Young, J. A., and Smith, B. (1988). Organizational change and the HR professional. *Personnel, 65*(10): 44–48.

6

The Antecedents, Consequences, and Correlates of Job Satisfaction

Srinika Jayaratne

University of Michigan, Ann Arbor, Michigan

Job satisfaction has been a matter of public concern and research interest since Robert Hoppock published *Job Satisfaction* in 1935. The five and a half decades since have seen an explosion of material on the topic, with hundreds of books, journal articles, magazine reviews, and television programs addressing the phenomenon. In fact, Locke (1976), writing a major review on the nature and causes of job satisfaction, stated that a survey using the key words *job satisfaction* yielded approximately 3350 articles or dissertations. When a computer search was conducted on PSYCINFO using the same key words in 1991, the yield was 6247 articles or dissertations.

In view of this plethora of relevant material, it is clearly impossible to provide a comprehensive review. For the most part, an attempt has been made to reference critical articles, but, at the same time, an effort has been made to represent the breadth of available material. Therefore, what is presented in this chapter are reviews of selected articles, chapters, and books, which, in the opinion of this author, provide good illustrations of the issues being raised. In addition, an effort has been made to contain the review to the literature of the last two decades. However, works prior to 1970 have been included on occasion when they were considered to be seminal publications or particularly salient examples.

This chapter will begin with a brief overview on the current theoretical underpinnings of job satisfaction. This will be followed by an examination of the empirical literature on the antecedents and correlates of job satisfaction, paying particular attention to selected demographic and dispositional factors. The third section will provide a brief overview on the consequences of job dissatisfaction. The final section will raise questions for future research.

This chapter will not examine the epistemological roots of the concept of job satisfaction, nor will it explore the relationship of job satisfaction to other similar concepts. However, this brief review emphasizes the various theories that have been presented in the context of job satisfaction, by way of orientation and overview. The reader is referred to Edwin Locke's (1976) excellent review on these issues in the article titled "The Nature and Causes of Job Satisfaction," and a somewhat earlier publication by Edward Lawler (1973) titled *Motivation in Work Organizations*.

The extant theories have not changed sufficiently nor have dramatically new theories emerged to justify an extensive reanalysis. Most critics argue vehemently that the job satisfaction literature is not based sufficiently in theory. It is perhaps fair to state that this criticism would be applicable to a large proportion of the domains currently being studied in the organizational literature, such as job performance, turnover, motivation, and any number of other related concepts. However, the following discussion draws attention to the dominant nature of two perspectives.

I. THEORIES OF JOB SATISFACTION

In discussing the theories of job satisfaction, one common thread becomes obvious: Virtually all theories subscribe to the notion that "satisfaction" is an affective state, which is a function of an interaction between a person and his or her environment. The differences lie in explaining the nature and character of the interactions. On the one hand, this degree of basic consensus is rather astounding given the thousands of research studies reported in the literature. On the other hand, as Lawler (1973) and others have pointed out, the research on job satisfaction has been typically atheoretical. Thus, more than a half century after the introduction of the term job satisfaction, we are still undecided about its theoretical underpinnings and remain critical of the research.

Despite these debates, two major theoretical perspectives have dominated the job satisfaction literature. Note that I have used the term *theoretical perspective* rather than theory, since the reference is to a class of theories or world views; that is, several researchers and theoreticians have proposed paradigms that are essentially promulgating similar or substantially overlapping views within a particular perspective, albeit with different elements. Rather than address each constituent theory at length, I have drawn a broad brush over the two relevant theoretical perspectives that subscribe to common themes in order to provide the reader with an overview of the paradigms that have either explicitly or implicitly played a significant role in the job satisfaction literature, namely, *expectancy theory* and the *two-factor theory*.

As points of historical reference to the perspectives presented here, consider the major reviews of the theories of job satisfaction. Lawler (1973) identified four different theoretical approaches: fulfillment theory (e.g., Schaffer, 1953; Vroom, 1964), equity theory (e.g., Adams, 1965), discrepancy theory (Katzell, 1964; Locke, 1969), and two-factor theory (Herzberg, Mausner, and Sniyderman, 1957). Locke (1976) distinguished between process theories (or causal models of job satisfaction) and content theories. Included in the process theories by Locke are the fulfillment, equity, and discrepancy theories. In both classification systems, the work of Herzberg and his colleagues are afforded a unique category: two-factor theory by Lawler and content theory by Locke. Clearly, the theory categorization in this review is very much in line with that of Locke (1976), however, I did not draw out the distinctions suggested by Locke between expectancies, needs, and values. These differences are more a matter of emphasis and method variance than a major substantive difference. Undoubtedly this is a simplification, but hopefully one that reiterates the overlapping nature of many theories. The interested reader should make every effort to go the original sources for explications of the individual theories.

A. Expectancy Theories

This perspective argues that an individual's assessment of job satisfaction is a function of the discrepancy between what an individual expects from the job and what the individual receives. In most formulations of this theory, that which is received is viewed as having either some tangible value or intrinsic value. For example, Vroom (1964) proposes two types of expectancies: the belief that effort will lead to good performance, and the expectation that good performance will lead to rewards. Similarly, Katzell (1964) emphasizes the discrepancy between actual amounts of outcomes received and outcomes expected. Hollenbeck (1989) presents a more cognitive model, arguing that an individual's affective responses are guided by perceived discrepancies between their sense of the present condition and some comparative reference. Locke (1969) represents the majority perspective by focusing on *perceived discrepancies* between that which is expected and that which is received. Because of the emphasis on discrepancy, some authors have preferred to distinguish between "discrepancy theory" and "fulfillment theory," in which the latter is the extent to which an individual's needs are satisfied (see Lawler, 1973; Schaffer, 1953).

The integration of expectancies with perceptions has created considerable debate with regard to the definition and measurement of "satisfaction." Locke (1976) argues for distinguishing between *expectancies* (a discrepancy between what is expected from the job and what is attained), *needs* (the extent to which an individual's objective requirements are fulfilled by the job), and *values* (the extent to which an individual acquires from the job that which he or she wants or desires). In a similar vein, Lawler (1973) notes that there are basically three different approaches to the study of expectancy: "the first looks at what people want, the second at what people feel they should receive, and the third at what people expect to receive" (p. 67). When expectancy theory is conceived in this manner, accurate representations of job satisfaction would require estimates of discrepancy between what an individual receives and wants (values), receives and needs, and receives and expects. In addition, one could generate other dimensions of expectancy—for example, what individuals believes they deserve and what others believe they should get. An individual's overall job satisfaction, then, would be determined by summing across these "dimensions" of discrepancies.

A classic model of this perspective is seen in the person-environment fit (P-E fit) theory (Caplan, 1979; 1987; French, Rogers, and Cobb, 1974; Pervin, 1968). In one of the more widely employed formulations of this perspective, "fit refers to the relationship between characteristics of the person (needs and abilities) and characteristics of the environment (resources and demands) measured along commensurate dimensions" (Caplan, 1979: 93). In some situations, behavior is determined mostly by the environment. However, even when environments are identical or nearly so, individual differences may result in different behaviors. In other instances, the person and environment will interact, producing a new dimension of the behavior or a totally new behavior or event that was not found either in the person or the environment prior to that interaction. The model, in effect, predicts changes in affective responses of individuals in the context of different environments. As Caplan (1979) points out, a person addressing the P-E fit theory should measure "all the variables necessary to determine whether a given population responds as a function of person, environment, or the interaction between the two" (p. 94)—which may constitute an impossible task.

While there are several different theories represented within the context of the general expectancy perspectives, there are also some common themes. Most important, these themes propose that attention be paid to: (1) differences between objective events and their perceptions; (2) needs, values, and expectations; and (3) difference or discrepancy scores.

B. Two-Factor Theory

The motivator-hygiene (or two-factor) theory was developed by Herzberg, Mausner, and Snyderman (1959). In its simplest form, the theory argues that job satisfaction is a result of the presence of *motivator* factors (elements of the work itself, such as promotion and recognition) and job dissatisfaction is the result of the lack of *hygiene* factors (elements of the context of work, such as supervision and interpersonal relations). By definition, then, to increase job satisfaction one must bring about changes in the motivator factors, and to decrease job dissatisfaction one must impact the hygiene factors. Thus, according to this theory, increasing job satisfaction does not necessarily mean that there will be a reduction in job dissatisfaction because dissatisfaction is tied to a different set of job dimensions. It is this presumed causal dichotomy that distinguishes the theory, and lends itself to the label of "two-factor theory." In attempting to distinguish the causes of dissatisfaction from the causes of satisfaction, this perspective opened itself to substantive criticism.

This controversial theory has many supporters and as many detractors. Dunnette, Campbell, and Hakel (1967) were straightforward: "It seems that the evidence is now sufficient to lay the two-factor theory to rest, and we hope that it may be buried peaceably" (p. 173). The primary criticisms of the theory are threefold: (1) it is method-bound—the only way to obtain the same results as Herzberg and his colleagues is to use the same methodology; (2) the factors for dissatisfaction and satisfaction overlap, and therefore the polar distinction does not hold true; and (3) the methodology employed by Herzberg et al. does not distinguish between "events" (what happened) and "agents" (who made it happen: see, e.g., Brayfield, 1960; Dunnette, Campbell, and Hakel, 1967; Ewen, 1964; Gaziel, 1986; Locke, 1976; Schneider and Locke, 1971; Soliman, 1970).

Despite heavy criticism, the two-factor theory remains a mainstay in the job satisfaction literature. The theory provides an important distinction between physical and psychological needs, and ties work to psychological well-being and growth by emphasizing the idea that job satisfaction is associated with the nature of work (Gaziel, 1986; Locke, 1976). This theory cannot, and should not, be summarily dismissed.

C. Summary

Virtually all studies on job satisfaction have used either expectancy theory or the two-factor theory either as an explicit or implicit basis for the research. This is not to say that the studies were based on one theory or that they adhered strictly to the formulations proposed by a given theory. As cited earlier, most critics of the literature lament the absence of any theory base. Many researchers tend to address some elements of a given theory, or employ measures or measurement strategies that are borrowed from a particular perspective. In doing so, the authors appear to implicitly accept the tenets of that perspective. Other researchers develop a blended approach, in which the emphasis is less on a conceptual framework and more on the intricacies of operationalization and measurement. The criticism holds in that few studies set out to specifically test the utility of any given theory. The segmented approach prevalent in the literature does not help theory development or theory testing.

Clustering so many different theories into two distinct perspectives, as I noted earlier, simplifies their nuances and even ignores some critical dimensions. The explicit purpose of this introduction, however, was to provide both a general overview and to argue for the existence of two major perspectives. This author is of the opinion that theory exists in the literature, but it exists between the lines in the form of implicit statements, models, hypotheses, and measures. A conscious effort should be made to articulate the underpinnings.

II. THE DEFINITION OF JOB SATISFACTION

A cursory look at some of the definitions of job satisfaction offered in the literature provides a perspective on its complexity and diversity

. . . any combination of psychological, physiological, and environmental circumstances that causes a person to truthfully to say, "I am satisfied with my job" (Hoppock, 1935).

. . . satisfaction is defined as the extent to which rewards actually received meet or exceed the perceived equitable level of rewards (Porter, 1968).

Job satisfaction may be defined as a pleasurable or positive emotional state resulting from the appraisal of one's job or job experiences (Locke, 1976).

Job satisfaction . . . measure men's satisfaction or dissatisfaction with those aspects of their jobs they deem important (Kohn and Schooler, 1983).

Two major approaches hold sway with regard to the conceptualization and definition of job satisfaction. The *first* approach provides more of a macro or global perspective, in which the concern is with general feelings about a job. Although job satisfaction itself is viewed as a multifaceted or composite phenomenon, the emphasis is on the global assessment or overall evaluation of job satisfaction. For example, Brayfield and Rothe (1951) developed an 18-item index that contained items such as: "I consider my job rather unpleasant"; "most days I am enthusiastic about my work"; and "I find real enjoyment in my work." These authors state that "items referring to specific aspects of a job were eliminated since an *overall* attitudinal factor was desired" in the construction of the scale (p. 308). Kunin (1955) and Dunham and Herman (1975) presented a series of faces ranging from happy to unhappy, and had respondents record their feelings about the job. Yet another global definition is provided by Ferratt (1981) using a single item: "Taking into consideration all the things about your job, how satisfied or dissatisfied are you with it?" The Gallup poll is less verbose: "Is your work satisfying?" The hallmark of the global definition is a unitary assessment. In effect, this approach to the definition of job satisfaction simply states that a positive response to the global question(s) indicates the degree of satisfaction or dissatisfaction with the job.

In contrast, the *second* approach emphasizes job facets. The extent to which an individual is satisfied with different aspects or facets of the job—for example, opportunities for advancement, salary, challenge—determines the degree of overall satisfaction. Overall job satisfaction becomes the sum of the expressed degree of satisfaction with different facets. For example, Herzberg, Mausner, and Snyderman (1959) proposed a variety of intrinsic (achievement, recognition) and extrinsic (company policy, supervision) factors that contribute to overall job satisfaction. Smith, Kendall, and Hulin (1969) developed the job descriptive index (JDI) to measure five facets: work, pay, supervision, promotion, and co-workers. Quinn and Staines (1977) identified a variety of organizational characteristics related to job satisfaction, such as role ambiguity, role conflict, and workload. The facet approach to measuring job satisfaction requires not only identifying critical components or facets of the job, but also determining the degree of satisfaction with each facet. An inability to identify and measure all relevant facets will result in a partial or incomplete assessment of job satisfaction (Scarpello and Campbell, 1983).

What is abundantly clear in these two types of definitions, which span a period of five decades, is the subjective nature of assessment. It is, in effect, what Locke (1976) refers to as "the appraisal made by a single individual of his job situation" (p. 1300). This subjectivity about assessment holds true regardless of whether one employs the global strategy or the facet strategy in the definition of job satisfaction.

Both procedures have their weaknesses. In employing the global approach, an individual assesses job satisfaction presumably by evaluating those aspects of the job which he or she finds salient and important. We do not, however, have any idea about the nature of these "implicit" or "relevant" facets, which may be important or even critical in looking for similarities between two or more satisfied individuals. Not only could these assessments be colored by individual and situational characteristics, they could also be influenced by current events and a host of other factors such as time of day and mood.

In contrast, the facet approach "predefines" for the individual a set of job dimensions that are deemed important according to some a priori logic. The tendency has been to view those facets as constituting a "universe of facets," which together provide an operational definition of job satisfaction. For example, Locke (1969) states that "overall job satisfaction is the sum of the evaluations of the discrete elements of which the job is composed" (p. 330). This approach provides only an illusion of complexity and completeness. That which is identified and measured becomes the definition. The facet-sum method, however, flies in the face of an idiosyncratic protocol, one that "truly" accepts the presence of individual differences. "People differ in what they view as satisfying and dissatisfying; what is one man's meat may be another man's poison" (Dunnette, Campbell, and Hakel, 1967: 143). On the other hand, this method allows for the construction of a theory-consistent definition, one in which the identified facets are gleaned from a known theory. But, the evidence in support of a simple summative model is still in need of further confirmation (see, e.g., Ferratt 1981).

This discussion leads me to the conclusion that the phenomenon of job satisfaction appears to defy a single definition. Because of the universal acceptance that job satisfaction is multi-faceted, although the unique facets remain arguable, the tendency in the literature has been to employ a facet-sum approach. Wanous and Lawler (1972), for example, conclude that not only is a facet-sum approach adequate, they also argue that it is unnecessary to assign individual weightings to different facets. Locke (1976) explicitly argued against individual facet weightings as well, noting that a high score on a given facet implies the importance of that facet relative to another. A question can be raised, however, as to whether the implied "other" facet is one that is being measured or a salient but unmeasured facet. Other researchers have supported the facet-sum argument on the basis that this type of linear model is parsimonious, and performs as well or better than nonlinear conjunctive and disjunctive models (Aldag and Brief, 1978; Rice, Gentile, and McFarlin, 1991). In fact, Ferratt (1981) concludes, that "the linear function (which explains 50%–60% of the variation in overall job satisfaction in this study) should be the standard for comparison" (p. 471). While this may be true, it still leaves us at least 40% short.

The statistical correlations reported in the literature between global and facet measures of job satisfaction tend to be relatively high, however, none of the research using facet measures (see, e.g., Blood, 1971; Evans, 1969; Ewen, 1967; Ferratt, 1981; Wanous and Lawler, 1972) explains more than 50% to 60% of the variance in global job satisfaction. The "whole" as currently measured appears to be more than the currently measured parts as suggested by Scarpello and Campbell (1983). Therefore, some authors such as Scarpello and Campbell (1983) are adamant: "global rating of overall job satisfaction is shown to be the most inclusive measure of overall job satisfaction" (p. 598). Thus, both conceptually and statistically, it appears that the two approaches to defining and operationalizing job satisfaction yield different results. Clearly, the high correlations between the two types of measures suggest significant overlap, but the meaning of this overlap methodologically and substantively is still unclear.

In light of these findings, one must necessarily conclude that: (1) job satisfaction is a purely subjective assessment or evaluation of one's work, (2) there exists no single satisfactory definition of job satisfaction, and (3) it is better to employ both a global definition and a facet definition in operationalizing job satisfaction.

III. THE MEASUREMENT OF JOB SATISFACTION

It is reasonable to argue that job satisfaction involves elements of individual personality, elements of the structural dimensions of the work environment or job context, elements of the nature of work or job content, elements of the "people" at work, and finally, elements of how the world at large may view a particular job or occupation. In addition, these elements may be idiosyncratic, culture specific, gender specific, and different across occupations. Bear in mind as well that there is no universal definition of job satisfaction.

The creation of a generic measure of job satisfaction, therefore, poses a formidable if not insoluble problem. In fact, Scarpello and Campbell (1983) posed the question: "Is the job satisfaction construct so broad that the identification of the major determinants of overall job satisfaction a futile task?" (p. 599). Portigal (1976) proposed a series of desirable characteristics for the development of a generic job satisfaction measure. Over 15 years later, they are still relevant:

1. Indicators should measure the level of satisfaction at different levels of aggregation and carry the same meaning. Thus, a particular "score" should mean the same thing for different groups at different times.
2. Measures should discriminate between groups with known differences, such as minorities and subsistence level workers.
3. Measures should be sensitive to changes in the content and context of work.
4. Measures should be applicable across different cultures and social classes, and be relevant to all segments of the workforce.
5. Measures should have sufficient validity, particularly construct and concurrent validity.
6. Measures should be tied to a theoretical base, preferably one that is broadly accepted.

7. Measures should have some normative data, such that improvement and deterioration can be judged on the basis of changes in scores.
8. The items in the indexes or measures of job satisfaction should be meaningful to the respondent.

To develop a single measure that can meet all of these demand characteristics may be a Herculean task. The issue becomes particularly relevant when employing a facet strategy. Consider the fact that job satisfaction studies have been conducted across an incredibly diverse set of occupations—business executives, home-care aides, police officers, product managers, railway employees, school psychologists, secretaries, social workers, stockbrokers, teachers, and university faculty, to name a few. Which facets of the job are universal? Locke (1976) identified job dimensions typically investigated in the research:

- Quality and quantity of work
- Satisfaction with pay
- Promotional opportunity and fairness
- Recognition and credit for one's work
- Benefits programs associated with the job
- Quality of working conditions
- Number and quality of co-workers
- Nature and style of supervision
- Company and management

What is missing from this list are two critical dimensions that have emerged over the years, but that have somehow been only sparsely investigated.

- Discriminatory behavior and attitudes
- Sexual harassment

Clearly, these are not "job facets" in the traditional sense, but they are environmental factors falling within the context of work and people-relations that could have a profound impact on the person. Discrimination and sexual harassment in the workplace may not be frequent, but when they do occur, they are not easily forgotten. Since such behaviors and attitudes are often subtle, and result in an affective response, they could easily influence a worker's general response and attitude toward a job. The extent to which an individual perceives and/or experiences discrimination or harassment then becomes an important element in the work environment. As such, some index of felt discrimination and harassment should be considered a job facet that would influence the quality of work life and job satisfaction.

Within the organizational literature, Cox (1990) noted "that despite the growing need for understanding the effects of ethnic and racial heterogeneity on organizations, the knowledge base for these issues is appallingly low" (p. 5). Only a handful of studies have explored the relationship between job satisfaction and racial discrimination, but the evidence reflects its importance in the assessment of job satisfaction. For example, Brabson, Jones, and Jayaratne (1991) noted that 64% of African-American human service workers reported they felt discriminated against on their job. In addition, numerous studies show that African-American workers feel less accepted in their organizations, report lower levels of promotability, feel more isolated, and experience lower levels of career satisfaction compared to their white counterparts (see, e.g., Beaty, 1990; Gold, Webb, and Smith, 1982; Greenhaus, Parasuraman, and Moch, 1980; Smith, 1977; Wormley, 1990). On the other hand, some studies of Hispanic workers report them to be more satisfied than white workers (Hawkes et al., 1984; McNeely, 1989). Clearly, no single monolithic picture can be presented with regard to all minorities. Different minorities may experience the work environment differently. Just as it would be an error to generalize the "white experience" to a minority population, it would be equally erroneous to generalize from one minority group to another.

The findings are equally compelling with regard to sex discrimination (see, e.g., Dalton and Marcis, 1987; Greenglass, 1985; Levitan, Quinn, and Staines, 1971; Matthews, Collins, and Cobb, 1974). There are virtually no empirical studies that have explored the relationship between job satisfaction and sexual harassment. The two empirical works this author found draw direct connections between sexual harassment and job satisfaction, but the work references only the experiences of blue collar workers. Both studies conclude that the experience of harassment is associated with a decrease in job satisfaction (Gruber and Bjorn, 1982; Kissman, 1990). With more and more women entering the workforce, and increasing evidence noting the negative consequences of such harassment on individuals, this dimension of the work environment must be considered more systematically in future research (see, e.g., MacKinnon, 1979; Maypole and Skaine, 1983).

In addition, measurement artifacts and pragmatics enter the picture. There is virtually nothing that is static in the work environment. As events unfold or change, evaluations of the workplace will most likely change as well. Thus, at the individual level, a psychological and subjective assessment of the work environment is essentially transitory and unstable (Portigal, 1976; Seashore, 1974.) This scenario has led to the measurement of groups, with little or no attention being paid to individual differences or longitudinal designs. As a result, what we have is a topographic description of job satisfaction—a description that tells us the form of the concept. Thus, we know that job satisfaction relates to a subjective appraisal and an affective response among specified groups of workers. In contrast, we know very little about its functional relationship to individual experiences and perceptions. These latter materials become important for the redesigning of work environments and the development of quality work programs, as well as in discussing linkages and overlap between similar theoretical concepts (Hackman and Oldham, 1980; Portigal, 1976).

A. The State of the Art in the Measurement of Job Satisfaction

The measurement of job satisfaction still remains a diverse and complex activity. While an excellent compilation of job-related scales is found in Robinson, Athanasiou, and Head (1969), the half century of research on the topic has not produced a consensus measure or even a consensus measurement strategy. A computer search of job satisfaction studies using PSYCINFO for 1990 and 1991 yielded 426 entries, a number of which were review articles. In order to obtain a reasonable perspective on current measures being employed, 75 articles were randomly selected. Table 1 lists the measures found in this review.

Other authors have documented a similar disarray in the measurement of job satisfaction. In a review on the relationship between job satisfaction and life satisfaction, Rain, Lane, and Steiner (1991) looked at 35 articles and noted that: "Before 1980, a variety of job satisfaction and life satisfaction measures were used, with no single measure dominating the research. Current research continues this trend" (p. 295). They reported that a "composite measure" was

Table 1   Job Satisfaction Measures Used in a Sample of Published Studies

Job Facets Global Measure (Quinn and Staines, 1977)	17
Single-item Global Measure (Quinn and Shepard, 1974)	13
Job Descriptive Index (JDI) (Smith, Kendall, and Hulin, 1969)	11
Minnesota Satisfaction Questionnaire (MSQ) (Weiss et al., 1967)	11
Hoppock Job Satisfaction Blank (Hoppock, 1935)	8
Brayfield and Roth Job Questionnaire (Brayfield and Rothe, 1951)	4
Action Tendency Measure (Hartman et al., 1986)	3
Job Diagnostic Survey (JDS) (Hackman and Oldham, 1980)	2
Female Faces Scale (Dunham and Herman, 1975; Kunin, 1955)	1
Index of Job Satisfaction (Kornhauser, 1965)	1
Other	4

Note: In many instances, the scales used were modified versions of the original.

used in 15 of the studies they reviewed, composite measures being identified as either facet-free or facet-specific measures. These would be similar to the first two items reported in Table 1. These authors also reported the JDI being used in four studies, the Minnesota Satisfaction Questionnaire (MSQ) in three studies, and other published measures being used in six studies.

The advent of meta-analysis has brought this issue to the forefront. For example, Spector (1986) conducted a meta-analytic study on the relationship between perceived control and a variety of outcome variables, including job satisfaction. He noted that many different measures of job satisfaction were used in the 88 studies included in the analysis, with the most popular being the JDI, MSQ, and the Job Diagnostic Survey (JDS). In addition, "many studies used single-item measures of overall satisfaction" (p. 1009). Loher et al. (1985) conducted a meta-analysis on the relation of job satisfaction to various job characteristics. They identified more than eight different measures of job satisfaction in 28 studies. Another meta-analysis conducted by Farrell and Stamm (1988) looked at job satisfaction as a correlate of absenteeism. These authors used 72 studies in their meta-analysis, but do not report the specific measures or indexes encountered. However, they discuss their findings within the context of "over-all job satisfaction," with the exact meaning being unclear. Clearly, the conclusions drawn in these meta-analyses could be affected by measurement issues such as method variance and multi-item and single-item measures of job satisfaction. For example, Iaffaldano and Muchin-sky (1985), who conducted a meta-analysis on the job satisfaction/job performance relation-ship, underscore this concern when they note that "higher correlations were obtained when general or global satisfaction measures were used" compared to measures of specific facets (p. 264).

Overall, the findings from existing literature reviews and meta-analyses are very similar to those reported in this review. The inability to develop a uniform or consensual strategy leaves the concept of job satisfaction in a tenuous position with regard to the use of newly developing methodologies such as meta-analysis. In addition, there appears to be a "better mouse trap" approach to the problem. New measures are constantly being developed, older measures are continually being modified, and other measures are being reconsituted. Consider the two following examples.

1. Multidimensional Job Satisfaction Scale

Shouksmith, Pajo and Jepsen (1990) developed the Multidimensional Job Satisfaction Scale (MJSS), which they state "can be used in studies comparing job satisfaction across sex, work locations, and occupations" (p. 363). These author specifically argue that they developed their scale because of shortcomings in the JDI (Smith, 1974), the Job Satisfaction Survey (Spector, 1985), and the MSQ (Weiss et al., 1967).

The MJSS essentially contains six work-related measures: (1) worker satisfaction with supervisors (from Warr and Routledge, 1969); (2) workers attitudes toward the physical conditions of the job (from Dunham, Smith, and Blackburn, 1977); (3) assessment of co-workers (from Warr and Routledge, 1969); (4) satisfaction with pay (from Cook et al., 1981); (5) satisfaction with promotion and advancement (from Weiss et al., 1967); and (6) a work motivation scale (from Shouksmith, 1989). In addition, the authors use a single-item global measure: "Taken all around, and considering all its aspects, your job is a very good one."

The MJSS represents a composite or amalgamated index rather than a new measure per se. All six dimensions are measured by items borrowed from other indexes. In effect, the authors argue that this particular configuration of existing items produces a better measure of job satisfaction than the items did in their original context. The authors propose this instrument as a short 36-item questionnaire measuring 11 job dimensions and overall job satisfaction.

In contrast to the reconfiguring strategy above, the Action Tendency Measure (ATM) represents an innovation based on criticisms of existing measures.

2. Action Tendency Measure

Hartman et al. (1986) developed the ATM, arguing that while the JDI and the MSQ have proven utility for monitoring attitudes of employees, they have served less well as predictors of job-related behaviors. Focusing on facets similar to those in the JDI, the "action tendency questionnaire asks how the respondent *feels like acting* in regard to various aspects of the job, instead of attempting to measure cognitive beliefs or to measure affects directly" (p. 319). One could, however, argue that statements about future actions are merely beliefs or cognitive representations of possible actions. The scale does not measure actual behaviors. In other words, the ATM may indeed be another way of assessing cognitive beliefs.

The authors state that they developed the ATM in keeping with Locke's (1976) proposal that an action tendency measure may provide a better frame of reference than some descriptive scale. The facets measured by the ATM are pay/promotion, supervision, co-workers, and work, and these dimensions are considered to be the core underlying elements of job satisfaction. The ATM consists of 23 items, three in the work scale, five in co-worker, seven in supervision, and eight in the pay/promotion scale.

Despite the stated liability of the JDI, the authors go on to employ the JDI for purposes of cross-validation, noting that "the reliability and validity of the JDI subscales had been documented as acceptable" (Hartman et al., 1986: 319). In comparing the findings from the JDI and ATM, it appears that the new mousetrap is similar to the old one in most ways. Given that the new approach neither utilizes a theory base nor anchors itself on a specific paradigm other than the possibility that it may provide a better frame of reference, a serious question can be raised about the development of yet another measure of job satisfaction.

B. Summary

While there have been attempts to distinguish between quality/quantity, subjective/objective, global/facet, and intrinsic/extrinsic factors in job satisfaction, no one measure has attained dominance in the field. The lack of consensus is in part related to conclusions reached in review articles. For example, Bamundo and Kopelman (1980) argue that a global single-item measure of job satisfaction correlates significantly with facet-specific satisfaction scores of the JDI. Similarly, Tait, Padgett, and Baldwin (1989) and Campbell, Converse, and Rodgers (1976) employed a global measure of job satisfaction in their reviews, arguing that it is more generalizable across studies. On the other hand, Ironson et al. (1989) state that global scales are not equivalent to summated facet scales, and Weaver (1980) suggests that the "global measure of job satisfaction has been very stable and may be somewhat unresponsive to changes in society" (p. 367). The debate will continue for some time to come. Given the status of measurement as discussed above, Seashore and Taber's (1975) conclusion is still pertinent: "no instrument exists for job satisfaction measurement that has, as yet, all of the properties and points of flexibility we assert to be achievable and desirable" (p. 344).

Self-report remains firmly entrenched as virtually the sole method of measurement in job satisfaction. Observational or physiological measures are nonexistent. Qualitative data of the "in-depth" type are virtually an anachronism. To some extent, the pervasive methodology may be both limiting the development of different measures and hampering the development of a different vision. Consider an analogy in clinical evaluation. For many years, experimental-control group comparisons utilizing pretest/posttest procedures held sway. Researchers then began to question the wisdom of comparing mean scores. Given that some individuals in the experimental groups did not do well, would it not be clinically important to find out why? This type of issue led to the development of single-case methodology and time-series measurement. As a result, there has been a radical change in the research question from "does the treatment work" to "when does the treatment work, with whom, under what conditions." The emphasis now is on individual differences, contextual changes, and the passage of time. Perhaps the methodology of job satisfaction measurement is in need of a different question. It would be shortsighted to let the method dictate the essence of the definition and its understanding.

IV. CAUSAL CORRELATES OF JOB SATISFACTION

In discussing the "causes" of job satisfaction, it is important to keep in mind that the vast majority of the available data are cross-sectional. Although the analyses for the most part are correlational, causal relationships are sometimes identified using a predetermined causal model. Time studies and longitudinal designs in the job satisfaction literature are the exception. While experiments and case studies can offer a different view of job satisfaction, perhaps one with more detail and depth, "the tendency in the job satisfaction area has been overwhelmingly to sacrifice depth in the interests of scope" (Locke, 1976: 1339). This scenario has not changed in the years since Locke's observation.

What is perhaps disconcerting about identifying the causes of job satisfaction is related to the very definition and measurement of job satisfaction. It is the general consensus that the measurement of job satisfaction requires the measurement of job facets *and* overall job satisfaction via a facet-free measure. One must then assume that the two methods are measuring essentially different aspects of the phenomenon of job satisfaction. Model I in Table 2 represents the facet-sum approach to the measurement of job satisfaction. It argues that an individual's overall job satisfaction is determined by summing across the levels of satisfaction with previously identified facets. The obtained value is the level of *overall* job satisfaction. If the summative score represents overall satisfaction, thus operationally defining job satisfaction, then a question must be raised about what causes satisfaction with the facets. Model III suggests an alternate scenario. It is possible, for example, for heredity, personality, and gender, to have an influence on perceptions of satisfactory relations with co-workers. In addition, these same elements may have other effects on all of the relevant job facets. Viewed collectively as antecedents, these elements would then become the causes of the different facets of job satisfaction, and therefore, by definition, the causes of overall job satisfaction. Under these circumstances, the job facets would play a mediating role.

In contrast, model II obtains an overall level of satisfaction, but makes no attempt to identify causes a priori. This model remains silent about causes by assuming but not specifying causes. Traditionally, overall job satisfaction has been predicted by employing a series of facets. But, as noted earlier, the facets themselves may have a series of different causes. In the absence of specified facets, developing a causal or rational model poses an impossible task.

It is here that theory appears to play a more significant role. In his discussion of the "causal factors in job satisfaction," Locke (1976) developed a category scheme in keeping with his facets: work, pay, promotion, verbal recognition, working conditions, self, supervisors and co-workers, and company and management. Each dimension or facet is then analyzed within the

Table 2 Hypothetical Causal Models of Job Satisfaction

Model I		
Satisfaction with co-workers	hi <———> lo	Overall satisfaction obtained
Satisfaction with supervision	hi <———> lo	by summing
Satisfaction with pay	hi <———> lo	across satisfaction
Satisfaction with promotions, etc.	hi <———> lo	with facets
Model II		
No identified facets	hi <———> lo	Overall satisfaction is rating on global scale
Model III		
Cause 1 (heredity)	———>	
Cause 2 (personality)	———>	Satisfaction with co-workers
Cause 3 (gender)	———>	

context of needs, expectancies, and values. For example, Locke (1976) notes that most workers *value* verbal recognition (praise), and the desire for recognition is tied to the *need* for self-esteem. Locke also identified recognition as "one of the single most frequently mentioned events causing job satisfaction and dissatisfaction" (p. 1324). Thus, the quality of supervision is not only a *cause* of job satisfaction, it is also a part of the *definition* of job satisfaction.

It is not unusual to find facets of job satisfaction being employed as independent variables and overall job satisfaction as the dependent variable. For example, Shouksmith, Pajo, and Jepsen (1990) established the internal validity of their scale by examining the correlations between 11 job facets (relations with supervisor, supervisor ability, work conditions, co-workers' attributes, co-workers' personalities, co-workers' ability, pay, promotion opportunity, promotion fairness, personal growth, job security) with one item on overall job satisfaction. Conway, Williams, and Green (1987) identified 17 job facets (promotion, training, supervisor, upper management, organizational structure, work environment, pay, work stress, challenge, staff distribution, merit pay, organization of work tasks, commitment, work group, affirmative action, benefits, job security), and used these to predict overall job satisfaction measured by four different global items. Rice, Gentile, and McFarlin (1991) measured satisfaction with 12 different job facets (pay, work hours, commuting time, promotion, co-workers, customer contact, opportunity to learn new skills, decision making, required physical effort, required mental effort, supervisor contact, control over schedule), and then predicted overall job satisfaction using six "facet-free items" based on the work of Quinn and Staines (1979). Taken overall, there appears to be little theoretical underpinning to the facet models, and furthermore, the development of facets are more idiosyncratic than general.

Stated simply, there is confusion and circular logic in the discussion of cause and effect or independent and dependent variables. A job facet cannot be a predictor (independent variable) of job satisfaction if it is also a dimension of a summative index of job satisfaction. There appears to be an implicit (and often explicit) assumption in the literature that a job facet index is only as good as the amount of variance it can explain in a global job satisfaction measure, typically a single item. At the same time, as Scarpello and Campbell (1983) have pointed out, some presume that single-item global measures are unreliable.

It is important to remember, however, that the two types of measures serve different purposes. A global assessment may provide a general affective statement, but it offers little information for interventions or management purposes. In contrast, a facet measurement model provides discreet information that may serve as the basis for administrative and policy changes, but that may not be all-inclusive. Thus, the advice to employ both types of measurement strategies makes both practice sense and research sense. Yet, if this analysis is correct, one must look for causes of job satisfaction outside the dimensions typically included as facets.

In his review, Locke (1976) also concluded that "one of the most unresearched subjects in the area of job attitudes is the individual's view of himself and the way in which this view affects what he seeks for pleasure on the job" (p. 1325). With this idea in mind, the causal factors discussed below take a somewhat different tack. The relationship of job facets with overall job satisfaction will not be discussed, partly because of the aforementioned methodogical argument, and partly because much of this discussion has already occurred. Rather, the focus will be on more current issues related to individual characteristics such as heredity, dispositional factors, race and ethnicity, gender, age, education, and marital status.

A. Heredity

Recently, heredity has been introduced (or reintroduced, as some would argue) as an important factor in the prediction of job satisfaction (see, e.g., Arvey et al. 1989; Buss, Plomin, and Willerman, 1973; Staw and Ross, 1985). The notions here are somewhat different from the concept of "hardiness" (Kobasa, 1979; Maddi and Kobasa, 1984.) Hardiness refers to the possession of commitment, control, and challenge, and is typically viewed as a mediator between stressful events and illness. Whether or not these characteristics are genetically perdetermined is unclear, although some may make this argument. In contrast, the proponents of a hereditary perspective argue that one's basic orientations to work are to some extent predetermined and "may reflect a biologically based trait that predisposes individuals to see positive or negative content in their lives" (Staw and Ross, 1985: 471). For example, Arvey et al. (1989) studied 34 pairs of monozygotic twins reared apart between 1979 and 1987 (25 female pairs and 9 male pairs). These authors argue that since job satisfaction is typically viewed as a multidimensional construct, that different elements may be differentially associated with genetic factors. The authors further argue that their data support the prediction that general job satisfaction has a strong genetic component, and noted that "approximately 30% of the observed variance in general job satisfaction was due to genetic factors" (p. 187). In fact, the authors noted that "these data are consistent with the hypothesis that these twin pairs seek out environments that are compatible with their particular genetic makeup" (p. 191). This research, however, presupposes a stable environment. Whether or not the twin differences would hold longitudinally given likely changes in environmental factors is not answered by the existing research. At one level, at least theoretically, this perspective pushes the person-environment fit perspective into its ultimate form. Perhaps Hoppock (1935) was not far from the "truth" when he said: "As an independent variable job satisfaction may not even exist. And if it does, the final definition may have to be made in terms of physiological chemistry" (p. 47).

Staw and Ross (1985) hypothesized the existence of "stable individual characteristics that predispose people to respond positively or negatively to job contexts" (p. 471). They conducted a secondary analysis of longitudinal data collected on 5000 men between the ages of 45 and 59. Based on their analyses, the authors argue that the "results show a much stronger case for dispositional effects than has been presented for many years in organizational psychology" (p. 477). The data provide partial support for the hypotheses that: (1) there is a significant relationship in individual attitudes over time, (2) there is a significant relationship in individual attitudes across situations, and (3) prior individual attitudes predict future attitudes.

Pulakos and Schmitt (1983) conducted a longitudinal study with high school students, and concluded that those students who expected jobs to be psychologically rewarding tended to be more satisfied than their less optimistic counterparts when they were eventually employed, 9 and 29 months later. This research effort was seen as presenting evidence demonstrating the stability of individual expectations, hence consistent with a dispositional component in the perception of job satisfaction.

The view that heredity and genetics play a significant role in the determination of job satisfaction has been challenged primarily on methodological grounds. For example, Gerhart (1987) presented evidence directly at odds with that of Staw and Ross (1985). Gerhart concludes that his research does not support the contention that "attitudinal consistency will equal or exceed the effects of situational factors in most contexts" (p. 372). Cropanzano and James (1991) take issue with the twin study presented by Arvey et al. (1989), arguing that the methodology not only has many validity threats, but also numerous problems associated with the quantification of the heritability of job satisfaction.

Few would argue about the existence of predisposing factors, but many would disagree that these factors have a genetic base, arguing more along the lines of learning and socialization history. Ultimately the issues may be political, and biased by the values and morals of the investigator and society. This author, for one, is not at all convinced that heredity has any role at all in the determination of job satisfaction.

B. Race and Ethnicity

Only recently have researchers paid attention to examining factors related to race and ethnicity with regard to job satisfaction. For the most part, exploration of possible racial differences was either ignored when minority populations were present, or the selected study samples were white. With the increasing number of minority scholars, and the raised concerns about the negative consequences of discrimination, a minority-relevant literature has begun to emerge in the field.

Given the "white" background of much of the job satisfaction literature, the question is whether or not the sources of job satisfaction typically identified for white workers will have a different impact on people of color. Even within minorities, the issues become somewhat clouded, since the vast majority of the available research studies employ samples of African-American respondents. Studies exploring other minority groups such as Hispanics and Asians are few and far between in these research endeavors, and these studies do show differences between minority groups (see, e.g., McNeely, 1987; 1989.)

The expectation that there may be minority/white differences is based on several justifiable assumptions: higher unemployment rates among minorities, minority overrepresentation in low-paying occupations, lower occupational returns for education among minorities, and discriminatory hiring and promotional practices, now as well as in the past (Tuch and Martin, 1991; Weaver, 1978). As Wilson and Butler (1978) state, "historically, racial issues have been major deterrents to fulfillment, through work, for minority group members" (p. 627). The question then, is whether or not this pattern of experiences is sufficiently homogeneous that it generates or encourages a distinctive orientation to the job.

That is, are the determinants of job satisfaction for people of color different from the determinants of job satisfaction for whites? Some authors take this as a given: "It may be assumed that minority group members approach their jobs with different frames of reference, especially to certain specific determinants of job satisfaction" (Milutinovich, 1977: 1085). While this may be true, the burden of proof remains with the researcher. On the other hand, Golembiewski (1978) and Smith, Smith, and Rollo (1975) both report the existence of similar factor structures in the JDI for African-American and white samples. In fact, Golembiewski (1978) argues that "the JDI seems to mean much the same for blacks and whites" (p. 578).

It would, however, be an error to generalize from one minority group to another. To lump all minorities together in this manner makes for confusion and stereotyping rather than clarification. For example, McNeely (1989) reported that Hispanic human service workers reported greater job satisfaction than non-Hispanic workers. McNeely (1987) also noted that Asian-American human service workers had similar levels of job satisfaction as non-Asian workers. Thus, job satisfaction issues pertinent to people of color are far more complex than the simplicity reflected in simple minority versus majority comparisons.

In terms of overall job satisfaction, the literature presents a mixed bag. A fair number of studies indicate that whites report higher levels of job satisfaction than African-Americans. With reference to black workers, Tuch and Martin (1991) note that "surprisingly little is understood about blacks' job satisfaction beyond the substantial evidence that they report lower absolute levels" (p. 104) in virtually all of the studies employing national probability samples. According to Weaver (1974), the data from five different Gallup polls report less satisfaction among African-Americans than whites. Quinn, Staines, and McCollough (1974) arrived at the same conclusion after reviewing 15 national surveys conducted between 1958 and 1973. Weaver (1980) presented additional national sample data collected between 1972 and 1978, and concluded that "job satisfaction among blacks is considerably lower than among whites" (p. 365). Similar results have been reported within different occupations as well: southern assembly line and packaging plant workers (Moch, 1980); mental health workers (Gold, Webb, and Smith, 1982); hospital employees (O'Reilly & Roberts, 1973); and certified public accountants (Slocum and Strawser, 1972).

However, some studies report the opposite finding; that is, that African-Americans report greater satisfaction with their jobs than whites. For example, Brenner and Fernstein (1984) reported this to be true with clerical employees; Katzell, Ewen, and Korman (1974) with blue collar workers; and Shiflett (1988) within the military. Other studies report little or no differences between races. For example, Weaver (1978) found no difference when other variables were controlled within a national probability sample. Beaty (1990) also found similar results with registered nurses, as did Jones et al. (1977) with navy personnel.

In other words, the data are inconclusive, and numerous explanations have been offered for these diverse findings. The dimension that has received the most attention relates to *intrinsic* (e.g., autonomy, authority) and *extrinsic* rewards (e.g., pay, promotions). The literature argues that there may be African-American versus white differences in the relative value of these rewards in increasing job satisfaction. Wilson and Butler (1978), for example, argue that "the types of experiences that produce black job satisfaction are of a markedly different nature from the traditional determinants of white job satisfaction" (p. 631). A number of studies note that African-American workers value extrinsic more than intrinsic rewards, while white workers value intrinsic more than extrinsic rewards (Bloom and Barry; Shiflett, 1988; Tuch and Martin, 1991). Other studies note that there are either no differences or minimal differences in this domain (Beaty, 1990; Konar, 1981; Weaver, 1978).

But not all is contentious. It is important to remember that *both* types of rewards increase job satisfaction, and workers higher on either of these rewards report higher satisfaction. And, most important, whites are significantly advantaged in the proportion of white collar jobs, education, and residence (more African-Americans reside in the south and urban areas), as well as in both intrinsic and extrinsic rewards (Tuch and Martin, 1991). All of these factors are associated with increased job satisfaction.

In sum, it is inaccurate to argue that race per se is a causal factor in job satisfaction. Rather, it appears to be part of a complex interaction. In fact, as a causal factor in job satisfaction, race *alone* is marginal (Shiflett, 1988; Tuch and Martin, 1991). Sources of job satisfaction are more uniform across race than different, despite some contrary findings, and the processes that produce worker satisfaction do not appear to differ systematically by race (Gavin and Ewen, 1974; Lincoln and Kallenberg, 1985; Shiflett, 1988; Smith, Smith, and Rollo, 1974; Tuch and Martin, 1991; Weaver, 1978). This brings me back to the beginning of this discussion. Race, for the most part, has been studied as a simple demographic. None of the studies cited here examined perceptions of discrimination, segregation, or harassment as issues worthy of measurement and inclusion in causal models. Furthermore, virtually no within-group studies exist. Most studies compare a minority with a white sample. Comparative approaches most surely apply measures and models based on majority research. The core issue, then, is the dearth of research and model development within minority populations (see Cox, 1990).

C. Gender

While there is some disagreement, the consensus of opinion is that there are no male-female differences in job satisfaction. This fact appears to hold both in studies with national representative samples (Campbell, Converse, and Rodgers, 1976) and specific occupations, as well as varying occupational positions (see, e.g., Golembiewski, 1977; Jayaratne and Chess, 1983; McNeely, 1986; Miller, 1980; Mottaz, 1986; Quinn, Staines, and McCullough, 1974; Weaver, 1977). In general, workers of both sexes in higher level occupations (higher status) report greater satisfaction than workers in lower level (lower status) positions (see, e.g., Kanter, 1977; Mottaz, 1986; Northcott and Lowe, 1987; Neil and Snizek, 1988). To the extent that occasional gender differences do appear, the findings seem to be related more to differences in organizational power, promotional structure, and job status, rather than gender per se (Golding, Resnick, and Crosby, 1983; Kanter, 1977; Neil and Snizek, 1988).

Feldberg and Glenn (1979) argue that two models have been employed in the study of work and gender. The *job model*, applied principally to men in the literature, posits a stucturalist perspective, and argues that working conditions shape an individual's perceptions of work. In contrast, the *gender model* emphasizes personal attributes, and argues that men and women bring different perspectives in to the workplace by virtue of different socialization patterns (see Kanter, 1977; Mannheim, 1983; Regan and Roland, 1982; Sexton, 1977). Kanter (1977), for example, expects similarities, not differences, between men and women, and points out that the extent to which there are differences, these are a function of work experiences. She concluded that women's work attitudes are more a function of the status within an organization (job model) and not their socialization (gender model).

With some qualifications, the bulk of the evidence favors the job model. For example, Jurik and Halemba (1984) studied correctional officers, a traditionally male occupation. They found no differences between males and females in job satisfaction, and concluded that their findings tend to support the job model. Similar findings are reported by McNeely (1986) and Jayaratne, Tripodi, and Chess (1983) with human service workers and social workers, traditionally occupations dominated by women. Northcott and Lowe (1987), who conducted a study on mail carriers and mail sorters in Canada, concluded that their data "for the most part, support the job model for both men and women and offer little evidence to support the gender model" (p. 128). Thus, the overall consensus would be supportive of the *job model* rather than the *gender model* in examining the role of gender in job satisfaction.

In this discussion, an effort has been made to stay as much as possible within the confines of determining whether or not gender per se has an effect of job satisfaction. The answer, as noted earlier, is no. On the other hand, there is a diverse and contradictory literature addressing the possible differential causes of job satisfaction between men and women. Although this literature is not considered to be within the purview of this review, in general, some authors argue that the determinants of job satisfaction for both males and females are more similar than dissimilar (see, e.g., Mottaz, 1986; Northcott and Lowe, 1987; Voyandoff, 1980). In other words, "those job characteristics that provide satisfaction for men also lead to satisfaction for women" (Voyandoff, 1980: 126). Others, however, suggest that while the differences may be minimal, they are nonetheless important.

The careful reader will conclude that there seems to be a great deal of similarity in the arguments proposed for the existence of differences in job satisfaction between men and women, as well as for minorities and whites. The difference argument has its basis in the assumed effects of socialization, culture, and experience of being a minority or a woman. This argument posits the existence of a "view of work" and a value orientation among minorities and women, which somehow produce a lowering in job satisfaction. The research and the data do not support this perspective. Rather, the vast majority of the research, and particularly the more recent literature, suggest that the work environment is viewed similarly by all people. While individuals certainly, and possibly minorities and women as a group, may attach different values to different elements of work and the context of work, taken as a whole, there is more similarity than dissimilarity.

To the extent that women and minorities are affected in a similar manner by comparable aspects of the work environment, these factors may become important in the development of programs designed to increase job satisfaction. Therefore, research that can discern "true" differences and similarities that are facet-specific or universal, may play an important role in the creation of a better work environment. Race and gender cannot and should not be treated as mere demographics. Research must attempt to further elucidate within-group differences rather than cataloging between-group differences.

D. Age, Education, and Marital Status

Many earlier studies include "personal characteristics" as factors that influence job satisfaction—most commonly age, marital status, and education level (see, e.g., Campbell, Converse, and Rodger, 1976; Quinn and Staines, 1976). There is considerable agreement in the literature on two of these characteristics: As a group, older workers appear to report greater job satisfaction than younger workers (Gibson and Klein, 1970; McNeely, 1988; Quinn, Staines, and McCollough, 1974; Tuch and Martin, 1991; Weaver, 1978; 1980), and workers with higher education levels report greater satisfaction than workers with lower levels of education (Berk, 1985; Gaziel, 1986; King, Murray, and Atkinson, 1982; Mullis, Ellett, and Mullis, 1986; Quinn, Staines, and McCullough, 1974; Weaver, 1980). In fact, Weaver (1980) reports this positive association between education and job satisfaction has become increasingly apparent since 1969. Prior to that time, the satisfaction-education association seems to have been either negative or nonexistent. The relationship may not be linear, however. Campbell, Converse, and Rodgers (1976), for example, report high levels of satisfaction among the least educated (grades

0–8) and most educated (college degree), with those in between reporting lower levels of job satisfaction.

In contrast, the evidence is somewhat more complicated and convoluted with regard to marital status. A large number of studies across a wide array of occupations report that married workers are more satisfied than single workers (Amaro, Russo, and Johnson, 1987; Bersoff and Crosby, 1984; Dillard and Feather, 1991; Tait, Padgett, and Baldwin, 1989; Valdez and Gutek, 1987). On the other hand, a number of studies report no difference in job satisfaction between married and unmarried workers (Bray et al., 1974; Goode, 1970; Lottinville and Scherman, 1988; Nichols, 1971; Rahim, 1982), and still other studies report the existence of gender differences in this regard. For example, Jayaratne and Chess (1983) report greater job satisfaction among married female social workers compared to single females, but no difference among males. On the other hand, Wright, King, and Berg (1985) note that black single female managers report higher levels of satisfaction compared to their married counterparts.

The data, then, suggest that a first-order analysis should not hypothesize a positive correlation between marital status and job satisfaction. On the other hand, the indications are that there are strong positive relationships between age and job satisfaction, as well as between education and job satisfaction.

Several caveats need to be recognized in drawing even these tentative conclusions. First, the use of a global job satisfaction measure may not be a sensitive index of existing differences. There may indeed be facet differences that need to be explored and carefully elaborated. Second, the somewhat confusing data regarding the relationship between marital status and job satisfaction underscores the importance of exploring the marriage-work interface, a research agenda that is now in progress (see, e.g., Eckenrode and Gore, 1990; Crouter, 1984). The results also suggest that more attention be paid to the single worker and issues related to gender. Third, while the positive correlation between education and job satisfaction may not be universal, it is credible when qualified (see, e.g., Glenn and Weaver, 1982). This relationship is often moderated by "status." Those with higher levels of education are more likely to occupy higher-status jobs, and those occupying higher-status jobs, and those occupying higher-status jobs are more likely to report greater satisfaction than those occupying lower-sevel jobs. For example, Campbell, Converse, and Rogers (1976) speculate that pay may be more important to those with less education compared to those with higher levels of education, and that challenge may be more important to those with higher education compared to those with little formal education. The satisfaction-education relationship may be better explained by examining different job facets. But, while facet-based instruments alone may be insufficient measures of overall job satisfaction, the detailed examination of the relationship of demographic factors with job satisfaction makes the measurement of facet satisfaction imperative.

E. Dispositional Factors

In contrast to the studies exploring genetics and heredity per se, a considerable body of literature has paid attention to various dimensions of personality. However, the research has "barely scratched the surface on the ways in which personality constructs may enter into theoretical systems" (Weiss and Adler, 1984: 43). Typically, when they have been used, "dispositional factors" or "personality factors" have been viewed more as exogenous variables—variables having "values determined outside of the model and . . . taken as a given, i.e., the model does not explain the level of these variables" (Hanushek and Jackson, 1977). Locke (1970) and Arnold (1960), for example, discuss "emotions" and "felt urges to action," but they are viewed more as discreet responses.

Given the stance taken in most of the literature that job satisfaction is the result of the interaction between a person and his or her environment, it is difficult to relegate the value of personality measurement to a peripheral role in a causal model (Spector, 1982). Broad indicators or dispositional characteristics—for example, locus of control, type A behavior, and self-esteem—could conceivably add to our understanding of the person-situation configuration in job satisfaction. If dispositional factors are to be of any value in these analyses, they must be insensitive to transient fluctuations in the environment (Seashore and Taber, 1975).

This perspective is consistent with the view that a person is an active agent selecting and shaping situations (see, e.g., Pervin, 1987; Snyder, 1983; Wachtel, 1973). Thus, the disposition drives, to some extent, both the person's perceptions of the environment as well as his or her actions. Locke (1976) stated in his review: "one of the most unresearched subjects in the area of job attitudes is the individual's view of himself and the way in which this view affects what he seeks for pleasure on the job and how various job experiences and conditions affect him" (p. 1325). The only characteristic that Locke discussed at length in this regard was self-esteem. While there is an abundant array of dispositional variables that may have an effect on job satisfaction, only self-esteem, locus of control, and type A behavior have been included in this review. These dimensions appear to have received the greatest attention in the literature.

1. Locus of Control

While somewhat controversial, the concept of internal and external locus of control has been prominent in the organizational literature. Simply stated: "those who ascribe control of events to themselves are said to have an internal locus of control . . . and people who attribute control to outside forces are said to have an external locus of control" (Spector, 1982: 482). The research overwhelmingly supports the view that internals report greater job satisfaction than externals. This finding has been reported among national representative samples in the United States (Andrisani and Nestel, 1976) and Canada (King, Murray, and Atkinson, 1982), as well as among a wide variety of occupational groups such as nurses (Greenberger et al., 1989), white collar workers (White and Spector, 1987), police (Lester, 1987), teachers (Santangelo and Lester, 1985), and engineers (Sharma and Chaudhary, 1980).

The study of locus of control has been dominated by the I-E scale developed by Rotter (1966). The utility of this type of generalized locus of control measure has been debated frequently, with two major conclusions emerging. First, there is a need to develop domain-specific I-E measures rather than relying on generalized measures (see, e.g., Phares, 1976; Spector, 1988). As a result, Spector (1988) developed the Work Locus of Control Scale (WLCS) and Pettersen (1985) proposed another work-specific I-E scale. Neither scale has been widely used as yet, but certainly should be in the minds of future researchers. Second, there is the distinct possibility that the concept of locus of control is multidimensional, and that "people's ability to control things is more situation or topic specific" (Payne, 1988: 214). Thus, research efforts should focus less on generalized expectancies and more on relevant domains.

In contrast to the positive findings regarding the relationship between internality and overall job satisfaction, the relationship of locus of control with specific job facets has been virtually ignored (see Spector, 1982). Little research evidence is available in this regard. Dailey (1978) reported internal engineers and scientists to be less satisfied with co-workers than their external counterparts. Mitchell, Smyser, and Weed (1975) and Runyon (1973) noted that worker satisfaction with supervision is moderated by the style of supervision. Internals preferred a participative style and externals a directive style. Thus, to the extent that locus of control plays a role in job satisfaction, and to the extent that the job facets are key to understanding the nature of job satisfaction, then future research should contend with issues relating job satisfaction facets with locus of control.

In summary, there is substantial evidence relating internality to increased overall job satisfaction. Besides limited sample studies such as those noted above, little information is available on the relationship of I-E to the different facets of the job. In view of these findings, it seems critical that a comprehensive model of job satisfaction include the dimension of internal-external control.

2. Type A Behavior

Behavior that has been described by such characteristics as competitive, aggressive, preoccupied with deadlines, hard-driving, and chronically impatient has been labeled type A (Chusmir and Hood, 1988; Day and Bedeian, 1991; Fletcher, 1988). These behavior patterns have been tied to a variety of health symptoms, including coronary disease, although recent reviews have raised some questions (Mathews and Haynes, 1986). However, the literature also notes that type A behavior is more prevalent among those with higher socioeconomic and educational status— that is, among individuals who typically report higher levels of satisfaction. In view of these findings, it has been argued that type A's self-select into objectively stressful occupations. Still other researchers point out that type A's report their jobs are more stressful, regardless of the objective level of stress (see Payne, 1988). In effect, the assumption is that type A individuals perceive and respond in different ways to the work environment compared to their less hard-driven colleagues, and as a result, suffer more negative consequences.

Recently, researchers have begun to examine the relationship of job satisfaction and other job attitudes with type A behavior (Chusmir and Hood, 1988). Given the assumption that type A's have a different perception of their work environment and that they often self-select their occupations, then it is reasonable to argue for the existence of a positive relationship between job satisfaction and type A behavior. Following the prognostications of a person-environment model, an individual's active seeking of a specific work context so that it matches his or her personality should result in a positive match. Such as argument, of course, assumes a congruence between expectations and experience. At a theoretical level, then, one would assume the degree of match to moderate the levels of expressed satisfaction in these instances. What the research does point out, however, is that type A's who perceive greater control over their environment report greater job satisfaction (Lee, Ashford, and Bobko, 1990). It is difficult under these circumstances to tease out the effects of control per se from the effects of type A behavior.

The research on type A behavior and job satisfaction is at best a mixed bag. Most of the research evidence seems to indicate no relationship between personality type and job satisfaction (see, e.g., Frost and Wilson, 1983; Lester and Solis, 1980; Matteson, Ivancevich, and Smith, 1984; Day and Bedeian, 1990). On the other hand, a few research studies indicate either a positive (Ashford and Bobko, 1990; Muhammad, 1990) or a negative relationship (Chusmir and Hood, 1988; Bluen, Barling, and Burns, 1990). Thus, while it appears reasonable to argue that personality type will play a significant role in the determination of job satisfaction, its empirical utility remains an open question.

The general finding of a strong association between negative effects and illness with type A remains especially intriguing. Given similar work contexts, it appears that type A's compared to non-type A's not only perceive a more stressful environment, but also appear to suffer more negative consequences. Those events perceived and experienced negatively by an individual apparently have a direct impact on personal well-being, independent of job satisfaction. If this is correct, then an individual could very well be totally satisfied with work, yet experience a high level of strain. Thus, important questions can be raised about the paths relating type A behavior to job satisfaction, along with implications of direct and indirect effects. This argument simply asserts the importance and value of including personality dimensions in the study of job satisfaction.

3. Self-esteem

Self-esteem has been explored in a somewhat different manner in the literature than the other two dispositional variables discussed here. Much evidence supports the existence of a main effect between job satisfaction and self-esteem—that is, self-esteem is positively correlated with job satisfaction (see, e.g., review articles by Clarke, 1971; Mossholder, Bedeian, and Armenakis, 1981). Significant associations between self-esteem and job satisfaction have been found across a broad spectrum of occupations, for example, with in-home aides (Dillard and Feather, 1991), physicians (Mohan and Bali, 1988), teachers (Lopez and Greenhaus, 1978), and in a national sample of working women (Andrisani, 1978).

This straightforward finding has been rejected by a number of authors, however. In part, issues inhere in identifying self-esteem either as a dispositional variable or as a task-dependent variable. Some argue that self-esteem is really a task or domain *dependent* variable, and individuals acquire esteem by virtue of their performance in particular contexts. For example, Marcic, Aiuppa, and Watson (1989) argue that "people who *fit* the organizational norm more are getting more positive feedback, which in turn would tend to increase their self-esteem" (p. 918). Others argue that self-esteem is an *independent* dispositional attribute: "it reflects aspects of an individual's continuing psychological state more than it reflects the circumstances of a particular work situation" (Mossholder, Bedeian, and Armenakis, 1981: 226). As such, an individual's level of esteem influences his or her ability to perform as well as the pleasure derived from the performance. However, there appears to be little or no relationship between performance and job satisfaction. Based on a meta-analytic review, Ianffaldano and Muchinsky (1985) concluded that: "the satisfaction-performance relation qualifies as a long-standing fad among organizational researchers . . . despite a profusion of empirical non-support" (p. 269).

The assumed relationship between performance and satisfaction appears to have inspired many of the investigations of self-esteem. Korman (1968) argued that performance was correlated with work satisfaction for high self-esteem workers, but not for those with low self-esteem. Inkson (1978) tested Korman's hypothesis, and concluded that self-esteem moderated the performance-satisfaction relationship, but only with regard to intrinsic satisfaction. Howard, Bellenger, and Wilcox (1987) noted that high self-esteem effects job satisfaction indirectly by reducing role stress. Somers and Lefkowitz (1983) stated that self-esteem moderates the relationship between job satisfaction and need gratification. Thus, much effort in examining the role of self-esteem with reference to satisfaction focuses on its utility as an intervening or moderating variable. The use of self-esteem in this manner clearly presents it as a dispositional variable, one whose intensity or degree directly or indirectly influences job satisfaction.

Overall, self-esteem appears to be an important variable, but the extent to which self-esteem is stable or labile within the context of varying environmental pressures and the nature of the indirect and moderating effects of self-esteem on job satisfaction remain to be established. The assumption of the dispositional perspective is that self-esteem will remain fairly stable across diverse situations. In contrast, those who view self-esteem as task-specific and acquired, argue that it is a pliable characteristic. And, since esteem is positively associated with job satisfaction, organizational factors can be manipulated to maximize the potential for increasing self-esteem.

F.   Summary

In general, the field reflects dissention about the merits of examining dispositional variables. Staw and Ross (1985), for example, argue for the centrality of dispositional factors. They see job attitudes as determined primarily by dispositional dimensions, and that "neither changes in pay nor changes in job status accounted for nearly as much variance as prior job attitude" (p. 475). Others such as Gerhart (1987) note that "from an applied view, the impact of traits on global job satisfaction may have little relevance" (p. 371). Organizational determinants such as pay and status are indeed important and significant predictors of job satisfaction.

While the dispositional variables have been discussed as unique dimensions with unique effects in this overview, the research indicates that they are related and interdependent. For example, research has demonstrated a positive association between type A personality and internal control. Both in turn have been associated with intrinsic dimensions of job satisfaction (see, e.g., Bluen, Barling, and Burns, 1990; Day and Bedeian, 1991). Such findings have led researchers to argue that the value of personality dimensions may in some ways be tied to the structure of the job being investigated. Thus, for example, Frost and Wilson (1983), studying nurses, found that internality was positively correlated with job satisfaction, but type A behavior was not. These authors then go on to argue that "one must consider personality variables, especially in jobs where satisfaction is contingent upon individual autonomy and control" (p. 403).

Perhaps the strongest argument for the inclusion of personality variables in models of job satisfaction comes from the conceptual frameworks related to P-E fit. A considerable body of the *fit* literature provides evidence that "misfit . . . can threaten the individual's well-being and may result in various adverse effects upon his/her health and job satisfaction (Furnham and Zacherl, 1986: 454). But, if dispositional factors are to play a role in the job satisfaction arena, the relevant personality dimensions must be more broadly articulated than now; that is, rather than preselecting particular dispositional variables on an adhoc basis, more complete models need to be explored. This is particularly important given the documented overlap between the various types of dispositional factors. As Seashore and Taber (1975) note, "directly measured enduring personality characteristics have only rarely been employed in studies of job satisfaction" (p. 354). At first, this may be an exploratory venture. But these exploratory analyses may be necessary in order to identify relevant personality dimensions. In the opinion of this author, current use of personality factors appear to be guided less by an exploratory or theoretical agenda, and more by measurement popularity and availability.

V. CORRELATES OF JOB DISSATISFACTION

If an individual experiences job dissatisfaction, there is a high probability that there will be negative personal repercussions, as well as the likelihood that other areas of that person's life will be negatively effected. Seashore and Taber (1975) make a definitive statement in this regard:

> . . . job dissatisfaction is in the normal case a transitional or temporary state which prompts some sort of accommodative or adaptive behavior, and in this limited sense is a partial "cause" of that behavior. In contrast, the experience of positive job satisfaction tends to perpetuate the psychobiological behaviors that induced, or are otherwise associated with, the experience of satisfaction. These individual accommodative processes become significant at the organizational or societal levels to the degree that they are prevalent and to the degree that they affect the integrity of the organization and/or society (p. 358).

However, it is virtually impossible to isolate the consequences of job dissatisfaction from those related to job stress. Sometimes, job dissatisfaction is viewed as another consequence of job stress, and at other times, it appears to play a moderating role between stress and psychosocial symptoms. It is, however, an empirical fact that there is an abundant array of personal, organizational, and societal symptoms that have been loosely correlated with job dissatisfaction.

Consider some examples. At the *personal* level, a great deal of research has associated job satisfaction with well-being. For example, job dissatisfaction has been associated with psychosomatic illness (Quinn, Staines, and McCollough, 1974); heart disease risk factors (French and Caplan, 1972); substance abuse (Mangione and Quinn, 1973); anomie and hopelessness (Winefield et al., 1991); mortality (O'Toole, 1975); and depression (O'Brien and Feather, 1990). In fact, Winefield et al. (1991) conclude from their longitudinal study of young adults that from the perspective of psychological well-being, those who are dissatisfied with their job are similar to the unemployed when compared with those who are satisfactorily employed. In a sense, "we know . . . that satisfaction with work is related to general well-being" (Pottick, 1989: 489). What we don't know is the extent to which these negative consequences are *purely* a function of dissatisfaction.

In addition, considerable evidence suggests that dissatisfaction with the job results in a negative spillover to other areas of personal well-being. For example, job satisfaction is positively correlated with life satisfaction (see, e.g., Andrews and Withey, 1974; Campbell, Converse, and Rodgers, 1976; Near, Rice, and Hunt, 1987; Pottick, 1989), as well as with marital and family relationships (see, e.g., Bromet, Dew, and Parkinson, 1990; Lambert, 1990; Weiss, 1990; Zedeck et al., 1989). More and more, the domain of interpersonal interactions outside the workplace has become a central focus of research when examining issues related to job satisfaction and dissatisfaction.

At the *organizational* level, the empirical findings are equally viable. Job dissatisfaction has been associated with work-related fatigue and injury (Quinn and Sheppard, 1974); theft and sabotage (Mangione and Quinn, 1973); turnover (Lawler, 1973); and absenteeism (Lawler, 1973; Vroom, 1964), to a name a few. In considering these negative organizational consequences of job dissatisfaction, Locke (1976) noted that "in view of the numerous replications of the relationship between satisfaction and withdrawal from the job, it would seem that little would be gained from additional studies along the same lines" (p. 1332). Yet, from a management viewpoint, it is critical to be able to isolate those dimensions associated with turnover and absenteeism because of negative organizational implications. Thus, while research on main effects may be a redundant activity, certainly considerable effort should be expended in examining the moderators of job satisfaction.

In contrast, the relationships of job satisfaction with performance and productivity have shown no consistent negative or positive associations. The two appear to be unrelated, or at best, minimally associated (Iaffaldano and Muchinsky, 1985). On the one hand this may suggest that performance monitoring is all that is needed. If quality products are delivered on time, the exploration of the quality of work life is an unnecessary or at best an intellectual luxury. However, given the well-established relationships between absenteeism and turnover with job dissatisfaction, it would appear that the negative consequences to the organization may in some ways be hidden; that is, as contextual factors impact on individual well-being, related negative consequences may not be far behind. As a result, organizational responses may be slower than desirable, and the long-term consequences may be detrimental to the functioning of the organization.

As paradoxical as it may sound, the impact of job dissatisfaction at the *societal* level is best understood, and has been studied for the most part, in terms of the individual. For example, job dissatisfaction has been correlated with extremist political voting behavior (Sheppard & Herrick, 1972) as well as with lack of political and community participation (Quinn and Sheppard, 1974). In addition, of course, society will ultimately have to pay the price for the provision of services to those dissatisfied workers who engage in destructive behaviors such as substance abuse or sabotage, those who suffer from mental health and health problems, and those in marriages and families falling apart because of what goes on at work. In bad economic times, for example, as job options decrease, so does job mobility. The outcome may be a dissatisfied worker forced to stay in a position, possibly resulting in serious negative consequences both to the individual and the organization. The social and financial burden of job dissatisfaction under these circumstances may be an "invisible" economic pitfall.

A. Summary

It is an empirical fact that job dissatisfaction is associated with a variety of personal, organizational, and societal consequences that are essentially negative. However, whether or not these consequences are a direct function of dissatisfaction with the job is difficult to state. For example, there could be differential response patterns to the various job facets. The salience of a given facet at a given time may produce varying responses over time. In addition, we know little about the consequences in terms of temporary and long-term effects. Historically, the tendency has been to gather cross-sectional data on the individual and to draw inferences about organizational and societal impact. This tendency is more a result of study design, in which data are collected from individual respondents with an emphasis on individual perception. However, the literature makes a strong argument for the value of documenting the consequences of job satisfaction at all levels, and not simply focusing on the person. This would suggest a multimethod strategy for data collection, and a shift away from the heavy reliance on survey data.

VI. RECOMMENDATIONS FOR FUTURE RESEARCH

As a concept, job satisfaction has been the center of a tremendous research effort. Its practical importance has grown over the years, as evidenced by the flood of research documenting the relationship of job satisfaction with personal, organizational, and societal consequences. Given this practical concern, it is increasingly important to strengthen the research endeavors. In his 1976 review, Locke cited as his main concern the conduct of studies "aimed at identifying causal mechanisms and less use of correlation without explanation" (p. 1340). As an arena for the vigorous implementation of a research agenda, this assertion still holds. In his analysis, Locke identified a variety of causal factors worthy of pursuit, most of which would fall in the domain of dispositional variables—defensiveness, propensity for emotional generalization, ineffective coping, and the like. His suggestion was to include more factors related to individual differences that may contribute to perceptions of satisfaction and dissatisfaction.

Given the current base of research knowledge, it is difficult to argue against the inclusion of personality dimensions in the study of job satisfaction. While this author would agree about the theoretical utility of these dimensions, and in fact did so earlier in this chapter, serious questions can be raised about their *practical* importance. Consider, for example, the issues of measurement if one is to achieve a best fit between a person and his or her choice of occupation. It is perhaps easy to obtain an excellent description of the tasks and roles associated with a particular job. This would be a relatively simple task compared to determining what personality characteristics need to be monitored, let alone issues of measurement validity, the reliability of the related instruments, and the specification of the acceptable *level or degree of presence of the trait*. In addition, the recent proposals suggesting a genetic base to job satisfaction could portend an Orwellian future. An overemphasis on individual characteristics, with its connotations of fixed attributes, suggests an environment in which some *selected* qualities a person brings in to the workplace are considered to be more important than the context of work. The political danger of such an emphasis, especially given the limited research tools available to identify and match individuals to the job, certainly raises serious ethical questions.

Having said this, however, one cannot simply overlook the evidence demonstrating the potential importance of dispositional variables. What appears to be needed are more controlled studies, experimental analogs, and longitudinal studies. It is the opinion of this author that cross-sectional survey methods have reached their zenith with regard to the study of causes and effects of job satisfaction. Further cross-sectional research would merely add to the available database. These studies are unlikely to break new ground or provide new perspectives by virtue of the limitations of the methodology.

The facet approach is the favored method in the measurement of job satisfaction. Its significance lies in the potential for identifying factors associated with more or less satisfaction, and thereby, with enhancing the potential for facet-specific interventions. However, the jury is still out with regard to the utility or centrality of particular facets. The strategy of employing factors determined a priori for assessment of job satisfaction has its limitations. We are still not explaining as much of global satisfaction as we should if these facets were universally relevant. Perhaps the time has come to reexamine the appropriateness of a deductive approach. Studies with a more qualitative bent, ones that explore the rationales for satisfaction and dissatisfaction without prior restrictions, may lead to better and different information and conceptual models. Indeed, an inductive strategy of this sort may result in the delineation of organization-specific or even disposition-specific factors that contribute to perceptions of satisfaction.

Relationships of demographic factors to job satisfaction have been commonplace in the job satisfaction literature, with one exception: the examination of issues associated with race and ethnicity. The vast majority of job satisfaction studies have utilized samples that are essentially white. Those few studies that did examine minority workers often hinted at the existence of differences. Yet, many of these studies employed the same conceptual frameworks, and did not explore contextual variables such as discrimination or harassment. With the changing "color" of the workplace, the absence of minority-relevant research on job satisfaction is an anachronism. Only if all people are affected in much the same ways by environmental variables does this research agenda make sense. However, if minority individuals bring in to the work environment a set of different values and perceptions engendered by society, community, and family, these historically antecedent factors may play a crucial role in the determination of job satisfaction as well as on the consequences of job dissatisfaction. Just as the family and spouse have become relevant and critical components in the examination of the work-family interface, race and ethnicity must be accorded due respect in the development of better models.

Finally, the atheoretical nature of the job satisfaction literature remains a disturbing problem. The various expectancy theories have yet to be fully tested. The two-factor theory has been written off by some researchers, but still offers an optional perspective, and in the opinion of this author, has been criticized in part because it is distinctive. The P-E fit models probably offer the best frameworks for future research. They offer a balance of a theoretical framework with a potential for intervention design.

The future of job satisfaction research can take many different paths. Investigators could continue to conduct surveys and add to the existing body of knowledge, or they could make a radical turn toward experimental analogs and longitudinal studies. Researchers may choose to ignore the reality of a culturally diverse workplace, or seek to develop alternate culturally sensitive explanatory models. Most important, the field must continue to struggle with examining both the definition and measurement of job satisfaction.

REFERENCES

Adams, J. S. (1965). Inequity in social exchange. In *Advances in Experimental Social Psychology*, vol. 2 (L. Berkowitz, ed.), Academic Press, New York.

Aldag, R. J., and Brief, A. P. (1978). Examination of alternative models of job satisfaction. *Human Relations*, *31*:91–98.

Amaro, H., Russo, N.F. and Johnson, J. (1987). Family and work: predictors of psychological well-being among Hispanic women professionals. *Psychology of Women Quarterly*, *11*:505–52.

Andrews, F., and Withey, S. (1976). *Social Indicators of Well-Being*. Plenum Press, New York.

Andrisani, P. J. (1978). Job satisfaction among working women. *Signs*, *3*:588–607.

Andrisani, P. J., and Nestel, G. (1976). Internal-external control as contributor to an outcome of work experience. *J. of Applied Psychology*, *61*:156–165.

Arnold, M. B. (1960). *Emotion and Personality: Psychological Aspects*, vol. 1. Columbia University Press, New York.

Arvey, R. D., Bouchard, T. J., Segal, N. L., and Abraham, L. M. (1989). Job satisfaction: Environmental and genetic components. *J. of Applied Psychology*, *74*:187–192.

Ashford, C., and Bobko, S. J. (1990). Interactive effects of "Type A" behavior and perceived control on worker performance, job satisfaction, and somatic complaints. *Academy of Management Journal*, *33*:870–881.

Bamundo, P. J., and Kopelman, R. E. (1980). The moderating effects of occupation, age, and urbanization on the relationship between job satisfaction and life satisfaction. *J. of Vocational Behavior*, *17*:106–123.

Beaty, D. (1990). Re-examining the link between job characteristics and job satisfaction. *J of Social Psychology*, *130*:131–132.

Berk, L. E. (1985). Relationship of caregiver education to child-oriented attitudes, job satisfaction, and behaviors toward children. *Child Care Quarterly*, *14*:103–129.

Bersoff, D., and Crosby, F. (1984). Job satisfaction and family status. *Personality and Social Psychology Bulletin*, *10*:79–84.

Blood, M. R. (1971). The validity of importance. *J of Applied Psychology*, *55*:487–488.

Bloom, R, and Barry, J. R. (1967). Determinants of work attitudes among Negroes. *J. of Applied Psychology*, *51*:291–294.

Bluen, S. D., Barling, J., and Burns, W. (1990). Predicting sales performance, job satisfaction, and depression using the achievement strivings and impatience-irritability dimensions of type A behavior. *J. of Applied Psychology*, *75*:212–216.

Brabson, H. V., Jones, C. A., and Jayaratne, S. (1991). Perceptions of emotional support, stress, and strain among African-American human service workers. *J. of Multicultural Social Work*, *1*:77–102.

Brayfield, A. H. (1960). Review of F. Herzberg, B. Mausner & B. Snyderman: The motivation to work. *Personnel Psychology*, *13*:101–103.

Brayfield, A. H., and Rothe, H. F. (1951). An index of job satisfaction. *J. of Applied Psychology*, *35*:307–311.

Brenner, O. C., and Fernstein, J. A. (1984). Racial differences in perceived job fulfillment of white collar workers. *Perceptual and Motor Skills*, *58*:643–646.

Bromet, E. J., Dew, M. A., and Parkinson, D. K. (1990). Spillover between work and family: A study of blue-collar working wives. In *Stress between Work and Family* (J. Eckenrode and S. Gore, eds), Plenum Press, New York.

Buss, A. H., Plomin, R., and Willerman, L. (1973). The inheritance of temperaments. *J. of Personality*, *41*:513–524.

Campbell, A., Converse, P. E., and Rodgers, W. L. (1976). *The Quality of American Life*. Russell Sage Foundation, New York.

Caplan, R. D. (1979). Social support, person-environment fit, and coping. In *Mental Health and the Economy* (L. A. Ferman and J. P. Gordus, eds.), W. E. Upjohn Institute for Employment Research, Kalamazoo, Mich.

Caplan, R. D. (1987). Person-environment fit theory and organizations: Commensurate dimensions, time perspectives, and mechanisms. *J. of Vocational Behavior*, *31*:248–267.

Chusmir, L. H., and Hood, J. N. (1988). Predictive characteristics of type A behavior among working men and women. *J. of Applied Social Psychology*, *18*:688–698.

Clarke, T. E. (1971). The work environment and mental health. *Studies in Personnel Psychology*, *3*:83–96.

Conway, P. G., Williams, M. S., and Green, J. L. (1987). A model of job facet satisfaction. *J. of Social Work Education*, *23*:48–57.

Cook, J. D., Hepworth, S. J., Wall, T. D. and Warr, P. B. (1981). *The Experience of Work*. Academic Press, London, England.

Cox, T. (1990). Problems with research by organizational scholars on issues of race and ethnicity. *J. of Applied Behavioral Science*, *26*:5–23.

Cropanzano, R and James, K. (1990). Some methodological considerations for the behavioral genetic analysis of work attitudes. *J. of Applied Psychology*, *75*:433–439.

Crouter, A. (1984). Spillover from family to work: The neglected side of the work–family interface. *Human Relations*, *37*:425–442.

Dailey, R. C. (1978). Relationship between locus of control, perceived group cohesiveness, and satisfaction with co-workers. *Psychological Reports*, *42*:311–316.

Dalton, A. H., and Marcis, J. G. (1987). Gender differences in job satisfaction among young adults. *J. of Behavioral Economics*, *16*:21–32.

Day, D. V., and Bedeian, A. G. (1991). Work climate and type A status as predictors of job satisfaction: A test of the interactional perspective. *J. of Vocational Behavior*, *38*:39–52.

Dillard, B. G., and Feather, B. L. (1991). The association between attitudes and job satisfaction: A study of in-home care aides. *Educational Gerontology*, *17*:209–218.

Dunham, R., and Herman, J. (1975). Development of a female faces scale for measuring job satisfaction. *J. of Applied Psychology*, *60*:629–631.

Dunham, R., Smith, F. J. and Blackburn, R. S. (1977). Validation of the Index of Organizational Reactions with the JDI, the MSQ, and Faces Scale. *Academy of Management Journal*, *20*:420–432.

Dunnette, M. D., Campbell, J. P., and Hakel, M. D. (1967). Factors contributing to job satisfaction and job dissatisfaction in six occupational groups. *Organizational Behavior and Human Performance*, *2*:143–174.

Eckenrode, J., and Gore, S. (1990). *Stress between Work and Family*. Plenum Press, New York.

Evans, M. G. (1969). Conceptual and operational problems in the measurement of various aspects of job satisfaction. *J. of Applied Psychology*, *53*:93–101.

Ewen, R. B. (1964). Some determinants of job satisfaction: A study of the generality of the Herzberg theory. *J. of Applied Psychology*, *48*:111–163.

Ewen, R. B. (1967). Weighting components of job satisfaction. *J. of Applied Psychology*, *51*:68–73.

Farrell, D., and Stamm, C. L. (1988). Meta-analysis of the correlates of employee absence. *Human Relations*, *41*:211–227.

Feldberg, R. L., and Glenn, E. N. (1979). Male and female: Job versus gender models in the sociology of work. *Social Problems*, *26*:524–538.

Ferratt, T. W. (1981). Overall job satisfaction: Is it a linear function of facet satisfaction? *Human Relations*, *34*:463–473.

Fletcher, B. C. (1988). The epidemiology of occupational stress. In *Causes, Coping and Consequences of Stress at Work* (C. L. Cooper and R. Payne, eds.), John Wiley, New York.

French, J. R. P., and Caplan, R. D. (1972). Organizational stress and individual strain. In *The Failure of Success* (A. J. Marrow, ed.), AMACOM, New York.

French, J. R. P., Rogers, W. L., and Cobb, S. (1974). Adjustment as person–environment fit. In *Coping and Adaptation* (G. V. Coelho, D. A. Hamburg, and H. E. Adams, eds.), Basic Books, New York.

Frost, T. F., and Wilson, H. G. (1983). Effects of locus of control and A-B personality type on job satisfaction within the health care field. *Psychological Reports*, *53*:399–405.

Furnham, A., and Zacherl, M. (1986). Personality and job satisfaction. *Personality and Individual Differences*, *7*:453–459.

Gavin, J. F., and Ewen, R. B. (1974). Racial differences in job attitudes and performance: Some theoretical considerations and empirical findings. *Personnel Psychology*, *27*:455–464.

Gaziel, H. H. (1986). Correlates of job satisfaction: A study of the two factor theory in an educational setting. *J. of Psychology*, *120*:613–626.

Gerhart, B. (1987). How important are dispositional factors as determinants of job satisfaction? Implications for job design and other personnel programs. *J. of Applied Psychology*, *72*:366–373.

Gibson, J. L., and Klein, S. M. (1970). Employee attitudes as a function of age and length of service: A reconceptualization. *Academy of Management Journal*, *13*:411–425.

Glenn, N. D., and Weaver, C. N. (1982). Further evidence on education and job satisfaction. *Social Forces*, *61*:46–55.

Gold, R. S., Webb, L. J., and Smith, J. K. (1982). Racial differences in job satisfaction among White and Black mental health employees. *J. of Psychology*, *111*:255–261.

Golding, J., Resnick, A., and Crosby, F. (1983). Work satisfaction as a function of gender and job status. *Psychology of Women Quarterly*, *7*:286–290.

Golembiewski, R. T. (1977). Testing some sterotypes about sexes in organizations: Differential satisfaction with work. *Human Resource Management*, *16*:30–32.

Golembiewski, R. T. (1978). Testing the applicability of the JDI to various demographic groupings. *Academy of Management Journal*, *21*:514–519.

Greenberger, D. B., Strasser, S., Cummings, L. L., and Dunham, R. B. (1989). The impact of personal control on performance and satisfaction. *Organizational Behavior & Human Decision Processes*, *43*:29–51.

Greenglass, E. R. (1985). Psychological implications of sex bias in the workplace. *Academic Psychology Bulletin*, *7*:227–240.

Gruber, J. E., and Bjorn, L. (1982). Blue-collar blues: The sexual harassment of women autoworkers. *Work & Occupations*, *9*:271–298.

Hackman, J. R., and Oldham, G. R. (1980). *Work Redesign*. Addison-Wesley, Reading, Mass.

Hanushek, E. A., and Jackson, J. E. (1977). *Statistical Methods for Social Scientists*. Academic Press, New York.

Hartman, S., Grigsby, D. W., Crino, M. D., and Chhokar, J. S. (1986). The measurement of job satisfaction by action tendencies. *Educational and Psychological Measurement*, *46*:317–329.

Hawkes, G. R., Guagnano, G. A., Acredolo, C., and Helmick, S. A. (1984). Status inconsistency and job satisfaction: General population and Mexican–American sub-population analyses. *Sociology and Social Research*, *68*:378–387.

Herzberg, F., Mausner, B., and Snyderman, B. (1959). *The Motivation to Work*. Wiley, New York.

Hollenback, J. R. (1989). Control theory and the perception of work environments: The effects of focus of attention on affective and behavioral reactions to work. *Organizational Behavior and Human Decision Processes*, *43*:406–430.

Hoppock, R. (1935). *Job Satisfaction*. Harper, New York.

Howell, R. D., Bellenger, D. N., and Wilcox, J. B. (1987). *J of Business Research*, *15*:71–84.

Iaffaldano, M. T., and Muchinsky, P. M. (1985). Job satisfaction and job performance: A meta-analysis. *Psychological Bulletin*, *97*:251–273.

Inkson, J. K. (1978). Self esteem as a moderator of the relationship between job performance and job satisfaction. *J. of Applied Psychology*, *63*:243–247.

Ironson, G. H., Smith, P. C., Brannick, M. T., and Gibson, W. M. (1989). Construction of a job in general scale: A comparison of global, composite, and specific measures. *J of Applied Psychology*, *74*:193–200.

Jayaratne, S., and Chess, W. A. (1983). Job satisfaction and turnover among social work administrators: A national survey. *Administration in Social Work*, *7*:11–22.

Jayaratne, S., Tripodi, T., and Chess, W. A. (1983). Perceptions of emotional support, stress, and strain by male and female social workers. *Social Work Research & Abstracts*, *19*:19–29.

Jones, A. P., James, L. R., Bruni, J. R., and Sells, S. B. (1977). Black-white differences in work environment perceptions and job satisfaction and its correlates. *Personnel Psychology*, *30*:5–16.

Jurik, N. C., and Halemba, G. J. (1984). Gender, working conditions and the job satisfaction of women in a non-traditional occupation: Female correctional officers in men's prisons. *The Sociological Quarterly*, *25*:551–566.

Kanter, R. N. (1977). *Men and Women of the Corporation*. Basic Books, New York.

Katzell, R. A. (1964). Personal values, job satisfaction, and job behavior. In *Man in a World of Work* (H. Borow, ed.), Houghton-Mifflin, Boston.

Katzell, R. A., Ewen, R., and Korman, A. (1974). Job attitudes of black and white workers: Male blue collar workers in six communities. *Vocational Behavior*, 4:365–376.

King, M., Murray, M. A., and Atkinson, T. (1982). Background, personality, job characteristics, and satisfaction with work in a national sample. *Human Relations*, 35:119–133.

Kissman, K. (1990). Women in blue-collar occupations: An exploration of constraints and facilitators. *J. of Sociology & Social Welfare*, 17:139–149.

Kobasa, S. C. (1979). Stressful life events, personality, and health: An inquiry into hardiness. *J. of Personality and Social Psychology*, 42:168–177.

Kohn, M. L. and Schooler, C. (1973). Occupational experience and psychological functioning: An assessment of reciprocal effects. *American Sociological Review*, 38:97–118.

Konar, E. (1981). Explaining racial differences in job satisfaction: A reexamination of the data. *J. of Applied Psychology*, 66:522–524.

Korman, A. K. (1968). Task success, task popularity, and self-esteem as influences on task liking. *J. of Applied Psychology*, 52:484–490.

Kornhauser, A. (1965). *Mental Health of the Industrial Worker: A Detroit Study*. John Wiley, New York.

Kunin, T. (1955). The construction of a new type of attitude measure. *Personnel Psychology*, 8:65–78.

Lambert, S. J. (1990). Processes linking work and family: A critical review and research agenda. *Human Relations*, 43:239–257.

Lawler, E. L. (1973). *Motivation in Work Organizations*. Brooks/Cole Publishers, Monterey, Calif.

Lee, C., Ashford, S. J. and Bobko, P. (1990). Interactive effects of "Type-A" behavior and perceived control on worker performance, job satisfaction, and somatic complaints. *Academy of Management Journal*, 33:870–881.

Lester, D., and Solis, A. (1980). Type A personality, stress, and job satisfaction in police officers. *Perceptual & Motor Skills*, 51:890.

Lester, D. (1987). Correlates of job satisfaction in police officers. *Psychological Reports*, 60:550.

Levitan, T., Quinn, R. P., and Staines, G. L. (1971). Sex discrimination against the American working woman. *American Behavioral Scientist*, 15:237–254.

Lincoln, J. R. and Kalleberg, A. L. (1985). Work organization and workforce commitment: A study of plants and employers in the U.S. and Japan. *American Sociological Review*, 50:738–760.

Locke, E. A. (1969). What is job satisfaction? *Organizational Behavior and Human Performance*: 409–336.

Locke, E. A. (1970). Job satisfaction and job performance: A theoretical analysis. *Organizational Behavior and Human Performance*, 5:484–500.

Locke, E. A. (1976). The nature and causes of job satisfaction. In *Handbook of Industrial and Organizational Psychology* (M. D. Dunnette, ed.), Rand McNally, Chicago.

Loher, B. T., Noe, R. A., Moeller, N. L., and Fitzgerald, M. P. (1985). A meta-analysis of the relation of job characteristics to job satisfaction. *J. of Applied Psychology*, 70:280–289.

Lopez, E. M., and Greenhaus, J. H. (1978). Self-esteem, race, and job satisfaction. *J. of Vocational Behavior*, 13:75–83.

Lottinville, E. and Scherman, A. (1988). Job satisfaction of married, divorced, and single working women in a medical setting. *Career Development Quarterly*, 37:165–176.

MacKinnon, C. A. (1979). *Sexual Harassment of Working Women: A Case of Sex Discrimination*. Yale University Press, New Haven, Conn.

Maddi, S. R., and Kobasa, S. C. (1984). *The Hardy Executive: Health Under Stress*. Dow Jones-Irwin, Homewood, Ill.

Mangione, T. W., and Quinn, R. P. (1973). *Job Satisfaction, Counterproductive Behavior, and Self-Narcotizising Withdrawal from Work*. Institute for Social Research, Ann Arbor, Mich.

Mannheim, B. (1983). Male and female industrial workers: Job satisfaction, work role centrality, and work place preference. *Work and Occupations*, 10:413–436.

Marcic, D., Aiuppa, T. A., and Watson, J. G. (1989). Personality type, organizational norms and self esteem. *Psychological Reports*, 65:915–191.

Matteson, M. T., Ivancevich, J. M., and Smith, S. V. (1984). Relation of type A behavior to performance and satisfaction among sales personnel. *J. of Vocational Behavior*, 25:203–214.

Matthews, J. J., Collins, W. E., and Cobb, B. B. (1974). A sex comparison of reasons for attrition in a male-dominated occupation. *Personnel Psychology*, 27:535–541.

Matthews, K. A., and Haynes, S. G. (1986). Type-A behavior pattern and coronary disease risk: Update and critical evaluation. *American J. of Epidemiology*, 123:923–960.

Maypole, D. E., and Skaine, R. (1983). Sexual harassment in the workplace. *Social Work*, 28:385–390.

McNeely, R. L. (1986). Gender and job satisfaction: Similarities and differences in a comprehensive human services department. *J. of Mental Health Administration, 12*:27–33.

McNeely, R. L. (1987). Job satisfaction and other characteristics of Asian American human service workers. *Social Work Research & Abstracts, 23*:7–9.

McNeely, R. L. (1988). Age and job satisfaction in human service employment. *Gerontologist, 28*:163–168.

McNeely, R. L. (1989). Job satisfaction and other characteristics among Hispanic–American human service workers. *Social Casework, 70*:237–242.

Miller, J. (1980). Individual and occupational determinants of job satisfaction: A focus on gender differences. *Sociology of Work and Occupations, 7*:337–366.

Milutinovich, J. V. (1977). Black-white differences in job satisfaction: Group cohesiveness, and leadership style. *Human Relations, 12*:1079–1087.

Mitchell, T. R., Smyser, C. M., and Weed, S. E. (1975). Locus of control: Supervision and work satisfaction. *Academy of Management Journal, 18*:623–631.

Moch, M. K. (1980). Racial differences in job satisfaction: Testing four common explanations. *J. of Applied Psychology, 65*:299–306.

Mohan, J., and Bali, S. (1988). A study of job satisfaction of doctors in relation to their personality, values and self esteem. *J. of Personality & Clinical Studies, 4*:63–68.

Morthcott, H. C., and Lowe, G. S. (1987). Job and gender influences in the subjective experience of work. *Canadian Review of Sociology and Anthropology, 24*:116–131.

Mossholder, K. W., Bedeian, A. G., and Armenakis, A. A. (1981). Role perceptions, satisfaction, and performance: Moderating effects of self-esteem and organizational level. *Organizational Behavior and Human Performance, 28*:224–234.

Mottaz, C. (1986). Gender differences in work satisfaction, work-related rewards and values, and the determinants of work satisfaction. *Human Relations, 39*:359–378.

Muhammad, J. (1990). Relationship of job stress and type A behavior to employees job satisfaction, organizational commitment, psychosomatic health problems, and turnover motivation. *Human Relations, 43*:727–738.

Mullis, A. K., Ellett, C. H., and Mullis, R. L. (1986). Job satisfaction among child care workers. *J. of Child Care, 2*:65–75.

Near, J. P., Rice, R. W., and Hunt, R. G. (1987). Job satisfaction and life satisfaction: A profile analysis. *Social Indicators Research, 19*:383–401.

Neil, C. C., and Snizek, W. E. (1988). Gender as a moderator of job satisfaction. *Work and Occupations, 15*:201–219.

Nichols, G. A. (1971). Job satisfaction and nurses' intentions to remain with or to leave an organization. *Nursing Research, 20*:218–228.

Northcott, H. C. and Lowe, G. S. (1987). Job and gender influences in the subjective experience of work. *Canadian Review of Sociology & Anthropology, 24*:117–131.

O'Brien, G. E., and Feather, N. T. (1990). The relative effects of unemployment and quality of employment on the affect, work values and personal control of adolescents. *J. of Occupational Psychology, 63*:151–165.

O'Reilly, C. A., and Roberts, K. H. (1973). Job satisfaction among whites and non-whites. *J. of Applied Psychology, 57*:295–299.

Oskamp, S. (1984). *Applied Social Psychology.* Prentice-Hall, Englewood Cliffs, N.J.

O'Toole, J. (1975). *Work in America.* MIT Press, Cambridge, Mass.

Payne, R. (1988). Individual differences in the study of occupational stress. In *Causes, Coping and Consequences of Stress at Work* (C. L. Cooper and R. Payne, eds.), John Wiley, New York.

Pervin, L. A. (1968). Performance and satisfaction as a function of individual–environment fit. *Psychological Bulletin, 69*:56–68.

Pervin, L. A. (1987). Person-environment congruence in the light of the person–situation controversy. *J. of Vocational Behavior, 31*:222–230.

Pettersen, N. (1985). Specific versus generalized locus of control scales related to job satisfaction. *Psychological Reports, 56*:60–62.

Phares, E. J. (1976). *Locus of Control in Personality.* General Learning Press, Morristown, N.J.

Porter, L. W. (1961). A study of perceived need satisfaction in bottom and middle management jobs. *J. of Applied Psychology, 45*:1–10.

Portigal, A. H. (1976). *Towards the Measurement of Work Satisfaction.* the Organization for Economic Co-operation and Development (OECD), Paris.

Pottick, K. J. (1989). The work role as a major life role. *Social Casework, 70*:488–494.

Pulakos, E. D., and Schmitt, N. (1983). A longitudinal study of a valence model approach for the prediction of job satisfaction of new employees. *J. of Applied Psychology*, 68:307–312.

Quinn, R. P., and Sheppard, L. J. (1974). *The 1972–73 Quality of Employment Survey*. Institute for Social Research, Ann Arbor, Mich.

Quinn, R. P., Staines, G. L., and McCollough, M. R. (1974). *Job Satisfaction: Is There a Trend?* U.S. Department of Labor, Washington, D.C.

Quinn, R. P., and Staines, G. L. (1977). *The 1975–76 Quality of Employment Survey*. Institute for Social Research, Ann Arbor, Mich.

Rahim, A. (1982). Demographic variables in general job satisfaction in a hospital: A multivariate study. *Perceptual and Motor Skills*, 55:711–719.

Rain, J. S., Lane, I. M., and Steiner, D. D. (1991). A current look at the job satisfaction/life satisfaction relationship: Review and future considerations. *Human Relations*, 44:287–307.

Regan, M. C., and Roland, H. E. (1982). University students: A change in expectations and aspirations over the decade. *Sociology of Education*, 55:223–228.

Rice, R. W., Gentile, D. A., and McFarlin, D. B. (1991). Facet importance and job satisfaction. *J. of Applied Psychology*, 76:31–39.

Robinson, J. P., Athanasiou, R., and Head, K. B. (1969). *Measures of Occupational Attitudes and Occupational Characteristics*. Survey Research Center, Ann Arbor, Mich.

Rotter, J. B. (1966). Generalized expectancies for internal versus external control of reinforcement. *Psychological Monographs*, 80, whole no. 609.

Runyon, K. E. (1973). Some interactions between personality variables and management styles. *J. of Applied Psychology*, 57:288–294.

Santangelo, S., and Lester, D. (1985). Correlates of job satisfaction of public school teachers: Moonlighting, locus of control, and stress. *Psychological Reports*, 56:130.

Scarpello, V., and Campbell, J. P. (1983). Job satisfaction: Are all the parts there? *Personnel Psychology*, 36:577–600.

Schaffer, R. H. (1953). Job satisfaction as related to need satisfaction in work. *Psychological Monographs*, 67, no. 14 (whole no. 364).

Seashore, S. E. (1974). Job satisfaction as an indicator of quality of employment. In *Measuring Quality of Working Life* (A. H. Portigal, ed.), Information Canada, Ottawa.

Seashore, S. E., and Taber, T. D. (1975). Job satisfaction indicators and their correlates. *American Behavioral Scientist*, 18:333–368.

Sexton, P. C. (1977). *Women and Work*. U.S. Department of Labor, Employment and Training Administration, Washington, D.C.

Sharma, U., and Chaudhary, P. N. (1980). Locus of control and job satisfaction among engineers. *Psychological Studies*, 25:126–128.

Sheppard, H. C. and Herrick, N. Q. (1972). *Where have all the robots gone? Worker dissatisfaction in the '70's*. Free Press, New York.

Shiflett, S. (1988). Effects of race and criterion on the predictive ability of beliefs and attitudes. *Psychological Reports*, 62:527–535.

Shouksmith, J. (1989). A construct validation of a scale for measuring work motivation. *New Zealand J. of Psychology*, 18:76–81.

Shouksmith, J., Pajo, K., and Jepsen, A. (1990). Construction of a multidimensional scale of job satisfaction. *Psychological Reports*, 67:355–364.

Slocum, J. W., and Strawser, R. H. (1972). Racial differences in job attitudes. *J. of Applied Psychology*, 56:28–32.

Smith, P. C., Kendall, L. M., and Hulin, C. L. (1969). *The Measurement of Satisfaction in Work and Retirement: A Strategy for the Study of Attitudes*. Rand McNally, Chicago.

Smith, P. C. (1974). The development of a method of measuring job satisfaction: The Cornell Studies. In *Studies in Personnel and Industrial Psychology*, 3rd ed. (E. A. Fleishman and A. R. Bass, eds.), Dorsey Press, Homewood, Ill.

Smith, P. C., Smith, O. W., and Rollo, J. (1974). Factor structure for blacks and whites of the Job Descriptive Index and its discrimination of job satisfaction. *J. of Applied Psychology*, 59:99–100.

Smith, E. J. (1977). Work attitudes and the job satisfaction of black workers. *Vocational Guidance Quarterly*, 25:252–263.

Snyder, M. (1983). The influence of individuals on situations: Implications for understanding the links between personality and social psychology. *J. of Personality*, 51:497–516.

Soliman, H. M. (1970). Motivation-hygiene theory of job attitudes. *J. of Applied Psychology*, 54:452–461.

Somers, M. J., and Lefkowitz, J. (1983). Self-esteem, need gratification, and work satisfaction: A test of competing explanations from consistency theory and self enhancement theory. *J. of Vocational Behavior*, *22*:303–311.

Spector, P. E. (1982). Behavior in organizations as a function of employee's locus of control. *Psychological Bulletin*, *91*:482–497.

Spector, P. E. (1985). Measurement of human service staff satisfaction: Development of the job satisfaction survey. *Amn. J. of Community Psychology*, *13*:693–713.

Spector, P. E. (1988). Development of the work locus of control scale. *J. of Occupational Psychology*, *61*:335–340.

Staw, B. M., and Ross, J. (1985). Stability in the midst of change: A dispositional approach to job attitudes. *J. of Applied Psychology*, *70*:469–480.

Tait, M., Padgett, M. Y., and Baldwin, T. T. (1989). Job satisfaction and life satisfaction: A reevaluation of the strength of the relationship and gender effects as a function of the date of the study. *J. of Applied Psychology*, *74*:502–507.

Tuch, S. A., and Martin, J. K. (1991). Race in the workplace: Black/white differences in the sources of job satisfaction. *Sociological Quarterly*, *32*:103–116.

Valdez, F. and Gutele, B. (1987). Family roles: A help or hindrance for working women. In B. Gutele and L. Larwood (Eds.) *Women's Career Development*. Sage, Beverly Hills, CA.

Voydanoff, P. (1980). Perceived job characteristics and job satisfaction among men and women. *Psychology of Women Quarterly*, *5*:177–185.

Vroom, V. H. (1964). *Work and Motivation*. Wiley, New York.

Wachtel, P. (1973). Psychodynamics, behavior therapy, and the implacable experimenter: An inquiry into the consistency of personality. *J. of Abnormal Psychology*, *82*:323–334.

Wanous, J. P., and Lawler, E. E. (1972). Measurement and meaning of job satisfaction. *J. of Applied Psychology*, *56*:95–105.

Warr, P. & Routledge, T. (1969). An opinion scale for the study of manager's job satisfaction. *Occupational Psychology*, *43*:95–109.

Weaver, C. N. (1978). Black-white correlates of job satisfaction. *J. of Applied Psychology*, *63*:255–258.

Weaver, C. N. (1974). Negro-white differences in job satisfaction. *Business Horizons*, *17*:67–72.

Weaver, C. N. (1980). Job satisfaction in the United States in the 1970s. *J. of Applied Psychology*, *65*:364–367.

Weiss, D. J., Dawis, R. V., England, G. W., and Lofquist, L. H. (1967). *Manual for the Minnesota Satisfaction Questionnaire*. Industrial Relations Center, University of Minnesota, Work Adjustment Project, Minneapolis.

Weiss, H. M., and Adler, J. (1984). Personality and organizational behavior. In *Research in Organizational Behavior*, vol. 6 (B. M. Staw and L. L. Cummings, eds.), JAI Press, Greenwich, Conn.

Weiss, R. S. (1990). Bringing work stress home. In *Stress between Work and Family* (J. Eckenrode and S. Gore, eds.), Plenum Press, New York.

White, A. T., and Spector, P. E. (1987). An investigation of age-related factors in the age-job satisfaction relationship. *Psychology & Aging*, *2*:261–265.

Wilson, K. L., and Butler, J. S. (1978). Race and job satisfaction in the military. *Sociological Quarterly*, *19*:626–638.

Winefield, A. H., Winefield, H. R., Tiggemann, M., and Goldney, R. (1991). A longitudinal study of the psychological effects of unemployment and unsatisfactory employment on young adults. *J. of Applied Psychology*, *76*:424–431.

Wright, R., King, S. W. and Berg, W. E. (1985). Job satisfaction in the work place: A study of Black females in management positions. *J. of Social Service Research*, *8*:65–79.

Zedeck, S., Maslach, C., Mosier, K., and Skitka, L. (1989). Affective responses to work and quality of family life: Employees and spouses perspectives. In *Work and Family: Theory, Research, and Applications* (E. B. Goldsmith, ed.), Sage Publications, Newbury Park, Calif.

7
Organization Design

William B. Stevenson

Boston College, Chestnut Hill, Massachusetts

I. DESIGNING AND DEFINING ORGANIZATIONS

Do managers design organizations? To design implies creating procedures for pursuing collective goals. These procedures specify who is going to do what, how information is going to flow through the organization, who has the authority to make decisions, and who has the authority to specify and evaluate the job responsibilities of others.

Rarely does a manager or group of managers have the opportunity to start from scratch, to specify the division of labor and formal procedures in detail. Managers may have this opportunity during reorganizations or foundings of new units and organizations. However, once the new procedures are in place, they are modified and subverted by those who are affected by this new set of procedures. In addition, circumstances change, new problems arise, and the organization evolves in new directions as individuals are added and new procedures are developed to deal with new problems. Eventually the positions and procedures that the founding members had designed may be inadequate for the new situation, and the individuals' activities may not coincide with their organizational positions and job descriptions.

Do managers design organizations? Well, they try. However, as Peters and Waterman (1982) have described the actions of leaders, the manager's designs are more like snow fences designed to guide the drifting snow. Organizational structure, then, can be considered a method for directing a stream of events.

Managers try to build stability into the organization. Structure implies permanence and stability. We seek stability in the chaos of organizational life because we experience stress and anxiety without a level of certainty in our lives (Schein, 1985; Turner, 1988). Assuming that organizations are created to accomplish purposes that are beyond the capabilities of individuals, we would like some understanding of the part we are playing in the organization, and what part others are playing. We would like certainty about our roles and guidelines about who we should interact with to accomplish our job.

According to Burns and Flam (1987), the structural rules we create to stabilize social life accomplish a variety of purposes. These rules solve collective action problems by providing norms that enable actors to coordinate their activities for collective goals. Rules help interdependent actors to avoid negative unintended consequences such as "the tragedy of the Commons" or the inadvertent depletion of common resources through each individual pursuing his or her own self-interest while being oblivious to the effects on the collectivity. An organizational structure provides positions of authority so that individual contributions can be audited, reducing the temptation of becoming a "free rider" who experiences the benefits of being in the organization without putting forth adequate effort. Finally, as Burns and Flam (1987: 18) note, social rule systems are created by powerful actors to "institutionalize their power and status, resource control, and future strategic action capabilities."

There are two perspectives on how we create these rules to stabilize organizations. Proponents of the formal structure perspective emphasize the structuring of activities as specified by management. Proponents of the emergent structure perspective focus on the stable patterns of interaction that develop in organizations, sometimes independently of formal structure.

To specify the procedures for getting things done and to allocate people to positions is one definition of organizational design. An organizational structure is a relatively persistent, enduring set of agreements that transcends the idiosyncrasies of the individuals involved. However, these specified agreements—usually embodied in an organizational chart and manual of procedures—are constantly being modified by the individuals involved. As we all know, the organization chart is a poor reflection of who is interacting with whom, and who may have the power in the organization. It follows that we can make a distinction between the formal structure as chart and the informal structure as patterns of interaction. We could regard these patterns of interaction as relatively stable and having a stabilizing influence on the organization, and we could define structure as patterns of interaction rather than the organization chart. Thus the definition of structure depends on your definition of the organization.

A. Defining the Organization as a Structure

One definition of the organization is a collectivity that exists in an environment and engages in activities that are usually related to a set of goals (Blau and Scott, 1962). To pursue these goals a structure is needed. As Blau states (1974: 29): "The defining criterion of a formal organization—or an organization, for short—is the existence of procedures for mobilizing and coordinating the efforts of various, usually specialized, subgroups in the pursuit of joint objectives." Organizations need a division of labor and a set of procedures that guide interaction, communication, decision making, and the interpretation of ambiguous and uncertain goals.

As we shall see below, there is a variety of perspectives among those who believe that organizational structure is defined by formal procedures and organization charts. For example, the organization chart can be considered a concrete manifestation of a set of structural variables: complexity, formalization, centralization, and the horizontal and vertical differentiation of tasks. These structural variables are altered, sometimes consciously, sometimes in a more haphazard evolutionary fashion, by the managers of organizations in response to growth or decline in size, changing technology, and shifts in the environment. Furthermore, these combinations of variables cluster together into identifiable types of organizations such as bureaucracies, conglomerates, and adhocracies.

Why are there so many forms of organizations? The organizational ecologists argue that there are many forms because there are many environmental niches for different types of organizations to fill. These forms also vary across cultures as assumptions about organizing differ. Within cultures, organizations vary across institutional fields that define what is normal and legitimate in the environment.

B. Defining the Organization as a Process

As an alternative definition of structure, some theorists argue that an organization is made up of relatively stable patterns of interaction for information processing and influence in which goal pursuit becomes less important. From this perspective, organizations are coalitions of shifting interest groups that develop goals through negotiation (Scott, 1987). These patterns of interaction, traditionally referred to as the informal structure, are now referred to as networks. This structure is informal in that it is not managed from above but emerges through interaction. From this viewpoint, the formal structure as embodied in the organization chart is the outcome of behind-the-scenes bargaining among powerful individuals and groups. Some argue that formal structure inhibits interaction and communication, and what is needed is more democratic organizations or an organization design without hierarchy.

These differences in the definition of an organization lead to differing conceptions of what constitutes an organizational structure. This debate reflects an actor-structure duality that characterizes the study of social behavior (Burns and Flam, 1987): Do you emphasize the interaction of individuals or the structure of the system in which the individuals are situated?

As we shall see, some theorists prefer to emphasize the system. For them the organization is a system that adjusts to contingencies. From this perspective, in answer to our original question, managers do design organizations and redesign them to adjust to changing environments. Other theorists prefer to emphasize that organizational structure, like all social structure, is created and reproduced through the interaction of individuals. If the members cease to follow one path and pursue another, then the organizational structure has changed. All too rarely, theorists try to take into account how structure is designed and then reproduced or changed through interaction.

II. THE ORGANIZATION AS A STRUCTURAL SYSTEM

What do managers design? From the viewpoint of a top-down design of a system, managers group workers into departments, decide who will have responsibility and authority for the work, and put procedures into place that will guide people's efforts. The understanding of how this is accomplished in organizations has become more complex over the last 30 years. Before the 1960s, the study of organizations was dominated by case studies that provided insight into organizational functioning but that were limited in application. Beginning in the 1960s, organizational researchers began to think of organizations as having sets of structural variables that could be manipulated to design organizations. Early studies concentrated on how variables such as centralization and formalization covaried across a sample of organizations. Over time research became steadily more sophisticated in theory and technique.

A. Structural Features as Variable Dimensions

In the 1960s, with the advent of mainframe computer power and the use of multivariate statistics, empirical generalizations across samples of organizations became possible. Groups of researchers embarked on ambitious programs to study a number of organizations at once. The most prominent groups studying structure across samples of organizations included the Aston group, so called because it originated at the University of Aston, England; Blau and his students, who conducted studies of public bureaucracies; and Hage and Aiken, who studied a group of health care organizations.

These groups shared a common research strategy. They all began with Weber's (1958) essay on bureaucracy. Weber had written an essay describing the characteristics of modern bureaucracy and how it differed from older feudal forms of administration. He pointed out how bureaucracy is more efficient than the feudal organization because bureaucracies have certain properties such as a hierarchy of supervision with clearly defined job duties for occupants. By comparison, in the past a local person of wealth and social position administered an organization such as a local government as a part-time occupation and lacked the expertise of the full-time bureaucrat. See Dibble (1965) for a description of English county government of the 16th century as an example of the feudal form.

Those taking the structure-as-variables approach considered Weber's essay as a set of guidelines for defining the structural properties of organizations. There was a general agreement that at least three dimensions derived from Weber's essay could characterize organizations: (1) structural complexity as exhibited by the amount of vertical and horizontal differentiation of the hierarchy; (2) the degree of formalization of the procedures for work; and (3) the degree of centralization of decision making and authority.

In this early research, many in this structure-as-variables group concentrated on the antecedents of these bureaucratic properties, feeling that case studies had concentrated on the consequences of bureaucracy, and that the time had come to examine the relationship among variables at a more aggregate level of analysis that would have consequences for individuals (Blau, 1968). Accordingly, these researchers concentrated on the impact of contextual variables such as size and the type of work performed in the organization (the technology) on the structural variables that described organizations.

1.   Structural Differentiation

There are two dimensions for allocating people to tasks: vertical and horizontal differentiation. Grouping people together in organizational departments is often referred to as horizontal differentiation. Creating a large number of departments horizontally leads to problems of coordination and administration that have to be solved by adding levels of supervision or increasing the vertical differentiation. This hierarchical structural differentiation would seem to be a key ingredient of bureaucracy, according to Weber: "The principles of office hierarchy and of levels of graded authority mean a firmly ordered system of super- and subordination in which there is supervision of the lower offices by the higher ones" (Weber, 1958: 197).

The measurement of these structural dimensions in terms of the allocation of positions was straightforward. Horizontal structural differentiation was measured in terms of number of departments and specialities by many researchers, including Blau and Schoenherr (1971), Hall, Haas, and Johnson (1967), and Pugh et al. (1968). Vertical differentiation was measured in terms of the number of levels of supervision by a number of researchers such as Meyer (1968), Pugh et al. (1968), and Hall, Haas, and Johnson (1967).

However, as Hall (1991) points out, definitions of these dimensions of organizations were not universal. Conceptual confusion was generated by these researchers as some defined horizontal complexity as being an indicator of how much training and experience was required for a given job (e.g., Hage and Aiken, 1967). Using this definition, organizations with greater numbers of professionals would be considered to be more structurally complex.

Researchers in this tradition assumed that the type of work performed by the organization or the technology of the organization affected the structural differentiation of the organization. The addition of new jobs would lead to the creation of new departments horizontally, and an increase in horizontal differentiation would lead to a demand for more vertical levels of supervision (Blau and Schoenherr, 1971).

However, contradictory results were found when testing these assumptions. Pugh et al. (1969) found that technology defined as workflow integration had only a slight effect on the structuring of activities. This result was confirmed by a reanalysis of the data by Hickson, Pugh, and Pheysey (1969). By contrast, Aldrich (1972) pointed out that their cross-sectional correlational data could be arranged in a causal model in which technology appeared to have strong effects on structure. Further, Hilton (1972) and Heise (1972) pointed out that this cross-sectional data could be used to formulate a wide variety of alternative causal models.

Dewar and Hage (1978) overcame some of the difficulties of causal inferences based on measuring organizational variables all at once by analyzing data over three points in time. They found evidence that the scope of the organization's task, a technological dimension, had important effects on horizontal differentiation. They found that the addition of new occupational specialities results in greater horizontal differentiation, and that larger organizations added vertical levels when the task scope was enlarged.

Researchers also hypothesized that the size of the organization would have effects on structural differentiation. On the societal level, Kasarda (1974) argued that large size had the most impact on the communicative structure of social systems. As size increases, "disproportionately large amounts of human resources are drawn into the communicative components of institutions, communities, and societies" (Kasarda, 1974: 19). Professional and technical functions increase disproportionately, but not as much as the communication functions, according to Kasarda.

Similarly, researchers such as Blau (1970) hypothesized that as organizations grow larger, problems of coordination and control increase. These coordination and control problems lead to an increase in the administrative component of the organization and an increase in the vertical and horizontal differentiation of structure. In his study of employment security offices in the United States, Blau maintained in an oft-referenced generalization that because of economies of scale in administration, "Increasing size generates structural differentiation in organizations along various dimensions at decelerating rates" (Blau, 1970: 204).

This rather sweeping generalization on organizational dynamics was based on data collected at one point. A number of researchers proceeded to look at the relationship of size and structure over time. Meyer (1972), looking at government finance agencies in 1966 and 1971, argued that "The effects of size are ubiquitous" (Meyer, 1972: 437). Size, as measured by number of full-time employees, was found to lead to horizontal and vertical differentiation, and when size was controlled, relationships between vertical and horizontal differentiation disappear, and the effects of differentiation on size vanish. However, Holdaway and Blowers (1971) did not find a consistent relationship between ratios of administrators to other employees and organizational size when looking at 41 Canadian school systems over a 5-year period. Yet, Hendershot and James (1972) provided some empirical support for Blau's proposition that a negative relationship would exist between the proportion of administrators to employees and size by examining school districts at two points in time. These studies of the effects of size on organizations are extensively critiqued by Kimberly (1976).

2. Formalization

A major component of Weberian organization to many researchers of this era was the amount of formalization, defined as the extent to which written rules ensure conformity to the organization (Hage, 1965; Hage and Aiken, 1967; Pugh et al., 1968). This concept would seem to capture an important component of the design of bureaucratic organizations, as many define bureaucracy as an organization bound up in red tape or formal rules. Indeed, Weber insisted that written rules were an important identifying feature of bureaucracy: "The reduction of modern office management to rules is deeply embedded in its very nature" (1958: 198).

Researchers proceeded to determine what leads to variation in these rules. The most consistent finding was that the routineness of the work correlated with the formalization of organizational roles (Hage and Aiken, 1969; Blau and Schoenherr, 1971; Pugh et al., 1969). However, in many of these studies the correlation is small, and when organizational size is controlled, the relationships disappear (Gerwin, 1981).

3. Centralization

Weber stated in his essay that bureaucratic organizations are distinguished by a strict ordering of authority from the top to the bottom of the hierarchy as well as by systems of rules. Therefore, some researchers argued (Hage, 1965; Hage and Aiken, 1967; Blau and Schoenherr, 1971; Pugh et al., 1968), Weberian bureaucracies should have a strong correlation between formalization of work duties and centralization of decisions concerning work.

The results of research on the relationship between formalization and centralization were inconclusive. Hage and Aiken (1967) found weak support for the relationship of formalization and centralization. However, Mansfield (1973) in a reanalysis of both an Aston study (Pugh et al., 1968) and a replication of the study (Child, 1972a) found that when controlling for size, the relationship between formalization and centralization was weak but negative. Mansfield (1973) argued that this result indicates that large formalized bureaucratic organizations are more likely to have decentralized decision making as compared to small organizations. Mansfield speculated that this negative relationship does not indicate more discretion at lower levels in the large organization, but instead, that large organizations create more rules that narrow the range of discretion of subordinates who then are delegated the ability to make decisions within a narrow range of alternatives.

4.   Is This a Useful Approach to the Study of Organizational Design?

This review has been extremely brief and selective, but gives the reader a feeling for the general issues addressed in this early research. This research represented a first attempt to define the components of organization design and the factors affecting these variables.

What was learned from these early studies of organizations? As we have seen, weak relationships exist between variables such as routineness of work and formalization. Relationships that seemed to make intuitive sense (e.g., a strong correlation between formalizing work roles and centralizing authority) proved inconsistent. Were any major propositions conclusively substantiated through this research? We could say that these studies demonstrated that size has an overwhelming impact on the structuring of organizations, but I agree with Starbuck (1981) that this generalization was known in 1960 before these studies were undertaken.

Why were the results of these studies weak and inconsistent? A number of reasons have been proposed. I have glossed over the problems of measurement that plagued these studies. For example, Dewar, Whetten, and Boje (1980) analyzed the reliability and validity of the scales used by Hage and Aiken to measure organizational properties and found, among other things, that Hage and Aiken's indicators of formalization did not exhibit strong convergent and discriminant validity. Dewar, Whetten, and Boje (1980) speculated that the lack of relationship between formalization and routineness of technology found by Hage and Aiken (1969) may have been due to measurement problems rather than a lack of relationships between these concepts.

The sampling strategies of these researchers also posed problems of interpretation. Since the Aston researchers sought to discover principles that applied across all organizations, they sampled 52 organizations that ranged from manufacturing to retail stores to government agencies. As an unintended effect, this heterogeneous sampling had effects on the meaning of such variables as workflow integration. For example, Aldrich (1972) points out that the Aston group (specifically Hickson, Pugh, and Pheysey, 1969) used a measure of workflow integration or technology with scores ranging from 1 to 17. Service organizations in their sample of 46 organizations scored low on technology and manufacturing organizations scored high, leading Aldrich to suggest that the technology measure is really measuring type of organization.

Furthermore, relationships between variables may not have been constant within as well as across organizations. In one of the few studies of this genre that confronts the issue of whether or not bureaucratic characteristics might vary within organizations, Hall (1962) found that the type of work done in different parts of the organization affected measures of bureaucracy such as the use of rules and procedures.

The connections between the abstract variables describing organizations and the actions of individuals within the organization also get no attention. Variables such as formalization and centralization capture organizational-level characteristics of organizations, but this does not help us to understand how these properties affect the individuals within the organization. Yet, when many of these researchers explained why variables were linked, they resorted to elaborate explanations based on the assumed dynamics of individuals within the organization.

For example, Blau and Schoenherr (1971) found a positive correlation between both vertical and horizontal differentiation and the proportion of supervisors to other personnel, as well as a negative correlation of both types of differentiation with span of control. From these correlations, they infer that structural differentiation intensifies problems of coordination and control in organizations. Managers must spend more time on these problems, and this effort leads to an increase in the number of managers needed in more differentiated organizations as compared to less differentiated organizations. These managers would have less time for direct supervision of subordinates, so managers would need more narrow spans of control in more as opposed to less differentiated organizations. This reasoning requires many untested assumptions about human behavior in organizations.

To some extent this critique of the structure-as-variables perspective is unfair because problems of sampling, variable definition, and explanatory power affect any new line of research in organizational behavior. In addition, researchers have been responsive to critics. Researchers have tried to link broader variables directly to individual behavior in organizations. (See James and Jones, 1976, for a review.) Aston researchers also have altered their research to respond to critics by using more homogeneous samples, studying organizations over time, and looking at relationships between variables that cut across levels of analysis (Pugh, 1981).

Nonetheless, there is one criticism that the early structural approach to organizational design did not confront: the lack of theory to guide research. As discussed above, the early studies always featured Weber's essay on bureaucracy, as if it provided guidelines for empirical research. More theoretically oriented views of organizational design developed at roughly the same time as the structure-as-variables approach. In these approaches, theorists consider how and why individuals take an active part in creating organizational structures. The issues addressed expanded beyond the concern for Weberian bureaucracy into questions concerning why different forms of organizations exist, and how these forms evolve into new organizations.

B. Structure-as-Form

The structure-as-variables approach treated the organization as a collection of variables that differed across heterogeneous samples of organizations. A number of researchers have suggested that an assortment of forms or configurations exists for organizations. These configurations are collections of variables that are shaped by the organization's technology and environment, and organizations facing the same set of contextual constraints will have roughly the same configuration of variables. This approach is similar to the structure-as-variables perspective. However, rather than trying to identify what characteristics of bureaucracy correlate with each other, researchers using this perspective began to pay more attention to the contextual variables of environment and technology, and how these contextual factors make one organization or collection of organizations different from others. In addition, many began to base their analysis of form on theories of the actions and limitations of the actors in organizations rather than Weber's essay on bureaucracy.

1. Forms of Organization

A number of researchers have suggested that the contingencies presented by the environment and the technology used by the organization lead to a variety of forms other than Weberian bureaucracy. For example, Stinchcombe (1959) argued that the construction industry relied on the professional socialization of the manual labor force through training in a craft to ensure quality in the work process rather than the centralized decision making, communicating, and auditing of work through staff positions and administrators required in a bureaucracy. He maintained that this craft form of organization was necessary because of the environment of the construction industry. Stinchcombe suggested that the seasonal and unstable nature of construction requires the flexibility to hire subcontractors and their workers for limited periods of time, whereas bureaucracy requires relative stability of workflow and income to enable routinized communications from top to bottom and to justify the cost of the staff.

Joyce Rothschild-Whitt (1979) proposed the "collectivist" organization as an alternative to bureaucracy. She pointed out that Weber maintained there were various types of social action with associated bases for authority and types of organizations. For example, Weber suggested that instrumentally rational social action corresponded to a ration-legal basis for authority found in bureaucracy. However, Weber also suggested that value rational actions exist. Value rational actions are taken not to accomplish ends, but in the "belief in the value for its own sake . . . independent of its prospects for success" (Weber, 1968: 24, quoted in Rothschild-Whitt, 1979).

Although he acknowledged that there were conflicts between the abstract formalism of legal systems and the desire to satisfy substantive goals, Weber believed that formal rationality as embodied in bureaucracy would become the dominant form of organization in society. Rothchild-Whitt proposed that collectivist organizations, based more on value-rationality, were an alternative form that grew in numbers during the 1970s. These alternative organizations (e.g., free schools, free medical clinics, and food cooperatives), were based on an alternative set of values compared to the dominant instrumentally focused organizations of society. Alternative organizations differed from the dominant form in terms of authority, rules, social control, social relations, recruitment and advancement, incentive structure, social stratification, and differentiation. The core difference manifested in these alternative organizations was an assumption of the importance of social consensus and social homogeneity to guide the organization. Whereas bureaucracy rests on the assumption of hierarchical authority and rules to ensure goal-directed behavior, alternative organizations reduce the need for these formal mechanisms of control by ensuring homogeneity of beliefs through recruitment before any action is taken by the organization.

Burns and Stalker (1961), looking at 20 industrial firms in England and Scotland, found that the demands of the external environment led to two types of internal structure: mechanistic and organic. The mechanistic structure, found in the relatively stable environment, was more like the Weberian bureaucracy and relied on rules, procedures, and a hierarchy of authority. By contrast, organic organizations existed in a rapidly changing environment and were more adaptive and less structured. Rules were less important, the hierarchy of authority was less clear, and decision making was more decentralized in the organic organization.

The ultimate in the organic organization could be considered the matrix organization. Galbraith (1973), studying the aerospace industry, found that the constantly shifting environment and changing technology required the formation of project teams combining individuals across functional specialities that reported to both a project leader and a functional manager. This bifurcation of authority was a violation of the Weberian concept of a clear top-to-bottom hierarchy of authority.

Mintzberg (1979) synthesized current thinking regarding the effects of the environment and technology with the concepts of Weber and Burns and Stalker, and classified existing organizations into five types: the simple structure, the machine bureaucracy, the professional bureaucracy, the divisionalized form, and the adhocracy. The simple structure relies on direct supervision from the top, but is organic in structure. Simple structures tend to be small, run by entrepreneurs, and exist in placid environments so that environmental demands do not overwhelm centralized control from the top. Larger, more established organizations, such as mass production manufacturing organizations, may become machine bureaucracies that rely on Weberian control mechanisms such as standardization of the work and centralized control. Machine bureaucracies are best suited for uncomplicated, stable environments.

If the work is not amenable to standardization, then the professional bureaucracy may exist instead. Professional bureaucracies, such as law firms or universities, depend on the standardization of professional skills, and are often split into an administrative machine bureaucracy side and a more organic professional operating core. These organizations are found in more complex but stable environments. The divisionalized firm, typified by the large conglomerate, consists of a number of machine bureaucracies as divisions, each existing in a relatively stable environment and all administered by a central office. Finally, the adhocracy is the ultimate organic form in which all coordination is done by mutual consultation. Employees find themselves with project as well as functional supervisors as the organization tries to adapt to its extremely demanding complex and dynamic environment.

Miller and Friesen (1984) suggest that there are a number of archetypes of organizations that can be created, depending on the goals of the analyst. In considering the connection between strategy and structure, they propose ten archetypes, five for successful types of organizations and five for organizations that were unsuccessful in linking strategic goals to their structural configuration. As an example of an unsuccessful archetype, the "impulsive firm" (Miller and Friesen, 1984:91) pursues a rapid expansion strategy, but top management dominates the organization and fails to delegate authority or establish systems to monitor and control the complex organization. By contrast, the successful archetype "adaptive firm under moderate challenge" (Miller and Friesen, 1984:103) pursues a strategy of incremental innovation in a stable market. The organization is centralized, but the stable environment allows the leader to informally coordinate organizational functions.

Each of these attempts to define forms of organizations is descriptive, and many of these efforts seem to be heavily influenced by a desire to prove that other forms of organizations besides bureaucracy exist. What is needed is a more theoretically oriented attempt to categorize types of organizations. McKelvey (1982) has speculated that organizational "species" can be defined based on their dominant competence. A dominant competence is composed of a description of an organization's primary task and workplace–management competencies. Workplace-management competencies are a combination of knowledge and skills for measuring effectiveness, coordinating activities, and dealing with the environment. Organizational species are "groups of competence-sharing populations isolated from each other because their dominant competencies are not easily learned or transmitted" (McKelvey, 1982: 192). Despite McKelvey's ambitious beginning, there has been little effort to systematically define an ecology of organizational species.

2. Contingency Theory

Many of the theorists of organization design I have discussed have made reference to the effects of the technology and environment of the organization. In the 1960s a number of authors began to develop a contingency theory of organizations that focused on the effects of technology and environment on organization design. These contingency theorists assume that the technology used by the organization and the environment in which the organization is embedded present constraints and contingencies to which the organization must adjust by modifying organizational structure and procedures. According to Thompson (1967), technology and environment create uncertainties that have to be overcome by the organization. Organizations abhor uncertainty, like nature abhors a vacuum, so that the creation of uncertainty by a change in the environment or technology must be countered by alteration of the organization structure.

Thompson argued that organizations avoid uncertainty because, following the insights of Simon (1957), decision makers have limited cognitive abilities or "bounded rationality" that can be overwhelmed unless the situation for making decisions can be simplified. Following this logic, organizations are vehicles for processing information and making decisions. When faced with complex decisions, managers can break the decision down into a series of simpler decisions that are delegated down a hierarchy of decision makers.

a. Technology. In order to prevent decision makers from being overwhelmed with information, the constraints and contingencies of technology and environment have to be taken into account. Woodward (1965) identified technology as an important variable affecting the design of organizations in her study of 100 English manufacturing firms. She found that the type of technology employed—categorized as small batch and unit production, large batch and mass production, or continuous process production—had effects on structural properties such as the number of levels of management, the span of control of managers, and the amount of written communications.

From these early beginnings, researchers developed a myriad of measures of technology. Scott (1975), for example, cross-classified measures of technology on two dimensions. The first dimension was based on whether the technology is defined in terms of the inputs used by the organization, the transformation process used to produce the product, or the outputs of the organization. Following Hickson, Pugh, and Pheysey (1969), the second dimension was based on whether the technology is defined in terms of the nature of the materials used, the characteristics of the operations used to produce the product, or the extent of the knowledge about the production process. These complex cross-classifications can be simplified because, as Scott (1975) notes, the most popular way of characterizing technology has been in terms of the operations used to produce the product.

Regardless of the way the technology of the organization is operationalized, the concept is theoretically interesting because the constraints and contingencies produced by a technology result in uncertainty that can be reduced by organization design, according to contingency theorists. As Scott (1990) notes, most analysts consider that technological uncertainty is generated by problems of interdependence of individuals during the production process, or by the complexity or diversity of components managed during the production process, or by the uncertainties generated by the lack of knowledge of what problems to deal with or what procedures to carry out. These technological problems generate uncertainties that organizations must control.

Galbraith (1973; 1977) suggested that increasing the information available to decision makers will reduce uncertainties. Thus, faced with increases in uncertainty that would over-whelm the usual information-processing structural devices of hierarchy, formal rules, and goal setting, organizations must either reduce the need for information processing or increase their capacity to process information. Organizations can reduce the need for information processing by creating slack resources or self-contained tasks. Alternatively, organizations can increase information-processing capacity by expanding the vertical information systems or creating additional lateral relations between individuals and units.

b. Environment. Technology as a variable affecting structure was popular before the late 1960s development of contingency theory. However, the idea that the environment altered the structure of the organization, although certainly used by others such as the Aston group, has become a major consideration in theories of organizations. For example, Thompson asserted that organizations used "an open-system logic" (1967: 24).

Lawrence and Lorsch (1967) argued that different environments placed different demands on organizations that would result in different internal structures. They studied organizations in the plastics, container, and food-processing industries and found that the uncertain environment and rapid change of the plastics industry led to a more differentiated and decentralized organization compared to the container firms, which existed in a more placid environment. Even within organizations, some units of the organization faced different task environments than others and would develop a differentiated view of the world.

It is important to note that Lawrence and Lorsch (1967) use the term differentiation to describe differences in attitudes and views toward the world produced by being a member of a unit facing a particular environment, rather than using the term to describe the proliferation of organizational units. Thus, research and development personnel in the plastics industry, facing a more uncertain task environment than production, would be differentiated from production in the sense that research personnel would be less inclined to rely on formality of structure to accomplish goals and would have a longer task horizon compared to production.

This differentiation of viewpoints leads to problems of integration. According to Lawrence and Lorsch (1967), the more varied the environments that organizational units confront, the more differentiated in outlook the units must become, and the greater the problems of integrating these different units in the pursuit of overall goals. Thus, the characteristics of the organization's environment lead to problems of differentiation and coordination across the organization, and the characteristics of environments lead to differentiation of organizations across environments. This was the essence of what Lawrence and Lorsch (1967) called a "contingency theory" of organizations.

What problems or contingencies did the environment generate? Two viewpoints developed over time: the environment was a source of uncertainty that could be reduced with more information, or the environment was a source of resources that led to political bargaining and the unequal distribution of power. As discussed above, the early contingency theorists, such as Thompson (1967), maintained that uncertainty was the source of contingencies, but Galbraith (1973; 1977) argued that uncertainty could be reduced with more information. From this "information-processing" point of view, the demands of environments lead to structural changes for processing information such as the creation of boundary-spanning individuals and units (Adams, 1976; Aldrich and Herker, 1977) who funnel information into the organization.

However, Thompson (1967) also argued that organizations wanted to avoid dependence on other organizations as a way of reducing uncertainty. According to Thompson (1967), organizations engage in strategies such as building up inventories or forming joint ventures with others in order to protect the "core technology" of the organization from excessive fluctuations and turmoil.

This insight led to the resource-dependence perspective on organizational design. According to resource-dependence theorists (e.g., Pfeffer and Salancik, 1978), environments are sources of resources, and organizations engage in strategies such as joint ventures to reduce dependence on a source of resources. From this perspective, the focus shifts from designing organizations to process information to how organizational units handle strategic contingencies (Hickson et al., 1971) and how this ability to handle environmental contingencies gives some actors and subunits power in the organization.

Two perspectives then develop for explaining organizational structures. From the information-processing perspective, the question becomes how appropriate a given structure might be for coordinating efforts to accomplish organizational goals. Those adopting the resource-dependence perspective ask how a structure is the outcome of bargaining and influence, with the sources of power determined by the ability to handle strategic contingencies. This emphasis on the use of power to determine structures leads Pfeffer (1978) to maintain that centralized organizations are the "natural state of affairs" (1978: 54); decentralized organizations exist because top management has lost power because of the need for outside financial support, the need for expertise, or the need for some other resource that can be provided by exchanging power over decisions for that resource.

3. Transaction Cost Theory

In contrast to the power perspectives that developed in the 1970s, Oliver Williamson (1975; 1981; 1985), an economist, suggested that structural configurations exist because they are efficient in minimizing the costs of making transactions. He proposed a shift in the unit of analysis from the macro level organization avoiding uncertainties to the more micro level transactions taking place between individuals and organizations in the marketplace. He hypothesized, following Coase (1937), that markets and organizational hierarchies are alternative means for conducting transactions, and organizations would only replace markets when the cost of transacting business within organizational boundaries is less than the cost of doing business in the marketplace.

Williamson argued that all transactions could be accomplished by contractual agreements in the market if individuals were perfectly rational, had all the information necessary to make informed market decisions, and were unfailingly honest. However, Williamson, like Thompson, had been influenced by Simon (1957). He maintained that because of their bounded rationality, people are limited in their abilities to account for every contingency and state them in a contract. To this human failing he added the problem of opportunism, "which is a condition of self-interest seeking with guile" (1985: 30). The combination of bounded rationality and the possibility of the occasional instance of opportunism makes many transactions difficult and unreliable in a market. To these problems of the market Williamson adds the factors of uncertainty and asset specificity. Transactional arrangements are often uncertain because it is difficult to anticipate all future contingencies and specify them in contracts. Some individuals have asset specificity because they are not easily substitutable for each other in the marketplace because of their specialized skills.

Bounded rationality and opportunism are assumed to exist in many situations. When coupled with uncertainty and asset specificity, there are many instances of transactions that are more efficient if the organization's boundaries are placed around them. Under these adverse conditions, hierarchical governance is more efficient than attempting to write contracts in a market context because hierarchical authority relationships allow for more efficient communication and auditing of behavior, and organizational incentive systems discourage cheating.

According to Williamson, a range of structural configurations economize on bounded rationality and guard against the hazards of opportunism. For example, as organizations grow and expand into new markets, it becomes more efficient to change from the U-form or unitary form of simple hierarchy to the M-form of multiple divisions governed from a central headquarters (Williamson, 1975). The M-form is more efficient than the market at allocating capital, according to Williamson (1975), because the central office has superior auditing capabilities compared to market analysts.

Williamson's perspective has produced a much more sophisticated analysis of organization design than many other economists who were content to admonish managers to "maximize profits!" (Williamson, 1985: 32). As Scott (1987) notes, this is a departure from neoclassical economic models that only considered the optimal mix of resources, labor, and capital in a production function. However, the transaction cost model has been criticized for ignoring the effects of the unequal distribution of power to make decisions and dictate the terms for transactions within and between organizations. Perrow (1981), for example, points out that the M-form of organization may be extremely powerful in the marketplace by dominating its competitors rather than being efficient. (See also the exchange between Williamson and Ouchi and Perrow in Van de Ven and Joyce, 1981.)

Transaction cost economics has also been criticized for ignoring or downplaying the fact that business transactions are embedded in a social context. As Granovetter (1985) points out, recurring economic transactions lead to the development of social relationships with an accompanying level of trust, which mitigates problems such as opportunism over time. Companies may not have to place boundaries around suppliers and customers if they develop social relationships with them. Thus, large Japanese companies are famous for their *keiretsu* form of quasi-organization in which a number of companies do business with each other as independent companies rather than forming a conglomerate. Historically, these autonomous companies were part of conglomerates (e.g., Mitsubishi was broken into hundreds of smaller companies after World War II), but this does not alter the fact that the independent Mitsubishi companies are as efficient if not more efficient than conglomerates. The trust necessary for close cooperation and coordination of transactions in *keiretsu* is achieved through managers who are also constantly interacting with managers from other companies at social functions conducted after office hours.

4. Evaluating Contingency Theories

How has contingency theory fared in general? Opinions differ, although contingency theories were certainly a theoretical leap forward from the early descriptive studies that simply correlated characteristics of organizations. Ten years after the beginnings of contingency theory, Meyer et al. (1978) suggested that the status of contingency theory as a preeminent theory of organizational design was no longer controversial. However, 10 years later, the flaws of contingency theory moved Carroll (1988: 1) to state "Intellectually speaking, contingency theory is dead."

Although still a dominant form of theorizing about organization design, contingency theories suffer from shortcomings. For example, Schoonhoven (1981) points out that the empirical fit between the environment, technology, and organization design can be specified in a number of ways. She argues that most theories imply an interaction between variables such as technology and structure that produces effectiveness. However, theorists usually are mute on the functional form of this interaction. For example, as Schoonhoven (1981) notes, if both technological uncertainty and professionalization have to be present for effectiveness to be high, then the theorist is implicitly hypothesizing a multiplicative effect.

Theoretically, most forms of contingency theory assume a great deal of rationality and adaptiveness of the organization. Organizations seem to be constantly growing and adapting to contingencies; organizations do not downsize or fail in the contingency theories of Thompson (1967) or Lawrence and Lorsch (1967). All employees are assumed to be pursuing the same goals in most contingency theories, although we have seen the exception in the resource-dependence theory of organizational power.

How organizational managers achieve the fit between their structure and contingencies is left for speculation. Thompson's explanation for organizational actions: "We will argue that organizations do some of the basic things they do because they must—or else!"(1967:1) leaves many questions unanswered about the dynamics of structural change. For example, Child questioned the assumption of the early correlational studies and contingency studies that economic efficiency dictated that organizations adjust to contextual variables. He pointed out that power holders in organizations have "strategic choice" (1972b: 1) and can choose through a political process to engage in strategic actions to try to manipulate their environment and their performance standards rather than reflexively adapting their structure to contextual variables.

5. Change in Structural Form

The foregoing suggests that the creation and reorganization of structural forms is not as rational as was implicitly assumed by the early contingency theorists. The assumption that all structural changes are accomplished in response to contingencies to enhance efficient production is brought into question by those who have examined the microprocesses that lead to changes in structures. Idea champions may push for the creation of units, others sometimes resist organizational change, and temporary organizations reveal the minimum requirements of structure when faced with impermanence.

a. Idea Champions and Structural Creation. The actions of individuals provide an important bridge between the contingencies of the environment and technology and the structuring of the organization. For example, Downs (1967) discussed "bureau genesis" or the process by which new units of government are created and sustained. He argues that new units can be created to perform a new function that is demanded by the environment, or new units may break off from existing units. These dynamics of differentiation are perfectly compatible with contingency explanations. However, Downs also argues that new units start because of advocates and zealots who agitate for the new unit. Competition for resources between units can lead to a marketplace of structural units, in which new structures must rapidly expand and secure sources of external support in order to survive.

These new bureaus undergo a life cycle in which the zealots rapidly expand the unit and secure resources. Over time the units become more formalized and rule-bound, and the zealots are replaced with conservers who want to preserve the new status quo. Eventually the new bureau may be taken over by another unit. The idea that idea champions are the necessary intermediate link between environmental and technological demands and the creation of structure was confirmed by Daft and Bradshaw (1980), who found that idea champions were overwhelmingly responsible for the creation of 30 new departments in five universities.

b. Resistance to Structural Change. A number of studies have found resistance to the process of structural reorganization. Tushman, Newman, and Romanelli (1986) maintain that organizational history encompasses two phases: most of an organization's history is composed of convergence and fine tuning of structure and procedures, but occasionally there is a frame-breaking change in reaction to crisis.

During convergence periods, organizations refine their procedures in reaction to small environmental shifts. However, sudden shifts in the legal, political, or technological environment, such as deregulation, lead to major changes in power, status, values, and goals. These shifts require a reorganization of structure and procedures. This is not easily accomplished because the existing actors—the conservers in Down's terminology—have established procedures, political coalitions, and external constituencies that will be upset by the revolutionary change. For example, Biggart (1977), in her description of the change of the U.S. Post Office Department to the U.S. Postal Service in the early 1970s, pointed out that structural change is a destructive process, in which old ideology, power alliances, and leadership have to be replaced in order for the structural reorganization to be successful.

Not all change can be accommodated by altering organizational structure. Ultimately, organizations can become bound up in their outdated rules and procedures and fail. Stinchcombe (1965) has argued that new organizations are created with the social resources available at the time of founding. Over time the organization becomes closed to outside influences as procedures are established and political alignments are put into place. Thus, in contrast to the contingency theory assumption of efficient adaptation, the time of origin of an organization reveals a great deal about the type of structure and procedures that are used in it. In a study of governmental finance agencies, Meyer and Brown (1977) found that the time of founding was related to the formalization of hiring and evaluation procedures. For example, organizations established after 1940 relied on more formal civil service procedures to hire and evaluate personnel, compared to organizations founded in earlier eras.

c. Temporary Organizations. The difficulty of change in response to environmental conditions implies that structure is intimately bound up with existing power relationships, internal and external constituencies, and ideologies. These older units and organizations may be less innovative as a result. One organizational solution to this inertia inherent in existing units is to create temporary organizations such as task forces or project teams. A number of theorists have argued that temporary structures are the wave of the future because they can preserve the flexibility required to deal with increasingly turbulent environments.

Although little research has been done, a number of authors have speculated on how temporary organizations differ from permanent organizations. Palisi (1970), for example, argues that transitory organizations are likely to have democratic rather than authoritarian decision making. Palisi (1970) suggests that authoritarian, centralized decision making is more efficient than democratic participation in that it is faster than trying to democratically coordinate many views. Authoritarian decision making is more likely in the permanent organization because it is faced with a larger number of decisions concerning how to interact with other organizations, recruit new members, and deal with social change, according to Palisi (1970). Temporary organizations are more focused on a specific problem and have the luxury of greater member involvement in decisions.

In a similar manner, Palisi (1970) maintains that temporary organizations should have a flatter hierarchy. Without the need for administrative positions to coordinate departments and protect the norms and structure over long periods of time, Palisi (1970) argues that temporary organizations have less need for coordinating levels of hierarchy. As a by-product, according to Palisi (1970), social distance is less in temporary organizations as compared to permanent organizations, which generate levels of socially distant positions. Analogously, Miles (1964) argues that norms of egalitarianism develop in temporary organizations that would be violated by creating positions of greater social distance.

This lack of bureaucratic structure is not without its costs. Keith (1978), in a study of task forces of teachers in 24 schools, found great role strain and ambiguity in these temporary systems. Keith (1978) argues that these newly created roles of short duration lead to a lack of role clarity. In addition, performing temporary roles in a task force within a permanent organization may lead to anxiety and conflict as the individual has to balance competing demands from several groups at once.

It would appear that temporary organizations, lacking the clarity of duties and decision-making responsibilities provided by formal structure, would be inefficient and incapable of completing complex tasks. However, there are substitutes for the clarity of bureaucratic procedures used in temporary organizations. For example, Bryman et al. (1987) found in a study of construction projects that compatibility among members of the team was considered paramount. This bias was manifested in the tendency of site managers to transfer a core of members as a team from site to site.

In addition, a familiarity between contractors and subcontractors was extremely important to site managers, according to Bryman et al. (1987). Familiarity between relatively autonomous teams was necessary to facilitate communication and integrate work between interdependent groups who would only be on a site for relatively brief periods of time. In addition, familiarity and the possibility of further subcontracting enabled the contractor to more effectively control the quality of work of the subcontractors.

Bryman et al. (1987) point out that others have emphasized the organic, loose, informal organizational characteristics of task forces and project teams that lack any stable structure. However, their study of construction demonstrates that familiarity and recurring interaction over a series of projects leads to a stable structure of interaction that substitutes for the more formal use of memos and written directives. Furthermore, strong personal leadership of contractors, with the contractor's ability to control opportunism by not awarding subsequent contracts to subcontractors, guarantees efficient performance.

More research is needed to increase our understanding of how information about shifting environments and technologies are translated into organizational structures. A more finely grained analysis of the political processes surrounding organizational change would enable us to understand why some shifts in the environment result in the creation of idea champions who are successful at structural change and why some idea champions fail to institute change. In-depth examination of temporary structures could reveal the conditions that lead to democratic participation versus more centralized decision making in the temporary structure. Additional study of temporary structures embedded in formal structure could reveal how temporary structure influences more stable formal structure. For example, would an organization that creates lots of task forces have a tendency to rarely change its formal structure? In other words, does the constant creation of temporary structures stabilize the formal structure by absorbing change? These questions raise a host of issues concerning career paths, communication patterns, and shifts in power in the organization that need to be addressed.

C. Form Reflects Culture

Cultural assumptions underlie any decision to create or reorganize structure. Weber's concept of bureaucratic structure is embodied in the western tendency to develop a formal procedure to deal with every problem and to create a formal position to be responsible for the procedure. However, the assumption that formalization will solve all organizational problems may not be true across national cultures. Japanese organizations, for example, are highly efficient without resorting to the plethora of formal procedures of the western corporation.

1. Structure as a Cultural Assumption

Rather than enlarge roles and rely on informal relationships to conduct work, it has become a cultural assumption of many organizational theorists and managers that more ranks and positions need to be put into place to deal with problems. For example, implicit in much of the theorizing about organizational design, particularly in its contingency theory variant, is an assumption that formalization will solve all problems. As Scott says "The rational system response to increasing task demands is to shorten and strengthen the leash: provide superiors with more and faster information so they can more rapidly change the instructions to performers; increase the ratio of superiors to performers so that more information can be processed more quickly and revised guidelines supplied to performers" (1987: 231). Scott goes on to say that new roles are created and new connections are specified to increase flexibility and the capacity to change: "But the flexibility involved is designed, not spontaneous, and the changes reflect capacity to shift rapidly from one set of formal rules and roles to another" (Scott, 1987: 231).

As an example of this bias toward creating formal structure, Meyer, Stevenson, and Webster (1985), in a study of city finance agencies from 1890 to 1975, found that structure in terms of the number of separate units in the finance function grew exponentially and far exceeded any measures of demand for city financial services. Stevenson (1985) found that the reaction of these city officials to pressure for change and reform was to increase structural complexity by increasing the number of structural units.

Expanding upon the insights of Williamson, Ouchi (1980) has argued that there is an alternative to the reliance on the formal control of rules and hierarchy or the discipline of the price competition in the market. He suggests that clan organizations that rely on informal control through extensive socialization and long-term employment are an effective alternative to bureaucracies or markets. For example, clan-based organizations such as IBM or Hewlitt-

Packard rely more on tradition and a strong culture than on rules or prices to achieve goal congruence throughout the organization.

2. Structural Variation Across Cultures

Ouchi bases his model of clan organization on Japanese organizations. There has been a long debate in organizational theory about whether national culture alters organizational structure, or whether the contingencies of industrialization lead to convergence on similar organizational forms. According to the convergence hypothesis, industrialization leads to larger and more complex organizations, and these contingencies lead to greater job specialization, more reliance on rules, and decentralization of decision making (Child, 1981). However, Child's (1981) review of the cross-national organizational comparison literature indicates that contingencies form broad parameters within which a great deal of cross-cultural diversity in organizational forms is possible.

The most popular form of cultural study of structure in the 1980s was the study of Japanese organizations. Here, convergence theory—based on the idea that technological constraints would lead to similar organizational designs across cultures as they industrialized—has done a 180° turn (Lincoln, 1990). In the 1950s and 1960s, convergence theorists argued that Japan's labor practices (e.g., promotion based on seniority, lifetime employment, and the decoupling of rank and responsibility) were vestiges of feudalism that would fade in a more modern industrialized Japan (Abegglen, 1958). However, in the 1980s these same labor practices were trumpeted by theorists such as Ouchi as ideals for western firms.

Japanese organizations appear to solve many of the problems that contingency theorists, and particularly transaction cost theorists, have identified as endemic to western firms. For example, the practice of lifetime employment, slow promotion, and lifetime careers leads to identification with the organization instead of with a professional speciality. This relieves some of the conflict and integration problems that Lawrence and Lorsch (1967) identified when organizational units of specialists develop highly differentiated viewpoints. The emphasis on collective values and consensual decision making leads the Japanese to avoid transfer pricing and complex managerial accounting systems that western firms use in allocating individual rewards and reducing opportunism (Ouchi, 1981).

The Japanese reliance on cultural beliefs, traditions, rituals, and ceremonies instead of explicit rules and price mechanisms, would seem to lead to organizations without much hierarchical control. We would expect flatter organizational hierarchies with less need for middle managers as coordinators and integrators. However, paradoxically, according to a review of studies of Japanese organizations by Lincoln and McBride (1987), Japanese hierarchies at the plant level are taller than western organizations. Lincoln and McBride (1987) argue that this paradox can be resolved by considering the implications of the lifetime internal labor market of Japanese firms. These internal labor markets imply a need for constant, long stairways for upward mobility that is satisfied by fine distinctions of status in the organization. This has the important effect of linking workers in long chains of unequal status relations and reducing interaction between status equals.

These characteristics of Japanese firms would seem to argue against the convergence-contingency argument that the environment and technology will lead all organizations to be structurally similar. This view is reinforced by Florida and Kenney (1991). In a study of Japanese automobile assembly plants in the United States, they found successful transplantation of Japanese manufacturing techniques such as team-based work organizations, rotation of work tasks within the team, and "just in time" supplier relationships. Eighty-six percent of the respondents to their survey said that their manufacturing processes were "exactly the same" or "very similar" to a manufacturing plant in Japan (Florida and Kenney, 1991: 385).

D. Structure as Institution

Cultural studies weaken the contingency theory assumption of economic efficiency driving the connection between environment, technology, and structure. Institutional theories of organizational structure assume that the connection between environment and structure may have nothing to do with economic efficiency. Instead, according to Meyer and Rowan (1977), some organizations alter their structure to reflect the myths of the society in an attempt to gain legitimacy. Meyer and Rowan (1977) argue that units in organizations charged with missions such as affirmative action and environmental protection are attempts to satisfy outside constituencies, and these offices may have no real impact on the organization's practices. This is true because as technologies become more ambiguous to evaluate and performance evaluation becomes more difficult, organizations will search for other means of evaluation. Organizations with ambiguous technologies will adapt procedures and structures that will give them legitimacy in their environment. These structures may be irrelevant to the performance of the organization's tasks, and structures can become decoupled from activity.

1. Structure as a Means of Generating Trust

From the institutional perspective, organizational structure may be less a means of organizing for efficient production and more a means of generating trust (Zucker, 1986), which has critical salience in all interpersonal relationships. Structure can generate trust because the supposed stability of organizational structures and procedures reassures organizational actors that uncertainty has been reduced.

To explain how structure generates trust, Zucker argues definitionally. On the one hand, trust can involve the assumption that others will put aside their self-interests in the interest of the collectivity. On the other hand, trust can be defined as the actor's expectation that interactions can be taken for granted. Zucker argues, based on this second definition, that the development of hierarchical organization at the turn of the century in the United States was a way of generating a set of taken-for-granted procedures among a workforce that was undergoing instability due to immigration, population mobility, and business instability. She further argues that there is a trade-off between the two forms of trust; that is, formalized procedures can replace other-directed trust based on social ties.

This trade-off between interaction-based trust and formalized procedures provides an explanation for a number of forms of organization previously discussed. As discussed above, temporary organizations such as construction projects rely on the continuing interaction across projects that substitutes for bureaucratic written procedures as a means of assuring consistency. Japanese clusters of interacting organizations or keiretsus rely on social ties to supplement work ties as a way of knitting together suppliers and customers. From the institutional perspective, the implication must be drawn that there are alternative ways to organize transactions. Social ties may substitute for formal ties of hierarchical authority in some institutional settings as a means of producing the trust necessary to conduct transactions. In other settings, the production of trust through formal authority and chains of command may be legitimated.

Further research into the trade-offs between generating expectations through formal procedures as opposed to continuing social interaction is necessary. Additional research on the growing numbers of joint ventures and alliances between corporations should reveal some of the trade-offs between contracts and social agreements. Comparisons between organizations that bridge national cultures should be particularly revealing in terms of trade-offs between these vehicles for generating trust.

2. Structure in the Institutional Field

The choice of formal or socially based trust is not left entirely to the organization, according to institutional theorists. The environmental setting in which organizations are embedded will lead to similarities in structures and procedures across organizations. This perspective offers an institutional convergence theory to replace contingency-based convergence theories. According to DiMaggio and Powell (1983), if we look at maturing organizational fields composed of organizations producing similar goods and services in conjunction with suppliers, customers, and regulators, we will see organizations becoming more structurally similar.

This institutional convergence takes place over a period of time. Initially, according to DiMaggio and Powell (1983), structural similarity may be caused by the efficiency of new procedures. Over time, either through coercion, imitation, or the normative pressures of the professionalization of the actors in the field, organizations will become similar regardless of efficiency considerations. For example, Tolbert and Zucker (1983) found that early adoption of civil service reforms was related to government needs and could be predicted by characteristics of the city such as number of immigrants, political reform movements, and city size. However, these variables did not predict the use of civil service procedures in cities adopting the reforms in later periods. Tolbert and Zucker (1983) concluded that civil service reforms diffused to other cities as these procedures became institutionally defined as legitimate and proper ways to conduct government business.

An interesting question for further research is how far the structure can get out of line with the efficiency demands of the environment and still survive. Meyer and Zucker (1989) maintain that "permanently failing" organizations continue despite their failure to pursue their official missions. They argue that employees and external constituencies can divert the organization from its official agenda. Under certain conditions, such as ambiguous and multiple objectives, joint action by employees or external constituencies can lead to the perpetuation of organizations despite the fact that they are failing to fulfill their official missions.

E. The Internal Evolution of Structure

Institutional theorists examine the processes by which organizations adapt their structure to acquire the legitimacy that will increase the organization's survival chances. Strategic choice theorists maintain that organizations must adapt to changes of resources and opportunities in the environment to retain economic efficiency. Population ecologists argue that sometimes these attempts at adaptation do not matter. Organizations are not always able to adapt to their environment and sometimes fail.

1.   Structure as a Source of Inertia

Why do organizations fail? As Downs (1967) and other observers of organizations have long known, organizations develop inertia and can become unable to adapt to a changing environment over time. Political commitments, social alliances, claims to legitimacy, and sunk costs in equipment can make it difficult to change an organization. Most critically, organizations develop formal procedures, a stable division of labor, a hierarchy of authority—in short, structure—to guarantee the reliability and accountability needed to assure customers, suppliers, and employees that the organization will produce the good or service.

As Hannan and Freeman (1984) note, reliability and accountability are only possible if structure is "highly reproducible" (Hannan and Freeman, 1984: 154). Reproducibility of behavior every day is achieved through processes of routinization and institutionalization. However, the institutional and routine nature of these procedures makes them hard to modify.

Hannan and Freeman (1984) maintain that only small organizations can adapt quickly to environmental changes. Only small organizations that really are "the wills of dominant coalitions and individuals" (Hannan and Freeman, 1984: 158) can change structure and strategy as quickly as individuals can perceive environmental shifts. Larger organizations will inevitably have to delegate decision making and responsibility, and these larger organizations will respond more slowly to environmental shifts.

It would seem, then, that small organizations would be more successful. However, population ecologists and others have provided ample empirical documentation for the "liability of newness" (Stinchcombe, 1965) hypothesis: new, and presumably smaller, organizations are much more likely to fail than older organizations. Hannan and Freeman's (1984) solution to this dilemma is to propose that reorganizations to adapt to the environment lower reliability of performance as contending parties engage in conflicts. In addition, confusion and inefficiency occur while old and new rules of business briefly coexist. Thus smaller organizations reorganize more often but are more vulnerable to failure than larger organizations, which have the slack resources to endure reorganizations. Environmental selection favors old, large organizations that succeed in reliably providing goods and services. However, these larger organizations develop inflexible structures and become bound up in inertial pressures.

2. Evolution and Organizational Design

If we stay at the population level of organizational analysis to detect selection of entire organizations, then we would have little to directly say about organizational design. Hannan and Freeman (1989) believe this is a necessary research strategy. They suggest that the study of population ecology only provides an understanding of the context within which organizational processes take place. However, are there not ways to organize routines that are flexible and adaptable, and that evolve, or does structure by its very nature lead to inflexibility? In order to answer this question, I first consider what is genetically transmitted to new organizations that replace others in the shifting environment. Then I discuss how ecological variation in structure and procedures within organizations is possible.

a. Structural Routines as Genetic Material. A consideration of the inheritance of characteristics requires a shift in focus from the demise of organizations to the replacement of old organizations or old organizational structures by new organizations and internal structures. Many ecologists focus on the demise of organizations. In an initial statement of the population ecology paradigm, Hannan and Freeman (1977) emphasized the death rates of organizations that are selected for survival by the environment. However, as Carroll (1984) has noted, selection processes are also dependent on the birth of new organizations.

Nelson and Winter (1982) argue that the genetic material that is transmitted from organization to organization and that leads to the development of new branches of existing organizations is made up of the routines that guide work. Winter argues that routines are effective "methods of doing things" (Winter, 1990: 272) that lead to productive competence. These routines evolve, are inherited, and are spread to other organizations. Organizations diversify as the outcome of adding activities that require more of the same competencies. As Meyer noted when commenting on Winter, this implies that conglomerates that acquire unrelated businesses create "hopeful monsters" (Meyer, 1990: 310) that will be eliminated through environmental selection.

b. Loosely Coupled Structure as a Survival Mechanism. These routines are constantly being modified as environments and technologies change. The arrangement of these routines into a hierarchy of structure may help the organization to adjust and evolve in its environment. This proposition follows from the writings of Herbert Simon (1962), who argues that organizations are composed of units that handle small parts of the task of organizing for work. These units can be modified to adapt to a particular subenvironment and are loosely connected so that changes in one part of the organization will not disrupt the entire organization. These varying units are arranged in a hierarchy for the overall coordination of work, but form a nearly decomposable system of units that can be created, modified, or eliminated as demanded by contingencies.

Organizational structures, then, are composed of loosely coupled units to preserve variability in the organization (Orton and Weick, 1990; Weick, 1976). Although population ecologists such as Aldrich (1979) and Singh and Lumsden (1990) have advocated the study of internal variation and evolution of structure, few empirical studies have been done on the internal evolution of organizational structure through such processes as loose coupling.

The study of internal evolution within hierarchical structures requires detailed study of structural change over time. In one of the few studies of internal structural change, Meyer, Stevenson, and Webster (1985) found that the existence of structure at lower levels of the organization (e.g., departments having subordinate divisions, or divisions having subordinate sections), lowered the death rates of the higher-level structure. Stevenson (1985), analyzing the same data, found that the frequency of change in terms of the creation and dissolution of units increased at the lower levels of the hierarchy. Further, Stevenson (1985) found that the frequency of change in the size of the organization was more tightly coupled to change in the number of subunits at the lower levels of hierarchy. The results of these studies suggest that the loosely coupled hierarchical arrangement of units in organizations allows environmental fluctuations to be absorbed at lower levels of the organization. Further studies of internal ecological and evolutionary processes are necessary in order to understand the evolutionary advantages of various structural configurations.

III. STRUCTURE AS PROCESS

To this point, structure has been assumed to be the hierarchy of authority, differentiation of the organization, and formal procedures created by management, particularly top management, to guide the organization. There is an alternative view of structure that gives more weight to the intentions and actions of actors at all levels of the organization instead of focusing on the goals of top management. In this alternative view, structure is defined as the persisting interactions between individuals that give regularity to behavior in the organization.

A. Informal and Formal Structure

In early organizational studies, this distinction between formal structure and patterns of interaction was referred to as the formal and informal structure. As Scott (1987) noted, early organizational writers often assumed that informal structures only characterized the lower levels of the organization, and excluded managers. This assumption was made partly because informal structures were regarded as the expression of emotion and sentiment in the lower-level workgroups that would impede the orderly operations of the formal structure (Roethisberger and Dickson, 1939). Case studies such as Dalton (1959) revealed that managers engaged in extensive interactions beyond the hierarchically specified communication channels and were highly embedded in informal structures of interaction.

B. The Varieties of Structure

This acknowledgment that recurring interaction captures a great deal of organizational activity has led Karl Weick to advocate that we transform the nouns we use to describe organizations into verbs (Weick, 1979); that is, we should study the process of organizing, not organization— we should study structuring, not structure. For Weick (1979) what is relevant to the structure of the organization are the systems of interlocked behavior used by individuals for reducing equivocality. By processing information through interlocked behavior, equivocality can be reduced to the point at which organizational actions can be taken.

In this same vein of considering how the actor creates structure, Giddens (1984) has argued that the study of social structure is the study of structuration. Structuration is the process whereby structures are constantly being produced and reproduced. Using Gidden's insight that actors are constantly reproducing structure through their actions rather than having structural constraints imposed upon them, Ranson, Hinings, and Greenwood (1980) have argued that organizational members have provinces of meaning or interpretive frameworks that become embodied in formal structures. Advocates of competing interpretive frameworks struggle with each other over the interpretation of organizational activities. Some groups are able to dominate others within the organization and impose their interpretive scheme as an organizational structure, subject to the constraints of the organization's size, technology, and environment.

Strauss (1978) and Strauss et al. (1963) have argued that the actors in organizations create a negotiated order. Studying psychiatric hospitals, Strauss et al. (1963) found constant negotiation between physicians and among other groups of staff members created and maintained the social structure. However, negotiation does not take place in a vacuum—organizational actors cannot simply create the organization; that is, the formal structure has effects on the negotiated order. Strauss (1978) has been careful to maintain that the formal structure of the organization has an important influence on the micropolitics of the negotiated order. For example, negotiation takes place along preexisting lines of communication and structural change requires a renegotiation of the social order.

C. Emergent Structure as Network

This idea that patterned interactions exist as a level of structure coexisting with the formal structure is captured by social network theorists (e.g., Lincoln, 1982; Tichy, Tushman, and Fombrun, 1979). Relatively repetitive and stable interactions between actors constitute networks that develop within and between organizational units. These networks could be considered "emergent" structure in the sense that these patterns of interaction are not necessarily formally specified, and these interactions allow for a process of intentional action by actors rather than just the reproduction of the existing structure.

These networks serve a variety of purposes in the organization. Brass's (1984) empirical research has shown that network centrality can give actors influence far exceeding their formal position. Networks of connections also can stabilize the organization and substitute for formal structure. For example, there is an increasing trend toward joint ventures, strategic alliances, and partnerships between companies. These alliances rely on a network form of organization (Powell, 1990) in which coordination is conducted through a network of ties rather than market-based contracts or a hierarchy of formal authority.

However, viewing the organizational structure as a pattern of interaction raises questions. Foremost among the questions that can be raised is determining how any intentionality is attributed to the organization beyond the interaction and goal pursuit of individuals. Dow argues that a concern for the pursuit of collective goals is "excess baggage" (1988: 59) as far as many interaction-based theorists are concerned. Rather, interaction theorists rely on "invisible hand" explanations to explain organizational order and the accomplishment of organizational objectives. For example, interaction theorists are skeptical of the ability of top managers to manipulate organizational culture. They believe "that shared beliefs and values, like the patterns of behavior they support, emerge from processes of social interaction in which top management is only one player among many" (Dow, 1988: 60). Interaction theorists, according to Dow (1988), question whether or not any consensus exists beyond the limited agreements or subcultures generated through localized interaction.

D. Linking the Formal Structure and Emergent Structure

It is hard to deny that formal structures exist and have effects on patterns of interactions, although, as Finc (1984) has noted, some interaction-based theorists tend to emphasize the negotiated order at the expense of the formal structure. Interaction-based theorizing has brought to the forefront the intentionality of the actor, but a strong element of structural coercion still exists in organizations.

1. Interaction and Structure

There is an interplay between formal structure and interaction. For example, Cyert and March (1963) argued that structure is the outcome of past coalitional bargaining. Thus, the negotiation of order leads to the creation of structures, such as organizational boundaries and budgets, that are temporarily agreed upon and constrain action until resources shift or until a periodic reevaluation of objectives occurs. Pfeffer (1978) maintains that formal structure is created to reduce conflict and satisfy feuding constituencies within and outside the organization. Thus, interaction begets formal structures that then constrain interaction.

2. Formal Position as a Resource in the Emergent Structure

Position in the formal structure also provides social resources for actors to engage in interaction. Stevenson (1990) has shown how the hierarchical arrangement of formal positions in a transit agency created a status system with greater interaction among those at the top compared to other levels. This result is confirmed by other studies that have shown that higher-level managers spend more time engaging in communication compared to other levels (Jablin, 1987).

Formal structure can provide the framework within which interaction patterns were created. For example, Stevenson and Gilly (1991) traced information about patient complaints as it flowed through a hospital. They found a tendency for employees throughout the organization to send complaints to mangers, who would then forward the complaints to other managers until the problem was solved. This network of managers that "attracted" complaints and passed them among themselves was in operation despite the existence of a formal procedure dictating that complaints be sent to formally designated problem solvers.

3. Interaction Among Interpenetrating Levels of Structure

The foregoing suggests that levels of structure exist in an organization. Organizational members occupy formal positions that are differentiated vertically and horizontally. Within this framework individuals engage in interactions that lead to the formation of networks that influence the organization and may lead to changes in the formal arrangement of positions. From this perspective, the challenge is to explain the relationship among levels of structure as the organization produces the good or service and adapts or does not adapt to changes in the technology and environment.

As an example of the idea that structure exists at several levels in the organization, consider recent research on the impact of technology on the organization. Interest in the impact of technology on the organization had been relatively dormant since the days of the Aston group research and early contingency theory in the 1970s (Barley, 1988). As previously discussed, the early studies of technology emphasized the causal influence of technology on structure across samples of organizations. The search was for generalizations such as Woodward's (1965) finding that continuous process manufacturing leads to a more centralized and formalized structure compared to batch processing.

"New technologies" such as microelectronics, robotics, and computerized information systems have led to a surge in technology studies. These more recent studies (e.g., Burkhardt and Brass, 1990; Rice and Aydin, 1991) emphasize that the link between structure and technology is not as determinate as had been assumed by contingency theorists. Rather, the actions of those who find their relationships to others altered by technology intercede in the process of structural change.

For example, Barley (1990) studied the impact of the introduction of computerized tomography scanners into two hospitals. He found that the introduction of this new technology into the radiology departments altered the formal work roles of the groups, leading to an alteration of the network of relationships. Over time the introduction of such new diagnostic techniques as ultrasound and body scanning led to a split within the radiology department between the older x-ray technicians and the new technology specialists. According to Barley (1990), the older radiologist group was characterized by staff with less discretion and knowledge who were subject to more bureaucratic procedures. The young group of specialists in new techniques relied less on formalized procedures and were "more collegial and cooperative" (Barley, 1990:91). In our terms, the conversion to a new technology induced a change in formal roles that produced a shift in the emergent structure of the organization that was reinforced by the differences in the formalization of relationships.

IV. CONCLUSIONS

There has been a steady movement in theorizing about organizational design. Initially, a "rational" model of organizations was advocated in which an unspecified group at the top of a coalition adjusted and calibrated the formal structure of the organization to accomplish organizational goals. Those goals were assumed to be clearly defined and internal to the organization, but on closer inspection they were not entirely under the control of the organization. Rather, the organization was subject to the vagaries of its technology and environment. This rational paradigm was further undermined by the realization that organizations adjust their structures to the myths of the environment as well as to economic conditions. Furthermore, random chance may play a role in the success of the organization. Organizations exist in populations in which some organizations fail despite their best efforts in a given time period.

As part of this trend to demystify and dethrone top management as the total arbiters of strategy and structure, some have emphasized that actors aside from top management interpret and act in the organizational situation. From this perspective, structures are created at several levels of analysis in the organization. Formal structure may become decoupled from activities to satisfy larger institutional myths, but emergent network structures of interaction may arise to stabilize the organization.

A. Changing Methodologies of Research on Organizational Design

A change in research strategy has accompanied these trends in theorizing. The Aston group strategy had been to move away from early case studies of organizations in order to develop empirical regularities that would hold across populations of organizations. Researchers have moved into two directions away from this approach. On the one hand, the pendulum seems to have swung back to the case study for those studying emergent structures. However, the new case studies are conducted with more sophisticated analytical tools than the early case studies, and these new methods allow for the discovery of empirical regularities across multiple workgroups. On the other hand, the population ecologists have escalated the level of analysis to the population over time, arguing that studies of populations and communities of organizations will reveal the context within which managers have to make decisions.

Both groups advocate the necessity of looking at organizational change over time in order to understand the existing structures of organizations. It is necessary to look at the historical development of a given structure in order to understand the connection between the formal structure and the emergent structure of organizations. This is a strategy that is necessary in order to answer some of the questions that are raised by these new approaches to organizational design.

B. Unanswered Questions

Given that multiple types of structures exist in organizations, the relationship between levels of structures need to be clarified. For example, the type of organization may influence the relationship between formal and emergent structures. Formal position may dictate the amount of status, information access, and influence in a more mechanistic organization. In a more loosely coupled, organic organization, relational position in emergent networks may be a stronger determinant of status, information, and power.

Another important question is the extent to which emergent structure can substitute for formal organization. Popular writers and some organization theorists have long advocated reducing or doing away with formal structure. From this viewpoint, formal structure is seen as a form of hierarchical social domination, and internal boundaries between units are seen as an impediment to the free flow of information. Therefore, organizations should be "self-organizing systems" (Weick, 1977) without structure, and organizational work should be conducted with a great deal of networking.

In the self-organizing system does structural position become defined by the others that you work with? In network analysis terms, some individuals are defined as structurally equivalent to others because they engage in interactions with the same individuals. Even though the "structurally equivalent" never interact with each other, they have been found to act in similar ways because of the similarity of their role sets (Burt, 1987). Without formal structure to guide interactions, do these equivalent positions develop and lead to similarities in behavior for certain actors across the organization?

Ultimately, the question of how much managers design organizations has to be revisited. Theory and research in the last 30 years has made it clear that top management has much less formal control over the organization than had been assumed by many researchers. The search for knowledge of how the intentions of managers and others in organizations are translated into levels of organizational structure, how these levels are altered by contingencies such as technologies, environments, and social myths, and how these levels induce changes in each other provides a full agenda for research.

REFERENCES

Abegglen, J. C. (1958). *The Japanese Factory: Aspects of Its Social Organization*. Free Press, Glencoe, Ill.

Adams, J. S. (1976). The structure and dynamics of behavior in organizational boundary roles. In *Handbook of Industrial and Organizational Psychology* (M. D. Dunnette, ed.), Rand McNally, Chicago, Ill., pp. 1175–1199.

Aldrich, H. (1972). Technology and organizational structure: A reexamination of the findings of the Aston group. *Administrative Science Quarterly*, *17*: 26–43.

Aldrich, H. (1979). *Organizations and Environments*. Prentice Hall, Englewood Cliffs, N.J.

Aldrich, H., and Herker, D. (1977). Boundary spanning roles and organizational structure. *Academy of Management Review*, *2*: 217–230.

Barley, S. R. (1988). Technology, power and the social organization of work: Towards a pragmatic theory of skilling and reskilling. *Research in the Sociology of Organizations*, *6*: 33–80.

Barley, S. R. (1990). The alignment of technology and structure through roles and networks. *Administrative Science Quarterly*, *35*: 61–103.

Biggart, N. W. (1977). The creative-destructive process of organizational change: The case of the post office. *Administrative Science Quarterly*, *22*: 410–426.

Blau, P. M. (1968). The hierarchy of authority in organizations. *American Journal of Sociology*, *73*: 453–467.

Blau, P. M. (1970). A formal theory of differentiation in organizations. *American Sociological Review*, *35*: 201–218.

Blau, P. M. (1974). *On the Nature of Organizations*. John Wiley, New York.

Blau, P. M., and Schoenherr, R. A. (1971). *The Structure of Organizations*. Basic Books, New York.

Blau, P. M., and Scott, W. R. (1962). *Formal Organizations*. Chandler, San Francisco.

Brass, D. J. (1984). Being in the right place: A structural analysis of individual influence in an organization. *Administrative Science Quarterly*, *29*: 518–539.

Bryman, A., Bresnen, M., Beardworth, A. D., Ford, J., and Keil, E. T. (1987). The concept of the temporary system: The case of the construction project. *Research in the Sociology of Organizations*, *5*: 253–283.

Burkhardt, M. E., and Brass, D. J. (1990). Changing patterns or patterns of change: The effects of a change in technology on social network structure and power. *Administrative Science Quarterly*, *35*: 104–127.

Burns, J., and Stalker, G. M. (1961). *The Management of Innovation*. Tavistock, London.

Burns, T. R., and Flam, H. (1987). *The Shaping of Social Organization*. Sage, Beverly Hills, Calif.

Burt, R. S. (1987). Social contagion and innovation: Cohesiveness versus structural equivalence. *American Journal of Sociology*, *92*: 1287–1335.

Carroll, G. R. (1984). Organizational ecology. *Annual Review of Sociology*, *10*: 71–93.

Carroll, G. R. (1988). Organizational ecology in theoretical perspective. In *Ecological Models of Organizations* (G. R. Carroll, ed.), Ballinger, Cambridge, Mass.

Child, J. (1972a). Organization structure and strategies of control: A replication of the Aston study. *Administrative Science Quarterly*, *17*:163–177.

Child, J. (1972b). Organizational structure, environment and performance: The role of strategic choice. *Sociology*, *6*: 1–22.

Child, J. (1981). Culture, contingency and capitalism in the cross-national study of organizations. *Research in Organizational Behavior*, *3*: 303–356.

Coase, R. H. (1937). The nature of the firm. *Economica*, *4*: 386–405.

Cyert, R. M., and March, J. G. (1963). *A Behavioral Theory of the Firm*. Prentice Hall, Englewood Cliffs, N.J.

Daft, R. L., and Bradshaw, P. J. (1980). The process of horizontal differentiation: Two models. *Administrative Science Quarterly*, *25*: 441–456.

Dalton, M. (1959). *Men Who Manage*. John Wiley, New York.

Dewar, R., and Hage, J. (1978). Size, technology, complexity and structural differentiation: Toward a theoretical synthesis. *Administrative Science Quarterly*, *23*: 111–136.

Dewar, R. D., Whetten, D. A., and Boje, D. (1980). An examination of the reliability and validity of the Aiken and Hage scales of centralization, formalization and task routineness. *Administrative Science Quarterly*, *25*: 120–128.

Dibble, V. K. (1965). The organization of traditional authority: English County government, 1558 to 1640. In *Handbook of Organizations* (J. G. March, ed.), Rand McNally, Chicago, pp. 879–909.

Dimaggio, P. J., and Powell, W. W. (1983). The iron cage revisited: Institutional isomorphism and collective rationality in organizational fields. *American Sociological Review*, 48: 147–160.

Dow, G. K. (1988). Configurational and coactivational views of organizational structure. *Academy of Management Review*, 13: 53–64.

Downs, A. (1967). *Inside Bureaucracy*. Little, Brown and Co., Boston.

Fine, G. A. (1984). Negotiated orders and organizational cultures. *Annual Review of Sociology*, 10: 239–262.

Florida, R., and Kenny, M. (1991). Transplanted organizations: The transfer of Japanese industrial organizations to the U.S. *American Sociological Review*, 56: 381–398.

Galbraith, J. R. (1973). *Designing Complex Organizations*. Addison Wesley, Reading, Mass.

Galbraith, J. R. (1977). *Organization Design*. Addison Wesley, Reading, Mass.

Gerwin, D. (1981). Relationships between structure and technology. In *Handbook of Organizational Design*, vol. 2 (P. C. Nystrom and W. H. Starbuck, eds.), Oxford University Press, New York, pp. 3–38.

Giddens, A. (1984). *The Constitution of Society*. University of California Press, Berkeley.

Granovetter, M. (1985). Economic action and social structure: The problem of embeddedness. *American Journal of Sociology*, 91: 481–510.

Hage, J. (1965). An axiomatic theory of organizations. *Administrative Science Quarterly*, 10: 289–320.

Hage, J., and Aiken, M. (1967). Relationship of centralization to other structural properties. *Administrative Science Quarterly*, 12: 72–91.

Hage, J., and Aiken, M. (1969). Routine technology, social structure and organizational goals. *Administrative Science Quarterly*, 14: 366–377.

Hall, R. H. (1962). Intra-organizational structural variation: Application of the bureaucratic model. *Administrative Science Quarterly*, 7: 295–308.

Hall, R. H. (1991). *Organizations: Structures, Processes and Outcomes*, 5th ed. Prentice Hall, Englewood Cliffs, N.J.

Hall, R. H., Haas, J. E., and Johnson, N. (1967). Organizational size, complexity and formalization. *Administrative Science Quarterly*, 32: 903–912.

Hannan, M. T., and Freeman, J. (1977). The population ecology of organizations. *American Journal of Sociology*, 82: 929–964.

Hannan, M. T., and Freeman, J. (1984). Structural inertia and organizational change. *American Sociological Review*, 49: 149–164.

Hannan, M. T., and Freeman, J. (1989). *Organizational Ecology*. Harvard University Press, Cambridge, Mass.

Heise, D. R. (1972). How do I know my data? Let me count the ways. *Administrative Science Quarterly*, 17: 58–61.

Hendershot, G. E., and James, T. F. (1972). Size and growth as determinants of administrative–production ratios in organizations. *American Sociological Review*, 37: 149–153.

Hickson, D. J., Hinings, C. R., Lee, C. A., Schneck, R. E., and Pennings, J. M. (1971). A strategic contingencies theory of intra organizational power. *Administrative Science Quarterly*, 16: 216–229.

Hickson, D. J., Pugh, D. S., Pheysey, D. C. (1969). Operations technology and organization structure: An empirical reappraisal. *Administrative Science Quarterly*, 14: 378–397.

Hilton, G. (1972). Causal inference analysis: A seductive process. *Administrative Science Quarterly*, 17: 44–57.

Holdaway, E. A., and Blowers, T. A. (1971). Administrative ratios and organizational size: A longitudinal examination. *American Sociological Review*, 36: 278–286.

Jablin, F. M. (1987). Formal organizational structure. In *Handbook of Organizational Communication* (F. M. Jablin, L. L. Putnam, K. H. Roberts, and L. W. Porter, eds.), Sage, Newbury Park, Calif.

James, L. R., and Jones, A. P. (1976). Organizational structure: A review of structural dimensions and their conceptual relationships with individual attitudes and behavior. *Organizational Behavior and Human Peformance*, 16: 74–113.

Kasarda, J. D. (1974). The structural implications of social system size: A three level analysis. *American Sociological Review*, 39: 19–28.

Keith, P. M. (1978). Individual and organizational correlates of a temporary system. *J. of Applied Behavioral Science*, 14: 195–203.

Kimberly, J. R. (1976). Organizational size and the structuralist perspective: A review, critique and proposal. *Administrative Science Quarterly*, 21: 571–597.

Lawrence, P. R., and Lorsch, J. W. (1967). *Organization and environment: Managing differentiation and integration*. Graduate School of Business Administration, Harvard University, Boston.

Lincoln, J. R. (1982). Intra- (and inter-) organizational networks. *Research in the Sociology of Organizations, 1*: 1–38.

Lincoln, J. R. (1990). Japanese organization and organization theory. *Research in Organizational Behavior, 12*: 255–294.

Lincoln, J. R., and McBride, K. (1987). Japanese industrial organizations in comparative perspective. *Annual Review of Sociology, 13*: 289–312.

Mansfield, R. (1973). Bureaucracy and centralization: An examination of organizational structure. *Administrative Science Quarterly, 18*: 477–488.

McKelvey, B. (1982). *Organizational Systematics*. University of California Press, Berkeley.

Meyer, J. W., and Rowan, B. (1977). Institutional organizations: Formal structures as myth and ceremony. *American Journal of Sociology, 83*: 340–363.

Meyer, M. W. (1968). Automation and bureaucratic structure. *Administrative Science Quarterly, 74*: 256–264.

Meyer, M. W. (1972). Size and the structure of organizations: A causal analysis. *American Sociological Review, 37*: 434–441.

Meyer, M. W. (1990). Notes of a skeptic: From organizational ecology to organizational evolution. In *Organizational Evolution: New Directions* (J. V. Singh, ed.), Sage, Newbury Park, Calif., pp. 298–314.

Meyer, M. W., and Brown, M. C. (1977). The process of bureaucratization. *American Journal of Sociology, 83*: 364–385.

Meyer, M. W. et al. (1978). *Environments and Organizations*. Jossey-Bass, San Francisco.

Meyer, M. W., Stevenson, W. B., and Webster, S. (1985). *The Limits of Bureaucracy*. DeGruyter, Berlin.

Meyer, M. W., and Zucker, L. G. (1989). *Permanently Failing Organizations*. Sage, Newbury Park, Calif.

Miles, M. B. (1964). On temporary systems. In *Innovation in Education* (M. B. Miles, ed.), Columbia University Press, New York.

Miller, D., and Friesen, P. H. (1984). *Organizations: A Quantum View*. Prentice Hall, Englewood Cliffs, N.J.

Mintzberg, H. (1979). *The Structuring of Organizations*. Prentice Hall, Englewood Cliffs, N.J.

Nelson, R. R., and Winter, S. G. (1982). *An Evolutionary Theory of Economic Change*. Belknap Press of Harvard University Press, Cambridge, Mass.

Orton, J. D., and Weick, K. E. (1990). Loosely coupled systems: A reconceptualization. *Academy of Management Review, 15*: 203–223.

Ouchi, W. G. (1980). Markets, bureaucracies and clans. *Administrative Science Quarterly, 25*: 129–141.

Ouchi, W. G. (1981). *Theory Z*. Addison-Wesley, Reading, Mass.

Palisi, B. J. (1970). Some suggestions about the transitory-permanence dimension of organizations. *British Journal of Sociology, 21*: 200–206.

Perrow, C. (1981). Markets, hierarchies and hegemony. In *Perspectives on Organization Design and Behavior* (A. H. Van de Ven and W. F. Joyce, eds.), John Wiley and Sons, New York, pp. 371–386.

Peters, T. J., and Waterman, R. H. (1982). In *Search of Excellence*. Harper and Row, Cambridge, Mass.

Pfeffer, J. (1978). *Organizational Design*. AHM Publishing, Arlington Heights, Ill.

Pfeffer, J., and Salancik, G. R. (1978). *The External Control of Organizations*. Harper and Row, New York.

Powell, W. W. (1990). Neither market nor hierarchy: Networks of organizations. *Research in Organizational Behavior, 12*: 295–336.

Pugh, D. S. (1981). The Aston program of research: Retrospect and prospect. In *Perspectives on Organization Design and Behavior* (A. H. Van de Ven and W. F. Joyce, eds.), John Wiley and Sons, New York, pp. 135–166.

Pugh, D. S., Hickson, D. J., Hinings, C. R., and Turner, C. (1968). Dimensions of organization structure. *Administrative Science Quarterly, 13*: 65–91.

Pugh, R. S., Hickson, D. J., Hinings, C. R., and Turner, C. (1969). The context of organization structures. *Administrative Science Quarterly, 14*: 91–114.

Ransom, S., Hinings, B., and Greenwood, R. (1980). The structuring of organizational structures. *Administrative Science Quarterly, 25*: 1–17.

Rice, R. E., and Aydin, C. (1991). Attitudes toward new organizational technology: Network proximity as a mechanism for social information processing. *Administrative Science Quarterly, 36*: 219–244.

Roethisberger, F. J., and Dickson, W. J. (1939). *Management and the Worker*. Harvard University Press, Cambridge, Mass.

Rothschild-Whitt, J. (1979). The collectivist organization: An alternative to rational bureaucratic models. *American Sociological Review*, *44*: 509–527.

Schein, E. H. (1985). *Organizational Culture and Leadership*. Jossey-Bass, San Francisco.

Schoonhoven, C. B. (1981). Problems with contingency theory: Testing assumptions hidden within the language of contingency "theory." *Administrative Science Quarterly*, *26*: 349–377.

Scott, W. R. (1975). Organizational structure. *Annual Review of Sociology*, *1*: 1–20.

Scott, W. R. (1987). *Organizations: Rational, Natural and Open Systems*, 2nd ed. Prentice Hall, Englewood Cliffs, N.J.

Scott, W. R. (1990). Technology and structure: An organization-level perspective. In *Technology and Organizations* (P. S. Goodman et al., eds.), Jossey-Bass, San Francisco, pp. 109–143.

Simon, H. A. (1957). *Administrative Behavior*, 2nd ed. Macmillan, New York.

Simon, H. A. (1962). The architecture of complexity. *Proceedings of the American Philosophical Society*, *106*: 467–482.

Singh, J. V., and Lumsden, C. J. (1990). Theory and research in organizational ecology. *Annual Review of Sociology*, *16*: 161–195.

Starbuck, W. H. (1981). A trip to view the elephants and rattlesnakes in the garden of Aston. In *Perspectives on Organization Design and Behavior* (A. H. Van de Ven and W. F. Joyce, eds.), John Wiley and Sons, New York, pp. 167–198.

Stevenson, W. B. (1985). Organizational growth and hierarchical change in formal structure. *J. of Mathematical Sociology*, *11*: 287–306.

Stevenson, W. B. (1990). Formal structure and networks of interactions within organizations. *Social Science Research*, *19*: 113–131.

Stevenson, W. B., and Gilly, M. C. (1991). Information processing and problem solving: The migration of problems through formal positions and networks of ties. *Academy of Management Journal*, *34*: 918–928.

Stinchcombe, A. L. (1959). Bureaucratic and craft administration of production: A comparative study. *Administrative Science Quarterly*, *4*: 168–187.

Stinchcombe, A. L. (1965). Social structure and organizations. In *Handbook of Organizations* (J. G. March, ed.), Rand McNally, Chicago, pp. 142–193.

Strauss, A., Schatzman, L., Ehrlich, D., Bucher, R., and Sabshin, M. (1963). The hospital and its negotiated order. In *The Hospital in Modern Society* (E. Freidson, ed.), Free Press, Glencoe, N.Y.

Strauss, A. (1978). *Negotiations*. Jossey-Bass, San Francisco.

Thompson, J. D. (1967). *Organizations in Action*. McGraw-Hill, New York.

Tichy, N., Tushman, M. L., and Fombrun, C. (1979). Social network analysis for organizations. *Academy of Management Review*, *4*: 507–519.

Tolbert, P. S., and Zucker, L. G. (1983). Institutionalized sources of change in the formal structure of organizations. *Administrative Science Quarterly*, *28*: 22–39.

Turner, J. H. (1988). *A Theory of Social Interaction*. Stanford University Press, Stanford, Calif.

Tushman, M. L., Newman, W. H., and Romanelli, E. (1986). Convergence and upheaval: Managing the unsteady pace of organizational evolution. *California Management Review*, *29*: 29–43.

Van de Ven, A. H., and Joyce, W. F. (1981). *Perspectives on Organization Design and Behavior*. John Wiley and Sons, New York.

Weber, M. (1958). Bureaucracy. In *From Max Weber: Essays in Sociology* (H. H. Gerth and C. W. Mills, eds.), Oxford University Press, New York, pp. 196–244.

Weber, M. (1968). In *Economy and Society* (G. Roth and C. Wittich, eds.), Bedminster Press, New York.

Weick, K. E. (1976). Educational organizations as loosely coupled systems. *Administrative Science Quarterly*, *21*: 1–19.

Weick, K. E. (1977). Organizational design: Organizations as self-designing systems. *Organizational Dynamics*, *6*: 30–46.

Weick, K. E. (1979). *The Social Psychology of Organizing*, 2nd ed. Addison-Wesley, Reading, Mass.

Williamson, O. (1975). *Markets and Hierarchies: Analysis and Antitrust Implications*. Free Press, New York.

Williamson, O. (1981). The economics of organizations: The transaction cost approach. *American Journal of Sociology*, *87*: 548–577.

Williamson, O. (1985). *The Economic Institutions of Capitalism: Firms, Markets, Relational Contracting*. Free Press, New York.

Winter, S. G. (1990). Survival, selection and inheritance in evolutionary theories of organizations. In *Organizational Evolution: New Directions* (J. V. Singh, ed.), Sage, Newbury Park, Calif., pp. 269–297.

Woodward, J. (1965). *Industrial Organization: Theory and Practice*. Oxford University Press, New York.

Zucker, L. G. (1986). Production of trust: Institutional sources of economic structure: 1840 to 1920. *Research in Organizational Behavior*, 8: 55–111.

8
Risk Taking in Organizations

Myron L. Weber

University of Calgary, Calgary, Alberta, Canada

I. INTRODUCTION

Risk taking in organizations is an increasingly crucial activity. As organizations have grown in size and complexity, so have the demands on their decision makers. As the scale of operation of organizations has expanded, so have the potential sources of uncertainty faced by would-be organizational risk takers. Increased levels of expertise have become available for dealing with organizational uncertainty, but perhaps the responsibility of decision makers for distinguishing among the increasingly subtle and complex alternatives available to them has grown even more.

Current programmed, risk-oriented, and heuristically based approaches to decision making have not had the intended effect of simplifying the task of organizational decision makers. They have, in fact, often had the reverse effect, given the higher expectations for outcomes that frequently accompany advanced decision-making technology. The resultant tasks are now regularly more risky and less certain, with demands for ever improving effectiveness in their accomplishment.

This is, of course, a contentious statement and it will require considerable discussion to support it fully. The major points that will be dealt with in this chapter are the *concept* of risk, the *crucial* notion of the *context* in which risk taking occurs, and the *characteristics* of decision makers themselves.

Broadly, when we turn to the organizational risk-taking literature for guidance in better understanding the dilemmas faced by such decision makers, and the means by which their effectiveness on behalf of their organizations might be increased, we encounter a vast body of literature that is often ambiguous and contradictory. Research in risk taking encompasses an extraordinarily diverse domain, dealing with literally tens of thousands of references encompassing both the conceptual and operational, as well as the normative and descriptive, and including a focus on the rational versus the nonrational in risk taking. Research emphases range in level of analysis from the individual through the group to the organizational and strategic. The breadth of topics treated include financial, portfolio and risk management, hazardous plant siting, traffic safety, medical decision making, and education and child development, as well as political and defense scenarios. The dimensions of risk perception, propensity, adjustment, communication, and the situational context of risk taking are also explored. Indeed, an extensive literature even exists regarding animal risk-taking behavior.

II. THE CONCEPT OF RISK

An initial task, then, is to suggest a structure that will both delimit and bring some order to the chaos that currently exists. A fundamental understanding of the concept of risk in its diverse contexts must underlie such a taxonomic effort, and should assist measurably in an operationally useful organization and comprehension of the literature. The concept of risk has been employed in several often inconsistent and confusing contexts. It has served as a synonym for error, loss, regret, and uncertainty, among other usages.

In addition, understanding the concept of risk and of risk-taking behavior also requires examination of the context in which risk taking occurs; that is, the risk-taking situation. This topic is to be discussed in detail in Section III of this chapter, but some preliminary sense of context is relevant here.

Examining first the context of decision making, in traditional terms, a decision maker faces a situation offering a number of alternative possible responses to a problem. Each response, or decision alternative, is then associated with various outcomes (and accompanying consequences) whose probabilities of occurrence vary between zero and one (Figure 1). Risk, then, will be taken to refer to *uncertainty* regarding the outcome (and consequence) of making a decision; that is, choosing among alternative actions in a decision-making situation in which each outcome occurs with a probability whose value is known to the decision maker. The more certain the outcomes for an action alternative (i.e., the closer the probability of occurrence of the outcomes to one), the less risky that action becomes. A decision maker would, then, after examination of alternative outcomes of varying risk, choose the one whose outcomes are "best" by his or her criteria, a process to be discussed in detail in Section IV.

An important distinction between "personal" and "organizational" decision making should first be made. On a personal level, an individual might choose one of a number of decision alternatives (i.e., making a decision by choosing one action from among many). The decision maker would then experience (with a certain probability) a personal outcome, as shown in Figure 1; thus, an individual investor choosing from among available securities would eventually realize a change in the value of his or her investment, from complete loss to considerable appreciation in value. The risk associated with this personal investment would then be a function of the uncertainty associated with personal outcomes, each of which have different values for the investor.

The "classical" decision-making literature suggests that the "rational" decision maker would select the outcome whose *expected value* (or product of the probability of occurrence of an organizational outcome, and the value of that outcome to the individual) is greatest. The decision maker would then seek to *maximize* the expected value, or a variant of this value, of his choice. Individuals who prefer a higher level of risk, for example, may elect to maximize their potential gain from a situation, while those opting for a lower level of risk may attempt to *minimize* their potential loss in a similar circumstance, or opt for a lesser certain return.

Alternatively, from an organizational perspective, risky decision making might involve a

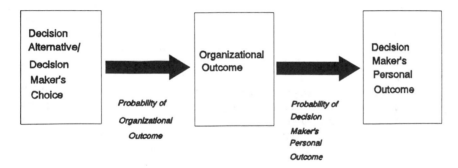

Figure 1   Decision-making context.

more complex and multistage process, in which the risk taker's personal outcome might be determined within an organizational context. If, for example, an investment advisor were acting on behalf of an organization, then her decision would first result, with a certain probability, in an outcome for the organization, followed by an outcome, also with a certain probability, for the individual. (See Figure 2.) In this situation, then, a financial officer of a corporation might now select securities that would (subsequently) generate for his organization a value within the range of more to less favorable potential portfolio values, or might instead opt for an assured organizational outcome. The officer would then experience personal outcomes as well. The risk associated with this corporate investment situation would then be a function of the differently valued outcomes available to both the organization and the individual risk taker.

III. DIMENSIONS OF RISK TAKING

A. Introduction

Risky decision making in organizations may then be portrayed as a scenario in which a decision maker selects one alternative with an associated outcome from among many of differential values and risks available to him or her in a decision-making situation. A useful model of risky organization decision making would then include three clusters of variables: the constellation of variables related to the *decision maker* (including such dimensions as demographics, level of risk-taking preferences, and other biases), the *situation* in which she makes such a decision (including such dimensions as the riskiness or uncertainty of the situation and the organizational context and resources, as well as the culture regarding risk taking, and the nature of the *decision* taken (including such properties as its level of riskiness). (See Figure 3.)

Our strategy for examining the literature then proceeds from research related to dimensions related to the decision maker, through the situation in which he performs, and then to the interaction of the two in determining the nature of the final decision realized.

B. The Decision Maker

1. Demographic Characteristics

The focus here on the decision maker has two emphases. Immediate attention goes to demographic features, and then to decision maker rationality.

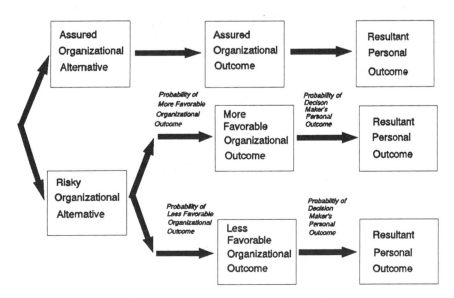

Figure 2 Decision structure.

Figure 3   Risky decision-making model.

Many demographic characteristics have received research attention; we must thus be harshly selective here. Brief attention is therefore devoted to age, gender, and education. Turning first to these personal characteristics, increasing age has been generally found to be inversely related to risk taking (Wallach and Kogan, 1961; Vroom and Bernd, 1971; Hutchinson and Clemens, 1980; McInish, 1982; MacCrimmon and Wehrung, 1986), although a few researchers (Cohn et al., 1975; Taylor and Dunnette, 1974) find older subjects to be as risky or riskier in their decision making as their younger colleagues. Further, in noting that elderly subjects are more risk-averse than college-age students, Kogan and Wallach (1967) stress the lack of longitudinal research on adults between college and retirement, and the consequent inability to describe shifts in riskiness during that period. Taylor and Dunnette (1974) find that although older managers are not less facile information processors or decision makers than younger ones, they seek more information, take longer to actually make decisions, diagnose information more accurately, have less ability to integrate information for accurate decision choices, have reduced confidence in their decisions, and are more willing to modify decisions in the face of adverse consequences.

The conclusions of research relating gender and risk taking have been ambiguous. Kogan and Wallach (1967) note little difference by gender among adults in their risk-taking tendencies. Muldrow and Bayton (1979), testing male and female executives, find few significant differences on a number of task and personal variables, but do find that women tend to take fewer risks than do men. Bartol (1976), finally, for the present purposes, suggests that decision-making models are weaker predictors for women than men and require additional demographic variables to increase their predictiveness for women.

The data relating education and risk taking are similarly unclear, with Watts and Tobin (1967), Hammon, Houston, and Melander (1967), Blume and Friend (1978), and MacCrimmon and Wehrung (1986) all finding a direct relationship between the two variables, but with Cohn et al. (1975), Laughhunn, Payne, and Crum (1980), and McInish (1982) reporting no significant relationship. Comparably ambiguous relationships are also apparent between intelligence and risk taking (Kogan and Wallach, 1967).

2.   The Rationality of Decision Making

A second major dimension of the present view of decision makers relates to their "rationality" or departure from it. As previously noted, rational decision makers will attempt to maximize the expected value of the outcome they seek; the "risk averter" or conservative decision maker will accept less than the expected value in exchange for reduced risk, and the "risk taker" will attempt to secure a value greater than expected value, although it might entail a greater risk.

Early mathematically oriented decision theorists (von Neumann and Morgenstern, 1947; Mosteller and Nogee, 1951; Davidson, Suppes, and Siegel, 1957) are prescriptive or normative and suggest that rational individuals should select outcomes in order to maximize expected values, assuring the attainment of "optimal" results. They specify a set of a priori axioms or postulates to facilitate such decision choices, including the formulation of notions of subjective probability and personal utility functions.

These theorists also suggest that the value to be maximized should be the product of a *subjective* or personally estimated probability of occurrence of an outcome and its *utility* or value to the decision maker. Such a *subjectively expected utility* (SEU) theory attempts to model the behavior of *rational* decision makers. Theorists posit various axioms designed to assure rational choice behavior and develop methodologies to obtain appropriate subjective probabilities and utilities from decision makers (Edwards, 1954; Edwards, Lindman, and Philips, 1965; Becker and McClintock, 1967; Mosteller and Nogee, 1951; Davidson, Suppes, and Siegel, 1957).

A parallel development in the social sciences is the development of the *expectancy valence theory*, which states generally that the force or motivation to complete a task is a function of six interacting factors: the likelihood that such effort will result in a given level of performance, the probability that task completion will be appropriately rewarded, the intrinsic and extrinsic valences associated with the task, the instrumentality of rewards for need satisfaction, and the variables dealing with individual differences, such as ability (Georgopoulos, Mahoney, and Jones, 1957; Vroom, 1964; Lawler, 1965; 1968; Galbraith and Cummings, 1967; Campbell et al., 1970).

Expectancy theory parallels SEU theory in its formulation. Like SEU, it assumes rationality in decision-making behavior. It also posits maximization of expectancy and valence, the expectancy theory equivalents of subjective probability and utility in SEU theory.

A number of studies in various arenas were initially supportive of both SEU and expectancy theories; that is, the rationality of individual decision making (Coombs and Komorita, 1958; Tversky, 1967; Lawler, 1968; Hackman and Porter, 1968; Wofford, 1971). These prescriptive models, which assume rational decision-making behavior, have been operationalized in a number of settings. For example, several financial and investment models have been suggested, some of which use variance as a measure of risk: Markowitz (1959), Sharpe (1964), Tobin (1965), Fama (1976), and others. Hertz (1964) and Magee (1964) both applied an expected value model to capital budgeting, and Swalm (1966) focused on utility-based decisions for corporate decision makers. Variations of these theories have also been employed in the examination of the risk assessment of disease by physicians (De Rivera, 1980; Christensen-Szalanski, 1983; Wallsten and Budescu, 1983).

However, a number of challenges to prescriptive theories of rational decision making have been made, with many of them centering on the underlying assumptions of the theories. As early as 1953, Edwards demonstrated that subjects often "prefer" some probabilities to others, making it difficult to speak of rationality in decision making, and indeed hard to even assign individual values to objects. Much controversy has also focused on the postulate of transitivity. It deals with the notion that for outcomes, actions, or probabilities X, Y, and Z, if X is preferred to Y and Y is preferred to Z, then X will be preferred to Z. Several researchers have reported studies in which instances of intransitivity abound (Edwards, 1954; 1961; Rapoport and Wallsten, 1972; Starke and Behling, 1975; Liddell and Solomon, 1977a, b).

The required independence of utility and subjective probability is also brought into question by the early research of Marks (1951), Irwin (1953), and Edwards (1953; 1955). See also the subsequent work by Starke and Behling (1975), as well as by Liddell and Solomon (1977b). Even the crucial assumption of maximization of expected utility has been contested, with such alternative criteria offered as minimizing the maximum potential loss (see, e.g., Montgomery and Adelbratt, 1982; Yates and Goldstein, 1983).

Similar concerns have been raised regarding a number of conceptual and empirical short-comings of expectancy theory. See, for example, Pritchard and De Leo (1971), Heneman and Schwab (1972), Wahba and House (1972a, b), and Kennedy, Fossum, and White (1983).

The direction of research then gradually shifted from the study of rational decision-making behavior to an exploration of departures from rationality; that is, risk taking and risk aversion. Theories became more *descriptive*, seeking to describe the process or mechanism through which actual decision making occurs. A prescriptive theory is often used as a starting point and modified until it is more descriptively accurate of the process under study. In an early study of corporate decision makers, Swalm (1966) noted that

> Businessmen do *not* attempt to optimize the expected dollar volume in risk situations involving what, to them, are large amounts . . . [Cardinal utility theory] offers a relatively simple way of classifying many types of industrial decision-makers . . . quite conservative—moderately conservative—a gambler. . . . If the decision-makers interviewed are at all representative of U.S. executives in general, our managers are surely not the takers of risk so often alluded to. . . . Rather than seeking risks, they shun them, consistently refusing to recommend risks that, from the overall company viewpoint, would almost certainly be attractive (pp. 135–136).

In a similar vein, Tobin (1965) distinguished between "risk lovers" and "risk averters," using a mean-variance approach to risk. A number of subsequent researchers have identified and characterized three classes of risk averters (conservative decision makers), risk neutrals (rational decision makers), and risk takers. The preponderance of research suggests that risk aversion predominates, not only among managers (MacCrimmon and Wehrung, 1986; Weber, 1986), but also among the international public (Bastide, Moatti, and Pages, 1989). This position has even been extended to include the notion of "societal risk aversion" (Sciortino, Hourton, and Spencer, 1988).

The suggestion has been made by some researchers that subjects are nonrational in their decisions because they have inadequate abilities to assess probabilities accurately (see, e.g., Svenson, 1984; Brehmer and Kuylenstierna, 1978; Christensen-Szalanski, 1983; Wallsten and Budescu, 1983; DeRivera, 1980). In response to this concern, other specialists have transformed probability measures within subjectively weighted utility theory in an attempt to improve their accuracy (e.g., Larson, 1980; Karmarkar, 1978).

In an effort to address some of these concerns, Brehmer and Kuylenstierna (1978) instructed subjects on the statistical nature of experimental tasks and determined that subjects did not adopt statistical strategies even when told to do so. They concluded, based upon their findings, that subjects' failure to improve performance was a function of their lack of cognitive capacity to implement statistical strategies. Schoemaker (1979), however, suggested that increased statistical expertise did reduce the cognitive complexity of assessing bets, increased the quality of risk assessment, and improved the likelihood that subjects followed a moment-based model of decision making. Other research, however, fails to confirm this view (Weber, 1987). In response to further exceptions to utility-based theories, Pollatsek and Tversky (1970) proposed a "theory of risk" attempting to remedy some of the exceptions raised. Once again, some studies supported the theory (e.g., Coombs and Huang, 1968), while others did not (e.g., Coombs and Bowen, 1971).

This example of criticism by critics of rationality notions and rejoinders by its defenders is just one of many illustrative of the dynamic that has governed the area of risky decision making for some time. The risky decision-making literature consists of two camps. One includes expectancy, expected value, subjectively expected utility, portfolio, and other theories, and emphasizes the role of rationality and maximization in decision making. Its proponents alter formulations when necessary to preserve the role of "reason" in decision making. The other major group is concerned with bounded rationality, satisficing, and the limitations of human information processing and decision-making capabilities. Scholars of this persuasion focus on violations of rationality principles.

Both groups have responded to the criticisms of their positions by the other. The "rationalists" contend that their position holds *if* a number of additional considerations are taken into account, including the costs of rationality, decision maker and situational characteristics, the notion of global maximization, and environmental feedback. They further suggest that the research of "nonrationalists" is not representative of actual decision situations and lacks information on actual subject perceptions of the situation.

The nonrationalists respond vigorously. They emphasize that behavior can always be "rationalized" by an appeal to a higher level of rationality, and that differences between experiments and reality may not matter.

The differences between the groups remain unresolved, but it might be concluded that *all* decision theories assume that boundaries exist to rationality in decision making. The essential difference is just a matter of *degree* and of research strategy. The advice of Rapaport and Wallsten (1972) is intended for specific application to utility theory, but it seems worthy of more general attention. They note in terms germane to the discussion above

> It seems then that the conflicting evidence pertaining to subjectively expected utility theory is presently irreconcilable. Consequently, the basic empirical question should not be whether to accept or reject subjectively expected utility theory as a whole, but rather to systematically discover the conditions under which it is or is not valid (p. 141).

In sum, incorporation of suggestions from several alternative approaches to risky decision making in organizations is a logical response to the current impasse. Students of expectancy, utility, and other prescriptive theories have been called to task for neglecting descriptive theories. On the other hand, descriptive theories have often minimized critical aspects treated in prescriptive models. An approach synthesizing a number of formulations should aid in reducing the "myopia" implicit in individual models and the ambiguities evident in the research based upon the disparate models currently employed.

3. Biases and Heuristics

Consequently, this conclusion warrants brief consideration of the most promising alternatives to prescriptive theories, as well as some discussion of their potential synthesis with more "rationally" based models. Among the approaches under consideration are those treating systematic biases in the perception or framing of risk situations.

Payne et al. (1980; 1981) examined the effect of specific target or reference points on risky decisions. It appeared to account for changes in risk preference, with risk seeking being dominant under conditions of nonruinous losses and risk aversion being dominant for ruinous losses, both under states of below-target returns. Such risk preferences were found to be stable over a wide range of experimental conditions. A related risk preference study suggested that decision makers tend to favor risk taking in loss situations, parallel to a portion of the Payne research (Kahneman and Tversky, 1979). The same authors also find risk aversion in settings yielding gains. Both of the Kahneman and Tversky results are generally supported in the literature (e.g., Kameda and Davis, 1990), although Budescu and Wallsten (1990) find results contrary to those predicted by Kahneman and Tversky in what they term their "prospect theory." Considerable ambiguity still exists, therefore, regarding risk preferences of decision makers.

Elaborating their prospect theory, Tversky and Kahneman (1974) cite the erroneous nature of intuitive judgments by decision makers facing uncertain situations. Based upon earlier work by Simon and his associates (Simon, 1956; 1957; Simon and Newell, 1970), they suggest that—given the "satisficing" nature of human decision making, as well as the constraint of "bounded rationality"—individuals use a limited number of "heuristics" in an effort to process and digest expeditiously the masses of data they encounter. This "decisional shorthand," which reduces the complexity of probability and value assessments to simpler judgmental operations, frequently results in severe systematic errors related to what is termed inadequate information coding. (See, e.g., Kahneman and Tversky, 1979; 1982, and Tversky and Kahneman, 1981, for amplification of these findings.)

Three special heuristics are described by Tversky and Kahneman (1974) as alternatives to rational decision-making models: representativeness, availability, and should be anchoring and adjustment. To briefly outline these examples of decision biases, *representativeness* describes a situation in which two items are similar, or one item is considered to be highly representative of the other. This circumstance may lead (often erroneously) to the judgment that it is highly probable that one item is generated from the other. Such an heuristic frequently results in insensitivity to the base rate of occurrence of outcomes, to sample size (i.e., "the law of small numbers"), to predictability, and to misconceptions regarding the nature of chance and regression, as well as to illusions of validity.

The *availability* heuristic, based upon relative familiarity with given events, can lead to biases in judgments of frequency. This error is related to several factors: the relative ease with which different instances can be retrieved from memory, the degree to which an event can be conceived by an individual, and the differential effectiveness with which the search for such events is conducted. Anchoring and adjustment, finally, refers to the mechanism whereby decision makers "anchor" themselves to an initial judgmental position, but then insufficiently adjust their view in response to subsequent information, resulting in such occurrences as overestimation of the likelihood of conjunctive events and underestimation of the probability of disjunctive events.

Prospect theory has been found to have broad applicability across a number of areas encompassing group policy decision making (Allison, Worth, and King, 1990), including those resulting in "groupthink" (Janis, 1972; Whyte, 1989); the impact of decision makers' general risk-taking propensity on decision framing (Qualls and Puto, 1989; Fagley and Miller, 1990); and the presence of decision bias in depressed subjects and stressful situations (Olszanski and Lewicka, 1988; Schaeffer, 1989). As in the case of the prescriptive theories, some research is supportive (e.g., Elliott and Archibald, 1989; Carlson, 1990), while other sources fail to confirm the predictions of the theory (Peterson and Lawson, 1989; Leon, 1989).

A synthesis of the many individual difference-based variables suggested by prescriptive and descriptive risky decision theories is imperative. Howell and Burnett (1978), in their development of a cognitive taxonomy of uncertainty measurement, suggested that neither statistical or heuristics notions were applicable to decision-making situations, depending upon the situation described. Even a composite of decision maker variables, however, can only account for a portion of the variance evident in risky decision-making behavior. This is a function of some crucial conceptual considerations that bear discussion immediately below.

C. The Decision-Making Situation

1. Preamble

Here, then, the discussion shifts to considering a number of aspects of the decision-making situation. Specific emphases include discussions of:

- Dimensions of decision alternatives and outcomes
- The group decision-making context
- Organizational and strategic dimensions

Much of the decision-making and risk-taking literature shares a common characteristic, one that provides reason for concern. The notions of risk, risk taking, and rational versus nonrational behavior are often discussed in isolation, without reference to the context in which they occur. This omission is understandable, given the enormous complexity that inclusion of the decision situation frequently generates. Unless, however, the value of outcomes and their consequences can be stated in *absolute* terms, the *operational* meaning of the above concepts in the absence of their setting must be called into question. MacCrimmon and Wehrung (1986), Baird and Thomas (1985), Weber (1986), and others have emphasized the importance of the context of decision making. The former have measured risk taking across a wide range of situations and noted the impact that setting has upon behavior.

This fundamental point can be carried an important step further. The level of risk and characterization of "rational" behavior can only be determined in the context of the situation in which they occur. It might be rational for a decision maker in a resource-rich multinational firm to select an alternative with a potentially high return, but also with a small but potentially disastrous downside. The same decision maker might be characterized as highly speculative were she or he to make the identical choice after the organization had undergone serious financial reverses.

The criticality of setting or situation can then be neglected only at great cost. Prescriptive theories implicitly assume that decision makers take such considerations into account in their deliberations. Descriptive approaches such as prospect theory suggest that individual biases overwhelm other factors. It is clear, however, that what is foolhardy in one setting can be embarrassingly conservative in another. Decision-making behavior that will yield a satisficing, if not an optimizing, result for an organization can only be determined given the organizational (and personal) situation in which the consequences of the decision will rebound. (See Figure 3.)

The literature discusses a variety of situational factors. Some authors describe contextual variables on a micro level (see, e.g., Weber, 1986), while at the opposite extreme, Baird and Thomas (1985) include industry, organization, and strategic variables in their research. Combining a number of levels of description, for example, Downey and Slocum (1975) suggest a taxonomy including perceived environmental characteristics, individual differences in cognitive processes, individual behavioral response repertoires, and societal expectations for the perception of uncertainty. Howell and Burnett (1978) include in situational factors whether the probabilities are frequency-based or nonfrequency-based, whether the situation is high or low in complexity and difficulty, and whether the decision is single- or multistage.

MacCrimmon and Wehrung (1986), in their monumental study of corporate decision makers, employ a series of questionnaires to tap a broad scope of situational dimensions. These include both naturally occurring risks and contrived experimental situations, personal and organizational payoffs that include both opportunities and threats, and both personal and business decisions.

2. Dimensions of Decision Alternatives and Outcomes

Proceeding from the micro to the macro in the examination of situational variables, the characteristics of the outcomes available to organizational decision makers will determine the risk implicit in their situation. The riskiness, or uncertainty, of a decision-making situation may be viewed in terms of the uncertainty contributed to the situation by each of its component dimensions. Increased situational risk should then be associated with a range of conditions, for example, increases in the number of decision alternatives and outcomes present, expansion in the range of values of decision outcomes, decreases in the value of the minimum or worst outcome, reductions in the number of iterations of the decision, and increasingly uniform probability distributions of decision outcomes. Situational risk increases with each of these changes in situational dimensions because they all represent an increase in uncertainty for situational dimensions (Weber, 1986).

a. Number of Decision Outcomes. A greater number of decision outcomes, for example, would be associated with increased risk in decision-making situations. Limitations would exist on the resources that could be devoted to the search for alternative choices, as would constraints that are imposed by bounded rationality. Given these, the likelihood of complete knowledge—that is, certainty—regarding a situation would diminish with an increasing number of decision alternatives (i.e., increasing situational complexity). By the earlier characterization of the risk concept, then, situational risk would increase with the number of decision alternatives available in that situation.

b. Probability Distribution of Decision Outcomes. Another situational dimension is related to the uniformity of distribution of decision outcome probabilities. The more nearly uniform the outcome probability distribution, the more risky would be the decision situation, since there would exist a reduced probability of only a single outcome occurring; that is, certainty (e.g., a probability distribution for four outcomes of 0.25, 0.25, 0.25, 0.25 describes a riskier situation than does one of 0.70, 0.10, 0.10, 0.10).

c.   Number of Decision Outcomes.   A third dimension related to the first two considers the number of decision outcomes. Situational risk would be related to the degree of knowledge available regarding a situation, knowledge aiding the decision maker in narrowing his alternative choices to a single one. By a rationale similar to that of the first situational dimension, then, an increased number of decision outcomes would also be associated with greater situational risk. In such (increased risk) situations, a decision maker would be less likely to possess complete certainty regarding alternatives containing the outcome than if the outcomes were fewer in number.

d.   Range of Decision Outcomes.   A fourth situational dimension encompasses the range of decision outcomes, or the difference between the least and most favorable outcomes that could occur in a situation. If certainty implies a knowledge of the decision situation *narrowing* the available choices to a single alternative, then *broadening* the range within which an action's outcomes may fall increases situational uncertainty. Specifically, a wider possible range of outcomes would make it less likely that complete knowledge or certainty of outcomes could be obtained. It is simply more difficult to characterize an action by a single (certain) outcome when the outcomes can take on a greater number of values (i.e., fall within a broader range).

e.   Minimum Value of Least Favorable Outcome.   A fifth critical dimension is the least favorable outcome result from a decision. The worse this outcome, the riskier would be the alternative associated with it, and therefore the decision situation. It should be noted that the consequences of this outcome occurring should be considered relative to the decision maker's resources, since for a given level of least favorable outcome, the lower the level of a decision maker's resources, the riskier the alternative containing that outcome and therefore the situation for the decision maker.

f.   Decision Repetitiveness.   A final dimension of the decision situation to be discussed here is the repetitiveness with which a decision is made. The literature suggests in general that unique decisions are difficult ones because of lack of knowledge available regarding the situation, or even of the inability to assign meaningful probabilities to outcomes if the usual frequency theory of probability is employed. A major consideration would then be that such statistical data as outcome means and variances have limited relevance to situations in which a decision occurs rarely. The riskiness, or uncertainty, of a decision-making situation must therefore be viewed in terms of the uncertainty contributed to the situation by each of its component dimensions.

3.   The Group Decision-Making Context

Here, the discussion turns briefly from one detailing aspects of decision outcomes to a broader context, group decision making, an arena that bears close attention. Research by Wallach and Kogan (1959; 1961), Kogan and Wallach (1967), Dion, Baron, and Miller (1970), and others examined what they termed the "risky-shift" phenomenon, in which groups purportedly made riskier decisions than did individuals.

Subsequent research using the Kogan and Wallach methodology, as well as alternative approaches, have lent support to the notion of risky shift, although conservative shifts have been observed as well. (See, for example, Belovicz and Finch, 1969; Taylor and Dunnette, 1974; Ziegler, 1977; Brockhaus, 1980; Cannetta, 1988; Whyte, 1989; and Hogg, Turner, and Davidson, 1990.) Such situational rootedness has proven suggestive. Some of the literature links shifts in risk to "groupthink" and to framing theory. A variant of risky shift, self-categorization theory, is also proposed. This theory uses "ingroups and outgroups" in formulating a number of predictions. For example, it is suggested that an ingroup confronted by a risky outgroup will shift toward caution; an ingroup confronted by a cautious outgroup will shift toward risk; and an ingroup confronted by both risky and cautious outgroups will converge on the mean of group members' original levels of risk (Hogg, Turner, and Davidson, 1990).

A number of questions have, however, arisen about the single measure of risk used in many of these studies—the choice dilemma questionnaire (CDQ), which measures a decision maker's risk preference by asking her or him to counsel hypothetical subjects in their choice of a risky alternative. The CDQ requests discrete, probability-based responses, but Balovicz and Finch (1969) suggest that continuous responses be permitted, and that its serious limitations restrict severely the use of the CDQ as an accurate measure of risk. Cartwright (1971) also criticizes the instrument as deficient in information, particularly about the utilities of alternative outcomes. The CDQ has its defenders, however.

MacKenzie (1971), in proposing that the CDQ is an inadequate measure of risk, suggests alternative measures that would simplify the experimental task to assure greater comparability of the questions asked of subjects. It should be noted that many of the sources (e.g., Cartwright, 1971; Vinocur, 1971) recommend that Wallach and Kogan's work and instrument could be neatly fitted into the prescriptive utility-based risky decision theories previously described.

4. Organizational and Strategic Dimensions

In a predominantly macro treatment of situational variables related to risk taking, Baird and Thomas's (1985) comprehensive example of a taxonomy of risk-taking factors, the authors present "A model of strategic risk taking incorporating environmental, industrial, organizational, decision maker, and problem variables" (p. 230). In "studying the risk-taking propensities of the decision makers as they interact with particular decision situations" (p. 231), they provide a compendium of variables under the five classifications listed above. These include risk taking as a function of:

- The external environment, encompassing the economy, governmental regulation, technological change, and the social value of risk taking
- Industry variables, with emphasis on the ratio of public to private sector firms, number of competitors, competitive rivalry, number of suppliers and customers, capital intensity, vertical integration, capacity utilization rate, mobility barriers, and life cycle
- Organizational variables, including life cycle/age, size in terms of sales or assets, financial strength, profitability/return measures, organizational slack, planning, incentive pay, divisionalized structure, market structure, aggressive goals, group decision making, and unionization.
- Strategic problems, incorporating complexity, ambiguity, rate of change of problem elements, importance of benefits, ruinous losses, reversibility, controllability, remote losses, probability of loss, and framing
- Decision maker characteristics, encompassing age, self-confidence, experience/knowledge, and preferences/biases/heuristics

The critical task is then to identify which of these and other potentially important contextual variables interact with the last of these dimensions, decision maker characteristics, to generate organizationally based risky decisions and strategies.

IV. THE INTERFACE AMONG DECISION MAKER, SITUATION, AND STRATEGY

A. Introduction

We have discussed in some detail both the characteristics of the decision maker and the dimensions of the risk situation. We have suggested that, subject to his or her personal attributes, including risk preference or orientation, the decision maker will, in the context of a decision situation, choose a decision strategy. The final step in the examination of risk taking in organizations, therefore, requires scrutiny of a few additional factors. We must first examine decision strategy and choice, or actual risk taking and other related behaviors. After a more detailed analysis of the concept of risk orientation or perference, we can then acquire some insight into the *actual nature* of the decision maker—situation interaction that results in the final organizational strategy and decision. A proposed mechanism for this mechanism will be suggested (Figure 3).

B.   Decision Strategy and Choice

Decision strategies may be characterized as rules for making decisions, specifying alternative actions in a decision-making situation. It is proposed, then, that a decision maker would examine a decision situation and assess its riskiness along several of the dimensions noted earlier. She or he would then select a strategy for use in the specific situation depending upon her risk preference or orientation, a concept that will be examined further shortly. The strategy applied to the situation would then vary with the riskiness of the situation encountered. Specifically, the risk attached to the application of a specific strategy in a given situation would be characterized as the uncertainty regarding the outcomes resulting from employment of the decision rule. As the riskiness of a decision situation increased, the decision maker would then adjust his decision strategy so as to hold the riskiness of the decision invariant.

A number of potential decision strategies would be available for use in a decision situation. These might include:

- Minimax loss (minimize the maximum potential loss)
- Equivalently, maximin gain (maximize the minimum potential gain)
- Minimax regret (minimize the maximum difference between the largest potential gain and the gain realized under the strategy employed)
- Minimize the probability of *any* loss
- Maximize the probability of *any* gain
- Maximax gain (maximize the maximum potential gain)

It is important to note here that decision strategies, and the specific alternatives chosen by decision makers as a result of their application, have a specific level of risk associated with them, as do each of the dimensions of the risk situation (and therefore the overall situation) to which the decision strategy is applied to generate the final alternative chosen. The riskiness incurred in making a decision would then be a function of both the decision strategy (and final decision) selected by the decision maker and the risky decision situation to which it is applied.

C.   Decision Strategy and Context

The preference of an organizational decision maker for a specific level of risk taking would then have a direct effect on his or her decision strategy. As a decision situation became more risky, therefore, he would adopt successively more conservative decision strategies in that context, the result of which would be progressively less risky decisions. The less risky decision making in the more risky situation would be necessary in order to hold the overall decision risk constant at the decision maker's predetermined level of preferred risk. For example, a decision maker applying a given decision strategy in a setting in which any potential loss were small relative to the resources available to him would find the same strategy inappropriate were the potential loss to increase well beyond his resources (i.e., were the decision situation to become more risky).

Since the situation is now riskier, the *same* strategy would lead to a higher level of loss. The decision maker would then be expected to adopt a new, more conservative strategy that is more protective of her assets in the changed decision situation, thereby restoring her original level of decision risk. As any other situational dimension varies with respect to risk, decision strategy would also be expected to change in a direction counter to that of the situation in order to hold the overall level of decision risk constant.

D.   Risk Orientation/Preference/Propensity

It has been suggested that a decision maker will strive to hold constant the level of decision risk in a decision situation/strategy association. This concept of constancy, and the *level* at which overall decision risk would be held constant, however, requires further examination, because these notions have become quite contentious ones, and both conceptual discussion and empirical support have been inconclusive. MacCrimmon and Wehrung (1986) have, for example, suggested that most research has failed to find a general risk-taking propensity across risk-taking measures and situations (see, e.g., Slovic, 1964; 1972; Kogan and Wallach, 1964; Alderfer and Bierman, 1970). They do report support for a concept of risk propensity for decision makers, with greater consistency across situations for risk averters than for risk takers. Jackson and Dutton (1988), however, identified a generalized willingness to take risks; and Weber (1987) found some commonality of risk preferences across differentially risky situations.

Some of the uncertainty regarding the constancy of risk preference is related to such difficulties of determining the preference of decision makers for risk taking as the multiplicity of measures for the construct. Risk-taking metrics include qualitative judgments of danger and supervisory assessments of the ability of subordinates to deal with "dicey situations," as well as abstract responses to experimental lottery scenarios.

It is suggested, then, that a decision maker possesses a generalized risk orientation or preference for a specific level of risk in his decision making. An individual's risk preference would then lead him to select a decision strategy of appropriate riskiness in a given situation. Such an association would result in a decision with an overall risk level determined by the decision maker's risk orientation or preference.

The value of risk orientation or propensity would describe a continuum from extreme aversion toward risk to extreme favorability with respect to risk. A conservative or risk-averse orientation would thus be associated with a tendency to select a specific decision strategy yielding a conservative or low level of risk in a particular situation. Note an important *caveat*, however. As suggested by the literature, risk orientation *may* vary by setting; and an individual who is risk averse in one context may therefore be risk taking in another.

E. The Nexus Among Risk Orientation, Situation, and Strategy

It is useful, then, to describe the suggested interaction between a decision maker's risk orientation and risk-taking behavior, or strategy, in the context of the decision-making situation in which he finds himself. If the decision maker favored a conservative risk-averse orientation in a given context, the decision strategy chosen would result in a conservative decision alternative; that is, one with a low potential for uncertainty or for loss (or minimum gain) in exchange for securing the gains offered by the alternative. If the *benefit* or gain available from a decision were to be virtually assured (consistent with risk aversion), an individual of conservative risk propensity would attempt to assure a low risk (or risk only a *low* cost) in order to obtain that benefit. In order to secure the gain or benefit, the decision maker must select from the available alternatives the one that offers no more than the desired risk specified by his or her risk orientation. An appropriate strategy would then be applied by the decision maker in order to choose from among the alternatives the one whose risk matches the minimum level acceptable to the decision maker (of conservative risk orientation, in this instance).

If an individual were less conservative in risk orientation, the level of risk he or she would be willing to incur in a decision situation would rise. The decision strategy he or she then employed in a decision situation of specified risk would also vary in a correspondingly less risk-averse direction. He or she might supplant a minimax loss strategy with a riskier one maximizing expected value; or, were the decision maker to become still less risk averse in risk orientation, replace the latter strategy with a maximax gain strategy. In each of these three instances, the application of increasingly risky strategies to a decision situation of fixed risk would result in decisions of increasingly higher risk levels consistent with correspondingly less conservative (or more risky) risk orientations on the part of the decision maker.

It should be *emphasized* that all of these decision-making activities occur within the context of a decision situation characterized by the level of risk perceived by decision makers. The dimensions of decision situations (e.g., Baird and Thomas, 1985), as well as decision behavior/

strategy, might also be ordered with respect to their riskiness for any decision maker. It is then the *combination* of risk orientation and behavior, as conditioned by an individual's risk orientation, that would describe the risk level of any given decision. As the riskiness of the situation changes in one direction, the riskiness of the most attractive strategy would vary in the opposite direction in order to preserve what is essentially a homeostatic equilibrium. The *final* equilibrium level for risk would then be specified by the risk orientation of the decision maker.

The compensatory interaction between risk situation and risk strategy/choice is reminiscent of the controversial "zero-risk theory" proposed by traffic safety researchers (e.g., Summala, 1988). It suggests that as transportation systems evolve to provide safer or less risky driving conditions, drivers adapt to the reduced risks of the road by driving both more rapidly and engaging in generally more hazardous driving behavior.

F. Buffering Activities

There is yet another important class of decision-making behavior in addition to determining strategies or choosing alternative actions that should also be described. These behaviors can best be characterized as "buffering" activities whose objective is to reduce the uncertainty faced by decision makers in organizational settings. One apparent means of diminishing uncertainty regarding a situation is securing additional information about that setting (Baird and Thomas, 1985; MacCrimmon and Wehrung, 1986). Another, termed "risk adjustment" by Wehrung et al. (1986; 1989), includes bargaining, spending additional resources, developing new options, and consulting supervisors.

Buffering activities can cover a very broad range. One variant of this approach might be to engage in risk communication with other stakeholders in the risky situation. This tactic has been widely employed in circumstances surrounding the siting of hazardous facilities and the development of potentially unsafe technology (Rayner, 1988; Kasperson, Penn, and Slovic, 1988; Weterings and Van Eijndhoven, 1989). One function of that interaction would be to secure information regarding reactions (e.g., from clients, public agencies, and interest groups or from other stakeholders that form an important part of an organization's decision-making environment). Another might be to influence those publics regarding future organizational decisions and thereby actually modify the decision environment in a less risky direction.

The use of insurance is another of many possible ways to reduce the risk present in a decision situation. Its reliance employment implies some degree of risk aversion on the part of the insured, since the insurer also attempts to secure a profit from the transaction. The net result of the transaction, however, is to reduce the risk encountered by the insured in exchange for the premium expended by decision makers or their organizations.

V. TOWARD A RISKY FUTURE

The extensive literature examining risk taking encompasses a great deal of information, but raises a correspondingly *greater* number of questions. A fundamental concern is the identification of a unified definition of risk, and creation of appropriate measures of the construct. Without these initial steps, both conceptual and empirical progress in the area will be severely limited.

Similarly, the cluster of individual difference variables that influence the decision maker must also be distinguished, and its impact on decision makers' risk preference or orientation must be determined. Of special concern here is the concept of risk preference or orientation. As suggested in an earlier discussion, the dilemma of whether this variable is constant over a range of conditions, or is even a meaningful personal construct, is unresolved. Some sources have associated the constancy of risk preference with the notion of optimal arousal, suggesting that risk taking represents a form of sensation seeking (Wehrung, 1986). They contend that decision makers at their "optimal" level of risk will resist *any* change in the status quo, modifying risk behavior in order to maintain an overall constancy. Counter to this view and the previously cited risk-homeostatic driving and smoking literature (e.g., Peltzman, 1975; Lee, 1979; Wilde, 1982) are those scholars who seriously question the validity of risk preference (e.g., Schoemaker, 1990). Once again, then, the existence of risk preference or orientation must be examined, and if verified, careful measures of the riskiness of decision maker predispositions must be developed. A number of researchers agree, however, that both the difficulty of isolating a universal risk preference effect and a necessarily crucial correlate are related to decision situation or context (e.g., Schoemaker, 1990; Sitkin and Pablo, 1992).

The taking of risk must then be explored in the context of the situation in which it occurs. The *definition* of risk requires an examination of context. Many sources contend that the very *existence* of risk requires the potential to suffer loss (e.g., MacCrimmon and Wehrung, 1986). If this tenet is accepted, then, for example, the notion of risk for a decision maker operating with benefit of a "cost-plus" arrangement or under conditions of guaranteed return on investment is meaningless.

In such circumstances, the divisive concept of risk preference is no longer contentious because a decision maker cannot be risk averse or risk favorable in the *absence* of risk. Carrying this same line of reasoning still further, the very significance of decision strategy or risk behavior without the specification of a situational context may be called into question. Can situational conditions be specified, for instance, under which the strategy of "minimizing the likelihood of a maximum loss occurring" loses the connotation of a risk-averse or conservative decision-making strategy?

The premises underlying the earlier discussion of rational-prescriptive versus descriptive orientations are then also open to question. The rational school of thought is vulnerable in view of the immediately foregoing comments. By parallel reasoning, such constructions of descriptive theory as heuristics may also be susceptible to challenge.

It might be suggested, for example, that rather than representing "universals," heuristics are also strongly situationally dependent. The application by a decision maker of the availability heuristic, for instance, is a function of the relative ease with which different events can be retrieved from memory and the comparative effectiveness of searching for such events. Situational effects might have a significant impact on event search and retrieval. The *density* of activity in different time periods could substantially influence the search and retrieval effectiveness for events that occur in differing intervals. Occurrences in periods of high activity might then be discriminated against in favor of those embedded in lower density intervals.

In view, then, of the central role of decision context or situation, it is evident that it should serve a pivotal function in future research. The unresolved role of risk preference in decision making, for example, relates to its stability, or at least predictability, across decision situations. It is clear that the decision-making situation *literally* forms the context in which decision makers determine final decisions and their level of riskiness.

An essential first step in clarifying the relationships among decision maker, decision situation, and decision riskiness is the identification of major dimensions, or classes of variables, that constitute the decision situation or context. Given the number and complexity of potential dimensions, the effort required to construct this taxonomy is prodigious but indispensable. It requires not only the description of the major dimensions of risk context, but also an ordering of their relative riskiness from the point of view of the decision maker.

Once this contextual taxonomy is in place, a number of other vital concerns can be addressed. The stability and predictability of risk preference across contextual dimensions could now be methodically examined. Schoemaker (1990), for example, in an elegant presentation, posits an inverse relationship between the relevance of risk preference and task or environmental complexity. Indeed, the effect of situation and other independent variables on the formation of risk preference or propensity would also be subject to systematic scrutiny (Weber, 1986; Sitkin and Pablo, 1992). Validated measures of risk preference would also have to be developed.

The contextual boundary conditions of rationality in decision making could also be better described within a systematic situational framework, as previously suggested. By way of illustration, Schoemaker (1990) notes that under certain conditions descriptive heuristics can closely approximate rationally oriented expected utility theory. The result of this endeavor, then, should be an enhanced understanding of the relative significance of prescriptive and descriptive theories, or more likely a synthesis of the two, in the understanding and prediction of risk-taking behavior.

Further examination of decision-making strategies and behavior would also be essential within the framework of situational context. Measures of the relative riskiness of decision-making strategies and other salient risk-taking behaviors, including risk-buffering activities, would permit exploration of the interaction of this outcome variable with those related to the decision maker and the decision-making situation.

Even a primitive knowledge of the identities, useful operational measures, and functional relationships among these three categories of variables would represent a significant advance in the state of knowledge of risk taking in organizations. The effort required to acquire even an incomplete answer to these questions will be considerable, but the benefits attainable from such information would be well worth the effort expended.

ACKNOWLEDGMENTS

I would like to acknowledge the important contributions of Robert T. Golembiewski, University of Georgia; Amy Pablo, University of Calgary; and Dov Zohar, Technion, toward completion of this chapter.

REFERENCES

Alderfer, C. P., and Bierman, H. Jr. (1970). Choices with risk: Beyond the mean and variance. *J. of Business*, *43*: 341–353.
Allison, Scott T., Worth, L. T., and King, M. C. (1990). Group decisions as social inference statistics. *J. of Personality and Social Psychology*, *58*(5): 801–811.
Baird, I. S., and Thomas, H. (1985). Toward a contingency model of strategic risk taking. *Academy of Management Review*, *10*: 230–243.
Bartol, Kathryn M. (1976). Expectancy theory as a predictor of female occupational characteristics and attitudes toward business. *Academy of Management Journal*, *19*: 669–675.
Bastide, Sophie, Moatti, Jean-Paul, and Pages, Jean-Pierre (1989). Risk perception and social acceptability of technologies. *Risk Analysis*, *9*(2): 215–223.
Becker, Gordon A., and McClintock, Charles G. (1967). Value: Behavioral decision theory. *Annual Review of Psychology*, *18*: 239–286.
Belovicz, Meyer W., and Finch, Frederick E. (1969). A critical analysis of the "risky shift" phenomenon, unpublished paper, University of Massachusetts, Amherst.
Blume, M. E., and Friend, I. (1978). *The Changing Role of the Individual Investor*. Wiley, New York.
Brehmer, Berndt, and Kuylenstierna, Jan (1978). Task information and performance in probabilistic inference tasks. *Organizational Behavior and Human Performance*, *22*: 445–464.
Brockhaus, R. H. (1980). Risk taking propensity of entrepreneurs. *Academy of Management Journal*, *23*: 509–520.
Budescu, David V., and Wallsten, James H. (1990). Dyadic decisions with numerical and verbal probabilities. *Organization Behavior and Human Decision Processes*, *46*(2): 240–263.
Campbell, John P., Dunette, Marvin D., Lawler, Edward E. III, and Weick, Karl E. (1970). *Managerial Behavior, Performance and Effectiveness*. McGraw-Hill, New York.
Cannetta, Aefano. (1988). Group atmosphere and collection decision. *Ricerched: Psicologis*, *12*(3–4): 159–170.
Carlson, Bruce W. (1990). Anchoring and adjustment in judgments under risk. *J. of Experimental Psychology, Learning, Memory and Cognition*, *16*(4): 665–676.
Cartwright, Dorwin (1971). Risk-taking by individuals and groups: An assessment of research employing choice dilemmas. *J. of Personality and Social Psychology*, *20*(3): 361.
Christensen-Szalanski, Jay J. J. (1983). Effects of expertise and experience on risk judgments. *J. of Applied Psychology*, *68*: 278–284.
Cohn, R. A., Lewellen, W. G., Lease, R. C., and Schlarbaum, G. G. (1975). Individual investor risk aversion and investment portfolio composition. *J. of Finance*, *30*: 605–620.

Coombs, C. H., and Bowen, J. N. (1971). A test of VE—Theories of risk and the effect of the central limit theories. *Acta Psychologica*, *35*: 15–28.

Coombs, C. H., and Huang, L. C. (1968). A portfolio theory of risk preference. *Michigan Mathematical Psychological Progress Technical Report 68-5*, University of Michigan, Ann Arbor.

Coombs, C. H., and Komorita, S. S. (1958). Measuring utility of money through decisions. *American Journal of Psychology*, *71*: 383–389.

Davidson, D., Suppes, and Siegel, S. (1957). *Decision-making: An Experimental Approach*. Stanford University Press, Stanford, Calif.

DeRivera, Daniel Pena Sanchez (1980). A decision analysis model for serious medical problem. *Management Science*, *26*: 707–718.

Dion, K. L., Baron, R. S., and Miller, N. (1970). Why do groups make riskier decisions than individuals? In *Current Advances in Experimental Social Psychology*, vol. 5, (L. Berkowitz, ed.), Academic Press, New York.

Downey, H. Kirk, and Slocum, John W. (1975). Uncertainty: Measures, research and sources of variation. *Academy of Management Journal*, *18*: 562–578.

Edwards, Ward (1953). Probability-preferences in gambling. *American Journal of Psychology*, *66*: 349–364.

Edwards, Ward (1954). The theory of decision-making. *Psychological Bulletin*, *51*: 389–407.

Edwards, Ward (1955). The prediction of decisions among bets. *J. of Experimental Psychology*, *50*: 201–214.

Edwards, Ward (1961). Behavioral decision theory. *Annual Review of Psychology*, *12*: 473–498.

Edwards, Ward, Lindman, H. L., and Philips, L. (1965). Emerging technologies for making decisions. In *New Directions in Psychology*, vol. 2 (T. M. Newcomb, ed.), pp. 259–325.

Elliot, Catherine S., and Archibald, Robert B. (1989). Subjective framing and attitudes toward risk. *J. of Economic Psychology*, *10*(3): 324–328.

Evans, L. (1986). Risk homeostasis theory and traffic accident data. *Risk Analysis*, *8*(1): 81–107.

Fagley, N. S., and Miller, Paul M. (1990). The effect of framing on choice, personality and social. *Psychology Bulletin*, *16*(3): 496–510.

Fama, E. F. (1975). *Foundations of Finance*. Basic Books, New York.

Galbraith, J., and Cummings, L. L. (1967). An empirical investigation of the motivational determinants of task performance. *Organizational Behavior and Human Performance*, *2*: 237–257.

Georgopoulous, B. S., Mahoney, G. M., and Jones, N. W. Jr. (1957). A path goal approach to productivity. *J. of Applied Psychology*, *4*: 345–353.

Hackman, J. R., and Porter, L. W. (1968). Expectancy theory predictions of work effectiveness. *Organizational Behavior and Human Performance*, *3*: 417–426.

Hammond, J. D., Houston, D. B., and Melander, E. R. (1967). Determinants of household life insurance premium expenditures: An empirical investigation. *J. of Risk and Insurance*, *34*: 397–408.

Heneman, H. G. III, and Schwab, Donald F. (1972). Evaluation of research on expectancy theory predictions of employee performance. *Psychological Bulletin*, *18*: 1–9.

Hertz, D. B. (1964). Risk analysis in capital investment. *Harvard Business Review*, *4*: 95–106.

Hogg, Michael A., Turner, John C., and Davidson, Barbara (1990). Polarized norms and social frames of preferences. *Basic and Applied Social Psychology*, *11*(1): 77–100.

Howell, William C., and Burnett, Sarah A. (1978). Uncertainty measurement: A cognitive taxonomy. *Organizational Behavior and Human Performance*, *22*: 45–68.

Hutchison, S. L. Jr., and Clemens, F. W. (1980). Advisement to take risk: The elderly's view. *Psychological Reports*, *47*: 426.

Irwin, R. (1953). Stated expectations as functions of probability and desirability of outcomes. *J. of Personality*, *21*: 329–335.

Jackson, S. E., and Dutton, J. E. (1988). Discerning threats of opportunities. *Administrative Science Quarterly*, *33*: 370–387.

Janis, I. L. (1972). *Victims of Groupthink: A Psychological Study of Foreign-Policy Decisions and Fiascos*. Houghton-Mifflin, New York.

Kahneman, D., and Tversky, A. (1974). Judgments under uncertainty. *Science*, *185*: 1124–1131.

Kahneman, D., and Tversky, A. (1982). The psychology of preferences. *Scientific American*, *246*: 160–173.

Kahneman, D., Slovic, P., and Tversky, A. (1982). *Judgments Under Uncertainty: Heuristics and Biases*. Cambridge University Press, London.

Kameda, Tatsuya, and Davis, James H. (1990). The function of the reference point in individual and group risk decision-making. *Organizational Behavior and Human Decision Processors*, *46*(2): 55–76.

Karmarkar, Uday S. (1978). Subjectively weighted utility: A descriptive extension of the expected utility model. *Organizational Behavior and Human Performance, 21*: 61–72.

Kasperson, Roger E., Renn, Orthwin, and Slovic, Paul (1988). The social amplification of risk: A conceptual framework. *Risk Analysis, 8*(2): 201–204.

Kennedy, Charles W., Fossum, John A., and White, Bernard J. (1983). An empirical comparison of within-subjects and between subjects expectancy theory models. *Organizational Behavior and Human Performance, 32*: 124–143.

Kogan, Mathew, and Wallach, M. A. (1967). Risk-taking as a function of the situation, the person and the group. In *New Directions in Psychology III* (G. Mandler, P. Mussen, N. Kogan, and M. Wallach, eds.), Holt, New York.

Kogan, N., and Wallach, M. A. (1964). *Risk-taking: A Study of Cognition and Personality.* Holt, Rinehart and Winston, New York.

Larson, James R. Jr. (1980). Exploring the external validity of a subjectively weighted utility model of decision-making. *Organizational Behavior and Human Performance, 26*: 293–304.

Laughunn, Dan J., Payne, John W., and Crum, Roy (1980). Managerial risk preferences for below-target returns. *Management Sciences, 26*: 1238–1249.

Lawler, E. E. (1965). Ability as a moderator of the relationship between job attitudes and job performance. *Personnel Psychology, 19*: 153–164.

Lawler, E. E. (1968). A correlational-causal analysis of the relationship between expectancy attitudes and job performance. *J. of Applied Psychology, 52*: 462–468.

Lee, R. N. (1979). Has the mortality of male doctors improved with the reduction in their cigarette smoking? *British Medical Journal, 2*: 1538–1540.

Leon, O. G. (1989). Influences of feedback on certainty effect. *Revista de Psicologia Generity Aplicada, 42*(4): 449–454.

Liddell, William W., and Solomon, Robert J. (1977a). A total and stochastic test of the transitivity postulate underlying expectancy theory. *Organizational Psychology and Human Performance, 19*: 311–324.

Liddell, William W., and Solomon, Robert J. (1977b). A test of two postulates underlying expectancy theory. *Academy of Management Journal, 20*: 460–464.

Loewenstein, George, and Mathew, Jane (1990). Dynamic processes in risk perception. *J. of Risk and Uncertainty, 3*: 155–175.

Lopes, L. (1987). Between hope and fear: The psychology of risk. In *Advances in Experimental Social Psychology*, vol. 20 (L. Berkowitz, ed.), Academic Press, San Diego, p. 255.

Mackenzie, Kenneth D. (1971). An analysis of risky shift experiments. *Organizational Behavior and Human Performance, 6*: 283–303.

Magee, J. F. (1964). Decision trees for decision making. *Harvard Business Review, 42*: 126–138.

March, James G., and Shapiro, Zur (1987). Managerial perspectives on risk and risk-taking. *Management Science, 33*: 1404–1418.

March, James G., and Shapiro, Zur (1990). Variable risk preferences and the focus of attention. *Psychological Review, 99*(1): 172–183.

March, James G., and Shapiro, Zur (1992). Variable risk preferences and the focus of attention. *Psychological Review*, in press.

Markowitz, H. M. (1959). *Portfolio Selection, Efficient Diversification of Investments.* Wiley, New York.

Marks, R. (1951). The effect of probability, desirability and "privilege" on the stated expectations of children. *J. of Personality, 19*: 332–351.

McInish, T. H. (1982). Individual investors and risk-taking. *J. of Economic Psychology, 2*: 125–136.

Montgomery, Henry, and Adelbratt, Thomas (1982). Gambling decisions and information about expectancy valence. *Organizational Behavior and Human Performance, 29*: 39–57.

Mosteller, Frederick, and Nogee, Philip (1951). An experimental measurement of utility. *J. of Political Economy, 59*: 371–404.

Muldrow, Tressie W., and Bayton, James A. (1979). Men and women executives and processes related to decision accuracy. *J. of Applied Psychology, 64*: 99–106.

Olszanski, Robert, and Lewika, Maria (1988). Risk preference for going and losses in depressed and non-depressed subjects. *Polish Psychological Bulletin, 19*(1): 77–89.

Peltzman, S. (1975). The effects of automobile safety regulation. *J. of Political Economy, 83*: 677–725.

Peterson, Steven A., and Lawson, Robert (1989). Risky business: Prospect theory and politics. *Political Psychology, 10*(2): 325–339.

Pollatsek, A., and Tversky, A. (1970). A theory of risk. *J. of Mathematical Psychology, 7*: 572–596.

Pritchard, R. D., and DeLeo, D. J. (1973). Experimental test of the valence-instrumentality relationship on job performance. *J. of Applied Psychology*, *57*: 264–270.

Qualls, William J., and Puts, Christopher P. (1989). Organizational climate and decision framing. *J. of Marketing Research*, *262*: 179–192.

Rapoport, A., and Wallsten, T. S. (1972). Individual decision-behavior. *Annual Review of Psychology*, *23*: 131–175.

Rayner, Steve (1988). Muddling through metaphors to maturity: The social amplification of risk. *Risk Analysis*, *8*(2): 201–204.

Schaeffer, Monica H. (1989). Environmental stress and individual decision-making. *Patient Education and Counselling*, *13*(3): 221–235.

Schneider, Sandra L., and Lopes, Lola L. (1986). Refection in preferences under risk: Who and when may suggest why. *J. of Experimental Psychology*, *12*(2): 535–548.

Schoemaker, Paul J. H. (1979). The role of statistical knowledge in gambling decisions: Moment versus risk dimension approaches. *Organizational Behavior and Human Performance*, *24*: 1–17.

Schoemaker, Paul J. H. (1990). Determinants of risk-taking, unpublished paper.

Sciortino, John J., Hourton, John H., and Spencer, Roger W. (1988). Risk and income distribution. *J. of Economic Psychology*, *9*(3): 399–408.

Sharpe, William R. (1964). Capital asset prices: A theory of market equilibrium under conditions of risk. *J. of Finance*, *19*: 425–442.

Simon, Herbert A. (1956). Rational choice and the structure of the environment. *Psychological Review*, *63*(2): 129–138.

Simon, Herbert A. (1957). *Administrative Review*, 2nd ed., Macmillan, New York.

Simon, Herbert A., and Newell, Alan (1970). Human problem-solving: The state of the theory in 1970. *American Psychologist*: 145–159.

Singh, J. (1986). Performance, slack and risk-taking in organizational decision-making. *Academy of Management*, *29*: 562–585.

Sitkin, Sim B., and Pablo, Amy L. (1992). Reconceptualizing the determinants of risk behavior. *Academy of Management*, *17*(1): 9–38.

Slovic, Paul (1964). Assessment of risk-taking behavior. *Psychological Bulletin*, *61*(3): 220–223.

Slovic, Paul (1972). From Shakespeare to Simon: Speculations and some evidence about man's ability to process information. *Oregon Research Institute Research Monograph*, *12*.

Stake, Frederick A., and Behling, Orlando (1975). A test of two postulates underlying expectancy theory. *Academy of Management Journal*, *18*: 703–714.

Summala, Heikki (1988). Risk control is not risk adjustment. *Ergonomics*, *31*(4): 491–506.

Svenson, Ola (1984). Process descriptions of decision-making. *Organizational Behavior and Human Performance*, *33*: 23–24.

Swalm, Ralph O. (1966). Utility theory—Insights into risk-taking. *Harvard Business Review*, *44*: 123–136.

Taylor, Ronald N., and Dunnette, Marvin D. (1974). Influence of dogmatism, risk-taking propensity and intelligence on decision-making strategies for a sample of industrial managers. *J. of Applied Psychology*, *59*: 420–423.

Tobin, J. (1965). The theory of portfolio selection. In *The Theory of Interest Rates* (Fitt, Hahn and R. R. F. Brechling, eds.), Macmillan, London.

Tversky, Amos (1967). Utility theory and additivity analysis of risky choices. *J. of Experimental Psychology*, *75*(1): 27–36.

Vinocur, A. (1971). Review and theoretical analysis of the effects of group processes upon individual and group decisions involving risk. *Psychological Bulletin*, *76*: 231–250.

Von Neumann, J., and Morgenstern, O. (1947). *Theory of Games and Economic Behavior*. Princeton University Press, Princeton, N.J.

Vroom, Victor (1964). *Work and Motivation*. Wiley, New York.

Vroom, Victor, and Pahl, B. (1971). Relationship between age and risk-taking among managers. *J. of Applied Psychology*, *55*: 339–405.

Wahba, Mohmoud A., and House, Robert J. (1972a). Expectancy theory in work and motivation: Some logical and methodological issues, unpublished paper, City College of New York, Baruch Center, New York.

Wahba, Mahmoud A., and House, Robert J. (1972b). Expectancy theory in managerial performance an motivation: An integrative model and empirical evidence, unpublished paper, City College of New York, Baruch Center, New York.

Wallach, M. A., and Kogan, N. (1961). Aspects of judgment and decision making: Interrelationships and changes with age. *Behavioral Science*, *6*: 23–26.

Wallsten, Thomas S., and Budescu, David V. (1983). Encoding subject probabilities A psychological and psychometric review. *Management Sciences*, *79*: 151–173.

Watts, H. W., and Tobin, J. (1967). Consumer expenditures and the capital account. In *Studies of Portfolio Behavior* (D. D. Hester and J. Tobin, eds.), Wiley, New York, pp. 1–39.

Weber, Elke V., Anderson, J., and Birnbaum, M. H. (1991). A theory of perceived risk and attractiveness. *Organizational Behavior and Human Decision Processes*, in press.

Weber, Elke V., and Bottom, William P. (1989). Axiomatic measures of perceived risk. *J. of Behavioral Decision-Making*, *2*: 113–131.

Weber, M. L. (1987). Risky decision-making: A conceptual model and empirical test, paper presented at the 7th International Symposium and Forecasting, Boston.

Wehrung, Donald A., Lee, K. H., Tse, D. K., and Vertinsky, I. B. (1989). Adjusting risky situations. *J. of Risk and Uncertainty*, *2*: 189–212.

Wetering, Rob A., and Van Eijndhoven, Jesse C. (1989). Informing the public about uncertain risks. *Risk Analysis*, *9*(4): 473–482.

Whyte, Glen (1989). Group think reconsidered. *Academy of Management Review*, *14*(1): 40–56.

Wilde, G. J. S. (1982). Incentive systems for accident-free and violation-free driving in the general population. *Ergonomics*, *25*(10): 879–890.

Wofford, J. C. (1971). The motivational basis of job satisfaction and job performance. *Personnel Psychology*, *24*: 501–519.

Ziegler, L. D. (1977). A study of differences in risk taking propensity between business and education students and practitioners, Ph.D. dissertation, University of Akron, Ohio.

9
Leadership Theory in Postmodernist Organizations

Karl W. Kuhnert

University of Georgia, Athens, Georgia

> The point is that the ways of nineteenth century thinking are becoming rapidly bankrupt . . . here I want to call attention to a condition of our time—that as the conventional ways of thinking about mind and life collapse, new ways of thinking are becoming available, not only to ivory tower philosophers but also to practitioners and the "man in the street."
>
> Gregory Bateson, *Mind and Nature*

Over the past five decades numerous authors have cast doubts on the legitimacy of organizational leadership research (Bennis, 1959; Kerr, 1977; Kerr and Jermier, 1978; Pfeffer, 1977). Researchers have been criticized for shoddy scientific approaches: lack of definitional focus, poor methodology, poor measurement, inappropriate assumptions, and reliance on outdated theories. Perhaps the most trenchant criticism has been toward researchers' almost total failure to link leadership theory with human resource practices (Russell and Kuhnert, 1992a). Although leadership is a permanently entrenched part of the socially constructed reality and we continue to have a "romance" with it (Meindl, Ehrlich, and Dukerich, 1985), the fact remains that at the level of theory, research, and method, the psychology of leadership suffers from a certain stuckness.

This chapter explores and attempts to relieve this stuckness. This is not another review of the myriad leadership studies published over the past decade (cf. reviews by House and Baetz, 1979; Van Fleet and Yukl, 1986), nor is it an examination of future organizational practice (e.g., Golembiewski and Kuhnert, in press). Rather, this chapter is an attempt to rise out of the morass and chart a direction for organizational leadership research that builds on past models, and at the same time, fosters an integrative understanding of leaders and the context in which they lead. Before such a course can be charted, however, it is important to look at the context in which any new theory of organizational leadership will be applied.

Many argue (e.g., Feyerabend, 1975; Mason and Mitroff, 1981) that we are in the midst of a paradigmatic struggle that is changing both the way that organizations are conceptualized and the manner in which they are structured. For example, there is a marked shift away from contingency approaches that view organizations as distinct units constrained and determined by the environment (Reed and Hughes, 1992) toward theories that define organizations as unique, interrelated cultures with complex symbolic dimensions as construed by their members (e.g., Turner, 1990). This change in thought has seen the corresponding fading of rationality and bureaucracy as predominant structures as well as the emergence of organizational forms that are based on diversity and that demand flexibility in their configuration. Fundamental to the success of these new organizations, leadership theories and practices must complement the emerging organizational forms.

This chapter explores new ways of looking at organizations as well as the implications of a postmodernistic view of organizations for leadership theory. In the first section, the concept of "postmodernism" is defined. In the second section, postmodernist organizations are contrasted with modernist organizations, and trends in the emergence of the former are identified. The third section offers a series of propositions for a leadership consistent with the characteristics of postmodern organizations, propositions intended to guide the future study of leadership. Finally, the implications of postmodernism for organizational theory and practice are discussed.

I. WHAT IS POSTMODERNISM?

Postmodernism (cf. Derrida, 1981; Habermas, 1984; Luhmann, 1976) is a cultural movement that has deep roots in art history and aesthetic theory (Featherstone, 1991). The term postmodernism means literally "that which comes after modernity," and is intended to communicate the inadequacy of the status quo as a way to deal with the future. While there is no agreement as to when postmodernism arrived, the concept can be traced to Focault (1980) and Lyotard (1984), and was expanded by Derrida (1981) and Baudrillard (1989). Postmodernism implies that new problems require new solutions—that the current questions cannot be answered through application of past methods. According to Clegg (1992), postmodernism responds to the fact that "there are now different phenomena to be analyzed, phenomena that are not simply a linear progression from the familiar past, but discontinuous with it" (p. 2).

Postmodernism has only recently begun to enter the literature of the social sciences (e.g., Boyne and Rattansi, 1990; Gergen, 1992) and organizations (Cooper and Burrell, 1988; Reed and Hughes, 1992). Unfortunately, a wide variety of confusing, contradictory, and discipline-specific interpretations can be attached to the terms modernist and postmodernist. For example, the term modernist is not synonymous with the word contemporary, but is used to characterize organizations of the past century from those of previous times. In this chapter the term modernist refers to a form of knowledge that is based on principles of rationalism, differentiation, and the "one-best" method. The term postmodernism, on the other hand, is closely allied with philosophical postmodernism inspired by Heidegger, Derrida, Wittgenstein, and other French thinkers. Their particular use of the term can be called deconstructive postmodernism because they deconstruct ingredients for a world view—for example, God, self, purpose, and meaning. The use of postmodernism in this chapter is constructive in that we seek to overcome the limitations of modernist organizations by constructing a postmodernist organization by reversing (revising) modernist principles of organization. Being postmodernist thus refers to a moving away from those principles of the modernist, and toward forms of knowledge based on nonrational, interrelatedness, and dedifferentiation.

The most thorough treatment of the impact of postmodernism on organizations, that of Clegg (1990), used its principles to understand the organizational forms and innovative management practices emerging throughout the world. In this work, Clegg challenges the entrenched rationalistic, deterministic, and bureaucratic view of organizations, and replaces it with the concept of a values-driven organization that is characterized by flexibility and fluidity and is based on principles of interaction and synthesis. The focus on Clegg is not to say that others have not made similar recommendations (cf. Argyris and Schön, 1978; Torbert, 1976). However, it is only recently that a confluence of events such as corporate restructuring, intense global competition, and a worldwide recession have required leaders to rethink organizational forms and processes.

II. MODERNIST VERSUS POSTMODERNIST ORGANIZATIONS

Just as there was an end to the preindustrial (premodern) period of organizations, there can be an end to the "modern" or industrial period. The modernist paradigm served organizations well when the primary focus was on making simple machines and manufacturing mass-produced goods, and it also made possible the technological explosion of which we are both beneficiaries and victims. There is a growing sense, however, that we should leave modernist organizations behind—that we can no longer afford to emphasize form over substance, structure over people, and power over working relationships. If organizations are to survive, producing something of value and meeting the needs of their workers, new structures and forms must emerge (Zaleznik, 1990).

Principles of modernist organizations can be traced to the seminal works of Max Weber, Emile Durkheim, and Fredrick Taylor, whose compelling organizational theories and acute understanding of industrialization framed 20th century understanding. While other modernists—for example, Chester Barnard (cf. Golembiewski and Kuhnert, 1992)—shared their outlook, these earlier observers contributed the basic principles that served to define and shape modernist organizations. Fundamental to the development of modernist organizations are the notions that: (1) there exists an "ideal" bureaucratic structure through which behavior in an organization can be controlled; (2) successful performance is based on simplified and efficient work; and (3) there is one best way to organize, plan, and perform work. It is argued here, however, that these principles must be replaced—in fact are being replaced—as the dominant organizational themes.

A. The Ideal Bureaucracy

Weber's contribution to modern organizational thought is the concept of a rationalized "ideal bureaucracy" (Bendix, 1962), in which strict procedures regulate behavior, facts and knowledge are the bases of decisions, authority is limited, and power is distributed according to position rather than social status and traditions. This model of organizational rationality has become the standard to which most private and public organizations aspire, if not emulate. Since Weber's time, the term *rational organization* has been used to describe functioning in which: (1) means-ends relationships are prescribed and processes result in certain outcomes, (2) efficiency is maximized, and (3) decision making follows facts and a certain and logical form (Zey-Ferrell, 1981).

As popular and successful as this concept of an ideal bureaucracy has been in the past, there is overwhelming evidence that neither organizations, nor their leaders and workers, can be rational (Simon, 1987; Kahneman, Slovic, and Tversky, 1982). As Zey (1992) points out

> people who make up organizations do not always act rationally in the interest of the dominant coalition or the collective unit. If they do choose to act in the interest of the collective good, they seldom have a consistent ordering of goals; they do not always pursue systematically the goals they do hold; there are inconsistencies of individual preferences and beliefs; they have incomplete information; they have an incomplete list of alternatives, they seldom conduct an exhaustive search of alternatives; and they do not always know the relationships between the organizational means and ends. Effective action in pursuit of goals is difficult and often impossible because of unexpected and uncertain events external to the organization (p. 25).

In postmodernist thinking a broader conceptualization of rationality is emerging; one that includes models of decision making based largely on the values, emotions, and preferences of individuals and only secondarily on the basis of logical-empirical considerations (Etzioni, 1988). Moreover, decision making is not an individualized event that takes place in isolation, nor are the designated "leaders" solely responsible for successful attainment of goals. Group norms, work structures, individual expectations, and informal leaders are recognized as having impacts on decisions made within organizations. Thus, postmodernist organizational thought uses a broader conceptualization of "bureaucracy" to allow for nonrational and nonauthoritative bases for decisions.

B. Division of Labor

Another major influence on modernist organizational theory is Emile Durkheim, who saw the division of labor as a fundamental principle of industrial organization. Division of labor essentially is the separation of work into its constituent elements, with each worker being assigned a limited range of tasks and responsibilities. What was so profound about the concept of division of labor and Durkheim's sociological analysis was not simply that the work should be differentiated, but that workers themselves would become specialized and isolated. Durkheim believed that, if taken to its extreme, division of labor would result in idealized bureaucracies—authoritative and hierarchical organizations—that would eventually lead to social dislocation and disorganization (Clegg and Dunkerley, 1980).

While division of labor contributed to the efficiency of individual jobs and raised the overall level of productivity in many industries, numerous organizational problems can be traced to the differentiation of work. These difficulties range from poor communications, confusing bases of authority, dispersed or abandoned responsibility, boredom, and poor employee morale (Child, 1984). To cope with differentiation, organizations have been forced to develop integrative mechanisms and procedures to ensure successful production and to enhance cooperation. Modernist organizations, however, must rely on management oversight, planning, and standardization as techniques for integration. These mechanisms work best only under conditions that are stable and predictable, and the added costs of such functions are substantial (Thompson, 1967).

The objective of the postmodern paradigm is to reverse the trend toward differentiation—to dedifferentiate, or structurally reunite organizations. Postmodernist organizations, for example, reject hierarchical bureaucratic design in favor of a more organic organizational design. Postmodernist organizations also look at the logical interrelatedness among jobs and tasks, assigning responsibility and demanding accountability on the basis of the "whole" rather than the parts of a job. Postmodern organizations also reward employees for flexibility and creativity in response to the rapidly changing environment in which they must operate.

C. The One-Best Way

Fredrick Taylor, the father of scientific management, left a substantial legacy to the structure of modern organizations. In his relatively short lifetime, Taylor introduced to organizations the concepts of the 40-hour week, time and motion studies, piece-rate compensation systems, as well as a "fair day's work for a fair day's pay." Although each of these has had a major influence on the structure of modern work, Taylor's notion that there is a "one-best way to organize" is the bedrock of all modern work designs (Braverman, 1974).

Taylor's axiom of one-best way subsumes the notion that organizational efficiency and productivity could be maximized by adopting scientific procedures such as observation, analysis, and control. He believed that there existed a single objective technique or method that best served the goals and needs of an organization. Through the application of scientific method, the single best approach to production, organization, and management could be identified and replicated in organizations (Wren, 1987).

Identification of the one-best way to organize and perform work requires scientific or analytic thinking. Analytic thinking is a three-step process whereby that which is to be understood is dissected or taken apart, each part is understood separately, and the parts are put back together in order to understand the whole.

Taylor's approach has real limitations. While analytic thinking reveals the structure of a system and results in understanding, it is not sufficient to *explain* why systems operate the way they do (Ackoff, 1991). Explanation requires a second type of thought—synthesis. According to Ackoff (1991), analytic and synthetic thinking are profoundly different

> Synthetic thinking, like analysis, involves three steps, but they are the reverse of those involved in analysis. In the first step of analysis, the thing to be understood is taken apart; in synthesis it is taken to be a part of a larger whole. The larger containing whole(s) is/are identified. In the second step of analysis the behavior of each part is explained separately; in the second step of synthesis the behavior of the containing whole is explained. In the last step of analysis, the understanding of the parts is aggregated in to an understanding of the whole; in synthesis, the understanding of the containing whole is disaggregated to explain the behavior of that part which is to be explained. The behavior and properties of that part are explained by revealing its role of function in the larger whole of which it is part (p. 91).

Postmodernist organizations seriously question the idea that there is a one-best way and that analysis is the way to get there. Leaders of postmodernist organizations champion the idea of diverse paths to achieve a desired state; and they realize that while analytic thinking is relevant to understanding, synthesis is required in order to understand why a system operates the way it does. While there is no example of a prototypical postmodernist organization, there are emerging management trends that illustrate postmodernist principles.

D. Trends Toward Postmodernist Organizations

Postmodernist organizations, in contrast to modernist organizations, tend to be less bureaucratic, more integrated, and more flexible in their structure. According to Clegg (1990)

> Where the modernist organization was rigid, postmodern organization is flexible. Where modernist consumption was premised on mass forms, postmodernist consumption is premised on niches. Where modernist organization was premised on technological determinism, postmodernist organization is premised on technological choices made possible through "de-dedicated" microelectronic equipment. Where modernist organization and jobs were highly differentiated, demarcated and de-skilled, postmodernist organizations and jobs are highly de-differentiated, demarcated and multi-skilled (p. 181).

Thus, the postmodern dedifferentiated organization not only suggests new forms of organization, but new ways to think about human resources and how they are managed. Table 1 shows in broad outline some of the differences in organizational practices between modernist and postmodernist organizations.

Perhaps the best example of the encroachment of postmodernist thought on current organization functioning is the proliferation of total quality management (Garvin, 1988). Total quality management (TQM) is a management philosophy based upon: (1) commitment to "continuous" improvement; (2) the analytical evaluation of work; (3) development of a "quality" culture; and (4) the empowerment of employees. Total quality management emphasizes a shift from vertical to horizontal structures, and rests on understanding of the total environment in which the organization competes, giving attention to understanding *interactions* among customers, competitors, suppliers, and regulators. From this perspective, quality is embedded within all the functions of the organization, rather than something external to be considered and evaluated at a later time. Both of these critical issues—attention to the environment and recognizing interconnections among people—have pointed to a new way of thinking about organizations and the management of performance in organizations. The TQM approach requires a form of organization and management that is far more flexible, empowering to workers, and more adaptable than the structures and processes designed to support modernist organizations. Thus, TQM reverses the modernist organization.

Another example of trends toward postmodern thinking comes out of Japan. The Japanese tend not to adopt the divisional model that is more common to large corporations in the U.S.; rather, their strategy is to develop *keiretsu* or a business group concept, that enables Japanese

Table 1 Organizational Practices of Modernist and Postmodernist Organizations

Modernist	Postmodernist
1. Mission goals, strategies, and main functions: specialization	Diffusion
2. Functional alignments: bureaucracy	Democracy
3. Coordination and control: disempowerment	Empowerment
4. Accountability: extraorganizational	Intraorganizational
5. Work-role relationships: structured	Unstructured
6. Planning: short-term strategies	Long-term strategies
7. Motivation: rewards and punishments	Commitment and trust
8. Quality improvement: externalized	Internalized
9. Relation of performance and reward: individualized	Team-based
10. Interpersonal relations: degenerative	Regenerative

Source: Adapted from Clegg (1990) and Golembiewski (1992).

companies to work out common business strategies in order to be competitive in the world market. Although criticized in this country for being a monopoly or quasi-trading block (Thurow, 1992), this strategy is effective and is postmodernist in its understanding of interactions and flexibility in organization.

III. A POSTMODERN LEADERSHIP THEORY

Under modernist organizations, the study of leadership was focused primarily on the effects, rather than the process, of leadership (Landy, 1989). Modernist studies of leadership show tendencies consistent with modernist organizations, including: restricting the study of leadership only to those who hold positions of authority within the bureaucracy; narrowing the examination of leadership to the restricted viewpoint of the leader or the leader-follower dyad; and developing theories and models of leadership that are static and assume consistency in both leaders and their followers. The result has been that we have learned some about how to manipulate people to get something accomplished, but not much about the nature of leadership.

If Clegg (1990) and others are correct in identifying a shift toward a postmodernist paradigm for organizations, there should be a corresponding shift in the theories of how organizations function—including leadership. Emerging organizational forms need new leadership and leaders who pursue an agenda more consistent with the postmodern principles of nonrationality, dedifferentiation, and synthesis. In other words, postmodern organizations require postmodern theories of leadership. As with postmodern organizations, we are now seeing the emergence of trends toward postmodern conceptualizations of leadership.

Listed below are five propositions that outline the contours of the postmodern study of leadership. The propositions have been made on the basis of three criteria. First, is the proposition consistent with the principles of postmodern organizations? Second, does the proposition suggest new directions of investigation for leadership researchers or a new way to think about leadership in organizations? Third, does the proposition call into question precisely those tenets of modernist leadership theory that are not regularly made the object of systematic examination? Together these propositions are intended to set the stage for a postmodern approach to leadership whose time has come.

A. Proposition One: Rational Leadership Models Must Be Complemented with Nonrational Models

The successful postmodernist study of leadership will not rely exclusively on rational models of leadership, but will also embrace nonrational concepts. The trend toward nonrational models of leadership has implications both in terms of the individuals who form the subject of leadership and for the assumed mechanisms through which leadership happens.

Organizational theories of leadership have tended to focus narrowly on those individuals who, by the nature of their positions in the hierarchy of the organization, hold positions of power (Landy, 1989). Although this focus has taught us much about how managers manage, it has failed to shed much light on how leaders lead. Interestingly, Weber himself was among the first to distinguish between rational and nonrational authority by proposing three types of organizational power: one based on legal precepts, the second on traditional role definitions, and the third on individual characteristics (Weber, 1947). In other words, Weber recognized that not all *leaders* hold bureaucratic authority and that individuals with such authority are not *necessarily* leaders. Under postmodern organizations, where work is less differentiated and structures are more flexible, more workers will hold authority and the bureaucratic structure will be less useful in identifying the positions of true leaders. Thus, postmodern leadership theory must look beyond the organizational chart and strive to identify and study leaders, regardless of the positions they hold.

In addition to a focus on managers, the past 50 years of leadership theories have in large part been transactional in nature. Terms like vertical dyad linkages, contingencies, social exchange, and path-goal carry the notion that leaders influence others through the exchange of something valued. For example, Hollander's exchange theory assumes that in order to be allowed to continue in a leadership position, the leader must be responsive to the needs of followers (cf. Hollander and Julian, 1969). Similarly, path-goal theories, which stem directly from the expectancy theories of motivation, assert that subordinates will do what leaders want if leaders do two things: (1) ensure that subordinates understand how to accomplish the leader's goals; and (2) ensure that subordinates can achieve their personal goals in the process (House, 1971). These "if you take care of me, I'll take care of you" models of leadership are clearly based on the rational notion that behavior is goal-directed.

One noticeable exception to this approach is the early theory of charismatic leadership, again proposed by Weber (1947). Under this theory, leadership was not based on position or methods of exchange, but on the personal qualities of the leader and the leader's ability "to exercise diffuse and intense influence over the beliefs, values, behavior, and peformance of others" (House, Spangler, and Woycke, 1991: 366). Today, this distinction between rational and nonrational approaches to the study of leadership is subsumed under the headings of transactional versus transformationsl leadership (Burns, 1978; Bass, 1985).

Research by Bass and his colleagues (e.g., Bass and Avolio, 1990; Avolio, Waldman, and Einstein, 1988) shows that transactional leaders are mostly concerned with maintaining the status quo, or with marginally improving the quality of performance through the management of the superior-subordinate exchange relationship. In contrast, transformational leadership involves influence through shared beliefs and values. Transformational leadership is nonrational because it assumes that individuals lead and followers follow on the basis of emotion and value judgments, and only secondarily on the basis of logical-empirical considerations. This recognition of the central role of beliefs, values, and emotions for the success of organizational leaders directs us to the second proposition of postmodern leadership theory.

B. Proposition Two: Leadership Is Fundamentally About Human Values

The essence of the modernist approach to leadership is the assumption that leaders are antecedent to as well as independent of their followers, and that individuals are primarily self-interested and motivated by their own perception of what is good. Similarly, modernist theories of decision making have assumed that leaders consciously and logically think through the causes of problems, the available alternatives for solving the problems, criteria for choosing among alternatives, and the plans through which the chosen alternative will be implemented (Vaill, 1992).

As noted above, however, there is a growing body of research that shows that some leaders lead through an appeal to shared beliefs and values. Moreover, there is overwhelming evidence to suggest leaders don't make decisions through logical analysis. Chester Barnard probably had it right when he said that true executive abilities involve "matters of feeling, judgment, sense, proportion, balance, and appropriateness" (1964: 235).

How then should the postmodern study of leadership and the decision-making processes of leaders proceed? One way is to pursue the study of emotions and personal values that leaders hold and pursue, rather than focus on skills and task performance (Russell and Kuhnert, 1992b; Fisher and Torbert, 1991). As used here, the term values refers to the conception, explicit or implicit, of that which is desirable to an individual or a group and which influences the selection from among available modes, means, and ends of action (Brion, 1989). In other words, values indicate preferred end states and are the standards by which choices are made (Burns, 1978).

Burns (1978), for example, distinguished between two kinds of values. End values determine a leader's purposes for leading. Modal values are those that reflect a "mode of conduct," such as an exchange of trust and respect between a subordinate and a superior. Modal values involve personal conduct and therefore are more related to style of leadership than to making fundamental organizational changes. Successful leadership based on modal values results in engaging in activities that are mutually beneficial to the interests of both the leader and the led. End values, such as integrity and justice, cannot be negotiated or exchanged between individuals and therefore are fundamentally different from modal values. The source of end values resides in the deeply held beliefs of the leader. By expressing these beliefs, leaders can unite their followers and create a climate for real organizationwide change.

In postmodern organizations, the study of values makes a marked departure from the past by assuming that integrity and the collective good can provide the basis for leaders' actions and that leaders' actions are interdependent and inseparable from those of their followers. It is the ability to articulate and impart the values shared by individuals, organizations, and the society that will give rise to effective postmodern leadership. In other words, postmodern leaders must recognize that leaders' motivations to lead and followers' reasons for following are multifaceted. Both are rooted not only in behaviors, but in individuals' personal beliefs and experiences. This point leads us to the third proposition of postmodern leadership theory.

C. Proposition Three: Searching for a Single Cause, or for a Single Model of Leadership, Does More Harm than Good

Researchers have been frustrated at attempts to measure leadership effectiveness, despite the belief that we know good leadership when we see it (Rosenbach and Taylor, 1989). This proposition asserts that the problem does not inhere in the absence of leadership definitions or models. Rather, the problem lies in our attempts to isolate cause from effect and to determine the single characteristic(s) or behavior(s) responsible for certain outcomes. This "single bullet" approach has characterized the way that studies of organizational leadership have historically been, and continue to be, conducted—in spite of the fact they have not been much help, either in generating theory or in identifying practices useful to organizations.

Indeed, our attempts to tease out the causes and effects of each piece of the multifaceted leadership puzzle may lead one to the conclusion that no observable behaviors, attributes, or motivations on the part of leaders are responsible for rises (or declines) in performance in organizations. In other words, the hundreds of studies that have attempted to distinguish effective from ineffective leaders have yielded only limited insight into what makes good leaders (Yukl, 1981). The problem arises from the fact that there are many ways to lead, and even more ways *not* to lead.

As the postmodernist principle of dedifferentiation suggests, there are many ways to effectively get there from here. One way to advance postmodern leadership theory, therefore, follows the advice of Marshall Sashkin (1989) to consider the leader's personal characteristics, behaviors, and situation *simultaneously*. This is not to be confused with the well-worn interactionist perspective of leadership, which separates "leader characteristics" from "exogenous situational variables," or treats person variables and context variables as independent and distinct entities. Rather, the approach offered by Sashkin demands that the person-context relationship be the unit of analysis. Such a relationship assumes that the person and context mutually influence each other in ways that result in qualitative changes in both the person and the context of which they are a part.

Recently, Bowen, Ledford, and Nathan (1991), in developing a new model for personnel selection, proposed, hiring for the organization, not the job. Conventional selection practices rely mainly on fitting employee knowledge, skills, and abilities to defined requirements of the job. Brown, Ledford, and Nathan, however, expand the traditional selection model to include employee attributes that fit the characteristics of the organization. This enlarging of the unit of analysis from the "person-job" to "person-organization" fit places the selection process in the context of a "rich interaction between the person and the organization, both of which are more broadly defined and assessed than in the traditional selection model" (p. 37). Brown, Ledford, and Nathan's ideas about personnel selection are consistent with a postmodern approach because the focus is on the "whole" person and how that person fits the organization, rather than on those "parts" of a person that relate only to specific job requirements.

Other scientists also have recognized the importance of expanding the unit of analysis in leadership research and have promoted the study of leaders in the context in which they lead (e.g., Dansereau, Graen, and Haga, 1975; Graen and Scandura, 1987). Most modernist leadership research has viewed the leader as autonomous and self-directing rather than as interactive and interdependent.

Embracing the person-context as the unit of analysis and the notion of leadership as a series of interrelated processes can only prove fruitful if leadership researchers are willing to implement innovative measurement strategies. Thus, examination of dedifferentiation requires a break from the "old" mode of thought and procedures for scientific inquiry. The need for such innovation yields the fourth proposition for postmodern leadership theory.

D. Proposition Four: Research Methods Must Rely on Synthesis as Opposed to Analysis

Research strategies are never chosen independent of the hypotheses they are designed to test nor of the variables they are designed to measure. In fact, a research strategy reflects a whole network of assumptions and practices that tie the researcher to the phenomenon being investigated. For these reasons, the leadership theory that is based on postmodern organizational principles must be developed and tested through the application of postmodern research strategies.

As noted above, modernist approaches to the study of organizations and leadership adopted analytic research strategies. Generally, such approaches are designed to discover linear and continuous relationships among select variables in the search for causes. Although there are many characteristics of analytic research, Miller and Mintzberg (1983) have identified four that fundamentally characterize the modern study of leadership: (1) a focus on bivariate relationships that gives way to a sharply circumscribed multivariate analysis; (2) assumptions that relationships are generally linear and that causation is unidirectional; (3) measures that are cross-sectional or taken at isolated, discontinuous points in time; and (4) reliance on questionnaires or other "objective" measurement devices.

For the reason cited below, and undoubtedly many others, the analytic approach to leadership has proven inadequate. For example, bivariate correlational techniques and many multivariate analyses are inadequate for demonstrating complex interrelationships among multiple measures. Furthermore, the assumption of linear and unidirectional change is being called into question by research that shows that organizational change and decision making is discontinuous by nature (e.g., Golembiewski, Billingsley, and Yeager, 1976). Cross-sectional research is equally inadequate primarily because it is incapable of showing both how events unfold over time and of highlighting long-term effects (Yukl, 1981). Finally, one of the strongest criticisms of past leadership research has been the overreliance on self-reports and questionnaires, in effect, distancing researchers from the phenomenon they are studying (McCall and Lombardo, 1978; Yukl, 1981).

Advances in postmodern leadership theory will require research methods that allow scientists to overcome these deficiencies—techniques that are based on principles of synthesis. Three properties of synthesis proposed by Miller and Mintzberg (1983) are particularly useful for postmodern leadership research. The first of these is that a large number of attributes be studied simultaneously in order to yield a detailed, holistic, integrated image of the organization. The point here is to use as inclusive a set of variables as possible when conducting leadership research, looking at the larger organizational context as well as at other technical and social systems that impact the leader. Lewin was on this track more than 40 years ago when he said

> structural properties are characterized by relations between parts or elements themselves . . . throughout the history of mathematics and physics problems of constancy of relations rather than of constancy of elements have gained importance and have gradually changed the picture of what is essential. The social sciences seem to show a very similar development (1947: 192).

Second, postmodern research techniques must take both time and process into account wherever possible. Very little research has been devoted to understanding how leaders change and develop in their careers, and past leadership research has been unable to address the long-term impact of leadership in organizations. Synthesis-based research favors longitudinal designs in which processes are studied along with end states, and in which researchers flesh out their findings, pursue leads and lags, and generally provide depth to their understanding of why leaders behave as they do.

Finally, synthesis advocates data analysis and theory building that are geared to finding common natural clusters among the attributes studied (Kuhnert, McCauley, and Golembiewski, 1992; Zammuto and Krakower, 1991). In other words, synthesis requires that we carefully sample behaviors, events, outcomes, and attitudes and look for larger wholes or patterns within these data. The units of analysis of postmodern leadership, therefore, would be those configurations, gestalts, or holistic patterns that reveal leaders' integrative, configurative, and longitudinal thinking. Such an approach gives rise to the fifth and final proposition of postmodern leadership.

E. Proposition Five: The Objects of Study Must Include the Observable as Well as the Representational or Symbolic

One of the grand debates in philosophy and psychology is whether the assumption can be made that there is "one true reality" or whether reality is constructed by the observer (cf. Gergen, 1985). The modernist paradigm takes as a given that what we experience is a direct reflection of the "real" world as that what is real is observable. As a result, much leadership research has examined that which is observable—behavior.

Since the early 1980s and without much fanfare, however, there has been a growing recognition that we need to do more than to look at observable behavior to understand the dynamics of leadership. This recognition has come in the form of a growing body of research on individual cognitive schema as well as on the shared meaning of events for individuals and groups (Bartunek, 1984; Gray, Bougon, and Donnellon, 1985; Martin and Meyerson, 1988; Smircich, 1983; Shrivasta and Schneider, 1984). The basic idea underlying these approaches is that if we understood what gives rise to behavior (e.g., cognitions), we would develop better theories of leadership. Cognitions, then, became representative or substitutes for the behaviors themselves. Unfortunately, most research in the recent "cognitive revolution" has been limited by the assumptions (e.g., linearity) and characteristics (e.g., cross-sectional methods) of the modernist research paradigm (Valsiner, 1991).

One stream of research that breaks with the modernist paradigm is that of Kuhnert and

Lewis (1987), who apply constructive/developmental research techniques to organizational leadership. Based on a theory of interpersonal understanding outlined by Kegan (1982), part of the theory assumes that individuals construct a subjective understanding of the world that shapes their experiences, as opposed to their directly experiencing an objective "real" world. The developmental part extends the constructivist view by highlighting sequential regularities or patterns in ways that people construct meaning during the course of their lives, and by showing how individuals progress from simple to more complex modes of understanding. Kegan argued that these regularities generate people's thoughts, feelings, and actions in the same way that linguistic deep structures generate grammatical language (Chomsky, 1968).

The relevance of constructive/developmental theory to postmodernist thinking lies in the underpinnings of the theory. Specifically, constructive developmental theory: (1) stresses the interaction between individuals and their social context; (2) liberates researchers from a static view of leadership; (3) emphasizes development of leaders over their lives; (4) is value-based; and (5) integrates multiple models of leadership into one framework. Although not the only way to approach postmodernism in organizations, the principles of the constructive/developmental perspective must be met by any successful theory of postmodern leadership.

IV. CONCLUSIONS

Organizational theorists have shown how many of our conventional ideas about organizations and management are built on a small number of fundamental assumptions that say much about the structure of jobs, leadership, communications, and administration. It is through the uncovering of these assumptions that we are directly informed about the behavior of an organization's members. Thus, progress in understanding the impact of leadership in organizations can only be made through understanding our perspectives of (and on) organizations (cf. Morgan, 1986).

It is argued here that postmodernism is reframing the conceptualization and study of organizations. This shift is characterized by a departure from restricted, differentiated, and hierarchical structures to those that are more flexible, less bureaucratic, and more integrated. The impact on these changes for organizational leaders is significant.

Postmodern organizations, for example, will require leaders who base their decisions not only on logic and fact, but increasingly on their own (and their followers') beliefs, convictions, and preferences. Postmodern leaders will need better understanding of the complex internal relationships among worker's jobs, organizational units, and related organizations as well as the external relationships between the organization and its environment. Postmodern leaders also must be able to manage flexibly and foster diversity and creativity among their employees.

If leadership theory is to assist postmodern organizations and leaders in adapting to these changes, it must also undergo a similar transformation. Some fundamental characteristics of postmodern theories of leadership have been proposed. While there may arguably be others that should be included, these tenets—nonrational bases for decisions, human values, multiple causes and effects, "synthetic" thought, and constructed realities—must be accepted and integrated into our conceptualizations of leadership if we are to get "unstuck" and provide useful insight into effective leaders. In short, the continuation of our "romance" with leadership depends on our ability to develop theories consistent with postmodern organizational thought— that is, with the changing structures and conditions of the organizations in which leaders lead.

ACKNOWLEDGMENT

Special thanks to Mary Anne Lahey for her critical comments on an earlier draft.

REFERENCES

Ackoff, R. A. (1991). *Ackoff's Fables: Irreverent Reflections on Business and Bureaucracy*. John Wiley & Sons, Inc., New York.

Argyris, C., and Schön, D. A. (1978). *Organizational Learning: A Theory of Action Perspective*. Addison-Wesley Publishing Co., Reading, Mass.

Avolio, B. J., Waldman, D. A., and Einstein, W. O. (1988). Transformational leadership in management game simulation. *Group and Organization Studies, 13*: 59–80.

Barnard, C. (1964). *The Functions of the Executive*. Harvard University Press, Cambridge, Mass.

Bartunek, J. M. (1984). Changing interpretive schemes and organizational restructuring: The example of a religious order. *Administrative Science Quarterly, 29*: 355–372.

Bass, B. M. (1985). *Leadership and Performance Beyond Expectations*. Free Press, New York.

Bass, B. M., and Avolio, B. J. (1990). The implications of transactional and transformational leadership for individual, team, and organizational development. In *Research in Organizational Change and Development*, vol. 4 (R. W. Woodman and W. P. Passmore, eds.), JAI Press, Greenwich, Conn.

Baudrillard, J. (1989). *America*. Verso Press, New York.

Bendix, R. B. (1962). *Max Weber: An Intellectual Portrait*. Doubleday & Co., Inc., New York.

Bennis, W. (1959). Leadership theory and administrative behavior: The problem of authority. *Administrative Science Quarterly, 4*: 259–301.

Bowen, D. E., Ledford, G. E. Jr., and Nathan, B. R. (1991). Hiring for the organization, not the job. *The Executive, 5, 4*: 35–51.

Boyne, R., and Rattansi, A. (1990). *Postmodernism and Society*. St. Martin's Press, New York.

Braverman, H. (1974). *Labor and Monopoly Capital: The Degradation of Work in the Twentieth Century*. Monthly Review Press, New York.

Brion, J. M. (1989). *Organizational Leadership of Human Resources: The Knowledge and the Skills* (part 1). JAI Press, Greenwich, Conn.

Burns, J. M. (1978). *Leadership*. Harper & Row, New York.

Child, J. (1984). *Organization: A Guide to Problems and Practice*. Harper & Row, London.

Clegg, S. R. (1990). *Modern Organizations: Organization Studies in the Postmodern World*. Sage Publications, London.

Clegg, S. R. (1992). Postmodern management? Paper presented at the Academy of Management Meeting, Las Vegas, Nev.

Clegg, S. R., and Dunkevley, D. (1980). *Organization class and control*. Routledge and Kegan Paul, London.

Chomsky, N. (1968). *Language of the Mind*. Harcourt, Brace & World: New York.

Cooper, R., and Burrell, G. (1988). Modernism, post modernism, and organizational analysis: An introduction. *Organizational Studies, 9*: 91–112.

Dansereau, F. Jr., Graen, G., and Haga, W. J. (1975). A vertical dyad linkage approach to leadership within formal organizations: A longitudinal investigation of the role making process. *Organizational Behavior and Human Performance, 13*: 46–78.

Derrida, J. (1981). *Dissemination*. University Chicago Press, Chicago.

Etzioni, A. (1988). *The Moral Dimension: Toward a New Economics*. The Free Press, New York.

Featherstone, M. (1991). *Consumer Culture and Postmodernism*. Sage Publications, London.

Feyerabend, P. (1975). *Against Method*. New Left Books, London.

Fisher, D., and Torbert, W. R. (1991). Transforming managerial practice: Beyond the achiever stage. In *Research in Organizational Change and Development*. Vol. 5 (R. W. Woodman and W. A. Passmore, eds.), pp. 143–173, JAI Press, Greenwich, Conn.

Foucault, M. (1980). *The History of Sexuality. Volume 1: An Introduction*. Random House, New York.

Garvin, D. A. (1988). *Managing Quality: The Strategic and Competitive Edge*. the Free Press, New York.

Gergen, K. J. (1985). The social constructivist movement in modern psychology. *American Psychologist, 40*: 266–275.

Gergen, K. J. (1992). Organizational theory in the modern era. In *Rethinking Organization: New Directions in Organizational Theory and Analysis* (M. Reed and M. Hughes, eds., Sage Publications, London.

Golembiewski, R. T. (1992). *Approaches to Planned Change*. Transaction, New Brunswick, N. J.

Golembiewski, R. T., Billingsley, K., and Yeager, S. (1976). Measuring change and persistence in human affairs: Types of change generated by OD designs. *J. of the Applied Behavioral Sciences, 12*: 133–157.

Golembiewski, R. T., and Kuhnert, K. W. (1992). *Barnard Recessed: Authority, the Zone of Indifference, and Several Possible Influences*. Academy of Management Meeting, Las Vegas, Nev.

Golembiewski, R. T., and Kuhnert, K. W. (in press). Looking toward 2000, and beyond: Some developmental tendencies in organizations. In *Organization Theory 2000* (R. T. Golembiewski and K. W. Kuhnert, eds.), International Journal of Public Administration.

Graen, G. B., and Scandura, T. A. (1987). Toward a psychology of dyadic organizing. In Research in Organizational Behavior, vol. 9 (L. L. Cummings, and B. M. Staw, eds.), JAI Press, Greenwich, Conn.

Gray, B., Bougon, M. G., and Donnellon, A. (1985). Organizations as constructions and destructions of meaning. *J. of Management*, *11*: 83–95.

Habermas, J. (1984). *The Theory of Communicative Action. I: Reason and the Rationalization of Society.* Beacon Press, Boston.

Hollander, E. P., and Julian, J. W. (1969). Contemporary trends in the analysis of leadership processes. *Psychological Bulletin*, *71*: 387–397.

House, R. J. (1971). A path goal theory of leader effectiveness. *Administrative Science Quarterly*, *16*: 321–339.

House R. J., and Baetz, M. L. (1979). Leadership: Some empirical generalizations and new research directions. *Research in Organizational Behavior*, *1*: 341–423.

House, R. J., Spangler, W. D., and Woycke, J. (1981). Personality and charisma in the U.S. presidency: A psychological theory of leader effectiveness. *Administrative Science Quarterly*, *36*: 364–396.

Kahneman, D., Slovic, P., and Tversky, A. (1982). *Judgement Under Uncertainty: Heuristics and Biases.* Cambridge University Press, Cambridge, NY.

Kegan, R. (1982). *The Evolving Self: Problems and Process in Human Development.* Harvard University Press, Cambridge, Mass.

Kerr, S. (1977). Substitutes for leadership: Some implications for organizational design. *Organizational and Administrative Sciences*, *8*: 135–146.

Kerr, S., and Jermier, J. (1978). Substitutes for leadership: Their meaning and measurement. *Organizational Behavior and Human Performance*, *22*: 374–403.

Kuhnert, K. W., and Lewis, P. (1987). Transactional and transformational leadership: A constructive/developmental analysis. *Academy of Management Review*, *12*: 648–657.

Kuhnert, K. W., McCauley, D., and Golembiewski, R. T. (June, 1992). A cluster-bloc analysis for the study of employee attitudes in organizations, presented at the American Psychological Association, San Diego.

Landy, F. J. (1989). *Psychology of Work Behavior.* Brooks/Cole, Pacific Grove, Calif.

Lewin, K. (1947). Group decision and social change (1944). In *Readings in Social Psychology* (T. Newcomb and E. Hartley, eds.), Holt, New York.

Luhmann, N. (1976). A general history of organized social systems. In *European Contributions to Organization Theory* (G. Hofstede and M. S. Kassem, eds.), Van Gorcum, Amsterdam, pp. 96–113.

Lyotard, J. F. (1984). *The Postmodern Condition: A Report on Knowledge.* Manchester University Press, England.

Martin, J., and Meyerson, D. 1988. Organizational cultures and the denial, channeling, and acknowledgment of ambiguity. In *Managing Ambiguity and Change* (L. R. Pondy, R. J. Noland, and H. Thomas eds.) Chichester, England, pp. 93–125.

Mason, R. O. and Mitroff, I. I. (1981). *Challenging strategic planning assumptions.* John Wiley, New York.

McCall, M. W. Jr., and Lombardo, M. M. (1978). *Leadership: Where Else Can We Go?* Duke University Press, Durham, N.C.

Meindl, J. R., Ehrlich, S. B., Duderich, J. M. (1985). The romance of leadership. *Administrative Science Quarterly*, *30*: 78–102.

Miller, D., and Mintzberg, H. (1983). The case for configuration. In *Beyond Method* (G. Morgan, ed.), Sage Publications, Newbury Park, Calif.

Morgan, G. (1986). *Images of Organization.* Sage Publications, Beverly Hills, Calif.

Pfeffer, J. (1977). The ambiguity of leadership. *Academy of Management Review*, *2*: 104–112.

Reed, M., and Hughes, M. (1992). *Rethinking Organizations: New Directions in Organizational Theory and Analysis.* Sage Publications, Newbury Park, Calif.

Rosenbach, W. E., and Taylor, R. E. (1989). *Contemporary Issues in Leadership.* Westview Press, Boulder, Colo.

Russell, C. J., and Kuhnert, K. W. (1992a). New frontiers in management selection systems: Where measurement technologies and theory collide. *The Leadership Quarterly*, *3*: 109–136.

Russell, C. J., and Kuhnert, K. W. (1992b). Integrating skill acquisition and perspective taking capacity in the development of leaders. *The Leadership Quarterly*, *3*: 335–353.

Sashkin, M. (1989). Visionary leadership: A perspective from education. In *Contemporary Issues in Leadership* (William E. Rosenbach and Robert L. Taylor, eds.), Westview Press, Boulder, Colo. pp. 222–234.

Shrivastva, P., and Schneider, S. (1984). Organizational frames of reference. *Human Relations*, *37*: 795–809.

Simon, H. A. (1987). Making management decisions: The role of intuition and emotion. *Academy of Management Executive*, *1*: 57–64.

Smircich, L. (1983). Organizations as shared meanings. In *Organizational Symbolism* (L. R. Pondy, P. Frost, G. Morgan, and T. Dandridge, eds.), JAI Press, Greenwich, Conn., pp. 55–65.

Thompson, J. D. (1967). *Organizations in Action*. McGraw-Hill, New York.

Thurow, L. (1992). *Head to Head: The Coming Economic Battle Among Japan, Europe, and America*. William Morrow and Company, Inc., New York.

Torbert, W. (1976). *Creating a Community of Inquiry: Conflict, Collaboration, Transformation*. John Wiley: New York.

Turner, B. (1990). *Organizational Symbolism*. de Gruyter, Berlin.

Vaill, P. (1992). Notes on "running an organization." *Journal of Management Inquiry*, *1*: 130–138.

Valsiner, J. (1991). Construction of the mental: From the "cognitive revolution" to the study of development. *Theory and Society*, *1*: 477–494.

Van Fleet, D. D., and Yukl, G. A. (1986). *Military Leadership: An Organizational Behavior Perspective*. JAI Press, Greenwich, Conn.

Weber, M. (1947). *The Protestant Ethic and the Spirit of Capitalism*. (tr. A. M. Henderson and Talcott Parsons; Talcott Parsons, ed.), Free Press and Falcon's Wing Press, Glencoe, Ill.

Wren, D. (1987). *The Evolution of Management Thought*. John Wiley and Sons, New York.

Yukl, G. A. (1981). *Leadership in Organizations*. Prentice-Hall, Inc., Englewood Cliffs, N.J.

Zaleznik, A. (1990). The leadership gap. *Academy of Management Executive*, *4*: 7–20.

Zammuto, R. F., and Krakower, J. Y. (1991). Quantitative and qualitative studies of organizational culture. In *Research in Organizational Change and Development*, vol. 5 (R. W. Woodman and W. A. Passmore, eds.), pp. 83–114.

Zey, M., ed. (1992). *Decision Making: Alternatives to Rational Choice Models*. Sage Publications, Newbury, Calif.

Zey-Ferrell, M. (1981). Criticisms of the dominant perspectives on organizations. *Sociological Quarterly*, *22*: 181–205.

Part II
Some Themes Requiring Enhanced Emphasis

10
Race and Ethnicity

Taylor Cox, Jr.

University of Michigan, Ann Arbor, Michigan

Stella Nkomo

University of North Carolina at Charlotte, Charlotte, North Carolina

I. INTRODUCTION

This chapter addresses the impact of racial and ethnic diversity on organizational processes and behavior. There are several reasons for devoting a chapter to this subject. First, in American society at large, race has been shown to influence many categories of life experience, including economic well-being (Morishima, 1981), psychological health (Thomas and Hughes, 1986), availability of health services (Eggers, 1988), sentencing in criminal cases (LaFree, 1980), and housing patterns (Massey and Denton, 1988). It seems reasonable therefore to expect race to also have an impact on behavior and processes in organizations. Second, previous research on the effects of race in the organizational context has generally shown that the work experience of employees varies systematically by race. For example, in our review of 145 empirical studies of the effects of race on organization behavior topics, significant main effects were found in 71% of the studies (Cox and Nkomo, 1990). Third, the workforce in the United States and throughout the world is becoming increasingly more diverse in terms of race and ethnicity (Johnston and Packard, 1987; Johnston, 1991; Horwitz and Forman, 1990). Because of this increase in racial heterogeneity in workgroups, the need to understand how race as well as racial and ethnic differences influence work behavior is greater than ever before.

This chapter will address theory and research on race/ethnicity as a factor in organization behavior (OB). Throughout the chapter, we will use the term racioethnicity, as suggested by Cox (1990), to refer to the combination of physical and cultural differences that distinguish Euro-Caucasian members of organizations from minority groups such as African-Americans, Hispanic Americans, Asian-Americans, and American Indians.

Following this introduction, we will review and analyze previous literature on the intersection of racioethnicity with central subject areas in the OB domain.

II. REVIEW AND ANALYSIS OF PREVIOUS RESEARCH

In this section we review five central subject areas in OB: job satisfaction/attitudes, performance appraisal, leadership, motivation, and careers (entry and upward mobility). These are the subject areas that have historically been addressed in the literature on racioethnic issues in organizations. For example, in a recent review of 20 of the leading OB journals we found that 88% of all articles dealing with racioethnic effects did so in terms of one of these five traditional

OB topics, excluding articles on the legal aspects of EEO/AA (Cox and Nkomo, 1990). We have taken this topical approach because work in this area is not yet sufficiently developed to organize our discussion around alternative theoretical paradigms. Throughout the review, we will offer an assessment of the literature focusing on strengths and shortcomings of the work and also offer suggestions for extending it. We conclude the chapter with additional suggestions for future research, focusing on some of the recent work on racioethnic effects that we consider to be particularly promising or important for researcher attention in the coming decade.

A. Job Satisfaction and Job Attitudes

Research in the area of job satisfaction has largely focused on two interrelated questions: Are there racial differences in job satisfaction; and are there racial differences in the importance attached to the facets that determine job satisfaction? There were a number of studies conducted during the 1970s and early 1980s, with a decreasing number appearing during the period from 1986 to 1991. Virtually all of this research addressed satisfactional attitudes of blacks compared to whites. Despite the sizable quantity of this research, the results are largely inconsistent. Some studies report whites as more satisfied than blacks, while other studies report the opposite.

O'Reilly and Roberts (1973) examined the differences in job satisfaction among a matched sample of white and nonwhite females performing the same job in a hospital setting. Using the job description index, the GM faces scale, and the Bayfield-Rothe index, they reported that whites were more satisfied with their jobs and that whites associated overall satisfaction more closely with promotion than nonwhites. The authors concluded that whites and nonwhites approach their jobs with different frames of reference. They argued that since socialization of school, work, and social behaviors is different for whites and nonwhites, it may be expected that attitudes and behaviors toward work will reflect these subcultural differences. The authors do acknowledge the difficulty of explaining differences without theoretical notions to explain cultural differences.

Consistently, Milutinovich and Tsaklanganos (1976) found significant differences in job satisfaction for workers living in communities with different levels of prosperity. Workers from poor neighborhoods were less satisfied with work, supervision, promotion, and total jobs than middle-income workers. In addition, they reported a significant interaction effect between the race of the worker and community prosperity. For example, blacks from middle-income communities were more satisfied with their work than blacks from either poor or high middle-income communities, while whites from poor communities were less satisfied with their work than whites from either middle-income or high middle-income communities. It would seem that this finding merely underscores the interaction between race and class and the likelihood that workers from poor neighborhoods are more often employed in jobs with lower pay and benefits.

Weaver (1978) found differences in the correlates of job satisfaction factors for whites and blacks. Using data drawn from national surveys he found that family income, supervisory position, and occupational prestige correlated with job satisfaction for whites but were not significant for blacks. Veechio (1980) examined data from the National Opinion Research Center for over 2000 full-time male workers and found significant main effect differences between blacks and whites on measures of job satisfaction. There were also differences in the manner in which these variables related for blacks relative to whites. A comparison of relationships between age and job prestige and between education and job satisfaction suggested the operation of different labor market processes between the two groups.

In contrast to the aforementioned studies, Gavin and Ewen (1974) compared job satisfaction of black and white male semiskilled employees in the same company. The instrument used to measure job satisfaction examined satisfaction with advancement, job and company, supervision, cooperation among co-workers and supervisors, and pay and working conditions. They found that blacks were more satisfied than whites on all but the supervision dimension; however, the size of the effect was small. The authors interpret their findings to indicate that the work perceptions of blacks may be influenced by external considerations—for example, reference groups or prior personal experiences. Similarly, Jones et al. (1977) compared the job satisfaction of black and white sailors assigned to the same shipboard divisions and found that while there were no differences in general satisfaction levels, black sailors were more satisfied with pay, rules and regulations regarding appearance, opportunities to get a better job, and attitudes toward the navy than their white counterparts. The satisfaction measures used by Jones et al. were the same as those employed by Gavin and Ewen (1974).

Two studies during the early 1980s attempted to explain racial differences in employee job satisfaction (Moch, 1980; Konar, 1981). Moch (1980) measured structural, cultural, social, and social psychological explanations for differential employee satisfaction by race. In addition to race, his analysis distinguished: racial composition of the employee's workgroup; the importance the employee placed on interpersonal relationships, on extrinsic rewards, and on intrinsic rewards; and the employee's social integration and perceived relative deprivation. He found that blacks reported less satisfaction than whites and that Mexican-Americans were more satisfied than whites. Race accounted for 21% of the variance in satisfaction beyond that accounted for by all the other factors. The other factors, however, accounted for only 4% of the variance in satisfaction beyond that accounted for by race. Moch concluded that structural, cultural, social, and social psychological factors did not significantly contribute to explaining racial differences in job satisfaction. In a review of the work, Konar (1981) differed with Moch's conclusion and argued that more research was needed on the structural factors affecting job satisfaction.

The most recent studies examining racioethnic effects on job satisfaction also report mixed results. Dalton and Marcis (1986) examined 1980 youth cohort data from the National Longitudinal Survey and found that satisfaction with the job for males compared to females was closely linked to general background characteristics, including race and ethnicity. Shiflett (1988) investigated the extent of job satisfaction and the importance of various job facets and performance outcomes for white and black enlisted men. He reported that black soldiers rated all facets of job satisfaction substantially more positively than did whites. Blacks seemed to derive greater satisfaction from extrinsic factors while whites tended to be more satisfied by intrinsic rewards. Wright et al. (1987), in a study of job satisfaction among black female public-sector managers found that organizational measures (organization size, type of position, level of government, etc.) accounted for most of the explained variance in satisfaction. Their study did not focus on racial differences per se, but used a sample of black women to test a model of job satisfaction.

Studies examining the relative importance of the different facets making up job satisfaction also report mixed findings. Slocum and Stawser (1972) examined whether or not intrinsic and extrinsic job factors vary as a function of racioethnicity. The black CPAs in their sample reported more need deficiency than white CPAs in the areas of opportunity to help people, opportunity for friendship, feeling of self-esteem, opportunity for independent thought and action, opportunity for growth and development, and compensation. Black CPAs generally felt that their needs were less satisfied by their jobs.

Weaver (1975) investigated preferences for job characteristics among black and white workers and found that blacks prefer high income more than whites, and were less likely to prefer important work and a feeling of accomplishment. Weaver (1975: 441) argued that because a black worker knows that having a job is at best tenuous, he may focus on the tangible, immediate security of income and be less mindful of the intrinsic satisfactions with work. Alper (1975) explored racioethnic differences in desired job characteristics among newly hired college graduates in sales and engineering positions. Overall, there were no differences in the relative importance attributed to job and work characteristics. However, black college graduates gave the hygiene factors (e.g., benefits, job security, and starting salary) significantly higher ratings than did the white sample. Alper (1975) concluded that while newly hired college graduates are highly future-oriented, the newly hired minority college graduate might still have security concerns beyond those of their white counterparts.

Beaty (1990) examined the link between job characteristics and job satisfaction for black and white nurses. He found no differences between black and white nurses on the extrinsic and intrinsic satisfaction measures and overall satisfaction. On the other hand, Shiflett (1988) reported that black soldiers derived greater satisfaction from extrinsic factors while white soldiers tended to be more satisfied by intrinsic factors. For blacks, satisfaction with extrinsic factors was related to intention to reenlist. For whites, satisfaction with work and supervision were related to reported effort and intention to reenlist. Shifflett (1988) also reported that blacks were more optimistic that good performance would lead to a desirable outcome.

Few studies have addressed racioethnic groups other than blacks and whites. Moch (1980) reported that the Mexican-Americans in his sample were more satisfied than blacks. McNeely (1987) investigated 336 black, Hispanic, and white female human service workers to determine whether or not racial/ethnic status was related to job satisfaction among managerial, supervisory, and professional employees. There were no significant differences among the three race groups on either overall or intrinsic satisfaction. Data indicated that blacks and whites were similar in patterns predictive of their satisfaction, and that Hispanics were influenced by concerns peculiar to those achieving recent professional status. The emphasis for Hispanics was on satisfaction with teamwork. The authors are cautious about their results because of the relative small sample of Hispanics in the study ($N=20$). Chusmir and Koberg (1990) examined ethnic differences in the relationship between job satisfaction and sex-role conflict among Hispanics and non-Hispanic white individuals. Hispanic subjects scored significantly lower on satisfaction with pay, supervision, and co-workers than did non-Hispanic whites. There was no significant link to any of the five facets of job satisfaction and sex role conflict for Hispanics. The authors did not address the possibility that the sex role conflict scale used in their study may be culture-bound. Since other research has demonstrated that sex roles and gender roles among Hispanics may be unique to their culture (Williams, 1988), this omission is potentially crucial.

In summary, research in this domain is plagued by inconsistency on how (if at all) racioethnic identity affects job satisfaction. There was also a lack of consistency in the instruments used to measure job satisfaction. In addition, only a few studies attempted to identify the underlying factors that might contribute to racioethnic differences in satisfaction. More attention needs to be paid to the social or psychological phenomena that have led researchers to predict or explore intergroup differences in job satisfaction. In this regard, the work of Moch (1980) and the suggestions of Komar (1981) should be revisited and extended.

There are some notable patterns in the approach to studying racioethnic effects on job satisfaction in the studies reviewed. In those studies in which differences were reported in facets of job satisfaction between black and white workers, the finding was that blacks placed more emphasis on hygiene or extrinsic factors than whites. There is a potential danger that the results could be interpreted as a cultural deficiency in that blacks are oriented toward fulfilling lower-order needs. An alternative interpretation may rest in examining the overall economic and historical context of work for black workers. Scholars must also be aware of potential differences in the meaning of the job satisfaction construct as well as in the reference point used by groups. In this regard, it would be helpful to know if the pattern of differences in job satisfaction facets holds across organizational levels and types of jobs.

B. Performance Evaluation

A number of studies have addressed the issue of rater and ratee racioethnic effects in performance ratings. The relatively large amount of research in this area is evidenced by the existence of three comprehensive literature and research reviews on the subject. Landy and Farr (1980) published a traditional literature review in 1980. Dipoybe (1985) offered a critical discussion of the limitations of both the theoretical framework and research methodology employed in most studies. Finally, Kraiger and Ford (1985) reported the results of a meta-analysis of over 70 studies. A brief summary of the major results of the research in this area is presented below rather than attempting to discuss each published study individually.

Several research studies have examined the effect of the racioethnicity of the ratee on job performance ratings. Early findings were often tentative and contradictory. Some studies found that ratees received significantly higher ratings from evaluators of their own race (Cox and Krumboltz, 1958; Dejung and Kaplan, 1962; Crooks, 1972; Landy and Farr, 1976; Schmitt and Lappin, 1980). Other studies reported results that indicated a complex interaction between ratee racioethnicity and ratee performance. Hamner et al. (1974) found that black performance may be rated as average by whites regardless of the actual level of performance. Similarly, Bigoness (1976) found bias even when objective performance standards had been implemented. Contrary to these findings, other studies failed to support the existence of significant racioethnic effects on performance evaluations (Bass and Turner, 1973; Schmidt and Johnson, 1973; Mobley, 1982; Brugnoli, Campion, and Basen, 1979). A notable distinction in the study by Brugnoli et al. was that race-linked bias was not evident when evaluations were based on observations of relevant job behavior.

Kraiger and Ford's 1985 meta-analysis of this research helped to clarify earlier results. They reported the following findings. First, the racioethnicity of the ratee does have an impact on performance ratings. Racioethnicity explained approximately 3.7% of the variance in job performance ratings. Ratees tend to receive higher ratings from raters of the same race. This tendency is equally strong for both black and white raters. The mean correlations between ratee racioethnicity and ratings for white and black raters were 0.183 and –0.220, respectively. Second, racioethnic effects were more likely in field settings than in laboratory studies. Third, racioethnic effects were more likely when blacks composed a small percentage of an organization's workforce.

Research since the Kraiger and Ford analysis has again produced contradictory results. Pulakos et al. (1989) examined ratings collected for 8642 first-term army enlisted personnel and found that racioethnic effects on ratings were minimal (less than 1%). They reported that blacks were rated higher on military bearing but lower than whites on the other two performance dimensions (technical skill and job effort and personal discipline). However, the authors did not explore why blacks were rated higher on military bearing, which was defined as appropriate military appearance and staying in good physical condition. Pulakos et al. (1989) strongly underscored how their results contradicted the findings of Kraiger and Ford (1985). From one perspective, however, their results do not really contradict those of Kraiger and Ford (1985) but are actually consistent with them. Blacks have good representation in the army among enlisted men and this could have moderated the racioethnic effects on performance ratings.

Greenhaus, Parasuraman, and Wormley (1990), in a matched sample of black and white managers in three companies, reported significant racioethnic effects in performance evaluations. Supervisors rated blacks lower than whites on both the relationship and task components of performance. In their study, racioethnicity accounted for 2.5% of the variance in the relationship component and 5.5% of the variance in the task component. Kleiman, Biderman, and Faley (1987) sought to identify factors related to employee perceptions of the accuracy of subjective performance ratings. The study also examined if perceived fairness and accuracy was moderated by employee sex and/or racioethnicity. They found that the black females in their study perceived the appraisal process as less fair and accurate compared to white males and females. These perceptions were affected by job experience. Black females with more job experience perceived the system as being fair and accurate.

While the studies often contradict one another, the accumulated evidence does indicate that racioethnicity plays a part in performance ratings. The remaining research issues revolve more around how much impact racioethnicity has on performance ratings and in understanding the processes underlying race effects. A few articles have explored this latter issue (Cox and Nkomo, 1986; Dipboye, 1985; Ilgen and Youtz, 1985; Pettigrew and Martin, 1987; DeMeuse, 1987). Cox and Nkomo (1986) explored the possibility that the meaning of performance ratings and the weighting of criteria may differ for members of different racioethnic groups. Data from performance appraisal ratings of 125 first-level managers revealed that among the top 10 correlates of performance ratings, blacks and whites had only one item in common. Overall results indicated that social behavior factors were more highly correlated with the overall job performance rating of black ratees than for white ratees. These findings suggest the use of different criteria and information based on racioethnicity, and hence black ratees may be confronted with the task of meeting a more complex set of performance criteria than their white counterparts. This point of view is reinforced by survey research suggesting that many black managers believe they are subjected to different performance expectations and criteria (Fernandez, 1981; Jones, 1986; Dickens and Dickens, 1982).

Ilgen and Youtz (1986) discussed the factors affecting the evaluation and development of minorities in organizations. Because their work represents one of the most thorough (and we believe thoughtful) discussions of the *causes* of difference, we will comment on it in some detail here. Drawing heavily from theoretical concepts in social psychology, they examine three possible explanations for the existence of racioethnic effects in the performance evaluation process: (1) rater bias; (2) lost opportunities and (3) self-limiting behavior.

C. Rater Bias

The first and most obvious explanation for the existence of racial differences is rater bias based on stereotypes of minorities. However, Ilgen and Youtz (1986) argue that the biases that exist in ratings may be the result of complex judgment processes of person perception rather than the simple minority group stereotypes. More subtle effects of group membership on attributions about the causes of performance, the attention that obvious membership in a particular minority group draws to the person, and beliefs about the conditions under which the person was hired for the job are also likely sources of rater bias. For example, good performance for minorities may be attributed to external factors (e.g., luck or the task) rather than ability, while that of majority group members may be more likely attributed to ability or effort (Greenhaus and Parasuraman, in press). Ilgen and Youtz (1986) also argue that the cognitive processing view of performance appraisals suggests that the search for information about ratee performance may be biased. Hypothesis-confirming ratee behaviors tend to be more salient to raters, and thus are more likely to be noticed and recalled by them. For example, if a rater believes that blacks are lazy he or she is more likely to notice instances of "laziness" on the part of black ratees (Ilgen and Youtz, 1986).

Cox and Nkomo's (1986) study also supports the view of differential use of information by raters when rating blacks. Jussim et al. (1987) examined predictions derived from three theories of stereotyping: complexity-extremity theory, assumed characteristics theory, and expectancy-violation theory. They found that the range of whites' evaluation of black applicants was larger than the range of their evaluations of white applicants. In a similar fashion, DeMeuse (1987) argues for more attention to the role of nonverbal cues on person perception. Nonverbal cues are defined as "all communication except that which is contained in words" (DeMeuse, 1987: 208). He suggests that this also includes demographic indicators (e.g., gender, race, and age) that may communicate systematic images to perceivers (raters). Demographic cues often possess widely understood and socially shared meanings (e.g., stereotypes of blacks and other racioethnic groups).

Another possible source of rater bias may simply be due to the novel or "solo" status of the minority group member (Pettigrew and Martin, 1987). In the case of a single minority group member among a majority group, the minority group member stands out. When racioethnicity is a very salient feature, it may be credited with far more relevance with respect to performance judgment than it deserves. This observation, noted by Ilgen and Youtz (1986) and Pettigrew and Martin (1987), is reinforced by Kraiger and Ford's (1985) finding that racioethnic effects in performance ratings are more likely in field settings when blacks are few in number.

D. Lost Opportunities

The second possible source of racioethnic effects in performance evaluation cited by Ilgen and Youtz (1986) was lost opportunities. Lost opportunities as a concept focuses on the role of the treatment of minorities in creating actual differences between groups (Ilgen and Youtz, 1986).

These lost opportunities include the absence of mentors, less interesting or challenging work as a result of being in the outgroup, and being left out of the informal social network. While these lost opportunities do not directly affect performance ratings, according to Ilgen and Youtz (1986) they may lead to *actual* differences in performance between groups over time. Similar explanations have also been posited by other researchers. For example, Alderfer et al. (1980), in their landmark study of race relations in organizations, found that the greatest disagreement between black and white managers was on the topic of promotions. In their study, white managers reported sharing career-relevant information with black managers at more than twice the rate that black managers reported receiving such information from white managers. Similarly, Greenhaus, Parasuraman, and Wormley (1990) found that compared to white managers, black managers felt less accepted in their organizations and perceived themselves as having less discretion on their jobs.

E. Self-Limiting Behavior

The final explanation presented by Ilgen and Youtz (1986) is self-limiting behavior on the part of minority group members, which they discuss as a long-term effect of experiencing rating biases and lost opportunities. According to their analysis, self-limiting behavior operates in a two-pronged fashion. First, if minorities continually experience lower performance ratings, negative stereotypes, and fewer job opportunities, they may come to believe that they are less competent and develop a negative self-concept. Second, minority employees continually placed in routine, unchallenging work assignments outside the normal career path may fall behind majority employee cohorts in terms of job knowledge, skill development, and performance. Self-limiting behavior developed as a result of lost opportunities will tend to perpetuate performance differences. We add to their discussion of self-limiting behavior that the extent to which racioethnic minorities engage in such behavior may be influenced by one's level of racioethnic identity. Those minority group members with a strong sense of identity will more likely resist internalizing negative feelings and their self-esteem would remain in tact.

In our view, all of these possible explanations warrant further study and research and underscore the importance of focusing research on understanding the processes that lead to differences in peformance ratings between minority and majority group members in organizations. Research is also needed on effective ways of minimizing negative rater behaviors and in testing performance evaluation systems that control rater errors grounded in stereotypes and bias.

F. Leadership

Studies examining racioethnicity and leadership have typically focused on differences in leader behavior between blacks and whites, as well as on the effects of racioethnicity on subordinate perceptions of leader behavior. One of the earliest studies on leadership and racioethnicity was Delbecq and Kaplan's (1968) investigation of interactions between black leaders and predominantly black subordinates in a government-sponsored program. They found that the leaders generally reacted by dominating the decision-making process, resorting to coalitions and authority of the office to resolve conflicts, and concentrating on safeguarding their own status and self-image. Unfortunately, there were no comparisons made with white leaders.

Richard and Jaffe (1972) investigated the behavior of biracial workgroups when blacks supervise whites. Results indicated that the performance ratings of black supervisors were significantly poorer than those of white supervisors. Subordinates supervised by blacks behaved differently from subordinates supervised by whites, and some of these behaviors appeared to hinder the effectiveness of the black supervisor. For example, subordinates with a black supervisor gave more suggestions and opinions and disagreed more than subordinates with a white supervisor. Finally, subordinates with negative racial bias gave poorer ratings to black supervisors than subordinates with liberal racial attitudes.

Beatty (1973) used the leader opinion questionnaire to measure supervisor consideration behavior and initiation behavior of black supervisors. Results indicated that the employer's perception of the black supervisors' social behavior tended to be the most important influence in evaluating black supervisors. Interpersonal attributes and cultural awareness were key determinants of perceptions.

Bartol, Anderson, and Schneier (1981) examined the motivation to manage among business students and found that blacks had a lower orientation toward imposing wishes on others and were less assertive. Shull and Anthony (1978), in a study of participants in a supervisory training program, examined black and white supervisory problem-solving styles. Little difference was found in all measures except attitudes toward received discipline. Blacks were less willing to accept harsh criticism for violation of rules, especially if performance was otherwise high. Bartol, Evans, and Stith (1978) conducted an extensive review of the research on black/white differences in leadership between 1964 and 1977, and found that ethnic factors affected leader behavior, leader potential, and leader performance, although blacks and whites were similar in many respects. They argued for more studies of ethnicity in all aspects of leadership research.

Adams (1978) examined attitudes and perceptions of subordinates toward minority versus majority group managers. Black males were perceived as exhibiting more "consideration" behavior compared to other groups. There were no related effects on satisfaction. Ivancevich and McMahon (1977) used the path-goal leadership model to examine the moderating impact of racioethnicity on task-goal attributes and task-effort and performance. They found that blacks reported different goal attributes associated with task effort and performance on an assigned goal. Goal challenge was related to performance for whites but not for blacks. Parker (1976), using Bowes and Seashore's four dimensions of leadership, explored black and white differences in leader behavior as perceived by black, white, and Chicano subordinates. Black supervisors were seen by subordinates as more effective leaders than white supervisors on the dimensions of managerial support, goal emphasis, and work facilitation. There was no evidence that subordinates viewed supervisors of the same racioethnic group more favorably than supervisors of a different race. However, white subordinates of white supervisors in workgroups that were predominantly black saw their supervisors more favorably than white subordinates of white supervisors in workgroups that were predominantly white. Parker (1976) speculated that the differences may have been due to the fact that majority group subordinates are not accustomed to being in the minority. Chicano subordinate rankings differentiated between black and white supervisors only on the goal emphasizing dimension, where black supervisors were rated higher.

Using Allport's intergroup contact theory, Hill and Fox (1973) tested hypotheses of differences in the way black and white supervisors feel and act toward black, white, and Puerto Rican subordinates on dimensions of work that are not task-prescribed. The sample consisted of Marine rifle squads. White leaders praised whites more than blacks. Black leaders showed no differences in the use of praise. Whites gave higher ratings of performance to black versus white subordinates. In general, racioethnic effects were found for white leaders but not for black leaders. Although white leaders often were more favorable to black subordinates, the authors speculated that this finding was affected by a recent emphasis on racioethnic harmony in the army.

Kipnis, Silverman, and Copeland (1973) examined the use of coercion by supervisors with black and white subordinates. First-line supervisors at a steel mill described an incident in which they used delegated powers to correct subordinate behavior. Analysis of these incidents revealed that supervisors used more coercion with black than white subordinates. It was assumed that heightened emotional responses caused by prejudice in the case of black subordinates induced the use of coercion.

It is perhaps noteworthy that we were unable to locate studies of racioethnicity and leadership published in the last 10 years. The amount of research done seems to have peaked in the late 1970s. As evidenced from the review above, there is a good deal of disparity in the nature of the effect of racioethnicity on leader behavior and subordinate reactions. Clearly, there is a profound need for more research in this area, given the forecast of an increasing diversity of racioethnic groups in the labor force. Research is needed that will more fully examine leadership styles of leaders of different racioethnic groups and in different supervisor-subordinate dyads.

In recent years leadership research has focused on examining "substitutes" for leadership. According to Kerr and Jermier (1978), "This research explores factors that neutralize leader behavior—the nature of the task, subordinate ability, and the organizational situation." Future research should take a multivariate approach using these factors in addition to racioethnicity.

Also needed is research that examines the relationship between transformational leadership (Kimberly and Quinn, 1984) and racioethnicity. For example, how do race and ethnicity influence one's ability to be a transformational leader?

Finally, we must incorporate theories of power and domination in understanding racioethnicity and leadership. Ultimately, leadership must be understood as an influence process and we cannot overlook the impact of the historical dominant and subordinate positions of whites and nonwhites in the larger societal context. What does it mean for a white employee who has grown up in society in which he or she holds a dominant and superior status vis-à-vis nonwhites to be in a situation in which he or she is now "subordinate?" Alternately, what are the social-psychological implications of a racioethnic minority manager functioning in a role that places him or her in a superior position relative to members of the white majority group? Traditional examinations of differences in leader behavior do not address the individual, group, societal, and historical factors that may impact leader or subordinate behavior in mixed racioethnic dyads.

G.   Motivation

Previous work on racioethnic effects on employee motivation has centered on cross-group comparisons of need structures and on expectancy theory. This focus is consistent with that of motivation theory generally, since it is frequently categorized as *content* (need structure theories such as Maslow's need hierarchy) and *process*, the most prominent being expectancy theory (Arnold and Feldman, 1986).

H.   Need Structure Studies

The need structure studies have generally used either Herzberg's motivation-hygiene theory (Herzberg, Mausner, and Snyderman, 1959) or McClelland's achievement, power, and affiliation theory (McClelland, 1961) as their basic framework. The primary research question addressed in this body of research is whether or not the need structures of workers are systematically related to racioethnicity. Two early studies examined growth/higher-order needs (challenging work, advancement, etc.) and hygienic factors (fringe benefits, job security, salary, etc.). Alper (1975) studied need structures among a sample of 70 newly hired African Americans and 179 newly hired whites. Although the study had no formally stated hypotheses, the author employed a Maslow-hierarchy logic (Maslow, 1954) suggesting that the history of economic disadvantage of nonwhites might lead to a greater emphasis on hygiene factors among nonwhites compared to whites. His results supported this line of reasoning, in that racioethnicity had no effect on the priority assigned to the growth factors, but whites gave significantly lower scores to hygiene factors.

However, a study by Feldman (1973) using the same conceptual framework but a sample of hard-core employed and working-class men, produced contradictory results. Feldman's data did show significant racioethnic effects on certain individual work outcomes, but did not support the pattern of higher priority on hygiene factors for nonwhites. The contradictory findings may have been due to slight differences in operational definitions of some variables. For example, Alper defined the pay variable as the importance of starting salary to initial employment decisions while Feldman defined it as a rating of good pay as a work outcome using a scale of 1 (most positive) to 9 (most negative). In the latter study respondents may have focused on postemployment concerns rather than the initial job decision. One interpretation, therefore, is that pay is a more prominent outcome in the initial employment decision whereas other factors, such as advancement, become more salient in the frame of reference of ongoing employment.

In another interesting study of racioethnic effects using the Herzberg framework, Kahoe (1974) found that patterns of correlations between intrinsic and extrinsic job incentives scales differed for black males compared to whites. In particular, he found that although working conditions are normally treated as an extrinsic factor in theory and research, scores on working condition scales correlated highly with the intrinsic scales in the black male sample. Kahoe offers the interpretation that the data indicate that working conditions may hold different meanings for members of different racioethnic groups. He suggests that working conditions may have self-actualization implications for persons with a history of poor and unequal conditions. Although the description of his work is not sufficiently detailed in the article to judge whether or not his argument is convincing, the idea that members of different racioethnic groups may assign different psychological meanings to job incentives is an intriguing one that we think deserves further exploration.

Several studies have also made cross-race comparisons using the McClelland framework. Watson and Barone (1976) studied achievement affiliation and power motivation levels in a sample of 64 black and 64 white managers using the thematic apperception test (TAT). No a priori predictions were offered about how racioethnic identity would affect the need structures. Their results indicated a significant effect of racioethnicity for power (higher for whites) but not for achievement or affiliation. They concluded that "black managers, as a class, have a remarkably similar need pattern to their white counterparts" (p. 47). Lefkowitz and Fraser (1980) essentially replicated the findings of Watson and Barone (1976) on achievement but did not find any racioethnic effects on power motivation. Their sample was college students and was quite small (31 blacks and 32 whites). Lefkowitz and Fraser (1980) also found that the racioethnicity of the test administrator had a significant effect on verbal productivity scores of both nonwhite and white respondents. Their discussion of this result provides an interesting insight into racioethnic influence. They note that McClelland found this same result and commented as follows on its meaning:

> If interactions (of administrator and respondent racioethnic group) were the rule, the concept of "race" for purposes of interview research could be reduced to the much simpler psychological concepts of same and different. Uniform reactions to black and white interviewers by respondents of both races necessitate conceptualization of race into black and white, concepts much less explicable and understandable psychologically than same and different (McClelland, 1974: 395).

This observation by McClelland has important implications for racioethnic research and for work on the broader concept of workforce diversity. The generic diversity concept is more appropriate when the group phenomena under study are accurately reducible to the notions of same and different, but there are many phenomena for which the specific racioethnic identities (and roles) of the interacting parties will be crucial. As McClelland has suggested, much of the work on diversity effects will therefore require attention to the social and psychological meaning of specific racioethnic groups represented in a transaction.

An additional implication of the use of the work of both Watson and Barron (1976) and Lefkowitz and Frazer (1980) is that their findings highlight the importance of acknowledging that minority-group managers in corporations are not necessarily representative of the overall population of their group. This was relatively less important when only a few nonwhites were being hired, but with workforce demographic trends indicating that more and more nonwhites will be hired, the profiles of the overall group becomes more important. Research that is limited to the present cohort of managers and professionals in organizations may not inform us well about the racioethnic issues of the future.

I. Expectancy Theory

Another prominent theoretical framework in the employee motivation area is expectancy theory (Vroom, 1964; Porter and Lawler, 1968). This theory holds that motivation to work will be high when: (1) a person believes that effort and good performance are tightly linked (effort-performance expectancy), and (2) a person believes that a good performance will lead to the outcome that he or she values (performance-outcome) expectancy). A series of studies in the 1970s examined the possibility that one or both of these "expectancies," or their ability to predict actual job performance, vary by racioethnicity.

All such studies that we were able to locate focused on comparisons between whites and blacks. Greenhaus and Gavin (1972) explored expectancy-theory differences in a sample of 390 white and 81 black male blue-collar employees of a major airline. They combined the two expectancies into a single variable called effort-reward expectancy. They also examined possible differences in the importance placed on various work rewards. Findings indicated no differences between blacks and whites on the value of rewards. The effort-reward expectancies were significantly different in only 2 of 12 reward categories, and in all cases they were higher for blacks. Perhaps most intriguing, the correlation between expectancies and supervisor ratings of job performance was more often significant for whites than for blacks. However, the correlations were low for both samples, and differences in correlations between blacks and whites were not significant.

Orpen and Nkohande (1977) studied relations between self-esteem, locus of control, and expectancy beliefs in a sample of 59 black and 61 white low-level managers from 10 South African companies. They predicted that whites would have both higher self-esteem and higher internal control scores than blacks, and that both self-esteem and internal control would have a positive relationship with effort-performance and performance-outcome expectancies. Although they did not explicitly address it, this theoretical scheme implies that blacks would have lower expectancies by virtue of lower self-esteem and more external locus of control. Their findings confirmed that the white managers had significantly higher self-esteem and internal locus of control scores, but these variables were significantly correlated with expectancies only in the white sample. Unfortunately, this study was not as informative as it could have been because the authors did not report how the expectancies themselves compared for the two groups, and failed to provide a test of statistical significance for the differences in correlation coefficients between blacks and whites.

In a related study, Feldman (1973) tested the following hypotheses: (1) blacks would have lower performance-outcome expectancies for the behavior of work itself; and (2) blacks would have stronger performance-outcome expectancies for the behavior of not working. His data supported neither hypothesis, however he did find significant effects of racioethnic group on expectancies. Blacks generally had higher expectancies of positive outcomes from working and less negative outcome expectancies of not working than whites. Feldman offers some thought-provoking speculation about the reasons for these results. In part, he argues that blacks may view not working less negatively because of a more realistic view of unemployment (because of their greater experience with it as a group), more ingenuity in finding alternatives to full-time continuous employment as sources of income, and less emphasis on one's work role as the basis of personal respect.

While we would not support an interpretation that the availability of regular, full-time work is relatively unimportant to blacks compared to whites, it does seem plausible that the different sociocultural histories of blacks and whites may convey different meanings for work in terms of personal respect and self-esteem. For example, since blacks were barred from participation in high-status jobs in racioethnically integrated settings for hundreds of years, to accept one's work role as the basis of esteem would have been to severely diminish self-esteem to the entire group. Under these circumstances it seems rational for blacks to resist the use of work roles as the basis for personal respect.

Collectively, these studies seem to suggest that relationships of the expectancy theory framework (i.e., the theory itself and related theories such as linkages with self-esteem and internal control) are not as reliably predicted for nonwhite samples as they are for whites. Feldman (1973: 20) puts it this way: "These data, while not supporting the original hypotheses, strongly suggest that race and economic class are associated with different views of the world of work."

This leads to questions about why the theory seems to operate differently for different racioethnic groups. Consideration of these questions offers some interesting ideas for further research. For example, one interpretation of the Greenhaus and Gavin (1972) study reviewed above is that the lesser correlation between expectancies and performance ratings indicates that performance ratings are less reflective of work effort for nonwhites compared to whites. As a second example, Orpen and Nkohande (1977) speculated that self-esteem could have been a better predictor of effort-performance expectancy for whites than for blacks because work is less central to the self-concept for the latter group. Still another explanation is suggested by Fernandez (1987), who observes that need structures may vary for people of different races. To the extent that they do, the valence-of-outcomes dimension of expectancy theory will be affected.

While researchers need to continue to give attention to new theoretical schemes for racioethnicity effects in the context of expectancy-theory, we believe that the theory of differential effort-performance expectancies for nonwhites compared to whites deserves special attention. Effort-performance expectancies may be lower for nonwhites because: (1) they have less confidence that their efforts will be recognized with high performance ratings; (2) they have control over fewer resources; and (3) they may have lower self-confidence for performance in organizations that are dominated by whites. The first point is supported by research indicating that some minority groups have a more external orientation to locus of control (Orpen and Nkohande, 1977; Helms and Giorgis, 1980), by research indicating that nonwhites tend to receive lower performance ratings than whites (Greenhaus, Parasuraman and Wormely, 1990), and also by the possibility of bias against nonwhites in performance evaluation processes (Pettigrew and Martin, 1987). The second point is supported by research indicating that nonwhites tend to have less overall responsibility and fewer subordinates than whites at comparable job levels (Mueller, Tanaka, and Parcel, 1989). The third point is supported by research on the self-confidence of nonwhites when there is a history of discrimination against their particular group (Brett and Morse, 1975; Orpen and Nkohande, 1977; Lefcourt and Ladwig, 1965).

One possible explanation for the failure of the previous studies to support the theory of lower expectancies for nonwhites is that these studies were all conducted during the early 1970s when equal opportunity and affirmative action were first emphasized in corporate America. It was a time of optimism for many minorities as the first decade under the Civil Rights Act of 1964 unfolded. Many organizations were sponsoring research and other activities around equal opportunity, which tended to raise expectations of positive change. At such a point in history, nonwhites may have been more likely to express strong belief in the meritocracy norm that underlies expectancy theory.

J. Careers: Entry

Research on whether or not white decision makers are less likely to select nonwhites for jobs has produced inconsistent results. Mullins's (1982) study of hiring decisions using white business students to rate hiring favorability of black and white applicants found that the black applicants were actually rated higher than the white applicants and that blacks performing poorly in the interview were rated higher than the low-performing white applicants. A similar conclusion was reached in two studies of racioethnic differences in recruitment that utilized the controversial methodology of sending fictitious resumes of black and white applicants to prospective employers (Newman, 1978; McIntyre et al., 1980). Newman (1978) investigated possible discrimination in recruitment by an analysis of responses of 207 companies to unsolicited resumes from fictitious black and white applicants. Findings indicated a tendency for large companies to favor black applicants. Using a similar methodology, McIntyre et al. (1980) essentially replicated the Newman findings.

Research using different methodologies has produced contradictory results. For example, using a policy-capturing approach, Barr and Hitt (1986) found that both managerial and student decision makers gave higher hiring favorability ratings and recommended higher starting salaries for white applicants than for black applicants. A careful analysis of the Barr and Hitt (1986) study suggests that several methodological differences may have accounted for the contradictory findings. First, in order to reduce the possibility of random or inconsistent decision patterns, they eliminated responses when the R^2 for a given ratee fell below a specified threshold (0.33). Second, they employed a policy-capturing data analysis approach that has a greater likelihood of identifying "theories used" rather than espoused theories (Slovic and Lichtenstein, 1971). Third, they included a visual (video) presentation of candidates as well as written dossiers. These steps may have increased the probability of detecting racioethnic impact. This research suggests that attention should be given to these methodological issues in future research designs testing racioethnic effects on hiring decisions. This is especially true for the issue of whether or not expressed theories and beliefs accurately reflect behavior. The problem of socially desirable responses is especially acute with racioethnic research because unfavorable responses toward nonwhites may be interpreted as racist behavior.

There has also been a considerable amount of research on racioethnic effects in interviews and tests employed in hiring decisions, but the studies we located were inconsistent as to whether or not there is racioethnic bias in interviews. Jackson (1979) studied the factors that affected the selection of managers in government jobs and concluded that interviewees with darker complexions may be at a disadvantage in the hiring process. Mullins (1982) used videotaped stimulus materials to examine interviewer ratings of high- and low-quality candidates role-played by black and white males. This laboratory experiment used business undergraduate students to rate applicants. Results indicated that the most important variable influencing interviewer ratings was applicant quality, but that the black applicant was significantly favored over the white applicant. Finally, Parson and Liden (1984) examined actual interview ratings of candidates for jobs in an amusement park. They found that blacks were rated significantly lower than white applicants on a number of interview dimensions.

The contradictory results in these studies on interviews may be related to the type of methodology employed. Much of the research using lab experiments has found that blacks received higher ratings than whites in interview situations, while studies using field data tend to show the opposite. The confusion here underscores the methodological dilemma faced by researchers. Laboratory experiments facilitate the creation of comparisons in which the candidates differ only by racioethnicity, but they may well increase the likelihood of socially desirable responses. On the other hand, nonexperimental field studies may be less subject to socially desirable response bias (i.e., when actual decisions are examined), but it is more difficult to assure that white and nonwhite applicants in the sample have the identical qualifications.

Research has also shown that interaction effects between the racioethnic identity of the interviewer and the interviewee sometimes influence the interview process. For example, Word, Zanna, and Cooper (1974) and Weitz (1972) found that white interviewers displayed more negative behaviors (e.g., physical distancing or low eye contact) with black interviewees than with white interviewees. Such behaviors can account for less adequate performances of black interviewees (Word, Zanna, and Cooper, 1974).

Additional research is needed in this area, especially on the implications of racioethnic interactions for the interview behavior of both interviewers and interviewees. Such research should include the situation in which whites are interviewed by nonwhites. The potential effectiveness of interviewer training to avoid subtle influences of racioethnic dynamics should also be explored. Traditional interviewer training in organizations has concentrated on the kinds of interview questions that are illegal under Title VII guidelines, with less attention to the possible unconscious behaviors of interviewers toward applicants of other racioethnic groups.

K. Research on Test Validation

A considerable amount of research has been done on the validity of various employment tests for people of different racioethnic groups. The prototypical question in this area has been: Does differential validity exist for specific groups? Once again, nearly all of this research has focused on blacks and whites. The term differential validity is used to describe the hypothesis that employment tests are less valid for nonwhites than for whites (Gatewood and Field, 1990). To a lesser extent, researchers have also focused on the single group validity issue—when a test is valid for one group and not the other.

Like most areas of research on racioethnic effects, results on test validity have been mixed. In one of the first studies, Lopez (1966) examined data on 865 black and white female toll collectors, and found that the best method for predicting job performance for the white group of employees differed from the best method for black employees. Kirkpatrick et al. (1968) also found differential validity in tests for different ethnic groups. Carter and Swanson (1990) addressed the extent to which the Strong interest inventory is psychometrically valid for black samples. After citing research supporting the validity of the Strong inventory for predicting the vocational interests of white samples, the authors review eight studies involving its use with black samples. They conclude that vocational interests are influenced by racioethnic group and also that little evidence supports the Strong inventory as a valid measurement device for black samples. They suggest that the different applicability of the Strong may be due to cultural differences among racioethnic groups.

Other research supporting the differential validity hypothesis for various tests includes Dugan (1966), Bayroff (1966), Ruda and Allrights (1968), Bartlett and O'Leary (1969), Lefkowitz (1972), Toole (1972), and Moore and MacNaughton (1979). In the 1970s, these studies were so influential that the Equal Employment Opportunity Commission altered its guidelines to recognize the possible existence of differential validity (Arvey and Faley, 1988).

Despite the considerable research supporting the existence of differential validity of hiring tests, the evidence is by no means unanimous. Boehm (1972; 1977) reviewed 31 studies involving the differential validity hypothesis and concluded that a majority of the reported findings of differential prediction could be regarded as methodological artifacts resulting from small sample sizes and inappropriate job performance measures. Similarly, Schmidt, Berner, and Hunter (1973) concluded from their review of the research that differential validity is found only by chance. An additional finding was that differential validity was more likely to be found in those studies that used subjective criterion measures (e.g., supervisory ratings).

Finally, three comprehensive reviews of the research available in the mid-1970s concluded that there was no support for the differential validity hypothesis (Hunter and Schmidt 1978; Hunter, Schmidt, and Hunter, 1979; Schmidt, Pearlman, and Hunter, 1980). The Schmidt, Pearlman, and Hunter study was exceptional in that it included Hispanics.

Unfortunately, much of the research and analyses of research on differential validity concentrates on methodological issues in conducting validity studies. More careful and extensive consideration needs to be given as to why one would expect differential validity to occur and why test score differences among certain racioethnic groups for certain types of tests persist (e.g., test differences between blacks and whites on many standard cognitive ability tests; Arvey and Faley, 1988). An idea that we believe deserves further exploration is that differences between minority and majority group members on paper-and-pencil employment tests result from cultural differences. The line of reasoning is that the content of most employment tests is based on white middle-class culture and therefore persons from that culture may be advantaged in taking such tests. A few writers have developed so-called culture-fair tests (e.g., the black intelligence test of cultural homogeneity developed by Williams, 1975, and the Chicano intelligence scale of cultural orientation developed by Ramirez, 1989). However, culture-fair tests have not had wide application (Arvey and Faley, 1988).

In sum, the available research about racioethnic effects on employment tests and interviews does not support concrete generalizations about the presence or absence of such effects. It would therefore seem prudent for organizations to take great care to ensure that the suitability and interpretation of selection tools are specifically assessed for racioethnic effects. It is also important to note that the research to date has been directed toward blacks and whites and has done little to examine validity for Hispanic, Asian, or other nonwhite populations. Finally, research to date has emphasized tests, and to a lesser extent, interviews. There is a need for research on other selection tools, such as assessment centers.

L. Careers: Promotion/Upward Mobility

The effect of being a racioethnic minority on promotion opportunity has been the subject of much commentary but relatively little empirical research or detailed theory construction. The most prevalent theoretical premise of the published material is that racioethnic minorities have lower opportunities for advancement in white-majority organizations than do whites and especially white males. The most obvious evidence in suppport of this conclusion is the relative absence of nonwhites from the highest levels of management in U.S. organizations. For example, 995 of the CEOs listed in the *Business Week* 1000 for 1990 are white, and a recent Department of Labor study of senior managers in nine *Fortune* 500 companies found that only 2.6% of the top managers were nonwhite (U.S. Department of Labor, 1991).

Since management jobs were effectively closed to racioethnic minorities until fairly recently, it is appropriate to distinguish the issue of arrival at the top from progress toward it. In this regard, Jones (1976; 1986) and Fernandez (1987) report survey data indicating that despite affirmative action, a large percentage of nonwhite employees believe that their race has hindered their advancement. Research that compares actual promotion rates of different racioethnic groups is scarce. Cox and Nkomo (1986) found no significant differences in promotability ratings between black and white lower-level managers in a large public-sector firm. However, in a study comparing the career progress of 26 black MBAs to that of 680 white MBAs of comparable career tenure, Brown and Ford (1977) found that only 31% of the blacks had reached middle-management or higher compared to 73% in the white sample. Similarly, in their study of 849 managers in three large corporations, Greenhaus, Parasuraman, and Wormley (1990) found that black managers had lower promotability ratings and were more likely to be plateaued (more than 7 years in their current jobs) than their white counterparts. They found that the lower promotion ratings of nonwhites mainly occurred indirectly through lower performance ratings, whereas the plateauing seemed to be a direct effect of racioethnicity.

A small amount of research and discussion has addressed possible causes of lower upward mobility of nonwhites compared to whites in predominantly white organizations. For example, Fine, Johnson, and Ryan (1990) studied 242 employees of various levels in a regional agency of the federal government. Factors cited as obstacles to the upward mobility of nonwhites included the impact of a white/male culture and negative stereotyping of nonwhites.

Another study addressing factors that may underlie upward mobility problems for nonwhites is the work by Greenhaus and Parasuraman (in press) on the effects of race on peformance attributions. Their data, taken from 1628 managers in three companies, indicate that the racioethnicity of employees does affect the types of performance attributions made about their work. In working relationships of less than 1 year, they found that supervisors were more likely to attribute good performance to ability if the subordinates were white instead of black. They also found that supervisors were more likely to attribute good performance to help from others and to job ease if the subordinate was black rather than white. Moreover, they found that advancement prospects for all managers were better if good performance was attributed to ability rather than luck, ease of job, or amount of help from others. This combination of findings strongly suggests that racioethnic effects on performance attributions is a significant cause of glass-ceiling effects on the upward mobility of nonwhite managers in predominantly white organizations. There has been much discussion in recent years about "subtle" discrimination. However, empirical verification that such discrimination actually occurs, and of how it occurs, is scarce. The work of Greenhaus and Parasurman makes an important contribution in this regard. We strongly urge additional research to replicate and extend their work.

A number of writers have argued that nonwhites have difficulty gaining promotion in predominantly white organizations because of more limited access to the types of job assignments and organizational experiences that are needed for promotion (Nkomo and Cox, 1990; Fernandez, 1975, 1981; Jones, 1986). Although published accounts of empirical research on this argument are scarce, several will be cited here. Mueller, Tanaka, and Parcel (1989) studied spans of both responsibility and control in a sample of 621 white male and 142 black male supervisors. They found that black managers had lower spans of control and less authority over the pay and promotion of subordinates than white managers. This finding suggests that blacks may not be as likely as whites to be selected for middle and senior manager positions because they do not have the same opportunity as whites to control resources at lower levels of management.

The control of resources is important for multiple reasons. First, the ability to control more resources may enable one to accomplish better work results and thereby create a more impressive track record. Second, jobs that control more resources are more likely to gain the attention of senior managers whose support is needed for promotion. Third, demonstrating the ability to handle resources well should improve one's probability of being selected for jobs of greater responsibility.

Another result from the Mueller, Tanaka, and Parcel study that is germane to our purpose here was their finding that social psychological variables, such as achievement orientation and interpersonal trust, were important predictors of spans of control for black supervisors but not for white supervisors. They interpret these results as evidence that nonwhites must be more qualified than whites to gain advancement in predominantly white organizations. Our own conclusion hinges on the interpretation of the phrase "more qualified." To the extent that it refers to judging minority managers on a broader range of criteria than is used with majority managers, we agree with their interpretation. In this respect, their results are reminiscent of our own finding cited earlier that social behavior factors were important predictors of overall performance ratings for black managers but not for white managers (Cox and Nkomo, 1986). Despite the obvious unfairness of such apparent "double standards," it is explainable on both rational and emotional grounds. If senior managers believe that nonwhite supervisors encounter more resistance than whites from peers, subordinates, and perhaps even from some customer constituencies, they may conclude that only very exceptional candidates will be able to succeed in such a position. Also, to the extent that the senior managers themselves (the vast majority of whom are white) feel more comfortable with racioethnically similar peers and direct reports, they may be more prone to give white candidates "the benefit of the doubt" in such areas as achievement motivation and interpersonal trust.

The double standard discussion inevitably raises the issue of affirmative action. Some would argue that the presence of affirmative action creates a double standard in which nonwhite candidates are subject to *less* rigorous evaluation criteria. Responding fully to this argument would require a lengthy and complicated discussion that is beyond the bounds of this chapter. One response however, is that whatever advantage affirmative action offers to nonwhites must be viewed within the context of the various forms of adverse discrimination that it is designed to address.

Several studies have addressed the extent to which nonwhites are segregated into certain kinds of jobs in predominantly white organizations. In a lab experiment using fictitious job applicant resumes, Terpstra and Larsen (1980) found that some jobs were stereotyped according to racioethnic identities of the applicant. Similar findings are reported by Stone and Stone (1987). Finally, Collins (1989) addressed the question of whether or not nonwhite managers tend to be segregated into staff jobs and particularly human relations, personnel, and community affairs. Based on interviews with 76 of the highest-ranking black managers in majority-white organizations, she determined that 66% of the sample entered and advanced through the managerial ranks in "racialized" jobs (i.e., jobs created to handle black consumer issues or civil rights-related matters). For a majority of the sample (51%), their last job held in the predominantly white sector was a racially oriented personnel or public relations job. Collins notes that nearly a third of these managers were working in more mainstream functions of their organizations when requested by superiors to accept racially oriented jobs. She further argues that the emphasis on these career paths for black executives made them unlikely candidates for further advancement because top managers in the private sector are rarely drawn from human relations or community affairs functions. Examination of the career paths of CEOs of large American firms (such as is provided in the 1990 annual *Business Week* 1000 profile) makes it clear that the critical career path for senior management positions has historically been finance (24%), marketing (25%), or operations/engineering (26%), but cetainly not human resources, (0%) and community relations (0%). Therefore, Collins' premise that functional segregation of nonwhites is a major cause of their absence from top management seems well founded.

M. Additional Suggestions for Future Research

Much of our thinking on the implications of past research for future theory and research has already been communicated in the process of reviewing the literature. Further, we have noted elsewhere (Cox and Nkomo, 1990) that previous organizational research on racioethnicity has suffered from: (1) an absence of theory or the use of overly simplistic and underdeveloped theoretical frameworks; (2) incomplete or inappropriate operationalizations of the concept of race itself (especially ignoring the cultural significance of race and intragroup differences in levels of racioethnic identity); and (3) failure to use multigroup samples and to address nonwhite samples other than blacks.

This said, we will address here several promising directions for future work that were not identified earlier. As suggested in the introduction to our review, previous work on racioethnicity in the OB literature has tended to address traditional OB topics for two biologically differentiated racioethnic groups (e.g., differences in motivational structures between blacks and whites). We believe that the quest to understand how organizational processes are influenced by racioethnicity will be well served if future work gives added emphasis to: (1) cultural dynamics of race, (2) intergroup theory, (3) the intersection of racioethnicity and gender, and (4) the theory of everyday racism. Each of these will be briefly discussed.

III. THE CULTURAL DYNAMICS OF RACE

While the biological aspects of racioethnicity are undeniably important, a considerable literature in social-psychology suggests that African-Americans, Chinese-Americans, Mexican-Americans, native Americans, and other minority groups also represent distinct cultural groups. For example, Cox, Lobel, and McLeod (1991) have noted differences in cultural traditions among black, Asian, Hispanic, and white Americans in the extent to which individualistic versus collective behaviors are favored. They found that from a knowledge of these differences they could predict that members of these nonwhite groups would display higher levels of cooperative versus competitive behavior in a two-party mixed motive game. Another example is Kochman's work (1981) on differences in communication styles between cohorts of white and black Americans born in the late 1940s and 1950s. He shows numerous examples of how ignorance of these differences creates potential for misunderstanding and leads to unsatisfying cross-group interactions. Numerous other writers have also addressed the cultural distinctiveness of different racioethnic groups (e.g., Fernandez, 1981; Triandis and Malpass, 1971; 1976; Foeman and Pressley, 1987; Leung and Bond, 1984; de Forest, 1984). Since organizations also represent specific cultural constellations (Denison, 1990; Sales and Mirvus, 1984; Meyerson and Martin, 1987), the issues of cultural intersection and potential culture clash deserve attention. Examples of emerging work that addresses these issues include the work of

Bell (1990) on bicultural identity, Cox and Nickelson's (1991) theory of intraorganizational acculturation, and empirical studies that apply ethnology research to the organizational context (e.g., Cox, Lobel, and McLeod, 1991; Farh, Dobbins, and Cheng, 1991; James and Khoo, in press). Additional work of this type is needed.

IV. INTERGROUP THEORY

Various branches of intergroup theory also hold a wealth of relatively untapped potential for work on racioethnic effects on organization behavior. We will mention two that we believe are especially promising. The embedded group theory (Alderfer, 1987; Alderfer and Smith, 1982) has been successfully applied to race-relations research in the organizational context. Alderfer and Smith (1982) argue that relationships between people are embedded in a network of affiliations that include both personal identity groups (e.g., ethnicity, gender, age) and task groups (e.g., organization level, functional specialization). These affiliations, in turn, occur in a context that is a mixture of intraorganizational and external environment. Understanding transactions between individuals therefore requires an understanding of the group affiliation profile of the parties as well as the social-political backdrop within which the parties interact. The theory acknowledges that individuals have multiple identities, and that the meaning of these identities must be understood in the context of the organizational and societal history of interaction of the identity groups. For example, the theory would predict that the relationship between a black manager and a white subordinate would be hindered by the fact that relationships between blacks and whites in America have historically featured the domination of whites over blacks. Understanding the interaction is further complicated by the other group affiliations of the respective parties. For example, if the manager is also a woman and the subordinate is a man, successful interaction will be even more difficult unless there is special attention to the relationship by both parties.

A second line of work within the domain of intergroup theory that we find especially promising for work on racioethnicity in OB is that on minority group density (Kanter, 1977a, b; Blalock, 1967; Pettigrew and Martin, 1987). In general, this work seeks to explicate the impact of proportional representation of a particular minority group identity in the larger group (density) on behavior and work outcomes. Kanter's thesis, which was developed from empirical work on gender and not racioethnicity, is that organizational experience of minorities will become more positive as their density increases. Blalock (following logic originally suggested by Key's studies of voting behavior of whites in the South, 1949; 1964) found that the experience of minorities may actually become more negative as density increases if the majority group feels threatened by the greater representation. Both arguments have received some empirical support. Additional research is needed not only to clarify how density affects behavior in organizations but also to provide guidance on how to respond to these effects. For example, if the Kanter thesis is correct, is affirmative action the most effective response? If the Blalock thesis is correct, how can perceived threat among majority group members be minimized?

V. RACIOETHNICITY AND GENDER

Few studies have examined the intersection of racioethnicity and gender effects on organizational experiences. Nonwhite women are typically subsumed alternately under the category "women" or "minorities." Their combined identity as black, Asian, or Hispanic women is often invisible, as they fall between the cracks of the two streams of research (Nkomo, 1988). There is an emerging body of literature that indicates that the combined and interactive effects of racioethnicity and gender have a pervasive impact on the lives of nonwhite women (Leggon, 1980; Bell, 1986; Nkomo and Cox, 1989; Thomas, 1989; Greenhaus, Parasuraman, and Wormley, 1990). A central issue in much of this early work has been whether or not the combined effects of racioethnicity and gender produce a double advantage or double disadvantage. While most researchers have recognized the effect as cumulative, they differ on whether it is positive or negative (Bell, Denton, and Nkomo, forthcoming). The double advantage view holds that minority women enjoy positive effects from their dual identities (Epstein, 1973), while the double whammy hypothesis suggests the net effect of racioethnicity and gender is negative for minority women (King, 1988; Benjamin, 1982).

In a study of black professionals, Nkomo and Cox (1989) examined the validity of the double advantage and double whammy hypotheses for black women managers. Although overall results supported neither hypothesis, the researchers did find that the black women had higher job performance ratings and were at about the same hierarchical level as the black men, but that the women received significantly lower pay.

Woo (1985) examined the notion of advantaged status of Asian-American women. In her study of census data, she found that while education enhanced earnings capability, the relative gains made by Asian-American women were not as great as those made by other women and were well below parity with white males.

Romero (1986) tested the double advantage hypothesis for Chicano women and found that the slow pace of the movement of Chicanos into higher-paying managerial and skilled positions did not support the claim of "preferential treatment." Other organizational researchers using cross-race, cross-gender designs, have reported significant interaction effects of racioethnicity and gender (Greenhaus, Parasuraman, and Wormley, 1990; Thomas, 1989). The available research suggests that the intersection between race and gender is complex and problematic and that we cannot assume that the experience of nonwhite women is similar to the experiences of nonwhite men, nor can we assume that the experiences of nonwhite women are the same as white women. Therefore, organizational scholars must increase the utilization of research designs that examine the interactive effects of racioethnicity and gender.

VI. EVERYDAY RACISM

Essed (1991) has developed what she calls a theory of everyday racism which combines the daily experiences of individuals with a more structural account of racism. Her theoretical framework draws on work from the literature of macro- and microsociology, social psychology, discourse analysis, race relations theory, and women's studies. According to Essed (1991: 50)

> Everyday racism is the integration of racism into everyday situations through practices (cognitive and behavioral) that activate underlaying power relations. This process must be seen as a continuum through which the integration of racism into everyday practices becomes part of the expected, of the unquestionable, and of what is seen as normal by the dominant group.

According to her analysis, racist beliefs and actions permeate everyday life and become embedded in human systems so that they tend to reproduce themselves. Essed (1991) identifies three main mechanisms of everyday racism: marginalization, problematization, and containment. Marginalization is a process in which a sense of "otherness" is perpetuated, while problematization refers to ideological constructions legitimizing exclusion and repression of certain groups. For example, problematization involves the hierarchical ordering of differences between groups according to biological, cultural, or value differences (e.g., European culture as superior to African or Asian culture). Containment suggests efforts by the dominant group to suppress the efforts of dominated groups for equality, justice, and power.

The theory of everyday racism suggests that research on racioethnicity in organizations must identify and examine the rules, policies, conditions, and power relations that tend to reproduce racism in "everyday organizational situations." Concomitantly, we need to explore how racism is systematically represented in events and language (often assumed to be neutral) in the daily routine of organizations. An example of language use is the often-stated emphasis on the word "qualified" when seeking a minority job candidate. Often the hidden belief behind the use of the word is the assumed pervasiveness of the inferiority of members of racioethnic groups.

Everyday racism also suggests that individuals in organizations are involved differently in the process of racism because of their position in the power structure. Gender, class, and other factors determine the content and structure of racism. For example, the experience of racism for African-American women, while similar to that of African-American men, may have qualitatively different features. Essed (1991) has labeled the experience of racioethnic women as gendered racism. In like fashion, the racism of dominant group women may be qualitatively different than that of dominant group men because of the position of women in the power structure. Research drawing upon the concepts of everyday racism may help unmask the subtle and covert nature of racism today and should contribute toward identifying both individual and structural strategies for eradicating racism in organizations.

VII. CONCLUSION

This chapter has reviewed and analyzed organizational literature on racioethnicity. Suggestions for future research have been described. In conclusion, we offer several summary comments. First, it seems clear that the base of knowledge about how racioethnic diversity impacts behavior in organizations remains woefully underdeveloped. Second, there is a considerable base of knowledge about the effects of racioethnicity in the society at large that has not been adequately applied to the organizational context. Finally, there is a great need for work that more adequately reflects the complexity of racioethnic phenomena in organizations. We are encouraged that several streams of work in the OB domain have emerged in the last few years that we believe address long-neglected, but critical dimensions of that complexity.

REFERENCES

Adams, A. V., Krislov, J., and Lairson, D. R. (1972). Plantwide seniority, black employment, and employer affirmative action. *Industrial and Labor Relations Review, 26*: 686–690.

Adams, E. F. (1978). A multivariate study of subordinate perceptions of and attitudes toward minority and majority managers. *Journal of Applied Psychology, 63*(3), 277–288.

Alderfer, C. P., Alderfer, C. J., Tucker, L., and Tucker, R. (1980). Diagnosing race relations in management. *J. of Applied Behavioral Science, 16*: 135–166.

Alderfer, C. P., and Smith, K. K. (1982). Studying intergroup relations embedded in organizations. *Administrative Science Quarterly, 27*: 35–65.

Alper, S. W. (1975). Racial differences in job and work environment priorities among newly hired college graduates. *J. of Applied Psychology, 60*: 120–134.

Arnold, H. J., and Feldman, D. C. (1986). *Organizational Behavior*. McGraw-Hill, New York.

Arvey, R. D., and Foley, R. H. (1988). *Fairness In Selecting Employees*. Addison-Wesley Publishing Company, Reading, Mass.

Barr, S. H., and Hitt, M. A. (1986). A comparison of selection decision models in manager versus student samples. *Personnel Psychology, 39*: 599–617.

Bartlett, C. J., and O'Leary, B. S. (1969). A differential prediction model to moderate the effects of heterogeneous groups in personnel selection and classification. *Personnel Psychology, 2*: 1–18.

Bartol, K. M., Anderson, C. R., and Schneier, J. (1981). Sex and ethnic effects on motivation to manage among college business students. *Journal of Applied Psychology, 66*: 40–44.

Bartol, K. M., Evans, C. L., and Stith, M. (1978). Black versus white leaders: A comparative review of the literature. *3*: 294–304.

Bass, A., and Turner, J. (1973). Ethnic group differences in relationship among criteria of job performance. *J. of Applied Psychology, 7*: 101–109.

Bayroff, A. (1966). Test technology and equal employment opportunity. *Personnel Psychology, 7*: 191–209.

Beatty, D. (1990). Re-examining the link between job characteristics and job satisfaction. *J. of Social Psychology, 130:* 131–132.

Beatty, R. W. (1973). Blacks as supervisors: A study of training, job performance, and employers' expectations. *Academy of Management Journal, 16*: 196–206.

Bell, E. (1986). The power within: Bicultural Life structures and stress among black women, Ph.D. dissertation, Case Western Reserve University.

Bell, E. L. (1990). The bicultural life experience of career-oriented black women. *J. of Organizational Behavior, 11*: 459–477.

Bell, E., Denton, T., and Nkomo, S. M. (1993). Women of color in management: Towards an inclusive analysis. In *Women in Management: Trends, Perspectives and Challenges* (E. Fagenson, ed.), Sage Publications, Newbury Park, Calif.

Benjamin, L. (1982). Black women achievers: An isolated elite. *Sociological Inquiry, 52*: 141–151.

Bigoness, W. (1976). Effect of applicants' sex, race, and performance on employers' ratings: Some additional findings. *J. of Applied Psychology, 61*: 80–84.

Blalock, H. Jr. (1967). *Toward a Theory of Minority-Group Relations*. John Wiley & Sons, New York.

Boehm, V. R. (1972). Negro-white differences in validity of employment testing and training selection procedures. *Journal of Applied Psychology, 57*: 101–109.

Boehm, V. R. (1977). Differential prediction—a methodological artifact. *J. of Applied Psychology, 62*: 146–154.

Brett, E. A., and Morse, S. J. (1975). A study of the attitudes of middle-class Africans. In *Contemporary South Africa: Social Psychological Perspectives* (S. J. Morse and C. Orpen, eds.), Juta, Cape Town, pp. 154–167.

Brown, H. A., and Ford, D. L., Jr. (1977). An explanatory analysis of discrimination in the employment of black MBA graduates. *J. of Applied Psychology, 62*: 50–56.

Brugnoli, G., Campion, J., and Basen, Jr. (1979). Racial bias in the use of work samples for personnel selection. *J. of Applied Psychology, 64*: 119–123.

Carter, R. T., and Swanson, J. L. (1990). The validity of the strong interest inventory with black Americans: A review of the literature. *J. of Vocational Behavior, 36*: 195–209.

Chusmir, L. H., and Koberg, C. S. (1990). Ethnic differences in the relationship between job satisfaction and sex-role conflict among Hispanics and nonhispanic white individuals. *Psychological Reports, 66*: 567–578.

Collins, S. M. (1989). The marginalization of black executives. *Social Problems, 36*:(4): 317–331.

Cox, J. A., and Kruboltz, J. D. (1958). Racial bias in peer ratings of basic airmen. *Sociometry, 21*: 292–299.

Cox, T. H. (1990). Problems with research by organizational scholars on issues of race and ethnicity. *The Journal of Applied Behavioral Science, 26*(1), 5–24.

Cox, T. H., and Finley-Nickelson, J. (1991). Models of acculturation for intra-organizational cultural diversity. *Canadian Journal of Administrative Sciences, 8*(2): 90–100.

Cox, T. H., Lobel, S., and Mcleod, P. (1991). Effects of ethnic group cultural difference on cooperative versus competitive behavior in a group task. *Academy of Management Journal, 34*: 827–847.

Cox, T. H., and Nkomo, S. M. (1986). Differential appraisal criteria based on race of the ratee. *Group and Organizational Studies, 11*: 101–119.

Cox, T. H., and Nkomo, S. M. (1990). Invisible men and women: A status report on race as a variable in organizational behavior and research. *J. of Organizational Behavior, 11*: 419–431.

Crooks, L. A., ed. (1972). *An Investigation of Sources of Bias in the Prediction of Job Performance: A Six Year Study*. Educational Testing Service, Princeton, N.J.

Dalton, A. H., and Marcis, J. G. (1986). The determinants of job satisfaction for young males and females. *Atlantic Economic Journal, 14*: 85.

deFrost, M. E. (1984). Spanish-Speaking Employees in American Industry. *Business Horizons, 27*: 14–17.

Dejung, J. E., and Kaplan, H. (1962). Some differential effects of race of rater and ratee on early peer ratings of combat aptitude. *J. of Applied Psychology, 46*: 370–374.

Delbecq, A. L., and Kaplan, S. D. (1968). The myth of the indigenous community leader within the war on poverty. *Academy of Management Journal, 11*: 11–25.

DeMeuse, K. P. (1987). A review of the effects of nonverbal cues on the performance appraisal process. *J. of Occupational Psychology, 60*: 207–226.

Denison, D. (1990). *Corporate Culture and Organizational Effectiveness*. John Wiley & Sons, New York.

Dickens, F., and Dickens, J. B. (1982). *The Black Manager*. Amacom, New York.

Dipboye, R. L. (1985). Some neglected variables in research on discrimination in appraisals. *Academy of Management Review, 10*: 116–127.

Dugan, R. (1966). Current problems in test performance of job applicants: II. *Personnel Psychology, 19*: 18–24.

Epstein, C. F. (1973). Positive effects of the multiple negative: Explaining the success of black professional women. *American Journal of Sociology, 5*: 913–935.

Essed, P. (1991). *Understanding Everyday Racism: An Interdisciplinary Theory*. Sage Publications, Newbury Park, Calif.

Farh, J. L., Dobbins, G. H., and Cheng, B. S. (1991). Cultural relativity in action: A comparison of self-ratings made by Chinese and U. S. workers. *Personnel Psychology*, 129–147.

Feldman, J. (1973). Race, economic class, and perceived outcomes of work and unemployment. *J. of Applied Psychology, 58*: 16–22.

Fernandez, J. P. (1975). *Black Managers in White Corporations*. John Wiley, New York.

Fernandez, J. P. (1981). *Racism and Sexism in Corporate Life: Changing Values in American Business*. Lexington Books, Lexington, Mass.

Fernandez, J. P. (1987). *Survival in the Corporate Fishbowl*. Lexington Books, Lexington, Mass.

Fine, M. G., Johnson, F. L., and Ryan, M. S. (1990). Cultural diversity in the workplace. *Public Personnel Management, 19*(3): 305–318.

Foeman, A. K., and Pressley, G. (1987). Ethnic culture and corporate culture: Using black styles in organizations. *Communications Quarterly, 35*: 293–307.

Gatewood, R. D., and Feild, H. (1990). *Human Resource Selection*. The Dryden Press, Chicago.

Gavin, J., and Ewen, R. (1974). Racial differences in job attitudes and performance—some theoretical considerations and empirical findings. *Personnel Psychology, 27*: 455–464.

Greenhaus, J. H., and Gavin, J. F. (1972). The relationship between expectancies and job behavior from white and black employees. *Personnel Psychology, 25*: 449–455.

Greenhaus, J. H., and Parasuraman, S. (in press). Job performance attributions and career advancement prospects: An examination of gender and race effects. In *Organizational Behavior and Human Decision Processes*.

Greenhaus, J. H., Parasuraman, S., and Wormley, W. (1990). Effects of race on organizational experiences, job performance evaluation, and career outcomes. *Academy of Management Journal, 33*: 64–86.

Hamner, W. C., Kim, J. S., Baird, L., and Bigoness, W. J. (1974). Race and sex as determinants of ratings by potential employers in a simulated work-sampling task. *J. of Applied Psychology, 59*: 705–711.

Helms, J. E., and Giorgis, T. W. (1980). A comparison of the locus of control and anxiety level of African, black American and white American college students. *J. of College Student Personnel,   *: 503–509.

Herzberg, F., Mausner, B., and Snyderman, B. B. (1959). *The Motivation to Work*. John Wiley & Sons, Inc., New York.

Hill, W. H., and Fox, W. M. (1973). Black and white marine squad leaders' perceptions of racially mixed squads. *Academy of Management Journal, 16*: 680–686.

Hunter, J. E., and Schmidt, F. L. (1978). Differential validity of employment tests by race: A critical analysis of three studies. *J. of Applied Psychology, 63*: 1–11.

Hunter, J. E., Schmidt, F. L., and Hunter, R. (1979). Differential validity of employment tests by race: A comprehensive review and analysis. *Psychological Bulletin, 85*: 721–735.

Ilgen, D. R., and Youtz, M. A. (1986). Factors affecting the evaluation and development of minorities in organizations. In *Research in Personnel and Human Resource Management: A Research Annual* (K. Bowland and G. Ferris, eds.), JAI Press, Greenwich, Conn., pp. 307–337.

Ivancevich, J. M., and McMahon, J. T. (1977). Black-white differences in a goal-setting program organization. *Behavior and Human Performance, 20*: 287–300.

Jackson, M. (1979). Racial factors in executive selection. *Public Personnel Management, 8*: 218–222.

James, K., and Khoo, G. (1991). Identity-related influences on the success of minority workers in primarily non-minority organizations. *Hispanic Journal of Behavioral Sciences*.

Johnston, W., and Packer, A. (1987). *Workforce 2000: Work and Worker for the 21st Century*. Hudson Institute, Indianapolis.

Jones, A. P., James, L. R., Bruni, J. R., and Sells, S. B. (1977). Black white differences in work environment perceptions and job satisfaction and its correlates. *Personnel Psychology, 30*: 5–16.

Jones, E. W. (1973). What's it like to be a black manager? *Harvard Business Review, 51*: 108–116.

Jones, E. W. (1986). Black managers: The dream deferred. *Harvard Business Review, 64*: 84–93.

Jussim, L., Coleman, L., and Lerch, L. (1987). The nature of stereotypes: A comparison and integration of three theories. *Journal of Personality and Social Psychology, 52*(3), 536–546.

Kahoe, R. D. (1974). A negro-white difference in psychological meaning of job incentives. *J. of Social Psychology, 92*: 157–158.

Kanter, R. M. (1977a). Some effects of proportions on group life: Skewed sex ratios and responses to token women. *American Journal of Sociology, 82*: 965–991.

Kanter, R. M. (1977b). *Men and Women of the Corporation.* Basic Books, New York.

Kerr, S., and Jermier, J. (1978). Substitutes for leadership: Their meaning and measurement. *Organizational Behavior and Human Performance, 22:* 375–403.

Key, V. O. Jr. (1949). *Southern Politics.* Random House, Inc., New York.

Key, V. O. Jr. (1964). *Politics, Parties, and Pressure Groups.* Thomas Crowell Co., New York.

Kimberly, J., and Quinn, R. (1984). *New Futures: Managing Corporate Transitions.* Dow-Jones-Irwin, Homewood, Ill.

King, D. (1988). Multiple jeopardy, multiple consciousness: The context of a black feminist ideology. *Signs, 14:* 42–72.

Kipnis, D., Silverman, A., and Copeland, C. (1973). Effects of emotional arousal on the use of supervised coercion with black and union members. *J. of Applied Psychology, 57:* 38–43.

Kleiman, L. S., Biderman, M. D., and Faley, R. H. (1987). An examination of employee perceptions of a subjective performance appraisal system. *J. of Business and Psychology, 2:* 112–121.

Kochman, T. (1981). *Black and White Styles In Conflict.* University of Chicago Press, Chicago.

Konar, E. (1981). Explaining racial differences in job satisfaction: A reexamination of the data. *J. of Applied Psychology, 66:* 522–524.

Kraiger, K., and Ford, J. (1985). A meta-analysis of ratee race effects in performance ratings. *J. of Applied Psychology, 70:* 56–65.

LaFree, G. D. (1980). The effect of sexual stratification by race on official reactions to rape. *American Sociological Review, 45:* 842–854.

Landy, F. J., and Farr, S. L. (1976). Police performance appraisal, *JSAS Catalog of Selected Documents in Psychology, 6:* 83 (ms. No., 1315).

Landy, F. J., and Farr, S. L. (1980). Performance rating. *Psychological Bulletin, 87:* 72–107.

Lefcourt, H. M., and Ladwig, G. W. (1965). Effect of reference group upon negroes' task persistence in a biracial competitive game. *J. of Psychology & Social Psychology, 1:* 668–671.

Lefkowitz, J. (1972). Differential validity: Ethnic groups as a moderator in predicting tenure. *Personnel Psychology, 25:* 223–240.

Lefkowitz, J., and Fraser, A. W. (1980). Assessment of achievement and power motivation of black and white, using a black and white TAT, with black and white administration. *J. of Applied Psychology, 65(6):* 685–696.

Leggon, C. B. (1980). Black female professionals: Dilemmas and contradictions of status. In *The Black Women* (La Frances Rodgers–Rose, ed.), Sage Publications, Beverly Hills, Calif.

Lueng, K., and Bond, M. (1984). The impact of cultural collection on reward allocation. *J. of Personality & Social Psychology, 47(4):* 805–811.

Maslow, A. H., (1954). *Motivation and Personality.* Harper & Row, New York.

Massey, D. S., and Denton, N. A. (1988). Suburbanization and segregation in U.S. metropolitan areas. *American Journal of Sociology, 94:* 592–626.

McClelland, D. C. (1961). *The Achieving Society.* Van Nostrand, Princeton, N.J.

McClelland, D. C. (1974). Effects of interviewer-respondent race interactions on household interview measures of motivation and intelligence. *J. of Personality and Social Psychology, 29:* 392–397.

McIntyre, S., Moberg, D., Posner, B., and Newman, J. (1980). Discrimination in recruitment: An empirical analysis–comment–reply. *Industrial & Labor Relations Review, 33:* 543–550.

McNeely, R. L. (1987). Predictors of job satisfaction among three racial/ethnic groups of professional female human service workers. *J. of Sociology & Social Welfare, 14:* 115–136.

Meyerson, D. E., and Martin, J. (1987). Culture change: An integration of three different views. *J. of Management Studies, 24:* 623–647.

Milutinovich, J. S., and Tsaklanganos, A. (1976). The impact of perceived community prosperity on job-satisfaction of black and white workers. *Academy of Management Journal, 19:* 49–65.

Mobley, W. (1982). Supervisor and employee race and sex effects on performance appraisals: A field study of adverse impact and generalizability. *Academy of Management Journal, 25:* 598–606.

Moch, M. (1980). Racial differences in job satisfaction: Testing four common explanations. *J. of Applied Psychology, 65:* 299–306.

Moore, C. Jr., and MacNaughton, J. (1979). Ethnic differences within an industrial selection battery. *Personnel Psychology, 22:* 473–482.

Morishima, J. (1981). Special employment issues for Asian Americans. *Public Personnel Management Journal, 10(4):* 384–392.

Mueller, C. W., Tanaka, K., and Parcel, T. L. (1989). Particularism in authority outcomes of black and white supervisors. *Social Science Research, 18:* 1–20.

Mullins, T. W. (1982). Interviewer decisions as a function of applicant race, applicant quality and interviewer prejudice. *Personnel Psycology, 35*: 163–174.

Newman, J. M. (1978). Discrimination in recruitment: An empirical analysis. *Industrial and Labor Relations Review, 32*: 15–23.

Nkomo, S. M. (1988). Race and sex: The forgotten case of the black female manager. In *Women's Careers: Pathways and Pitfalls* (S. Rose and L. Larwood, eds.), Praeger, New York.

Nkomo, S. M., and Cox, T. Jr. (1989). Gender differences in the factors affecting the upward mobility of black managers. *Sex Roles, 21*: 825–835.

Nkomo, S. M., and Cox, T. H. Jr. (1990). Factors affecting the upward mobility of black managers. *Review of Black Political Economy, 18*.

O'Reilly, C. A., and Roberts, K. M. (1973). Job satisfaction among whites and nonwhites: A cross cultural approach. *J. of Applied Psychology, 57*: 295–299.

Orpen, C., and Nkohande, J. (May 1977). Self-esteem, interval control and expectancy beliefs of white and black managers in South Africa. *J. of Management Studies*: 192–199.

Parker, W. S. (1976). Black white differences in leader behavior related to subordinates' reactions. *J. of Applied Psychology, 61*, 140–147.

Parson, C. K., and Liden, R. C. (1984). Interviewer perceptions of applicant qualifications: A multivariate field study of demographic characteristics and nonverbal cues. *J. of Applied Psychology, 69*: 557–568.

Pettigrew,T. F., and Martin, J. (1987). Shaping the organizational context for black American inclusion. *J. of Social Forces, 43*: 41–78.

Porter, L., and Lawler III, E. E. *Managerial Attitudes and Performance*. Dorsey Press, Chicago.

Pulakos, E. D., Oppler, S. H., White, L. A., and Borman, W. C. (1989). Examination of race and sex effects on performance ratings. *J. of Applied Psychology, 74*: 770–780.

Ramirez, A. (1989). Racism toward Hispanics: The culturally monolithic society. In *Eliminating Racism* (P. A. Katz and D. A. Taylor, eds.), Plenum Press, New York, pp. 137–153.

Richards, S. A., and Jaffee, C. L. (1972). Blacks supervising whites: A study of interracial difficulties in working together in a simulated organization. *J. of Applied Psychology, 56*: 234–240.

Romero, M. (1986). Twice Protected? Assessing the impact of affirmative action on Mexican-American women. In *Ethnicity and Women* (W.A. Van Horne and T. V. Tonnesen, eds.), pp. 135–156.

Ruda, E., and Allrights, L. (1968). Racial differences on selection instruments related to subsequent job performance. *Personnel Psychology, 2*: 31–41.

Sales, A. L., and Mirvis, P. H. (1984). When cultures collide: Issues of acquisition. In *Managing Organizational Transitions* (J. R. Kimberly and R. E. Quinn, eds.), Irwin, Homewood, Ill., pp. 107–133.

Schmidt, F. L., and Johnson, R. H. (1973). Effect of race on peer ratings in an industrial setting. *J. of Applied Psychology, 57*: 237–241.

Schmitt, N., and Lappin, M. (1980). Race and sex as determinants of the mean and variance of performance ratings. *J. of Applied Psychology, 65*: 428–435.

Shiflett, S. (1988). Effects of race and criterion on the predictive ability of beliefs and attitudes. *Psychological Reports, 62*: 527–535.

Shull, F. Anthony (1978). Do black and white supervisory problem solving styles differ? *Personnel Psychology, 56*: 28–32.

Slocum, J. Jr., and Strawser, R. (1972). Racial differences in job attitudes. *J. of Applied Psychology, 56*: 28–32.

Slovic, P., and Lichtenstein, S. (1971). Comparison of Bayesian and regression approaches to the study of information processing in judgement. *Organizational Behavior & Human Performance, 6*: 649–711.

Stone, D. L., and Stone, E. F. (1987). Effects of missing application blank information on personnel selection decisions: Do privacy protect strategic bias the outcome? *J. of Applied Psychology, 58*: 16–22.

Terpstra, D., and Larsen, M. (1985). A note on job type and applicant race as determinants of hiring decisions. *J. of Occupational Psychology, 53*: 117–119.

Thomas, D. (1989). Mentoring and irrationality: The role of racial taboos. *Human Resource Management, 28*: 279–290.

Toole, D. (1972). The differential validity of personality, personal history, and aptitude data for minority and non-minority employees. *Personnel Psychology, 25*: 661–672.

Triandis, H. C., and Malpass, R. S. (1971). Studies of black and white interracial and job settings. *J. of Applied Social Psychology, 1*: 107–117.

U.S. Department of Labor (1991). A report on the glass ceiling initiative.

Vecchio, R. (1980). Worker alienation as a moderator of the job quality–job satisfaction relationship: The case of racial differences. *Academy of Management Journal, 23*: 479–486.

Vroom, V. H. (1964). *Work and Motivation.* Wiley, New York.

Watson, J. G., and Barone, S. (1976). The self-concept, personal values, and motivational orientation of black and white managers. *Academy of Management Journal, 19*: 36–48.

Weaver, C. N. (1975). Black-white differences in attitudes toward job characteristics. *J. of Applied Psychology, 60*: 438–441.

Weaver, C. N. (1978). Black-white correlates of job satisfaction. *J. of Applied Psychology, 63*: 255–258.

Weitz, S. (1972). Attitude, voice and behavior: repressed affect model of interracial interaction. *J. of Personality and Social Psychology, 24*: 14–21.

Williams, N. (1988). Role making among married Mexican American women: Issues of class and ethnicity. *J. of Applied Behavioral Science, 24*: 203–217.

Williams, R. L. (1975). The Bitch-100: A culture-specific test. *J. of Afro-American Issues, 3*: 103–116.

Woo, D. (1985). The socioeconomic status of Asian American women in the labor force: An alternative view. *Sociological Perspectives, 28*: 307–338.

Word, C. O., Zanna, M. P., and Cooper, J. (1974). The nonverbal mediation of self-fulfilling prophecies in interracial interaction. *J. of Experimental Social Psychology, 10*: 109–120.

Wright, R., King, S. W., Berg, W. E., and Creecy, R. F. (1987). Job satisfaction among black female managers: A causal approach. *Human Relations, 40*: 489–506.

11
Human Factors in Information Systems

G. David Garson

North Carolina State University, Raleigh, North Carolina

This chapter presents cases of "computer foul-ups" to illustrate the sociotechnical nature of what seems on the surface to be a technical matter. After this, social issues in workplace computerization are examined, including issues of deskilling, dehumanization, disemployment, and discrimination. Planning for sociotechnical change in an environment fraught with profound real and imagined social problems is treated next. The traditional information systems (IS) approach to planning, the systems development life cycle, is discussed with emphasis on new developments in its paradigm that provide an opening for organization development (OD). Implementation of IS initiatives using OD strategies constitutes the concluding section. The cognitive basis for employee resistance to IS is related to traditional OD themes, such as employee participation. The chapter concludes with a focus on developing a supportive information culture through a team approach.

It is said that "To err is human, but to really foul things up takes a computer." However, on inspection computer systems problems often are traceable primarily to human factors. Many of the problems associated with computer systems are attributable to subtle sabotage by members of employee cultures dissatisfied with how computerization is or might be affecting them (Metz, 1986). Information system failures are rarely merely of a technical nature. Rather, they often involve human factors and even political dimensions (see Morgan and Soden, 1973; Lucas, 1975). Tom DeMarco and Timothy Lister, for example, collected data on nearly 500 management information systems (MIS) projects and found that among the larger ones, fully 25% failed. "We've been contacting whoever is left of the project staff to find out what went wrong. For the overwhelming majority of the bankrupt projects we studied," they wrote, *"there was not a single technological issue to explain the failure"* (DeMarco and Lister, 1987: 4; emphasis in original).

Although IS problems relate to technical, data, conceptual, people, and complexity dimensions (Alter, 1980), in fact even technical and data problems may well involve people factors. Psychological factors associated with computing have been studied at least since the early 1970s (Weinberg, 1971; Shneiderman, 1980; Minsky, 1986; Turnage, 1990). Studies have shown that most IS problems are nontechnical in nature: conceptual (people have selected software that is inappropriate for the problem); social (personnel and interpersonal problems); and complexity-related (people find the system is too difficult to understand and use; Lucas, 1975; Alter, 1980; Lyytinen, 1987b). For these reasons, behavioral science rather than computer science may be more relevant to understanding and addressing the problem of computer foul-ups (Turner, 1982; Dawson, Cummings, and Ryan, 1987).

I. GREAT COMPUTER FOUL-UPS: THE HUMAN FACTORS ROLE

Before reviewing human factors issues in IS, some examples may be cited to bolster the premise that such factors are central to IS implementation. Noted computer scientists, such as Carl Hammer, readily acknowledge this. Hammer, for instance, told a governmental MIS conference, "Let us look at the all too frequently mentioned 'computer goofs.' Upon closer examination they always turn out to be human errors which greatly upset the life and tranquility of the office" (quoted in McGraw, 1988a: 7). Hammer cited a number of illustrations of his point, to which we can add others.

A. The Case of the Lost Password

In one instance, a financial analyst with the District of Columbia decided, after policy disagreements with superiors, to change the computer access code to the district's financial database. He then "forgot" the new code, causing many days of turmoil in city administration. While widely publicized as a computer foul-up, in actuality the issue of password management is one having to do with human factors. Management must make the decision whether to require a system that keeps password control under plural accountable individuals, or whether to leave such decisions to single lower-level employees (McGraw, 1988a: 7).

B. New York City's Welfare Management System

Computer foul-ups are often not due to computer technology per se but rather to the failure to take account of the fact that in the end it is human beings who have to run them and use their results. A major example was New York City's welfare management system, mandated in 1976 by the state legislature as an efficiency measure. Conceived as a way of creating a massive, centralized multipurpose integrated database, it was implemented in a top-down manner. The city had only written input to the contractor. Not only did subsequent testing in the field over 2 years yield some 3000 errors, but the welfare service error rate rose from 1% to 2% to an unacceptable 20%. The major problems were traced to not taking account of the capacities and motivation of the end users responsible for data input. While computerization doesn't require nonparticipatory system design, the two are associated all too frequently, often with disastrous results.

It is easily possible for MIS systems to become so complex they lose effectiveness. A common reason for complexity is the desire to create a giant integrated system for an entire jurisdiction, centered on a database holding all the information that might be used by dozens of agencies for quite varied purposes. A 1987 report on New York City's experience stated, "The chaos and rampant error rates in NYC's new Welfare Management System appear to be due to a tremendous increase in the number of codes it requires for data entry and the consequent difficulty for users in learning to use it" (Roman, 1987: 1).

The new system consolidated welfare databases across the city, but it also led to a dramatic increase in the error rate. In order to provide full integration, it was necessary to create a system with over 100 data screens. Social work staff had to enter codes from long lists: employee codes, client codes, case codes, and so on. The overall system was not designed with an appreciation for human nature: the tendency of employees not concerned with certain aspects of the database to ignore or treat arbitrarily for speedy disposal those data entry fields not of interest and relevance to their own work.

While it is conceivable that training, oversight, and rewards are salvaging New York's system, its early failures nonetheless illustrate a major principle of MIS. Good MIS design takes account of the capacities and incentives of the staff who actually control the data at its entry point. Design of MIS is not separable from broader concerns of organization design and OD (Roman, 1987: 1, 17).

C. The IRS Entity System

Many of the problems of implementing MIS systems are traceable to the attempt by management to use computing to increase the level of supervision over employees, abolishing human relations approaches to staffing. Such tendencies hark back to the "scientific management" era earlier in this century. An example was the attempt to implement the "Entity" system in the Internal Revenue Service (see McGraw, 1987). Entity software assigned priorities to IRS officers' cases on the basis of all tax forms and all tax years related to a single business or individual as an entity. Although it could have been used for decision support for the officers, in fact it was used to remove officers' discretion by forcing case assignment through computer-generated prioritizing.

Previous to Entity, IRS officers could prioritize cases partly on the basis of their analysis of the ability to pay and their establishment of payment schedules. Entity tended toward lock-step case assignment, which some officials found resulted in overly harsh enforcement in some cases and in taxes going uncollected in other instances because the "wrong" cases were given priority. In addition to being deprofessionalizing vis-à-vis officers' roles, Entity also was a form of quantitative reporting of officers' casework. Like many other quantitative performance accounting efforts, Entity created stiff resistance. One user reported, "I have found nothing in this system that enhances the quality of my work. It is a time reporting system, plain and simple. The emphasis is on our time and what we do with our time" (McGraw, 1986: 2). Based on employee complaints such as these, the National Treasury Employees Union mounted a campaign in 1987 to stop the spread of Entity from its experimental site in Hartford, Connecticut.

Although eventually resolved by taking greater account of human factors, the introduction of Entity illustrates the temptation to use computing to enforce quantitative performance measurement on employees—an old concept predating computers and one that has frequently been counterproductive. Nonetheless, the management problems in such cases are not those of computing per se but rather deal with how quantitative information is to be used within an agency: will it enhance staff decision-making, or will it deprofessionalize staff by withdrawing discretion over decisions? (McGraw, 1987: 2).

D. Too Many Rabbis

Banker (1988) reports the case of too many rabbis in the 1984 Democratic presidential campaign. Shortly after the election, thank-you letters were sent to thousands of individuals who had contributed. In no time complaints and questions came flooding back from individuals who had been addressed as "Rabbi," "Colonel," or by some other title that did not apply to them. It turned out that the Democrats had used a computerized mailing list that was dependent on entering a code for the desired title (e.g., "02" was "Mrs." and "20" was "Rabbi"). If the keypunch operator started with an extra character, say a space, then all the codes were displaced by one character, in many cases causing "Mrs." to be coded as "Rabbi." Here the problem was partly technical: better error-trapping in the mailing list software could have helped the data-entry clerks to be more careful. But it was also a management problem: the system assumed there would be no data-entry mistakes, or at least that it was not worth paying anyone to perform a quality control role. With human beings making mistakes on the input side and with no human check on the output side, computer foul-ups were inevitable.

E. Accounting Can't Account

In 1989 it was reported by the General Accounting Office (GAO) that for over 4 years Customs Service officials had known their accounting software was defective and had been unable to account for $54 million in duty fees because the agency's automated commercial system lacked adequate accounting controls. "The Customs Service is basically saying," the GAO noted, "they have taken checks or cash under their control and sometime before that money was deposited with a bank, they have lost control. It appears, I underline appears, they have lost the money." Customs officials were reported in agreement that poor software was to blame. At one level, this is a technical problem having to do with software design and its lack of proper provision for audit trails, cross-checks, and other controls. At another level, however, this fiasco reflects an agency so preoccupied with drug enforcement that MIS was placed at the bottom of its priorities. Lack of rigorous software acceptance procedures, ongoing MIS evaluation, and just plain lack of investment characterized MIS in Customs. This is a problem that can be viewed as a technical problem, but it was also a management and people problem (Grimm, 1989).

F. The Soviets Lose a Satellite

The Phobos 1 satellite, launched by the Soviet Union in 1988 to gather information about Mars, went into a tumble and became lost. The error was traced to the transmission of a single character in a complex series of digital commands. This character triggered a test sequence meant to be activated only while the satellite was on the ground, before launch. Some labeled the error "bad luck," while others blamed system design for allowing minor code errors to translate into major and disastrous outcomes. Requiring verification of key commands, for instance, could have avoided the satellite becoming lost. The disaster was at one level a design error, but it was also a human factors problem—failure to design for the error-prone ways of human beings (Waldrop, 1989).

G. Summary

What all six examples have in common is the intertwining of human factors with technical ones. These examples are hardly exceptional. It is not surprising that DeMarco and Lister (1987) found few technological and many human critical factors in the hundreds of implementation disasters they studied. The point, however, is not to pit technological factors and human factors against each other in some sort of straw-man debate. Rather, the purpose of this section has been simply to convey in concrete terms that in discussing computer implementation we are discussing a truly integrated, *sociotechnical* phenomenon. The two dimensions cannot be separated. This should hardly have been surprising to academics since it has often been shown that how people use a computer, and not the machine's inherent features, determines how a computer will be used (in education, for instance: see Mehan, 1989). If this seems an obvious point, many MIS literature discussions still approach the software implementation problem as a technical one of how to accomplish a code conversion from one machine to another (e.g., Ayer and Patrinostro, 1986), or as equivalent technical perspectives that ignore human factors.

II. ISSUES IN WORKPLACE COMPUTERIZATION

The foregoing cases do not imply that all MIS problems are human factors problems. Some problems arise because the technology is not yet perfected. Perrow (1984) reports numerous military mishaps involving computers. Our NORAD missile defense system was registering 10 false alarms a day in 1980. On January 16, 1990, a computer code bug caused millions of Americans to receive the message "Sorry, all lines are busy" when they tried to dial long distance on the AT&T system. Other computer code bugs in the Ada language used by the Defense Department have created major problems in the development of "smart" weapons (Morrison, 1989).

Some shortcomings of MIS can be ameliorated simply through improved technology. The NCIC (National Crime Information Center) database, for example, was much criticized for "false hits"; that is, too many innocent individuals were matched to the descriptions of criminals in the databases. Consequently, in 1987 the NCIC board approved proposals to allow transmission of fingerprint images, photos, and composite drawings along with the descriptive text.

Such approaches require vast increases in data storage and transmission speed, technology not previously available at an affordable cost. Indeed the full automation of FBI fingerprint files itself requires new technology and is still a goal of the NCIC 2000 project. However, no amount of improved technology to build in greater safeguards will ever fully "solve" the problems of government databases in relation to individual rights (McGraw, 1988b). Moreover, many systems that seem to be technology-driven, such as the efficient Japanese just-in-time inventory system, on closer inspection turn out to depend critically on social bonds and relationships, not just computer hardware and software (Minabe, 1986). The larger and more integrated the MIS system (and this is the direction of the times), the more critical planning for human factors becomes (Walton and Susman, 1987).

The "human factor" in computer systems in the workplace has been the subject of a burgeoning body of literature. Literature reviews include Attewell and Rule (1984), Anderson (1985), Kaplinsky (1987), and the U.S. Office of Technology Assessment (1985; 1987; 1988), as well as syllabi and course descriptions on the subject (Shapiro and MacDonald, 1987; Behar, 1988). Anthologies include those edited by Kraut (1987a), Cyert and Mowery (1987), and Hartman (1987). Among the most important human factor issues from the employee viewpoint, are those dealing with the alleged dehumanization of computerized work, the possibilities for disemployment, and the differential effects of computing on women and minorities.

A. Deskilling: Does Computing Alienate Work?

Computerization arouses many fears, one of which is the fear that work will become "deskilled" or "alienated" from the employee viewpoint, and "dehumanized" from the client or customer viewpoint. Dealing with such fears is a critical element in the OD of an information culture supportive of IS initiatives, whether or not such fears are well founded. Before turning to OD strategies, however, it is important to assess the validity of fears of deskilling and dehumanization attributed to computerization.

The alienation argument focuses on the fear that computerization will mean that employees will lose discretion over their jobs and will become regulated by machines. Mowshowitz (1986), for instance, is among those who have found that computerization of clerical work sets the stage for the industrialization of professional work as well. This is a common theme in radical criticisms of automation, and has surfaced in conventional research as well (Kraut, 1987b; Garson, 1988), as in studies of the overcontrol of such rank-and-file employees as social workers (Karger and Kreuger, 1988: 115). The fear of reduction of performance appraisals to computerized formulas, or even a reduction of professionalism to a computer-checked piece-work quota system, is a particularly important specific focal point in the alienation debate (e.g., on faculty merit reviews by computer, see Hudson, 1989). Marx and Sherizen (1986), for instance, have published anecdotal evidence that workers may feel exploited when computer monitoring of performance is introduced, and Chamot (1987) has found that such monitoring increases job stress.

Computerization has been shown by such authors as Zuboff (1982) to degrade work at times. Studying white collar offices and the control room of a paper factory, Zuboff found that computerization led to withdrawal or anger in the workplace. Fear of dehumanization or alienation in the workplace has long been recognized as being an important obstacle to the implementation of MIS projects (Berkwitt, 1966). Conomikes (1967) even predicted that MIS would crush esprit de corps in organizations, creating a class of dispirited workers devoid of dedication to the organization.

Buchanan and Boddy (1983) found that in a bakery computerization was associated with deskilling from status as bakers to that of machine operators. Other studies, such as that by Zuboff (1982), have shown that even some managers may feel a loss of control when computerization is introduced, even to the point of frustration and anger. In a more recent study by Zuboff (1989), a worker is quoted as saying, "In the old way you had control over the job. The computer now tells you what to do. There is more responsibility but less control." Another worker says, "It's like driving down the highway with your lights out and someone else pushing the accelerator." Zuboff believes IS may well become instruments of comprehensive control over subordinates, at the same time eliminating the human element of face-to-face engagement.

The deskilling issue has been raised in partricular with regard to jobs held by women (Working Women, 1980), in spite of Servan-Schreiber's (1985) reasoning that computerization emphasizes mental over physical labor and therefore will mean greater work equality for women. There is considerable evidence that computerization tends to affect disproportionately positions usually held by women (Gutek, 1983; Form and McMillen, 1983; Gutek and Bikson, 1985; Mowshowitz, 1986; Gattiker, Gutek, and Berger, 1988). Some investigators argue that computerization reduces women workers to semiskilled levels, degrading their status (Morgall, 1983), a contention in line with Marxist analysis of work (Braverman, 1974).

A review of the literature on computer-related deskilling among women by Judith Perrolle (1987: 155, 167) found evidence supporting both sides of the debate. On the one hand, computerization of jobs such as typing does reduce skill levels needed (e.g., because of increased ease of correction) and may increase specialization (the word processor, unlike the typist, e.g., may never even see the printed product, which may be sent via a network to a desktop publishing station elsewhere). Moreover, in a study of *Fortune* 500 companies, Gattiker, Gutek, and Berger (1988) found the personal computer's perceived contribution to the quality of work life was lower for women than for men. Another study (Machung, 1988) found that word processing increased bosses' work turnaround expectations, sometimes to unrealistic levels, so that productivity advantages of computer did not benefit secretaries, who were found to lose interest in work processing after about 6 months and to decline in productivity.

On the other hand, the preponderance of evidence is that office automation benefits women employees. Perrole cites studies finding, for instance, that secretaries report feeling their jobs enriched and more fun as a result of word processing (Cassedy and Nussbaum, 1983: 91). Similarly, bank teller jobs have been enlarged to include more functions and problem solving (Bosch-Font, 1985). In general, other research shows office equipment is rarely associated with women's dissatisfaction with work (Form and McMillen, 1983). Frequently but not invariably, computerization may lead to work expansion: for example, data entry personnel may become involved with spreadsheet analyses, and typists may become knowledgeable about desktop publishing, with anecdotal evidence of resulting increased worker satisfaction (Piturro, 1989: 144). Likewise, Kling and Iacono (1989) found many social and technological contingencies in desktop computerization ignored by Zuboff, leading to complex ramifications rather than uniform effects in the direction of work degradation.

From the beginning, most researchers have found that computerization tends to increase rather than decrease skill levels in an organization (Mann and Williams, 1960; Anshen, 1960; Shaul, 1964; Delehanty, 1966). For instance, Danziger and Kraemer (1986) showed that for three-quarters of 2400 government workers, computing increased their sense of accomplishment, contradicting predictions that computing would be deskilling and would lead to alienating jobs. Apart from data-handling professionals, computing seemed to be associated with decreases in time pressure and therefore with a better working environment. A study of the electronics industry by Salzman (1987) also found little evidence of a deskilling effect, and studying inventory management, Kling and Iacono (1984) found computerization increased interdependence, which in turn increased peer involvement in work, a factor normally associated with self-actualization, not deskilling. These findings are more in line with expectations such as Servan-Schreiber's (1985) that computerization can lead to more interesting, challenging, humane, and rewarding work, allowing employees unprecedented access to information and greater control over their lives. Even among social workers, among the most vociferous in voicing fears of computerization, an empirical study by Gandy and Tepperman (1990) found that in practice social work staff affected by computerization voiced little concern after the initial implementation period. A majority of staff in people-changing organizations did not find computerization a threat to their discretion, autonomy, or relations with clients (Gandy and

Tepperman, 1990: 177). A substantial minority actually felt computerization increased their levels of discretion.

A recent review concluded that "Some of modern automation 'de-skills' the work place, but on balance it calls for a higher level of literacy, reasoning, and mathematical thinking" (Wolman, 1990: 16). The real problem may be not so much deskilling as the lack of skills-training among American workers. The Hudson Institute predicted in 1989 that by the year 2000, 40% of the workforce may need to read or write technical or scientific articles, whereas only 7% now have this ability. Some 59% are projected to need to know how to read computer and technology-related manuals and to write business communications, capacities held in 1989 by only an estimated 16%. As a consequence, organizations are being forced to increase the level of education and training (Wolman, 1990). It is in this context that a later section of this chapter treats the importance of training in development strategies for improving organizational information culture.

B. Automation and Control: Does Computing Dehumanize Work?

The dehumanization argument focuses on the client rather than worker viewpoint. It articulates fears that interactions will be stripped of their interpersonal component, deemed particularly essential in social services. Note that we are not talking here about the fact that artificial intelligence is in its infancy and that few computer programs adequately substitute for professional human services (e.g., online services substituting for librarians: see Azubuike, 1988). Rather, the dehumanization argument focuses on the inherent limitations of computerized services, even when software meets all empirical objectives.

Government workers and service professionals often fear that computerization will mean "people-processing" in a depersonalized and demeaning manner. This argument arises, for instance, in reference to impersonalization of relationships with clients such as library patrons forced to deal with computers rather than librarians (Raitt, 1986) or hospital patients monitored by computer rather than by nurses directly (Lynch, 1985). In a study of counseling services for college students, Arbona and Perrone (1989) concluded that students found human counseling more satisfying and helpful than interacting with a computer counsellor. It is noteworthy, however, that mixed computer/human counseling was found to be as satisfactory as all-human counseling, suggesting that computers can play an effective supplementary if not substitutionary role in service organizations.

Some arguments about the alleged dehumanizing effects of computing may be misplaced. Weizenbaum (1976), for example, sharply condemned the dehumanizing nature of computer-assisted psychotherapy, as diverting people into "fraudulent" computer-human interactions. Yet, as Erdman and Foster (1988: 77–78) note, Weizenbaum neglects several points: (1) while the program condemned by Weizenbaum did have the computer role-play a human therapist, many clinical programs employ structured approaches devoid of this element; (2) even when peopl do anthropomorphize computers, this does not mean they are defrauded; and (3) the overwhelming majority of users of such programs do not find use of such programs to be impersonal, and this approach may be less "dehumanizing" than the intimidation sometimes associated with interaction with high-paid, high status human professional.

The dehumanization argument is sometimes extended in a political dimension, to suggest that clients are not only dehumanized but are also exploited by control centralized through computing. This argument is expressed by Cnaan (1989), for instance, when he speaks of the need to develop practice-relevant software to protect and empower social work clients. Studies such as these focus on the potential centralizing effects of computing, on their use for purposes of mystification of clients, and on their potential use in reifying problems that otherwise would have to be dealt with in human confrontations. Several initiatives have placed computer power in the hands of "have-not" groups, much as Cnaan advocates (Cassell et al., 1988; Downing, 1989).

There appears, however, to be no study providing empirical evidence that policy outputs attributable to computing systematically disadvantage certain classes or social groups. On the contrary, it is very difficult to demonstrate any correlation of computerization with substantive policy change. Computing is only one of several variables affecting organizational outcomes (Thompson, Sarbaugh-McCall, and Norris, 1989). A common finding in the literature is the association of computerization with amplification, by which is meant the tendency of computing to reinforce existing power relationships within the organization, whether centralist or de-centralist. Computerization can force administrators to clarify goals as part of the process of determining indicators to be tracked in an IS. This goal clarification process depends on situational and human rather than technological factors. Thus, if a generalization is to be made about power and computing, it is that computing acts to amplify existing tendencies within an organization as goals become clarified and better achieved through new IS (Robey, 1977; 1981; Caporael and Thorngate, 1984: 11; Olson and Primps, 1984; Kraemer and King, 1986; Marx and Sheizen, 1986; Jackson, 1987; Calhoun and Copp, 1988).

C. Will Computers Increase Unemployment?

Another major obstacle to successful MIS implementation has to do with fears of disemploy-ment through automation. Computerization is associated with job elimination among, for example, typists and clerical workers in industries such as banking and insurance (Reinecke, 1982; 142; BIFU, 1982; FIET, 1980). Clerical workers were once predicted to take the brunt of computerization, decimating their ranks (Simon, 1960). Later predictions merely emphasized that the growth of the clerical class was slowed, not reversed, by computerization (Lee, 1967). Still later, empirical researchers could find no impact of MIS on clerical employment (Swart and Baldwin, 1971).

There were early fears that automation would lead to widespread unemployment. Simon (1960), for example, predicted that computerization would mean smaller human employment relative to the total workforce due to the comparative advantage of automated machines. In the British context, the automation of printing presses has disemployed printers, leading some writers to fear that any major national productivity effort involving computing would need to be accompanied by a national program of work creation (Laver, 1989; Ch. 5).

Overall there is little evidence to contradict the contention that in the long run computing creates as many jobs as it displaces (Uris, 1963; Hill, 1966; Kraemer and King, 1986), but the causes of employment are so complex that firm conclusions are impossible (Weber, 1988). There is little doubt, though, that computerization is associated with problems of worker displacement and retraining, if not of unemployment itself (Lund and Hansen, 1986). More-over, justified or not, the fear that the computer will replace humans is a major factor in resistance of employees to new information technology (e.g., among social workers: Smith and Bolitho, 1989).

D. Differential Impacts of Computerization on Women and Minorities

1. Gender

There is some evidence that computerization favors males. Many studies arising from educa-tional settings show male students are more likely to use computers, own computers, attend computer camps, and have more experience with computers (Lockheed and Frakt, 1984; Muira and Hess, 1984; Sanders, 1984; Schubert and Bakke, 1984; Gattiker and Nelligan, 1988; Badagliacco and Tannenbaum, 1989). Some 85% of children using computers in schools are males (Erdman and Foster, 1988). Males may also have more positive attitudes toward computers (Vrendenburg, 1984; Collis, 1985; Davis, 1985; Badagliacco and Tannenbaum, 1989; for contrary findings see Loyd and Gressard, 1984; Baylor, 1985); but this may simply reflect males having greater computer experience (Griswold, 1985; Kay, 1989) or opportunity

(Schubert, 1986). Moreover, students who show greater computer anxiety, women or men, may nonetheless be equally able to complete computer tasks (Lambert and Lenthall, 1989).

In summary, in school settings males may use computers more not because of more favorable attitudes toward computing but for other reasons—perhaps more role models or other encouragement (Fuchs, 1986). It does not appear that intrinsic sex-related reasons justify gender discrimination in computer-related tasks.

The small gender differences found in educational settings may be reflected in the workplace. In contrast to public schools, use of computers by women is much more common at work (Erdman and Foster, 1988: 83). Adele Platter (1988) studied 1980 data on 15,151 high school sophomores and seniors, comparing responses of the same individuals 4 years later when they were in college or the workplace. Platter found computing experience in work, school, and home is related to gender, race, socioeconomic status, father's education, and family income. Moreover, gender had control effects on several of these relationships; that is, relationships disappeared or were mitigated when gender was taken into account. Citing women's work roles and health needs, some authors have taken the view that governmental and business organizations have a responsibility to provide special programs for workers, particularly women, when computers are part of the work environment (Bradley, 1988). This issue has become the subject of public policy in Sweden.

Among the most-documented workplace illustrations of the impact of computing on women is that of computer-related industries. A December 1987 survey of 300 female and 700 male members of the International Communications Association (ICA) found few women who felt they had been discriminated against in their careers, but two-thirds felt they were *not* moving up fast enough (Wexler, 1988). Women cited barriers in this computer-intensive profession such as the prevalence of an "old boys' network" and stereotying women into clerical roles. In this survey some 29% of women were staff and 26% were managers but only 8% were directors, creating charges that women were stuck "at the third rung" in their careers. Some of the differential is explained by the higher educational level of males in the ICA sample. Although some studies show that the computer industry pays women less than it pays men with comparable education and job responsibilities (Wright, 1987), more recent data suggest rapid improvements in the late 1980s. Pay may now be roughly comparable between sexes for similar jobs and the real problem instead is that women are less likely "to get to the executive-level positions where salaries are higher" (Glenn and Tolbert, 1987; Altman, 1989: 25). When broad MIS work categories are considered (e.g., "computer programmers," "computer systems analysts"), women's earnings are 75% to 87% of those of men in the same category. Although a 1990 survey shows only 2.3% of CIOs (chief information officers) were women, this discouraging finding still compares favorably to the figure of women making up less than half of 1% of the highest-paid officers and directors of 799 companies surveyed by *Fortune* magazine (Myers, 1990: 38–39).

2. Minorities and Ethnicity

As with gender, race and ethnicity have been linked to less favorable attitudes toward and less experience with computers (Badagliacco, 1990). It is charged plausibly that wealthy school districts may familiarize white students more with computers than can be done in inner-city districts populated by minority ethnic groups, and that computerization is exacerbating cultural differentials in America (Ibrahim, 1985). Dutton et al. (1987) found that formal education, which is significantly lower among minorities, is a strong factor in explaining the adoption and use of computers in the home. As a corollary, it has been found that computer use in education declines dramatically when students are from families with low socioeconomic status (Becker, 1983; McGee, 1987). The correlation of computing and social class has been documented in other countries as well (Levy, Navon, and Shapira, 1991). The effects of gender, class, and race are cumulative, so that disadvantaged status in two or three categories is worse than disadvantaged status in any one. Thus poor black women are the most disadvantaged in computing (Frenkel: 1990:45).

Race and ethnicity, of course, correlate with socioeconomic status. Badagliacco and Tannenbaum (1989), for instance, found at an American college that ethnicity was correlated with computer experience and attitudes, with whites having the most experience and most favorable attitudes and Hispanics having the least, with gender and number of credit hours controlled. Race also appears as a correlate of computing experience in other studies (e.g., Gattiker and Nelligan, 1988; Platter, 1988). On the other hand, computer technology may reduce cultural differences as well. Some authors, for example, have found fewer interracial differences when intelligence tests are administered by computers rather than by humans (Johnson and Mihal, 1973).

E. Occupational Safety in IS

A special issue concerns whether or not computer displays and even computing itself are threats to occupational health and safety. From the employee's point of view this is a health issue pertaining to exposure to computers for long periods, but this in turn can lead to the organizational issue of whether or not harmful effects to individuals could lead to computer system failures. For example, can air traffic controllers be harmed by staring at monitors too long, and can this lead to disastrous mistakes?

There is a long history of research and legislation pertaining to video display terminals (VDTs) such as those used by computers. Possible damaging health effects include eye strain, rashes, and even miscarriage and birth defects. Sitting at the keyboard for prolonged periods can cause nerve damage in the hands in certain situations, and the *Los Angeles Times* has created alternative jobs for reporters disabled from apparent VDT-related repetitive stress injuries. As a result of these concerns, ergonomic safety standards have been set by the Human Factors Society and studies report few effects (*ERGO*, 1987), but the controversy continues in the pages of specialized journals such as *VDT News* (New York).

In the late 1980s, ergonomic standards become more important as the courts looked with increasing favor on employees' suits arising from repetitive stress claims. Repetitive stress injuries have led American firms to invest in new ergonomic computer furniture, monitor glare shields, eye-care insurance policies, and other strategies (Goff, 1989). In 1989 Suffolk County, New York, became the first American jurisdiction to pass legislation on such matters. Suffolk County's law regulates VDT usage by making training mandatory for situations in which employees use VDTs more than 26 hours per week. Mandated training must include informing new employees within 30 days how to recognize VDT-related symptoms and measures to alleviate them. An additional provision that companies pay for periodic eye exams and correction of visual problems has been blocked in the courts (as of 1989). Though limited in nature, the Suffolk County law may be the tip of the iceberg.

Beyond the direct threats to health in the form of VDT usage, there is the issue of "technostress." Technostress is, of course, only one aspect of stress on the job, which in turn is increasingly recognized as a major organizational problem. The National Council on Compensation Insurance has found that stress accounts for 10% of occupational illness claims, averaging $15,000 each, and this rate doubled in the 1980s (McPartlin, 1990: 30).

While only a portion of job stress is atttibutable to technostress, there is little doubt that computing contributes its share. Occasionally, the computer factor is external to the worker, as in stress associated with computer monitoring of performance. However, there is evidence that computer use by the employee himself contributes to higher blood pressure and mood responses similar to "anger" components of certain psychological tests (Emurian, 1989). Coined by Craig Brod, a psychologist and author of *Technostress: The Human Cost of the Computer Revolution* (1982), technostress is characterized by high-intensity involvement with computer interactions, leading to interaction with humans producing stress in the computer-involved individual. For many workers, the intense human-machine relationship is both draining and addictive, leading to "keyed-up" behavior, expecting machinelike immediate results from co-workers, and generating intolerance toward nonlogical social and "gray area" aspects of the work environment.

F. Summary

When the various issues of workplace computerization are assessed objectively, one finds a mixed picture. There is some objective basis for fears that computerization may deskill, dehumanize, disemploy, discriminate, and psychologically and physically harm workers. However, in each area the findings are mixed, with the preponderance of evidence often pointing in the opposite direction. Computerization also increases skill levels, enhances feelings of satisfaction, and can empower workers who, with minimal precautions, can minimize or avoid computer threats in the area of occupational safety.

Many of the seemingly opposing results obtained in studies of IS in relation to deskilling and dehumanization can be accounted for in terms of amplification, life cycle, and intersubjectivity. The amplification effect, one of the most pervasive findings on IS, means that computerization augments preexisting organizational tendencies. If an organization is oriented toward tight, quantitative performance measurement of employees, computerization will increase that and make workers feel even more regulated. If an organization is oriented toward openness and social interaction, computer networking will enhance that, too. Second, there are life cycle differences. Negative attitudes toward IS initiatives are at a low point on announcement; perceptions improve as workers experience OD, training, and attention during implementation (assuming the organization doesn't neglect these). Later, the novelty wears off, indifference sets in, and perceptions of "no difference" become common. Third, the IS implementation experience is intersubjective in the phenomenological sense; that is, the perception of the experience has to do with the definition of the situation as it emerges from the social interaction of the participants. The cognitive basis of IS implementation interacts directly with results as measured by researchers interested in deskilling and dehumanization. These results can be misinterpreted easily if attributed solely to objective factors while ignoring the subjective element.

While much more research needs to be done in each of these areas, the lesson is clear from the point of view of OD. While one cannot convincingly sustain sweeping generalizations on computerization as deskilling, dehumanizing, exploitative, and discriminatory, often there will be enough exceptions and anecdotal evidence to feed employees' fears along these lines. A strategy of OD to promote an information culture supportive of IS initiatives has its work cut out for it.

III. PLANNING FOR HUMAN FACTORS IN IS

The traditional approach to planning MIS systems is called the systems development life cycle (SDLC) method. The SDLC model has been a staple in MIS texts since the 1960s (cf. Davis and Olson, 1985; Ahituv and Neumann, 1986) and is based on the idea of a product life cycle (Hammer, 1981). It can be summarized as a linear checklist of activities that must be undertaken in a series of phases that begin with planning and end with system termination. To put it another way, SDLC is a planning process that decomposes an MIS system problem into its constituent parts, treats each step separately, and recomposes the whole at the end (Langefors, 1973). Different authors include different labels for the steps in SDLC, but the underlying common idea is that "there exists a generic, structured, linear, and iterative process for computer systems development" (Overman, 1988: 57). In general, the SDLC model evolves from an engineering background that has traditionally not given human factors a major place in planning priorities, although this is changing. There has been increasing recognition of the need for flexibility in applying SDLC methods (e.g., Ahituv, Neumann, and Hadass, 1984; Rubin, 1986).

A. Systems Development Life Cycle Management

SDLC is, above all, a planning model that assumes rational planning by decision makers in control of all factors (Keen and Morton, 1978; Lanzara, 1983). As such, it reflects such values as stability, predictability, and control. Its weaknesses can be inflexibility, a too-technical scope, and neglect of psychological, social, political, and cultural aspects of planning (Lyytinen, 1987a: 14). Though conceived in terms of large mainframe applications, SDLC can be applied to smaller microcomputer-based applications as well (cf. Overman, 1988).

Early conceptions of SDLC emphasized the phases of problem definition, system design, and implementation. Later writers added prerequisite stages (strategic planning, system planning) and follow-up stages (evaluation, termination/divestment). The SDLC concept is not static but has evolved considerably since its early formulations in weapons systems research (see Davis, 1974). Recent writers have called attention to the need for feedback loops from later stages to earlier ones (e.g., applying implementation criteria at the problem definition stage; see Schultz and Slevin, 1975), implying an iterative approach. By 1990 the iterative approach was officially embodied in the work of the committee on iterative software development of the Office of Innovation Systems of the GAO's Information Resource Management Service (Power, 1990). The concepts of feedback and iteration open SDLC to the possibilities of teamwork, participation, and other concepts associated with the OD tradition.

Another concept adopted relatively recently in SDLC thinking is that of prototyping. Prototyping is the process of creating quickly all or part of a system in the form of a simulation of that system, typically with limited functionality, then extending that functionality a step at a time until the system is complete. Prototyping of intermediate versions of a final system is explicitly purposed for feedback objectives (see the review in Jenkins and Lauer, 1983; see also Shah and Davis, 1988: 472). The advantage of prototyping is that it allows user feedback early enough to accommodate major structural changes before extensive development investments are committed. Prototyping is seen as a team process overcoming earlier and simpler versions of SDLC. These early SDLC models are now seen as too linear, lacking a group planning orientation, and not reflecting actual experience in the real world. The broadening of the SDLC concept was discussed extensively in the 1980s (see McCracken and Jackson, 1981; Appleton, 1983; King and Srinivasan, 1988).

Factors that facilitate successful SDLC implementations are those common in organizational change generally, with a few special IS concerns added in. For an early influential inventory of 22 success factors, see Ein-Dor and Segev, 1978; for a review of 16 studies of success factors in implementation, identifying some of the above-cited factors, see Caudle, 1988; on the limits of success factor studies, see Lyytinen, 1987a: 25. A synthesis of the literature suggests the following list of success factors:

1. Obtain strong top management support before and during implementation (see Bruwer, 1984; Sanders and Cortney, 1985), and it helps if the IS unit is highly placed within the organization and if IS responsibilities are under one unit rather than split among many.
2. Obtain the support of key political actors who can be advocates for change; often this means making sure that IS planning flows from organizational mission goals or other expressions of the vision of the organization's leadership; if possible, work with people who are already familiar with and predisposed toward what is to be implemented.
3. Help obtain support by having credible staff with prestigious training by basing implementation on established, respected theories and models, and/or by having a high-quality IS product to sell.
4. Help obtain support also by having a conscious "sales" effort, tailoring what is to be implemented to the needs of the decision makers first and also to the needs of the users. It is also helpful if there are specific champions who shepherd the development, sales, training, and maintenance efforts with a view to pleasing decision makers and users; awareness and articulation of a felt need must be encouraged among both decision makers

and users; top management must see the information to be provided as relevant, economical, accurate, and motivating users to promote the organization's objectives.

5. Avoid offending other powerful political actors; do your homework; try to maintain a neutral stance in organizational politics; and use "neutral" third-party consultants to help ease politically difficult decisions. These may mean the IS designed will provide managers information on a need-to-know basis (e.g., access only to data on one's own unit).

6. Employ a strong project mananger and clear lines of responsibility with commensurate authority; the manager must be able to set limits on the MIS, not only to contain cost but also to prevent information overload and to tailor reports to needs as perceived by upper management.

7. Provide budget for the planning process as well as later stages of implementation—implementation on a shoestring may be worse than none at all; if costs are to be recovered by fees, the fees must be reasonable, encourage initial investment, treat different types of clients differently as appropriate, and take account of competitive alternatives; have a realistic time frame (e.g., at least a year).

8. Assemble a planning team representing management, technical staff, and end users; emphasize end-user participation, understanding that user involvement and commitment are critical (see Adelman, 1982; Ives and Olsen, 1984); rotate membership to assure widespread participation; make sure there is adequate release time to participate.

9. Develop and use success measurement indicators to document your progress and justify your budget; later make sure there is a clear plan for evaluation.

10. Make sure critical users have the proper incentives as well as duties in the MIS system; ask if the staff who enter data have the incentive to take proper care in collecting and verifying it, or if their incentive is to minimize hassles by not worrying about such considerations.

11. Consider departmental and interpersonal fairness and cost issues—i.e., do productivity benefits of the overall MIS system accrue fairly to the departments suffering the burden of work and change?

12. Allow a flexible process and seek consensus one step at a time; avoid the all-or-nothing plan approval strategy.

13. Avoid top-down mandates; give departments and users a chance to object and take protests seriously; do invest in OD.

14. Software should be user-friendly; ergonomics and the human-machine interface should not be ignored.

15. Keep all affected departments informed; give regularly scheduled formal reports; have open meetings and minutes; commit to a substantial investment in training employees; identify employees to be impacted by the MIS early, and target special efforts toward them; avoid MIS jargon and a "semantic gap" between implementers and the organizational rank and file (see DeBrabander and Thiers, 1984).

16. Make sure the needed computer power and other technology are available, appropriate to the task, and accessible within the budget; likewise one must have high-quality data and trained staff for the application in question (ideally an in-house development staff may be best—see Raymond, 1985); be aware that inadequate investment in input-output hardware has been a common bottleneck and cause of MIS failures.

All of these success factors simply indicate what has long been known—that MIS is not just a technical area, nor can SDLC plans be based solely or even mainly on technical factors. Instead this is an area in which human factors are critical. Organization development approaches are important in accomplishing change effectively in an environment in which, unfortunately, objectives of managers and other key actors are often diverse and conflicting (Montague, 1986). On the other hand, researchers have identified a very large number of success factor variables but there is no adequate underlying theory to relate them.

As Martin and Overman note (1988: 56), "research on successful system development does not show any single set of factors to determine success or failure of computer systems." In any given situation, some factors may not be necessary at all and others may be of only marginal importance; that is, the situational perspective common in OD seems almost inevitably to be the applicable viewpoint for SDLC as well, a viewpoint that moves it not a small distance from the engineering to the social and behavioral sciences. Unfortunately, nearly all the success factor literature arises from case studies of an eclectic, descriptive nature. Progress on the critical success factors theory depends on going beyond this to a more rigorous and systematic measurement of the success factors with a view to the application of these measures in various multivariate analytic techniques. Not only this, but there is a need to do so for an unbiased sample of IS interventions, in contrast to the present basis of this literature largely on self-reported success models.

B. Training for Information Systems

Training, though often neglected, is a crucial and expensive part of overall MIS implementation. Although it is clear that a great deal of technical knowledge is diffused through informal contacts and person-to-person networking (Kearns, 1989) that do not require programming or formal computer literacy on the part of end users (Allerbeck and Hoag, 1989), formal training can play a critical role in changing end-user attitudes about computing (Gattiker and Paulson, 1987). For instance, researchers have found that the major factor associated with users' perceived responsiveness of computer IS to management needs (other than simply larger numbers of MIS professionals available for service) was adequate training programs for managers ($r = .55$, $p < .001$; Stevens and LaPlante, 1986). Training has effects that go well beyond the implementation stage. A study of accountants and microcomputers found that training accounted for 41% of the variance of users' subsequent satisfaction with computer systems on their jobs (Ulinsky, 1987).

Training is generally perceived by management as something that staff members need when new systems are introduced. Perhaps the most serious training challenges, however, concern educating managers to be aware of what can be accomplished with computers and to be aware of their hidden costs in time and resources. Although it is relatively straightforward to teach novice users how to turn on a computer, how to format disks, and how to find their way back to the program after ending up in the disk operating system, leaving even these simple training objectives to a peer learning is a mistake. Training employees to be truly productive and to exploit the potential of powerful software requires an expensive, ongoing formal training program (Stone, 1988: 38).

Training, moreover, is complicated by frequent upgrades and software changes, poor product documentation, software bugs, different command and function key structures for each software product, and general lack of standardization. Perhaps the most significant training complication is simply user expectations. Having heard the wonderful promises and hype associated with end-user computing, novices often feel mastery should come without effort and that a 40-billion-character mainframe dataset ought to be analyzable without difficulty on their personal computer, *if* only the trainer were more knowledgeable and a better communicator. The training unit, in sum, is very apt to be overworked and underappreciated when it comes to MIS support (Karten, 1988: 82).

Although training facilities may be able to support large classes, most trainers prefer to keep class size under 15 students. Many consider six to eight to be optimal for novices. Thus, even with one 3-day class every week, it would take well over a year to train 1000 users in just the basics. A department with several thousand potential computer users may never reach the end of entry-level training, much less provide for intermediate and advanced training. Moreover, training is not a matter to be done by programmers in their spare time. IBM found, for instance, that an extensive 1-year course was needed to properly prepare an experienced programmer to present a 2-week course (Pietrasanta, 1989). One consequence of constraints on training resources is that self-administering computerized training is seen as a major need, combining authoring systems, expert systems, hypertext, and other tools (Carr, 1988).

A president of a training firm has offered the following list of the "10 biggest mistakes" of training implementation (Ware, 1990):

1. *Scheduling training at the wrong time*: there is a 90% loss of a new askill if it is not utilized within 30 days after training.
2. *No preplanning the course*: training goals of the course must be closely coordinated with career goals of the individual, including at least 10 minutes of one-to-one discussion of this relationship.
3. *Training before problem analysis*: if the problem isn't analyzed carefully, the wrong subject matter or even the wrong individuals may be the focus of training.
4. *Not training users*: efficient management encourages lean support staffs, but this requires trained end users.
5. *Not training MIS managers and liaisons*: even MIS personnel need training, often on such topics as presentation skills, motivation and control methods, and project estimation and evaluation techniques.
6. *Not choosing training on a cost-benefit basis*: clear objectives and measurable performance improvement targets should be set for planning, so that management can know when training is successful.
7. *Choosing training only on the basis of cost*: training tends to lose out when general cost cutting occurs, but it should be viewed in terms of value gained.
8. *Selecting generic courses*: courses should deal with the specific problems encountered by the trainees. Analogous problems, however equivalent in general terms, lack the motivational power of tailored examples.
9. *Buying lecture-oriented training*: the ratio of lecture to hands-on should be 1:2 or 1:3. Lectures without practice may involve little real learning.
10. *Killing the messenger*: be prepared that training needs analysis may reveal significant organizational and individual weakness, and see this as an opportunity rather than an insult.

Beyond mere technical training, part of training for MIS is a recognition that personal computers (PC) users can become too technical for their own good. It is all too possible to become fascinated with PC expertise, neglecting other more important agency tasks or requiring undue support from computer center staff. Part of the training function is not simply to help employees learn how to apply computing resources to their tasks but also to avoid interest in technology for technology's sake. Frequently, state-of-the-art technology has little to do with the agency's mission. The focus should be on appropriate technology. The more important training function is to help users go sufficiently beyond simple use of computer products to have a long-range view of how computing fits into the information needs of the agency. This is particularly important for MIS officers and other agency officials who are responsible for providing decision support.

C. Improving the User-Friendliness of Software

This is, of course, a major IS planning objective. The Committee on Human Factors—a unit of the Commission on Behavioral and Social Sciences and Education established by the National Research Council—made this a priority several years ago (Carroll and Olson, 1987). Today's integrated management software has several design characteristics that illustrate strategies to improve user-friendliness:

1. Relational databases are used, allowing multiple data files to be linked for purposes of a single report.
2. Modular design is employed, so that the functional parts of the software are documented

and their relation to each other is easily understood; this not only facilitates software maintenance but modules may be reused in other applications.

3. Standard interfaces are used, such as standard budget codes or standard personnel codes, or the social security number is used as a link across data files.

4. Data redundancy is kept to a minimum; instead, relational databases are used to look up data not found in a given file but located elsewhere in the IS.

5. User-friendly design features are incorporated, including the ability to "back up" in command sequences, the ability to use menus rather than commands if desired, a menu of predefined standard views (screens) and reports, and standard data files allowing import/ export of data vis-à-vis other applications, such as microcomputer spreadsheets.

Integrated MIS tend to be popular with users, who like instant access to the latest online facts, the ability to get various report printouts at a moment's notice, and the ability to access information from remote locations (Harralson, Sheldon, and Wilson, 1988). More recently, graphical user interfaces (GUI) have been promoted as a way of making human-computer interaction even more intuitive. Mixed modality interfaces, which supplement GUI icons with verbal representation, appear to be more user-friendly than either text or pictorial interfaces alone (Guastello, Traut, and Korienek, 1989).

What is user-friendly to one is not to another, particularly when occasional or novice users are compared to "power" or advanced users. The appropriate user interface depends on the user's cognitive strengths and limitations (Norcio and Stanley, 1989). Occasional users prefer menus, for example, whereas regular users—already familiar with what they want to do—want to have command words available to do directly what they want. Better systems provide both. For instance, new users of CompuServe, the largest general-purpose telecommunications network, may work their way through layers of menu choices to find what they wish. Later, as they become more experienced, these users may wish to drop to the command level and issue a simple command such as "GO AP" to go, say, to the AP News section directly. "You end up doing a lot more input work to get the same results after you've learned the program. Give me familiar keys. Give me one-word English commands," says one experienced user (Vizachero, 1988: 40).

Why did dBASE become the market leader among microcomputer databases? It was neither the first nor the most user-friendly. What it did provide was a programming environment that enabled applications developers to tailor their dBASE software into reusable, "canned" packages for clients. This ability to develop stand-alone applications meant that in many cases the programmer needed to do little more than provide a human interface to the power built into the dBASE package. Today, most leading database packages provide such programmable applications development environments. Yet it is these very powerful programmable features on which "power users" depend that are criticized as being too complex and "not user-friendly" by others.

Some vendors claim several times faster learning time for software based on menus with icon-symbol choices selectable by a mouse (a roller device for pointing to choices rather than having to type). Others claim that as they become more experienced and desire quicker direct-command alternatives, users have to "unlearn" the menu system to move over to the more powerful command mode. From this viewpoint, it is more user-friendly simply to start with the command mode even as a novice.

The subjective element of user-friendliness is illustrated by the not infrequent need to make "irrational" concessions to user preferences. For example, in implementing a computerized land development system, MIS planners in Austin, Texas, consciously targeted certain tedious manual reports for replacement with computer-generated reports, implementing the printed computer output replacements early in the implementation process even though the eventual purpose was to replace all paper reports with online access. "By identifying strategic manual tasks that required time-consuming and tedious clerical effort and then replacing them with computerized reports," the MIS planners wrote, "clerical resistance to the new system gradually dissolved. What seemed at first as redundant work received their allegiance only after it began to produce tangible benefits" (Arbeit, Heald, and Szkotak, 1987: 175).

Sometimes overcoming resistance to changer may involve concessions to special needs of the stakeholders affected by a given project. In the same project discussed above, the planners found employees highly committed to handwritten project logs. When work backed up, employees placed priority on the manual logs, leaving the computer system as much as 2 weeks behind the data in the logs. To solve this problem, the planners created a computerized emulation of the handwritten logs, capable of generating similar written reports. Employees accepted this familiar format and abandoned manual logs, eliminating duplication of data entry.

Overcoming resistance to change often requires de-emphasis of the "astounding technical wonders" of new packages and upgrades. Increasingly, software vendors have found that what is perceived as user-friendly is continuity with the past, not innovation. Software is seen as user-friendly if it will leave their lives unchanged. Since training costs often exceed purchase costs of new software, the fear of change is not necessarily irrational. "The more things change, the more they remain the same. That's the message PC hardware and software vendors are now sending to their customers as they introduce new or advanced products" (LaPlante and Parker, 1989: 1).

IV. IMPLEMENTATION ISSUES IN INFORMATION SYSTEMS

Although improved technology must always be considered as a strategy in any MIS problem, it is even more often the case that human factors will (or should) take up most of the time of MIS designers and managers. It has been a well-established fact for over a quarter century that human problems cause more MIS failures than do technical problems (Megginson, 1963; Holmes, 1970). Much is known about the nature of human error, the conditions that encourage error, or software designs that are error-resistant (Norman, 1983; Perrow, 1984; Petroski, 1985; Norman, 1990), and much of this is now well established in MIS training literature (Helander, 1988).

A. Employee Resistance

The seminal work in the 1970s of Lucas (1976) showed the importance of human behavior in IS, notably employees' resistance and the importance of their participation in the implementation process. A typical survey of major firms, for instance, showed that the primary problems arising in MIS implementation were associated not with technical factors but with lack of top management support, poor planning, and/or employee opposition (Cerullo, 1979). Surveys of users also generally show negative employee attitudes toward organizational computer services (Lucas, 1981; Turner, 1982; however, see Senn, 1980). Consultants routinely find that organizational surveys of computer user satisfaction average from only 5% to 40% satisfied, and are almost never above 50% (Reditt and Lodahl, 1989). There is voluminous literature now available on dealing with resistance to factory automation and other computerization efforts (Majchrzak, 1988). For instance, in human service agencies it has been found that employees are alienated by IS, and that they perceive them as technical efforts developed for administrators rather than for the "real" needs of clients and social workers (Brower and Mutschler, 1985; Mutschler and Hasenfeld, 1986). Resistance to computer-related change has been reported in numerous other settings, including educational institutions (Talley, 1989).

Employee resistance is one of the major factors accounting for the fact that IS innovations are not adopted simply by force of example. For instance, even though studies have shown that computer-assisted diagnosis is at least as effective as clinical diagnosis (Hedlund et al., 1980), resistance by practicing clinicians has severely impeded its utilization (Goodman, Gingerich, and de Shazer, 1989: 65). Not only do IS projects not spread merely by example, but computer system implementation can become an occasion for breakdowns in employee morale or even for employee opposition to change (Frederickson, Riley, and Myers, 1984). In some cases, employee resistance to introduction of computer systems has led to their actual abandonment (Hedlund, Vieweg, and Cho, 1985).

In any large organization, people tend to resist change, and reaction to IS is no exception (Keen, 1981). The more the features of the MIS differ from the features of the organizational setting in negatively valued ways, the more the resistance (Markus, 1984). Computerization efforts often require job redefinition and some employees may resent reduced (or increased) responsibilities, or may dislike being moved to another unit, or may dislike changes in the decision-making system and other impacts of IS. Employees may perceive computerization as being imposed from above in an inflexible manner. A leading organizational psychologist, Chris Argyris (1971), has described the syndrome of "psychological failure" associated with negative confrontations of employees with IS implementation: resistance, shielding, withdrawal, and self-orientation. These dysfunctional behaviors can result, Argyris notes, because IS may undermine employees' feelings of being essential, either by restricting their freedom of movement, or because IS emphasizes leadership based more on competence than formal authority and this, too, may threaten the perceived status or promotion chances of the employee or manager. While Argyris's conclusions were based largely on employees who were keypunchers, the same sociotechnical syndrome can affect other types of workers as well.

B. Cognitive Aspects of IS Implementation

Overcoming employee resistance is a problem in cognitive change. Themes concerning cognition and employee resistance were dominant in a major study of MIS implementation in three of Canada's provincial governments (Alberta, Saskatchewan, and Manitoba), each of which had been making major investments in computing. It was found that computerization alters the flow and content of information, changes job content, and affects relationships between organizational members. A key finding in this study was that the primary issue is not computing itself, but rather perceptions of the method of implementing it. Of paramount importance are the consequences of the intentions, philosophies, and values that are at play when computer-based systems are designed and implemented (Alexander, 1987). It is precisely in this area that human factors and OD become important.

Likewise, in a study of two other MIS cases, John Martin and E. Sam Overman concluded that the "origins of MIS inadequacy lie in their failure to explicitly integrate information needs and cognitive expectations with the management activities and behaviors present in organizations" (1988: 69). In one case involving automation of an existing compensation system, implementation went smoothly. In another case involving establishment of a new MIS to track salaries in terms of gender, implementation became mired in controversy and the system did not become integrated into organizational decision making. Thus, to the extent that MIS interventions threaten or seem to threaten the prevailing system of values and expectations within complex organizations, the more attention must be paid to human factors.

As some authors have noted (see Mead and Trainor, 1985), MIS projects must overcome four common employee perceptions: (1) that automation is being mandated arbitrarily; (2) that the new computer system will be unreliable; (3) that the new system will increase rather than decrease the work burden; and (4) that employees will not understand the system or be able to operate it. Free and open communications throughout the MIS implementation process is an important avenue for reducing employee resistance over these issues. For example, Elliot (1958) came to these conclusions over a quarter century ago in his study of computerization at the Detroit Edison Company. Computer systems generated and influenced primarily by central management are often seen as costly to create and to maintain, and at the same time they may be viewed by individual managers as remote, inflexible, and imposed from above.

Likewise, Marchand and Kresslein (1988) have set forth the following six major cognitive obstacles to implementation of information research management (IRM) projects:

1. *Conceptual*: the belief that agency processes are too intangible and dynamic to lend themselves to automation, or that if automated, IRM will lead to undue manipulation and centralization of power.
2. *Methodological*: the belief that in MIS, social values must predominate in decision making, not measurable economic criteria, and therefore in all important matters computerization is largely irrelevant.
3. *Political*: the belief that sunk costs in the status quo prevent the extensive changes that full implementation of IRM concepts would involve.
4. *Structural-functional*: the belief that the rapid growth and flux associated with information technology prevent IRM development.
5. *Fiscal*: the belief that funds are not available to finance IRM.
6. *Social*: the belief that personal computer phobia, fear of job loss, retraining obstacles, and other people issues will overwhelm IRM development (Marchand and Kresslein, 1988: 429–433). Many studies confirm that employees, rightly or wrongly, perceive computerization as a tool for increasing control over workers and an obstacle to delivery of quality services (e.g., social workers in Mandell, 1987).

Although employees' attitudes tend to be against change, attitudes will adapt (Larwood, 1984) *if* new technology is seen as bringing desired benefits, as is the intent in OD efforts. In particular, acceptance is much more likely when computing is presented as complementary to human skills, enhancing rather than replacing them (Rosenbrock, 1977; 1981; Petheram, 1989). Changing employee attitudes is all the more important since word-of-mouth is a critical aspect of the process by which technological innovations are spread (Czepiel, 1974). Since bureaucracy often encourages units to compete with one another and even to hide information, successful MIS implementation requires giving each unit a stake in the outcome. As Dickson, a pioneer in the study of human relations and MIS, noted, when it comes to MIS it is essential to "involve people as a component, knowledge of their behavior as a part of the system is important to the success of the entire field" (Dickson, 1968: 24).

Each person must feel the reward structure of the organization encourages collecting and sharing of information, even when such efforts are not intrinsically part of one's job in the narrow sense. Majchrzak and Cotton (1988), for instance, in a longitudinal study of the introduction of computer-automated batch production, found the most important set of factors determining adjustment was actual changes to individual jobs. The central goal of MIS implementation is to convince employees that the actual changes proposed will lead to beneficial changes in the reward structure, which include not only income but control over the task, information providing the "big picture," training, status, and recognition. An illustration is the practice of using the implementation of MIS projects as the occasion to redefine and upgrade job descriptions of employees and managers, thereby giving them a direct career stake in the success of MIS (redefining managerial roles during implementation has long been advocated, e.g., by Horton, 1974).

Stake-holding may account for findings that managers and professionals are significantly more positive in their perceptions of computers than are rank-and-file employees (Safayeni, Purdy, and Higgins, 1989). An example of an intervention addressing this issue, described by Namm (1986), is the formation of interdepartmental planning groups whose mandate it is to develop "key reports" on data utilization for the organization as a whole, showing managers and professionals how computerization will benefit them individually. However, the stake-holding concept potentially can be applied to all employees. At a general level, for instance, Drummond and Landsberger (1989) have detailed a "shared vision methodology" for participative IS planning, involving early formation of work groups that develop explicit scenarios depicting their vision of how their future work environment will be after implementation.

C. Participation and IS Implementation

Employee participation and involvement are leading approaches to laying the cognitive foundation for successful MIS implementation, especially when employee resistance is a recognized factor. Psychologists sometimes divide people into those with an "external locus of control" and those with an "internal locus" (Rotter, 1966). The former, to simplify, are individuals who believe events are under the control of luck, fate, or powerful others, and so are outside their own control. Various studies have shown that such individuals are particularly likely to react negatively to computer environments (Swanson, 1974; Robey, 1979; Baroudi, Olson, and Ives, 1986). Hawk (1989) has shown, however, that when high user involvement is introduced, external-control individuals react the same as internal-control individuals; that is, participation can be instrumental to removing psychological predispositions against MIS interventions.

When employee "ownership" of the change process is encouraged, productivity may rise. For instance, Rocheleau found in a study of acceptance of urban transportation models, "The same people who are skeptical of quantitative models and answers arising out of 'distant' centralized MIS systems may be much less cautious about the models they themselves have developed on user-friendly microcomputers" (Rocheleau, 1985: 267). Rocheleau found that in contrast to remote mainframes, use of decentralized microcomputers under the direct control of planners led staff to develop a personal interest in the reliability and validity of data as well as favorable attitudes toward computer modeling for decision making. To give a different illustration, Metz (1986) has used participative decision making effectively for this purpose and other studies have shown the importance of user participation in implementation as a way of securing involvement, commitment, and success (Baroudi, Olson, and Ives, 1986).

D. Generalists as Facilitators

If it is recognized that human factors and information culture are central to IS implementation, the role of technical specialists is diminished. Illustrative was the strategy of John Ferro, microcomputer coordinator for the House Information System (HIS) in Congress. When faced with the challenge of selecting personnel for the development of extensive new database applications for congressional offices, Ferro decided not to use programmers for the bulk of his development. Instead he selected those with a broad, nontechnical orientation toward MIS.

"The office automation consultants we use are generalists," Ferro explained. "They know the work going on in the offices because that's where they usually came from and they listen. Experienced technicians have great strengths, too, but they generally prefer the cloistered life of a professional programmer" (Angus, 1987: 35). After teaching a database system to generalists, they were able to go into congressional offices and work effectively with end users on implementation. In this work the generalist strongly encouraged end users to become intimately involved in such issues as designing the data entry screens and reports in order to encourage a strong sense of end-user ownership. An important side benefit of this generalist approach to MIS OD was a more self-reliant universe of users, enabling Ferro to support 2000 users with only eight staff members—a 250:1 ratio considered unusually efficient by support service standards (Angus, 1987: 35; see also Callahan, 1985).

Ferro's approach has become common in American business. A survey of the top 500 IS companies found "In recent years MIS has been trading its lab coat for a suit jacket. What began in the transistor age as a 'techie' career is now frequently the domain of executives whose understanding of economics and business plans exceeds their knowledge of MIPS and through-put . . . Companies are looking for renaissance men (and women) then, and not technical wizards for IS jobs" (*InformationWEEK*, 1989: 113, 120). Managing MIS is mainly a matter of managing people and planning for business and governmental needs, not technical problem solving. Implementing MIS has more to do with OD than computers and software, encouraging traditional SDLC approaches to become integrated with human relations techniques associated with generalist managers.

E. Fostering an Information Culture

Organization development is a branch of administration that addresses the issue of working with people to effect organizational change in spite of obstacles. All OD strategies share the classic unfreeze-change-refreeze steps of change (cf. Albert, 1984). To take just one example of an OD intervention, managers can use organizational and employee surveys to provide information useful not only for management decision making but also for OD. Organization development surveys can play a role in the critical first stage of change processes by providing information that makes explicit the beliefs associated with the existing information culture. By making beliefs explicit (e.g., beliefs outlined above in relation to cognitive aspects of IS implementation), the basis is laid for their discussion through participative groups in the workplace or other means (e.g., Golembiewski and Hilles, 1979).

To reduce resistance to change, introduction of computer systems must be viewed not as a technical set of decisions alone but as decisions involving human factors. There must be a change in the "information culture" of the organization, a change that recognizes that the critical point in implementation concerns the responses of the users (Metz, 1986). New information technology affects employee skill levels and sets in motion a complex process of seeking and giving advice, and this process of advice giving may become institutionalized in formal structures (Barley, 1986). If implementation is poorly managed, as Zmud and Apple (1988) note, organizations may reject new technologies or merely routinize them (accommodate them but minimize their organizational impacts) rather than institutionalize them (provide organizational supports that help achieve higher levels of use).

However, fostering an information culture requires more than participation alone. Other factors of success involve extensive appropriate training and the design of user-friendly (and bug-free) software, combined with a willingness to absorb for a time the costs of parallel operation of the old and new systems. Above all, there must be a clear analysis of the benefits involved, those affected must share in the benefits, and all this must be communicated to employees in an open, informative, and plausible manner (Garson, 1987). If employees believe that computerization will make them more effective, they will more easily accept the change it involves (Gattiker and Larwood, 1986).

Social psychologists have found that beyond the actual need for money, the need for social affiliation and networking is a major motivation for employment. While computing can either enhance or disrupt social networks on the job, consideration of such networks is an important function of OD planning for MIS implementation (Argote, Goodman, and Schkade, 1983). In their study of the introduction of robots into a work environment, these authors found that one of the reasons for working was to maintain social networks. In another study, Kiesler (1987) found that the unofficial social aspects of computer networking were among its most significant. Workers often prefer oral and personal information sources to computer-based ones (e.g., social workers, Forrest and Williams, 1987: 3–10), but an emphasis on the role of computer networking in supporting similar types of communication may help mitigate this cause of resistance.

F. Teams and Information Culture

Various studies show the close connection between technological, organizational, and social aspects of IS implementation in forming an organizational culture that is supportive of IS (e.g., Wang, 1989). While most applications to IS concern interactions with employees, and sometimes other actors such as suppliers and clients, there is an important role for OD techniques within IS teams themselves. Those OD applications useful for enhancing the IS team include goal clarification exercises, management style assessments, trust-building activities, and democratic participation.

Constantine (1990) has criticized the traditional "closed model" of IS projects, wherein a single authority attempts to control a project through top-down hierarchical organization. Instead, Constantine advocates "structured open teams." In these there is still a "technical leader/project manager" role, but decision making is by consensus, treating all team members as equals. A "scribe" role records the decision-making process of the group. The "information manager" role expands on this by providing group memory. The "facilitator" role helps keep meetings productive (avoiding sidetracking, encouraging participation, summarizing). The "critic" role is commissioned to play devil's advocate. This consensual approach may slow IS development from a short-term perspective, but by its utilization of the resources of all group members, Constantine believes that structured open teams lead to better solutions as well as more "solution ownership," leading to better and faster development in the long run.

The "group memory" role advocated by Constantine has great importance. The implementation of IS frequently involves the attempt to recreate in one place a system that already exists in another. Rettig (1990: 26) cites the example of a regional telephone company attempting to do precisely that, relying only on word-of-mouth planning without formal group memory of the system that was to be replicated.

In this example the project manager for the new facility to be created focused solely on technical aspects, ignoring OD aspects of the original implementation. The MIS managers at the new site were not even consulted. A formal group memory role would have prevented "soft" aspects of the original project implementation from being forgotten. Second, formal group memory also can prevent technical mistakes. In the same example a particular software module, one that billed customers for installation charges, was inadvertently omitted. A technician installing the new system noticed something was missing but simply patched over the "hole" in the code. Customers, happy about not being charged, did not lodge complaints. For several months, the phone company failed to bill for installations, an oversight that would have been prevented by a written plan emerging from formal group memory in the original project.

Savage (1990) goes as far as to advocate dismantling traditional organizational departmentalization in favor of task-oriented teams as part of what he calls "fifth-generation management," making an analogy to fifth-generation computer software's association with parallel processing and artificial intelligence. In Savage's view, computer networks of task-oriented teams can become the hub of organizational activity in the twenty-first century.

However, one needn't embrace this revolutionary vision to acknowledge the importance of teams to fostering a more effective information culture. The rise of "groupware" is a more modest version of this, operating through a variety of software tools for group decision support, computer-supported meetings, teleconferencing, screen sharing, electronic presentation, team calendars, project management, group writing, and other task-oriented functions (Ellis, Gibbs, and Rein, 1991; Leibs, 1991). Even without groupware, team approaches are important to MIS implementation simply from a participative and cognitive viewpoint, as discussed in previous sections. However, networking software of many types may enhance team strategies in the coming decades well beyond past experience.

V. CONCLUSION

The people factor in MIS involves both teamwork and leadership. The importance of leadership is pointed up by findings that show some 70% of all MIS systems have been implemented largely as a result of their being championed by a single individual who provided the leadership and drive necessary for effecting the broad changes involved (Holland, Kretlow, and Lignon, 1974). If that leader attempts to bring about MIS change in an authoritarian manner, however, the result may be resistance, lack of effectiveness, and even outright failure.

Computerized IS make the human element more, not less, important. As Argyris (1966: 95) noted over 20 years ago, "the more management deals with complexity by the use of computers and quantitative approaches, the more it will be forced to work with inputs of many different people, and the more important will be the group dynamics of decision-making meetings." The involvement of end users is essential in the development of governmental computer systems. For example, assessing needs in relation to the NCIC 2000 crime database, the Mitre Corporation interviewed hundreds of users of the system, arriving at a list of 246 desirable features for the new one. End users are often the best and most prolific source of creative ideas about PMIS design (McGraw, 1988b: 88).

The implementation of MIS requires more than simply tapping the wealth of knowledge available in the employee rank and file, however. Human factors are ubiquitous in MIS implementation. Most computer foul-ups are human factors problems, not technical ones. Human factors issues in workplace computerization are complex, involving charges that computers lead to deskilling, dehumanization, disemployment, discrimination, and occupational hazard. While MIS need not be any of these things, a strategic organizational planning perspective is needed to avoid pitfalls that are common and major in nature. The SDLC approach, which has been the mainstay of MIS planning, has traditionally not provided adequately for human factors considerations, but now changes in the SDLC model (e.g., iteration, prototyping) are opening the doors for OD priorities that transcend the technical plane.

Investment in training and software design friendly to end users is part of the growing awareness of human factor needs. Implementation of MIS is best accomplished, however, if there is a recognition of the origins and importance of employee resistance to computer-related change. There must be a recognition that the long-run success of MIS rests on a cognitive base within the organization. Participatory and other organization development approaches, typically facilitated by nontechnical generalists, need to be mobilized to foster a supportive, team-based information culture within the enterprise or agency if MIS implementation is to achieve its greatest potential.

REFERENCES

Adelman, L. (1982). Involving users in the development of decision-analytic aids: The principal factor in successful implementation. *J. of Operation Research Society, 33*(4): 333–342.

Ahituv, N., Neumann, S., and Hadass, M. (June 1984). A flexible approach to information systems development. *MIS Quarterly, 8*(2): 69–78.

Ahituv, Niv, and Neumnan, Seev (1986). *Principles of Information Systems Management*, 2nd ed. W. C. Brown, Dubuque, Iowa.

Albert, S. (1984). A delete design model for successful transitions. In *Managing organizational transitions* (J. R. Kimberly and R. E. Quinn, eds.), Irwin, Homewood, Ill., pp. 169–191.

Alexander, Cynthia Jacqueline (1987). The administrative politics of EDP in the three prairie governments, Ph.D dissertation, Queen's University, Kingston, Canada.

Allerbeck, Klaus R., and Hoag, Wendy J. (February 1989). Utopia is around the corner: Computer diffusion in the USA as a social movement. *Zeitschrift fu Soziologie, 18*(1): 35–53.

Alter, S. (1980). *Decision Support Systems: Current Price and Continuing, Challenge* Addison-Wesley, Reading, Mass.

Altman, June (August 28, 1989). Women are the underdog candidates for senior MIS posts. *MIS Week*: 25.

Anderson, Ronald (1985). A classification of the literature on computers and social sciences. *Computers and the Social Sciences, 1*(2): 67–76.

Angus, Jeff (July 1987). Congress in accord over PC database solution. *InfoWorld, 13*: 35.

Anshen, M. (1960). The manager and the black box. *Harvard Business Review, 38*(6): 85–92.

Appleton, D. S. (1983). Data-driven prototyping. *Datamation, 29*(11): 259–268.

Arbeit, David, Heald, James, and Szkotak, James (1987). Development tracking in Austin, Texas: The land development review system. *URISA 1987, 3:* 169–180.

Arbona, Consuelo, and Perrone, Philip A. (1989). The use of the computer in counseling college students. *Computers in Human Services, 5*(3/4): 99–112.

Argote, L., Goodman, P., and Schkade, D. (1983). The human side of robotics: How workers react to a robot. *Sloan Management Review, 24*(3): 31–42.

Argyris, Chris (1966). Interpersonal barriers to decision-making. *Harvard Business Review, 44*(2): 84–97.

Argyris, Chris (1971). Management information systems: The challenge to rationality and emotionality. *Management Science, 17*(6): B275–92.

Attewell, Paul, and Rule, James (December 1984). Computing and organizations: What we know and what we don't know. *Communications of the ACM, 27*(12):1184–1192.

Ayer, Steve J., and Patrinostro, Frank S. (1986). *Software Implementation Documentation.* Software Development Documentation Series, vol. 5. Technical Communications Associates, Sunnyvale, Calif.

Azubuike, Abraham A. (1988). The computer as mask: A problem of inadequate human interaction examined with particular regard to online public access catalogues. *J. of Information Science, 14*(5):275–83.

Badagliacco, Joanne M. (Spring 1990). Gender and race differences in computing attitudes and experience. *Social Science Computer Review, 8*(1): 42–63.

Badagliacco, Joanne M., and Tannenbaum, Robert S. (1989). Computing: Gauging gender and race differences in experience and attitudes, and stratification in access, Paper delivered to the American Sociological Association, annual conference.

Banker, Stephen (August 1988). Great moments in computing: The best of the worst. *PC/Computing*: 156–157.

Barley, S. R. (1986). Technology as an occasion for structuring evidence from observations of CT scanners and the social order of radiology departments. *Administrative Science Quarterly, 31*: 78–108.

Baroudi, J. J., Olson, M. H., and Ives, B. (1986). An empirical study of the impact of user involvement on system usage and information satisfaction. *Communications of the ACM, 29*: 232–238.

Baylor, J. (1985). Assessment of microcomputer attitudes of education students. Mid-South Educational Research Association, annual meeting, Biloxi, Miss.

Becker, J. H. (1983). *National Survey Examines How Schools Use Microcomputers*, Report nos. 1–6. Center for the Social Organization of Schools, Johns Hopkins University, Baltimore.

Behar, Joseph (December 1988). Course syllabus: The social impact of computer information technology. *Science, Technology & Society, 69*(4): 7–12.

Berkwitt, G. J. (1966). The new executive elite. *Dun's Review, 88*(5): 40–42 ff.

BIFU (1982). *New Technology in Banking, Insurance, and Finance.* Banking, Insurance and Finance Union, London.

Bosch-Font, Francisco (1985). Retail Banking and Technology: An Analysis of Skill Mix Transformation, report 85-B3. Institute for Research on Educational Finance and Governance, School of Education, Stanford University, Palo Alto, Calif.

Bradley, Gunilla (1988). Women, work, and computers. *Women and Health, 13*(3–4): 117–132.

Braverman, Harry (1974). *Labor and Monopoly Capital: The Degradation of Work in the Twentieth Century.* Montly Review Press, New York.

Brower, A. M., and Mutschler, E. (1985). Evaluation systems for practitioners: Computer-assisted information processing. In *Advances in Clinical Social Work Practice* (C. B. Germain, ed.), National Association of Social Workers, Silver Springs, Md., pp. 223–250.

Bruwer, P. J. S. (1984). A descriptive model of success for computer-based information systems. *Information and Management, 7*(2): 63–67.

Buchanan, D., and Boddy, D. (1983). Advanced technology and the quality of working life: The effects of computerized controls on biscuit-making operators. *J. of Occupational Psychology, 56*: 109–119.

Calhoun, Craig, and Copp, Martha (1988). Computerization in legal work: How much does new technology change professional practice? *Research in the Sociology of Work, 4*: 233–259.

Callahan, J. (1985). Need for the systems generalist. *J. of Systems Management, 36*(1): 32–34.

Caporael, L., and Thorngate, W. (1984). Introduction: Towards the social psychology of computing. *J. of Social Issues, 40*(3): 1–13.

Carr, Clay (May 1988). Making the human-computer marriage work. *Training and Development Journal, 42*(5): 65–68,70,74.

Carroll, John M., and Olson, Judith Reitman, eds. (May 15–16, 1987). Mental model in human-computer interaction. Research issues about what the user of software knows. Workshop on Software Human Factors: Users' Mental Models, National Academy of Sciences National Research Council, Washington, D.C.

Cassedy, Ellen, and Nussbaum, Karen (1983). *Nine to Five: The Working Woman's Guide to Office Survival.* Penguin, New York.

Cassell, Catherine, Fitter, Mike, Fryer, David, and Smith, Leigh (March 1988). The development of computer applications by non-employed people in community settings. *J. of Occupational Psychology, 61*(1): 89–102.

Caudle, Sharon L. (July/August 1988). Federal information resources management after the Paperwork Reduction Act. *Public Administration Review, 48*(4): 790–799.

Cerullo, M. J. (1979). MIS: What can go wrong. *Management Accounting, 60*(10): 43–48.

Chamot, D. (1987). Electronic work and the white-collar employee. In (R. Kraut, ed.), pp. 22–34.

Cnaan, Ram A. (Fall 1989). Social work education and direct practice in the computer age. *J. of Social Work Education, 25*(3): 235–43.

Collis, B. (1985). Psychosocial implications of sex differences in attitudes toward computers: Results of a survey. *International Journal of Women's Studies, 8*(3): 207–213.

Conomikes, G. (1967). Computers are creating personnel problems. *Personnel Journal, 46*: 52–53.

Constantine, L. (1990). Teamwork paradigms and the structured open team. In *Proceedings of Software Development, '90*. Miller Freeman Publications, San Francisco.

Cyert, Richard M., and Mowery, David C., eds. (1987). *Technology and Employment: Innovation and Growth in the U.S. Economy*. National Academy Press, Washington, D.C.

Czepiel, J. A. (1974). Word of mouth processes in the diffusion of a major technological innovation. *J. of Marketing Research, 11*: 172–180.

Danziger, James N., and Kraemer, Kenneth L. (1986). *People and Computers: The Impact of Computing on End Users in Organizations*. Columbia University Press, New York.

Davis, G. B. (1974). *Management Information Systems: Conceptual Foundations, Structure, and Development*. McGraw-Hill, New York.

Davis, G. B. and Olsen, N. (1985). *Management Information Systems*. McGraw-Hill, New York.

Davis, L. V. (1985). Female and male voices in social work. *Social Work, 30*: 106–113.

Dawson, Gaye C., Cummings, William C., and Ryan, Lanny J. (Fall 1987). The human vs. computer conflict in community mental health agencies. *J. of Mental Health Administration, 14*(2): 30–34.

DeBrabander, B. and Thiers, G. (1984). Successful information system development in relation to situational factors which affect effective communication between MIS users and EDP experts. *Management Science, 30*(2): 137–155.

Delahanty, G. E. (1966). Office automation and the occupation structure. *Industrial Management Review, 7*(2): 98–108.

DeMarco, Tom and Lister, Timothy (1987). *Peopleware: Productive Projects and Teams*. Dorset House, New York.

Dickson, G. W. (1968). Management information–decision systems. *Business Horizons, 11*(6):17–26.

Downing, John D. H. (Summer 1989). Computers for political change: PeaceNet and public data access. *J. of Communication, 39*(3): 154–162.

Drummond, Marshall Edward, and Landsberger, Peter J. (Fall 1989). Defining the target environment: A "shared vision" methodology for information systems planning—a case study. *Information Resources Management Journal, 2*(4): 17–30.

Dutton, William H. et al. (April 1987). Diffusion and social impacts of personal computers. *Communication Research, 14*(2): 219–250.

Ein-Dor, P., and Segev, E. (1978). Organization context and the success of management information systems. *Management Science, 24*(1): 1064–1077.

Elliot, J. D. (1958). EDP—Its impact on jobs, procedures and people. *J. of Industrial Engineering, 9*(5): 407–410.

Ellis, C. A., Gibbs, S. J., and Rein, G. L. (January 1991). Groupware: Some issues and experiences. *Communications of the ACM, 34*(1): 38–58.

Emurian, Henry H. (1989). Human-computer interactions: Are there adverse health consequences? *Computers in Human Behavior, 5*(4): 265–275.

Erdman, Harold P., and Foster, Sharon W. (1988). Ethical issues in the use of computer-based assessment. *Computers in Human Services, 3*(1/2): 71–87.

ERGO (Fall/Winter 1987). Vision experts report VDT's not harmful to the eyes. *ERGO: An Ergonomics Digest:* 2.

FIET (1980). *Bank Workers and New Technology*. International Federation of Commercial, Clerical, Professional and Technical Employees, Geneva.

Form, W., and McMillen, D. B. (1983). Women, men, and machines. *Work and Occupations, 10*: 147–78.

Forrest, Jan, and Williams, Sandra (1987). *New Technology and Information Exchange in Social Services*. Policy Studies Institute, London.

Frederiksen, L., Riley, A. W., and Myers, J. B. (Winter 1984). Matching technology and organizational structure: A case study in white collar productivity improvement. *J. of Organizational Behavior Management, 6*(3/4): 59–80.

Frenkel, Karen A. (November 1990). Women and computing. *Communications of the ACM, 33*(11): 34–46.

Fuchs, Lucy (January 21–24, 1986). Closing the gender gap: Girls and computers, Florida Instructional Computing Conference, Orlando.

Gandy, John M., and Tepperman, Lorne (1990). *False Alarm: The Computerization of Eight Social Welfare Organizations*. Wilfrid Laurier University Press, Waterloo, Ontario, Canada.

Garson, Barbara (1988). *The Electronic Sweatshop: How Computers are Transforming the Office of the Future into the Factory of the Past*. Simon and Schuster, New York.

Garson, G. David (1987). *Computers in Public Employee Relations*. International Personnel Management Association, Alexandria, Va.

Gattiker, Urs E., and Larwood, Laura (1986). Resistance to change: Reactions to workplace computerization in offices, annual meeting of TIMS/ORSA, Los Angeles.

Gattiker, Urs E., and Paulson, D. (1987). Testing for effective teaching methods: Achieving computer literacy for end-users. *INFOR: Information Systems and Operations Research, 25*(9187): 256–276.

Gattiker, Urs E., Gutek, Barbara A., and Berger, Dale E. (Fall 1988). Office technology and employee attitudes. *Social Science Computer Review, 6*(3).

Gattiker, Urs E., and Nelligan, Todd W. (January 1988). Computerized offices in Canada and the United States: Investigating dispositional similarities and differences. *J. of Organizational Behavior, 9*(1): 77–96.

Glenn, Evelyn Nakano, and Tolbert, Charles M. (1987). Race and gender in high technology employment: Recent trends in computer occupations, Society for the Study of Social Problems, annual meeting, Chicago.

Goff, Leslie (July 1989). Lack of definitive VDT info has employers in quandary. *Management Information Systems Week, 31*: 28–29.

Golembiewski, Robert T., and Richard Hilles, (1979). *Toward the Responsive Organization*. Brighton Publishing, Salt Lake City, Utah.

Goodman, Hannah, Gingerich, Wallace J., and de Shazer, Steve (1989). BRIEFER: An expert system for clinical practice. *Computers in Human Services, 5*(1/2): 53–68.

Grimm, Vanessa Jo (May 1989). System blamed for $54m discrepancy at Customs. *Government Computer News*, 1: 80.

Griswold, P. A. (1985). Differences between education and business majors in their attitudes about computers. *AEDS Journal, 18*(3): 131–138.

Guastello, Stephen J., Traut, Mary, and Korienek, Gener (July 1989). Verbal versus pictorial representations of objects in a human-computer interface. *International Journal of Man-Machine Studies, 31*(1): 99–120.

Gutek, Barbara A. (1983). Women's work in the office of the future. In *The Technological Woman* (J. Zimmerman, ed.), Praeger, New York.

Gutek, Barbara A., and Bikson, T. K. (1985). Differential experience of men and women in computerized offices. *Sex Roles, 13*: 123–136.

Hammer, Jeffrey S. (1981). Life cycle management, *Information Management, 4*(4): 71–80.

Harralson, John, Sheldon, Robert, and Wilson, Robert J. (1988). Integrated management systems. In (J. Rabin and Jackowski, ed.),

Hartman, Heidi, ed. (1987). *Computer Chips and Paper Clips: Technology and Women's Employment*, vol. 2. National Academy Press, Washington, D.C.

Hawk, Stephen R. (1989). Locus of control and computer attitude: The effect of user involvement. *Computers in Human Behavior, 5*(3): 199–206.

Hedlund, J. L., Evenson, R. C., Sletten, I.W., and Cho, D. W. (1980). The computer and clinical prediction. In *Technology in Mental Health Care Delivery Systems* (J. D. Sidowski, J. H. Johnson, and T. A. Williams, eds.) Ablex, Norwood, N.J., pp. 201–234.

Hedlund, J., Vieweg, B., and Cho, D. (1985). Mental health computing in the 1980s: General information systems and clinical documentation. *Computers in Human Services, 1*(1): 3–33.

Helander, M. (1988). *Handbook of Human-Computer Interaction*. North-Holland, New York.

Hill, W. A. (1966). The impact of EDP systems on office employees: Some empirical conclusions. *Academy of Management Journal, 9*(3): 9–19.

Holland, W. E., Kretlow, W. J., and Ligon, J. C. (1974). Sociotechnical aspects of MIS. *J. of Systems Management, 25*(2): 14–16.

Holmes, R. W. (1970). 12 areas to investigate for better MIS. *Financial Executive, 38*(7): 24–31.

Horton, F. W. Jr. (1974). The evolution of MIS in government. *J. of Systems Management, 25*(3): 14–20.

Hudson, Walter W. (1989). Automated faculty merit reviews. *Computers in Human Services, 5*(3/4): 131–146.

Ibrahim, F. A. (1985). Human rights and ethical issues in the use of advanced technology. *J. of Counseling and Development, 64*: 134–135.

Information WEEK (September 19, 1989). Business before IS: Companies are seeking fewer "techno-nerds," more MBAs in IS recruiting. *Information WEEK*: 113–120.

Ives, B., and Olson, M. (1984). User involvement and MIS success: A research review. *Management Science, 30*(5): 586–603.

Jackson, Lee A. (1987). Computers and the social psychology of work. *Computers in Human Behavior, 3*(3–4): 251–262.

Jenkins, A. M., and Lauer, T. W. (1983). An annotated bibliography on prototyping. Discussion Paper 228, School of Business, Indianapolis.

Kaplinsky, Raphel (1987). *Microelectronics and Employment Revisited: A Review.* International Labour Office, Geneva.

Karger, Howard Jacob, and Kreuger, Larry W. (1988). Technology and the "not always so human" services. *Computers in Human Services, 3*(1/2): 111–126.

Karten, Naomi (Winter 1988). The myth of the sophisticated user. *Journal of Information Systems Management, 5*(1): 81–83.

Kay, Robin H. (Spring 1989). Gender differences in computer attitudes, literacy, locus of control and commitment. *J. of Research on Computing in Education, 21*(3): 307–316.

Kearns, Kevin P. (June 1989). Communication networks among municipal administrators: Sharing information about computers in local government. *Knowledge, 10*(4): 260–179.

Keen, Peter G. W. (January 1981). Information systems and organizational change. *Communications of the ACM, 24*(1): 24–33.

Keen, Peter G. W., and Morton, Michael S. Scott (1978). *Decision Support Systems: An Organizational Perspective.* Addison-Wesley, Reading, Mass.

Kiesler, Sara B. (Spring 1987). Social aspects of computer environments. *Social Science, 72*(1): 23–28.

King, William R., and Srinivasan, Ananth (1988). The systems development life cycle and the modern information systems environment. In (J. Rabin and Jackowski, ed.),

Kling, Rob, and Iacono, Suzanne (1984). Computing as an occasion for social control. *J. of Social Issues, 40*(3): 77–96.

Kling, Rob, and Iacono, Suzanne (1989). Desktop computerization and the organization of work. In *Computers in the Human Context: Information Technology, Productivity, and People* (Tom Forester, ed.), MIT Press, Cambridge, Mass.

Kraemer, Kenneth L., and King, John Leslie (November 1986). Computing and public organizations. *Public Administration Review, 46*, special issue: 488–496.

Kraut, Robert E., ed. (1987a). *Technology and the Transformation of White-Collar Work.* Lawrence Erlbaum Associates, Hillsdale, N.J.

Kraut, Robert E. (1987b). Social issues and white-collar technology: An overview. In *Technology and the Transformation of White-Collar Work* (Robert E. Kraut, ed.), Lawrence Erlbaum Associates, Hillsdale, N.J. pp. 1–22.

Lambert, Matthew E., and Lenthall, Gerard (1989). Effects of psychology courseware use on computer anxiety in students. *Computers in Human Behavior, 5*(3): 207–214.

Langefors, B. (1973). *Theoretical Analysis of Information Systems.* Student literature, Lund, Sweden.

Lanzara, G. F. (1983). The design process: Frames, metaphors, and games. In (Briefs, Ciborra, and Schneider, eds.), pp. 29–40.

LaPlante, Alice, and Parker, Rachel (May 1, 1989). PC vendors calm technology fears. *InfoWorld, 11*(18): 1, 117.

Larwood, L. (1984). *Organizational Behavior and Management.* Kent Publ., Boston.

Laver, Murray (1989). *Information Technology: Agent of Change.* Cambridge University Press, New York.

Lee, H. C. (1967). The organizational impact of computers. *Management Services, 4*(3): 39–43.

Leike, Scott (February 11, 1991). The promise and the pitfalls. *InformationWeek*, 307: 38–40.

Levy, D., Navon, D., and Shapira, R. (1991). Computers and class—computers and social-inequality in Israeli schools. *Urban Education, 25*(4): 483–499.

Lockheed, M. E., and Frakt, S. B. (1984). Sex equity: Increasing girls' use of computers. *The Computing Teacher, 11*: 16–18.

Loyd, B. H., and Gressard, C. (1984). The effects of sex, age, and computer experience on computer attitudes. *AEDS Journal, 18*(2): 67–77.

Lucas, H. C. Jr. (1975). Performance and the use of a management information system. *Management Science, 3*(4): 908–919.

Lucas, H. C. Jr. (1976). *The Analysis, Design, and Implementation of Information Systems.* McGraw-Hill, New York.

Lucas, H. C. Jr. (1981). *Implementation: The Key to Successful Information Systems.* Columbia University Press, New York.

Lund, R., and Hansen, J. (1986). *Keeping America at Work: Strategies for Employing the New Technologies.* Wiley, New York.

Lynch, R. K. (1985). Nine pitfalls in implementing packaged applications software. *J. of Information Systems Management, 2*(2): 88–92.

Lyytinen, Kalle (March 1987). Different perspectives on information systems: Problems and solutions. *ACM Computing Survey, 19*(1): 5–46.

Lyytinen, Kalle (1987b). Information system failure: A survey and classification of empirical literature. *Oxford Survey of Information Technology*, 4.

Machung, Annie (1988). Who needs a personality to talk to a machine?: Communications in the automated office. In *Technology and Women's Voices: Keeping in Touch* (Cheris Kramarae, ed.), Routledge and Kegan Paul, London.

Majchrzak, Ann (1988). *The Human Side of Factory Automation.* Jossey-Bass, San Francisco.

Majchrzak, Ann, and Cotton, John (Fall 1988). A longitudinal study of adjustment to technological change: From mass to computer-automated batch production. *J. of Occupational Psychology, 61*(1): 43–66.

Mandell, Steven F. (1987). Resistance and power: The perceived effect that computerization has on a social agency's power relationships, First International Conference for Human Service Information Technology Applications, Birmingham, U.K.

Mann, F. C., and Williams, L. K. (1960). Observations on the dynamics of a change to electronic data-processing equipment. *Administrative Science Quarterly, 5*(1): 217–256.

Marchand, Donald A., and Kresslein, John C. (1988). Information resources management and the public sector administrator. In (J. Rabin and Jackowski, eds.),

Markus, M. Lynne (1984). *Systems in Organizations: Bugs and Features.* Pitman, Marshfield, Mass.

Martin, John A., and Overman, E. Sam (Summer 1988). Management of cognitive hierarchies: What is the role of management information systems? *Public Productivity Review, 11*(4): 69–84.

Marx, G., and Sherizen, S. (1986). Monitoring on the job: How to protect privacy as well as property. *Technology Review, 89*(8): 62–72.

McCracken, D. D., and Jackson, M. A. (1981). A minority dissenting position. In (Cotterman, Couger, Enger, and Harold, eds.), pp. 551–553.

McGee, G. W. (1987). Social context variables affecting the implementation of microcomputers. *J. of Educational Computing Research, 3*: 189–207.

McGraw, Tim (January 1988a). Computer expert stresses ADP's role in the office. *Government Computer News, 8*: 7.

McGraw, Tim (January 1, 1988b). Board hashes out proposal for FBI's NCIC system. *Government Computer News*: 88.

McInerney, William D. (1989). Social and organizational effects of educational computing. *J. of Educational Computing Research, 5*(4): 487–506.

McPartlin, John P. (July 30, 1990). The terrors of technostress. *InformationWeek, 280*: 30–33.

Mead, Ron, and Trainor, Bill (October 25, 1985). New users require special attention. *Government Computer News*: 65.

Megginson, L. C. (1963). Automation: Our greatest asset—our greatest problem. *Academy of Management Journal, 6*(3): 232–244.

Mehan, Hugh (March 1989). Microcomputers in classrooms: Eduational technology or social practice? *Anthropology and Education Quarterly, 20*(1): 4–22.

Metz, E. (1986). Managing change towards a leading edge information culture. *Organizational Dynamics, 15*: 28–40.

Minabe, S. (1986). Japanese competitiveness and Japanese management. *Sciences, 233*: 301–304.

Minsky, M. (1986). *The Society of Mind.* Simon and Schuster, New York.

Montague, Steve (1986). Government MIS: the pregnant pyramid. *Optimum, 17*(2): 67–75.

Morgall, J. (1983). Typing our way to freedom. Is it true that new office technology can liberate women? *Behavior and Information Technology, 2*: 215–226.

Morgan, H., and Soden, J. (1973). Understanding MIS failures. *Data Base, 5*(1).

Morrison, David (January 14, 1989). Software crisis: The Pentagon is trying to cope with the costs and the bugs associated with the computer software that makes its "smart" weapons smart. *National Journal, 21*: 72–5.

Mowshowitz, A. (1986). Social dimensions of office automation. In (Yovits, ed.) pp. 336–404.

Muira, I.T., and Hess, R. D. (1984). Enrollment differences in computer camps and summer classes. *The Computing Teacher, 11*:22.

Mutschler, E., and Hasenfeld, Y. (1986). Integrated information systems for social work practice. *Social Work, 31*: 345–349.

Myers, Kara (August 27, 1990). Cracking the glass ceiling. *InformationWeek*, 284: 38–41.

Namm, J. (1986). The case of the changing technology: Impact of micro-computer technology on a *Fortune 500* company. In (Murphy and Pardeck, eds.), pp. 95–101.

Norcio, Anthony F., and Stanley, Jaki, (March–April 1989). Adaptive human-computer interfaces: A literature survey and perspective. *IEEE Transactions on Systems, Man, & Cybernetics, 19*(2): 399–408.

Norman, Donald A. (April 1983). Design rules based on analyses of human error. *Communications of the ACM, 26*(4): 254–258.

Norman, Donald A. (January 1990). Commentary: Human error and the design of computer systems. *Communications of the ACM, 33*(1): 4–7.

Olson, Margrethe H., and Primps, S. (1984). Working at home with computers: Work and nonwork issues. *J. of Social Issues, 40*(3): 97–112.

Overman, E. Sam (1988). Using the systems development life cycle for computer applications in human services. *Computers in Human Services, 3*(3/4): 55–69.

Perrolle, Judith A. (1987). *Computers and Social Change: Information, Property, and Power*. Wadsworth, Belmont, Calif.

Perrow, Charles (1984). *Normal Accidents: Living with High Risk Technology*. Basic Books, New York.

Petheram, Brian (1989). An approach to integrating technology in human service applications. *Computers in Human Services, 5*(1/2): 187–195.

Petroski, H. (1985). *To Engineer is Human: The Role of Failure in Successful Design*. St. Martins, New York.

Pietrasanta, A. (1989). Software engineering education in IBM. In *Issues in Software Engineering Education* (R. Fairley and P. Freeman, eds.), Springer-Verlag, New York, pp. 5–18.

Piturro, Marlene (October 1989). Redefining old jobs, creating new ones. *Personal Computing, 13*(10): 141–144.

Platter, Adele (June 1988). Computer experiences of young adults: An empirical analysis. *Social Indicators Research, 8*(3): 291–302.

Power, Kevin (April 2, 1990). DOD course might be used for Trail Bioss training. *Government Computer News*: 57.

Rabin, Jack, and Jackowski, Edward B., eds. (1988). *Handbook of Information Research Management*. Marcel Dekker, New York.

Raitt, D. I. (October 1986). Mini debate: Small is not necessarily beautiful: Advantages and disadvantages of microcomputer use in libraries. *4*(5): 248–257.

Raymond, L. (1985). Organizational characteristics and MIS success factors in the context of small business. *MIS Quarterly, 9*(1): 37–52.

Reddit, Kay, and Lodahl, Tom (July 24, 1989). The human side. *Management Information Systems Week*:

Reinecke, Ian (1982). *Electronic Illusions: A Skeptic's View of Our High Tech Future*. Penguin, New York.

Rettig, Marc (October 1990). Software teams. *Communications of the ACM, 33*(10): 23–27.

Robey, Daniel (1977). Computers and management structure: Some empirical findings re-examined. *Human Relations, 30*: 963–976.

Robey, Daniel (1979). User attitudes and management information system use. *Academy of Management Journal, 22*: 527–538.

Robey, Daniel (1981). Computer information systems and organization structure. *Communications of the ACM, 24*: 679–687.

Rocheleau, Bruce (1985). Microcomputers and information management: Some emerging issues. *Public Productivity Review, 9*(2–3): 260–270.

Roman, Susan (November 16, 1987). Code overload plagues NYC welfare system. *MIS Week*: 1, 17.

Rosenbrock, H. H. (1977). The future of control. *Automation, 13*.

Rosenbrock, H. H. (1981). Engineers and work that people do. *IEEE Control Systems Magazine, 1*(3).

Rotter, J. (1966). Generalized expectancies for internal versus external control of reinforcement. *Psychological Monographs, 80*(609).

Rubin, Barry M. (November 1986). Information systems for public management: Design and implementation. *Public Administration Review, 46*: 540–552.

Safayeni, Frank R., Purdy, R. Lyn, and Higgins, Christopher A. (March–April 1989). Social meaning of personal computers for managers and professionals: Methodology and results. *Behavior and Information Technology, 8*(2): 99–107.

Salzman, Harold (1987). Computer technology and the automation of skill: The case of computer-aided design, American Sociological Association, annual meeting, Chicago.

Sanders, G., and Courtney, J. (1985). A field of organizational factors influencing DSS success. *MIS Quarterly, 9*(1) 77–93.

Sanders, J. S. (1984). The computer: Male, female, or androgynous? *The Computing Teacher, 11*: 31–34.

Savage, Charles M. (1990). *5th Generation Management: Integrating Enterprises Through Human Networking*. Digital Press, Bedford, Mass.

Schubert, J.G. (1986). Ideas about inequality in computer learning. *The Monitor, 24*(7–8): 11–13, 26.

Schubert, J.G., and Bakke, T. W. (1984). Practical solutions to overcoming equity in computer use. *The Computing Teacher, 11*: 28–30.

Schultz, R. L., and Slevin, (1975). Implementation and organizational validity: An empirical investigation. In *Implementing OR/MS* (R. L. Schultz and Slevin, eds.), Elsevier, New York.

Senn, J. A. (1980). Management's assessment of computer information systems. *J. of Systems Management, 11*(9): 6–11.

Servan-Schreiber, Jean-Jacques (1985). On the computer revolution. *World Policy Journal, 2*: 569–586.

Shah, Arvind D., and Davis, Richard K. (1988). Defining end user requirements through service analysis. In (J. Rabin and Jackowski, eds.),

Shapiro, S. I., and MacDonald, Colin G. R. (Spring 1987). Computers and the human spirit. *Weaver* (Technology Studies Resource Center, Lehigh University, Pa.), *5*(2): 8–9.

Shaul, D. R. (1964). What's really ahead for middle management. *Personnel, 41*(6): 8–16.

Shneiderman, B. (1980). *Software Psychology: Human Factors in Computer and Information Systems*. Little, Brown, Boston.

Simon, Herbert A. (1960). The corporation—Will it be managed by machines? In *Management and Corporations 1985* (M. Anshen and G. L. Bach, eds.), McGraw-Hill, New York.

Smith, Norman J., and Bolitho, Floyd H. (1989). Information: The hydra-headed concept in the human services. *Computers in Human Services, 5*(3/4): 83–98.

Stevens, John M., and LaPlante, Josephine M. (November 1986). Factors associated with financial decision support systems in state government: An empirical examination. *Public Administration Review*, special issue, *46*: 522–531.

Stone, Paula S. (February 8, 1988b). Computer instruction for novices still a priority. *InfoWorld*: 38.

Swanson, B. E. (1974). Management information systems: Appreciation and involvement. *Management Science*: 178–188.

Swart, J. C., and Baldwin, R. A. (1971). EDP effects on clerical workers. *Academy of Management Journal, 14*(4): 497–512.

Talley, Sally A. (July 1989). A study of resistance to technological change: Principals and the use of microcomputers as a management tool. *Dissertation Abstracts International, 50*(1-A): 28–29.

Thompson, Lyke, Sarbaugh-McCall, Marjoire, and Norris, Donald (Winter 1989). The social impacts of computing: Control in organizations. *Social Science Computer Review, 7*(4): 407–417.

Turnage, Janet J. (February 1990). The challenge of new workplace technology for psychology. *American Psychologist, 45*(2): 171–178.

Turner, Judith (1982). Observations on the use of behavioral models in information systems research and practice. *Information Management, 5*(3): 207–213.

Ulinsky, Michael (1987). An analysis of the relationship of job need fulfillment and microcomputer training to microcomputer user satisfaction levels of public accountants, Ph.D. dissertation, New York University, New York.

Uris, A. (1963). Middle management and technological change. *Management Review, 52*(10): 55–58.

U.S. Office of Technology Assessment (1985). *Automation of America's Offices*. Superintendent of Documents, Washington, D.C.

U.S. Office of Technology Assessment (April 1986). *Intellectual Property Rights in an Age of Electronics and Information*, Report no. OTA-CIT-302. Congress of the U.S., Office of Technology Assessment, Washington, D.C.

U.S. Office of Technology Assessment (1987). *The Electronic Supervisor: New Technology, New Tensions*. (Superintendent of Documents, Washington, D.C.

U.S. Office of Technology Assessment (1988). *Technology and the American Economic Transition*. Superintendent of Documents, Washington, D.C.

Vizachero, Rick (January 8, 1988b). Mac believers shout icon but my reaction is I can't. *Government Computer News*: 40.

Vrendenburg, K. (1984). Sex differences in attitudes, feelings, and behaviors toward computers, American Psychological Association, annual meeting, Toronto, Canada.

Waldrop, M. M. (1989). Phobos at Mars: A dramatic view—and then failure. *Science, 245*: 1044–1045.

Walton, R., and Susman, G. (1987). People policies for the new machines. *Harvard Business Review, 65*: 98–106.

Wang, Zhong-ming (November 1989). The human-computer interface hierarchy model and strategies in system development. *Ergonomics, 32*(11): 1391–1400.

Ware, Robb (May 21, 1990). MIS managers are often responsible for training horror stories. *MIS Week, 11*(21): 36.

Weber, Ron (January 1988). Computer technology and jobs: An impact assessment and model. *Communications of the ACM, 31*(1): 68.

Weinberg, G. (1971). *The Psychology of Computer Programming*. Van Nostrand, New York.

Weizenbaum, Joseph (1976). *Computer Power and Human Reason: From Judgment to Calculation*. W. H. Freeman, San Francisco.

Wexler, Joanne (February 1988). Are women's telecom careers measuring up? *TPT: The Magazine for Networking Management*: 21–26.

Wolman, Rebekah (January 1990). Technology and the basic skills crisis. *Information Center*: 16–24.

Working Women (1980). *Race Against Time: Automation of the Office*. Working Women, Cleveland.

Wright, Barbara Drygulski (1987). *Women, Work, and Technology: Transformations*. University of Michigan Press, Ann Arbor.

12
Psychological Burnout in Organizations

Ronald J. Burke

York University, North York, Ontario, Canada

Astrid M. Richardsen

University of Tromso, Tromso, Norway

I. INTRODUCTION

The last 10 years have witnessed a growing interest in research and writing on psychological burnout in work settings. Writing in the popular press has often exceeded knowledge based on solid research conclusions. As a result of widespread colloquial usage of the term, occupational burnout has become somewhat of a faddish concept.

Burnout has been defined in various ways by different researchers. The broadest definitions (Freudenberger and Richelson, 1980) equate burnout with stress, connect burnout with an endless list of adverse health and well-being variables, and suggest it is caused by the relentless pursuit of success. Other definitions are narrower, relating burnout to human service professions with interpersonal stress as its cause (Maslach and Jackson, 1981); that is, psychological burnout is related to feelings experienced by people whose jobs require repeated exposure to emotionally charged interpersonal situations (Maslach, 1978).

One of the major obstacles to understanding burnout is that there is no single definition of burnout that is accepted as standard (Maslach, 1982b). Because there is little agreement among consultants, clinicians, researchers, managers, and administrators about what burnout is, our understanding of the concept, what produces it and what results from it, is still far from complete. While the widespread interest in burnout over the past two decades has resulted in more awareness and less denial of the problem, some researchers have cautioned against rushing into solutions before there is full understanding of the problem (Maslach and Jackson, 1984a). There is still limited information about what percentage of people experience burnout, and for how long; and we still need conclusive data on critical criterion outcomes, such as quality of work, turnover, and personal health.

Definitions of psychological burnout have been changed or modified as a result of increasing knowledge about it. In many cases the changes have been in the direction of including more rather than less (Freudenberger, 1983; Maslach, 1982b). As a result, there is a growing diversity in the applications of the concept (Pines and Aronson, 1988). While the term burnout originated in people-oriented, helping professions, which may have had the effect of limiting early research to human service professions (Maslach and Jackson, 1984a), research conducted over the past decade has extended the concept of burnout to many other occupations that also have a high degree of interpersonal stress (see Shirom, 1989). In addition, the concept has been expanded to include as causes of burnout several nonwork spheres of life, for example, the emotional strain of contact with people in one's personal life (Pines, 1987; 1988).

On one hand, a broadened concept of burnout allows us to compare a variety of settings and to increase our understanding of the basic characteristics of burnout. On the other hand, if the term is overextended and overused, implying a wide variety of causes and solutions, it may have diminished usefulness as a concept, making clear and meaningful discussion impossible (Freudenberger, 1983; Maslach, 1982b). A crucial issue for future research concerns defining and operationalizing burnout (Maslach and Jackson, 1984b). It is important to recognize that burnout is a multifaceted concept while at the same time limiting the number of psychological states that are considered part of it, and developing psychometrically sound measures that can discriminate among these states.

There is general agreement regarding some of the characteristics of burnout, but determining whether or not a worker is burned out may still be difficult (Farber, 1983). This is partly because of the lack of agreement concerning the extent to which burnout is purely a psychological condition or actual behavior, such as attempts to cope with negative stress conditions. Despite the many differences in definitions and approaches to burnout, Maslach (1982b) noted that there are also common threads. There is general agreement that burnout occurs at an individual level; that burnout is an internal psychological experience involving feelings, attitudes, motives, and expectations; and that burnout is a negative experience for the individual, in that it concerns problems, distress, and discomfort.

Understanding burnout is important for several reasons. First, it may be related to important individual, organizational, and client outcomes (Maslach and Jackson, 1981; Cherniss, 1980a). Second, it may be widespread; that is, it may be a large problem among helping professionals. Over the past 20 years our society has become increasingly professionalized. A growing number of individuals are being helped by professionals. The latter include: social workers, teachers, police officers, nurses, physicians, psychotherapists, counselors, psychiatrists, ministers, child care workers, mental health workers, prison personnel, legal services attorneys, psychiatric nurses, probation officers, and agency administrators. If these individuals are prone to burnout, it may be a widespread problem. Finally, it may be possible to reduce the prevalence of burnout if it were better understood.

Efforts have been made to identify causes of burnout. Some writing suggests that since individuals burn out, this implies some weakness or deficiency in the victims of burnout. A related position implicates clients of helping professionals as the cause of burnout; clients have weaknesses or deficiencies. Other writing (Pines and Kafry, 1981) has focused on the situations in which people find themselves; that is, burnout is best understood in terms of situational sources of job-related interpersonal stress. Recent research has shifted the emphasis to an identification of "bad" situations rather than "bad" individuals. Research findings accumulated over the past 20 years have shown few significant and consistent personality correlates of burnout, but many significant and consistent job, work setting, and organizational correlates of burnout (Maslach, 1982b).

There is voluminous literature on psychological burnout. This chapter provides a selective review of this material, providing enough content to draw valid conclusions and highlight issues that still need resolution. It addresses the following topics:

- Definitions of burnout
- Measures of burnout
- Models of burnout
- Conceptual and methodological issues
- Factors contributing to burnout
    Individual difference variables
    Organizational variables
- Consequences of burnout
- Interventions to reduce burnout
- Conclusions

II. DEFINITIONS OF BURNOUT

A. Freudenberger

Freudenberger (1974) is given credit for first using the term burnout. Burnout was defined as "to fail, wear out, or become exhausted by making excessive demands on energy, strength, or resources." Freudenberger and Richelson (1980) described burnout as a state of chronic fatigue, depression, and frustration brought about by devotion to a cause, way of life, or relationship that not only failed to produce expected rewards but also ultimately led to lessened job involvement as well as lowered job accomplishment. The definition limited burnout to individuals who are dynamic, charismatic, goal-oriented, high achieving, and highly dedicated an committed to everything they undertake.

Freudenberer's work (1974; 1980—with Richelson; 1983) was based on clinical observations and case studies and provided great insights into individuals dynamics of burnout, psychological reasons why it occurs, and processes by which it occurs. His writing stimulated efforts by other researchers who attempted to provide an empirical basis for the study of burnout (e.g., Maslach, Pines).

B. Cherniss

Cherniss (1980b) defined burnout as a transactional process consisting of job stress, worker strain, and psychological accommodation. More specifically, the development of burnout was conceptualized as consisting of three stages. The first stage involves an imbalance between work demands and an individual's resources to deal with these demands (stress). The second stage—an immediate, short-term emotional response to this imbalance—is characterized by feelings of anxiety, tension, fatigue, and exhaustion (strain). The third stage of burnout is marked by a number of changes in attitude and behavior. These include a tendency to treat clients in a detached or mechanical fashion, or a cynical preoccupation with gratification of one's own needs (defensive coping). Burnout, then, is defined as a process in which workers disengage from their work in response to stress and strain experienced on the job. The process begins when the helper experiences stress and strain that cannot be alleviated through active problem solving. The changes in attitude and behavior associated with burnout provide a psychological escape.

C. Pines and Aronson

Pines and Aronson (1988; Pines, Aronson, and Kafry, 1981) defined burnout as a state of physical, emotional, and mental exhaustion caused by long-term involvement in situations that are emotionally demanding. The emotional demands are caused by a combination of very high expectations and chronic situational stress. Burnout is accompanied by an array of symptoms that include physical depletion and feelings of helplessness, hopelessness, and lack of enthusiasm about work and even life in general. People who burn out develop negative self-concepts and negative attitudes toward work and toward other people (dehumanizing others). In addition to these detrimental psychological effects, burnout appears to be a major factor in low morale, absenteeism, tardiness, and high job turnover. Burnout usually affects those who go into helping professions with a strong desire to give of themselves to others, who are highly motivated and idealistic, and who have expectations that their work will bring a sense of meaning into their lives.

Pines, Aronson, and Kafry (1981) distinguished between tedium and burnout. While these two states are similar in terms of symptomatology, they are different in origin. Tedium can be the result of any prolonged chronic pressures (mental, physical, or emotional), whereas burnout is the result of constant or repeated emotional pressure associated with intense involvement with people, thus burnout is reserved for the helping professions. Although the intensity, duration, frequency and consequences may vary, both tedium and burnout are reactions that include emotional and mental exhaustion. For the reaction or experience to be labeled as burnout it has to have a certain degree of all three components.

D. Maslach and Jackson

Maslach (1982a; 1982b) and Maslach and Jackson (1981; 1984a; 1984b; 1986) have defined burnout as a syndrome of emotional exhaustion, depersonalization, and reduced personal accomplishment that occurs among individuals who work with people in some capacity. Emotional exhaustion refers to feelings of being emotionally overextended and drained by one's contact with other people. Depersonalization refers to an unfeeling and callous response toward these people, who are usually the recipients of one's service or care. Reduced personal accomplishment refers to a decline in one's feeling of competence and successful achievement in one's work with people.

Maslach and Jackson (1984a) have stressed the importance of viewing burnout as a multifaceted concept. The three components are considered to be conceptually distinct but are not assumed to be empirically uncorrelated (Jackson, Schwab, and Schuler, 1986). The components may share common hypothesized causes and therefore may be intercorrelated. The value of distinguishing among the three components of burnout is shown by findings of differential patterns of correlations between each component and other variables (Jackson, Schwab, and Schuler, 1986).

III. MEASURES OF BURNOUT

A. The Maslach Burnout Inventory

The most widely used measure of burnout is the Maslach burnout inventory (MBI; Maslach and Jackson, 1981; 1986). The scale consists of 22 items that measure three aspects of the burnout syndrome. The emotional exhaustion subscale (nine items) assesses feelings of being emotionally overextended and exhausted by one's work. The depersonalization subscale (five items) measures an unfeeling and impersonal response toward recipients of one's service, care, treatment, or instruction. The personal accomplishment subscale (eight items) assesses feelings of competence and successful achievement in one's work with people. Each item is rated on a seven-point scale ranging from "never" to "every day." In the first edition of the scale (Maslach and Jackson, 1981), each item was rated in terms of intensity as well as frequency, but these two dimensions were highly correlated when subscale scores were computed, and the current edition assesses only the frequency dimension.

The authors reported that internal consistency coefficients for the three subscales ranged from .71 to .90, and test-retest reliability was high as well (Maslach and Jackson, 1986). In terms of convergent validity, significant correlations were found between MBI scores and behavioral ratings by observers (e.g., co-workers and spouses); the presence of certain job characteristics that were expected to contribute to experienced burnout (e.g., large caseloads, direct contact with clients, feedback from the job itself, and task significance); and measures of various outcomes hypothesized to be related to burnout (e.g., dissatisfaction with opportunities for growth and development in the job, desire to leave job, as well as impairment of interpersonal relationships both on and off the job). Discriminant validity evidence included moderate correlations between MBI subscales and job dissatisfaction, and nonsignificant correlations with social desirability scores (Jackson, Schwab, and Schuler, 1986).

But other reliability and validity studies have yielded inconsistent results. Reliability estimates are usually found to be adequate (Corcoran, 1985; Powers and Gose, 1986), but factor analyses to confirm the proposed factor structure give only modest support for the three subscales (Gold, 1984; Iwanicki and Schwab, 1981; Koeske and Koeske, 1989; Powers and Gose, 1986). In general, the multidimensionality of the MBI has been demonstrated in that several factors emerged (Green, Walkey, and Taylor, 1991). The emotional exhaustion subscale seemed to be the most stable factor, but several items on the depersonalization subscale also loaded highly on other factors, raising questions about the independence and robustness of this factor. Several researchers have found that items on the personal accomplishment subscale also loaded on more than one factor, and therefore may not have simple structure (Corcoran, 1985; Powers and Gose, 1986).

In terms of convergent validity of the MBI, Koeske and Koeske (1989) found evidence of selective impact of antecedents (e.g., work stress, work load, and client contact). However, all three subscales of the MBI were strongly linked to job satisfaction and intention to quit, indicating support for burnout theory as far as consequences are concerned.

B. Tedium

The tedium measure was developed by Pines, Aronson, and Kafry (1981). It consists of 21 items rated on a seven-point Likert scale ranging from "never" to "always," and the overall tedium score is the mean value of the responses to these items. The items represent the three aspects of physical exhaustion (being tired, being physically exhausted, feeling wiped out and rundown, being weary), emotional exhaustion (feeling depressed, being emotionally exhausted, feeling burned out), and mental exhaustion (being unhappy, feeling worthless, disillusioned and resentful of people, feeling rejected). Burnout is identical to tedium in terms of definition and symptomatology, but is seen as resulting from work with people in situations that are emotionally demanding.

Unlike the MBI, the tedium measure makes no reference to work. The tedium measure was standardized on several samples of participants, and the authors reported acceptable test-retest reliability and internal consistency.

The MBI and the tedium measure are both widely used and well-standardized burnout measures. Two studies (Corcoran, 1985; Stout and Williams, 1983) compared the MBI with the tedium measure ot determine correlations between them and to correlate scores on both instruments with measures of job satisfaction and health problems. Test-retest reliability was higher for the tedium measure than for the MBI, and internal consistency coefficients were acceptable for both burnout measures. The tedium measure correlated significantly with all subscales of the MBI, and was also significantly correlated with both job satisfaction and health problems. The MBI emotional exhaustion and depersonalitzation components were significantly correlated with job satisfaction, but not with health problems (Corcoran, 1985). Personal accomplishment did not correlate with either of these two measures. The authors suggest that the tedium measure, utilizing just one score, may be a more suitable measure of burnout than the MBI. The MBI may be appropriate for more sophisticated use in organizational assessment, particularly in attempting to identify patterns of burnout and/or stages of its development.

C. Staff Burnout Scale

The staff burnout scale for health professionals (SBS-HP; Jones, 1980) is a 30-item inventory based on Maslach's conceptual approach, but also includes behavioral and physiological items. Twenty items measure the burnout syndrome as defined by Maslach and Pines, and ten items form a lie scale to detect tendencies to "fake good." While the MBI assesses a worker's psychological or affective experience of burnout, the SBS-HP assesses the adverse cognitive, affective, behavioral, and psychophysiological reactions that make up the burnout syndrome (Jones, 1981). Although the scale is scored to yield one total burnout score, Jones (1980) reported four factors. These were dissatisfaction with work, psychological and interpersonal tension, physical illness and distress, and unprofessional patient relationships. The SBS-HP measures acute stress reactions or how the examinee currently feels. Jones (1981) reported a reliability coefficient of 0.93. Validation evidence suggest that the SBS-HP is related to the same external stressors and stress reactions as the MBI, but correlations between the two burnout measures were not reported (Jones, 1981).

D. Other Measures

Several other scales to assess burnout have been developed but have not been widely used in research. The Matthews burnout scale for employees is a self-report instrument that measures the single construct of burnout by sampling a variety of behaviors from the cognitive, affective, and physiological domains (Matthews, 1990). The different types of behavior sampled are attitudes toward work, role adjustment, locus of control, coping skills, personal adjustment, and temperament. The scale discriminated between burned out and non-burned out employees (according to supervisor ratings) in a sample of 200 employees in a variety of people-oriented professions, and scale scores correlated significantly with each of the three MBI subscales.

Freudenberger and Richelson (1980) developed a scale intended as a self-assessment tool. It measures exhaustion, sadness, and withdrawal from routine activities. This scale does not have adequate psychometric properties and was not intended as a research tool.

IV. MODELS OF BURNOUT

One of the challenges in burnout research is to integrate research findings into a coherent and comprehensive framework that consistently and reliably reflects the dynamics of the burnout process in a variety of work settings. A comprehensive model of burnout must incorporate: (1) the various individual and organizational variables that constitute sources of stress and demands leading to the development of burnout; (2) the consequences of burnout in terms of personal, work-related, and organizational outcomes; and (3) a framework for multilevel interventions to alleviate burnout.

One of the advantages of viewing burnout as a process over time is that it allows us to track burnout's antecedents, particularly those features of the organization that contribute to the development of stress and then burnout. This has both theoretical and practical implications. By being able to specify more precisely those factors that contribute to burnout at a given time, we elaborate on the theoretical underpinnings of burnout and its development.

From a practical perspective, it is of great value to the organization and its managers to be able to specify just what the causes of burnout are at a given time. Assuming that there is access to, and means of, implementing appropriate intervention procedures, it is possible not only to improve the worker's morale but also to prevent physical and emotional harm.

In recent years, several developmental models of burnout have been proposed and have generated research activity that has contributed to our knowledge. Three such models will be reviewed here.

A. Cherniss

Cherniss (1980a) and his associates interviewed 28 beginning professionals in four fields (mental health, poverty law, public health nursing, and high school teaching). All were interviewed several times over a 1- to 2-year period. The process model he proposed is shown in Figure 1. The variables in the model were distilled from interviews with and observations of these new professionals.

This model proposes that particular work setting characteristics interact with individuals who enter the job with particular career orientations. These individuals also bring with them particular extrawork demands and supports. These factors, in concert, result in particular sources of stress being experienced to varying degrees by job incumbents. Individuals cope with these stresses in different ways. Some employ techniques and strategies that might be termed active problem solving while others cope by exhibiting the negative attitude changes Cherniss identified in his definition of burnout. Burnout, for Cherniss, occurs over time—it is a process—and represents one way of adapting to, or coping with, particular sources of stress.

Two studies have provided direct tests of the model. Burke, Shearer, and Deszca (1984b) designed a study to validate the Cherniss model among men and women in police work.

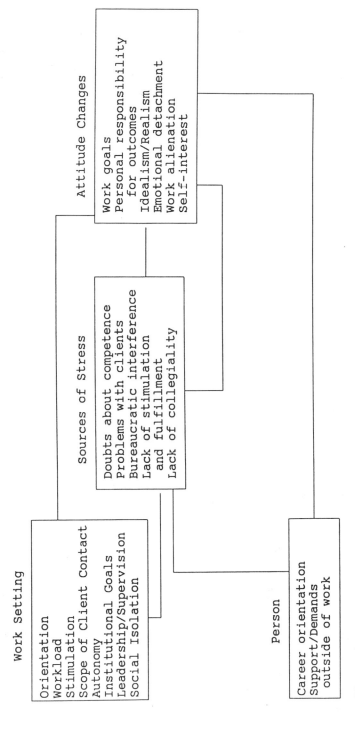

Figure 1 Cherniss process model of burnout.

Measures of Cherniss's concepts were created for the research, since none existed. Path analysis was used to examine relationships among pairs of variables, entered in such a way as to assume a causal order, but controlling for relationships with the other variables in the model. The model received considerable empirical support. Correlations indicated that proposed work setting and stress antecedents were significantly correlated with a measure of negative attitude change (or burnout) proposed by Cherniss, as well as with the most widely used measure of burnout, the MBI. In addition, extraorganizational variables had significant direct effects on reported levels of burnout. As proposed by Cherniss, burnout was also found to be associated with undesirable personal and organizational outcomes. More complex path analyses continued to provide empirical support for the Cherniss framework. These analyses revealed both a significant direct relationship of work setting characteristics to the burnout measures, and a significant indirect relationship of work setting characteristics to the burnout measures through experienced sources of stress.

Burke and Greenglass (1989a) examined psychological burnout among 833 men and women in teaching using the framework developed by Cherniss. The data provided strong preliminary support for the model and produced findings consistent with previous research (Burke, Shearer, and Deszca, 1984b).

B. Golembiewski

The second way in which burnout might be examined as a process involved the notion of phases within the burnout concept itself. Golembiewski and his colleagues (Golembiewski, Munzenrider, and Carter, 1983) began this line of research. They assigned different priorities or prepotencies to the three subscales of the MBI. Depersonalization was considered the least important contributor to burnout. Lack of personal accomplishment was rated a more important contributor to burnout. Finally, emotional exhaustion was considered to be the most important contributor to burnout. Dichotomizing the distribution of scores at the median as high and low generated eight phases of burnout (see Figure 2).

Previous research with the MBI has used scores on the three subscales as well as a total score. The phase approach uses the three subscales but transcends them. In addition, the phase approach involves a total score but orders phases having similar total scores in a theoretically based sequence. The phase approach thus has a theoretical richness not present in the more common uses of the MBI.

Golembiewski collected MBI data on 281 men and women from a product division of a large corporation, along with data on 22 work setting variables. These included: five dimensions of job satisfaction measured by the job description index (JDI) (Smith, Kendall, and Hulin, 1969); 10 facets of the job measured by the job diagnostic survey (JDS) (Hackman and Oldham, 1980); and an assortment of work attitudes and experiences (such as trust in supervisors and fellow employees and job involvement). Groups representing the eight progressive burnout phases were compared using analysis of variance (ANOVA). Significant F values were present on 20 of the 22 variables. Golembiewski replicated this study using 1535 employees from a single federal agency and identical measures (except for the JDI) with generally similar results (Golembiewski, Munzenrider, and Stevenson, 1986).

Research using the progressive phase notion has had two emphases. The first, and the largest body of work, has attempted to validate the notion of progressive phases itself. This

MBI Subscales	Phases							
	I	II	III	IV	V	VI	VII	VIII
Depersonalization	Lo	Hi	Lo	Hi	Lo	Hi	Lo	Hi
Personal Accomplishment	Lo	Lo	Hi	Hi	Lo	Lo	Hi	Hi
Emotional Exhaustion	Lo	Lo	Lo	Lo	Hi	Hi	Hi	Hi

Figure 2 Golembiewski phase model of burnout.

stream of research has compared individuals at various phases on a wide array of potential antecedents and consequences of psychological burnout (Burke and Deszca, 1986; Burke and Greenglass, 1989c; Burke, Shearer, and Deszca, 1984a; Golembiewski, Hilles, and Daly, 1986). This research has provided considerable support for the validity of the underlying notion of progressive phases of burnout; that is, individuals in the more advanced phases almost always report more negative work experiences (e.g., greater stress, less job autonomy) and more negative outcomes (e.g., less job satisfaction, more psychosomatic symptoms) than do individuals in less advanced phases.

The studies that have investigated worksite features in relationship to the phase model have been remarkably consistent. Advanced phases of burnout have been associated with a range of negative worksite features that seem to vary regularly phase by phase. As the phases progress from I through VIII, individuals see their worksites as less attractive and more depriving (Deckard, Rountree, and Golembiewski, 1986; Burke and Deszca, 1986; Burke and Greenglass, 1989c; Burke, Shearer, and Deszca, 1984a; and Munzenrider, 1984; 1988; Golembiewski, Munzenrider and Carter, 1983; Golembiewski, Munzenrider, and Stevenson, 1985; Janz, Dugan, and Ross, 1986); report less satisfaction and higher turnover intentions (Burke and Deszca, 1986; Burke and Greenglass, 1989c; Burke, Shearer, and Deszca, 1984a; Golembiewski and Munzenrider, 1988); report less job involvement and participation in decision making (Golembiewski and Munzenrider, 1984; 1988); report lower work-related psychological sense of community (Deckard, Rountree, and Golembiewski, 1986); report greater incidence of physical symptoms and negative feelings (Burke and Deszca, 1986; Burke and Greenglass, 1989c; Burke, Shearer, and Deszca, 1984a); and work-unit productivity tends to decrease (Golembiewski, 1984).

A second but considerably smaller stream of research has examined the advantages of three and four phases of psychological burnout over the eight-phase model initially proposed by Golembiewski (Cahoon and Rowney, 1984; Rountree, 1984). Cahoon and Rowney collapsed Golembiewski's eight phases into three; low (phases I, II, and III), moderate (phases IV and V), and high (phases VI, VII, and VIII). Using fewer phases is proposed as one way of dealing with entry-transition questions inherent with the full model (Rountree, 1984).

In terms of incidence of burnout in the various phases, Golembiewski (1984) reported that the distribution across organizations varies. For example, the range of respondents in phase VIII, in a "best" versus "worst" profile, varied from 6% to 29%. The range of scores in phase I varied from 41% (best) to 29% (worst). In a study of almost 9000 respondents from 26 organizations or work units, Golembiewski (1986) reported that 16 out of 26 organizations have 40% or more of the respondents in the three most advanced phases of burnout (VI-VIII). At an individual level of analysis, over 41% of the total sample of almost 9000 participants were classified in these three phases. These assignments tended to cluster in the extreme phases; approximately 43% were classified in phases I through III.

Several studies have investigated the stability of burnout and burnout phases. Golembiewski, Deckard, and Rountree (1989) measured burnout five times over a 7-week period. Correlation for each subdimension at five points in time varied substantially. The average percentages of variance explained were 34% for depersonalization, 32% for personal accomplishment, and 52% for emotional exhaustion. According to the authors, this is consistent with the properties of the phase model. Emotional exhaustion scores seemed more stable than scores on the other two subscales, and "this is consistent with the conceptual view of progressive virulence of the three subdimensions." Gamma estimates of stability of phase assignments indicated that approximately 48% of all the cases indicated no change over the time period. When phase assignments in groups of three phases were assessed, 65% indicated no change from phases I through III, and 74% indicated no change from phases VI through VIII. Similar results from scores collected at five different times over 1 year were reported by Golembiewski and Munzenrider (1988), and Golembiewski and Boss (1991) found a high degree of stability among phase assignments in an aggregate of three convenience populations tested at 1 and 2 years apart.

Burke and Greenglass (1991) studied the stability of burnout phases among teachers. Questionnaires were administered twice 1 year apart. Forty-three percent of the sample remained in the same burnout phase ($N = 132$); 32% moved to a lower phase ($N = 98$); and 25% moved to a higher phase ($N = 77$). These latter percentages (32% vs. 25%) were not significantly different. Individuals in the middle phases were more likely to change phases during the year than individuals at extreme phases in the first year of measurement. There was a negative relationship between magnitude of change in burnout phase and frequency; that is, the number of school-based educators who made small changes was greater than the number who made large changes in burnout phases.

An analysis examined the relationship between direction and degree of change in burnout phase, work experience, and well-being. This involved the creation of a new variable indicating both degree and direction of change in burnout phase. This variable had 15 categories based on degree and direction of change in burnout phase; that is, individuals could increase or decrease as much as seven burnout phases or remain the same. Correlations were then computed between this variable and change scores on the various antecedents and consequences (e.g., work experience, satisfaction, and health variables). Six of the 13 correlations reached statistical significance, and in each case individuals moving to a lower burnout phase reported corresponding improvements in antecedents (work setting characteristics, level of work stress) and consequences (greater job satisfaction and fewer psychosomatic symptoms). Interestingly, changes in burnout phase were not associated with changes in marital satisfaction or health and life-style behaviors.

It was also possible to compare these findings on persistence of psychological burnout phases over a 1-year period with those of Golembiewski and his colleagues. Very similar findings were evident in the two studies involving two different samples and settings. Thus, about 40% of the respondents remained in the same phase; about 30% moved to a less advanced phase; and about 30% moved to a more advanced phase. These data support the conclusion that psychological burnout, over time, is substantially a chronic condition; that is, a majority of individuals (but not all) will remain in the same burnout phase over a 1-year period.

C. Leiter

Leiter (1989; 1991a, b) has proposed and researched a process model of burnout based on two assumptions. The first is that components of burnout influence one another over time, and the second is that the three components have distinct relationships with environmental conditions and individual difference characteristics (Leiter, 1991b). Leiter used structural equation modeling in his analyses, which allows one to explore a process model of burnout while maintaining the MBI's three-factor structure (Leiter, 1991a). According to Leiter (1991b), this method also allows one to explore the impact of one component of burnout on the other two components, and to determine the distinct relationship of each aspect of burnout with environmental conditions.

Leiter's model places emotional exhaustion in a central position (see Figure 3). The sequencing of the three subscales in the development of burnout was described in Leiter and Maslach (1988). Emotional exhaustion develops first, as it is most responsive to demands and stressors of the job. Workers attempt to cope with feelings of exhaustion by depersonalizing their relationships with clients. As they lose this personal component of their work relationships, their feelings of accomplishment diminish, resulting in the state of burnout. Leiter (1989) argues that the positive correlations found among the MBI subscales support the view that depersonalization is an ineffective attempt to cope with exhaustion. If it were a successful coping response, depersonalization would be negatively correlated with emotional exhaustion.

The model defines emotional exhaustion as a reaction to occupational stressors, the impact of which is mediated through emotional exhaustion on various outcomes. The principal stressors he has considered are work overload and conflict with people in the work setting. These will have impact on depersonalization, accomplishment, and other outcomes to the extent that they have an impact on emotional exhaustion. Effective skill utilization and coping efforts are proposed to have buffering effects on exhaustion and personal accomplishment. Supervisor and co-worker support, positive client relationships, and autonomy are proposed to buffer other aspects of burnout.

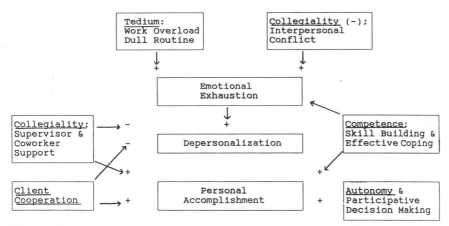

Figure 3 Leiter process model of burnout.

Leiter found considerable support for his model in several studies. However, in some studies (Leiter, 1988b; 1991a) the hypothesized direct link between depersonalization and personal accomplishment was not supported. It seems that the relationship of personal accomplishment with the other two MBI subscales could be better explained by their shared association with other measures, especially social support (Leiter, 1991b).

A recent study by Lee and Ashforth (in press) compared the phase model of Golembiewski and Leiter's model. They analyzed longitudinal data from human survey workers in two surveys separated by 8 months. The results supported the prediction of the Leiter model that emotional exhaustion was a precursor of depersonalization. However, consistent with Leiter's work, they did not find support for the prediction that depersonalization leads to diminished personal accomplishment. In the model derived by Lee and Ashforth, personal accomplishment emerged as a direct function of emotional exhaustion. This is in contrast to the role of personal accomplishment as a parallel construct found in Leiter's studies (1990; 1991a). However, the authors note that the relationship of personal accomplishment with the other burnout components may be subject to influence from various aspects of a work setting.

V. CONCEPTUAL AND METHODOLOGICAL ISSUES

Because the concept of burnout has not been identified as the province of a particular approach or way of thinking, there is a varied range of ideas about burnout and methodologies that can be used in research (Maslach and Jackson, 1984a). Many different researchers and practitioners have studied burnout employing a wide variety of methodologies and approaches, from clinical observations and case studies to sophisticated assessment tools and statistical analysis, as well as organizational interventions. Although this is promising for the future of burnout research, there are a number of issues that create problems in interpreting findings and that impede a full understanding of the concept.

Most research on burnout has focused on professionals in a variety of human service settings (e.g., teachers, lawyers, nurses, social workers, counselors, and police officers). A common assumption of such research has been that contact with people is a major source of emotional strain. Some researchers have even attempted to separate the concepts of work strain experienced in people-oriented professions versus work strain experienced in nonpeople-oriented professions (e.g., Pines and Aronson, 1981). The focus on people as a source of stress may be too narrow (Maslach and Jackson, 1984a). Burnout has also been increasingly investigated in a wide spectrum of occupations not oriented toward people (Shamir, 1989), as well as nonemployment-related settings (Pines, 1987; 1988). With such diverse applications of the term burnout, it may be difficult to compare research findings and to test theoretical models of the sources and consequences of experienced burnout in organizations. In addition, even within helping professions, there may be variations in patterns of relationships, depending on sample subgroup (Kahill, 1988). Helping professions may differ in terms of roles, power, and rewards; and direct contact with service recipients may be structured differently.

Several methodological issues are also of consequence in evaluating burnout research. Until recently, there have been few theories or models to guide research or interventions. This may in part be due to the fact that the main focus has been on burnout as a social problem rather than a theoretical issue (Maslach, 1982b). However, the lack of general models has resulted in a large number of research studies that typically are one-shot, correlational investigations of a limited set of variables with small populations (Kilpatrick, 1989; Paine, 1982). In a panel of 194 burnout studies published between 1973 and 1987, Kilpatrick (1989) found that 90% of the studies were surveys, 71% used convenience samples, almost 90% were one-shot studies, almost all obtained only self-report information, and almost all were descriptive studies. Some attempts have been made to develop more complex and interactive models that consider the influence of a multitude of factors (e.g., Cherniss, 1980a; 1980b; Leiter, 1988a, 1991a; Leiter and Maslach, 1988), and there are indications that burnout studies are increasing in methodological rigor (Kilpatrick, 1989). A growing number of studies are longitudinal (Burke and Greenglass, 1990; 1991; Cherniss, 1989; 1990; Golembiewski, Hilles, and Daly, 1987; Jackson, Schwab, and Shuler, 1986; Leiter, 1990); are employing true experimental designs (see Pines and Aronson, 1981; Golembiewski, Hilles, and Daly, 1987; Higgins, 1986); are focusing on interventions (Golembiewski, Hilles, and Daly, 1987; Higgins, 1986); and most issues related to construct validity are being addressed (Kilpatrick, 1989).

Another methodological issue concerns measures used to assess burnout. Because most studies have relied on self-report measures, and many have used different instruments to measure burnout, results from studies are not easily compared. Many researchers have noted the need for investigations in which multiple measures of burnout are employed (Kahill, 1988; Maslach, 1982b; Shinn, 1982). Instrumentation problems have special implications for determining the incidence of burnout. Burnout may be more common and widespread than previously thought, however, estimates based on existing research findings are difficult. For example, although the most frequently used measure of burnout is the MBI, researchers have used different operational definitions of what constitutes high or low burnout (Kilpatrick, 1989). In the studies reviewed by Kilpatrick (1989), burnout rates, when reported, ranged from less than 10% to over 80%. Golembiewski (1986) found, in a study sample of about 9000 participants in 26 work units, over 40% of respondents were classified in the three most advanced phases of burnout.

The stressors that contribute to burnout are generally well defined (Shinn, 1982). However, patterns of causality are difficult to determine, partly because studies have assessed variables at only one point in time, and partly because many of these variables are interdependent. Even when multivariate models are used, the results are ambiguous when the predictor variables are highly intercorrelated (Shinn, 1982). This creates problems at both theoretical and practical levels. It is difficult for administrators to use research findings to guide interventions aimed at changing work environments, and for researchers to entangle relationships and develop parsimonious explanations of burnout. The future of burnout research depends on the use of more sophisticated research designs to facilitate the development of comprehensive approaches (Kahill, 1988; Paine, 1982; Shinn, 1982).

Support for models of sources of burnout are often limited to the emotional exhaustion aspect of burnout (Kahill, 1988; Koeske and Koeske, 1989; Schwab, Jackson, and Schuler, 1986; Shiron, 1989). In general, the various job conditions and behavioral reactions studied so far are more strongly related to emotional exhaustion than to the other two subscales (Maslach and Jackson, 1984a). There may be other factors that are better predictors of depersonalization and personal accomplishment, but researchers have not been as successful in pinpointing causes and consequences of these two components of burnout. One aspect that may relate to depersonalization is the role of the client, including the type and severity of client problems and clients' reactions to the staff (Maslach, 1978). In several studies, Leiter (1991b) found that organizational demands and supports contribute differentially to the three burnout aspects. Emotional exhaustion is predicted mainly by occupational stressors, such as work overload, inadequate skill use, and interpersonal conflicts. Factors contributing to depersonalization and personal accomplishment include emotional exhaustion, supervisor and co-worker support, client cooperation, skill building and effective coping, and participative decision making. Koeske and Koeske (1989) suggested a reconceptualization of burnout that regards exhaustion as the essence of burnout, and that treats accomplishment and depersonalization as related variables, but not as elements of burnout. Leiter (1991b), on the other hand, argued that the relationship among the three subscales is intrinsic to understanding the burnout syndrome.

There are some major themes in different theories of what produces burnout and what results from it (Maslach, 1982b). Most causal analyses have emphasized difficult interpersonal relationships at work, job stress, and characteristics of the organizational setting. There has been more emphasis on situational and social causes than on individual aspects (e.g., expectations, personality traits). However, recent studies suggest that the primary sources of burnout are related to both organizational conditions and personal characteristics of the helping professional (Schwab, Jackson, and Schuler, 1986). Burke, Shearer, and Deszca (1984b) found support for the primary role of job and work setting characteristics in contributing to burnout, with the lesser role played by demographic factors. Burnout has been linked to various work-related behaviors (e.g., absenteeism and turnover). Some studies have found that the inclusion of extrawork variables, both social supports and extrawork demands, also appears to be useful in one's understanding of burnout at work. Other studies have clearly shown that occupational burnout does influence workers' functioning outside work (Jayaratne, Chess, and Kunkel, 1986; Maslach and Jackson, 1985; Zedeck et al., 1988).

Another problem in the burnout literature concerns the amount of variance explained by the job conditions measures. In many studies using regression analyses, the amount of explained variance was relatively low for each of the three burnout components. In addition, when variables were tested in sets, the unique contribution of specific variables was often insignificant. In order to understand fully sources and consequences of burnout, and individual differences that may exist, we may have to include cognitive variables (e.g., Leiter, 1990; 1991a; Meier, 1983; 1984), such as how work environments are appraised, and how coping resources are assessed and used.

It is important to establish the objective consequences of burnout for both individuals and organizations, and better research designs along with the development of comprehensive, multivariate models of the burnout phenomenon are needed in order to advance the field. As Maslach and Jackson (1984a) noted, better research will generate better ideas for interventions, and better understanding of the burnout concept may stimulate commitment to implementation and long-term evaluation of interventions.

VI. FACTORS CONTRIBUTING TO BURNOUT: INDIVIDUAL DIFFERENCE VARIABLES

A variety of individual demographic and situational variables has been considered, including sex, age, career orientations, and several personality characteristics. These factors have been found to generally have only modest or no correlation with levels of psychological burnout.

A. Sex

Several studies have found sex differences in the burnout response (Burke and Greenglass, 1989f; Cahoon and Rowney, 1984; Etzion and Pines, 1986; Greenglass, Burke, and Ondrack, 1990; Maslach and Jackson, 1984b; 1985; Ogus, Greenglass, and Burke, 1990; Schwab and

Iwanicki, 1982a; Schwab, Jackson, and Schuler, 1986). However, it is difficult to interpret such sex differences, because they may be confounded with a number of significant variables relevant to burnout, such as type of occupation, hierarchical rank, role overload, role conflict, and social support systems (Greenglass, 1991).

Maslach and Jackson (1985) examined sex differences among workers from a wide range of health and service occupations. They found that women scored significantly higher on emotional exhaustion and lower on personal accomplishment than men, while men scored higher than women on depersonalization. Although these findings support the notion that patterns of burnout may be the result of sex-role socialization, the investigators caution against such an explanation because, in their study, sex was confounded with type of occupation. For example, in their sample the physicians, psychiatrists, and police officers were mostly male, whereas nurses, social workers, and counselors were usually women. Therefore, any sex differences may actually have reflected differences in occupations.

While many researchere have asserted that women are more likely to suffer from burnout than men because of the role overload and role conflict (Pines, Aronson, and Kafry, 1981; Etzion and Pines, 1986), empirical evidence reviewed by Greenglass (1991) does not support the notion that multiple roles are necessarily associated with greater stress or illness in women. Some early studies (Pines and Kafry, 1981; Etzion and Pines, 1986) did find support for the view that women were more susceptible to burnout, but recent studies have found no differences in burnout among men and women. In a study of 126 dual-career physician couples, Izraeli (1988) found that women were not more burned out than men, and there were no sex differences in the relationship of burnout with work-family conflict, the need for achievement, and the amount of involvement in work. Similarly, no significant differences in burnout were found among male and female professional engineers (Etzion, 1988).

In fact, recent research evidence indicates that women may do slightly better than men. A number of studies have found that men score higher than women on depersonalization and have more negative attitudes toward clients than women. Higher scores for men than women on depersonalization have been reported among public contact workers (Maslach and Jackson, 1984b; 1985), among teachers (Burke and Greenglass, 1989f; Greenglass and Burke, 1988; Ogus, Greenglass, and Burke, 1990; Schwab and Iwanicki, 1982a), and among school personnel (Greenglass, Burke, and Ondrack, 1990). Cahoon and Rowney (1984) found that male managers were significantly more burned out than female managers, especially in their depersonalization response.

It is interesting that women often score lower on burnout than men. Socialization and societal expectation, internalized by women, result in women taking and maintaining major responsibility for the home and family, which contributes to women, more often than men, bearing the brunt of role conflict. Data support this, as seen, for example, in a study by Sekaran (1986), in which women who were part of dual-worker couples, suffered more interrole conflict than men. Additional data indicate that stress from conflicts between job and family responsibilities in managerial women was related to higher incidence of irritation, anxiety, and depression (Greenglass, 1985). Burke and Greenglass (1989f) found that women teachers reported more work-family conflict as well as more problems with time management than men, yet reported less burnout. Men experienced more work stress than women and also had less peer support. The data suggested that while both men and women were experiencing stress, the kinds of stresses differed. It is possible that in teaching as well as in other female-dominated professions, women have more peer support from similar women in the organization. Social support may protect an individual experiencing high strain from the deleterious effects of these stressful events (Burke and Greenglass, 1989f).

Greenglass (1991) has offered several possible explanations for gender differences in the experience of burnout. One explanation is rooted in accepted norms associated with the masculine role, which emphasizes strength, independence, and invulnerability. Since it is socially unacceptable for men to openly express vulnerability, depersonalization may be the result of an inability of men to cope with work strain. Ogus, Greenglass, and Burke (1990) found that high depersonalization in men was associated with lack of collegiality, higher absenteeism, greater medication use, and a lower-quality life-style. Another possible explanation is that women may have greater ability to cope with interpersonal stress than men (Greenglass, 1991). Women may be less likely to respond to people and their problems in an impersonal and callous manner since the traditional female role emphasizes caring, nurturance, and concern for others (Maslach and Jackson, 1985). Communication patterns that are high on responsivity and emotional involvement may indicate more effective communication (Greenglass, 1991). What has been seen as characteristic behavior of women and labeled as a weakness in the past, may in fact constitute a strength in terms of coping with job strain.

B. Age and Other Background Variables

Other background variables include age, marital status, and level of education (Schwab, Jackson, and Schuler, 1986). The variable of age in teachers or helping professionals has been linked to burnout; younger professionals tend to experience higher levels of emotional exhaustion and fatigue (Schwab and Iwanicki, 1982a). Among public contact workers, there was also a consistent pattern of lower burnout with older age (Maslach and Jackson, 1984b).

Studies have generally found weak relationships between other demographic variables and burnout (Burke, Shearer, and Deszca, 1984b; Maslach and Jackson, 1984b). Marital status, type of community, level of education, and number of years of experience did not relate to burnout (Schwab and Iwanicki, 1982a). However, Burke, Shearer, and Deszca (1984b) found that single police officers had higher burnout scores than did married ones, and a similar pattern was found by Maslach and Jackson (1984b) in a sample of public service employees. Kilpatrick (1989) indicated that studies that have reported associations between marital status and burnout in general find that single, widowed, and divorced persons were more burned out than married people. Studies that investigated relationships among burnout and tenure in occupation or current position suggest that those with less than a year of experience or with fewer years in their current position tend to report higher burnout. Results from studies including the number of years in an organization were mixed.

C. Personality Characteristics

There is general agreement that burnout-prone individuals are empathic, sensitive, dedicated, idealistic, and people-oriented, but also anxious, obsessional, overenthusiastic, and susceptible to overidentification with others (Cherniss, 1980b; Farber, 1983; Freudenberger and Richelson, 1980; Pines and Aronson, 1981). Most researchers have emphasized the central role of work-related stresses in the etiology of burnout (Farber, 1983). However, several studies have found relationships between various personality characteristics and burnout. McCranie and Brandsma (1988) found that higher burnout scores among physicians were significantly correlated with a number of Minnesota multiphasic personality inventory (MMPI) scales measuring low self-esteem, feelings of inadequacy, dysphoria and obsessive worry, passivity, social anxiety, and withdrawal from others. Studies have also found relationships between type A personality characteristics and burnout (Farber, 1983).

Several studies have found significant relationships between burnout and anxiety. Jayaratne, Chess, and Kunkel (1986) found that child welfare workers who scored high on the burnout scales were more likely to report higher levels of anxiety; Gold and Michael (1985) found that high levels of anxiety were related to the emotional exhaustion and depersonalization subscales among practice teachers; and Morgan and Krehbiel (1985) found that burned-out teachers of emotionally disturbed children reported significantly higher tension and anxiety than teachers who were not burned out. Cherniss (1980a) stated that a person with neurotic anxiety is much more susceptible to burnout. Richardsen, Burke, and Leiter (1992) found evidence that trait anxiety contributed significantly to burnout among nurses.

D. Career Orientations

Career orientation refers to the meaning of work for the individual. It includes goals, values, wants and outlooks, career-related aspirations, and desired rewards. Cherniss (1980a) proposed that for each career orientation there is an optimal work setting. The degree of stress, strain, and burnout is influenced by the fit between individual career orientation and work setting. Cherniss (1980a) observed four career orientations in his sample of early-career helping professionals.

Social activists want to do more in their work than just help individual clients. Their major purpose in their jobs is to bring about social and institutional change. They are idealists and visionaries who seek their work more as a crusade than as a career or job. They are often highly critical of their profession and hope to transform it through their work. Personal security and status are relatively unimportant to them.

Careerists pursue success as traditionally defined. Prestige, respectability, and financial security are important to them. Careerists want to impress their supervisors in order to advance their careers. They are interested in credentials, comparing themselves with other performers, and competing with them.

Artisans are more interested in the intrinsic quality of their work than in career advancement and financial success. Meeting their own internal standards is important to them along with professional development and growth. Artisans seek jobs that provide opportunities for challenge, new experiences, and the development of professionals skills, as well as the chance to use technique in a skillful manner. They want jobs that leads to an inner sense of accomplishment and growth.

Self-investors are more involved in their personal lives outside work. They are not strongly engaged in their present work. Families and personal exploration and discovery are central interests. They do not want to change the world while at work, do not want career advancement or success, and do not have high internal standards of performance. They are minimally committed to their work and look to activities outside their careers to satisfy strong needs.

Burke, Deszca, and Shearer (1986) examined these four career orientations and burnout in police officers. Social activists reported greater burnout, greater stress, and the least satisfying work setting. In addition, social activists exhibited poorer individual well-being (e.g., they reported more psychosomatic symptoms, greater use of alcohol and drugs, smoked more, drank more coffee). Self-investors reported the least job satisfaction as well as the fewest negative impacts of job demands on personal, home, and family life. Careerists and artisans reported the greatest work satisfaction, the least burnout, the least stress, and the most satisfying work settings. Social activist and careerist orientations weakened over time while the artisan orientation became stronger.

Similar results were obtained in a study (Burke and Greenglass, 1988) that considered the effects of initial career orientations on psychological burnout in teachers. The four career orientations were also related to measures of satisfaction and well-being among the same men and women in teaching using a longitudinal study design. One year later, self-investors, a type of nonwork orientation, reported greater burnout and greater experienced stress, and the least satisfying work setting. In addition, self-investors reported greater psychological burnout and work alienation (less job satisfaction, greater absenteeism). Social activists reported the poorest emotional and physical well-being. Careerists reported the least marital satisfaction, with the greatest conflict between work, parental, and self roles. Artisans exhibited the most positive work *and* life experiences. The concept of person-job or person-culture fit has been proposed to explain the distress of the self-investors and social activists (Burke and Deszca, 1988; Burke and Greenglass, 1989b).

The findings, as a whole, provide support for the hypothesis that individuals who begin their careers with a social activist orientation run a greater risk of experiencing a more negative work setting, heightened stress, greater degrees of burnout, and poorer well-being. In addition, social activists are currently pursuing a life-style (increased drinking, drug use, smoking, drinking of coffee, and taking of medication) that is more destructive to their health.

Some interesting findings concerned the self-investors. These individuals, consistent with their low commitment to work, exhibited a higher intention to leave policing or teaching, were relatively dissatisfied with their jobs, took off more sick days in the preceding 6 months than the other career orientations, and reported that their job demands have less of a negative impact on home and family and on their weekends and vacations. In addition, demands for exemplary behavior as a member of the larger social community posed less of a problem for them.

In general, self-investors fell in between the social activists and the careerists and artisans. The self-investors may be alienated from their work, but given their low commitment to work, appear to be paying a less heavy price than the social activists. The careerist orientation and the artisan orientation, to a lesser degree, are characterized by a more positively viewed work setting, less stress, less burnout, and greater job satisfaction. On the negative side, this career orientation is associated with greater negative impact of job demands on home and family life and with more type A behavior.

Burke and Deszca (1987) compared work experiences, satisfaction levels, and well-being of police officers who had changed their career orientations with police officers who had not. Two hundred and eighteen men and women in police work provided data by completing questionnaires. About half the sample had changed their career orientations. Police officers who had changed their career orientations were significantly less satisfied and reported poorer psychological well-being than police officers who did not change their career orientations.

Career orientations emerge as a useful concept in helping to explain incidences of professional burnout among men and women in police work and teaching. Career orientations, as proposed by Cherniss (1980a), encompass an element of fit between one's vision and aspirations and the stresses and rewards of one's job. When a poor fit exists, tension and dissatisfaction result. In some cases, individuals adapt to the job by changing their career orientations. In other cases, individuals reported a more negative attitude change as embodied in burnout. It would seem that by considering both the demands and rewards of jobs and the career orientations of individuals in those jobs, one would be better able to understand, predict, and alleviate burnout.

VII. ORGANIZATIONAL VARIABLES

Research on organizational variables related to burnout has generally followed the social psychological and organizational perspectives outlined by Maslach (1982a). Two different emphases have dominated the study of burnout (Maslach and Jackson, 1984a). One focus has been the employee-client relationship, looking at variables such as the type of client problem involved and the nature of the employee's personal relationship with the client. The second emphasis has been on the employee-organization relationship, studying the role of feedback, control and role clarity, social support, and expectations.

A. Client Factors

Complaints from clients about the bureaucratic structure surrounding the delivery of human services are often directed at the staff with whom they are dealing (Maslach, 1978). This serves as an added source of stress in the work of human service professionals, with the common result that staff try to establish some psychological distance from clients; that is, depersonalize their relationships with clients. According to Maslach (1978), client factors that may be stressful include the type of client problem (e.g., being in trouble, the seriousness of an illness, and the probability of change or cure); the personal relevance of client problems (e.g., staff person may overidentify with clients and share in their feelings and frustrations); the rules governing the staff-client relationship (both implicit and explicit); and client stance (e.g., being passive and dependent, thereby placing a tremendous burden of responsibility on staff). In addition, negative feedback, complaints and criticisms, and anger and frustration from clients about the staff or the institution may be stressful for staff to hear.

Studies have shown that the sheer number of clients seen also contributes to burnout (Jackson, Schwab, and Schuler, 1986; Maslach and Jackson, 1984b). Maslach and Jackson (1984b) found significantly higher burnout scores among public service employees with the largest caseloads. The type of client seen also was related to burnout, particularly depersonalization. The more stressful the contact with clients was, the higher the burnout scores. In general, burnout was not related to client characteristics such as age, sex, ethnicity, and socioeconomic status. However, emotional exhaustion was higher for those with predominantly black caseloads from a lower socioeconomic class than for those with predominantly white caseloads.

A study of school board principals, department heads, and teachers indicated that principals experienced less stress and burnout than teachers and department heads (Burke and Greenglass, 1989d). The lower burnout in principals may be the result of their spending fewer hours of contact with students than teachers and department heads and having more resources (power, autonomy, etc.).

Grade level may also influence burnout. Schwab and Iwanicki (1982a) found that high school teachers had more negative attitudes toward students and less personal accomplishment than elementary school teachers. Burke and Greenglass (1989e) also found that elementary teachers and administrators exhibited significantly less burnout than junior high and secondary teachers and administrators. Similar patterns of differences were present on theoretically based antecedents and consequences of burnout. Secondary teachers reported a more negative work setting, were more dissatisfied, and were in greater distress.

B. Workload

Several measures of quantitative workload have been related to burnout. Leiter (1988b; 1991a, b) has consistently found that work overload is significantly related to emotional exhaustion, but does not contribute to depersonalization or personal accomplishment. Similar findings have been reported by several other researchers (Jackson, Schwab, and Schuler, 1986; Jackson, Turner, and Brief, 1987).

C. Role Conflict and Role Ambiguity

Numerous studies have identified role conflict and role ambiguity as important contributors to the development of burnout (Schwab, Jackson, and Schuler, 1986). Role conflict is the simultaneous occurrence of two or more sets of inconsistent, expected role behaviors (Farber, 1983; Rizzo, House, and Lirtzman, 1970) representing multiple sources of demand (Jackson, Turner, and Briet, 1987). Role ambiguity is the lack of clear, consistent information regarding the rights, duties, and responsibilities of the job, and how these duties and responsibilities can best be performed.

Studies have found that where high levels of role conflict are present, professionals experienced high levels of emotional exhaustion and fatigue as well as negative attitudes toward recipients (Jackson, Turner, and Briet, 1987; Schwab and Iwanicki, 1982b; Schwab, Jackson, and Schuler, 1986). Schwab, Jackson, and Schuler (1986) found that both role conflict and role ambiguity contributed significantly to emotional exhaustion, and role conflict also predicted depersonalization.

D. Professional Expectations

Most professionals enter into a job with expectations about what the job will be like and what can be accomplished on the job. Most human service professionals enter their profession with a commitment to helping people, with expectations of making a difference, and perhaps with clearly defined career goals (Schwab, Jackson, and Schuler, 1986). When these expectations are not met and the goals are not reached, the individual will likely experience a sense of failure. The match between initial job expectations and actual job experiences partly determines employees' reactions to their jobs, and there is some evidence to suggest that unmet job expectations are associated with burnout (Schwab, Jackson, and Schuler, 1986). Conflicting expectations (current situation worse than expected) contributed significantly to emotional exhaustion, but not to the other two burnout components. However, in a longitudinal study of teachers, Jackson, Schwab, and Schuler (1986) found no support for the hypothesis that unmet expectations are important to the etiology of burnout. The authors suggested that no conclusions about the role of expectations should yet be drawn.

In general, role conflict and ambiguity were not associated with personal accomplishment. For example, Friesen and Sarros (1986) found that role clarity did not predict any of the three burnout aspects among Canadian teachers and administrators.

E. Participation in Decision Making

Lack of control or autonomy in one's job may also contribute to burnout (Pines, Aronson, and Kafry, 1981). Control involves the perception of being able to influence decision making in important aspects of the job, for example, work scheduling and development of policies that directly affect the work environment (Schwab, Jackson, and Schuler, 1986). It is possible that increasing participation in the decision-making process will enhance the control employees have over their work environment, and it may be an effective way to reduce job-related strain (Jackson, 1983).

In several studies, participation in decision making contributed significantly to depersonalization, but not to the other two burnout components (Jackson, Turner, and Briet, 1987; Schwab, Jackson, and Schuler, 1986). Autonomy in terms of job content was related to personal accomplishment among teachers (Jackson, Schwab, and Schuler, 1986). However, Landsbergis (1988) found among health care workers that job decision latitude contributed to all three components of burnout. Jobs that combined high workload demands with low decision authority were associated with higher burnout and more job strain (job dissatisfaction, sleeping problems, depression/life satisfaction, and physical/psychosomatic strain).

A study by Burke and Greenglass (1989d) observed that among school-based educators, stress and burnout increased as their hierarchical level decreased. Principals reported a more positive work setting, less experienced stress, less burnout, and better emotional health than did teachers. Department heads had an intermediate level of stress. At the same time, there were few effects due to one's administrative position associated with other variables such as physical health, medication use, life-style, marital satisfaction, and role conflict. The data suggest that superior organizational position may enable greater participation in decision making. The lower levels of stress observed among principals may be a function of increased decision-making power.

F. Social Support

There were indications that lack of social support may lead to burnout (Pines, Aronson, and Kafry, 1981; Leiter and Maslach, 1988). An effective support group includes people who can (1) provide emotional comfort; (2) confront people in humane ways when behavior is inappropriate; (3) provide technical support in work-related areas; (4) encourage individual growth; (5) serve as active listeners; and (6) share similar values, beliefs, and perceptions of reality (Pines, Aronson, and Kafry, 1981). Support may come from various sources—from administration, co-workers, or others outside the work environment. Two kinds of social support have been studied in relation to burnout. One is social support at work from co-workers and supervisors, and the other is social support outside of work, primarily from family.

Research has clearly shown that there is a relationship between the quality of the interpersonal environment of an organization and workers' psychological involvement in their work (Leiter, 1988a, b; Leiter and Maslach, 1988). Aspects of work settings that contribute to burnout often involve contact with other people, and these may include both clients and co-workers. Social support from colleagues in the form of friendship and help may be an important element in a worker's satisfaction with the job and experience of burnout. Interactions with co-workers may not always be supportive, however; sometimes interpersonal contacts at work are negative because of conflicts and disagreements among people (Leiter and Maslach, 1988). A number of studies have shown that lack of peer support is correlated with burnout (Burke, Shearer, and Deszca, 1984b; Jackson, Schwab, and Schuler, 1986; Leiter, 1988a; 1991a; Ross, Altmeier, and Russell, 1989; Schwab, Jackson, and Schuler, 1986), and some have suggested that interactions with co-workers may be the most important sources of job stress and burnout (Leiter and Maslach, 1988). Unpleasant interpersonal contact with co-workers contributed significantly to emotional exhaustion, and positive co-worker relationships were inversely related to both depersonalization and personal accomplishment. Poor co-worker relations were also related to all aspects of burnout among public service employees (Maslach and Jackson, 1984b). Leiter (1991a) has consistently found that workers who are experiencing emotional exhaustion are more likely to depersonalize perceptions of clients or diminish feelings of accomplishment if they lack supportive relationships with co-workers as well as with their immediate supervisors.

A great deal of research evidence also indicates that supervisor support is important in the experience of burnout (Constable and Russell, 1986; Jackson, Schwab, and Schuler, 1986; Jackson, Turner, and Briet, 1987; Leiter, 1988b; 1991a; Leiter and Maslach, 1988; Ross, Atlmaier, and Russel, 1989; Russell, Altmaier, and Van Velzen, 1987; Seltzer and Numerof, 1988). In all these studies, lack of supervisor support seemed to be a major determinant of burnout. Some have argued that the relationship with one's supervisor may be more strongly associated with emotional exhaustion, because supervisors are often the source of work demands (Beehr, 1985; Constable and Russell, 1986; Leiter and Maslach, 1988). On the other hand, supervisor contact may involve praise, guidance, and promotions (Leiter and Maslach, 1988), which serve to communicate to the worker that his or her efforts are appreciated. Therefore, supervisor support may be more closely associated with personal accomplishment. Several studies have found that support from one's supervisor was significantly correlated with personal accomplishment, but not with the two other aspects of burnout (Jackson, Schwab, and Schuler, 1986; Jackson, Turner, and Brief, 1987). Similar findings have also been reported by Leiter (1991a).

Social support has been postulated as a buffer against job strain and burnout (Russell, Altmaier, and Van Velzen, 1987). However, Leiter's work as well as the work of other researchers (e.g., Cummins, 1990; Etzion, 1984; Fisher, 1985; Jayaratne and Chess, 1984; Jayaratne, Himle, and Chess, 1988; Ross, Altmaier, and Russel, 1989) have shown little evidence of social support as a buffer or moderating variable between job stressors and work strain such as burnout, but have indicated direct links between social support and burnout. That is, lack of supportive relationships contributes directly to higher burnout. However, the existence of support may help the worker cope with stress and burnout better. Social support was found to have important main effects in reducing the level of unmet-expectations stress facilitating positive adjustment outcomes in newcomers to the nursing profession (Fisher, 1985).

The evidence for the role of extra work supports in developing or alleviating burnout is not clear. Several studies have indicated that lack of home and family supports is associated with increased burnout in the helping professions (Burke, Shearer, and Desca, 1984b; Jayaratne, Chess, and Kunkel, 1986; Leiter, 1990; Zedeck et al., 1988). However, other studies have found no relationships between burnout and family support or support from friends and relatives (Constable and Russell, 1986; Ross, Altmaier, and Russell, 1989; Russell, Altmaier, and Van Velzen, 1987). However, different measures were used to assess family supports and may have affected the results.

G. Reward Structure

Related to the topic of supervisor support is the issue of how feedback about performance is communicated to the worker. Reward and punishment structures may have impact on personal accomplishment and depersonalization (Schwab, Jackson, and Schuler, 1986). When employees do not get information and feedback on how well they are doing and what others think of their work, it may constitute a source of stress that contributes to burnout.

Schwab, Jackson, and Schuler (1986) studied the effects of contingent and noncontingent rewards and punishments on burnout. The only variable that had a significant relationship to burnout was punishment contingent on poor performance. In a study of public service lawyers, job conditions that imply one's efforts are ineffective and/or unappreciated (performance-reward relationship, social support from co-workers, and autonomy) did not contribute to personal accomplishment (Jackson, Turner, and Briet, 1987). Ratings of job training and evaluation of co-workers indicated that poor job preparation was correlated significantly with all three aspects of burnout (Maslach and Jackson, 1984b).

VIII. CONSEQUENCES OF BURNOUT

One of the difficulties in research on consequences of burnout is that outcome variables may be confounded with aspects of the burnout syndrome (Garden, 1991; Lazaro, Shinn, and Robinson, 1984; Shinn, 1982). For example, there is potential confounding of the relationship between reduced personal accomplishment and job performance (Garden, 1991). Another example of confounding burnout with its consequences is seen in research on the relationship of burnout to turnover (Lazaro, Shinn, and Robinson, 1984). In addition, various concepts that have been proposed as consequences of burnout may themselves be interrelated (Shinn, 1982). Shinn (1982) used example of turnover, and argued that while several studies have indicated relationships among burnout and both turnover and intentions to leave one's job, other studies have indicated that several other variables are also consistently related to turnover.

Many studies have shown that various job conditions (e.g., work pressure, participation in decision making, and feedback from clients) have differential effects on the three aspects of burnout measured by the MBI. A similar pattern of differential effects is evident with regard to behavioral reactions. Behavioral reactions—such as job withdrawal, absenteeism, and turnover—are often more strongly related to emotional exhaustion than to depersonalization or feelings of personal accomplishment (Maslach and Jackson, 1984b).

A. Attitude Changes

As individuals try to cope with the stresses of a professional career, negative attitudes may develop toward clients, work, oneself, and life in general. Cherniss (1980a) found that in the first 6 months of their careers, over 70% of new professionals in nursing, teaching, law, and social work experienced negative attitudes toward clients, the system, or themselves. The negative attitude changes outlined by Cherniss (1980a) included reduced work goals, reduced personal responsibility for outcomes, less idealism, more emotional detachment, work alienation, and greater self-interest. These six areas of attitude change are the elements included in Cherniss's (1980a, b) concept of burnout, and research has indicated that they are highly correlated with another measure of burnout (the MBI), as well as with such burnout outcomes as job satisfaction and turnover intentions and with several measures of individual well-being and health (Burke, 1987; Burke and Greenglass, 1989a; Burke, Shearer, and Deszca, 1984b).

B. Job Satisfaction

Job satisfaction has received considerable research attention, and most studies have found that burnout is clearly associated with reduced job satisfaction (e.g., Berkeley Planning Associates, 1988; Burke, 1987; Burke and Greenglass, 1989a; Burke, Shearer, and Deszca, 1984b; Duxbury et al., 1984; Golembiewski and Munzenrider, 1988; Jayaratne and Chess, 1983; Justice, Gold, and Klein, 1981; Maslach and Jackson, 1984b; Stout and Williams, 1983; Wolpin, Burke, and Greenglass, 1991; Zedeck et al., 1988). Satisfaction with the job and work in general has been studied, as has satisfaction with various aspects of the job—for example, satisfaction with co-workers and supervisors, with caseload, autonomy or control, promotion, pay, and specific work activities (Kahill, 1988). While the relationship between overall job satisfaction and burnout is well established, the evidence for an association between reduced satisfaction with particular aspects and burnout seems less clear because of a limited number of independent studies (Kahill, 1988).

The strength of the relationship between these two variables (e.g., Brookings et al., 1985; Duxbury et al., 1984; Jayaratne and Chess, 1983; Justice, Gold, and Klein, 1981; Lindquist and Whitehead, 1986; McDermott, 1984; Rimmerman, 1989), indicates that they are overlapping (Harrison, 1980; Karger, 1981; McNeely, 1983) yet not identical dimensions (Drory and Shamir, 1988; Landsbergis, 1988; Maslach and Jackson, 1981; Riggar, Godley, and Hafer, 1984). This should be expected since both are affective work responses. Despite this relatively firm association, the nature of the link between job satisfaction and psychological burnout is still unclear.

Some researchers have considered psychological burnout to be a cause of job satisfaction (e.g., Burke, Shearer, and Deszca, 1984b; Burke and Greenglass, 1988; Cunningham, 1983; Iwanicki, 1983; Jayaratne, Chess, and Kunkel, 1986), while others have considered job satisfaction to be a cause of psychological burnout (e.g. Dolan, 1987; Kilpatrick, Magnetti, and Mivis, 1991; Leiter, 1988a; Penn, Romano, and Foat, 1988; Pines, Aronson, and Kafry, 1981; Rafferty et al., 1986; Rottier, Kelly, and Tomhave, 1984; Stout and Williams, 1983). In addition, although most studies have found significant relationships between the two, some (e.g., Belcastro and Hays, 1984; Pines and Kafry, 1981; Quattrochi-Tubin, Jones, and Breedlove, 1982; Whitehead, 1986) have reported no relationship. Almost all of the studies reviewed were cross-sectional and correlational. The majority used the MBI to measure psychological burnout, but job satisfaction was measured by a wide variety of scales.

One of the few studies using a longitudinal design in studying the relationship between burnout and job satisfaction is that of Wolpin, Burke, and Greenglass (1991). Teachers and administrators responded to questionnaires given 1 year apart. Path analyses of the data from both times of measurement indicated that psychological burnout appeared to be a cause of reduced job satisfaction, and not vice versa. However, the researchers also found strong direct links between sources of work stress and job satisfaction. Other studies, using multiple regression analyses, have found that burnout, and particularly emotional exhaustion, could significantly predict job satisfaction (Greenglass and Burke, 1990; Richardsen, Burke, and Leiter, 1992), although the amounts of variance accounted for by these regression models was not large. Taken together, the results are suggestive of a causal relationship between burnout and job satisfaction.

C. Organizational Commitment

Organizational commitment is a complex construct that includes behavioral as well as attitudinal components (Mowday, Porter, and Steers, 1982). It includes the extent to which workers incorporate the values of the organization, as well as their intention to remain a part of the organization. It is often assumed that a typical newcomer to a human service profession enters with a high degree of commitment (Jackson, Turner, and Briet, 1987). Over time, if there are negative affective reactions to a job, the desire to leave may grow and eventually turnover may occur. Organizational commitment may be related to the process by which turnover intentions get translated into actually leaving. Several researchers have therefore investigated the relationship between burnout and organizational commitment, on the assumption that lowered commitment is an early indication of turnover intentions (Jackson, Turner, and Briet, 1987). Studies focusing on organizational commitment in relation to burnout have generally used the organizational commitment questionnaire (OCQ) developed by Mowday, Steers, and Porter (1979).

A series of studies by Leiter (Leiter, 1988b; 1991a; Leiter and Maslach, 1988) have provided support for a model in which burnout is a mediating variable between organizational demands and organizational commitment. The effects of organizational stressors in the form of work overload and interpersonal conflict on commitment were mediated mainly through emotional exhaustion (Leiter, 1991a). Organizational supports, such as skill utilization and supervisor support, showed direct links with organizational commitment, whereas depersonalization and personal accomplishment seem to affect commitment through shared relationships with skill utilization and coping styles.

This central role of emotional exhaustion has not been found in other studies. A study of public service lawyers also indicated lowered organizational commitment as a consequence of burnout (Jackson, Turner, and Briet, 1987). In that study, all three burnout components explained significant variance in organizational commitment, and the combined variance accounted for was 51%. These results may show the importance of the burnout components when entered separately. Two of Leiter's studies (Leiter, 1988b; Leiter and Maslach, 1988) indicated that all three components of burnout were significantly correlated with commitment, but when they were entered in regression analyses along with organizational demands and supports, the results suggested the more important role of emotional exhaustion as a mediator between organizational stress and commitment.

D. Intention to Quit

There is evidence that turnover is a special problem for human service organizations (Lazaro, Shinn, and Robinson, 1984). Professionals in social work and rehabilitation leave their jobs at about twice the rate per year of professionals in nonservice fields. Most studies have investigated turnover intentions and have found that desired or intended turnover was significantly related to burnout (e.g., Maslach and Jackson, 1984a, b; Quattorchi-Tubin, Jones, and Breedlove, 1982; Pines, Aronson, and Kafry, 1981; Taylor ct al., 1990). Actual turnover has also been linked to burnout in a few studies (e.g., Berkeley Planning Associates, 1977; Jones, 1981). Models of turnover (e.g., Mowday, Porter, and Steers, 1982) have suggested a process in which job attitudes such as dissatisfaction may influence the intent to leave, and that intent in turn is predictive of actually leaving. However, a variety of other variables may intervene at each stage in the process. In a study of public contact workers, the data clearly supported the relationship of burnout to both dissatisfaction and desires to change work or quit (Maslach and Jackson, 1984b).

The role of burnout as a mediating affective response between perceived stress and dropout intentions among sports officials was investigated by Taylor et al. (1990). A cross-sectional path analysis provided evidence that fear of failure, role-culture conflict, and interpersonal conflict had only indirect effects, through burnout, on turnover intentions. However, a longitudinal path analysis failed to support a causal relationship. The strongest predictor of turnover intention at time 2 was in fact turnover intention at time 1.

Schwab, Jackson, and Schuler, (1986) found that only emotional exhaustion predicted turnover intentions among teachers. The amount of variance explained by this factor was only 6%, however, suggesting that other variables not included in the regression may be better predictors of turnover intentions. In a longitudinal study of teachers, emotional exhaustion measured at time 1 was significantly related to subsequently considering a new teaching job; and both emotional exhaustion and depersonalization predicted having considered leaving education in the past 6 months (Jackson, Schwab, and Schuler, 1986). However, they found a low rate of actual turnover in the sample during the year of the study.

E. Absence from Work

The evidence linking burnout to absenteeism is not consistent (Kahill, 1988). Several authors have found measures of burnout to be related to tardiness, frequency of breaks, and absenteeism (Maslach and Jackson, 1981; Pines, Aronson, and Kafry, 1981; Schwab, Jackson, and Schuler, 1986). However, the relationships rarely account for large amounts of variance in turnover (Lazaro et al., 1984). For example, emotional exhaustion contributed to self-reported absence among teachers (Schwab, Jackson, and Schuler, 1986), but only 3% of the variance was accounted for. Maslach and Jackson (1981) found a moderate correlation between absenteeism rated by co-workers and depersonalization. Other studies have found no relationship between absenteeism and burnout (Lazaro, Shinn, and Robinson, 1984; Quattrochi-Tubin, Jones, and Breedlove, 1982). For example, Lazaro et al. (1984) found that absenteeism was not correlated with any burnout measure after controlling for age and sex, which they concluded was surprising in light of previous research.

F. Job Performance

While there is little empirical literature on burnout and job performance (Lazaro, Shinn, and Robinson, 1984), studies have generally found positive relationships between burnout and poor job performance (Kahill, 1988). For example, Quattorchi-Tubin, Jones, and Breedlove (1982) found that burned-out workers were more likely to neglect job duties, committed more on-the-job mistakes, and were more likely to receive discipline by supervisors. Jones (1981) reported that burned-out telephone crisis counselors received poorer evaluations from supervisors than did counselors who were not burned out. Among teachers, those experiencing high emotional exhaustion and reduced personal accomplishment exerted less effort on the job (Schwab, Jackson, and Schuler, 1986). Similar findings have been reported in commercial and industrial settings (Golembiewski and Munzenrider, 1988).

Some studies indicate that it may be useful to make a distinction between perceived and actual performance. Scores on the MBI often correlate significantly with self-ratings of performance, whereas performance ratings by the supervisor are not consistent (Lazaro, Shinn, and Robinson, 1984). Among midcareer MBA students, Garden (1991) found significant positive relationships between burnout and items that assessed perceived performance, particularly those affecting self-esteem. However, there was no significant association between burnout and actual performance. Similar results were obtained by Lazaro et al. (1982) in a study of child care workers. Results of hierarchical multiple regressions indicated that the burnout measures accounted for 48% of the variance in self-rated job performance, but only 8% of the variance in performance rated by the supervisor.

G. Quality of Personal Life

There is evidence that burnout may affect workers' home life. All three burnout components contributed significantly to lowered quality of personal life among teachers (Schwab, Jackson, and Schuler, 1986), although combined, the three aspects accounted for only 12% of the variance. Among police officers, emotional exhaustion has been linked to coming home tense, anxious, and angry; complaining about work problems; and beng more withdrawn at home (Jackson and Maslach, 1982). Studies have indicated that workers experiencing burnout are more likely to have unsatisfactory marriages (Burke and Greenglass, 1989a; Jackson and Maslach, 1982), and that they indicate a greater negative impact of the job on home and family than workers who are not burned out (Burke, 1987; Burke, Shearer, and Deszca, 1984b; Zedeck et al., 1988).

Burnout has been related to having fewer friends and preferring to avoid people (Jackson and Maslach, 1982; Maslach and Jackson, 1981); and burnout may also affect the quality of personal relationships with friends (Kahill, 1988). In addition, among mental health workers, Maslach and Jackson (1981) found that depersonalization correlated with the frequency of complaints to co-workers.

Evidence indicates that burnout is related to poor health; for example, fatigue and physical depletion or exhaustion, sleep difficulties, and specific somatic problems such as headaches, gastrointestinal disturbances, colds, and flu (Kahill, 1988). However, the relationship to major illness has not been consistently demonstrated. Burnout may also lead to health-related problems (e.g., insomnia, increased use of medications and alcohol). In a study of men and women in police work (Burke, Shearer, and Deszca, 1984b), individuals scoring higher on two burnout measures reported more psychosomatic symptoms (e.g., poor appetite, headaches, heart pains); more negative feelings (e.g., impulse to aggression, anger, depression, insomnia); and less job satisfaction. High burnout scores were also related to life-style practices associated with poorer health (e.g., consuming alcohol, smoking, little exercise), and tangible signs of poorer health (e.g., high blood pressure, absenteeism resulting from illness, and currently taking medication). Similar results were found in another study of police officers (Burke, 1987), and in a study of teachers (Burke and Greenglass, 1989a). Emotional exhaustion contributed significantly to subsequent somatization in a longitudinal study of teachers (Greenglass and Burke, 1990).

In addition, burnout has been linked to a number of emotional symptoms; for example, depression (Firth et al., 1987; Jayaratne and Chess, 1983; Jayaratne, Chess, and Kunkel, 1986), guilt (Pines, and Aronson, and Kafry, 1981; Pines and Kafry, 1981), and anxiety and tension (Fimian and Cross, 1986; Gold and Michael, 1985; Morgan and Krehbiel, 1985). In a longitudinal study of teachers, Greenglass and Burke (1990) found that burnout contributed significantly to subsequent depression for both men and women. For women, emotional exhaustion and depersonalization were significant predictors, whereas emotional exhaustion and reduced personal accomplishment predicted depression for men. Burnout did not contribute to any variation in anxiety scores.

Greenglass, Burke, and Ondrack (1990) examined the relatinship between burnout, work stress, and coping in female and male school personnel. Results indicated that men, compared to women, scored significantly higher on depersonalization. Men were experiencing significantly greater work stress than women, but were less likely than their female counterparts to employ particular coping techniques such as investing in friends and participating in cultural activities. Further results suggested that women were better able to use coping strategies to reduce burnout than men. Similar findings were obtained by Ogus, Greenglass, and Burke (1990) in a study of factors contributing to burnout in female and male teachers. Additional results in their study indicated that in men only was high depersonalization associated with lessened collegiality and unclear institutional goals. High depersonalization in men was also associated with higher absenteeism, greater medicinal use, and a lower-quality life-style (e.g., greater smoking and consumption of alcohol and caffeine). These relationships were not significant in women. The results suggest that men are more likely to experience depersonalization than women because of greater work stress and less adequate coping strategies. The data further suggest that depersonalization is more salient in men and is more debilitating in them than in their female counterparts.

IX. INTERVENTIONS TO REDUCE BURNOUT

Although little empirical evidence of the incidence of burnout exists, many researchers and workers have considered it a serious and pervasive workforce problem (Golembiewski, 1984). There is a growing awareness that stress is a costly problem, frequently associated with declining productivity and significant health consequences, yet reviews of the literature note that there are few scientific studies evaluating stress reduction and management procedures (Bruning and Frew, 1986; Farber, 1983; Matteson and Ivancevich, 1986). Farber (1983) also noted that efforts to formulate and validate treatment approaches to burnout have been hindered by such factors as the lack of clear distinctions between the concepts of stress and burnout, the lack of a commonly accepted etiological model, and the tendency to focus interventions on a limited number of variables. In addition, approaches to treating burnout often vary as a function of the training and orientation of individual burnout consultants (Farber, 1983), and consequently the field lacks an accepted framework for interventions.

Some researchers have provided evidence that burnout is particularly prevalent in human service professions. In a study comparing various occupational groups (banking, industry, postal service, health services, education, social services), employees in social services scored significantly higher on the emotional exhaustion subscale on the MBI than did postal workers, and scored significantly higher on the Matthews burnout sale for employees than did workers in banking and industry (Matthews, 1990). This finding supports research by Maslach (1982a) indicating high burnout rates among social service workers.

Golembiewski's work, and that of others (e.g., Burke and Greenglass, 1991), have provided some indications of incidence and of stability of burnout scores. If such estimates of stability and persistance are valid, alleviating burnout through interventions may be a considerable but necessary challenge. If nothing is done, levels of experienced psychological burnout remain unchanged.

Cherniss (1992) explored the long-term consequences of burnout in terms of the relationship between the degree of burnout experienced during the first year of the career and career adaptation during the next decade. His respondents were 25 human service professionals originally working in the fields of public service law, public health nursing, high school teaching, and mental health. They were studied during the first year of their careers and again 12 years later. Early career burnout was assessed via ratings of interviews that were highly correlated with the MBI. Career adaptation variables included career stability, work satisfaction, attitudes toward recipients, and flexibility as measured at the time of follow-up. Each of these variables was measured via interview ratings, a questionnaire, and ratings made by confidants of the subjects. Results showed that respondents who were more burned out early in their careers were less likely to change careers and more flexible in their approach to work as rated by confidants at the time of follow-up. The results suggest that early career burnout does not seem to lead to any significant long-term negative consequences. However, burnout occurring later in the career might have more serious long-term effects.

One important implication of this study was that human service professionals *can* recover from early career burnout. Interestingly, some of the conditions that helped these professionals recover from burnout were the same ones that helped to prevent burnout. These were: new work situations that provided more autonomy, organizational support, and interesting work. In most cases these changes came about through turnover or promotion.

It may be possible to reduce the prevalence of burnout after we develop a more complete understanding of the problem and evaluate the effectiveness of various interventions in the workplace.

Over the years writers have suggested a number of interventions that can be used to reduce burnout in the workplace. Most of these interventions were aimed at reducing burnout at the source; that is, changing the work environment in order to reduce the potential for burnout among workers. Specific examples include staff development and counseling (Cherniss, 1980b); increasing worker involvement and participation in decision making (Schwab, Jackson, and Schuler, 1986); improving supervision through clarification of work goals (Maslach and Jackson, 1984b; Schwab, Jackson, and Schuler, 1986); and facilitating the development of social support (Schwab, Jackson, and Schuler, 1986); among others.

Although most of these suggestions were based primarily on correlational evidence of associations between such work variables and burnout, and few of the interventions were tested empirically, the notion of organizational-level interventions aimed at environmental sources of stress has received attention in the intervention literature (Kilpatrick, 1986). In the past decade a number of well-designed studies of organizational-level interventions have appeared (e.g., Golembiewski, Hilles, and Daly, 1986; 1987). An intervention program that incorporated many of Cherniss's (1980b) ideas for reducing burnout was also carried out (Falconer and Hornick, 1983).

A.   Reducing Psychological Burnout Through Worksite Changes

Golembiewski, Hilles, and Daly (1987) reported on an organization development (OD) effort using theory-driven interventions with a 31-member human resources staff of a single organization. They used the phase model to assess levels of psychological burnout as well as measuring various proportions of the work environment. The researchers gathered data over a 2-year period, administering the survey five times. The group scored high on burnout, work pressures, and turnover. A traditional OD intervention involving data collection, feedback, and action planning was used. The level of burnout, initially high among the human resources staff, fell and remained lower for at least 4 months after the last planned intervention. This improvement diminished somewhat after 9 more months, despite a major reorganization. Improvements in group cohesiveness and in the rate of turnover persisted and even improved over this time.

B. Reducing Psychological Burnout by Changing Orientation

The Children's Aid Society (CAS) of metropolitan Toronto developed an interesting intervention to reduce burnout among entering frontline social workers in child welfare (Falconer and Hornick, 1983). This program was radically different in many ways from their traditional orientation practices, and involved: (1) hiring frontline workers in batches; (2) keeping these newly hired workers in small groups of five or six individuals for their first 6 months of employment; (3) gradually increasing their caseload so that it eventually reached 60% of the normal caseload by the 6-month point; (4) enhancing the supervisor's role by emphasizing education (accompanied by a reduction of other supervisory duties); (5) improving the training program (1 to 2 days of training every 2 weeks); (6) increasing social support for the groups; and (7) attempting to deal with stressors found to be associated with burnout in previous research (e.g., promoting clear, consistent, and specific feedback; clarifying rules, policies, and roles; allowing for autonomy and innovation).

The research employed a pretest extended posttest design with a nonequivalent comparison group. The project, designed to run for 2 1/2 years, was cut short because of budget cutbacks resulting from the general economic recession. The resulting samples sizes rendered the quantitative data of little use. Qualitative data indicated general satisfaction with the program and beliefs that the goals of the program were realized. Supervisors felt that frontline workers in the program achieved a level of skill during the 6 months comparable to that achieved in 1 year under the traditional orientation program.

C. Organizational- Versus Individual-Level Interventions

Several studies have indicated the effectiveness of individual-level interventions in reducing stress and burnout. Bruning and Frew (1986) evaluated three intervention strategies in a longitudinal study of supervisors, managers, engineers, and support personnel in a manufacturing facility. The three intervention strategies were cognitive skills training, relaxation/meditation training, and exercise training. Participants were randomly assigned to one of three experimental groups and a control group. Attitudinal measure were manifest anxiety, job satisfaction (with work, supervisor, co-workers, pay, and promotion), and self-esteem, measured before the experiment and again after 13 weeks. The original treatment groups were then split and assigned a second treatment, and the control group received all three types of training. Ten weeks later the attitudinal measures were given again. Analysis of covariance using time I scores as covariates, indicated that four of the seven attitudinal measures showed significant change due to treatments: these were self-esteem and satisfaction with supervisor, co-worker, and promotion. Analysis of covariance using time II scores as covariates indicated that the combination strategies did not lead to any further change in the attitudinal measures. Tests to determine if any treatment or treatments were superior in improving attitudes showed that improvements in self-esteem were apparent for all the treatment groups, and that the meditation/relaxation group showed the greatest improvements in the satisfaction measures. The results suggest that improvements in attitudes were directly related to broad-based stress-intervention strategies in a longitudinal field setting. In addition, improvements on two physiological measures were observed 13 weeks after training. These were reductions in pulse rate and systolic blood pressure. The authors concluded that there may be support for broad-based stress-intervention strategies.

Golembiewski and Rountree (1991) studied the effects of quality of work life interventions on burnout and attitude measures among nursing directors and their CEOs. The intervention was derived from OD theory and consisted of an off-site training session combining group work and collaborating in pairs on how to build an ideal team. Dependent measures were burnout, reactions to supervision, and a work-related sense of community. Results indicated a sharp shift in the burnout phase distribution of the participants. Reaction to supervision scores were significantly different between treatment and control groups after the intervention, but not prior to it. Sense of community also increased for nursing directors who were in the treatment group. The authors concluded that the success rate of interaction-centered interventions was quite impressive, and suggested further use of regenerative interaction designs in ameliorating burnout.

Higgins (1986) evaluated the effectiveness of two stress-reduction programs among working women. One program consisted of progressive relaxation and systematic desensitization; and the other involved instruction in time management, rational-emotive therapy, and assertiveness training. Dependent measures were emotional exhaustion, personal strain, and absenteeism. Each stress-reduction program consisted of seven sessions. Analysis of covariance indicated no significant differences between the two treatment groups, and both treatment groups were significantly different from the control group. Emotional exhaustion and personal strain scores decreased significantly from pretest to posttest in both treatment groups, but both scores increased in the control group. There were no differences in absenteeism among the three groups. The author concluded that both programs were effective. At the conclusion of the study, the participants of both programs reported less stress than nonparticipants. Contrary to claims made by other researchers that long-term interventions are necessary for change of any significant magnitude to occur, the results from this study suggested that relatively brief programs can produce significant reductions in self-reported stress.

Coping may be defined as efforts to reduce stress and strain such as burnout (Shinn et al., 1984). Many authors have pointed out the limitations of individual coping (e.g., Pines and Aronson, 1981). Most individual coping strategies used by human service professionals had either no association or positive associations with burnout. However, in a study of mental health workers that distinguished between escape coping (avoiding or ignoring difficult situations) and control coping (utilizing strategies to confront or address difficulties), Leiter (1991a) found that both coping styles were significantly related to emotional exhaustion, and control coping was also associated with personal accomplishment. Mental health workers who used cognitive and action control strategies to address difficulties at work were less likely to experience exhaustion and had more positive assessment of their personal accomplishment. Those who used escapist cognitive and action control strategies tended to experience greater levels of emotional exhaustion. A longitudinal study by Leiter (1990) also found that control coping was positively related to subsequent personal accomplishment.

The importance of organizational-level interventions aimed at environmental sources of professional and managerial stress, rather than individual-level interventions, emerges from a field experiment conducted by Ganster et al. (1982). They evaluated a stress management training program in a field experiment with 99 public agency employees randomly assigned to treatment ($N = 60$) and control ($N = 39$) groups. The training program consisted of 16 hours of training spread over 8 weeks. Participants were taught progressive relaxation and cognitive restructuring techniques. Dependent variables were epinephrine and norepinephrine excretion at work, anxiety, depression, irritation, and somatic complaints, all measured at three times (pretest, posttest, and 4 months after treatment). Treatment participants exhibited significantly lower epinephrine and depression levels than did controls at the posttest, and 4-month follow-up levels did not regress to initial pretest levels. However, the treatment effects were not found in a subsequent intervention on the original control group.

Research conducted by Shinn et al (1984) leads to similar conclusions. They collected data from 141 human service workers using questionnaires assessing job stressors, coping strategies, and various aspects of strain (alienation, satisfaction, symptomatology). Coping efforts to reduce stressors and strain were assessed at three levels: by individual workers, by groups of workers to help one another (social support), and by their employing human service agencies. Although many more individual coping responses were mentioned than group- or agency-initiated responses, only the group responses were associated with low levels of strain. Unfortunately, there were not enough agency-initiated responses identified to undertake a meaningful analysis. Thus it appears that in the work setting individual coping responses may be less useful than higher-level strategies involving groups of workers or entire units or organizations. Other researchers (Leiter, 1991b; Pearlin and Schooler, 1978) also conclude that chronic, organizationally generated stressors may be resistant to reduction through individual coping efforts.

Ivancevich and Matteson (1987) made the point that organization-based stress management intervention programs incorporating well-designed evaluations have rarely been undertaken. They (along with Murphy, 1987) offer suggestions for increasing researcher interest in scientifically designing, implementing, and evaluating organizational-level stress management intervention programs. Murphy (1988) found few well-designed evaluations of interventions aimed at reducing work stressors. Of those he identified, all were found to consistently show benefits. Yet stressor reduction represents the most direct way to reduce stress since it deals with the source (Golembiewski, Hilles, and Daly, 1987). This has been termed "primary prevention" in the stress management literature.

X. CONCLUSIONS

The quantity of psychological burnout research has grown markedly in recent years, as has general interest in the subject. Yet in spite of this larger volume, our understanding of the burnout phenomenon remains limited. This results from the complexity of the burnout process itself as well as a variety of dilemmas and ambiguities facing burnout researchers. The latter involve issues of definition, measurement, references from data collected at one time, small and often unrepresentative samples, the absence of integrated models, and overly simplistic research design and data analysis approaches.

A continuing commitment to psychological burnout research will almost certainly be the case over the next decade. Burnout is now beginning to be examined in cross-cultural settings with findings consistent with those found previously in North America (Golembiewski et al., in press; Shirom, 1989; Richardsen, Burke, and Leiter, 1992). The magnitude and complexity of the problem warrants this attention and investment. The number of researchers now interested in psychological burnout has grown. Some advances in conceptualization have already taken place (Cherniss, 1980a; Leiter 1991b; Golembiewski and Munzenrider, 1988), but much more systematic research is needed to elucidate the factors involved in the experience and manifestations of psychological burnout. It appears that an increase in our understanding of psychological burnout will only come slowly.

A. Research and Practice: Two Cultures?

There is a large gap between psychological burnout researchers and practitioners—between the producers and consumers of burnout research findings. The most obvious illustrations of this gap can be seen in the following: little awareness of research findings by practitioners (managers, consultants, as well as clinicians), little intervention being undertaken at the organizational level, little research being undertaken to determine the effectiveness of individual-level interventions, and only modest use of burnout research findings for intervention and policy development. Bridging this gap would appear to be particularly important for readers of this handbook. The results would be better-informed research *and* practice.

This gap is not unique to the area of psychological burnout, however (Kilman, 1983). The field of organizational behavior is currently examining research methods that are useful for both theory and practice (Beyer, 1982; 1983; Lawler et al., 1985). Both researchers and consumers of research findings would benefit from an examination of this literature. It is possible to combine research and intervention in the area of psychological burnout (Gardell, 1982) to produce findings of value for policy formation and improving the quality of work life (Kahn, 1987). The following strategic targets for research and application should be given high priority: more comprehensive research projects, greater use of longitudinal research design, and attempts to build intervention efforts using action research approaches.

ACKNOWLEDGMENTS

Preparation of this manuscript was supported in part by the Faculty of Administrative Studies, York University. We would like to thank Doug Turner and Bruna Gaspini for assistance in preparing the manuscript, and Bob Golembiewski for helpful comments.

REFERENCES

Beehr, T. A. (1985). The role of social support in coping with organizational stress. In *Human Stress and Cognition in Organizations* (T. A. Beehr and R. S. Bhagat, eds.), Wiley, New York.

Belcastro, P. A., and Hays, L. C. (1984). Ergophilia . . . ergophobia . . . ergo . . . burnout? *Professional Psychology: Research and Practice, 15*: 260–270.

Berkeley Planning Associates (1977). Project management and worker burnout. In *Evaluation of Child Abuse and Neglect Demonstration Projects, 1974–1977*, Vol. 9. National Technical Incorporation Service, Springfield, Va.

Beyer, J., ed. (1982). The utilization of organizational research (special issue, part I). *Administrative Science Quarterly, 27*: 588–685.

Beyer, J., ed. (1983). The utilization of organizational research (sepcial issue, part II). *Administrative Science Quarterly, 28*: 63–144.

Brookings, J., Bolton, B., Brown, C., and McEvoy, A. (1985). Self-reported job burnout among female human service professionals. *J. of Occupational Behavior, 6*: 143–150.

Bruning, N. S., and Frew, D. R. (1986). Can stress intervention strategies improve self-esteem, manifest anxiety, and job satisfaction? A longitudinal field experiment. *J. of Health and Human Resources Administration, 9*: 110–124.

Burke, R. J. (1987). Burnout in police work: An examination of the Cherniss model. *Group and Organization Studies, 12*: 174–188.

Burke, R. J., and Deszca, E. (1986). Correlates of psychological burnout phases among police officers. *Human Relations, 39*: 487–502.

Burke, R. J., and Deszca, E. (1987). Changes in career orientations in police officers: An exploratory study. *Psychological Reports, 61*: 515–526.

Burke, R. J., and Deszca, G. (1988). Career orientations, satisfaction and health among police officers: Some consequences of person-job misfit. *Psychological Reports, 62*: 639–649.

Burke, R. J., Deszca, G., and Shearer, J. (1986). Career orientations and burnout in police officers. *Canadian Journal of Administrative Science, 1*: 179–194.

Burke, R. J., and Greenglass, E. R. (1988). Career orientations and psychological burnout in teachers. *Psychological Reports, 63*: 107–116.

Burke, R. J., and Greenglass, E. R. (1989a). Psychological burnout among men and women in teaching: An examination of the Cherniss model. *Human Relations, 42*: 261–273.

Burke, R. J., and Greenglass, E. R. (1989b). Teachers: Orientations, satisfaction and health: Some consequences of person-job misfit. *International Journal of Career Management, 1*: 4–10.

Burke, R. J., and Greenglass, E. R. (1989c). Correlates of psychological burnout phases among teachers. *J. of Health and Human Resource Administration, 12*: 46–62.

Burke, R. J., and Greenglass, E. R. (1989d). It may be lonely at the top but it's less stressful: Psychological burnout in public schools. *Psychological Reports, 64*: 615–623.

Burke, R. J., and Greenglass, E. R. (1989e). The clients' role in psychological burnout in teachers and administrators. *Psychological Reports, 64*: 1299–1306.

Burke, R. J., and Greenglass, E. R. (1989f). Sex differences in psychological burnout in teachers. *Psychological Reports, 65*: 55–63.

Burke, R. J., and Greenglass, E. R. (1990). Career orientations, satisfaction and health: A longitudinal study. *Canadian Journal of Administrative Sciences, 7*: 19–25.

Burke, R. J., and Greenglass, E. R. (1991). A longitudinal study of progressive phases of psychological burnout. *J. of Health and Human Resources Administration, 13*: 390–408.

Burke, R. J., Shearer, J., and Deszca, G. (1984a). Correlates of burnout phases among police officers. *Group and Organization Studies, 9*: 451–466.

Burke, R. J., Shearer, J., and Deszca, G. (1984b). Burnout among men and women in police work: An examination of the Cherniss model. *J. of Health and Human Resources Administration, 7*: 162–188.

Cahoon, A. R., and Rowney, J. I. A. (1984). Managerial burnout: A comparison by sex and level of responsibility. *J. of Health and Human Resources Administration, 7*: 249–263.

Cherniss, C. (1980a). *Professinal Burnout in Human Service Organizations*. Praeger, New York.

Cherniss, C. (1980b). *Staff Burnout: Job Stress in the Human Services*. Sage, Beverly Hills, Calif.

Cherniss, C. (1989). Burnout in new professionals: A long-term follow-up study. *J. of Health and Human Resources Administration, 12*: 11–24.

Cherniss, C. (1990). Natural recovery from burnout: Results of a 10-year follow-up study. *J. of Health and Human Resources Administration, 13*: 132–154.

Cherniss, C. (1992). Long-term consequences of burnout: An exploratory study. *J. of Organizational Behavior, 13*: 1–11.

Constable, J. F., and Russell, D. W. (1986). The effects of social support and the work environment upon burnout among nurses. *J. of Human Stress, 12*: 20–26.

Corcoran, K. J. (1985). Measuring burnout: A reliability and convergent validity study. *J. of Social Behavior and Personality, 1*: 107–112.

Cummins, R. C. (1990). Job stress and the buffering effect of supervisory support. *Group & Organization Studies, 15*: 92–104.

Cunningham, W. G. (1983). Teacher burnout-solutions for the 1980's: A review of the literature. *Urban Review, 15*(1): 37–51.

Deckard, G. J., Rountree, B. H., and Golembiewski, R. T. (1986). Worksite features and progressive burnout phases: Another replication cum extension. *J. of Health and Human Resources Administration, 9*: 38–55.

Dolan, N. (1987). The relationship between burnout and job satisfaction in nurses. *J. of Advanced Nursing, 12*: 3–12.

Drory, A., and Shamir, B. (1988). Effects of organizational and life variables on job satisfaction and burnout. *Group and Organizational Studies, 13*: 441–455.

Duxbury, M. L., Armstrong, G. D., Drew, D. J., and Henly, S. J. (1984). Head nurse leadership styles with staff nurse burnout and job satisfaction in neonatal intensive care units. *Nursing Research, 33*(2): 97–101.

Etzion, D. (1984). Moderating effect of social support on the stress-burnout relationship. *J. of Applied Psychology, 69*: 615–622.

Etzion, D. (1988). The experience of burnout and work/non-work success in male and female engineers: A matched pairs comparison. *Human Resources Management, 27*: 117–133.

Etzion, D., and Pines, A. (1986). Sex and culture in burnout and coping among human service professionals. *J. of Cross Cultural Psychology, 17*: 191–209.

Falconer, N. E., and Hornick, J. P. (1983). *Attack on burnout: The Importance of Early Training*. Children's Aid Society of Metropolitan Toronto, Toronto.

Farber, B. A. (1983). Introduction: A critical perspective on burnout. In *Stress and Burnout in the Human Service Professionals* (B. A. Farber, ed.), Pergamon, New York, pp. 1–22.

Fimian, M. J., and Cross, A. H. (1986). Stress and burnout among preadolescent and early adolescent gifted students: A preliminary investigation. *J. of Early Adolescence, 6*: 247–267.

Firth, H., McKeown, P., McIntee, J., and Britton, P. (1987). Professional depression, "burnout" and personality in longstay nursing. *International Journal of Nursing Studies, 24*: 227–237.

Fisher, C. D. (1985). Social support and adjustment to work: A longitudinal study. *J. of Management, 11*: 39–53.

Freudenberger, H. J. (1974). Staff burnout. *J. of Social Issues, 30*: 159–164.

Freudenberger, H. J. (1983). Burnout: Contemporary issues, trends, and concerns. In *Stress and Burnout* (B. A. Farber, ed.), Pergamon, New York, pp. 23–28.

Freudenberger, H. J., and Richelson, G. (1980). *Burn-out: The High Cost of High Achievement*. Anchor Press, New York.

Friesen, D., and Sarros, J. (1986). Sources of burnout among educators. *J. of Organizational Behavior, 10*: 179–188.

Ganster, D. C., Mayes, B. T., Sime, W. E., and Tharp, G. D. (1982). Managing occupational stress: A field experiment. *J. of Applied Psychology, 67*: 533–542.

Gardell, B. (1982). Scandanavian research on stress in working life. *International Journal of Health Services, 19*: 31–40.

Garden, A. M. (1991). Relationship between burnout and performance. *J. of Applied Psychology, 69*: 615–622.

Gold, Y. (1984). The factorial validity of the Maslach Burnout Inventory in a sample of California elementary and junior high school classroom teachers. *Educational and Psychological Measurement, 44*: 1009–1016.

Gold, Y., and Michael, W. B. (1985). Academic self-concept correlates of potential burnout in a sample of first-semester elementary-school practice teachers: A concurrent validity study. *Educational and Psychological Measurement, 45*: 909–914.

Golembiewski, R. T. (1982). Organization development interventions. In *Job Stress and Burnout* (W. S. Paine, ed.), Sage, Beverly Hills, Calif., pp. 229–253.

Golembiewski, R. T. (1984). An orientation to psychological burnout: Probably something old, definitely something new. *J. of Health and Human Resources Administration, 7*: 153–161.

Golembiewski, R. T. (1986). The epidemiology of progressive burnout: A primer. *J. of Health and Human Resources Administration, 9*: 16–37.

Golembiewski, R. T. (1989). A note on Leiter's study: Highlighting two models of burnout. *Group and Organization Studies, 14*: 5–13.

Golembiewski, R. T., and Boss, R. W. (1991). Shelving levels of burnout for individuals in organizations: A note on the stability of phases. *J. of Health and Human Resources Administration, 13*: 409–420.

Golembiewski, R. T., Deckard, G. J., and Rountree, B. H. (1989). The stability of burnout assignments: Measurement properties of the phase model. *J. of Health and Human Resources Administration, 12*: 63–78.

Golembiewski, R. T., Hilles, R., and Daly, R. (1986). Ameliorating advanced burnout: A design for the easier of two modes and some consequences. *J. of Health and Human Resources Administration, 9*: 125–147.

Golembiewski, R. T., Hilles, R., and Daly, R. (1987). Some effects of multiple OD interventions on burnout and work site features. *J. of Applied Behavioral Science, 23*: 295–313.

Golembiewski, R. T., and Munzenrider, R. (1984). Active and passive reactions to psychological burnout: Toward greater specificity in a phase model. *J. of Health and Human Resources Administration, 7*: 264–268.

Golembiewski, R. T., and Munzenrider, R. F. (1988). *Phases of Burnout: Developments in Concepts and Applications*. Praeger, New York.

Golembiewski, R. T., Munzenrider, R., and Carter, D. (1983). Phases of progressive burnout and their work-site covariants. *J. of Applied Behavioral Science, 13*: 461–482.

Golembiewski, R. T., Munzenrider, R., and Stevenson, J. (1985). *Stress in Organizations*. Praeger, New York.

Golembiewski, R. T., and Rountree, B. (1991). Releasing human potential for collaboration: A social intervention targeting supervisory relationships and stress. *Public Administration Quarterly, 15*: 32–45.

Golembiewski, R. T., Scherb, K. and Boudreau, R. (in press). Burnout in cross-sectional settings. In W. B. Schaubeli, T. Marek and C. Maslach (Eds.) *Professional Burnout*. Hemisphere Publishing, New York.

Green, D. E., Walkey, Fott, S., and Taylor, A. J. W. (1991). The three-factor structure of the Maslach burnout inventory: A multicultural, multinational confirmatory study. *J. of Social Behavior and Personality, 6*: 453–472.

Greenglass, E. R. (1985). Psychological implications of sex bias in the work place. *Academic Psychology Bulletin, 7*: 227–240.

Greenglass, E. R. (1991). Burnout and gender: Theoretical and organizational implications. *Canadian Psychology, 32*: 562–572.

Greenglass, E. R., and Burke, R. J. (1988). Work and family precursors of burnout in teachers: Sex differences. *Sex Roles, 18*: 215–229.

Greenglass, E. R., and Burke, R. J. (1990). Burnout over time. *J. of Health and Human Resources Administration, 13*: 192–204.

Greenglass, E. R., Burke, R. J., and Ondrack, M. (1990). A gender-role perspective of coping and burnout. *Applied Psychology: An International Review, 39*: 5–27.

Hackman, J. R., and Oldham, G. R. (1980). *Work Redesign*. Addison-Wesley, Reading, Mass.

Harrison, W. D. (1980). Role strain and burnout in child-protective service workers. *Social Service Review, 54*(1): 31–44.

Higgins, N. C. (1986). Occupational stress and working women: The effectiveness of two stress reduction programs. *J. of Vocational Behavior, 29*: 66–78.

Ivancevich, J. M., and Matteson, M. T. (1987). Organizational level stress management interventions: A review and recommendations. In *Job Stress: From Theory to Suggestion* (J. M. Ivancevich and D. C. Ganster, eds.), Howarth Press, New York, pp. 229–248.

Iwanicki, E. F. (1983). Toward understanding and alleviating teacher burnout. *Theory into Practice, 22*(1): 27–32.

Iwanicki, E. F., and Schwab, R. L. (1981). A cross validation study of the Maslach burnout inventory. *Educational and Psychological Measurement, 41*: 1167–1174.

Izraeli, D. N. (1988). Burning out in medicine: A comparison of husbands and wives in dual-career couples. Special issue: Work and family: Theory, research, and applications. *J. of Social Behavior and Personality, 3*: 329–346.

Jackson, S. E. (1983). Participation in decision making as a strategy for reducing job-related strain. *J. of Applied Psychology, 68*: 3–19.

Jackson, S. E., and Maslach, C. (1982). After-effects of job related stress: Families as victims. *J. of Occupational Behavior, 3*: 63–77.

Jackson, S. E., Schwab, R. L., and Schuler, R. S. (1986). Toward an understanding of the burnout phenomenon. *J. of Applied Psychology, 71*: 630–640.

Jackson, S. E., Turner, J. A., and Brief, A. P. (1987). Correlates of burnout among public service lawyers. *J. of Occupational Behavior, 8*: 339–349.

Janz, T., Dugan, S., and Ross, M. S. (1986). Organization culture and burnout: Empirical findings at the individual and department levels. *J. of Health and Human Resources Administration, 9*: 78–92.

Jayaratne, S., and Chess, W. A. (1983). Job satisfaction and burnout in social work. In *Stress and Burnout in the Human Servce Professions* (B. A. Farber, ed.) Pergamon Press, Elmsford, N.Y. pp. 129–141.

Jayaratne, S., and Chess, W. A. (1984). The effects of emotional support on perceived job stress and strain. *J. of Applied Behavoral Science, 20*: 141–153.

Jayaratne, S., Chess, W. A., and Kunkel, D. A. (1986). Burnout: Its impact on child welfare workers and their spouses. *Social Work, 31*: 53–59.

Jayaratne, S., Himle, D., and Chess, W. A. (1988). Dealing with work stress and strain: Is the perception of support more important than its use? *J. of Applied Behavioral Science, 24*: 191–202.

Jones, J. W. (1980). *The Staff Burnout Scale for Health Professionals (SBS-HP)*. London House Press, Park Ridge, Ill.

Jones, J. W., ed. (1981). *The Burnout Syndrome: Current Research, Theory, Interventions*. London House Management Press, Park Ridge, Ill.

Justice, B., Gold, R. S., and Kelin, J. P. (1981). Life events and burnout. *J. of Psychology, 108*: 219–226.

Kahill, S. (1988). Symptoms of professional burnout: A review of the empirical evidence. *Canadian Psychology, 29*: 284–297.

Kahn, R. L. (1987). Work stress in the 1980's: Research and practice. In *Work Stress: Health Care Systems in the Workplace* (J. C. Quick, R. S. Bhagat, J. E. Dalton, and J. D. Quick, eds.) Praeger, New York, pp. 311–320.

Karger, H. J. (1981). Burnout as alienation. *Social Service Review, 55*: 270–283.

Kilman, R. H. (1983). *Producing Useful Knowledge for Organizations*. Praeger, New York.

Kilpatrick, A. O. (1986). Burnout: An empirical assessment, Ph.D. dissertation, University of Georgia, Athens.

Kilpatrick, A. O. (1989). Burnout correlates and validity of research designs in a large panel of studies. *J. of Health and Human Resources Administration, 12*: 25–45.

Kilpatrick, A. O., Magnetti, S. M., and Mirvis, D. P. (1991). Burnout and job satisfaction among public hospital administrators: Preliminary findings. *J. of Health and Human Resources Administration, 13*: 470–482.

Koeske, G. F., and Koeske, R. D. (1989). Construct validity of the Maslach burnout inventory: A critical review and reconceptualization. *J. of Applied Behavioral Science, 25*: 131–144.

Landsbergis, P. (1988). Occupational stress among health care workers: A test of the job demands control model. *J. of Applied Behavioral Science, 25*: 131–144.

Lawler, E. E., Mohrman, A. M., Mohrman, S. A., Ledford, G. E., and Cummings, T. G. (1985). *Doing Research That is Useful for Theory and Practice*. Jossey-Bass, San Francisco.

Lazaro, L., Shinn, M., and Robinson, P. E. (1984). Burnout, performance, and job withdrawal behavior. *J. of Health and Human Resources Administration, 7*: 213–234.

Lee, R. T., and Ashforth, B. E. (in press). A longitudinal study of burnout among supervisors and managers: Comparisons between the Leiter and Maslach (1988) and Golembiewski et al. (1986) models. In *Organizational Behavior and Human Decision Processes*.

Leiter, M. P. (1988a). Burnout as a function of communication patterns. A study of multidiscipinary mental health team. *Group & Organization Studies, 13*: 111–128.

Leiter, M. P. (1988b). Commitment as a function of stress reactions among nurses: A model of psychological evaluations of work settings. *Canadian Journal of Community Mental Health, 7*: 115–132.

Leiter, M. P. (1989). Conceptual implications of two models of burnout: A response to Golembiewski. *Group & Organization Studies, 14*: 15–22.

Leiter, M. P. (1990). The impact of family resources, control coping, and skill utilization on the development of burnout: A longitudinal study. *Human Relations, 43*: 1067–1083.

Leiter, M. P. (1991a). Coping patterns as predictors of burnout: The function of control and escapist coping. *J. of Occupational Behavior, 12*: 123–144.

Leiter, M. P. (1991b). The dream denied: Professional burnout and the constraints of human service organizations. *Canadian Psychology, 32*: 547–555.

Leiter, M. P., and Maslach, C. (1988). The impact of interpersonal environment on burnout and organizational commitment. *J. of Occupational Behavior, 8*: 297–308.

Maslach, C. (1978). The client role in staff burnout. *J. of Social Issues, 34*: 111–124.

Maslach, C. (1982a). *Burnout: The Cost of Caring*. Prentice Hall, Englewood Cliffs, N.J.

Maslach C. (1982b). Understanding burnout: Definitional issues in analyzing a complex phenomenon. In *Job Stress and Burnout: Research, Theory and Intervention Perspectives* (W. S. Paine, ed.), Sage, Beverly Hills, Calif., pp. 29–40.

Maslach, C., and Jackson, S. (1981). The measurement of experienced burnout. *J. of Occupational Behavior, 2*: 99–115.

Maslach, C., and Jackson, S. E. (1984a). Burnout in organizational settings. In *Applied Social Psychology Annual*, vol. 5 (S. Oskamp, ed.), Sage, Beverly Hills, Calif., pp. 133–153.

Maslach, C., and Jackson, S. E. (1984b). Patterns of burnout among a national sample of public contact workers. *J. of Health and Human Resource Administration, 7*: 189–212.

Maslach, C., and Jackson, S. E. (1985). The role of sex and family variables in burnout. *Sex. Roles, 12*: 837–851,

Maslach, C., and Jackson, S. E. (1986). *Maslach Burnout Inventory Manual*, 2nd Ed. Consulting Psychologists Press, Inc., Palo Alto, Calif.

Matteson, M. T., and Ivancevich, J. M. (1986). An exploratory investigation of CES as an employee stress management procedure. *J. of Health and Human Resource Administration, 9*: 93–109.

Matthews, D. B. (1990). A comparison of burnout in selected occupational fields. *Career Development Quarterly, 14*: 30–36.

McCranie, E. W., and Brandsma, J. M. (1988). Personality antecedents of burnout among middle-aged physicians. *Behavioral Medicine, 36*: 889–910.

McNeely, R. L. (1983). Organizational patterns and work satisfaction in comprehensive human service agency: An empirical test. *Human Relations, 36*(10): 957–972.

Meier, S. T. (1983). Toward a theory of burnout. *Human Relations, 36*: 899–910.

Meier, S. T. (1984). The construct validity of burnout. *J. of Occupational Psychology, 57*: 211–219.

Morgan, S. R., and Krehbiel, R. (1985). The psychological condition of burned-out teachers with a nonhumanistic orientation. *J. of Humanistic Education and Development, 24*: 59–67.

Mowday, R. T., Porter, L. W., and Steers, R. M. (1982). *Employee-Organization Linkages: The Psychology of Commitment, Absenteeism, and Turnover*. Academic Press, New York.

Mowday, R. T., Steers, R. M., and Porter, L. W. (1979). The measurement of organizational commitment. *J. of Vocational Behavior, 14*: 224–247.

Murphy, L. R. (1987). A review of organizational stress management research: Methodological considerations. In *Job Stress: From Theory to Suggestion* (J. M. Ivancevich and D. C. Ganster, eds.), Howarth Press, New York, pp. 215–227.

Murphy, L. R. (1988). Workplace interventions for stress reduction and prevention. In *Causes, Coping and Consequences of Stress at Work* (C. L. Cooper and R. Payne, eds.), John Wiley, New York, pp. 301–339.

Ogus, E. D., Greenglass, E. R., and Burke, R. J. (1990). Gender-role differences, work stress and depersonalization. *J. of Social Behavior and Personality, 5*: 387–398.

Paine, W. S. (1982). Overview: Burnout stress syndromes and the 1980s. In *Job Stress and Burnout: Research, Theory and Intervention Perspectives* (W. S. Paine, ed.), Sage, Beverly Hills, Calif., pp. 11–29.

Pearlin L., and Schooler, C. (1978). The structure of coping. *Journal of Health and Social Behavior, 19*: 2–21.

Penn, M., Romano, J. L., and Foat, D. (1988). The relationship between job satisfaction and burnout: A study of human service professionals. *Administration in Mental Health, 15*: 157–165.

Pines, A. (1987). Marriage burnout: a new conceptual framework for working with couples. *Psychotherapy in Private Practice, 5*: 31–43.

Pines, A. (1988). *Keeping the Spark Alive: Preventing Burnout in Love and Marriage.* St. Martin's Press, New York.

Pines, A, and Aronson, E. (1981). *Burnout: From Tedium to Personal Growth.* The Free Press, New York.

Pines, A., and Aronson, E. (1988). *Career Burnout: Causes and Cures,* 2nd ed. the Free Press, New York.

Pines, A., Aronson, E., and Kafry, D. (1981). *Burnout: From Tedium to Personal Growth.* the Free Press, New York.

Pines, A., and Kafry, D. (1981). Tedium in the life and work of professional women as compared with men. *Sex Roles, 7*: 117–134.

Powers, S., and Gose, K. F. (1986). Reliability and construct validity of the Maslach burnout inventory in a sample of university students. *Educational and Psychological Measurement, 46*: 251–255.

Quattrochi-Tubin, S., Jones, J. W., and Breedlove, V. (1982). The burnout syndrome in geriatric counselors and service workers. *Activities, Adaptation and Aging, 3*: 65–76.

Rafferty, J. P., Lemkau, J. P., Purdy, R. R., and Rudisill, J. R., (1986). Validity of the Maslach burnout inventory for family practice physicians. *J. of Clinical Psychology, 42*: 488–492.

Richardsen, A. M., Burke, R. J., and Leiter, M. P. (1992). Occupational demands, psychological burnout and anxiety among hospital personnel in Norway. *Anxiety Research, 5*: 55–68.

Rimmerman, A. (1989). Burnout among beginning rehabilitation workers in Israel and its relationship to social support, supervision, and job satisfaction. *Rehabilitation Counselling Bulletin, 32*(3): 243–247.

Rizzo, J. R., and House, R. J., and Lirtzman, S. I. (1970). Role conflict and ambiguity in complex organizations. *Administrative Science Quarterly, 15*: 150–163.

Ross, R. R., Altmaier, E. M., and Russell, D. W. (1989). Job stress, social support, and burnout among counseling center staff. *J. of Counseling Psychology, 36*: 464–470.

Rottier, J., Kelly, W., and Tomhave, W. K. (1984). Teacher burnout—small and rural school style. *Education, 104*: 72–79.

Rountree, B. H. (1984). Psychological burnout in task groups: Examining the proposition that some task groups of workers have an affinity for burnout, while others do not. *J. of Health and Human Resources Administration, 7*: 235–249.

Russell, D. W., Altmaier, E., and Van Velzen, D. (1987). Job-related stress, social support, and burnout among classroom teachers. *J. of Applied Psychology, 72*: 269–274.

Schwab, R. L., and Iwanicki, E. F. (1982a). Who are our burned out teachers? *Educational Research Quarterly, 1*: 5–16.

Schwab, R. L., and Iwanicki, E. F. (1982b). Perceived role conflict, role ambiguity and teacher burnout. *Educational Administration Quarterly, 18*: 60–74.

Schwab, R. L., Jackson, S. E., and Schuler, R. S. (1986). Educator burnout: Sources and consequences. *Educational Research Quarterly, 10*: 15–30.

Sekaran, U. (1986). *Dual-Career Families.* Jossey-Bass Publishers, San Francisco.

Seltzer, J., and Numerof, R. E. (1988). Supervisory leadership and subordinate burnout. *Academy of Management Journal, 31*: 439–446.

Shinn, M. (1982). Methodological issues: Evaluating and using information. In *Job Stress and Burnout: Research, Theory and Intervention Perspectives* (W. S. Paine, ed.), Sage, Beverly Hills, Calif., pp. 61–82.

Shinn, M., Rosario, M., March, H., and Chestnut, D. E. (1984). Coping with job stress and burnout in the human services. *J. of Personality and Social Psychology, 46*: 864–876.

Shirom, A. (1989). Burnout in work organizations. In *International Review of Industrial and Organizational Psychology* (C. L. Cooper and I. T. Robertson, eds.), John Wiley, New York, pp. 25–48.

Smith, P. C., Kendall, L. M., and Hulin, C. L. (1969). *The Measurement of Satisfaction in Work and Retirement*. Rand McNally, Chicago.

Stout, J. K., and Williams, J. M. (1983). Comparison of two measures of burnout. *Psychological Reports, 53*: 283–289.

Taylor, A. H., Daniel, J. V., Leith, L., and Burke, R. J. (1990). Perceived stress, psychological burnout and paths to turnover intentions among sport officials. *Applied Sport Psychology, 2*: 84–97.

Whitehead, J. T. (1986). Job burnout and job satisfaction among probation managers. *J. of Criminal Justice, 14*: 25–35.

Wolpin, J., Burke, R. J., and Greenglass, E. R. (1991). Is job satisfaction an antecedent or a consequence of psychological burnout? *Human Relations, 44*: 193–209.

Zedeck, S., Maslach, C., Mosier, K., and Skitka, L. (1988). Affective response to work and quality of family life: Employee and spouse perspectives. Special issue: Work and family: Theory, research, and applications. *J. of Social Behavior and Personality, 3*: 135–157.

13

Work-Family Role Conflict and Employer Responsibility

An Organizational Analysis of Workplace Responses to a Social Problem

Paul M. Roman

University of Georgia, Athens, Georgia

Terry C. Blum

Georgia Institute of Technology, Atlanta, Georgia

For the past decade, much public attention has been directed to conflicts between the demands of work and the demands of family responsibilities among adults in American society. A central concern is the proper role of American employers in alleviating or resolving work-family role conflicts. While debate surrounding this concern has generated much steam, some smoke, and a little fire, the progress that has been made in defining employers' proper roles in this arena is not impressive.

The goal of this chapter is to address questions surrounding employers' proper roles in this arena. We attempt to define the context of employer/organizational responsibility, and examine issues of work-family linkages within that context. We review rather selectively and at some points quite minimally the very large (and growing) literature that describes the nature and scope of the work-family conflict "problem." We also look at a sampling of the literature that describes (and occasionally evaluates) alternative designs for family-linked interventions. Extensive reviews of these two bodies of literature can be found elsewhere, and the review tasks are not duplicated here (Fernandez, 1986; Ferber and O'Farrell, 1991; Goldsmith, 1989; Googins, 1991).

In a chapter such as this, one might undertake to describe the interface between work-family conflicts and organizational behavior, or between programmatic interventions and organizational dynamics. Instead, our analysis has a somewhat peculiar center within organizational theory. Our focus is upon organizations functioning within complex environments that include vectors and forces with which organizations must contend (Thompson, 1967; Aldrich, 1979; Aldrich and Marsden, 1988). These include particular stresses and problems that employees bring into organizational life as part of their day-to-day work and as part of their life careers. They include other specialized organizations that define personal and social problems in particular ways; such organizations may market both definitions and solutions for these problems that are suggested for workplace adoption. The environments surrounding organizations also include governmental and political organizations that mandate problem definitions and solutions. We utilize the framework that organizations behave within complex environments, and we use organizational and sociological analysis to understand several different categories of organizational behavior vis-à-vis work-family role conflicts.

We also shed light on a neglected set of increasingly important issues for understanding organizations as workplaces. Within the young field of organizational behavior, little conceptual attention has been given to the provision of "fringe benefits" for employees. "Benefits" seem rather obvious, hardly worthy of detailed conceptual analysis. Fringe benefits often are "taken for granted," as can be witnessed in the increasingly rare efforts by the mass media to draw public attention to the fringe benefit packages that are at the center of major labor-management disputes.

What are fringe benefits? They can be as narrowly defined as specific indirect-compensation items included in the compensation package as part of a collective bargaining agreement. Benefits also can be defined as broadly as all of those items (both concrete and ephemeral) provided by employers that contribute to the well-being or betterment of employees, the community, an the broader society (cf. Mitchell, 1989; Fishman and Cherniss, 1990).

Benefits are typically seen as values added to the employment contract to attract or retain the workforce or certain classes or categories of employees. Yet when we view the diversity of fringe benefits across American workplaces, it is obvious that their adoption and implementation capture a wide range of organizational motives and desired outcomes that extend beyond hiring and turnover concerns. It may also be the case that different benefit provisions add to or alter inequalities in the workplace through the low visibility of the economic value that may be attached to them (O'Rand, 1986).

Rein (1982) has recognized the crucial importance of fringe benefits provided by private sector employees in addressing a wide array of issues affecting individual and collective welfare. He points out that the "welfare state" concept supports the false notion of a dichotomy between the government and the private sector in providing for "welfare." As a beginning typology for what might be a macrosociology of fringe benefits, Rein suggests that "social objectives" (commonly embedded in employee fringe benefits) of the government may be implemented through private enterprise by different procedures: mandate, regulation, stimulation, or support.

One way of addressing work-family role conflicts is through employers' provision of added fringe benefits. There can be little argument that perceived conflicts generated between employees' joint commitments to workplace roles and to family roles have escalated in the 1990s. The escalation has reached what numerous observers call a crisis. But under the conditions of this and other crises, workplaces must continue to function. What can be reasonably defined as employers' responsibilities or irresponsibilities vis-à-vis employees' welfare in the face of societal dysjunctions? In this instance the dysjunctions of concern are changes in family structure and process that may impact dramatically communities, society, and established features of culture. We attempt in this chapter to use organizational analysis to provide some answers to the fundamental question of who should be doing what.

I. ORGANIZATIONAL RATIONALES FOR RESPONDING TO WORK-FAMILY ROLE CONFLICTS

There are several interrelated reasons why work organizations may desire policies and fringe benefits to deal with work-family role conflicts. The first is reduction in turnover. Turnover may be the result of (1) employees seeking employment in settings in which family-related fringe benefits are better; (2) the need to quit work because of the unbearable strains of work-family conflicts; (3) the need to resign because the personal financial costs involved in providing for family-related needs come to outweigh the economic benefits of employment. Provision of family-related fringe benefits thus may not only reduce the attraction of employees to other work settings, but also can reduce the "pull" of those employees back to the home.

A related but somewhat different reason for employer response to work-family conflicts is to enhance productivity. This may occur through reducing disruptions produced by employees attending to family issues in manners that produce off-the-job and on-the-job absenteeism (Trice and Roman, 1972). Such issues might be ameliorated by organization-provided policies or fringe benefits. Productivity enhancement might also result from reduction in employees' preoccupations with family issues that are brought to the job, adversely affecting both concentration and interpersonal relations. Related is the enhancement of productivity through improved morale produced among employees who perceive value in their employers' attention to family needs.

A third rationale is more proactive. It operates from the premise that provision of family-related fringe benefits contributes to a positive organizational culture that should be maintained for its own sake (Deal and Kennedy, 1982). Many employers provide safe and healthy working environments for their employees independent of either responding to or anticipating government regulations about health and safety. Likewise there are some work settings in which it is simply "natural" to accommodate to the changing demography of the workforce by providing family-oriented programs and fringe benefits without a primary concern about their economic payoff (cf. Morgan and Tucker, 1991). This implies that considerable organizational slack would be necessary to provide such fringe benefits without concern for payoff, but such fringe benefit provision may be a direct reflection of the hierarchy of values within management.

Regardless of these possible motives for adopting different family-related fringe benefits or human resource management policies, most employers have little guidance in being able to decide what investments need to be made to deal reasonably with work-family role conflicts. Various forms of environmental scanning can inform an organization of the extent to which other organizations competing in the same labor market are providing such fringe benefits. Such observations do not, however, assure that these particular fringe benefit provisions create an edge in competing for labor.

The overall lack of guidance can be problematic, reflecting what happens when social problems are dealt with through a patchwork of loosely defined "private policies." Anecdotes have described how inadequate or misdirected scanning of the environment led to embarrassment in some workplaces where pains were taken to introduce particular family-oriented fringe benefits that then were not utilized and had to be withdrawn (cf. Kossek, 1990: 788–789). Thus, ascertaining what might be effective in addressing work-family role conflicts is not a foolproof process. By the same token, some scanning of the environment is a more appropriate procedure than simply responding to what appear to be national trends in benefit provision, or being guided by demands of particular constituencies within a given workplace.

II. THE EXISTING LITERATURE ON WORK-FAMILY ISSUES

The amount of published literature on work and family issues has exploded during the past decade. Much of it is oriented toward statistical observations of the extent to which work involvement has disrupted "traditional" family life in the United States (Freedman, 1988), together with anecdotal reports of what major corporations have done to help resolve these problems (Galinsky and Stein, 1990). Despite the initial excitement and optimism one gains from reading about "family-friendly" corporate programs and policies (Morgan and Tucker, 1991), rarely do these reports about large companies acknowledge the difficulties in implementing similar strategies in smaller work settings, settings in which most Americans are employed.

In terms of scientific documentation, many descriptions of the "extent of the problem" can be found. These repeatedly center on the scope of women's involvement in the labor force. There has also emerged a fairly extensive social science literature on the division of labor in the home that occurs when the wife and mother is involved in labor force participation (Geerken and Gove, 1983), much of which has been afforded by the availability for secondary analyses of several major sets of national survey data collected at different times. Numerous media-based and scientific attitudinal surveys are used to confirm the high prevalence of perceived conflicts between the demands of work and family. These reported perceptions are not necessarily linked with measures that validate the existence or describe the distribution of these conflicts (Greenhaus, 1989).

Many semipopular and academic sources can be found advocating adoption of this or that programmatic intervention on the basis of its apparent success in alleviating work–family role conflicts in other nations. Especially prominent are descriptions of state-based policies in Western Europe and Scandinavia, where it is asserted that work-family problems have been minimized (Aldous, 1990). Finally, numerous publications illustrate the pressure found in state and federal governments for legislation that will mandate various types of workplace responses to facilitate reduction of work-family role conflicts (Zigler and Frank, 1988).

Despite its bulk and range, this is neither a comprehensive nor an intellectually satisfying accumulation of knowledge. In a rare critique of this literature, Kingston (1989) observes that it is atheoretical and that it exaggerates the interdependence of the institutional spheres of work and of the family.

At least two significant topics are largely missing from this literature. One cannot find a representative empirical overview of the variety of means by which work organizations deal with work-family role conflicts. While there are many case study-type descriptions (and some statistics) about the work-family programmatic interventions undertaken within major corporations (cf. Galinsky and Stein, 1990), substantial research cannot be found that adequately describes the distribution of attention to work-family role conflict issues across the wide range of worksites in which Americans are employed, especially smaller workplaces. Indeed, when one scans available data about benefit provision in smaller work settings, one is struck by the severe gaps in the provision of what most regard as the most fundamental fringe benefits; that is, health insurance (Ferber and O'Farrell, 1991).

The second gap of major significance is the lack of empirical analysis of the impact of various types of work-family interventions, programs, or policies (Raabe, 1990). Where these impacts have been considered, the research designs usually have multiple shortcomings for drawing generalizations to an overall population of work organizations. Therefore, while there is no shortage of proactive reviews and descriptive literature about the different types of policies or interventions that might be undertaken to deal with work-family conflicts, we know practically nothing about impact. The relative "value" of any of these strategies, measured in any systematic way, thus remains unknown.

"Impact" and "value" are of course very broad concepts. One can hardly suggest common criteria for measuring impact or value that would generate consensus across employers, employee groups, intellectual leaders, consultants, or other constituencies. But within the body of literature on the reduction of work-family role conflicts, one finds that nearly all of it is written from perspectives that are presumed to be those of employees. It is suggested that these perspectives significantly reflect the assumptions and ideologies of scholars who view themselves as advocates of the family, of rights of individuals, or of equality for women (cf. Kline and Cowan, 1989). Relatively little has been heard from the perspective of work organizations.

Implicit in this employee-level orientation is an assumption that extant workplace policies and workplace practices are not supportive of families or of women's equality. From a scientific perspective, there is a troubling and pervasive implication that managers have shown or will show substantial resistance to supporting pro-family actions in the workplace. One finds, for example, a prominent family sociologist asserting that from an international perspective, American employers are clearly "laggards" in introducing policies to deal with work-family conflicts, explained in part by the lack of power of women and by employers' failure to recognize that such policies may serve their self-interests (Aldous, 1990).

With notable exceptions (Googins, 1991: 63–103), this literature implies that conflicts between work and family demands are very recent historical developments. There is a temptation to view this arena of concern as a second-generation product of the social movement for women's equality (Kingston, 1989). There is no doubt that the issues embed strong political concerns. To some extent, these writings are characterized by a narrow focus on stress and pressure placed on wives and mothers, rather than by a broad focus on the welfare of family units.

III. THE BROADER CONTEXT OF EMPLOYERS' RESPONSES TO WORK-FAMILY ROLE CONFLICT ISSUES

There is little disagreement over the presence or significant extent of work-family role conflicts, but at the same time it is clear that there is little unity among the advocates for particular directions or for changes in work-family policies. There is no identifiable national organization that is singularly pressing for action on these issues. Despite what might appear to be an obvious linkage, there is minimal evidence of concerted involvement or leadership for organized labor around these issues. Thus if it could be said that constituencies exist, they are widely fragmented. This absence of unity is an empirical curiosity.

Thus, while there is a great deal of attention to alleviation and resolution of work–family role conflict issues, in reality little progress has been documented, regardless of yardsticks one might use to gauge program implementation or program outcome. However, work-family conflicts offer a stage for raising (but not necessarily answering) broader questions about the role of work organizations in responding to social problems and social issues. These and related questions may advance a macrosociology of "fringe benefits" in work organizations:

- Are there general principles regarding the involvement of workplaces in the implementation of policies to resolve broader social problems (Fishman and Cherniss, 1990)?
- Does the accumulation of private policies across workplaces come to constitute de facto public policies in regard to certain issues (cf. Rein, 1982)?
- Is there reasonable equity emanating from these kinds of "bottom-up" generated public policies? In many respects, the current set of dilemmas and strains in health care distribution, management, and costs in the United States is a consequence of the implicit assignment to workplaces of what might be seen as a public responsibility. Should these experiences, and the observations of the inequities that have been created, affect judgments in considering whether or not a similar pattern should be followed in policies directed at work–family role conflicts?
- Are there issues of deeper significance in allowing workplace-based decisions to possibly alter or restructure the pattern of family life in the United States (Coltrane, 1990)?

We base the following observations on perspectives of organizations rather than perspectives of employees of organizations, recognizing that in some orientations organizations cannot be empirically separated from their "members." We are concerned with basic questions of why and how work organizations may appropriately address such issues within the context of contemporary American society. A basic concern is equity, a fundamental feature of bureaucratic organization (cf. Edwards, 1979). Such an analysis can offer insights into the limits on workplaces' provision of such services and interventions, and raise fundamental questions about the overall involvement of work organizations in dealing with this set of issues.

To begin, let us critically consider the typical characterization of "the problem." At first, the issues seem clear-cut. Even the most cursory examination of contemporary writings about human resource management, the sociology of the family, or women's studies reveals a consensus: work-family conflicts are serious, important, and worthy targets of deliberate social action and intervention (Goldsmith, 1989). The basis for concern in cherished values is also evident. American tradition calls for strong commitments to preserving the institutions of parenthood and the nuclear family, with those supporting alternative arrangements rarely suggesting intolerance of these valued and honored structures.

But contrary to the simple consensus that work-family role conflicts constitute "a problem," any attempt to grasp the essence of organizations' attempts to address work–family conflict issues will reveal the vagueness of the entire topical area. Five dimensions of such murkiness include:

1. The boundaries of work-family conflicts are not well defined. Virtually any personal problem or issue expressed by or projected upon employees either stem from or impacts relationships with their spouses, children, and/or parents. Definitions of the scope of

work-family conflicts can include the workforce's entire panoply of troubles and personal woes.

2. As mentioned in the preceding section, consensus is hard to find on "outcome criteria" appropriate for evaluating organizational policies geared to alleviate work-family conflicts. The range of such possible goals could include improved productivity of workers, decreased absenteeism, decreased use of leave time, improved morale, decreased job-related stress, lower rates of divorce, higher levels of marital satisfaction, improved functioning of children, or a better prepared workforce of the future. Obviously, measures of achievement of these different goals are not necessarily correlated with one another. Further, achievement of some of these goals may preclude achievement of others.

3. As mentioned, one seeks in vain for a well-defined "movement" focused upon either addressing or resolving work-family conflicts. Many voices, however, claim authority about these issues. Curiously, however, these is little evidence of any effort to try to bring together these various interests into a single structure that might prove to be viable in implementing some form of strategically planned political and/or organizational change. This lack of political focus may be a fundamental barrier to hoped-for developments of additional programs and fringe benefits. As Dobbin (1992) has recently found in regard to private social insurance, organized interest groups may be critical in stimulating benefit provision action by both employers and government.

4. While there is no clearly organized movement to resolve these problems, there are remarkably active mini-industries growing up around these issues. Two of these are the most visible: the increasingly competitive enterprises of providing child care for working families and the mushrooming number of small firms, "institutes," "centers," and other expert-sounding organizations providing a variety of informational and consulting services to work organizations as to how they might best cope with work-family conflicts. Interestingly, there does not appear to be any collaborative involvement between these two groups. While impressive in their growth and expansion, both of these mini-industries are localized and fragmented, with little base for unity in either marketing or political activism. Further, we find the emergence of "eldercare" as yet a third mini-industry, seemingly separate and independent from the existing activities, despite what would seem to be a logical linkage with child care.

5. The various analysts of work-family conflicts point toward either the government or the workplace as the necessary fountainhead of proactive action toward alleviating work–family conflicts. Despite many pronouncements, there is sparse evidence that—as the targets or potential recipients of these programs and services—working women and men are enthusiastic about such innovations. An even more important question is the level of enthusiasm within the workforce if the offering of such services were to be paired with increased taxes and/or indirect levies on employees associated with particular conditions of employment.

IV. THE INCREASE IN WOMEN'S WORKFORCE PARTICIPATION AND ITS IMPACTS

What are the origins of the high prevalence of work-family role conflicts that seems evident in contemporary American life? The disobedience leading to the ejection of Adam and Eve from the Garden of Eden for some explains the social institutions of both work and family. In the Book of Genesis, these central foci of human existence originated as God's punishments for disobedience. Pain and stress associated with work and the family are as old as written history, and only their forms change over time.

The major characteristics of the contemporary set of issues in the U.S. center on the increase in the rate of employment of women at formal jobs in formal organizations. As Googins (1991) has pointed out, this major change was certainly not the first to produce strains between work and family demands in American society. However, the high rate of women's employment outside the home will likely continue indefinitely. Forces that might reverse this trend cannot be identified at present.

The intermingling of issues related to gender with those related to the family characterizes portions of the literature (Fogarty, Rapoport, and Rapoport, 1971; Kessler-Harris, 1982; Sacks and Remy, 1984; Auerbach, 1990). From one perspective, women's opportunity for full participation in the workforce can be seen as liberating. From the perspective of the women's equality movement, such participation reflects the reduction of discriminatory behaviors associated with gender as an ascribed status. On the other hand, such workforce participation can be seen as enslaving, removing women from more desirable roles in the household.

Although not immediately obvious, substantial conflicts and cross-pressures exist among the goals of improvement in gender equality, of stability for the nuclear family, and of maximizing the welfare of children, to cite only three of several possibilities. Further, women's employment is not necessarily an index of desire to abandon or never adopt the roles of housewives, to say nothing of the relationship between employment and attitudes toward parenthood.

There is more than a touch of irony in viewing formal workforce entry as a sign of liberation. Over the course of history, different social groups (including women in some instances), using a range of political maneuvers, have attempted to reduce or eliminate their participation in the workforce. The most recent example is the diminution of employment of the elderly, made possible by both public and private financial support of retirees. This was antedated by a few decades by the successful struggle to minimize child labor.

As many have commented, there are lasting impacts that may assure the long-term continuation of women's large-scale workforce participation.

First, employment by women is quickly becoming a sociocultural norm (Kessler-Harris, 1982; Sacks and Remy, 1984). The social desirability of such employment appears stronger within the middle and upper classes where available work is more physically and socially desirable. This creates pressure for the middle- and upper-middle class young woman completing her education to decide upon a course of employment that may lead to a career. The participation inevitably has effects on the timing or sequencing of activity within the normative structures of the family. Bearing children and/or forming a nuclear family unit has become less of a normative priority as adulthood is achieved (cf. Coltrane, 1990). In addition to women's labor force participation as an impediment to the decision to bear children, the nonwork demands on men that have increased as their spouses remain in the labor force also bear on such decisions.

These emergent normative structures may also affect mate selection, with both men and women seeking partners who also are employed or who have promise of a career. Mate selection is also affected by the need for compatibility and/or compromises in the individual partners' career aspirations or commitments. Further, these employment patterns and partner selection criteria lead to the workplace being a setting for mate selection.

Third, in settings in which married women are employed, standards of living become adjusted to the dual incomes of both partners, assuming the male adult is also employed (Eggebeen and Hawkins, 1990). Becoming accustomed to a comfortable level of income creates an ongoing economic pressure to sustain employment on the part of both partners. Furthermore, changes that affect the income of one spouse may create pressure for accommodation through income increases on the part of the other spouse.

Fourth, the various types of programmatic interventions and work-related benefits focused on work-family stress reduction inevitably create additional pressures for sustaining women's employment. Such structures both directly and indirectly support the normative nature of women's employment and two-breadwinner couples. In a sense, it could be argued that a new "ethic" has been created by which women are supposed to enter the workforce, at least for some significant period of their adult life. Reinforcing this ethic is the negative image that may be increasingly associated with housewifery in certain social class and subcultural groups.

From the perspective of labor force dynamics, widespread entry of women into the American workforce is another wave of "new employees," paralleling immigrants as a group of new workforce entrants that have more or less shared social statuses and experienced deprivations at different points in history. Historians have traced these various influxes to the needs of American industrialists and to rapid expansions in construction and public works (Brandes, 1976; Jacoby, 1985; 1991). Unlike this recent wave of women, however, most immigrant workers started at the bottom of work hierarchies. Inexperience with formalized workplaces, external pressures to seek and maintain employment, and willingness to perform duties that were seen as less desirable by other members of the labor force were all more or less viewed as attributes of the various waves of immigrants entering the American workforce which made them attractive hires to many established employers.

The emphasis upon equal employment opportunities for American minorities, especially blacks, accelerated their entry into organizationally based jobs in the American labor force in a variety of different patterns beginning in the 1940s and extending up to the present. This was at least a partial parallel to the earlier waves of immigrant workers. It was not, however, the initial entry of blacks into the labor force. Blacks and other minorities have been afforded limited assistance by governmentally mandated employment policies in obtaining entry into better jobs in middle and upper-middle levels of the workforce, including some placement in managerial positions.

Within this context of earlier changes, the influx of women in the 1970s, 1980s, and 1990s into the American workplace involved a mixture of some earlier employment experiences of immigrants and minorities. In part, and in contrast to men as a group, women employees offered employers a pool of less experienced, less skilled and less expensive employees. However, women have not been necessarily placed in the "dirty work" jobs of earlier waves of new entrants. But it is very important to note that women employees may be more willing to accept unconventional work arrangements that sometimes have been the only work arrangements that can fit with family demands.

Part-time and temporary work statuses allow employers of women to avoid perquisites given to male employees in full-time, long-term positions (Ferber and O'Farrell, 1991: 101–111). Particularly notable is the lower rates at which women workers receive complete fringe benefits packages, if they receive any fringe benefits at all. Having access to a pool of potential employees who do not qualify for employers' fringe benefits provisions can be an incredible boon to employers when the cost of fringe benefits constitutes such a large and growing proportion of the compensation package for "regular" employees. Thus, without fringe benefits and with scheduling that would likely be unacceptable to many men, many of the jobs taken by women may indeed be the contemporary version of the dirty work of the earlier decades of the century.

This in part describes the historical context of today's concern with work organizations' responses to work-family role conflict issues. Over history, there has been a pattern of organizational responses to influxes of waves of new workers. These responses are captured in historians' concept of welfare capitalism (Brandes, 1976; Zahavi, 1988), and included programs and interventions such as the provision of housing, health care, recreation, and a range of educational activities, including home economics, learning to speak and read English, and preparation for American citizenship.

Policies and programs focused on work-family conflicts may be conceptualized as the primary set of reactions of social concern to the large-scale influx of women into the workforce. To a certain extent, affirmative action policies may also represent responses to the wave of women workers. While these policies originally facilitated the earlier wave of minority group members into improved employment opportunities, the entry of women helped reinforce and sustain the protections that might be afforded by these regulations.

V. EFFECTS OF THE ABSENCE OF A NATIONAL FAMILY POLICY

While many entertain different perspectives on the issue, the widespread employment of both men and women of child-bearing and child-rearing age has dramatic impacts on the well-being of children. It may also affect soon-to-emerge workforces and the demographic structure of future generations of American society.

Unlike many other nations, the United States lacks a national family "policy." The use of the term *policy* here is misleading, but this is the prevailing terminology that will be used for the remainder of this chapter. A more accurate description is a "deliberately affirmed cultural value."

National family "policies" do not represent solutions per se to work-family role conflict issues. The essence of such policies is that they guide legislative decisions as well as voluntary actions of workplace and other leaders, suggesting that when resource allocation decisions are made, priority should be given to those outcomes that will maximize the solidarity of the nuclear family as a fundamental social unit as well as to outcomes that will maximize the welfare and well-being of dependent children (Zigler and Frank, 1988; Ferber and O'Farrell, 1991). Where such policies exist, they are reportedly supportive rather than coercive, and their presence does not mean intolerance of life-styles other than the nuclear family, nor do they necessarily bear upon what may be seen as personal issues such as abortion rights.

To some extent this void in the United States reflects a persistent cultural value on the woman's "place" in the home, nurturing children and supporting the male partner's employment and employment-related aspirations. The prospects for adoption of such a policy in this country in the near future are not good. Despite the appearance of widespread positive sentiments for dealing with work-family role conflicts, there is, as we have already mentioned, no well-organized work-family constituency. There are poorly coordinated attempts from many directions to influence legislation to support or mandate one or another "family-friendly" policy (cf. Schroeder, 1988). It is difficult to envision how these piecemeal efforts can eventuate in a coherent and equitable national family policy, the absence of which places employers in a position in which they must determine the kind of "policy" that they desire to design, support, or ignore. Thus the accumulation of workplace-specific policies constitutes a patchwork, created in response to different constituencies that speak with different voices from different sectors of the workplace.

How has the United States avoided having a family policy? In regard to a variety of social problems, time-honored traditions in this country support an abundance of rhetoric and homiletics that emanates from high levels of political and business leadership. The facile and ephemeral qualities of most of this verbiage are typically reinforced by the absence of specific mandates, policies, or funding support. In such a context, the absence of a national family policy in the United States can be easily trivialized, avoided, or denied. It is our argument here that in the absence of such a policy, work organizations, somewhat by default, are now viewed by many influential persons as responsible for direct participation in resolving work-family role conflicts. Such an approach creates many problems, the most important of which is the lack of equity for families and employees who must deal with these conflicts.

VI. THE PROSPECTS OF INTERINSTITUTIONAL SUPPORT

A national family policy is similar to any developmental tool intended to improve the functioning of a social system in a direction that reflects specific, consensual values. As was previously mentioned, a national family policy is not a program, but a guide for formulating specific programs. A national family policy encourages mutual support across social institutions rather than having them work at cross-purposes. It also encourages the assessment of capabilities so that new programs are placed in settings in which they are most likely to flourish.

A negative example may elucidate this process. From an institutional perspective, where is the proper assignment of responsibility for resolving work-family role conflicts? Where are the resources and expertise most readily available? Insight into particular organizational processes may be found in considering why the range of child care responsibilities associated with working parents has not been assigned to public school systems but instead is being delegated to workplaces. The logic of the former approach is practically overwhelming. However, the use of public schools for these purposes has received very little attention in contrast to the campaigns that have been waged for work organizations' participation in dealing with these issues.

In contrast to the workplace—in which little or no expertise, skills, or physical facilitation are found in regard to child development—public school systems are thoroughly equipped with the physical facilities and the staffing that could assure that children of working parents are properly cared for while the parents are at work. With some modest augmentation of facilities and professional expertise, such care could include extended day care for small children and infants. Of equal if not greater importance, such facilities could also accommodate pre- and after-school opportunities for youth who are now "latchkey" children (Googins, 1991), spending large amounts of time without supervision or involvement in appropriate activities that will promote healthy development.

The expertise to plan, design, schedule, and provide these and other types of care are clearly lodged within the public education system. Furthermore, these systems have already been established under varying degrees of public scrutiny such that their physical environments are designed to assure health and safety for children of all ages. The buildings, programs, policies, and procedures have a very high degree of uniformity across the nation, assuring that standardized and equitable services for working parents could be developed on a very broad scale. Finally, it is evident that despite the existence of these publicly supported and maintained buildings and grounds in virtually every American urban neighborhood, suburban community, and rural town, the facilities are used for only a tiny part of the 24-hour day, and even to this extent are used fully for only three-quarters of the calendar year.

Historically, the invention and near-universal implementation of kindergartens within U.S. public school systems during the 20th century demonstrates that public schools' technology can be extended in an age-downward direction without accompanying radical disruption. There is no reason that the extended use of such facilities for the care and supervision of children that is suggested here be compulsory or coercive, but rather that it be available as a voluntary choice for working parents.

The argument for extending the current use of the public school system to deal with the child care problems of employed parents is even more compelling when one examines the alternative systems that have emerged. There has been minimal regulation of the physical facilities or environmental conditions associated with privately operated day care. Meaningful educational or training standards for personnel to engage in direct care of children have not been developed (cf. Belsky, 1988). Further, despite the well-established norms that have been developed over many decades across the United States that the maintenance of public education is taxpayers' responsibility regardless of their status as parents, payment for child care has emerged as a private responsibility of parents, except for making a portion of these payments exempt from federal taxes under certain conditions.

The perspective of this chapter is not advocacy for a change to school-system responsibility for the care of children of employed parents, but rather to analyze the rationale for the assignments of institutional responsibilities that are currently in place. There is little novelty to suggestions for greater involvement of public schools in child care, and in some settings, school systems offer extended days for children. But the implementation of the potential for this remarkably effective use of public facilities is very limited.

This can be understood through a brief organizational analysis. As formal organizations, public school systems have successfully although perhaps unintentionally provided several means of defense against broadening their span of activity to include forms of appropriately enriched supervision of the children of employed parents.

As a first and perhaps primary explanation, as providers of public services, public school systems have protected themselves from intrusions from the external environment, such as being assigned new roles in child care, by successfully claiming that resources to perform the roles already assigned to them are woefully inadequate.

Second, this perception is reinforced by an associated public attitude that the schools are generally inefficient and ineffective in performing their assigned functions. Curiously school system administrators and professional educators seem to accede remarkably by their silence to these hostile, intense, and fundamental criticisms.

Third, and of great importance, although public school systems have a very high level of organizational and functional uniformity across the nation, school systems almost universally remain under local control. Governance is locally elected and taxation occurs at the local level. School board members are tacitly the stewards of educational quality but they are also the elected representatives of taxpayers whose only clear feedback about the operation of the local school system may be their annual tax bill.

Thus there is little support for motivations on the part of this governance to broaden the system's responsibilities and jeopardize school board members' elected status by increasing taxes to support these new functions. In such a context there can be little reward associated with demonstrating innovative ideas to the broader society unless the implementation of such innovations involves rewards at the local level, rewards other than external recognition. These factors, coupled with the local governance's operational acceptance of the premise of a chronic shortage of resources, precludes the adoption of broad visions on the solutions of future problems.

Fourth, there is no natural linkage between workplaces and the public educational system other than through workplaces' responsibility for property taxes that support schools. Indeed, in many parts of the nation this linkage is utterly trivialized by using exemption from local taxes (primarily used to support schools) as the basis for attracting new industry to communities. Thus there is no vehicle through which workplaces could form an alliance with public school systems in working to bring about effective ways for the latter to take a lead role in child care.

Only recently has corporate leadership in the United States demonstrated an interest in public education, albeit with a visible coating of rhetoric (cf. Dunn, 1991). A well-publicized part of this interest has involved corporate leaders' attention to the schooling of the underprivileged. However, in light of the discussion here, it is perhaps predictable that another, perhaps equally substantial part of this relatively tiny level of interest, is being directed toward the development of private school systems for organizations' employees as a new form of benefit; that is, an alternative to what are perceived as unacceptable local school systems as a means of attracting and retaining employees (Ward, 1991). In contrast to such a remarkably narrow and "selfish" vision of corporate social responsibility, the proposal for increasing the utilization of public school facilities to address child care issues could benefit employees without regard to the size, benefit structure, or corporate social involvement of their employer.

From an organizational viewpoint, it seems evident that a clear-cut national family policy is the only means by which the value of public school systems' involvement in reducing work-family role conflicts could be considered in an objective way. With guidance from a national family policy that delineated roles of the entire complex of social institutions, dialogues could begin between workplaces and public school systems in which their mutual interest in child care issues could be explored. Otherwise there is no basis for such interaction.

VII. COPYING THE POLICIES OF OTHERS

Ambiguity created by the absence of a U.S. national family policy is also reflected in a number of prominent discussions centered on the means that American workplaces should undertake to aid in the reduction of work-family role conflicts. These are based upon observations of what are described as generous and appropriate workplace policies supporting the coexistence of work and family roles in other nations, especially in Western Europe (Kamerman and Kahn, 1981; Kamerman, 1988; Allen, 1988; Frank and Lipner, 1988; Haas, 1990; Ferber and O'Farrell, 1991: 155–178). While certainly of interest and perhaps suggesting possible employer responses to work-family issues, the international comparisons perhaps have their greatest value in describing what occurs in nations with distinctive national policies supporting child well-being and family life.

What is frustrating in many of these presentations is the implication of the ease of transferring these employer policies to the United States, the only alleged barrier being the shortsightedness and lack of concern for the family endemic to American culture (cf. Aldous, 1990). While the cross-national descriptions recognize the critical presence of a national family policy, this necessity is not always included with the optimistic projections of the positive value of adoption of specific "family-friendly" workplace policies.

Further, such implications fail to recognize the interdependent nature of culture and social institutions, and the relative futility of transferring desired outcomes from the adoption of one culture's practices in another culture. Again, strategies of organizational analysis can highlight the complexities and potential adverse side effects of attempted cross-cultural diffusion of simple health practices (Paul, 1955), to say nothing of detailed human resource management policies to be mandated across employment settings.

Such discussions recall recommendations advanced some years ago for the prevention of alcohol problems in American society by introducing children to drinking at a young age (Chafetz, 1962). This recommendation was based on the observation that alcoholism was rare in Orthodox Jewish cultures where children's participation at early ages in ritual-based drinking was nearly universal. Alcoholism was likewise rare in rural Italy, where young children were introduced to wine at meals. Somewhat of a parallel is found in the enamoring of some American consultants and managers to Japanese management practices during the 1970s and 1980s (Waring, 1991). While the potential of cross-cultural transfer of outcomes seems somewhat greater in the latter case, analyses of both instances demonstrate that direct transfers of ideas and practices are not simple, and that desired outcomes are lodged in complex systems of interdependencies.

Were these systems to be successfully transferred, likely they would bring with them trade-offs that would be viewed with alarm by many among the potential adopters of the new practices. Thus Orthodox Jewish drinking customs in adulthood are characterized by intense normative proscriptions against drunkenness (Bales, 1946), Japanese workers and managers hold remarkably different attitudes toward their careers an their relationships to their employers than those in American culture (Waring, 1991), and Western European cultures that offer structured resolutions to work-family conflicts are characterized by very high degrees of social equality and few opportunities for the kinds of upward mobility that are central to the motivations of many American workers.

VIII.   OTHER CONTRIBUTIONS TO THE "CRISIS"

Beyond the absence of a national family policy, there are two somewhat more subtle contributors to the "crisis" that has been defined around work-family role conflicts in the United States.

In a very real sense, the conflicts between work and family have been present in many social class segments for long periods of time, well before the current "crisis" was realized. In many working class and poor households, both partners or single household heads have had formal jobs, motivated by the sheer necessity of providing an adequate level of living. What is notable is the extent to which conflicts between work and family roles eventually came to permeate the middle and upper middle classes. At the same time that women were entering the workforce in record numbers and proportions, rates of divorce were skyrocketing in these social classes, producing single-parent households also in record numbers (Googins, 1991).

Impacted by working women in their own households or families and/or by divorce, male decision makers became much more likely to have been affected by a work-family conflict than they had been in the distant past. When they observe the consequences and conflicts of the employment of their own wives and daughters (including the impacts of marriage and divorce), these decision makers have rather suddenly perceived a large-scale societal crisis, calling for determined and sometimes expensive organizational actions (Fernandez, 1986). This situation parallels the incredibly dramatic societal response to illegal drugs in the early 1970s (Roman and Blum, 1992), with observers then arguing that the depth and scope of those responses were a direct consequence of drug use appearing among youth in the middle and upper-middle class segments of society (i.e, the children of organizational decision makers). This created a new awareness of illegal drugs that implied that the presence of the drugs themselves was a novelty, despite the fact that marijuana and cocaine had been present in society for decades, eliciting little social response or concern as long as the usage patterns remained outside the social class environments of societal decision makers.

Finally, the definition of a "crisis" in work-family conflicts is propelled by emerging vested interests. In looking at new social issues, it is typical to view their roots within combinations of sociohistorical forces that have created a "need" for a societal response. Sometimes such explanations include the potency of "social movements" as sociopolitical forces in pressing for the implementation of change. As was previously mentioned, it is tempting to point to the social movement advocating equal rights for women as a prime force behind the growth of attention to work-family role conflict issues, although the lack of any consensual center in the advocacy for programming or change speaks against the validity of such an observation.

Distinct from the concept of social movements, sociologists have refined a notion of organizational "claims making" that is used to account for variations in the attention cycle to different social issues and problems (Spector and Kitsuse, 1977). For example, in our earlier work one of us anticipated this notion by describing the growth and entrepreneurialism of an "alcoholism industry" (Trice and Roman, 1972). This industry flourished during the 1970s and 1980s, promoting the dual notions that alcoholism was a hidden and extremely costly behavior but that it also was a health problem that could be treated successfully. Campaigns generating public awareness were successful, and the demand for the treatment programs that were the entrepreneurial heart of the industry escalated. This in turn has led to institutionalization of alcoholism as a health problem, and has assured longevity for at least part of the for-profit treatment system that was practically unknown prior to 1970 (Roman and Blum, 1992).

As what might be seen as a spin-off of the women's equality movement, leaving behind much of the altruistic motivation, there has arisen a distinctive set of entrepreneurs focused on work-family role conflicts. Their services center on providing a range of advice to the workplace, delivered through conferences, workshops, newsletters, books, and especially on-site consultation. Suggestions delivered through these media center on what particular organizations might do to most effectively deal with their employees' work-family role conflicts, the profile of which these specialists will readily provide.

This collection of providers marketing their services to human resources management does not make up anything close to a large "industry"; its primary products are information and advice that is sold to workplaces. For human resource managers, however, it constitutes a very visible and persistent presence. Unlike many forms of professional consultation to organizations, this advice is distinctively value-laden with its purveyors' perspectives on the importance of policy-driven "action" toward work-family role conflicts. The advice may or may not have a firm scientific base. From the perspective of this "industry," the derivation and promotion of one or another "facts" about the nature or resolution of work-family role conflicts may be critical in sustaining both popular and workplace attention to work-family role conflicts.

IX. PRIVATE POLICIES AS SUBSTITUTES FOR PUBLIC POLICY

In the absence of a national family policy, the workplace becomes a natural setting for the reduction of work-family conflicts. It is difficult to conceive how "the family" could be conceived in a parallel manner as a setting for solutions, other than through the not uncommon public cheerleading by political leaders when people are urged to "buck up," work harder, and generally persist in the face of adversities. However, as is described in the following section, it is clear that some work-family conflicts are definitely family problems while others are more appropriately classified as work problems. Without guidance from public policy, there are no available means for making these distinctions in a manner that builds consensus rather than fuels conflict.

Looking at the most prominent and fundamental arena for such conflicts, the care of household dependents—young, old, or impaired—government-provided services clearly are not adequate to meet these needs. In an era in which the tax base is perceived as inadequate to support expansion of such services, employers are "tapped" as logical providers of the means to reduce these problems. After all, goes this logic, employers are the primary beneficiaries of parents' employment, and thus employers should provide the means for dealing with resultant difficulties.

A less obvious reason for perceived employer responsibility for dealing with work–family conflicts is the precedents that have been set by employers' provision of coverage for health care expenses, together with their involvement in pension plans to supplement the government's provision of retirement benefits through Social Security (cf. Rein, 1982; Dobbin, 1992).

There is a generalized perception that employers' involvement in health care and retirement benefits, two crucial indirect supports for family functioning, has proven quite effective. Such generalizations typically overlook the gaps created by these largely voluntary provisions of fringe benefits. While a large proportion of employed people and their dependents enjoy a reasonable level of third-party coverage for health care costs through employer-sponsored insurance, the majority of small private sector employers do not offer such critical fringe benefits to their employees, often because of prohibitive costs (Ferber and O'Farrell, 1991). This places many employees and their families at high risk of personal economic catastrophe should they require extensive health care. Despite a variety of legislative attempts, U.S. public policy essentially ignores the issue of coverage of health care costs for the employees of smaller work organizations. This of course should adequately foreshadow the dubious success of assigning smaller workplaces the task of alleviating work-family role conflicts in some fashion.

Accepting that the combination of these rather recent "traditions" of benefit provisions, public expectations, and default by various levels of government require some formalized workplace response to work-family role conflicts, workplace managements have a choice of providing direct or indirect services for aiding and dealing with dependent care issues. The most well-known example is the provision of child care. Experience indicates that it is very difficult for work organizations to meet employees' needs through the provision of direct child care services. Child care can be provided, yet it is almost impossible to meet the diversity of needs and concerns presented by working parents with small children at home. For a few examples: the services that are offered may fail to meet employees' needs in terms of location, hours of operation, staffing by persons who are acceptable to employees, use of child care or educational techniques that are acceptable to employees, or providing care to a group of children who some employees accept as suitable for interaction with their children. Regardless of the match that is made between some employees' needs or desires and the direct services that an employer provides, some or many needs or desires will not be met or fulfilled.

If direct services for care of employee dependents are not feasible, then what about indirect services? Some form of voucher system is attractive here, allowing the employee to select services that meet particular needs. But provision of such fringe benefits to only a portion of the workforce may be effective only if a carefully designed system of flexible benefits is in place, adoption of which is far from universal and especially difficult for smaller employers.

These issues highlight American employers' inconsistent involvement in providing fringe benefits across a range of different kinds of disruptions of employees' productivity and careers. In an important way, these individual problems collectively comprise the impacts of broader social problems. What are employers' appropriate responsibilities?

To highlight the essence of some of the dilemmas presented by these issues, consider the "devil's advocate" suggestion to eliminate and outlaw all fringe benefits, including those previously established by governmental mandate. Were fringe benefits eliminated, then individuals would be responsible to resolve problems of health care, retirement income, child care, life insurance, and all the other fringe benefits one's employer might have fully or partially provided. Such an arrangement would base all employment contracts on wages or salaries. Such a change might introduce considerably more equity than exists under present arrangements (cf. O'Rand, 1986). Without fringe benefits, which vary greatly in terms of their actual and potential economic value to employees, universal no-benefit would offer an open and visible means for evaluating and comparing the relative worth of different types of employment.

This obviously unpopular and likely unworkable suggestion highlights the erratic and inconsistent ways that employers presently offer fringe benefits. These "patterns" represent employers' responses to at least four categories of economic and social factors (not necessarily mutually exclusive):

1. Labor market conditions, which may require the offering of particular types of fringe benefits in order to attract and/or retain certain types of employees.
2. Paternalism, or the generalized notion that employee productivity can be enhanced, employee loyalty can be cemented, and perhaps employee dependence on the employer can be embedded by the offering of a wide range of fringe benefits, including ones that are unusual and personalized, such as housing and off-job recreational activities (Jacoby, 1985; 1991).
3. Collective bargaining agreements with representatives of certified groups established to represent employees on issues of wages, benefits, welfare, and rights. Where such bargaining is established, different fringe benefits provisions typically obtain for the levels and/or categories of the workforce that are inside and outside the bargaining units.
4. Corporate social responsibility, a concept centered on the range of roles that organizations may play in maintaining or enhancing the quality of life of employees as well as impacting the broader community in which the organization is based. This idea, dealt with again at the close of the chapter, offers both vagueness and complexity in the organizational motives it may represent (Mitchell, 1989).

How employers interpret their responsibilities to provide for employee welfare beyond wages deserves much more investigation than it has ever received (Rein, 1982). The near-universally perceived necessity of employer-provided benefits demonstrates their institutionalization. Clearly our political leadership, the general public, and many employers do not believe that employees would deal adequately with personal health insurance or save enough for retirement without direction, guidance, and even coercion from the employer. The resulting patchwork of fringe benefits creates inequities for both employees and employers.

Such inequity is not easily corrected. Fringe benefits easily become "out of control," in a broad sense. Contingencies perceived in the external environment may trigger certain individual benefit provisions. Employers may even copy one another's benefit provisions without a logic for defining the appropriateness of a particular benefit. But adopted fringe benefits do not disappear when the contingency dissipates or the attraction of other organizational "role models" wanes (cf. Dobbin, 1992). Fringe benefits tend to accumulate. Except in times of severe exigencies, rarely are they reduced or withdrawn.

These generalizations need not suggest that employers avoid taking steps to alleviate work-family role conflicts. But on the basis of the reasoning that is offered here, work organizations should exercise considerable caution in adopting programs or interventions that appear to address work-family issues. Such programming, where it occurs, should be based in a context of voluntarism and should embody some form of strategic plan. It should not be an issue casually delegated to a task force, nor should these policy questions be quickly resolved in response to constituency pressures, as conformity to what are perceived as the new norms for benefit provision, or in response to anticipated governmental regulations.

X. QUESTIONS OF PROGRAM EFFECTIVENESS

Many of these observations beg for empirical studies on the impact of organization-based work-family role conflict reduction mechanisms (Raabe, 1990), but the utility of such studies may be more limited than one might expect. This is because the question of impact or effectiveness is nearly impossible to answer.

Contrary to what seems to be common sense, there is rarely a single consensual criterion for judging the effectiveness of ameliorative efforts introduced into the workplace. Thus, for example, employers may desire to "improve productivity" through the introduction of a particular policy or program. What does this mean? Improved employee attendance, rate of productivity, job satisfaction, life satisfaction, profits, product quality, consumer satisfaction, market share, or shareholder confidence?

It is quickly evident that this little list of criteria includes a common theme of improvement, yet each of the individual items defies straightforward measurement. Absenteeism, for example, is notoriously sensitive to a range of environmental influences that may cloud any measure of program impact. *Quality* is a management buzzword of relatively recent vintage, a concept that itself begs for criteria. Further, if one is looking for a comprehensive impact, multiple measures of multiple criteria become necessary. Are such criteria common across a large or even a reasonable number of workplaces? If so, can comparable measures be drawn across these settings? Finally, the Achilles' heel of practically any attempt at program evaluation in work organizations is the proper attribution of cause and effect. Without carefully controlled experimental or quasi-experimental designs, or without measurement of the principal factors that may comprise alternative explanations of outcomes, attempted evaluations are generally left with measures of association that may or may not be spurious.

While it is thus logical and responsible to call for the development of a body of sound research to support the efficacy of work-family role conflict policies and programs, only approximations with very limited generalizability can be expected. Of course such a dilemma is not unique to examination of the impact of these types of innovations, but describes the obstacles to investigating specific impacts of human resource management innovations generally.

Of the available studies, the vast majority are extremely limited in terms of both scope and methods. Indeed, the bulk of the literature centered on the impact of work-family policies on employees and worksites does not appear in refereed publications, but in symposia, as book chapters, or in special issues of journals in which manuscripts are typically invited. It may, however, be useful to focus briefly on examples of good-quality research and consider some of the broad implications of its findings.

We selected two research reports from recent literature that come closest to meeting standards for acceptable research methods. These examples provide a flavor of the methodological problems of such research (Kossek, 1990; Goff, Mount, and Jamison, 1990). The findings of these studies, limited as they may be, do support some of the notions advanced in this chapter. This brief review suggests that good studies do not produce strong testimony for the efficacy of a very central work-family role conflict reduction device, child care.

Using data collected from a sample of employees in a large midwestern public utility, Kossek (1990) examined the kinds of child care assistance that employees with children would find helpful in reducing conflicts between job and family demands. Her findings indicated that there was a considerable diversity of needs within this single population. It was not likely that a single child care service set up by the employer would be adequate to reach this range of needs. This study's conclusions, based on a single organization with what might be characterized as a fairly specific core technology, are not optimistic about the effectiveness of direct child care services in meeting perceived needs, and of course the data say nothing as to whether or not such services would produce any significant or desirable impacts within the organization.

In a complementary data collection and analysis, Goff, Mount, and Jamison (1990) also used a single midwestern firm, in this instance dealing in electronics and communications, that had established an on-site child day care center for employees: "No support was found for the hypothesis that use of a child care center at work would reduce the amount of work/family conflict and absenteeism of employed parents" (p. 793). However, the study did find that employed parents' satisfaction with their children's day care arrangements, wherever such care was located, was associated with reduced work-family conflict that was in turn associated with lower levels of absenteeism.

These data clearly point to the possible futility of employers' attempts at providing direct services to reduce work-family role conflict. The data suggest that a wide range of options are necessary to satisfactorily meet such needs across a diverse workforce. The demonstrated association between role conflict reduction and employee attendance points to the potential values of such attention by employers, but does not specify the appropriate nature of that attention.

Although it may be appropriate to take a broader perspective in order to understand why some employers have adopted interventions and policies related to work-family conflict reduction, it is even more appropriate to understand that cost-benefit or cost-effectiveness judgments are not *the* necessary foundation for all human resources management practices. In several respects, the question of the "impact" of different work-family conflict interventions is the wrong question to ask.

It is the wrong question because it presumes that these interventions are primarily focused on individual outcomes; that is, the resolution of the problems of a cumulative number of individuals. Indeed, the significance of these policies may be their symbolic availability and their demonstration that the employer "cares." This is not necessarily cynical, for indeed some employers may have little concern about the cost of a certain benefit or service as long as they are made aware that it is useful to some employees and is viewed favorably by those who do not need to use it. But it also should be recognized that there is little standardization in design and process across different work-family conflict-related interventions, creating great difficulty for the application of typical "program evaluation" strategies. There are at least two basic reasons for this variation.

First, such policies or interventions should be adapted to both the workforces they serve and the workplaces within which they are developed, defying standardization in either structure or process. Customization is essential for effective program implementation, for adaptation to organizational cultures, and for integration with other preexisting practices. Such lack of standardization, however, makes most generalizations problematic.

Second, under current conditions, such work-family conflict reduction policies can only be implemented voluntarily by employers who make independent decisions about the level of investment they desire to make. Given the absence of a well-developed group of consultants who might introduce uniformity into such policies, standards for the design of such policies are unlikely in the foreseeable future.

Asking about the efficacy of a work-family conflict reduction policy is similar to asking about the efficacy of employers' provision of health insurance benefits. Such a question seems absurd because the immediate and obvious responses are, "efficacious for accomplishing what?" and, perhaps, "what kind of health insurance coverage?"

Concepts of program evaluation assume common program ingredients and common goals across programs. This usually allows for some form of quasi-experimental design to ascertain program impact. The results of such evaluations ideally guide funding agencies' future decisions. Workplaces do not typically treat their human resource management strategies in this manner, but this does not mean that their "efficacy" is to be ignored or simply assumed on faith.

The more appropriate approach is to examine the effectiveness of the structure and process of an individual program, often called an "audit." An audit of a work-family conflict reduction program in a given workplace would begin with a clear understanding of what the organization hoped to accomplish when program adoption occurred. An audit requires on-site examination of the presence and quality of program ingredients, including a review of data generated through management information systems wherein auditors can examine the efficiency of the use of resources assigned by the work organization to the particular program.

An audit may center on the extent to which management's goals are being achieved. It is very unlikely that all of these goals could be readily translated into quantitative data, leading to the observation that outcomes of an audit are often impressionistic. An audit should also offer an explanation for perceived shortfalls in goal achievement. But unlike an evaluation, an audit may conclude that the pattern of operation of a program or the impact of a policy is limited by the political economy of a given workplace rather than concluding that a particular policy decision has proven not to be "cost-effective." In contrast to outcome data generated by an evaluation, an audit provides a firmer base on which to assess the realities of a different alterations that might be made to the program that is being examined.

XI.   THE VALUE OF THE EMPLOYEE ASSISTANCE PROGRAM MODEL IN ALLEVIATING WORK-FAMILY ROLE CONFLICTS

On the basis of our observations about policy and the allocation of responsibility, and drawing from the minimal research available, it is most effective for employers to provide only indirect services related to the alleviation of work-family conflicts. If designed and used appropriately, the employee assistance program (EAP) may provide a reasonable means for organizations of all shapes and sizes to be responsive to work-family role conflict issues. This can happen without compromising employees' choices and responsibilities, and also without creating inequities.

From the perspective advanced in this chapter regarding the appropriate roles of the employment setting in facilitating reductions of work-family role conflicts, the model offered by the EAP has considerable promise for providing a meaningful and equitable level of service. In a nutshell, the EAP's salience as an indirect service to aid in work-family role conflict reduction lies in their established practices of:

1. Aiding in employees' identification and understanding of problems that adversely affect work performance and/or discomforts that arise in conjunction with carrying out their jobs
2. Linking employees with the most appropriate service for dealing with the identified problem
3. Balancing the referral advice with the appropriateness of the costs of the services that may be utilized—costs that may be covered by the employer fully, partly, or not at all, depending upon the employees' applicable benefits coverage (Blum and Roman, 1989; Sonnenstuhl and Trice 1986)

In order to assess the possible roles of an EAP in dealing with work-family role conflicts, it is important to consider some of the assumptions underlying EAP operation. Ideally, a philosophy of employee responsibility pervades all levels of EAP activity: employees voluntarily go the EAP for assessment, employees decide whether or not to pursue the referral suggested by the EAP counselor, and the employee is responsible for "following through" with the regimen prescribed or suggested by the external service provider. The professional responsibility resting with the EAP (and thus the implied responsibility of the employer) is to provide the employee with an objective and accurate assessment of the nature of the presenting problem. Following suggestions for assistance made by the EAP is the responsibility of the employee. A key skill of the EAP is laying out such choices in a context that emphasizes that the employee's job performance is always the bottom line. Extensively versed in the operation, costs, and effectiveness of different community resources, the EAP counselor should be able to make a referral that best fits the employee's problem, work demands, geographic location, and copayment responsibility. The effectiveness of this strategy in dealing with substance abuse problems has been well established (Trice and Beyer, 1984; Walsh et al., 1991).

Informally, the EAP can also undertake "follow-up" of employees who have undergone the diagnosis and referral process to ascertain how the recommendations produced positive results. By supporting the action recommendations made by the referral agency, EAP follow-up increases the likelihood of a long-term payoff associated with the employer's investment (Foote and Erfurt, 1991). A crucial distinction is for follow-up to provide ongoing support for employees' problem resolution rather than coercive "Big Brother" monitoring.

Within this ideal model, the EAP is equally available to all members of the workforce. As mentioned, this equity reflects also in the fact that payments for any services received from external providers in association with the employee's acceptance of EAP referral advice are based upon the existing fringe benefits provisions or on the client's ability to make a copayment. Finally, if leave is required in order to follow the regimen prescribed for an employee's dealing with a particular personal problem, such leave must remain within the definitions and limits of sick leave or personal leave. When these limits are reached, leave without pay takes effect.

Needless to say, all EAPs do not follow this ideal philosophy. For example, in some settings, confrontation of a poorly performing employee requires that the employee undertake a diagnostic interview with the EAP and follow the EAP counselor's referrals. Noncompliance may lead to discipline. Such a strategy removes responsibility from the employee. Substituted is the employer's implied commitment that the diagnosis and prescription will be successful in resolving the problem, a not-so-obvious invitation for later litigation (Blum and Roman, 1989).

Elsewhere EAPs provide direct services through formal counseling sessions with employees affected by familial, psychiatric, or substance abuse problems. Such direct service may be given at the discretion of the EAP counselor, but in some instances the organization specifically urges the EAP's direct involvement in "short-term counseling" as a cost containment measure, assuming that such use of the counselor's time is more cost-effective than an external referral. This also undermines the philosophy of employee responsibility by essentially making the employer both judge and jury vis-à-vis the employee's problem (Blum and Roman, 1989).

The EAP model does, however, offer significant possibilities for organizational responses to alleviating the conflicts associated with work-family roles. First, it should be mentioned that EAPs may be already much more involved in dealing with these problems than has been appreciated by advocates pressing for the implementation of other program innovations. Our own recent research concerning all new intakes to 81 different private sector-based EAPs indicates that as many as 50% of these caseloads involve some aspect of family problems (Roman and Blum, 1992). The medicalized orientation of EAPs tends to limit description of these "family" cases to circumstances of dealing with troublesome children or marital conflicts and breakdowns. The data do not specify the sources of the problems, nor do these data necessarily include "advice" given in regard to child care or help with other household dependents.

In addition to already providing help for family-related issues, EAPs have critical advantages in developing and maintaining a reasonable, but limited, level of involvement of the workplace in family-related issues:

1. EAPs are a "benefit" equitably available to all employees rather than useful only to those with certain family configurations. This equity is demonstrated further by the financial coverage for the use of services that may be defined as health-related, such coverage being extant "across-the-board" fringe benefits. We of course recognize typical variations (often inequities) in such benefit packages betewen hourly and salaried employees, as well as their regressive nature of deductibles and copayments vis-à-vis income.
2. EAPs do not involve the organization in the provision of direct services. Direct service provision involves potential conflicts of interest for the employer, does not necessarily meet the needs of most employees with a particular problem, may be inequitable in that the elected styles of some employees' lives preclude their ever needing particular services, and may put the organization in a position of attempting to manage services about which there is no managerial expertise.

    By contrast, EAPs link individuals with services that they may or may not elect to use. This is their right. If the suggested treatment is to resolve the underlying problems that led to a job performance decrement, it is the employee's responsibility to cooperate with the treatment to meet the obligations of the implicit contract. Should employees' preoccupations and involvements with personal problems continue to adversely affect their ability to perform their assigned jobs, the prescribed consequences of poor performance kick in.

    In other words, referral to treatment in no way absolves the individual from the expectation that job performance will return to an acceptable level within a reasonable period of time. While the ramifications of the Americans with Disabilities Act have not yet been realized by EAPs, at present the receipt of EAP advice or services does not classify the employee as disabled and thus exempt from adverse action.
3. Lest the concept be inappropriately minimized, EAPs are distinctively designed to help employees deal with personal problems that affect their work either directly or through preoccupations. EAPs offer far more than a semiguided tour through the yellow pages. These services intend to maximize the efficiency of employees' attempts to deal with

personal problems by using expert knowledge of the pros and cons of particular service provider arrangements in deciding upon these linkages. Thus EAPs constitute a distinctive service, although most of the services that are provided are indirect.

Numerous potential problems need to be considered before organizations implement an EAP-type solution to address work-family role conflict issues. The foregoing discussion alludes to many of these problems. Should a work-family problem identification and referral service be incorporated into an existing EAP, or should a new system be developed? There are several reasons to argue in favor of the latter.

1. According to our own unpublished survey data, many if not most EAP counselors currently claim that they are overworked and overtaxed. These include victims of a peculiar type of success, the effective diffusion through the workplace of information about the EAP helping individuals with particular problems. This leads to more new intakes, a pattern that may spiral. Why is this a problem? Because few organizations immediately accede more resources to the EAP, so that work overload for the EAP staff commonly persists for a long period, taking its toll in staff stress, dissatisfaction, and turnover.

Further, such growth in caseload occurs through self-referrals of problems for which employees readily admit the need for assistance. From the viewpoint of the workplace, these may not be necessarily the problems that exact the greatest costs in terms of poor job performance or other disruptions. No doubt channeling these self-referrals to services that aid them with their problems and that are cost-effective from the organization's perspective result in substantial cost savings as compared to employees' seeking such help on ther own. But the demand that a heavy flow of self-referrals can place upon the EAP may preclude its staff from using the time-consuming techniques necessary to identify and ferret out these other, more costly problems.

As compared to alcoholism or severe depression, one might view work-family conflicts as trivial problems, paralleling many self-referrals. Further, an EAP could easily and quickly become swamped by requests for assistance in resolving work-family conflicts. The costs this may create for the organization are default costs; that is, the EAP will by necessity neglect other, perhaps more costly, problems that it otherwise would have attended to were it not for these new demands.

Given the typical human desire for maximum positive feedback about successful performance, EAP staff might move in the direction of giving greater emphasis to work–family problems if it appeared that these problem resolutions were much more tractable than other problems in its typical caseload. In other words, EAP staff could feel much better about their own success if they dealt primarily with things that could be readily fixed.

2. Employee assistance program counselors may not possess the appropriate skills to alleviate work-family role conflicts. A medicalized perspective dominates EAP work wherein problems in functioning and job performance are initially interpreted as stemming from individual-level pathologies such as substance abuse or psychiatric illness (Roman, 1980; Conrad and Schneider, 1980). For better or worse, using the methods developed by psychiatrists in their *Diagnostic and Statistical Manual of Mental Disorder*, diagnostic scrutiny of almost anyone can reveal behavioral and psychological malfunction. In such a framework, the outcomes of stresses rather than their sources may become the prevailing focus. The EAP's involvement with work-family issues could lead to a broadening of the application of such diagnoses and explanatory frameworks to employees in work-family role conflict situations, an outcome of dubious value indeed.

This reasoning leads to the conclusion that while the EAP model may have useful application to alleviating work-family role conflict issues in the workplace, adding this responsibility to an existing EAP could lead to many undesirable side effects. However, a new but coordinated service built around the EAP model offers considerable promise. This may not be as easy as it sounds, for anecdotal information indicates that in some settings work-family role conflict reduction already is an EAP responsibility, the assignments made by human resource managers without any addition of resources or competencies. The disjunction of such new assignments from the core of what EAPs can most effectively accomplish occurs because of a lack of adequate "consumer education" for executives in both line management and in the human resources function about EAPs (Roman et al., 1987). Such poor understanding of the purpose of an EAP can result in the EAP becoming an organization's generic social problem reduction unit, a sort of trashcan toward which work-family issues would be automatically directed.

A pitfall in developing a new work-family-oriented activity is the lack of a clear definition of the skills appropriate for providing such services. The haphazard way in which EAP activities have evolved over the past 20 years has meant that only recently have clear standards of job performance for EAP administrators and counselors begun to emerge. A work-family assistance role would have to go through this developmental process.

If not organized in a way that is clearly separate from the EAP, such a new service might easily undermine the EAP by its attraction to EAP personnel. From our own work we have found that much "core" EAP work involves dealing with different personal and interpersonal problems affecting employees' lives, especially in the areas of substance abuse and psychiatric disorder. In light of this and other job stresses such as occupational isolation, perceptions of organizational inequity, and ambiguous supervisory relationships spawned by the lack of EAP workers' supervision by those with EAP skills, EAP workers are rather easily "drawn away" from their core activities and attracted to roles in which client problems are solved quickly and positive feedback about one's impact is readily available.

However, the EAP model does offer a means for a reasonable and equitable pattern of involvement for employers to aid with reducing work-family role conflicts. An existing EAP offers an ideal setting for nurturing the development of a new referral service for work–family role conflicts, but care must be taken to assure that while both use a similar model and cross-referral opportunities should be assured, their functions are essentially separate.

XII. DISAGGREGATING THE WORK-FAMILY ROLE CONFLICT ISSUE

Instead of lumping together all issues involving work-family role conflicts, it may be useful to partially disaggregate them. This allows us to consider "degrees of appropriateness" of assigning alleviation of these conflicts to the workplace or to the individual employee who is experiencing the conflict.

A first "cut" that is immediately apparent stems from the fact that increased women's participation in the labor force has not been matched by decreased male participation. This leads to a void in many households of available time to maintain the home and care for children. Thus the necessity to continue to accomplish these tasks is one seedbed for role conflicts, perceived or real.

A second such seedbed derives from the fact that while household/child care roles may become strained or partially "empty," they are supplanted by the new roles of the female adult in the household functioning as an employee, in some instances oriented toward developing an occupational career. Working at a job, employed by an organization, and developing a career comprises a new and potentially complex set of roles. The seedbed for conflict is the contingencies for the female adult's role partners, both the male spouse as well as children, and possibly other family members. The contingencies center on the location of employment of the two adult workers. Locations may be chosen in order for each partner to try to maximize work, career, familial, and life satisfaction. If not, various types of negotiated orders may develop, or the family system may continue to adapt to the strains that result from choices of location that might be called "unbalanced."

Many arguments can be marshaled against the idea that employers should bear responsibility for dealing with issues resulting from the first seedbed, but there may be equally compelling arguments for organizational responsibility for dealing with role conflicts from the second seedbed.

One way of viewing employer/organizational responsibility looks at emergent "stressors" as more or less contingencies of employment. From such a perspective, illustration can be drawn from employer responsibility for physical injuries or illnesses stemming directly from the demands of work. Critical is the contrast between this work-health arena and the work-family arena. Through a variety of pieces of federal and state legislation, the United States has a national "worker compensation policy" that places employees outside the mercy of their employer should they become injured, sick, and/or unable to continue working. Indeed, employers bear all or some of the responsibility for the consequences of workplace injuries or illnesses.

But one does not need a depth of legal sophistication to be aware of the scope and intensity of litigation centered on whether or not certain injuries or illnesses indeed result from contingencies of employment (Nelkin and Brown, 1984; Rosner and Markowitz, 1987). A whole set of occupational activity centers on various forms of detective work to establish or contest whether employers' negligence versus employee's physical condition, their drug use, their carelessness or their knowledge of work rules, validates or nullifies employer responsibility for costs associated with injuires or illnesses alleged to be caused by some aspect of the organization of work or the work environment.

Might such contentiousness come to surround the question of family-related contingencies associated with employment contracts? Illustrative are the consequences flowing from an employer's decision to hire both members of a married couple. As both members of a professional couple are committed to careers, it is increasingly common for the hiring of both to be a contingency for the hiring of one. While good "fits" for both partners in the organization are possible, this is not likely. Experience in academia indicates that this almost always involves a situation in which one member of the couple is the desired hire, and accommodations are made to include the partner. Obviously, this can be a polarized situation in which one partner is badly wanted and the other "barely fits." Such an imbalance might be a function of the intensity of the desire for one of the hires. Parenthetically, experience in the organization after employment can reverse the desirability of the respective partners.

Regardless of outcome, within the current context of understanding of the employment contract, such hiring is an attempt by the organization to maximize. In so doing, it creates obligations for itself. Likely it will try to contain those obligations. This calls for strategic planning on the part of the job candidates. During employment negotiations the couple might be wise to anticipate contingencies they may face as a consequence of their own projected family plans. In the highly charged atmosphere of the employer's promises in the attempt to "close the deal," the couple might make a parallel attempt to extract specific commitments from the employer to deal with these future events.

Does such a pattern of hiring involve a long-term organizational commitment to resolve the work-family role conflicts that eventually emerge for either or both members of this couple? Such hires imply such a commitment, with the consequence that it would be expected for the employer to avoid placing new role demands on one member of the couple to such an extent that family life was notably disrupted. While deliberate avoidance of creating or exacerbating work-family role conflicts with such hires seems a reasonable expectation, how far should such a principle extend? Specifically, does it apply two work-family role conflicts of a couple that reflect voluntary choices on their part, such as the arrival of children or changes in the couple's responsibility for the care of dependents such as elderly parents?

Over time, the troublesome side effects of such employer commitments can grow. In the context of such commitments, for example, special treatment can readily lead to perceived inequities among other employees over both the short and long term. Further, experience may disprove the earlier wisdom of the investment in the dual hire. The perceived value of one or both members of the couple may not "pan out," or their presence as a couple may prove demoralizing for other organizational members with partners employed elsewhere. The impact on the couple of life-cycle changes may have all sorts of reverberations (Lobel, 1991), but we would persist with the observation that this may represent a situation in which the organization's hiring actions committed it to a path of minimizing work-family role conflicts for the dually employed couple.

How does this scenario apply to the couple established from among the existing employees in a work organization; that is, the consequences of "Cupid on the job?" The increased workforce participation of women has significantly increased both the role of the workplace as a setting for mate selection as well as the prevalence of dual-employed couples in workplaces in which the couples were formed after employment. Parenthetically, the use of the work organization as a site for mate selection may have some unrecognized and remarkable values in enhancing the quality of mating decisions. Sharing a workplace can enhance the information the potential members of the couple have about each other, information that may usefully inform their decision to commit to one another (e.g., what their potential partners' job role requirements really entail, their prescribed interaction partners, and how their potential partners treat their peers, superiors, and/or subordinates at work).

Consistent with the logic about employer responsibility for couples hired together, there may be little or no obligation on the part of an employer to accommodate to the work–family role conflicts of those who become married after employment. Why? Obviously because the members of the couple were exercising free choice in selecting a mate from within the workplace. There is no reason why persons making such choices should enjoy advantages over those whose partners are employed elsewhere or are not employed at all.

These examples and their implications for employer responsibility can be expanded to other combinations of dual employment. Some employers become actively involved in facilitating the employment in another organization of a partner of someone they want to hire. When there has been this active involvement in "setting up" a dual employment arrangement for a couple, does the proactive employer have an obligation relative to the spouse should the arrangements sour? Similarly, what obligations exist when an individual in a dual career marriage is hired with the employer's full awareness of the contingencies that this individual faces in regard to continuity of his or her spouse's employment? If the employer finds it necessary to geographically transfer the employee at a later date, is there an obligation to attempt to find placement for the spouse in the new community?

The bottom line in the present cultural setting is that employers are obligated to the extent that they have made binding legal commitments relating to how employment arrangements bear upon family arrangements. Such legal agreements are certainly a possibility, but when they are not made, the employer is bound only by ethics.

Following the logic of such contingencies and agreements, we can consider employer responsibility for role conflicts that emerge between the household and the job. For example, an employer would be expected to provide child care benefits if having children was a contingency of employment. Further, an employer could be expected to provide eldercare benefits if having an elderly relative in residence was a contingency of employment. These examples demonstrates the absurdity of attempting to coerce employers to provide family-related fringe benefits that are going to be of equal benefit to all employees.

XIII. CONCLUSION

The important conclusion derived from this discussion is that in the absence of a national family policy, in a limited number of employment decisions (a number that may escalate in the future for those organizations hiring professional-level employees) the employer may be obligated to respond to work-family conflicts in a legalistic context. Otherwise, there is no formal responsibility relative to employees who decide to bear and raise children or decide to include in their residential arrangements other dependents. This also holds true for couples that are created in an organization after their employment.

This provides a general logic for considering the issue of workplace responsibility for providing child or other dependent care services. In addition to the problems that have already been mentioned in styling such services to adequately meet the needs of all employees, it is obvious in derivations from these examples that provision of such fringe benefits is not equitable to employees who do not make certain choices, unless of course they are offered a benefit of equal value that is of utility to them.

These conclusions seem harsh, and support the antifamily caricature of employers that was criticized earlier in this chapter. To look in a quite different direction, the example of the couples created subsequent to employment points towards a nonobligatory approach for organizations to use in approaching work-family role conflict issues. How does the example make this point?

While employers have no particular obligations to employees who became a couple with the same employer subsequent to employment, it is absurd to suggest that employers should refuse to recognize such emergent family situations or should ignore the conflicts that are generated between work and family obligations. Organizational cultures can be supportive of individual welfare without inappropriate involvement in direct services. In terms of a positive cultural response to employees' personal integrity and well-being, the marriage of two employees should engender organizational acknowledgment, support, and even celebration. The same thing holds true for the joyful support that should accompany employees' new parenthood, and the sympathetic support for employees who become burdened with disabled or impaired dependents.

In any employment situation, any type, level, or combination of fringe benefits can be reasonably offered in response to labor market competition or as a deliberate exercise in demonstrating corporate social responsibility. There are certainly a significant number of large and relatively wealthy American corporations wherein management and ownership assign high priority to family-related outcomes. Providing these services as a means of enhancing a particular organizational culture is distinctively different from responding to perceived or real external pressures. Providing these fringe benefits as a specific vehicle for cherished corporate values demonstrates a proper workplace role, and serves to help sustain an important distinction of the role of American workplaces in resolving broader societal and community problems. Barriers to duplicating such direct services in smaller workplaces have already been noted, but there are fewer barriers for support of a family-positive organizational culture in such settings.

In terms of the "second seedbed" described above, work organizations may respond to the "voluntary" work-family role conflict issues within the context of organizational social responsibility. Such an attitude stands as a practical alternative to workplaces serving as societal vehicles for implementing some hodgepodge version of a currently nonexistent national policy supportive of the nuclear family and the welfare of all children. As pointed out early in the chapter, Rein (1982) suggests that "social objectives" of the government may flow through private enterprise by governmental mandate, regulation, stimulation, or support. It is difficult to see where any of these processes are really in place relative to work–family conflict resolution. The fact that there is no national family policy should be the foundation for consideration of these issues. Planned change can await the arrival of such a policy in the United States while constituencies might organize to press for its enactment.

Our goal in this chapter has been to examine work-family linkage issues in the context of employer/organizational responsibility. Our reflections on a series of fundamental concerns, concluding with reflections on organizational social responsibility, suggest that employers may smooth performance and productivity through offering information and referral services vis-à-vis work-family role conflict reduction. This is a conceptually based recommendation, for it embeds principles that need to be considered before organizations become deeply involved in direct services.

Despite their attraction in some respects, the provision of direct services by employers has not met with any documentable degree of success on any criterion yet reported from systematic research. There is little such quality research to consider at present. The value of additional research should be recognized, and directed more broadly than program evaluation. An important question is how such research could be funded.

It is no surprise that in the absence of a national family policy, there is also no funding agency to support family-oriented research. Exceptions are projects that might touch upon family issues that meet the standards and goals of the National Institutes of Health. Research directed toward pathologies among children may be supported by the National Institute on Child Health and Human Development, and research on problems of the elderly might be supported by the National Institute on Aging. It is somewhat ironic that there is also no designated federal agency for research on workplace issues, save a tiny amount of research funding available through the U.S. Department of Labor or very limited support offered by the National Institute on Occupational Safety and Health for projects directed toward workplace safety or occupational health hazards. Otherwise, family and worksite research proposals must compete on their general scientific merit with the vast range of projects submitted to the National Science Foundation.

Research studies also may be supported by private agencies and foundations. An examination of the support acknowledged in published studies reviewed for this chapter suggests private foundation support is prominent. Such support is very limited compared to federal funding, and is not directly accessible by most researchers. Finally, it is possible for work organizations to support directly studies related to work-family role conflict issues. While such sources of support are also very limited, it may also be the case that such support would be primarily concerned with limited evaluations centered on the supporting work organization. Given this overall picture of limited and narrow support available for research, there is not a good base for optimism about the development in the near future of a strong database to support either macro or micropolicy decisions affecting work organizations.

Despite these shortfalls, a wealth of demographic data supports some other final observations. Of all the criteria that might be used to demonstrate the existence of costly problems associated with work-family role conflicts, attention should be drawn to the impact of child welfare today on the workforce of tomorrow. While seeming high-blown and rhetorical, this kind of practical demography is about as concrete as one can get, despite the reluctance of American leadership to move away from their self-absorption and consider the future outcomes of today's choices and behaviors.

This is not to minimize the immediate pains felt by parents and children caught between work and home responsibilities, but to underline that these problems are indeed subject to "intergenerational transmission." The absence of policies today may be evident in the next decades when the costs of ignoring the efficacy of the future workforce become evident. Using organizational analysis for a final time, failures to develop serious support for a national family policy may represent a failure to tap into concepts that are meaningful in the "strategic planning" of workplace leaders who are repeatedly urged to implement "quality" and to look toward the future. It may be that focus on the workforce of tomorrow and beyond is a considerably more effective means for garnering the attention of key influential persons other than a focus on those who, while they may be troubled by role conflicts and strains, are continuing to seek employment and come to work.

ACKNOWLEDGMENTS

Partial support from research grants R01-AA-07250 and R01-AA-07218 from the National Institute on Alcohol Abuse and Alcoholism and grant no. R01-DA-07417 from the National Institute on Drug Abuse is gratefully acknowledged. The comments of Dr. Joan Kraft and Dr. Robert T. Golembiewski on an earlier draft are much appreciated.

The perspectives of the first author (PMR) have been shaped in part by appointment from 1988 to 1991 as a member of the Panel on Employer Policies and Working Families of the National Research Council/National Academy of Sciences. Recommendations from that panel's deliberations are found in Ferber and O'Farrell (1991), pp. 179–201.

REFERENCES

Aldous, J. (1990). Specification and speculation concerning the politics of workplace family policies. *J. of Family Issues, 11*: 355–367.

Aldrich, H. E. (1979). *Organizations and Environments*. Prentice Hall, Englewood Cliffs, N.J.

Aldrich, H., and Marsden, P. V. (1988). Environments and organizations. In *Handbook of Sociology*. (N. J. Smelser, ed.), Sage Publications, Newbury Park, Calif., pp. 361–392.

Allen, J. P. (1988). European infant care leaves: Foreign perspectives on the integration of work and family roles. In *The Parental Leave Crisis: Toward a National Policy*. (E. F. Zigler and M. Frank, eds.), Yale University Press, New Haven, Conn.

Auerbach, J. D. (1990). Employer-supported child care as a women-responsive policy. *J. of Family Issues, 11*: 384–400.

Bales, R. F. (1946). Cultural differences in rates of alcoholism. *Quarterly Journal of Studies on Alcohol, 6*: 480–499.

Belsky, J. (1988). A reassessment of infant day care. pp. 100–119. In *The Parental Leave Crisis: Toward a National Policy* (E. F. Zigler and M. Frank, eds.), Yale University Press, New Haven, Conn.

Blum, T. C., and Roman, P. (1989). Employee assistance programs and human resources management. In *Research in Personnel and Human Resources Management*, vol. 7 (K. M. Rowland and G. R. Ferris, eds.), JAI Press, Greenwich, Conn., pp. 259–312.

Brandes, S. D. (1976). *American Welfare Capitalism: 1880–1940*. University of Chicago Press, Chicago.

Chafetz, M. (1962). *Liquor: The Servant of Man*. Little Brown, Boston.

Coltrane, S. (1990). Birth timing and the division of labor in dual-earner families. *J. of Family Issues, 11*: 157–181.

Conrad, P. and Schneider, J. (1980). *Deviance and Medicalization*. C. Mosby, St. Louis.

Deal, T. E., and Kennedy, A. A. (1982). *Corporate Cultures: The Rites and Rituals of Corporate Life*. Addison-Wesley, Reading, Mass.

Dobbin, F. (1992). The origins of private social insurance: Public policy and fringe benefits in America, 1920–1950. *American Journal of Sociology, 97*: 1416–1450.

Dunn, J. (1991). Revolution in education. *Georgia Tech Alumni Magazine, 67*: 40–44.

Edwards, R. C. (1979). *Contested Terrain: The Transformation of the Workplace in the Twentieth Century*. Basic Books, New York.

Eggebeen, D. J., and Hawkins, A. J. (1990). Economic need and wives' employment." *J. of Family Issues, 11*: 48–66.

Ferber, M. A., and O'Farrell, B. (1991). *Work and Family: Policies for a Changing Work Force, A National Research Council Report*. National Academy Press, Washington, D.C.

Fernandez, J. (1986). *Child Care and Corporate Productivity: Resolving Family/Work Conflicts*. D. C. Heath, Lexington, Mass.

Fishman, D. B., and Cherniss, C., eds. (1990). *The Human Side of Corporate Competitiveness*. Sage Publications, Newbury Park, Calif.

Fogarty, M. P., Rapoport, R., and Rapoport, R. N. (1971). *Sex, Career and Family*. Sage Publications, Beverly Hills, Calif.

Foote, A., and Erfurt, J. C. (1991). Effects of EAP follow-up on prevention of relapse among substance abuse clients. *J. of Studies on Alcohol, 52*: 241–248.

Frank, M., and Lipner, R. (1988). History of maternity leave in Europe and the United States. In *The Parental Leave Crisis: Toward a National Policy* (E. F. Zigler and M. Frank, eds.), Yale University Press, New Haven, Conn.

Freedman, J. (1988). The changing composition of the family and the workplace. In *The Parental Leave Crisis: Toward a National Policy* (E. F. Zigler and M. Frank, eds.), Yale University Press, New Haven, Conn.

Galinsky, E., and Stein, P. J. (1990). The impact of human resource policies on employees: Balancing work/family life. *J. of Family Issues, 11*: 368–383.

Geerken, M., and Gove, W. (1983). *At Home and at Work: The Family's Allocation of Labor*. Sage Publications, Beverly Hills, Calif.

Goff, S. J., Mount, M. K., and Jamison, R. L. (1990). Employer supported child care, work/family conflict, and absenteeism: A field study. *Personnel Psychology, 43*: 793–809.

Goldsmith, E. B., ed. (1989). *Work and Family: Theory, Research, and Applications*. Sage Publications, Newbury Park, Calif.

Googins, B. K. (1991). *Work/Family Conflicts: Private Lives, Public Responses*. Auburn House, New York.

Greenhaus, J. H. (1989). The intersection of work and family roles: Individual, interpersonal, and organizational issues. In *Work and Family: Theory, Research, and Applications* (E. B. Goldsmith, ed.), Sage Publications, Newbury Park, Calif.

Haas, L. (1990). Gender equality and social policy: Implications of a study of parental leave in Sweden. *J. of Family Issues, 11*: 401–423.

Jacoby, S. M. (1985). *Employing Bureaucracy: Managers, Unions and the Transformation of Work in American Industry, 1900–1945.* Columbia University Press, New York.

Jacoby, S. M., ed. (1991). *Masters to Managers: Historical and Comparative Perspectives on American Employers.* Columbia University Press, New York.

Kamerman, S. B. (1988). Maternity and parenting benefits: An international overview. In *The Parental Leave Crisis: Toward a National Policy* (E. F. Zigler and M. Frank, eds.), Yale University Press, New Haven, Conn.

Kamerman, S. B., and Kahn, A. J. (1981). *Child Care, Family Benefits and Working Parents: A Study in Comparative Policy.* Columbia University Press, New York.

Kessler-Harris, A. (1982). *Out to Work: A History of Wage-Earning Women in the United States.* Oxford University Press, New York.

Kingston, P. W. (1989). Studying the work-family connection: Atheoretical progress, ideological bias, and shaky foundations for policy. In *Work and Family: Theory, Research, and Applications* (E. B. Goldsmith, Sage Publications, Newbury Park, Calif.

Kline, M., and Cowan, P. A. (1989). Re-thinking the connections among "work and family" and well-being: A model for investigating employment and family work contexts. In *Work and Family: Theory, Research, and Applications* (E. B. Goldsmith, eds.), Sage Publications, Newbury Park, Calif.

Kossek, E. E. (1990). Diversity in child care assistance needs: Employee problems, preferences and work-related outcomes. *Personnel Psychology, 43*: 769–791.

Lobel, A. S. (1991). Allocation of investment in work and family roles: Alternative theories and implications for research. *Academy of Management Review, 16*: 507–521.

Mitchell, N. J. (1989). *The Generous Corporation.* Yale University Press, New Haven, Conn.

Morgan, H., and Tucker, K. (1991). *Companies that Care: The Most Family-Friendly Companies in America—What They Offer, and How They Got That Way.* Simon and Schuster, New York.

Nelkin, D., and Brown, M. S. (1984). *Workers at Risk: Voices from the Workplace.* University of Chicago Press, Chicago.

O'Rand, A. (1986). The hidden payroll: Employee benefits and the structure of workplace inequality. *Sociological Forum, 1*: 657–683.

Paul, B. D., ed. (1955). *Health, Culture and Community: Case Studies of Public Reactions to Health Programs.* Russell Sage Foundation, New York.

Raabe, P. H. (1990). The organizational effects of workplace family policies: Past weaknesses and recent progress toward improved research. *J. of Family Issues, 11*: 477–491.

Rein, M. (1982). The social policy of the firm. *Policy Sciences, 14*: 117–135.

Roman, P. (1980). Medicalization and social control in the workplace: Prospects for the 1980s. *J. of Applied Behavioral Sciences, 16*: 407–422.

Roman, P., and Blum, T. C. (1992). Employee assistance and drug screening programs. In *Treating Drug Problems*, vol. 2 (D. Gerstein and H. J. Harwood, eds.), National Academy of Sciences Press, Washington, D.C., pp. 197–244.

Roman, P., Blum, T. C., and Bennett, N. (1987). Educating organizational consumers about employee assistance programs. *Public Personnel Management, 16*: 299–312.

Rosner, D., and Markowitz, G. (1987). *Dying for Work: Workers' Safety and Health in Twentieth Century America.* Indiana University Press, Bloomington.

Sacks, K. B., and Remy, D. (1984). *My Troubles Are Going to Have Trouble with Me: Everyday Trials and Triumphs of Women Workers.* Rutgers University Press, New Brunswick, N.J.

Schroeder, P. (1988). Parental leave: The need for a federal policy. In *The Parental Leave Crisis: Toward a National Policy* (E. F. Zigler and M. Frank, eds.), Yale University Press, Conn.

Sonnenstuhl, W., and Trice, H. (1986). *Strategies for Employee Assistance Programs: The Crucial Balance* (Key Issues no. 30). ILR Press, Ithaca, N.Y.

Spector, M., and Kitsuse, J. (1977). *Constructing Social Problems.* Cummings Publishing Company, Menlo Park, Calif.

Thompson, J. (1967). *Organizations in Action.* McGraw-Hill, New York.

Trice, H. M., and Beyer, J. M. (1984). Work-related outcomes of the constructive confrontation strategy in a job-based alcoholism program. *J. of Studies on Alcohol, 45*: 393–404.

Trice, H. M., and Roman, P. M. (1972). *Spirits and Demons at Work: Alcohol and Other Drugs on the Job.* ILR Press of Cornell University, Ithaca, N.Y.

Walsh, D. C., Hingson, R. W., Merrigan, D. M., et al. (1991). A randomized trial of treatment options for alcohol-abusing workers. *New England Journal of Medicine, 325*: 775–782.

Ward, B. (April 1991). Corporations and kindergartens. *Sky, 20*: 28–39.

Waring, S. P. (1991). *Taylorism Transformed: Scientific Management Theory Since 1945*, University of North Carolina Press, Chapel Hill.

Zahavi, Gerald. (1988). *Workers, Managers and Welfare Capitalism*. University of Illinois Press, Urbana.

Zigler, E. F., and Frank, M., eds. (1988). *The Parental Leave Crisis: Toward a National Policy*. Yale University Press, New Haven, Conn.

14

Management Training and Development

Dorothy Olshfski

Rutgers University, Newark, New Jersey

Deborah Ann Cutchin

Rutgers University, New Brunswick, New Jersey

The quality of American private and public sector executives is critical to the maintenance of the American quality of life. Global competition and technological and scientific advances, as well as comunication and transportation innovations, make a chaotic and complex world. Coping will be difficult; managing will be challenging. Senior business and government executives will face the challenge of designing and implementing policies to respond to the problems and opportunities accompanying these changes. These executives must assume major roles in ensuring that their organizations are positioned for success.

Quality, excellence, productivity, and results are the current dominant themes in business management (Deming, 1986; Peters and Waterman, 1982). The public sector echoes these concerns while adding a customer-driven emphasis, often heard in business circles but a new element in public management (Osborne and Goebler, 1992). Business and government managers are exhorted to steamline their operations because, even with limited resources, their organizations are still expected to produce superior results. The trends in executive education mirror these directions in business and government, both in the topics covered and in current thinking about how to link education to business strategy or results (Schaeffer and Thomson, 1992; Bolt, 1989; Nilsson, 1987).

To assess how management education is responding to these challenges, this chapter examines management training programs, paying special attention to executive development. To distinguish among the array of programs packaged and marketed for managers, we categorize management training according to the extent to which the program integrates individual and organizational goals in its design. We also pay close attention to the evaluation processes used in the various training programs. The chaotic management training market that presently exists makes it difficult to make careful, reasoned decisions about management education. This chapter attempts to make some sense out of management education by presenting a clear picture of the available programs.

I. TRADITIONS IN MANAGEMENT EDUCATION

Understanding about executive behavior and education has changed to reflect both our knowledge and understanding about what executives do and what skills they need in order to do it. In the 1950s and 1960s the emphasis was on the "organization man" (Whyte, 1956), who specialized in who-you-know connections and relations between mentors and subordinates (Jennings, 1971). The management development programs, initiated after World War II, were built upon the success of training foremen during the previous quarter century. These early training programs, which originally dealt with specific technical detail, eventually included more and more material dealing with the effective management of people and principles of organization, thus helping break down the belief that good managers were born, not made (Bridgman, 1959, cited in Porter and McKibbin, 1988). Specific management education was further stimulated by Frederick Taylor's influential enphasis on the theme that managing was a higher-level skill than production (Zuboff, 1989). Easier access to college created by the GI Bill further strengthened the linkage between a college degree and entrance into private or public sector management.

Training administered by private companies grew from about 5% in 1946 to 50% of all large firms by the 1950s. It was largely conducted in-house and the content and format of the courses laid the basis for the management development activities that occur today (Bridgman, 1959, cited in Porter and McKibbin, 1988). However, the training effort often neglected program evaluation. In a time of surplus and American business success, perhaps, the training coordinators paid scarce attention to cost-effectiveness or measurable outcomes resulting from management education (Thayer, 1989).

In the late 1960s emphasis shifted in the nature of training as well as in the general view of executive behavior. Alvin Toffler's (1970) *Future Shock* signaled the emergence of a new concern: stress associated with trying to cope with too many changes in too short a time. Other researchers identified shifts in motivation away from extrinsic rewards (pay, benefits, and job security) to such intrinsic satisfactions as self-development and self-actualization (Katz and Georgopoulous, 1971). Adapting to fast-paced change, minimizing the negative effects of rapid change on organizational relationships and process, and accommodating changing patterns of needs and motives became the foci of training. Training was organized around the growing discipline of organizational behavior (OB) and the resulting increasingly sophisticated understanding of individual and group behavior. The shift in training was evident by including in the training program new topics and techniques such as team-building, T groups, sensitivity training, and the use of psychological self-assessment instruments (Golembiewski, 1972; 1979). Teaching management skills began to reflect the complexity that characterized the interactive nature of managing and leading people.

But not everyone at this time was impressed with training departments. Indeed, Robert Townsend (1970) characterized training as a "corporate kindergarten" and recommended elimination of the "babysitters."

Recently, Porter and McKibbin (1988) proposed that management development programs have built upon the content and format of the late 1960s. They have grown both outward to include a larger number of companies, as well as upward to include a larger percentage of middle- and upper-level managers. Drawing on a survey of senior business and government executives, Bolt (1985) made two points. Senior executives were playing a more directive role in shaping the training curricula, and the training emphasized results and the implementation of company strategy and objectives.

Organizationally supported training in the public sector, also grew, although with much less support than training has received in the private sector. In 1986, federal training programs alone cost an estimated $633 million a year (Spindler, 1992). At the federal level, the establishment of the Senior Executive Service in 1978 included a provision requiring executive development for the upper ranks of the career service. At the state and local level, training efforts concentrate on first-line supervisors and middle managers due to the preponderance of direct service delivery (Flanders, 1989). The support of state management training is reflected in the trend to adopt the certified public manager program (CPM) as an important training vehicle. Begun in Georgia in 1976, CPM is a successful training program in supervision and middle management skills. Eleven states operate as full-fledged members of the CPM consortium and seven additional states are in various stages of the accreditation process (Van Wart, 1992). Some evidence suggests that municipal managers believe that training has the strongest potential for improving productivity in their organizations (Poister and Streib, 1989).

Although concern over falling productivity and Japanese competition were present during the Reagan years, the 1980s were largely characterized by a boom economy. The linkage between strategy and outcome was not closely monitored. Porter and McKibbin (1988) observed that the business community vocalized strong support for executive development, but generally did not follow through with concrete action.

The 1990s find the business community concerned with survival in a fiercely competitive economic market. No less affected, the public sector tries to do more with less, and government officials are repeatedly faced with citizen dissatisfaction and tax revolts. This difficult environment generates compelling reasons for giving close attention to the linkage between strategy and outcome in both sectors. Under this pressure, management education is focusing on measurable results.

II. LOCUS OF TRAINING PROGRAMS

Management development programs are designed and implemented by universities, consulting firms, or in-house training departments. Porter and McKibbin's (1988) extensive survey of university providers and corporate executives found that the vast majority of all firms used all three types of training.

In recent years, executive training has become the fastest growth area for universities (Watson, 1988). Between 1962 and 1985, the number of executive development programs fielded by business schools increased by 770%, and both business and university executives expect that participation to increase in the next 10-year period (Porter and McKibbin, 1988).

Public and private sector organizations employ university-based training to fill niches that in-house programs cannot accommodate. Corporate directors of management development identified the advantages of university programs as presenting the opportunity for the participants to interact with managers from other organizations and to gain the broadest exposure to new ideas in a field (Porter and McKibbin, 1988). Nonetheless, these programs vary widely among universities with respect to clientele, faculty qualifications, and program focus. Furthermore, there is no agreement on what precisely constitutes leadership or executive development, nor is there any commonality among the universities concerning whether to focus on skills or concepts (Spindler, 1992).

Training programs provided by consulting firms, which operate under pressure to make money and without the support provided by university backing, vary wildly in their quality, design, implementation, and level of sophistication. Independent vendors are attractive to organizations because they tend to be able to provide highly specialized programs or unique services (Porter and McKibbin, 1988). Consistently, the main advantage of the consulting firms, as seen by the client's in-house development expert, is their ability to offer a level of expertise unavailable elsewhere (Porter and McKibbin, 1988). Management education firms range from the Center for Creative Leadership in North Carolina—which provides research support and high-quality programs—to transient firms or individuals that offer programs pulled together by unqualified executives. Quality control is one of the key issues for commercial vendors since entry into the field is easy and enforceable standards of quality do not exist. Word-of-mouth has to do as a regulating force.

Finally, firms presently utilize in-house management development centers more extensively then any other format, and over the next 10 years that use is expected to increase. The perceived advantage of corporate in-house programs is their ability to provide training specific to organizational needs in a cost-effective manner using company expertise (Porter and McKibbin, 1988). Increasingly, in-house management development programs are considered to be powerful tools to initiate organization change (Tichy, 1989; Nilsson, 1987). In-house residental training facilities are a component of many company development programs. For example, GE's Crotonville facility services approximately 8000 participants per year, and is seen as an important lever for change at GE (Tichy, 1989). Similarly, the federal government utilizes the Office of Personal Management's (OPM) executive development centers to conduct residential training for federal executives, but on a modest scale.

Regardless of the locus of the educational effort, tremendous variance exists in measures of quality, content, and delivery of executive development programs. The three types of providers participate in all the categories of executive development programs outlined below.

III. CATEGORIES OF MANAGEMENT DEVELOPMENT

We categorize management development programs according to the extent to which the program involves a conscious effort to link individual and organizational goals. The first two categories, indoctrination and traditional programs, do not make an explicit attempt to create these linkages. Instead, they focus on either individual or organizational goals, but not both in a conscious fashion. The latter categories, especially the tailored program and process models, make a conscious effort to integrate these two goals while using real-world problems to focus the learning experience.

The choice between categories can be consequential in many ways. Generally, for example, the less integrated the program goals, the less labor intensive the effort. Hence, more students can be accommodated by a single instructor. Conversely, the more integrated the program, the fewer the number of students that can be accommodated by a single instructor.

The appropriateness of each of the categories of management development is dependent upon the goals of the participants and/or the organization that sponsors them. If the goals are clear and the expectations of the participants are aligned with those goals, then there is a better chance that the management program will be effective.

A. Indoctrination Programs

This category will always be with us. If nothing else, every organization needs to communicate to new managers how-we-do-things-here information. In addition, experienced employees also need to learn information about new organizational policies or processes. Furthermore, an increasingly diverse workplace in the United States and a multicultural management operation globally both require indoctrination programs to provide an overview of an organization's standard operating procedures, as well as an introduction to the organization's culture. The most efficient way for the organization to communicate this type of information is to hold large classes. These sessions are strictly to inform, sometimes in great detail, where an organization stands on a particular point and what behaviors are expected from the organization's members.

Typical programs in this category include introductory programs on company or agency philosophy, rules and procedures, employee rights and responsibilities, and employee benefits. This category also includes programs in affirmative action, ethical decision making, sexual harassment, and AIDS policy.

Virtually all organizations use indoctrination programs as a relatively simple form of management training with direct and explicit aims. This type of program is not labor intensive and at different times is used at all levels of all organizations.

Evaluation of the training effectiveness depends, as always, on the goals of the indoctrination. If the program is informational, presented in oral and written form, then a formal training evaluation may be quite simple. If the indoctrination training is concerned with implementing a company policy that requires specific behaviors, then the inclusion of measures of the desired behavior on the managers' performance appraisal would be part of an adequate evaluation strategy. For example, placing affirmative action hiring and promotion goals on a manager's performance contract, or list of yearly objectives, can provide a yardstick to measure the success of an affirmative action program and the manager's progress in implementing agency policy.

B. Traditional Management Training

This second category of management development refers to training organized to parallel the academic disciplines in universities. The goal is to impart knowledge using typical classroom practices—lecture and discussion—as the primary mode of delivery. The subject matter, not an organizational problem, drives these programs. And although the treatment of the topic may be highly sophisticated and detailed, the linkage between the topic and the issues and problems in a specific organization are largely or entirely left to the learner to uncover.

This format is appropriate for members at all levels in the organization, although the subject matter will change to suit the hierarchical and educational level of the participants. This type of training is a cost-effective way to convey knowledge, since many participants can work with a single instructor. Machine-guided and taped instruction are included in this category and further enhance cost-effectiveness. Also, the traditional training format is excellent for teaching or improving technical skills, as well as for informing participants about current thinking in a discipline. At the executive level, this is an appropriate format to inform top managers about subjects of current interest: international economics, information about a specific foreign country or region of the world, the impact of changes in government tax or regulatory policy, or current statistical measurement techniques.

At the individual level, the goals relate to acquiring knowledge, skill, or information, so tests are the standard method of evaluation. Teachers rate the participants according to how well they demonstrate that the knowledge has been acquired. At the organizational level, a traditional training program designed to teach a skill that has direct and current applications in the organization often can be evaluated in terms of measures of increase in operating efficiency.

The linkage between increased nontechnical individual knowledge and organizational outcomes is harder to pin down. Unlike improving technical skills, which can lead directly to increased organizational effectiveness and which can be easily tested, goals associated with mastering softer skills—for example, strategic thinking or planning, business ethics, or public policy making—provide a more tenuous and not-so-easily-testable linkage between individual skill and organizational outcomes. Nonetheless, if the participants and the instructor understand the need being addressed, the traditional method of training works very well, especially at the individual level for skill or knowledge enhancement.

C. Insight

Management programs designed to convey or develop insight rely on the assumption that a good manager knows his or her individual strengths, weaknesses, skills, and likely behaviors. Further, possessing this knowledge allows the manager to deploy him- or herself and subordinates to the best advantage. Consequently, typical programs aim to help generate this self-knowledge or insight concerning such topics as leadership and thinking style, communication, interpersonal orientation, and team-building skills. Development programs that fit into this category include outdoor experiences, like Outward Bound (Bolt, 1989), an assessment center designed as a managerial development exercise (Boehm and Hoyle, 1977; Thornton and Byham, 1982), and programs built around the Meyers-Briggs type indicators (Meyers, 1962; Keirsey and Bates, 1984) and life-styles inventories (Lafferty, 1989).

Insight programs may stand alone, or be part of a broader development program. They are also appropriate and commonly employed at all levels of management. These programs range from low to medium in labor intensiveness. Generally, outdoor experience programs and assessment center exercises have a higher participant-instructor ratio than pen-and-paper psychological test programs.

The knowledge offered by these programs is not limited to a single academic subject, although the vehicle for insight may be drawn from a particular discipline. The debriefing discussions and the ultimate applications of that knowledge often can extend to a wide range of management activities. Insight programs frequently link individual development with organizational improvement only through the implicit assumption that individual knowledge or skill improvement will produce organizational improvements. This transfer problem has received scant research attention.

The linkages here are difficult for measuring both individual and organizational improvements. Over time, it is possible to measure individual skill improvement through the use of individual development plans based on managerial weaknesses or problems identified through insight-based development programs, but the research data are scarce. Also in this category, Golembiewski (1972) identified substantial and consistent personal changes, especially with respect to sensitivity training as a vehicle to provide skills and attitudes appropriate for team building, although the linkages to enhanced organizational performance were not as strong. Outdoor-type experiences are popular, but much of the supporting evidence is anecdotal (Bolt, 1989).

As far as evaluating organizational outcomes, if the managers accept the assumptions undergirding these programs, and the insight-based program does provide self-knowledge (this is testable), then that may be acceptable until further research is available. Insight-based management development programs ideally endeavor to transfer the training into the texture and contours of specific management systems. This requires subtle evaluation measures.

D. Trend-Related Programs

Trend-related programs are organized around a current managerial problem or a process, not a particular discipline. This type of management training usually draws from a number of disciplines so it typically does not fit a single academic subject matter. Trend-related programs have a more interdisciplinary focus than the traditional program format. They are linked to issues that are looming out there in the environment that have been picked up in the business or popular literature as a trend in management. Some recent trend-related programs include programs dealing with managing diversity, total quality management (TQM), quality circles, or managing your boss.

The presentation format used in trend-related programs is similar to the traditional category but with greater likelihood that case studies and packaged simulations will be used. The simulations and case studies are generic, not organization-specific. These programs tend to be slightly more labor intensive than the traditional format because the simulations may limit the size of the group that can be accommodated. Simulations tend to limit size either because of limitations of the technology, as in the case of computer simulations, or in order to provide maximum opportunity for interaction among the participants, as in the case of all-person simulations.

These programs are excellent for disseminating cutting-edge knowledge, as well as for providing the participants with the vocabulary associated with the new or current process or progam. At the individual level, the knowledge-based component of these programs is measureable. The instructor may evaluate the participants by using tests that ask the participants to demonstrate their knowledge by answering questions about the topic, or by using projects that ask the participants to demonstrate their knowledge by applying the concept or process to a problem in the workplace and then documenting the attempt.

Measuring organizational outcomes is more problematic. The key issues for this type of format is that on-the-job applications of much of the material taught in the trend-related programs frequently require systemic interventions. For example, a successful TQM program requires top-level support for an organizationwide effort. Hence, a single manager working in a single department, or even a single division, often will become frustrated. Also, because these programs concentrate on breadth rather than depth, and because they tend to be generic rather than agency-specific, they often expend little effort to help the participants make linkages between ongoing organizational efforts and the new program or process.

Trend-related program participants are asked to think about something differently and to acquire new skills, but without a specific plan accepted at the top levels of the organization about implementation of the processes and programs discussed in the development sessions, implementation of the trend-related program often will be thwarted. The level of integration of individual development and organizational goals depends upon whether or not there is top-level organizational support for these large-scale efforts. Trend-related programs do an excellent job of teaching managers and executives to talk the talk; but walking the walk is frequently neglected.

E. Tailored Programs

Using real work problems as grounding for the training, tailored programs emphasize improving individual-level managerial skills and knowledge in pursuit of solving an organizational problem. The focus is on thinking, doing, problem solving, and long-term organizational strategies, the hope being that the knowledge gained and skills developed will have broad applications to organizational problems.

The tailored program model is designed around an unresolved, carefully packaged policy or strategy problem. Prior to the beginning of the program, the problem is identified and defined and the program is built around that problem. The executive-learners are given basic data and analysis concerning the problem they are to address. They are also given access to the key organizational participants as well as to other resource experts in the substantive area of the problem or associated management processes and behaviors. The participants then work as a consulting group to produce analysis and recommendations; that is, while they go about solving an organizational problem, they are also analyzing *how* they are solving the problem. Ultimately, the executive-participants are supposed to solve an organizational issue, and in the process, they are to analyze, evaluate, and hone their managerial skills and behaviors.

Examples of the tailored program model include the Rocky Mountain Program at the University of Colorado (Bauman and Weschler, 1992); the Tennessee Government Executive Institute in Tennessee (Cunningham and Olshfski, 1988); the New Jersey Municipal Managers Program (Cutchin, 1990); and the executive program at the GE Crotonville facility (Tichy, 1989). Although these programs are ongoing, the structure of the management development exercise changes each session to reflect the new problem.

The Tennessee Government Executive Institute, during different sessions, tackled the development of a state plan for managing solid waste, planning a youth employment strategy, and designing a state plan for managing state parks. In each of these cases, the problem was defined prior to the arrival of the participants and in consultation with the relevant state department secretary. The state department secretary agreed to become involved, usually by presenting a session or sending the relevant state administrator. The administrator also agreed to provide some access to the department's documents and data files, as well as to be present for the presentation of the completed final report. The report ultimately was sent to the governor.

The executive-participants, acting as a consulting team (or teams, depending upon the project), were required to collect and analyze data, consider alternatives and consequences of the proposed actions, and make recommendations to resolve the problem. Throughout the process, and in addition to the substantive assistance provided, the participants were provided with numerous occasions to examine and evaluate their own behaviors with respect both to working with the other managers and to contributing to the solution of the problem.

Well-designed tailored programs aim to produce what Argyris and Schön (1978) have termed double-loop learning. The goal of double-loop learning is to connect the detection of errors not only to strategies and assumptions for effective performance but to the very norms that define performance. It goes beyond simply correcting the problem. Double-loop learning attempts to correct the behaviors or processes that caused the original error (Argyris, 1991; Argyris and Schön, 1978). The tailored program format explicitly links individual learning with organization change by requiring the manager-as-organizational-analyst to make adjustments both at the organizational and individual levels.

Tailored programs are more labor intensive than those mentioned above because of the extensive use of experts in both the substantive field of the group's problem as well as in the self-analysis and individual skills part of the program. Tailored programs also require full-time administrators who act to ensure the participants are able to integrate the separate sections of the development program into a coherent picture. This requires a substantial commitment of time and energy on the part of the program administrators (Bauman and Weschler, 1992; Cunningham and Olshfski, 1988).

These programs emphasize practice over theory, and actual experience rather than vicarious experience; they also are flexible and multidisciplinary. The topics and skills addressed in the training do not fit into any standard academic categories. Each tailored program is custom-made for each executive development cohort. Unlike the other training categories mentioned above which can be used many times, all or most of the tailored program can be used only once; specifically, those sections of the program devoted to the specifics of the organizational problem can not be reused.

Tailored programs accommodate both individual and organizational goals. The finished plan generated by the program can be evaluated in terms of the quality of the analysis and innovativeness of the solution, in addition to a longitudinal evaluation of the long-term effectiveness of the plan in solving the original problem. Individual level outcomes ae more difficult to assess because, like the insight type of training programs, the knowledge gained about managerial skills and behaviors is extremely personalized.

F. Tailored Process

The tailored process executive development model explicitly intertwines individual and executive development. It aims to produce double-loop learning by continual assessment of organizational and individual performance as well as of the linkages between the two. This type of program provides for maximum flexibility because, unlike the tailored program format, tailored process programs expect the participant-executive to define the problem to be resolved. And this is the key difference between this management development strategy and the tailored programs mentioned above. The tailored process training design allows organizational problems to be defined and redefined as the executive-participant and the training consultant interact.

Few of the problems facing top executives are simple, unambiguous ones. If they were, they would have been solved at lower levels of the organization. Problems facing top-level excutives are complex, ambiguous, interrelated to other issues in the environment, and rife with controversy over how the situation should be characterized. Mason and Mitroff (1981) have identified these as wicked problems. In support of the important and complicated nature of problem identification, Richard Reich (1991) identified problem identification, along with problem solving and brokering, as the three skills needed to steer organizations in the 1990s environment. Tailored process programs assume problem definition as a critical, yet difficult, issue for top executives.

Tailored process models can be used to describe the experience of the managers and consultants involved in some recent large-scale projects. The building of the rapid rail system in Atlanta (MARTA) followed this pattern (Golembiewski, 1983). It was also the format used to facilitate the creation of Centerton, a high-involvement organization emphasizing individual involvement and high-quality organizational level results (Perkins, Nieva, and Lawler, 1983). Large management consulting companies, such as Arthur Anderson or McKinsey, frequently employ this model when a firm partner establishes a paid one-on-one relationship with the CEO of a private firm. In each of these cases, the consultant works for organizational success by helping the executive to be more effective. There is an expectation that the goals of the programs will be modified as the project progresses, and that attention is focused on management skills and knowledge improvement while in the course of accomplishing the organizational objective.

Unlike the tailored program model, the tailored process model of executive development defines the consultant's job in a less structured, more intense way. The consultant is to act as sounding board, confidant, reality tester, gadfly, and generally a good, technically competent, articulate, and supportive albeit critical friend to the key decision makers in the organization. The consultant's role is to help the participant think through the problems, to raise questions, and to encourage problem solving. Overall, the consultant is to create support for evaluation and change, both personal and organizational.

The consultant normally comes from outside the participant's organization, and the consultant's pay and status are roughly equal to but outside the control of the executive-participant. The consultant has no vested interest in the company except that the participant succeed, so the advice is deemed to be independent and impartial. Although the functions are similar, the consultant is not a mentor, and this is for two reasons: the consultant is paid to act as confidant and friend; and the executive is not expected to reciprocate by offering similar services to the consultant.

This is the most personalized and expensive type of executive development and because of its cost and intensity, is employed mainly at the higher levels, or when a project is large, new, untested, and critical for the success of the organization in charge of the project. Consultants are free to advise and provide feedback to executives because they have no vested interest in the organization, and typically have access to a range of independent sources of advice within their own firms.

Evaluation of the success of this type of program can be estimated on the organizational level by the overall success of the organization, as well as at the individual level by subjective judgments concerning how well the relationship is working. Organizational- and individual-level evaluations are complicated, because at this level of training, the goals of both the company and the manager are so intertwined that it is difficult to sort out and clearly target causality. Further, since the goals are amenable to change over the course of the project, linking evaluation to goal accomplishment may just confuse the issue.

IV. SUMMARY

An emerging theme in executive and management development is that business and government organizations are increasingly taking their development functions very seriously. There are compelling reasons for this attention: money expended on managerial development is expected to yield a return, times are too competitive, and resources are too limited. Yet the management training community is chaotic, characterized by wide variation in content, quality, and delivery format.

The models of executive development presented here should help classify and even clarify the types of management training and development being conducted in business and government organizations. The categories of executive development are organized according to the amount of integration of individual- and organizational-level goals in the training program. Management training and development ranges from the simple and direct type of indoctrination format to the sophisticated and intense tailored process and program models of executive development. There is extreme variation in the content, delivery, and focus of executive development programs offered within and among the three categories. A successful match between a management team and the provider of the development effort depends upon (1) clear identification of the goal expected as a result of the training; (2) analysis to discover if the chosen goal can be accommodated by a particular program; and (3) clear thinking about how to measure results. Ultimately, it is the responsibility of the purchaser to be clear on the goals—individual and organizational—that are to be accomplished through this training as well as to consider the avenues available to measure the results.

REFERENCES

Argyris, C. (1991). Teaching smart people how to learn. *Harvard Business Review*, *69*: 99–109.
Argyris, C., and Schön, D. (1978). *Organizational Learning: A Theory of Action Perspective*. Addison-Wesley, Reading, Mass.

Bauman, P., and Weschler, L. (1992). The Rocky Mountain program: Advanced learning for the complexities of public management. *Public Productivity and Management Review, 15*: 463–475.

Boehm, V., and Hoyle, D. (1977). Assessment in management development. In *Applying the Assessment Center Method* (J. L. Moses and W. Byham, eds.), Pergamon Press, New York, pp. 203–225.

Bolt, J. F. (1985). Tailor executive development to strategy. *Harvard Business Review*: 168–175.

Bolt, J. F. (1989) *Executive Development: A Strategy for Corporate Competitiveness.* Harper & Row, New York.

Bridgeman, D. S. (1959). Company management development programs. In *The Education of American Businessmen* (F. C. Pierson, ed.), McGraw–Hill, New York, pp. 536–576.

Cunningham, R., and Olshfski, D. (1988). Designing an executive development program for State Department executives, unpublished paper presented to National Association of State Training and Development Directors, Atlanta, Ga.

Cutchin, D. (1990). Municipal executive productivity: Lessons from New Jersey. *Public Productivity and Management Reivew, 13*: 245–270.

Deming, W. E. (1986). *Out of the Crisis.* MIT, Cambridge, Mass.

Flanders, L. R. (1989). Developing executive and managerial talent. In *Handbook of Public Administration* (J. L. Perry, ed.), Jossey–Bass, San Francisco.

Golembiewski, R. (1972). *Renewing Organizations: The Laboratory Approach to Planned Change.* Peacock Press, Ithica, Ill.

Golembiewski, R. (1979). *Approaches to Planned Change, Part 1: Orienting Perspectives and Micro-Level Interventions.* Marcel Dekker, New York.

Golembiewski, R. (1983). Lessons from a fast-paced public project: Perspectives on doing better the next time around. *Public Administration Review, 43*: 547–556.

Jennings, E. E. (1971). *Routes to the Executive Suite.* McGraw-Hill, New York.

Katz, D., and Georgopoulous, G. (1971). Organizations in a changing world. *Applied Behavioral Science, 7*: 349–351.

Keirsey, D., and Bates, M. (1984). *Please Understand Me: Character and Temperment Types,* 4th ed. Gnosology Books, Del Mar, Calif.

Knowles, M. S. (1987). Adult learning. *Training and Development Handbook* (R. L. Craig, ed.), McGraw-Hill, New York.

Lafferty, J. C. (1989). *Level I: Life-Style Inventory Self-Description.* Human Synergistics, Plymouth, Mich.

Mason, R. O., and Mitroff, I. I. (1981). *Challenging Strategic Planning Assumptions.* John Wiley, New York.

Meyers, I. (1962). *Manual: The Meyers-Briggs Type Indicators.* Consulting Psychologist, Palo Alto, Calif.

Nilsson, W. P. (1987). *Achieving Strategic Goals Through Executive Development.* Addison-Wesley, Reading, Mass.

Osborne, D., and Gaebler, T. (1992). *Reinventing Government.* Addison-Wesley, Reading, Mass.

Perkins, D. N., Nieva, V., and Lawler, E. (1983). *Managing Creaton.* John Wiley, New York.

Peters, T., and Waterman, R. (1982). *In Search of Excellence.* Harper & Row, Cambridge, Mass.

Pierson, F. C. (1959). *The Education of American Businessmen.* McGraw-Hill, New York.

Poister, T. H., and Streib, G. (1989). Municipal managers' concerns for productivity improvement. *Public Productivity and Management Review, 8*: 3–11.

Porter, L. W., and McKibbin, L. E. (1988). *Management Education and Development.* McGraw-Hill, New York.

Reich, R. (1991). *The Work of Nations.* Knopf, New York.

Schaeffer, R. H, and Thomson, H. A. (1992). Successful change programs begin with results. *Harvard Business Review, 70*: 80–91.

Spindler, C. J. (1992). University-based public sector management development and training. *Public Productivity and Management Review, 15*: 439–448.

Thayer, P. W. (1989). A historical perspective on training. In *Training and Development in Organizations* (Irwin Goldstein et al., eds.), Jossey-Bass, San Francisco.

Thornton, G., and Byham, W. (1982). *Assessment Centers and Managerial Performance.* Academic Press, New York.

Tichy, N. M. (1989). GE's Crotonville: A staging ground for corporate revolution. *The Academy of Management Executive, 3*: 99–106.

Toffler, A. (1970). *Future Shock.* Random House, New York.

Townsend, P. (1970). *Up the Organization*. Fawcett Crest, Greenwich, Conn.

Van Wart, M. (1992). Connecting management and executive development in the states. *Public Productivity and Management Review*, *15*: 477–486.

Watson, R. (1988). New visions for university-sponsored executive education programs. *Academy of Management Executive*, *2*: 321–324.

Whyte, W. H. (1956). *The Organization Man*. Doubleday Anchor, New York.

Zuboff, S. (1988). *In the Age of the Smart Machine*. Basic Books, New York.

15
Valuing Differences
Organization and Gender

Allan R. Cahoon and Julie Rowney

University of Calgary, Calgary, Alberta, Canada

I. INTRODUCTION

Ideally, organizations are designed to facilitate the accomplishment of both their task as well as their process goals. In the 1990s, the organization must maximize the contributions of its most valuable resource, its people. Historically overlooked, and often deliberately neglected, is the role that gender differences play in the organization's effective human resource management. This chapter will review the relationship between gender difference and organizations. First it will focus on the reality of the workplace for women, particularly as it relates to the management of organizations, and identify the problems and issues they face. This chapter starts with a historical overview focusing on research studies of women in organizations and the nature of management, which resulted in considerable optimism for change in the early 1980s. The achievements of the 1980s are reviewed and assessed in light of the historical issues raised and the initial optimism developed in the literature. The failure of the efforts in the 1980s to achieve significant breakthrough is then assessed and evaluated. The chapter will conclude with the challenges organizations now face in dealing with gender differences as well as provide some suggestions about what can be done to address these issues.

The literature reviewed comes primarily from that focused on developments in the United States and Canada. A review of the research from other developed countries complemented much of the North American research, and references are made to international studies when significant differences were discovered, or to reinforce the commonality of issues women in organizations generally face. Discouragingly, no women-friendly countries can be identified in spite of apparent cultural stereotypes of countries with reputations for more enlightened treatment of women (e.g., Israel and the countries of Scandinavia). The challenge to value gender differences and to effectively incorporate the contributions women make to organizations remains universal and compelling.

A. The Evolving Workplace

The role of men and women at work is changing. Work remains a central activity in the lives of most people. It is a major mechanism for positioning people in society and for allocating social status and power. The work we do determines how and where we live, with whom we associate, and to a great degree, how we feel about ourselves and how well we interact with others. It

339

directly bears on our level of satisfaction and the degree of stress we perceive, and is directly related to the level of burnout we experience. Work patterns affect our behavior in organizations, therefore any attempt to improve or change the behavior of individuals within organizations requires an appreciation of both the relationship between people and their organizations, and how this relationship is changing as the representation of women continues to increase. As long as women were effectively excluded from intellectual inquiry in organizations, a gender-related basis of organization behavior was not widely recognized; organization culture and the way of thinking about organizations were shaped by male perspective.

This same reality of management continues today. It is male dominated, in spite of the important findings of the past decade stressing the need to confront sex discrimination in the workplace, particularly at lower and middle management ranks (Cahoon and Rowney, 1988). The progress that women have achieved in certain careers continues to be limited and restricted to the lower levels of the organization hierarchy. The higher women are promoted in organizations, the more obvious are the limitations that they encounter (Morrison et al., 1987).

It is easier for women to obtain positions at lower levels these days, but these positions often prove to be holding patterns for them (Cahoon and Rowney, 1988). Appointment and promotion to lower levels of management are based upon objective criteria, the proven ability and obvious competency to undertake the required identifiable tasks. Indeed, the rise in the labor force over the past 10 years is largely due to a dramatic increase in the participation of women in the workforce. In the United States, as of 1988, women made up over 45% of the workforce, compared with 38.5% in 1973 (Bureau of Labor Statistics, 1989). In Canada, 94% of the employment growth between 1981 and 1986 was caused by increased participation by women (Statistics Canada, Labour Force Activity Report, 1986). By 1988, the participation rate of women in the Canadian workforce had reached 56%, compared to 75% for males.

According to Statistics Canada, women now occupy 32% of managerial and administrative positions, an increase of approximately 12% in 10 years. In the United States, close to 40% of all managerial positions are held by women, compared with 20% in 1974 (Bureau of Labor Statistics, 1989). Unfortunately, despite these figures, the picture is not that positive. Most women are still concentrated in lower management levels and include both part-time and full-time positions (Cahoon and Rowney, 1988; Morrison and Von Glinow, 1990; Schein, 1989). It was much easier for women to obtain leadership positions at the lower ranges of the organizational hierarchy, but it was difficult for them to reach middle levels of management and rarer to attain senior management positions (Cahoon and Rowney, 1988). Women hold only 2% of senior management positions in American's largest companies (Berlin, 1988), and in a 1992 study of the *Fortune* 500, only 3.6% of board directorships and 1.7% of corporate officerships were held by women.

Women do not fare any better in public or educational institution management. The U.S. government reported only 8.6% women in its senior executive service (U.S. Office of Personnel Management, 1989). In education, the position of women in senior administrative positions has remained relatively constant and low in spite of the large percentage of teachers who are women—6% versus 55%, on average (Canadian Teachers Federation, 1988).

The growth in the participation rates of women in the workplace has been in the more traditional female occupation categories and at the entry level of management (Cahoon and Rowney, 1988). Many authors suggest that although social movements and legislation have provided the impetus for women to enter the managerial ranks, few females have become top-level managers (Buono and Kamm, 1983; Morrison, 1990; Schein, 1989). Women are still caught between emerging corporate and traditional roles, and may remain so for a considerable period of time as it is more difficult for those severely underrepresented in upper-level policy-making positions to effect changes. Kanter (1977) has suggested that three simultaneously interacting variables determine the likelihood of movement up through the managerial ranks: (1) the extent of a particular position's power; (2) the degree of opportunity or mobility inherent in a particular position; and (3) the extent of tokenism versus realistic representation in a given position. Limited numbers of token management positions having little power or opportunity for advancement are peripheral to the mainstream of influence in organizations.

However, according to Harlan and Weiss (1981), merely increasing the number of women in particular management positions does not alleviate the problems women face once they are in these positions.

Those women who have advanced into management find reward differentials. There is evidence that at higher occupational levels, women are less satisfied with their pay than are men (Varca, Shaffer, and McCauley, 1983). The explanation is that at lower levels of management, women are often unaware of the wage and salary differentials between women and men in similar positions. However, once these differences become overt and known, dissatisfaction occurs.

The business world is male-dominated and androcentric; prevailing forces view the world and shape reality from a male perspective. As such, that world systematically discriminates against women. Although in an enlightened 1990s view of the world obvious conscious and intentional discrimination against women is completely unacceptable, discrimination still prevails. Women do not get the same opportunities as men in organizations, and the higher they go in the organization, the more obvious this becomes.

Probably the major conclusion to be reached in perusing the literature on gender and work is the pervasiveness of the effect; gender interacts on organizational, individual, and personal levels, sometimes positively, but more often negatively. The research topics range across psychological, social, and economic areas. The findings can be confirmations or contradictions. Given the complexity and developmental nature of the topic, is it necessary to begin with the historical antecedents of the 1970s, and present the optimistic forecasts and trends of the 1980s, and then the challenges of the 1990s. The organizational context as it relates to gender, the changing nature of work, and the profile of employees all must be considered.

II. TRADITIONS OF ORGANIZATIONS AND MANAGEMENT

A. The Nature of Organizations

The organization of the 1970s was a relatively stable, hierarchical entity that could rely on its experiences to predict its future. The strategic planning process was an extrapolation of the past into the future. The computer costs were primarily in hardware, the time dimensions lengthy, and change slow. There was stability, rationality, and a dominant view of organizations as being closed systems.

The traditions of organizations emphasized formal rules and procedures and a strong commitment to productivity, management control, authority, and compartmentalization. Organizational achievement and success are paramount, and both employees and the nature of work emphasized the achievement of the organization's objectives. Structure was studied in order to identify operating procedures. Highly bureaucratic systems were valued, and this emphasized uniformity, conformity, and a chain of command. Organizations emphasized the need to develop a strong corporate culture, which required strong socialization processes and continual reinforcement.

Despite a rather tranquil context, stereotyping of the sexes had been documented by Anastasi and Foley (1949), Maccoby (1966), and Schein (1971; 1973; 1975), to cite only a few. The Equal Pay Act of 1963 mandated equal pay for equal work, the Civil Rights Act of 1964 prohibited employment discrimination based on sex, and two executive orders (in 1965 and 1967) prohibited private firms with government contracts from employment discrimination based on racial, religious, ethnic, or sexual grounds. In 1970 organizations were required to undertake affirmative action on behalf of women and minorities. The Equal Employment Opportunity Act of 1972 prohibited government agencies at all levels from employment discrimination. Thus it can be concluded that discrimination based on gender had been perceived as a serious problem and remedial action was initiated through legislation.

The nature of the work and the nature of the workers conformed to the bureaucratic model. The focus on structure, productivity, and management control resulted in an emphasis on large-scale efficiencies, assembly line production, and increased worker specialization. It reflected a highly instrumental approach to work that required data, results, ideas, and tasks. The work in these traditional organizations was routine, highly competitive, and unfriendly to women in anything other than stereotypic work. Employees were expected to be obedient, compliant, and rational, and were viewed impersonally as instruments of production. Although many identified the obvious barriers and obstacles women faced, this recognition did not result in any significant change in the treatment and utilization of women (Kanter, 1987; Schwartz, 1992; Fierman, 1990).

B. The Nature of Managers

In 1967 Douglas McGregor (1967: 23) described the "model of the successful manager in our culture" as "masculine." He explained

> The good manager is aggressive, competitive, firm, just. He is not feminine, he is not soft or yielding or dependent or intuitive in the womanly sense. The very expression of emotion is widely viewed as a feminine weakness that would interfere with effective business processes. The fact is that all these emotions are part of the human nature of men and women alike. Cultural forces have shaped not their existence but their acceptability, they are repressed, but this does not render them inactive. They continue to influence attitudes, opinions, and decisions.

McGregor was not alone in defining management as a male domain. Much of the research of the 1960s and 1970s demonstrate that men were seen as better suited for management than women (Bowman, Worthy, and Greyson, 1968).

Various studies shows that in the absence of any information other than their gender, women were considered less competent than men (Rosenkrantz et al., 1968; Sheriffs and Jarrett, 1953). Research also showed that male success was more likely to be attributed to ability than was female success (Deaux and Emswiller, 1974). Further studies illustrated that performance records attributed to women were often evaluated less favorably than the identical items attributed to men (Goldberg, 1968; Mischel, 1974; Rosen and Jerdee, 1973). Schein's findings (1973; 1975) on attitudes of female and male executives supported the masculine profile for successful management.

In 1965, a *Harvard Business Review* survey of 2000 business executives found that 31% of the male respondents described women as temperamentally unfit for management. Within organizations, the image of the powerful person was inescapably male. Stereotypic images of leaders result from leaders soliciting replacement who were similar to themselves (Dalton, 1951; Pfeffer, 1977; Wilson and Lupton, 1959). A large number of studies found a positive correlation between the amount of verbal participation in groups and leadership (Stein and Heller, 1979).

Since men talked more than women in mixed groups, women were more likely to yield to a man's opinion. Men allocated a higher portion of their behavior to task-related areas (Lockheed and Hall, 1976) and emerged as leaders even in informal settings. Nonverbal actions also impacted on the leadership appearance of men and women, with men using higher-status or dominant nonverbal behaviour (smiled less, acted more relaxed, etc.), than women.

The informal organization played a crucial role in understanding how organizations really functioned, and was often cited as one of the major stumbling blocks for women in their efforts to climb the corporate ladder (Lips, 1981). The emphasis on the informal organization was a reaction to the dominance of the formal structure focus, and included a recognition of the lateral and other relationships and processes not governed by the rules and regulations of the formal organization. The power coalitions of the formal organization clearly excluded women, and its rules were based on male behaviors, modes of communication, and common experiences (Hennig and Jardim, 1977).

Traditional organization structure often resulted in interactions between men and women across status lines. Power, leadership, decision making, and control was considered the male domain, while support or nurturance, hostessing, and "organizational housework" were considered the domains of women (Kanter, 1977b). Productivity, motivation, and career success was largely determined by organization structure and the very nature of the social circumstances in which employees found themselves (Kanter, 1977a). Accordingly, Kanter believes that success and the observed differences in behavior were directly a result of the nature of the organization itself, its structure, and its processes. When men and women were provided equal opportunity, and evaluated on equally objective criteria, they behaved in very similar ways and they had similar successes.

In the 1970s, gender was an important variable in determining who did what in the organization. Many occupations were sex-typed, and considered the exclusive territory of one sex, and came to be defined in ways considered appropriate for that sex (Schein, 1989). This organizational sex-typing affected the sex ratio of those with whom employees interacted, which in turn defined the appropriate role models, norms of behavior, and criteria used for evaluation and promotion.

Women introduced into traditionally male work environments faced a number of problems (Pecorella, 1986). The reaction they receive is frequently hostile and based on stereotypic attitudes about the nature of the work and the role of female employees. Sex-role stereotyping portrayed men as more competent, but as less warm or expressive than women (Broverman et al., 1972). Thus, competency was labeled as a masculine characteristic, whereas female characteristics were more often related to warmth and expressiveness. Bem (1974; 1975; 1979) developed an instrument (the Bem sex-role inventory; BSRI), to measure perceived masculinity and femininity of managers. Her intent was to advocate an androgynous view of management as the model of the "good manager," which will be explored in Section III.

Until the 1970s the managerial position was obviously a male sex-typed one. The ratio of men to women managers was extremely high, and there was a widespread belief that this was the way it should be (McGregor, 1967; Schein, 1973; 1975). A woman, by virtue of her gender alone, was perceived as less qualified and less capable of being a manager. Not only did the structure and culture of organizations discriminate against women, but they were required to work harder (Colwil, 1982), were required to have greater qualifications and skills (Schein, 1989), were ignored in the recruitment process (Cohen and Bunker, 1975), and were passed over for promotion simply on the basis of sex-role stereotypic thinking on the part of organizational decision makers.

III. BREAKTHROUGH: THE 1980s AND THE ADVANCEMENT OF WOMEN

A. The Rationale For Failure

By the end of the 1970s, the reality of women in organizations and the issues they faced in achieving success had become far more visible. Research identified two primary explanations as to why women were not achieving a more equal status with men in organizations. At one extreme were those researchers who claimed that women hadn't been successful because of the external obstacles and barriers they faced. At the other end of the continuum were those who pointed to the internal barriers women faced in achieving success.

The former focused on challenging the discriminatory nature of the male-dominated "system," and androcentric nature of organization processes, the pervasiveness of sex-role stereotypes, and the isolation of women at higher levels of management (Loring and Wells, 1972; Colwil, 1982; Kanter, 1977; Schein, 1989). The work of these writers demonstrated that women's limited participation in organizations was wrong. Such research showed that women and men were not being treated equally, and that the barriers needed to be acknowledged and altered if women were to have equality of opportunity in the workplace. Morrison et al. (1987) argued convincingly that women had to meet a far more stringent set of behavioral criteria than men in order to make it into the executive suite; they were allowed less flexibility and had a narrow range of acceptable behaviors available to achieve executive success.

Others argued that men in power tended to have lower expectations of women, and as a consequence, women were ghettoized into traditional female roles, to jobs with little real power and limited opportunities for advancement (Kanter, 1978; Feuer, 1988). According to the external cause viewpoint, women lacked mentors and effective role models, and when required to be "gender pioneers" they risk alienation and have considerably more difficulty than men (Pecorella, 1986; 1988).

The "internal" school looked to the debilitating stereotypes associated with women, the impact of feminine traits on perceived management performance, the culturally reinforced dependency, and the self-defeating behaviors women exhibited, consciously or unconsciously, on the job (Bem, 1977; Sargent, 1981).

The social behaviors of women differ from men in the workplace, especially as they relate to communication, interpersonal skills, and assertiveness (Feuer, 1988). Women are considered to be good listeners with highly developed verbal skills. Men, on the other hand, tend to talk more, for longer periods of time, interrupting women up to five times as often as women interrupt men. Other limiting characteristics of females that have been proposed are that women are often overly task-oriented (Colwil, 1982), tend to delegate less effectively, and overly control subordinates' work—often finishing their work and cleaning up after them (Schein, 1989; Feuer, 1988). Other negative characteristics in the stereotype of female managers is their tendency to become obsessed with technical competence and to become job-focused rather than career-focused. According to those who offer an internal explanation for the lack of progress for women in the 1980s, certain stereotypic behaviors have had significantly limited effects on women. Women often associate achievement with affiliation (the need for approval and acceptance), whereas men are less concerned about making friends. Success has been perceived as being unfeminine (Braiker, 1986).

Women tend to focus on achieving excellence in performance at the job, whereas men more commonly view achievement as a way to be competitive. Women often attribute success to good luck, failure to a lack of ability; men are more likely to attribute success to ability, and failure to the difficulty of the task. Finally, women tend to distort feedback in a negative way.

More recently, sex differences in management styles and practices are acknowledged as a particular advantage women bring to management (Loden, 1985; Lamkin, 1986). According to Loden, women have the characteristics necessary to succeed in the future: concern for people, interpersonal skills, and decision making and creative problem-solving skills. Recognizing women's natural strengths and capitalizing on them is the expectation of these authors.

The 1980s saw the emergence of organizations facing significant challenges and changes. The nature of the workforce changed, bringing with it demands for increased participation in decision making and fairer and less paternalistic human resource practices, as well as the increased recognition of the need for organizational flexibility. Organizations moved to empower their employees, to involve them on task forces, and to structure them in matrix formats as well as in strategic business units. They faced problems of mergers and acquisitions, global competition, downsizing, flattening with limited opportunity for advancement, and increasing demands on management for team leadership. Instead of the amount of leisure time increasing, employees, and particularly managers, were forced to work more (Rowney and Cahoon, 1990; Engdahl, 1988).

B. The Promise of Androgyny

What emerged early in the 1980s was an emphasis on androgynous management. Androgyny was used to explain the behavioral changes expected as the gender balance in managerial ranks changed. The ideal of the androgynous manager was someone who would integrate traditional "male" roles and values along with traditional "female" ones. According to Alice Sargent (1981), the increasing numbers of women entering management should ensure that the definition of what constitutes good management would change from the traditional masculine one to an androgynous one that would incorporate the strengths of both the feminine as well as the masculine traits.

There was to be a shift from the male model as characterized by rugged individualism, autonomy, and independence to a more feminine model that focused on interdependence, mutuality, networking, and teams. The objective of this new management was to capitalize on the necessary male characteristics: dominance; independence; orientation on achievement; rational, analytical decision making; forceful communication; and competition. But these would be blended with the effective female traits: concern for people; attention to the nonverbal cues; increased interpersonal sensitivity and awareness; creative, intuitive decision making; and empowering leadership (Sargent, 1983; Powell and Butterfield, 1979; Sargent and Stupek, 1989.)

Powell and Butterfield (1989) reviewed earlier research on androgyny, to see if the expected changes had occurred, and whether the "good manager" had indeed become an androgynous one. What they discovered, however, was that over the 10 years since their previous study, there had been a slight strengthening in support for the masculine manager. The idealism of those advocating an androgynous approach to management was not justified, and the male model of management continues to prevail. Powell and Butterfield conclude that androgynous management is not the panacea that it was expected to be.

The advice women received in the late 1970s to act more like men in order to succeed in the corporate world appears misguided. Adopting the male model has not served women particularly well (Cohen, 1989). Korabik and Roya (1989) reported that women who had adopted a more masculine style of management were less effective than women who adopted a more androgynous style in decision making, problem solving, and listening skills.

What happened to the androgynous ideal indicates the disillusionment that followed much of the idealism that accompanied the start of the 1980s. Virginia Schein's initial research in the 1970s (Schein, 1971; 1973; 1975) was revised (Brenner, Tomkiewicz, and Schein, 1989). The results of Brenner, Tomkiewicz, and Schein (1989) show that the attitudes of male managers toward the role of women in management remained remarkably similar to those held by male managers 15 years earlier. Although the perception generated in the 1980s was that men held an increasingly positive attitude toward female managers, the reality appears to be that men's unconscious attitudes toward women in organizations have in fact changed little over the previous 15 years (Dubno, 1985).

On the other hand, female managers' attitudes differed from their earlier counterparts, and they did not share the view that managers are seen as possessing characteristics more commonly ascribed to men. Understandably, women seem more aware of the positive contributions being made by female managers than are their male counterparts. Successful women have had to develop their own strategies for achieving success and continue to be outstanding in order to be recognized and promoted.

C. The Failure Is Universal

The 1980s heralded new approaches to management development that were designed to improve the situation of both men and women in the organization. Concepts included a learning cycle theory (Kolb, 1974), action learning, manager self-development, and even outdoor training. Firms recognized the need to facilitate the advancement of women into managerial positions (Boeker et al., 1985).

These development attempts designed to increase the number of women in management have had a very limited impact (Armstrong, 1989). Significant changes in the gender composition of management, especially at upper levels, will occur only if structures and practices are more inclusive of women's issues and concerns. Research has indicated that management development programs for women should include: (1) gaining an awareness of the political and cultural aspects of the organization; (2) identifying and building on personal management and leadership style; (3) instituting stress management; and (4) developing career/life planning (Hammond, 1986).

Barriers against women, especially in the upper levels of management, continue. All the data indicate that women currently hold less than 5% of senior executive positions (Rowney and

Cahoon, 1990; Gallese, 1989; Quaglieri and Pecenka, 1985). Women continue to receive lower compensation than their male counterparts (Jefferson, 1989; Dubno, 1985; Stephan, 1987; Lynagh and Poist, 1985). They continue to receive fewer promotional opportunities (Gold and Pringle, 1988; Dubno, 1985; Lynagh and Poist, 1985). Companies may wait to discriminate against women until the time of their promotion by moving women into staff jobs of functions that are not central to the core of the business, or by the use of creative job titles that sound prestigious, but that have few important responsibilities. Another explanation for the lack of parity between men and women in organizations is that they receive differential socialization. Men find it difficult to see women as "fitting in" (Stephan, 1987). Most companies have been slow in changing the aspects of corporate life that to date have driven women out (Taylor, 1986).

The situation experienced by women in organizations during the 1980s in North America is not unlike that experienced by women in other countries. A 1987 study by the British Institute of Management showed that women held 5.5% of all executive positions and 10.8% of senior positions in junior management (Williams, 1987). While it appears relatively easy for women to obtain employment at the lower levels of the organization, it is increasingly difficult to move up the hierarchy. This puts increasing pressure on women, both at home and at work, as compared to their male counterparts' experience (Davidson and Cooper, 1985). According to the analysis of the study, societal expectations, the lack of role models, and the predominance of "masculine virtue" in organizations are the bases of the discrepancies. An Australian study (Gold and Pringle, 1988), showed that in spite of similarities in profiles of male and female managers, women received fewer promotions. A major hindering factor cited in the study was the organizational attitudes toward women in the predominantly male management environment.

The situation seems similar elsewhere. In Canada, women are entering management at junior levels, but have not been able to penetrate senior management successfully (Rowney and Cahoon, 1990; Wentem, 1985). Similarly, discouraging results have been reported from Germany (Antal and Krebsbach-Gnath, 1986–1987), Japan (Steinoff and Tanaka, 1986–1987), and Israel (Izaeila, 1986–1987).

The 1980s were unable to deliver to organizations on the promises implicit in the optimism that surrounded the late 1970s and early 1980s. Although the structures of organizations changed significantly, the practice of management, as it relates to gender, did not—this in spite of extensive government legislation, increased public awareness, and the determination of many women. Although intentions may have been honorable, the effects of the 1980s did not significantly improve opportunities for women in organizations. This reality is conveniently ignored by most organizations, which overlook the data in preference to specific examples or anecdotes, and even by many women who would prefer not to see gender as the significant obstacle that it is proving to be for them in organizations.

IV. RECONCEPTUALIZATION AND CHANGE: THE 1990s

A. Organizational Reality and the 1980s

The 1990s have proven to be a time for the reconceptualization of the issues of gender in organizations. Although in many ways the 1980s created an organizational revolution, and even with the significant changes in the management practices, the 1980s did not deliver on the promises made to women as well as other minorities.

A number of paradoxes have been created for organizations and their management. A strong organizational culture was prescribed for "excellent organizations" (Peters and Waterman, 1982), but organizations found that they had to be flexible, "right-sized," and responsive to change. Relatedly, organizational growth based on acquisitions and mergers and survival of the fittest in a global economy often occurred along with an emphasis on small, self-contained "strategic business units." Advancing technology and the explosion of specialized knowledge and information technology were injected into organizations that were flatter, less hierarchical, and operated as more specialized, autonomous units. A loose–tight coupling was advocated for management, in which certain functions or operations of the organization were decentralized in order to ensure maximum flexibility, creativity, individual responsiveness, and customer/client focus. At the same time, other functions were being centralized to ensure uniformity, standardization, economies of scale, and other efficiencies.

Management was challenged with decision making in flatter and leaner organizations. These provided limited opportunity for advancement, and also increased demands resulting from increased worker participation, autonomy, and the uncertainties in the environment. Change produced uncertainty within organizations, which in turn produced more conservative decision making involving "safe choices." Consequently, appointing women into areas previously occupied by men seemed to become more risky for many managements, and a corresponding employee disinvestment with organizations and management occurred. Women at the executive level dropped out as fast as they joined (Kanter, 1987).

Managers were challenged to be more creative and innovative in their decision making, but high-risk strategies often had uncertain consequences. Many managers came to feel that they operated in environments that were largely out of control, and they were forced to be reactive crisis managers, rather than the strategic, visionary leaders that they had been challenged to be. They faced uncertainty and complexity, and significant value changes toward security within organizations and among employees.

In retrospect, it is perhaps most noteworthy that so many initiatives were extended, despite setbacks. Organizations emphasized empowerment, increased individual ownership, participation, and greater openness and communication. Human relations practices were revised to reflect a "social contract" with employees that provide greater autonomy, more team responsibility, and an emphasis on performance management, with its increased attention to individual goals, career development, and feedback as well as personal and professional development.

B. The Glass Ceiling

In 1987, Morrison, White, and Van Velsor published "Breaking the Glass Ceiling: Can Women Reach the Top of America's Corporations?" They effectively conceptualized the dilemma discovered by an increasing number of women in organizations, that there existed a transparent barrier at the highest levels of organizations, a barrier that only a handful of women have been able to break.

Even those who manage to break this invisible ceiling continue to encounter androcentric traditions and stereotypes that restrict their movement within the inner sanctum of senior management (Friedman, 1988; Little, 1991). In spite of the best organizational and mangement intentions of the 1980s, coupled with the range of equal employment opportunity and affirmative action programs implemented by governments and companies themselves, women continue to encounter personal, situational, and institutional obstacles and barriers (Auster, 1988). The explanations for their lack of success continue to be attributed to internal (person-centered) views or external (situational) explanations (Morrison and Von Glinow, 1990; Tharenou, 1991; Crawford and Marecek, 1989).

Other researchers have examined the barriers to the career aspirations of managerial and professional women. Horgan (1989) examined the hypothesis that cognitive learning theory may hold the clue to women breaking the glass ceiling. According to her, two underlying reasons explain why women continue to be largely unsuccessful in organizations: it is much more difficult for women to gain managerial expertise and related social learning than men, due to the differences in their social systems; and most women's management experience must be analyzed and evaluated for sex appropriateness and how it will be perceived. All the data women receive must be recoded to eliminate the sex bias in order for women to be recognized and to perform, in sum. Women inevitably have more difficulty obtaining feedback, will receive less helpful feedback, and will often be presented with ambiguous expectations as to appropriate behavior on the job. Such factors lead to a tough conclusion: in order for women to succeed, they often will need to be brighter, more able to learn the ropes without special help, may take longer to do so, and will ultimately need special circumstances or assistance in order to effectively move to the top of our organizations (see, e.g., Horgan, 1989).

Sex-role stereotyping continues to result in different standards being used to judge the qualifications and successes of women. Often, women's success is attributed to luck instead of ability (Ragins and Sundstrom, 1989), whereas men's success is attributed to innate qualifications and ability. The assumption that "what is skill for the male is luck for the female" continues into the 1990s. Presenting "hard" data about women's abilities often will have little effect; typically, "soft" data, in the form of anecdotes or case studies, will have more impact (Horgan, 1988). As long as women continue to be perceived as having different capabilities than men, and these perceived differences are not challenged consistently and demonstrably, women will remain disadvantaged and underutilized in our organizations. For example, research by Morrison et al. (1987) reported that contradictory expectations of women often derail their careers. For example, they are expected to be tough but not "macho," to take responsibility but also follow orders, and to be ambitious but not expect to receive equal treatment. Women who have succeeded in breaking the glass ceiling have had to make more personal sacrifices (Friedman, 1988), and have had to experience greater psychological conflict and stress (Rowney and Cahoon, 1999).

That women continue to be discriminated against in employment is incontestable: discrimination occurs in the selection, interviewing and hiring process, assignment of work responsibilities, and promotions and pay. Continued denial of this reality will do nothing to contribute to our understanding of the fundamental and indisputable elements responsible for its existence or to develop the corrective initiatives that are required to reduce and ultimately eliminate the inequities and inefficiencies inherent in discrimination. The 1990s require organizations to own the problem of discrimination and its effect, in spite of the good intentions, to address the issue manifest at least since the 1980s.

Much needs doing, then. For example, organizations need to identify all the reasons for the obstacles women face and to develop action plans to address them. For starters, this means changing the attitudes and behavior of men, as well as providing programs to help women learn the skills required to succeed as gender pioneers.

Organizational structures also must be changed to reflect the changing nature of the work, to reflect the modifications in the profile of the average employees (increasingly female or minority), and to focus more on process rather than on simply be concerned with getting things done. Company-sponsored training for both men and women is needed to help them develop more positive qualities required to manage workforce diversity. The norm is that women in executive positions are an anomaly, and in order to reach these positions, they have had to be strategists and survivors, intent on being different from the stereotype. In many cases these characteristics simply brought them to the edge of, but would not get them through, the glass ceiling (Collins, 1988).

Moreover, women have the most to gain by cultivating organizationally sanctioned mentors, whose availability has been directly linked to career advancement, higher pay, and greater career satisfaction (Kram, 1985; Kram and Isabella, 1985). Thus, the mentoring relationship seems critical to the advancement of women in organizations (Kanter, 1977; Morrison et al., 1987), but the costs will be great. For example, research suggests the particular importance of mentoring for women, but also highlights their difficulty in finding mentors (Ragins, 1989). Organizations must, as much as possible, move to formalize mentoring relations, particularly in light of sex differences and cross-sex effects on the mentor-protégé relationship (Burke, McKeen, and McKenna, 1990).

One explanation posited for the failure of women to break the glass ceiling is that they lack access to informal networks and are excluded from informal relations with male colleagues, usually referred to as "old boys' networks" (Ragin and Sundstrom, 1989). Women tend to be less aware of the informal networks and their importance and potential usefulness. There has been little support (in both time and resources) provided to women to build informal networks. Both men and women generally prefer to communicate with others similar to themselves; and men, being the dominant group in almost all organizations, typically maintain their dominance by excluding women from informal interactions. Organizations committed to addressing the obstacles women face in organizations must provide more support and assistance to women in forming and being included in informal networks, because it is in these networks that critical human resources decisions such as promotion and acceptance often are in effect made and validated.

C. The Dilemma Remains

What can women expect from their organizations in the 1990s? Catalyst (1991) conducted a survey of large American corporations to examine the current status of women in their organizations, the perceptions of executives on the qualities women needed to succeed, and also the nature of the programs and services offered to assist women in overcoming the obstacles and barriers they face. The results are not all that promising. In spite of the fact that nearly 60% of the companies surveyed responded that women constituted over 50% of their hourly employees, they represented less than 5% of senior management in over half of the companies. Women remained clustered in traditional female areas (human resources, communications, and public affairs). Although over half believed that their managerial women had the competencies and skills necessary to compete with men for senior management positions, developing women was not one of the top human resource strategies—this in spite of the fact that most chief executive respondents (79%), believed that there were identifiable barriers to the advancement of women, and an even greater proportion (91%) believed it was the company's responsibility to help remove these barriers.

One of the greatest paradoxes of the past two decades is that in spite of the huge influx of women into management, inequity and discrimination continue. Women represent close to 50% of the workforce and will be an even more significant component in the future, but organizations are slow to recognize this reality and capitalize on the full potential of their women employees. Organizations that accept the challenge must recognize the costs associated with continued inaction. They then must accept collectively the responsibility for this lack of opportunity and success of women, and work with women and men within their organizations to find the necessary solutions. Underutilized resources in our organizations cannot be left underdeveloped in a competitive organization and world economy; it is important that managers and organizational leaders recognize the valuable resource women represent to management.

V. THE ISSUES AND CHALLENGES FOR MANAGING DIVERSITY IN THE 21ST CENTURY

Organizations and management in the 21st century will be very different from what we inherited in the 1980s. The world will face unparalleled demographic challenges and a workforce that will be increasingly cynical of cosmetic and superficial change. In the 1980s and now the 1990s, the labor force will fall to its lowest level since the 1930s. Surviving the baby bust will require that organizations draw on women, ethnic minorities, and the disabled. The effective workforce will be a much more diverse workforce (Morrison and Von Glinow, 1990). The challenge facing organizations in the 1990s is to assimilate a more diverse labor force into high-status, high-skill management roles.

Preparing for the challenges of the 21st century is no small task. A major difficulty is that increasingly, factors external to the specific remedies required may affect the outcomes more than the necessary remedies themselves. Organizational cultures will have to be transformed, and the track record for successful cultural transformation has not been very impressive. Konrad calls for the reinforcement of women-friendly companies (Konrad, 1990). This *Business Week* survey identified major corporations in which women made up at least 20% of senior management positions. The survey identified only six organizations, but did identify some additional organizations that they felt were on the way. The analysis of these women-friendly companies, however, did not result in any agreement as to what was required in order to improve opportunities for women.

It appears that there is no easy solution to the obstacles and barriers that women face in achieving success in organizations. It requires that organizations recognize that the problem exists, and that it is their responsibility to do something about it. Most critically, women themselves must take the initiative to bring about these essential changes. Achieving effective workforce diversity requires action, the sooner the better. There is a significant challenge to undertake research that clearly shows that women-friendly organizations are successful and effective.

There are obvious steps organizations can take to ensure continued commitment of all their workers, including women. These include: increasing job satisfaction by matching workers' expectations with appropriate rewards, increasing the meaningfulness of the work that women do in the organization, and encouraging as well as valuing the participation of women in decision making. Of particular interest to women, organizations can offer more flexible working hours, provide child care support, and implement obvious practices that show they value a diverse workforce.

Organizations and their leaders must address the issues that women face in the workplace, especially stress and burnout, work and family, dual-career families, and workplace flexibility—for matters will only get worse. By 1995, the U. S. Department of Labor predicts that 81% of all marriages will be dual-career partnerships (Reynolds and Bennett, 1991). The changing nature of the workforce and demographics will require women-friendly settings that formally recognize time off for child and eldercare for both men and women (Falkenberg, Monachello, and Edlund, 1991). These organizations will move to identify critical tasks and measure performance on them. Women-friendly companies will initiate policies that eliminate unnecessary stress caused by role conflicts and unreasonable time pressures (e.g., power breakfasts, lunches, and compulsory after-hour meetings and functions). Career development will increasingly be focused on lateral promotions for individuals who are balancing other responsibilities, and also will provide for career opt-outs for temporary periods of time (Falkenberg, Monachello, and Edlund, 1991).

Management education must take some initiative in revising curricula to reflect awareness of gender issues in the workplace and examine issues of sex-role stereotyping (Rosener and Pierce, 1989). Role models of successful women in senior positions must be available. Increasingly, organizational culture and the quality of work life must be addressed by organizations. Although the impetus for such attention is directed toward improving the opportunities that women face in organizations, the successful resolution will result in more effective and progressive human resource practices that will benefit all members of the organization. Research efforts must be expanded to show why gender differences are desirable and positive for competitive organizations in a world economy.

Some positive signs do exist, of course. According to women in the executive search field, companies today are increasingly recognizing the value of promoting women to executive positions for pragmatic business reasons, not just to fulfill equal employment obligations (Overman, 1991). They realize that in order to attract and retain competent women, a supportive culture must be developed and models provided.

Plenty of initiatives remain, clearly. Haskell (1991) identified some of the impenetrable barriers that women continue to face in the 1990s:

- An old boys' network that continues to stereotype women and excluded them
- The pain of being a gender pioneer, created by the dilemmas that women face in balancing career, personal, and family life and in being the first of their gender to break into the old boys' network
- The need for women to continue to prove their competence as a result of training, experience, knowledge of the business, internal systems, etc.
- The commonly held view that there are in fact no real barriers to women in organizations today

- Exclusive organizational politics and the requirement that successful women executives must have access to them to build alliances and support
- The backlash phenomenon, the retaliation or punishment leveled against women who have become successful by men and women who may once have been supportive

Work role transitions are significant, yet largely misunderstood (Nicholson and West, 1988). This is particularly true for the transition from middle management to senior management, and the impact this has on an individual's career, self-concepts, and organizational adjustment. Organizations have a particular responsibility to recognize work role transitions, especially for gender pioneers.

Human resource practices for organizations committed to breaking these barriers will involve useful programs, for example, spousal placement services (Buhler, 1991) and flexible hours in order to facilitate dual-career families with children—but spirit and value—infusion must dominate. Executive leadership in the future will increasingly be made up of visionary team builders, motivated by a view of the nature of work that is inclusive rather than authoritative, that values diversity, and that believes that the way to be competitive in an increasingly global economy is to attract and retain the best people. These transformational executives will more often be women who have developed the strengths to work in flatter, more consensual organizations in which the organizational chart will look much more like a spider web than the traditional pyramid. Their new style of leadership will focus on empowerment and nuturing relationships across the organization and from different levels of management (Allan, 1991). The awareness of reality and the "value-added" contribution focus of women in organizations must increasingly continue to be an important, relevant, and significant emphasis of current organization research.

REFERENCES

Allan, Jane (1991). Managing: When women set the rules. *Canadian Business, 64*(4): 40–43.

Anastasi, A., and Foley, J. P. Jr. (1949). *Differential Psychology*. Macmillan, New York.

Antal, Ariane Berthoin, and Krebsbach-Gnath, Camilla (1986–1987). Women in management: Unused resources in the Federal Republic of Germany. *International Studies of Management and Organization, 16*(3/4): 131–151.

Armstrong, Pat (1989). Is there still a chairman of the board?, *J. of Management Development, 8*(6): 6–16.

Auster, Ellen R. (1988). Behind closed doors: Sex bias at professional and managerial levels. *Employment Responsibilities and Rights Journal, 1*(2): 129–144.

Bem, S. L. (1974). The measurement of psychological androgyny. *J. of Consulting and Clinical Psychology, 42*: 155–162.

Bem, S. L. (1975). Sex role adaptability: One consequence of psychological androgyny. *J. of Personality and Social Psychology, 42*: 634–643.

Bem, S. L. (1979). Theory and measurement of androgyny: A reply to the Pedhazur–Testenbaum and Locksley-Colten critiques. *J. of Personality and Social Psychology, 37*: 1047–1054.

Berlin, R. K. (September 12, 1988). Women beat the corporate game. *Fortune*: 128–138.

Boeker, Warren, Blair, Rebecca, Vanloo, M. Frances, and Roberts, Karlene (1985). Are the expectations of women managers being met?, *California Management Review, 27*(3): 148–157.

Bowman, G. W., Worthy, N. B., and Graysen, S. A. (1968). Are women executives people? *Harvard Business Review, 43*(4): 14–30.

Braiker, Harriet B. (1986). The secret of psychological stamina. *Working Woman, 11*(9); 129–132.

Brenner, O. C., Tomiewicz, J., and Schein, V. E. (1989). The relationship between sex role stereotypes and requisite management characteristics revised. *Academy of Management Journal, 32*(3): 662–669.

Broverman, I. K., Vogel, S. R., Broverman, D. M., Clarkson, F. E., and Rosenkrantz, P. S. (1972). Sex role stereotypes: A current appraisal. *J. of Social Issues, 28*(2): 59–78.

Buhler, Patricia (1991). The impact of women in business in the 90's. *Supervisor, 52*(11): 21–23.

Buono, A. F., and Kamm, J. B. (1983). Marginality and the organization socialization of female managers. *Human Relations, 36*(2): 1125–1140.

Bureau of Labor Statistics (1989). *Statistical Report*. U. S. Government Printer.

Burke, Ron J., McKeen, Carol A., and McKenna, C. S. (1990). Sex defferences and cross-sex effects on mentoring: Some preliminary data. *Psychological Reports, 61*(7): 1011–1023.

Cahoon, Allan R., and Rowney, J. I. A. Individual and Organizational Characteristics of Women in Managerial Leadership Roles, *Proceedings: Women in Management Research Symposium,* Mount Saint Vincent University, Halifax, Nova Scotia, April 1988.

Canadian Teachers Federation (1988). *Women in Education: Progress as Paradox—A Profile of Women as Teachers.* Canadian Teachers Federation.

Catalyst (1991). *Women in Corporate Management: Results of a Catalyst Survey.* New York.

Cohen, Sharon S. (1989). Beyond macho—The power of womanly management. *Working Woman, 14*(2): 77–81.

Cohen, Stephen L., and Bunker, Kerry A. (1975). Subtle effects of sex role stereotypes on recruiters' hiring decisions. *J. of Applied Psychology, 60*(5): 566–572.

Collins, Anne (1988). Why we're not number one: A position paper from Canada's top corporate women. *Canadian Business, 61*(11): 32–39, 141–153.

Colwil, Nina L. (1982). *The New Partnership: Women and Men in Organizations.* Mayfield Publishing. Palo Alto, Calif.

Crawford, M., and Marecek, J. (1989). Psychology reconstructs the female. *Psychology of Women Quarterly, 13*: 147–165.

Dalton M. (1951). Informal factors in career achievement. *American Journal of Sociology, 56*: 407–415.

Davidson, Marilyn, and Cooper, Gary (1985). Women managers: Work stress and marriage. *International Journal of Social Economics, 12*(2): 17–25.

Deaux, K., and Emswiller, T. (January 1974). Explanations of successful performance on sex-linked tasks: What is skill for the male is luck for the female. *J. of Personality and Social Psychology, 29*: 80–85.

Dubno, Peter (Spring 1985). Is corporate sexism passe?, *Business and Society Review, 53*: 59–61.

Engdahl, Lora (1988). Beat the clock. *Executive Financial Women, 3*(3): 18–23.

Falkenberg, Loren E., Monachello, Mary L., and Edlund, L. Connie (1991). What is needed to balance work and family responsibilities? *Equal Opportunities International, 19*(3/4): 33–37.

Feuer, Dale (1988). Who women manage. *Training, 25*(8): 23–31.

Fierman, Jaclyn D. (July 30, 1990). Why women still don't hit the top. *Fortune*: 40–62.

Friedman, Dana E. (1988). Why the glass ceiling. *Across the Board, 25*(7/8): 32–37.

Gallese, Liz R. (1989). Corporate women on the move: Here are the women to watch in corporate America. *Business Month, 133*(4): 30–56.

Gold, Una O'C., and Pringle, Judith K. (1988). Gender-specific factors in management promotion. *J. of Managerial Psychology, 3*(4): 17–22.

Goldberg, P. A. (1968). Are women prejudiced against women? *Trans-Actions, 5*(5): 28–30.

Hammond, Valarie (1986). Management training for women. *J. of European Industrial Training, 10*(7): 15–22.

Harlan, A., and Weiss, C. (1981). *Moving Up: Women in Managerial Careers.* Centre for Research on Women, Wellesley College, Wellesley, Mass.

Haskell, Jean R. (1991). A new look at women executive. *Executive Excellence, 8*(1): 13–14.

Hennig, Margaret, and Jardin, Anne (1977). *The Managerial Woman.* Doubleday, Garden City, N.Y.

Horgan, Dianne D. (1989). A cognitive learning perspective on women becoming expert managers. *J. of Business and Psychology, 3*(3): 299–313.

Izaeli, Dafna N. (1986–1987). Women's movement into management in Israel. *International Studies of Management and Organization, 16*(3/4): 76–107.

Jefferson, Vivian V. (1989). Compensation: The gender gap continues. *Association Management, 41*(1): 56–64.

Kanter, Rosabeth Moss (1977a). *Men and Women of the Corporation.* Basic Books, Inc., New York.

Kanter, Rosabeth Moss (1977b). Women in organizations: Sex roles, group dynamics, and change strategies. In *Beyond Sex Roles* (A. G. Sargent, ed.), West Publishing Company, New York, pp. 371–387.

Kanter, Rosabeth Moss (March 1987). Men and women of the corporation revisited. *Management Review*: 14–16.

Kolb, D. A. (1974). Four styles of managerial learning. In *Organizational Psychology: A Book of Readings*, 2nd ed. (D. A. Kolb, I. M. Rubin, and J. M. McIntyre, eds.), Prentice Hall, Englewood Cliffs, N.J.

Konrad, W. (1990). Welcome to the women friendly company. *Business Week, 30*: 165–172.

Korabik, Karen, and Ayman, Roya (1989). Women managers have to act like men. *J. of Management Development, 8*(6): 23–32.

Kram, K. E. (1985). *Mentoring at Work.* Scott Foresman, Glenview, Ill.

Kram, K. E. and Isabella, L. A. (1985). Mentoring alternatives: The role of peer relationships in career development. *Academy of Management Journal, 28*(1): 110–132.

Lamkin, Martha D. (1986). Power: How to get it, keep it, and use it wisely. *Vital Speeches, 53*(5): 151–154.

Lips, Hilary M. (1981). *Women, Men and the Psychology of Power.* Prentice-Hall, Inc., Englewood Cliffs, N.J.

Little, Danity M. (1991). Women in government: Shattering the glass ceiling. *Bureaucrat, 20*(3): 24–28.

Lockheed, M. E., and Hall, K. P. (1976). Conceptualizing sex as a status characteristic: Applications to leadership training strategies. *J. of Social Issues, 32*(3): 111–124.

Loden, Marilyn (1985). *Feminine Leadership: How to Succeed in Business Without Being One of the Boys.* Times Books, New York.

Loring, Rosalind, and Wells, Theodora (1972). *Breakthrough: Women into Management.* Van Nostrand Reinhold Co., New York.

Lynagh, Peter M., and Poist, Richard F. (1985). Women: A difference of opinion. *Distribution, 84*(8): 90–93.

Maccoby, E. E. (1966). *The Development of Sex Differences.* Stanford University Press, Stanford, Calif.

McGregor, D. (1967). *The Professional Manager.* McGraw-Hill, New York.

Mischel, H. N. (1974). Sex bias in the evaluation of professional achievements. *J. of Educational Psychology, 66:* 157–166.

Morrison, Ann, and Von Glinow, M. A. (Fall 1990). Women and minorities in management. *American Psychologist, 45:* 200–208.

Morrison, A. M., White, R. P., Van Velsor, E., and the Center for Creative Leadership (1987). *Breaking the Glass Ceiling: Can Women Reach the Top of America's Largest Corporations?* Addison-Wesley, Reading, Mass.

Nicholson, Nigel, and West, Michael (1988). *Managerial Job Change: Men and Women in Transition.* the Press Syndicate of the University of Cambridge, Cambridge, U.K.

Overman, Stephanie (1991). In search of women achievers. *Human Relations Magazine, 36*(6): 60–61, 116.

Pecorella, Robert F. (1986). Gender integration in the public sector: From sanitationman to sanitation worker. *Urban Resources, 3:* 15–21.

Peters, Thomas J., and Waterman, Robert H. Jr. (1982). *In Search of Excellence: Lessons From America's Best Run Corporations.* Harper & Row, New York.

Pfeffer, J. (January 1977). The ambiguity of leadership. *Academy of Management Review:* 104–112.

Powell, Gary N., and Butterfield, D. Anthony (1979). The good manager: Masculine or androgynous? *Academy of Management Journal, 22*(2): 395–403.

Powell, Gary N., and Butterfield, D. Anthony (1989). The "good manager": Did androgyny fare better in the 1980's? *Group and Organization Studies, 14*(2): 216–233.

Quaglieri, Philip L., and Pacenka, Joseph O. (1985). Making it to the top. *Leadership and Organization Development Journal, 6*(1): 25–26.

Ragins, B. R., and Sundstrom, E. (January 1989). Gender and power in organizations: A longitudinal perspective. *Psychological Bulletin, 105:* 51–58.

Reynolds, Calvin, and Bennett, Rita (March 1991). The career couple challenge. *Personnel Journal, 70*(3): 46–48.

Rosen, B., and Jerdee, T. H. (1973). The influence of sex-role stereotypes on evaluators of male and female supervisory behavior. *J. of Applied Psychology, 57:* 44–48.

Rosener, Judy B., and Pearce, Catherine L. (1989). Men and women in organizations: Are future managers exposed to the issues? *Organizational Behavior Teaching Review, 13*(2): 55–67.

Rosenkrantz, P., Vogel, S., Bee, H., Broverman, I., and Broverman, D. M. (1968). Sex-role stereotypes and self concepts in college students. *J. of Consulting and Clinical Psychology, 32:* 287–295.

Rowney, J. I. A., and Cahoon, A. R. (1990). Individual and organizational characteristics of women in managerial leadership. *J. of Business Ethics, 9*(4/5): 293–316.

Sargent, Alice G. (1981). *The Androgenous Manager.* Amacom, New York.

Sargent, Alice G. (1983). Women and men working together: Toward androgyny. *Training and Development Journal, 37*(4): 70–76.

Sargent, Alice G., and Stupak, Ronald J. (1989). Managing in the '90s: The androgynous manager. *Training and Development Journal, 43*(2): 29–35.

Schein, V. E. (1971). The woman industrialist psychologist: Illusion or reality. *American Psychologist, 26*(8): 708–712.

Schein, V. E. (1973). The relationship between sex role stereotypes and requisite management characteristics. *J. of Applied Psychology, 57*: 95–100.

Schein, V. E. (June 1975). The relationship between sex role stereotypes and requisite management characteristics among female managers. *J. of Applied Psychology, 60*: 340–344.

Schein, Virginia E. (1989). Sex role stereotypes and requisite management characteristics past, present and future, working paper NC. 89-26, National Centre for Management Research and Development, School of Business Administration, the University of Western Ontario, Canada.

Schwartz, Felice N. (March/April 1992). Women as a business imperative. *Harvard Business Review, 70*(2): 105–113.

Sheriffs, A. C., and Jarrett, R. F. (1953). Sex differences in attitudes about sex differences. *J. of Psychology, 35*: 161–168.

Statistics Canada (1986). Labour Force Activity Report.

Stein, R. T., and Heller, T. (1979). An empirical analysis of the correlations between leadership status and participation rates reported in the literature. *J. of Personality and Social Psychology, 37*(11): 1993–2002.

Steinhoff, Patricia G., and Tanaka, Kazuko (1986–1987). Women managers in Japan. *International Studies of Management and Organization, 16*(3/4): 108–132.

Stephan, Paula E. (1987). The career prospects of female MBA's. *Business, 37*(1): 37–41.

Taylor, Alex III (1986). Why women managers are bailing out. *Fortune, 114*(4): 16–23.

Tharenou, P. (1991). The relative importance of work and home environments, early and later experiences and cognitions for men and women managers' progression, Academy of Management Best Paper Proceedings, (J. L. Wall and L. R. Jauch, eds.), Miami Beach.

U.S. Office of Personnel Management (1989). *Report on Minority.* Group and Sex Pay Plan and Appointing Authority, report no. 40, Washington, D.C.

Varca, P., Shaffer, G. S., and McCauley, C. D. (1983). Sex differences in job satisfaction revised. *Academy of Management Journal, 26*(2): 348–353.

Wente, Margaret (1985). The woman who never was. *Canadian Business, 58*(6): 253–259.

Williams, Shirley (1987). Women: Liberation's hostages? *Director, 41*(3): 156–160.

Wilson, C., and Lupton, T. (1959). The social background and connections of top decision makers. *Manchester School of Economics and Social Studies, 27*: 33–51.

Part III
Some Themes with Great Potential

16
On the Wisdom of Making Values Explicit in Organizational Behavior Research

Gordon A. Walter

The University of British Columbia, Vancouver, British Columbia, Canada

A variety of values provide a powerful impetus to social science research. However, objectivity is such a strong ideal for all science that values are generally left implicit, denied, or obfuscated. Moreover, implicit value issues impose more significant problems for the social sciences than for most of the physical sciences. *Values deserve far more explicit consideration* in research. For example, why are certain implicit values concentrated in a given subfield and not in another? Varying popularity of research has been documented to be remarkably independent of the accumulation of rigorous research results (Dunnette and Brown, 1968; Nord and Durand, 1978). It is likely that the popularity of research is substantially related to the values attached to the subject matter, but we often cannot even be sure what those values are. This is only one of many reasons explored in this chapter about the significance of making values explicit in organizational behavior (OB) research. This chapter offers one view of why the field would benefit from scrutinizing the value aspects of research with the same rigor that is directed toward theoretical and methodological aspects. Specific value questions about pivotal issues in the field are explored to make some fundamental issues more explicit. These issues include the people OB research is supposed to serve, the world OB research is helping to enact, and the power the field relies upon to make a point.

This chapter explicitly emphasizes one value, freedom (Walter, 1984). Freedom is argued to be worthy of researcher care and attention. The freedom value carries the ethical imperative to anyone communicating with others to provide the information necessary for those individuals to exercise informed choice. The freedom value is, therefore, the basis for this chapter's call for more explicit value reporting in research. Explicit value reporting is a critical prerequisite of informed choice among readers (Walter, 1984).

Wisdom is needed, as well as technical competence, to make values explicit in OB research (Kaplan, 1964; Rokeach, 1968; 1973). Unfortunately, the social sciences do not generally cultivate the forms of discourse usually associated with wisdom's calling, such as that of Kaplan and Rokeach or such as is available in historical analysis and philosophy (two exemplars here are Wildavsky, 1979; McIntyre, 1981). In fact, social science seldom seems to aspire to wisdom. This chapter offers one view of the nature of wisdom and contrasts this with what is generally assumed to be the endpoint of research striving. The chapter returns periodically to question why borrowing from the physical sciences has not worked out as well as intended.

In this chapter I try to speak plainly and simply about issues that are anything but plain and simple. My hope is that the chapter will open doors for some readers to be more responsive to the "will of wisdom" in dealing with values in research and practice. Equally strong is my hope that I have the wisdom to deal well with such an elusive topic (Kaplan, 1964). Wisdom is a word seldom used in OB. Instead, we generally concentrate on "validated knowledge." Nevertheless, wisdom is what we must aspire to if we are to unravel fundamental value issues in research. This chapter begins by focusing on wisdom. It then moves on to several value-laden issues at the heart of the field.

I. WHY IS WISDOM NEEDED TO ILLUMINATE VALUES IN OB RESEARCH?

Social science research seems to be more difficult than physical science research in several ways. Two particular burdens in social science research are the subjectivity of the variables and the complexity of the interrelations among them. Moreover, humans act on their environment differently than do physical things (e.g., atoms) or even other species (e.g., insects). Humans are less programmed and less tightly determined by a dominant law, or tied up by genetic programming. Quite simply, the variables of relevance to any OB study are profound, subtle, complex, and imbedded within the phenomenon and method in ways unheard of in the physical sciences.

Rigorous measures and methods in social science can subdue but not eliminate these difficulties. However, social science does not need to be defensive or defeatist about these subjectivities; we need "wisdom" to penetrate them. Ironically, while OB is beginning to see the relevance of wisdom in management and management development, "social scientists have largely ignored this topic" (Bigelow, 1992: 144). First we need to overtly acknowledge the sources of ambiguity and vagueness that research with humans involves. Indeed, Dunnette (1966) used the term *incurable vagueness* in his diagnosis of psychology.

Dunnette's judgment seems chillingly appropriate to OB today, despite substantial progress on many fronts. Our progress in applying the scientific analytical method to the issues of organizations has been impressive, but it also has left reflective epistemologists profoundly concerned (Phillips, 1976; Astley, 1985). Further, the growing divergencies in results and paradigms prompted Pfeffer (1988) to comment that the field today is more like a weed patch than a well-tended garden. When one contemplates matrices with hundreds of variables on each axis, one yearns for some way to create a synthesis. Is a daunting pile of often incompatible information the inevitable by-product of analytical decomposition research in OB?

Rather than seek immediate synthesis or an all-encompassing paradigm, this chapter suggests viewing the field from a different perspective. Unfortunately, what becomes apparent is *a need to increase decomposition*. However difficult this strategy might seem in the short run, it just may also open the door to wisdom. The next three sections offer the reader a unique perspective from which to consider "progress" in OB research. Wisdom provides the unifying theme for developing this perspective.

II. SCIENCE AND WISDOM

Physical scientists protest that social science is not really science because "it has no laws." One response to this pressure has been the adoption of the scientific method: the use of rigorous tests for research design, measurement, and data analysis. Another response has been to advance ideas that have strong face validity, a sense of reasonableness, and popular appeal. (Both issues are addressed later.)

This alleged deficiency has been nettlesome to social science from the start. For once let us not be defensive in the face of this criticism. Let's accept it (Machlup, 1961). Then, given our dilemma, let's ask: "What is the best way for social science to advance that is consistent with the *spirit and purpose of the physical sciences?*" First, we would pay particular attention to laws or at least lawlike truths.

Two obvious candidates for social science laws are the "law of effect" and the "law of supply and demand." The well-known law of effect is, of course, the central law of behaviorism. It asserts that behavior is a function of its consequences (rewards and punishments). The second law, the law of supply and demand, is the central law in economics. It asserts that increased demand for a good or service is positively correlated with increased price.

We know that even these two laws do not hold 100% of the time, but they serve well over time and at the aggregate level of analysis. We also know that both of these laws are in many ways weaker than physical laws, such as the "law of gravity" and the "second law of thermodynamics." However, the two behavioral laws do capture strong tendencies in human affairs and have a high degree of generalizability. They *are* lawlike truths.

OB research usually measures variables and models that are less perfect than the laws of supply and demand and effect. As already noted, confounding complexities and subjectivities arise in social science because humans have intentionality, unlike inanimate objects, which are the prime focus in physical science (Quine, 1960). The absence of laws does not invalidate application of inductive/analytic/reductionistic research strategies to OB issues. Quite the contrary. In the absence of comprehensive laws, many have concluded that seeking objective truth via highly decomposed phenomena is even more imperative because of the field's vulnerability to polemics. Decomposition is accepted as specific to unique variable subsets and conditions (Phillips, 1976). Unfortunately, reductionism as a research strategy yields increasing fragmentation of results within and especially between different schools of thought. And information fragments do not aggregate as well in the social sciences as they do in the physical sciences. The fact that various paradigms are competing for the position of "framing" the overarching questions between fields may in the long term bring some significant resolution, but in the short term they actually increase the problems. Pfeffer's (1988) weed patch metaphor is not one that comforts those working in a scientific field.

How do we sort the weeds and the fruits of our garden? If one OB paradigm yields slightly better correlations than another, should it be considered superior? What if one paradigm concentrates on "harder" (more measurable) variables? What if the results from one paradigm assault another paradigm's cherished values? What if one group's cherished values are used to suppress scientific research results from an unpopular or awkward paradigm? What criterion should be used to choose between incompatible facts when the informational component of research results is less important than value questions? For example, crime is a problem for society. Can there be any doubt that ferocious policing, prosecution, and punishment would reduce the crime rate? Would proving this via a rigorous research design, measurement, and data analysis make any difference? Would acting on this proof yield a "good" society by Western cultural standards, emphasizing individual freedom?

Is the worth of research in its applications or in the excitement it generates within a constituency (Davis, 1971)? Consider again the law of effect. The real shortcoming of the law of effect is not its invalidity. It is as close to a real law as behavioral science will ever get. The law approaches truth, is scientifically respectable, and is also of practical value. But, let's face it, the law of effect is not very exciting to a large portion of the field. The law of effect is useful but not fascinating, effective but tedious, pragmatic but uninspiring! No wonder our own epistemologists and many outside social sciences view the conduct of social science with scepticism (Astley, 1985).

However, social science has established increasingly clearly defined methods in its drive for scientific adequacy and respectability. Adherence to these methods is yielding increasingly valid information, although at times there is a tendency to ask smaller questions in an effort to create research control. Thus behavioral science is rising above the "B.S." epithet attributed to it by bad-tempered critics. Unfortunately, scientific methods alone do not a science make. A discipline that finds correlation coefficients of 0.2 noteworthy and 0.4 impressive (as long as there is statistical significance) is a long way from fulfilling the purpose of science: prediction and control. Are we really getting closer to lawlike truths?

Thus far I have described how the dominant research paradigm in OB seems to impel a perpetual and perhaps growing state of disaggregated results. Some assert an urgent need for synthesis (Pfeffer, 1988) but progress here has been less than perhaps once was hoped for. Since no simple laws are identifiable, "wisdom" may provide a mechanism by which we can at least *prioritize results*. A digression into nature of wisdom seems useful at this point.

III. INFORMATION, KNOWLEDGE, AND WISDOM

Wisdom involves prudence and sound judgment, but wisdom is more than this. Note that wisdom has linked, but distinct, etymologies from information and knowledge. Information comes from the Latin *forma*, the shape of data. Knowledge is to know (how). Wisdom is from the Latin *vide* (to see) and refers to perceiving sacred knowledge (Partridge, 1966). Bigelow concluded from a review of the "wisdom literature" (e.g., Ben Franklin) that the essentials of wisdom include: (1) movement to longer-term strategies; (2) ability to learn from experience; (3) expanding practical knowledge; (4) metaknowledge: knowledge of the limits of knowledge; and (5) value and orientation shifts toward emphasis on increasing "interiority" (e.g., peace of mind), as well as toward external action geared to the common good (Bigelow, 1992: 145–147). This section of the chapter extends both concrete and more illusive aspects of wisdom.

According to ethicists, while the objective of science is prediction and control, the objective of wisdom is maintaining and enhancing the "good" (Frankena, 1963). Wisdom is thought and action in the service of specific values. Personal wisdom is often equated with the personal discipline that enables one to live according to guiding precepts or a guiding vision. Still, wisdom is simultaneously *more abstract and more action oriented* than mere prudence. A Zen master explains wisdom

> If we are prepared for thinking, there is no need to make an effort to think. This is called mindfulness. Mindfulness is, at the same time, wisdom. By wisdom we do not mean some particular faculty or philosophy. It is the readiness of the mind that is wisdom. So wisdom could be various philosophies and teachings, and various kinds of research and studies. But we should not become attached to some particular wisdom, such as that which was taught by Buddha. Wisdom is not something to learn. Wisdom is something which will come out of your mindfulness. So the point is to be ready for observing things, and to be ready for thinking. This is called emptiness of your mind. Emptiness is nothing but the practice of zazen (Suzuki, 1975: 115).

This view contrasts with Bigelow's (1992) which is essentially that of wisdom as a metaskill. Bigelow sees wisdom to be developed through coping with complex challenges and making other practical efforts, through ascending in value clarity, and through transcending short-term selfishness. While OB is concerned with the *right information*, one has a sense from both perspectives that wisdom is fundamentally about *using and experiencing* different "truths" in a *right way*. A wisdom perspective should give pause to young scholars who are cramming as many ideas as possible into their heads. Retrieval and utilization mechanisms are equally important. Mature scholars might reflect whether or not they have become overly identified with or attached to a particular paradigm.

Physical science has been successful in transforming information into knowledge. This is partially because of the clarity and tangibleness of many variables and tests in physical science. For example, my master's thesis was in solid state physics and seems like a dream of simplicity, graphic measurement, and access to direct extensions of powerful laws and relations. The last 200 years stand as a tribute to the power of science for bringing the physical world into the service of humanity. Sceptics and critics cannot destroy the powerful position of science in our social order. Social science rightly builds on that tradition. However, in the social sciences, transforming information into knowledge is often more difficult, plus the aggregation problem persists.

Still, isn't the Zen notion of emptiness just Eastern mysticism? One need not go to the mystical East to access judgments about wisdom that also confront our assumptions about the aggregation of knowledge as the way to wisdom. Take, for example, the autobiography of Henry Adams, who was the son of the U.S. ambassador to France during the Civil War, the grandson of John Quincy Adams (the fourth president), and the great-grandson of John Adams (the second president). At the end of a brilliant career at Harvard and as an advisor to a series of presidents, Henry Adams concluded

> The object of education for that mind should be the teaching itself how to react with vigour and economy . . . education should try to lessen the obstacles, diminish the friction, invigorate the energy, and should train minds to react, not at haphazard, but by choice, on the lines of force that attract . . . Accidental education could go no further, for one's mind was already littered and stuffed beyond hope with the millions of chance images stored away without order in the memory. One might as well try to educate a gravel-pit (Adams, 1963: 314–316).

Ironically, the Zen master quoted earlier draws an almost identical conclusion to that of Henry Adams: "It is quite usual for us to gather pieces of information from various sources, thinking in this way to increase our knowledge. Actually, following this way we end up not knowing anything at all . . . Instead of gathering knowledge, you should clear your mind" (Suzuki, 1975: 84–86).

The central point of this section links directly with the message about the limits of the scientific method noted in Section II. Still, wisdom appears to be even more illusive and subjective than assumed or implied by most OB research. Wisdom seems to confound simple notions of knowledge advancement through information specification and accumulation. The challenge, then, is for the field to learn how to develop and draw upon wisdom in improved ways. The field of ethics offers a specific focal point to improve our ability in drawing on wisdom.

IV. THE VIRTUES TRADITION IN ETHICS: WISDOM IN ACTION

Wisdom, both in the West and the East, involves *a way of being* rather than an amount of data storage. Ethicists refer to such personal characteristics as *virtues* (McIntyre, 1981), and consistently, they see wisdom as a virtue. The virtue of wisdom enables one to perceive ephemeral "goods" and to utilize subtle truths in human affairs. The distinction between Eastern and Western thought is not about wisdom being a virtue but about how to cultivate wisdom in oneself.

Henry Adams's notion of "lines of force that attract" implies that wisdom comes from winnowing and refining knowledge through a combination of thought and action. This idea is consistent with Bigelow's (1992) recommendations for a management development pedagogy, and this idea seems quite reasonable to most Westerners. Adams appears to believe in intellectually understanding the underlying principles that govern human affairs. In this sense, Adams was a man of the emerging scientific age in which we are now even more firmly rooted.

The principles by which a wise person lives are, virtually, personal laws. Principles of life cannot be proven, but they can be experienced. If the experience is good, the necessary validation is provided in the form of a good life. Further, saying "lines of force that attract" implies a need to go beyond fragmented information toward a *pattern of knowledge* that is consistent with underlying "laws." This means that wisdom *does not come from evermore precise information*, but from a comprehensive grasp of something more abstract, more enduring, more holistic (Bigelow, 1992). In this sense Adams reflects a classical education as well as a scientific one. Moreover, wisdom comes at the nexus of knowledge and practice.

Wisdom in Zen is equally clearly seen not to be attained through an accumulation or a refinement process. However, even in Zen, wisdom does involve striving toward a very similar state to that implied by Adams. In Zen, constant meditation increases *both* self-awareness and self-detachment. For example, this "skill" gives the individual an opportunity to see his or her own distortions, projections, and other follies. As Suzuki explains (1975: 84–86)

> If your mind is clear, true knowledge is already yours. When you listen to our teaching with a pure, clear mind, you can accept it as if you were hearing something which you already knew. This is called emptiness, or omnipotent self, or knowing everything. When you know everything, you are like a dark sky. Sometimes a flashing will come through the dark sky. After it passes, you forget all about it, and there is nothing left but the dark sky. The sky is never surprised when all of a sudden a thunderbolt breaks through. And when the lightning does flash, a wonderful sight may be seen. When we have emptiness we are always prepared for watching the flashing . . . The usual translation of the Japanese word *nin* is "patience" but perhaps "constancy" is a better word. You must force yourself to be patient, but in constancy there is no particular effort involved—there is only the unchanging ability to accept things as they are. For people who have no idea of emptiness, this ability may appear to be patience, but patience can actually be non-acceptance. People who know, even if only intuitively, the state of emptiness always have open the possibility of accepting things as they are . . . We should always live in the dark empty sky. The sky is always the sky. Even though clouds and lightning come, the sky is not disturbed. Even if the flashing of enlightenment comes, our practice forgets all about it. Then it is ready for another enlightenment. It is necessary for us to have enlightenments one after another, if possible moment after moment. This is what is called enlightenment before you attain it and after you attain it.

In short, wisdom is self-mastery. Perhaps the pivotal element of self-mastery in Zen is the wisdom not to succumb to the cognitive tendency of trying to force experience into schema, preconceived theories, and personal motive-driven projections and distortions (e.g., Alba and Hasher, 1983). If so, then wisdom in Zen has parallels to the psychological concepts of accurate perception and nondefensive ego boundaries. This is *not* a very mystical mode of functioning, although it is a difficult one. Virtue in Zen is to be *free* from the self-delusions that arise from desires and preconceived thoughts and is remarkably similar to Western notions of psychological health and even vibrancy. It takes great virtue to be sufficiently wise to avail oneself of the "obvious," but perhaps not a great deal of information and knowledge.

Why is it that social science is so entranced with information and so oblivious to wisdom and to virtue? McIntyre asserts that the entire twentieth century has been involved in a broad renunciation of the "virtues" tradition of the previous several thousand years: "In most of the public and most of the private world the classical and medieval virtues are replaced by the meagre substitutes which modern morality affords" (McIntyre, 1981: 225). That is, the orientation in this scientific age has shifted from mastering self (wisdom) to directing and controlling external objective reality, both physical and social. It has also moved away from explicit attention to values and toward explicit attention to mechanisms, formulas, and models of manipulating that external world.

Have the social sciences taken a wrong turn somewhere in their development? Today research within a given paradigm often generates information that is incongruent with findings in another paradigm. Paradigms compete for dominance in framing the basic issues of the day. This competition is intense and earnest, but also in a sense, it is a charade, because paradigmatic differences are not likely to ever be scientifically resolved.

Perhaps more than ever, information may distract thought from wisdom, and more important, may deflect action from other virtues. How can we tame the thicket and thereby move beyond debates in which information is always talked about but the value positions actually driving competing paradigms are suppressed? One way is for researchers to be more explicit about the values that inspire their work or are served by it. Another is to document key value aspects of research design and methodology. To this end, we now ask some basic questions. First among these are questions about the people who benefit from the knowledge that OB research generates.

V. WHOM DO WE SERVE?

Who uses the knowledge that OB research generates? To whom does it have value and how is it applied? The answers to these questions are not obvious.

By contrast, the field of finance has both clarity and simplicity here. Finance is dedicated to the holders of capital and their agents. Why does OB claim to serve both everybody (organizational participants and managers) and nobody (systems and procedures improvement)? Does OB primarily serve managers or owners? By concentrating on descriptions of external social dynamics and ignoring making values explicit, researchers shroud their results in a kind of mystery. If we are to serve university students, should they learn more about building the system or merely competing within (or with) it? Porter and McKibben (1989) indicate that students do not need more information. They need skills and other "how-to" capacity development. However, little OB research has been directed toward skill and capacity specification and development. Why?

Does OB serve the human resources function? Most decidedly yes. Is OB for big companies or small, manufacturing or service? Most new jobs have been created in small companies and in service industries. Why has OB paid so little attention to these sectors? Has OB slowed or accellerated the decline of many large corporations relative to international competition?

Is OB knowledge for managers? Yes and no. OB research is increasingly technical and unfortunately requires considerable translation to be of value to managers; that is, it is often not directly useful (Lorsch, 1979; Miner, 1984). There are many exceptions to this observation, but OB research often makes one think of the Sufi story about the idiot savant, Nasrudin. Nasrudin was looking for his keys under a streetlight. When a helpful bystander asked where the keys were lost, Nasrudin replied that it was hundreds of yards away. Unfortunately, it was much too dark to search in that area. So he was (re?)searching where he could *see clearly*.

Organizational behavior seems to ask a preponderance of questions near certain lights, such as a convenient sample that is quickly approachable within various acceptable research conventions. Most researchers stick close to ideas that link well to established theoretical models and positions. In this sense OB is as much the prisoner of its theoretical roots as it is a beneficiary of them. Organizational behavior doesn't seem very concerned about, or excited at, the prospect of *disproving a theory*. We seek to justify and even repackage traditional theories. We do this in the face of the obvious fact that many of these theories are mutually incompatible. Why don't we focus research questions so that we can really test theories against one another (MacKenzie and House, 1978; Pfeffer, 1988)? What values of science have we missed in copying the form but not the spirit of physical science?

Should OB help construct good lives for people who must spend substantial proportion of their time within utilitarian organizations? Isn't it remarkable that the field has asked so few questions about what really constitutes a good life in organizations and relies on writers like Schrank and Turkel to focus attention? A good OB counterexample is found in Nord and Durand, 1978. Why do so many articles tell us so little about life in organizations? Does OB really have a commitment to thinking first about people living their lives in organizations rather than having jobs in organizations? Has OB contributed to the decline of organized labor in the United States? What values have really been served and what values have been diminished by OB research in the past 20 years?

Finally, perhaps OB primarily serves itself; that is, OB may have become a field in which academic *information* is primarily generated by and for academics to promote their careers and to create actualization opportunities for themselves (Astley, 1985). Some businesspersons attend various conferences, but most of the time they seem out of place. Several concerns have been raised about the incongruence between OB academic interests and business needs in recent years (e.g., Thomas and Tymon, 1982; Maher, 1990). In ancient Greece the decline of academe occurred when academics turned inwardly and communicated only with each other, rather than with their communities (Durant, 1944; also see Rimler, 1976). Have OB academics started such a process? If this is true, what values are being actualized by various research projects?

VI. WHAT KIND OF A WORLD DO WE HELP TO ENACT?

Organizational behavior has been built on an open secret. Many people in OB are fascinated by the chance to understand the complexities of human interaction, and harbor hopes of contributing to a better order. The definition of "better" evidently varies a great deal, if one reflects on research themes and "camps." To some, it is a world of finely honed administrative systems that bring bureaucracy to its zenith. To some it is an "empowering" social context. To some it is a system that is fair, where "fair" can be defined as a crisp meritocracy, or mellow equalitarianism, in terms of various ideologies, or in terms of redressing a specific sense of injustice felt by a segment of society. Sometimes these values are very explicit and the images evoked are linked with the content of the theory. Oftentimes the researcher's values are more covertly imbedded in the research.

The point is that various value priorities are closely linked to the central images of most subdisciplines in OB (Astley, 1985). The fact that some research is more rigorous than other research should not deflect us from asking questions about the pivotal values fostered by each piece of work; being wrongly rigorous has little to recommend it.

Organizational behavior also involves a kind of elitism that is value-laden and may not be what many would gladly embrace, on reflection. Twenty years ago Gouldner (1973) asserted that value-free social science was a myth. At that time he also encouraged social scientists to be bold in efforts to actualize various values. This was done out of a sense of purpose, rather than elitism. Much of that purpose was humanistic and dedicated to social egalitarianism. Ironically, the effect is one of *designing the values* of a social order, a decidedly elite enterprise.

This form of elitism seems to be broadly held in all the social sciences and has been insightfully analyzed by Wildavsky (1979). Wildavsky draws a dichotomy between "intellectual cogitation" and "social interaction" as alternative styles of policy formulation (Wildavsky, 1979: 123; also see Table 1). Wildavsky explains that intellectual cogitation is favored by people who see themselves as the definers, designers, and directors of the evolving social order. These elites see themselves as having the right infromation, the right attitude, and the right power to direct progress. This *is* a value position.

The social interaction model is more Adam Smithian in character. It says that people will pursue their own desired outcomes through politics. Wildavsky argues that "policy analysis makes more sense as an aid to (rather than substitute for) the politics of social interaction . . . merely to say that something should be done—without saying anything about how is an abdication of responsibility . . . social forces use analysis to *advance as well as to understand their own interests*. The task of policy analysis, therefore, is the weighty and *ancient one of speaking truth to power*." (emphasis added, Wildavsky, 1979: 125–126).

Wildavsky's remarks may perhaps shed some light on why so many businesspersons perpetually complain that academics do not understand business. Academics typically focus on a narrow slice of reality and from these results advocate answers and formulas. Successful businesspersons report that the interactive flow of business life is more complex than is treated

Table 1   Alternative Styles of Policy Analysts

	Social interaction	Intellectual cogitation
Institutions	Markets and politics	Planning
Calculations	Partial	Comprehensive
Calculators	Many minds interacting	Single-minded decision
Decision making	Exchange and bargaining	Comprehending and deciding
Error	Correction	Avoidance
Criteria	Agreement	Right
Administration	Reactions	Orders

Source: From Wildavsky, 1979:123.

by academics. These dynamics mean that a purely analytic approach *invariably fails*. Metaphorically, consider a business issue to be a ball of yarn. A businessperson faces various tasks, such as winding the ball of yarn or making it tighter. Academic research tends to slice through the ball and expose a whole set of "ends" of cut yarn.

The academic "slice approach" doesn't help the interactive, dynamic, action-oriented manager. It does not matter how brilliant the data analysis or the modeling; nor is measurement accuracy of the density of cut ends all that important. Quite simply, the information generated is not usable (Beer, 1992). Businesspersons report that it is better to stumble along with "common sense" than to defer to expert/academic formulas that are based on such research (Thomas and Tymon, 1982). Bigelow (1992) defines common sense as the most basic form of wisdom.

At the same time, scholars need to be mindful of a trap in analytical science. This trap is attributing scientific motives, values, and agendas to businesspersons and government. This error is compounded when defenses against business or government critiques also focus on the analytic (Miner, 1984). Managers are primarily pragmatists and they are boggled by the fragmented and incongruous scientific knowledge they are exhorted to implement. For example, motivation research suggests technique A or B, leadership research may call for technique C, while negotiation research suggests technique D. When asked why they do not implement, say, a specific leadership prescription, those in business and government often report that they cannot separate leadership from a host of other simultaneous factors. These different action agendas are not separable in practice, according to businesspersons. Because they are interwoven, they require consistency of practice. But fragmentation and the technical demands of the field create growing risks of inconsistencies that "systems" models cannot overcome.

Can OB scholars learn to strike a balance between simply usable and tightly delineated/highly decomposed information? Are we dedicated to *appearing rational and detached* in the scientific sense to the exclusion of *being rational* about our purpose (Wildavsky, 1979)? One businessperson confided to me that one of his greatest fears was to be trapped in a presentation by a pure academic. The problem: boredom. This technically advanced and sophisticated person reported that he often had to withdraw from listening to an academic speaker's pedantry and trivia. To keep his mind active he concentrates on something more interesting—like counting the number of holes in the ceiling tiles! Yes, yes—they can bore us too. But how much power do we have when we meet with such a reaction from our key constituency?

VII. THE ISSUES THAT ARE EXPLORED OR IGNORED

Organizational behavior *seems* to study everything and to do so from almost every imaginable perspective. With closer scrutiny, however, one can easily identify blind spots, systematic exclusions, and fads. The field seems to gravitate toward dominant models and issues for substantial periods. For example, leadership research was developing fairly well-defined research norms in the mid-1970s, and at about the same time, it seemed to reach a dead end. Why was there a rebirth of leadership research in the late 1980s and how did it break the boundaries of earlier research conventions? Did previous methodological constraints die with the research stream? Why didn't this happen a decade earlier?

Organizational behavior has always demonstrated interest in and concern about conflict, yet OB has paid almost no attention to the conflict between management and owners. This conflict was ignored in OB until it became the centerpiece of agency theory in the fields of finance and accounting (Jensen and Meckling, 1976; Fama and Jensen, 1983). Agency theory delineates concerns identified over half a century ago by Berle and Means (1932) about dysfunctions in the separation of capital from control, and is directed at helping owners of firms with management problems. Agency theory argues that this conflict between absentee owners and professional managers can be addressed by contracts and "incentives." Organizational behavior research is just beginning in this area (see Tosi and Gomez-Mejia, 1989), and only a few OB researchers are trying to explore agency questions in greater depth (Walsh, 1990).

The questions tumble forth. How is it that an issue of such great significance was ignored by OB for so long? Was it incompatible with key values held by researchers? Would most OB researchers rather not think that Berle and Means had identified a significant or relevant issue? Do OB researcher values create blind spots, or is something more ideologically driven occurring? Could something akin to true narrow-mindedness be the real explanation?

VIII. THE POWER WE IN OB RELY UPON TO MAKE A POINT

Both scientific rigor and successful application are important sources of power for OB, although they do not always sit well together. Science seeks eternal truths, while applications imply a pressing need or unique problem. Science proceeds slowly but relevant applications often exist only for relatively brief periods. For example, consider the issue of faddishness in social science (Dunnette, 1966). Almost anything that generates excitement with audiences finds devotees in OB, and Abrahamson (1991) documents that faddishness has not fallen out of fashion in more recent years. Face validity often seems to be as compelling as solid scientific evidence or long-term business practice. A topic may be accepted at face value because it appeals to a prejudice, wishful thinking, or because it fits with a popular paradigm.

Marketing to some need or desire in a client group or an audience often can and does prevail over scientific rigor. At the present moment self-managing work teams are a "hot" variant of/alternative to the popular total quality management (TQM) model. How much do we really know about the long-term consequences of removing "real" supervisors/leaders?

Further, there is a strong tendency in OB to apply findings before there is proof (Pinder, 1977). This probably reveals a strategy of proving via application rather than through scientific means, and it may be a reasonable strategy for an individual scholar. Unfortunately, the scientific credibility of the field is reduced when applications yield poor results, since managers seldom are in a position to judge scientific rigor and rely on the discipline to provide screening. Premature application of scientific knowledge may even be unethical because of the implicit claim that scientific proof exists when it does not (Pinder, 1977). The point is, what values are really driving the field? Is this a science or an elaborate dance that legitimizes career adventurers in their dealings with nonscientists?

A second and contradictory problem involves style of communicating to audiences. Journalists are not inhibited by the canons of science, and in fact, a large proportion of the ideas actually absorbed by managers comes from "popular" sources, such as *Business Week* and *Fortune*. Journalistic writing can dominate over scientific rigor in popular sources, but one is struck by other differences between it and much of academic research. For example, journalists *really try to communicate* to their business audience and try to show *how* a specific technique, action, or insight applies in a *real context*. While some accepted applications may be difficult to scientifically document in complex business and government environments, it may be more valuable to study *why they work* than to criticize them for lacking rigorous analytic support.

Are we scientists, or more highly organized how-to columnists? Are we really rational? Earlier, this chapter relied on Wildavsky's observations on the "intellectual cogitation" proclivities of social planners. He states "In reality, *planning* is not defended for what it accomplishes but for what it *symbolizes—rationality*" (Wildavsky, 1979: 190, emphasis added). One can say, by analogy, that OB makes substantial claims about the role of science in management and gathers information using systematic scientific methods *to symbolize a value* that human affairs should be dealt with rationally.

Research may *appear* more rational when values are not made explicit, but in fact, keeping values hidden has just the opposite effect. Rationality is reduced. To a great degree, even in analytical activities, believing *is* seeing. Thus, in a way, journalists are more rational than OB academics because they make their value position abundantly clear in the emotional slanting of their message. By the informed choice criterion, this too serves the freedom value. The point is, journalists appear less rational than social scientists but may actually not be less rational or "fair" to the readers. They organize their communications to be usable and thus testable in the audience's world. Their power derives from the vividness and recency of their reportage rather than from scientific authority.

Academics scratch their heads in bewilderment and frustration when business or government people value nonscientific information over academically sound research (Miner, 1984). Perhaps the field is up against the inherent limitations of the scientific method itself. Would it not be wise for the OB field to accept that journalism has proven useful and to learn from that field? Should OB not take into account the differences between concrete life and the abstractness of OB research?

We need to return to reductionist research methods at this point. Organizational behavior scholars seem so content to study parts that they miss what managers see as real-world tests of common sense (wisdom). For example, consider the art of Japanese management. Most of the classics on Japanese management emphasize people processes for participation. For someone with the most minimal curiosity about the history and culture of Japan, one striking fact predominates. Japan was a military dictatorship for the 350 years before 1945. For observers of Japanese society, one of the most striking features is the industriousness of its people. For observers of its financial system, the fact that the average Japanese saves 30% of his or her income predominates. For observers of its government, the absence of a welfare state and the fact that only one party has held power for the entire democratic (post-World War II) period are glaring realities. Why have these factors seldom been included in books on the art of Japanese management? Isn't it obvious that such factors dramatically define the meaning of participation? Have participation advocates been so enthusiastic to latch onto the Japanese example to advance their values that they missed or suppressed such pivotal interpretive factors? Alternatively, was their research rigorous?

Moreover, anthropological/sociological studies of Japan emphasize the group nature of the culture in contrast to the individualism that forms the basis of Western culture (e.g., Benedict, 1946). Can OB scholars really believe that such a distinct context as Japan is irrelevant to management processes? Can we really believe that "quick slice" research would identify universal processes that transcend context? Can alien researchers in a closed society be confident that the "upfront" attributions by the Japanese are accurate rather than self-presentational, communicative rather than obfuscating, helpful rather than dissembling?

Observers who have substantial contact with Japan and/or appreciate these complexities are shocked by superficial and oversimplified "theories" of Japanese effectiveness. It is not surprising that many managers conclude that academics do not understand business when OB completely misses the "blindingly obvious." Are we too pedantic for the world of action?

The point is that there are some definite liabilities in translating OB research into organizational reality. By ignoring value differences between academics and managers we undermine effective communication. If we were more overt about values we would take a step in the right direction—toward clarifying how various pieces of knowledge can be woven together into a practical whole. In the absence of better integrative efforts, Henry Adams's "gravel" accumulates year by year in the pit. We overlay previous deposits but *do not really "build"* toward well-developed principles of truth. The form of physical science is copied but its substance is not duplicated.

In short, there is a value incongruity in OB between seeking scientific truth and showing that truth to be useful in the short term. This gap contributes to the state of confusion and ambiguity that is a hallmark of the field and contributes to internal competition and tension that inhibit OB scholars from moving toward wisdom. An explicit value focus could supplant value neutrality as a scientific cannon that advances rationality in OB. An old saying has it that "The person who stands for nothing will fall for anything." When values remain implicit, "form" tends to predominate over logic. How else can one explain the OB field's vulnerability to fads, glib prescriptions, outright charlatans, and nonsense (Dunnette, 1966; Abrahamson, 1991)? Offerings that fit into the value set of a dominant paradigm are embraced with unseemly excitement and speed.

In Search of Excellence (Peters and Waterman, 1982) presented an "up with people" appearance and built upon values held by many subfields in OB in a way that led to the book's popularity in business and government. Many OB scholars discounted the work as methodologically weak, but slowly came to "appreciate" it as its popularity grew. Ironically, it was not scholars who effectively attacked the weaknesses of the book. Instead, *Fortune* and *Business Week* found the compelling evidence (*Business Week*, 1986). What are the real driving values in what we do and what we do not do?

IX. WHAT WE NEED

It will come as no surprise to readers that I believe what we need now is to make values explicit in OB research. Unfortunately, this is easier to advocate than to effect. First, the very concept of values is illusive and subjective, perhaps more so than nearly any other concept in the field. Second, values are related to beliefs, motives, perceptions, attitudes, and behavior in such complex ways that any active consideration of values is vulnerable to confusion.

At this point, it is consequently important to signal a clear starting point for making values explicit in OB research. To attempt to build such a starting point, I rely on the Rokeach (1971) view of values, a view that seems to have become quite pivotal in values research (Becker and Connor, 1986).

Rokeach builds his conception of values upon classic treatments—on Kluckhohn (1951), who defines values as "conceptions of the desirable," and on Kaplan, who states that values "refer to the standards or principles of worth" (Kaplan, 1967: 370). Rokeach specifies that values are "abstract ideals—not tied to any specific outcome or situation" (Rokeach, 1971: 24). Values are more basic and general than attitudes. One's attitude toward a specific object or situation is seen as an expression of one's values and beliefs; that is, attitudes are derived from values and pertain to concrete experience. Beliefs involve cognitive schema and patterns of means/ends relationships. Thus, while Posner and Schmidt (1984) explore "work values," Becker and Connor (1986) prefer to follow Rokeach's view that certain work attitudes and interests are situational expressions and extensions of the individual's core values. Becker and Connor summarize the multilevel relationship between values, attitudes, and behavior as seen in Figure 1, which shows the prime relationship as: values underlie attitudes which, in turn, underlie behavior. Influence in the opposite direction is shown by dotted lines that connote secondary importance.

Rokeach distinguishes between terminal and instrumental values. Terminal values refer to desirable end states and are divided into personal (e.g., an exciting life) and societal (peace). Instrumental values refer to modes of conduct that contribute to achieving the desired end states and are divided into moral values (honesty, responsibility, etc.) and competence values (behaving logically, intelligently, or imaginatively). Violation of moral values results in guilt about wrongdoing, while violation of competence values results in shame about personal inadequacy (Rokeach, 1971: 7–8). In colloquial society, such terms as sociopath are used to label people who function strictly on competency values (i.e, without moral values). The profound importance of making values explicit can be quickly and vividly illustrated with the help of Rokeach's categorization. For example, observe that most of the major issues in OB are "framed" largely in terms of competence. At the same time, much of the challenge for the field involves such politically charged issues as affirmative action and pay equity. Both affirmative action and pay equity revolve around equalitarianism, a moral value that is central to "liberal" ideology (Rokeach, 1971: 165–211). How can OB researchers ignore such value-laden factors in describing organizational processes?

The Rokeach research also shows a large proportion of such diverse ideologies as commu-

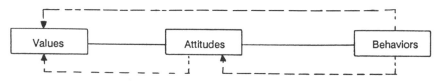

FIGURE 1 Schematic of values, attitudes, and behaviors. (From Becker and Connor, 1988: 4.)

nism, liberalism, fascism, and capitalism are explainable in terms of high or low degrees of two key values: equality and freedom. His research reinforces the insights of Whyte (1956) in *The Organization Man*. In that book, Whyte described the social ethic and the individualistic ethic as the emergent patterns of the post-World War II era. Ellis and Wildavsky (1989) used three ideologies (individualism, egalitarianism, and hierarchy or vertical control valuing) to analyze successes and failures of U.S. presidents from Washington to Lincoln. Ellis and Wildavsky brilliantly demonstrated the powerful clarification that can come from overt value analysis of the Rokeach variety. By contrast, isn't it remarkable that we seldom see OB researchers explicitly considering values in their analyses? Is this because OB scholars are generally so committed to bureaucratic assumptions (hierarchical values) that they cannot or will not acknowledge the importance of competing values such as equality and freedom (Quinn, 1988; Golembiewski, 1989)? Is this intentional or is it outside awareness? Is it fair? Is it wise?

Connor and Becker (1977) provide a crisp typology of the ways researcher values can introduce bias into results. These biases include: topic and subject selection, experimenter favor-seeking responses by experimental subjects, researcher blind spots and misperceptions due to cultural insensitivities, and interpretation biases. Consider some Rokeach data on value differences between males and females in the United States shown in Table 2. The displayed value rankings would lead one to predict that males in the United States with modal values would be more likely to research such topics as goal setting and peak performance while modal females would be more likely to research equity or group consensus. What would be the effect on research results if these phenomena were studied by individuals with radically different values?

Table 3 shows terminal values for whites and blacks in the United States. Both populations rank "a world at peace" first in their value priorities and have other striking value similarities (e.g., family security). Note, however, that equality is ranked second for blacks, but only eleventh for whites. What problems might arise in, say, using personnel selection-type questions involving team interaction if white researchers were looking at organizations with a large number of black participants? Can there be any doubt that many of the unresolved problems

Table 2 Instrumental Value Medians and Composite Rank Orders for American Men and Women

	Male	Female	
	N = 665	N = 744	p
Ambitious	5.6(2)	7.4(4)	.001
Broad-minded	7.2(4)	7.7(5)	—
Capable	8.9(8)	10.1(12)	.001
Cheerful	10.4(12)	9.4(10)	.05
Clean	9.4(9)	8.1(8)	.01
Courageous	7.5(5)	8.1(6)	—
Forgiving	8.2(6)	6.4(2)	.001
Helpful	8.3(7)	8.1(7)	—
Honest	3.4(1)	3.2(1)	—
Imaginative	14.3(18)	16.1(18)	.001
Independent	10.2(11)	10.7(14)	—
Intellectual	12.8(15)	13.2(16)	—
Logical	13.5(16)	14.7(17)	.001
Loving	10.9(14)	8.6(9)	.001
Obedient	13.5(17)	13.1(15)	—
Polite	10.9(13)	10.7(13)	—
Responsible	6.6(3)	6.8(3)	—
Self-controlled	9.7(10)	9.5(11)	—

Note: Figures shown are median rankings and, in parentheses, composite rank orders. *Source*: From Rokeach, 1973:58.

Table 3 Terminal Value Medians and Composite Rank Orders for White and Black Americans

Value	White N = 1,195	Black N = 202	p
A comfortable life	9.6(12)	6.6(5)	.001
An exciting life	15.4(18)	15.3(18)	—
A sense of accomplishment	8.8(8)	10.2(11)	.01
A world at peace	3.3(1)	3.5(1)	—
A world of beauty	13.5(15)	14.1(16)	—
Equality	9.6(11)	4.6(2)	.001
Family security	3.6(2)	5.1(4)	.001
Freedom	5.6(3)	5.0(3)	—
Happiness	7.6(4)	7.6(7)	—
Inner harmony	10.4(13)	10.9(12)	—
Mature love	12.1(14)	13.7(14)	.001
National security	9.1(9)	11.4(13)	.001
Pleasure	14.7(17)	14.3(17)	—
Salvation	8.5(7)	9.4(9)	—
Self-respect	7.7(5)	7.5(6)	—
Social recognition	14.6(16)	13.7(15)	.05
True friendship	9.3(10)	9.8(10)	—
Wisdom	7.9(6)	8.5(8)	—

Note: Figures shown are median rankings and, in parentheses, composite rank orders. *Source*: From Rokeach, 1973:67.

between blacks and whites in the United States are the result of value differences between the subcultures of the two populations? The point of the racial example is that organizations are not just a context of technical and performance problems; the problems are bigger. The solution to these problems is obviously *not* to throw up one's hands and say "only blacks can study (and understand) blacks." That's simply racism.

However, the solution does involve *not ignoring or suppressing systematic value differences* between various subcultures in society. Organizations are a context for a host of value problems, many of which are more subtle and difficult to penetrate than black/white differences. Golembiewski goes further to make clear that organization is not only the context of moral problems but that *organization is a moral problem* (Golembiewski, 1989). How can explicit value considerations be absent from organizational research in light of this?

Social science has pursued a strategy of making research as objective as possible in an effort to solve the value-bias problem. In so doing methodologists have made an elementary mistake—to assume that rigorous research would be transparent to values. Rokeach's research again provides some relevant illustrative data. Most academics rank religious values substantially lower than the typical member of U.S. society (Rokeach, 1971: 144–150). This makes sense, since academe is a virtual secular religion of scientific inquiry (Peck, 1978), but it has serious implications. For example, OB research proceeds *as if* religion were not a factor in day-to-day life in organizations. Is this assumption realistic? Does it show adequate respect for the role of religion in the lives of organizational participants or of the religious/moral values of those participants? Does OB research discount the fact that most organized religions actively influence their adherents toward cooperation, helpfulness, and honesty, tendencies of profound importance to effective organization (Barnard, 1938)? When is methodological rigor a Trojan horse for asserting a specific set of values? Is this the proper role of science? Is this value neutral? Is it even honest?

Transcending value narrowness and bias is an important step in the right direction for OB research, but we also need to go beyond preponderantly valuing quickness, accuracy, and cleverness in information generation. We need to approach research with full acknowledgment that in general, OB intentionally looks at a myriad of ongoing phenomena that attract real-world interest. Moreover, many OB scholars leap at opportunities to apply the current state of the science. It is both useful and important to be explicit about the values imbedded in a research paradigm. It is useful because it makes it easier for readers to judge the appropriateness of sample, analytical techniques, excluded variables, and other factors that could influence the validity of the findings. Further, explicit value statements help focus readers on possible research design issues such as subject selection and data gathering. Thus detailed value statements are as valuable for assessing the significance of the results as are detailed method-ological and data analysis descriptions.

X. THE FREEDOM VALUE

Organizational behavior research needs to be important in a value sense as well as in a theoretical sense. Significance beyond the statistical is needed. What values could have this power? A full answer to this question will require the field to engage in long debate. My suggested first step is to identify at least one value that is worthy of serious attention. Two possible values come immediately to attention: freedom and equality.

Freedom and equality are central to Western society in this century, with freedom gaining dominance in recent years (Rawls, 1971; Rokeach, 1973; Walter, 1984; Golembiewski, 1989). Proponents of the welfare state assert that equality has primary importance, and thus their attention is focused on redressing distributional inequalities that arise in an economy in which the rich get richer (Ellis and Wildavsky, 1989). The chief way the equality value has been expressed in OB is via participative management, since participation is a mechanism of power equalization (Strauss and Sayles, 1972). The freedom value has been advanced in the work of Rogers (1956) as a means to mental health, and by Maslow (1965) as the autonomy "need" and thus as an end in itself. In *The Organization Man*, Whyte (1957) expressed worries about the power of modern social control techniques and their erosive effects on individual freedom. Argyris echoed Whyte's insights in behavioral science terminology and focused the argument in *Personality and Organization* (1957) as did Walter (1984) about organizational development (OD) techniques. Golembiewski dealt with this theme more explicitly and comprehensively in *Men, Management and Morality* (1965, 1989). Thus the tradition of defending freedom goes back to the basic roots of OB. Further, the freedom issue has been in the ascent in scholarly circles since Rawls's (1971) clarification of its centrality for justice.

In *Freedom vs. Organization* Bertrand Russell (1962) explains that freedom has had an uneasy relationship with *order* throughout history. Most societies have gone through a triad of social conditions: anarchy, democracy, totalitarianism. Russell posits a cycle: anarchy to democracy to totalitarianism to anarchy again, and so on. Rising world competition in the 1980s seemed to legitimize aggressive "top-down" coercion by corporate leaders. For example, Hirsch (1988) reports that 250,000 managers lost their jobs due to merger and acquisition restructurings in only 5 years. Does this signal the rise of coercive management in organizations and increased totalitarianism in society? Has recent organizational "toughening up" been good or bad? By definition, a meaningful answer requires explicit value considerations.

According to Russell, a variety of mechanisms (such as commitment building) are utilized to create order during the advance from anarchy to democracy. Advanced civilizations facilitate the development of complex economies which, in turn, free the individual from the perpetual struggle for survival. As affluence continues, democratically created structures for establishing order become a force unto themselves. Order is sought for order's sake. The means-ends relationship, in which order *serves* the freedom value, becomes inverted. *Control as a value becomes more important than freedom.* Eventually, zealous striving for control becomes oppressive (Russell, 1962). Oppression grows until the human spirit is crushed and the energy in the system collapses. World political events seem far away from OB, but they create the zeitgeist that heavily influences the agenda for all the social sciences. The former USSR serves as a contemporary example of a totalitarian system collapsing under its own oppressive weight. The former giant is teetering on the brink of anarchy, and it is impossible to predict if it will move successfully to democracy without the intervening anarchy or if it will revert to totalitarianism. Clearly, freedom versus control constitutes one of the profound issues for this age.

Section II noted that laws are the bedrock of science and that the illusiveness of laws in social science are of key importance. One physical law, the second law of thermodynamics, has poignance for the subject of freedom versus organization. This law states that "energy naturally flows from a state of greater organization to a state of lesser organization" (Peck, 1978: 263–264). We call this phenomenon entropy. Thus, heat energy flows from higher-temperature bodies and spaces to lower ones. Why doesn't the universe "run down?" Because the four forces—gravity, magnetism, and the strong and weak atomic forces—produce order and countervail against chaos. We cannot simply analogize between these physical truths and the totalitarianism/anarchy polarity, but we should at least pause and contemplate the parallels. The fact that such a profound issue as the relation between control and freedom has received such scant attention in OB is striking. When Golembiewski (1989) writes of organization as a moral problem, he effectively states that this is the central issue of OB. At the very least, we should increase the overtness with which we consider this issue.

Organizational behavior needs wisdom to adequately deal with the dilemma of control versus freedom; data alone will not do the job. Classical Greeks emphasized the need to strike a balance, to seek the golden mean between competing ideals. So too did Hegel. It is unlikely that the golden mean is reducible to a statistic. Organizational behavior cannot achieve wisdom while ignoring the need for balancing relevant values. Advancement is not for those who have the "right" information, but for those who have the "right stance" toward information. If OB scholars can resist the elitist (antiegalitarian) urge to prescribe "solutions," perhaps they can develop a more meaningful role within an interactonist approach (as suggested by Wildavsky, 1979).

An explicit value focus should supplant value neutrality as a stepping stone toward rationality in OB. The old saying mentioned in Section VIII has it that "The person who stands for nothing will fall for anything." There is a substantial lack of recognition in OB about the pervasive and value-laden self-selection by subfield and paradigm.

XI. CONCLUSION

Organizational behavior has never been a value-free science and it never will be (Gouldner, 1973; Rokeach, 1973; Connor and Becker, 1977). Our discipline has made impressive strides in adapting and extending the scientific method to the challenges of our equivocal subject matter. We OB scholars need to continue to adapt the field. Organizational behavior needs to be more than an "almost science." Merely wrapping OB in the "emperor's clothes" of symbolic science serves little enduring purpose and fools few besides ourselves.

If OB scholars are to play a constructive role in building the era that has been coming into being for at least 200 years, we must tackle complex, subjective, and profound problems. These problems are inevitably enmeshed in value questions. Making our values explicit will clarify discussion. If we settle for an antiseptic approach, or if we merely concentrate on measuring less and less with greater and greater accuracy, we reduce ourselves from scientists to mere technocrats. We will have failed to fulfill our responsibility. Sadly, we also will have missed a unique opportunity to shape the institutions that are likely to define the lives of billions of people for an extended period of the emerging *Pax Americana* era (Kennedy, 1988).

The great peace of Rome lasted three centuries and there are reasons to believe that the era we are entering will be even more successful. If OB scholars meet wisdom's challenge they will contribute to the vitality and quality of the era that is evolving. Wisdom's path along "the lines of force that attract" inevitably involves pivotal values. We need to extend our scientific method to embrace *the spirit as well as the letter of science*. Making values explicit in OB research would strengthen OB as a science and simultaneously improve our communication with nonscientists.

ACKNOWLEDGMENT

The author would like to acknowledge collegial comments on previous drafts of this chapter and many helpful suggestions from Patrick Connor, Melvin McKnight, and Craig Pinder.

REFERENCES

Abrahamson, E. (1991). Managerial fads and fashions: The diffusion and rejection of innovations. *Academy of Management Review, 16*(3): 586–612.

Alba, J. W., and Hasher, L. (1983). Is memory schematic? *Psychological Bulletin, 93*: 200–231.

Argyris, C. (1957). *Personality and Organization*. Harper Row, New York.

Astley, G. W. (1985). Administrative science as socially constructed truth. *Administrative Science Quarterly 30*(4): 497–513.

Barnard, C. (1938). *The Functions of the Executive*. Harvard University Press, Cambridge, Mass.

Becker, B. W., and Connor, P. E. (1988). On the status and promise of values research. *Management Bibliographies and Reviews, 12*(2): 3–17.

Beer, M. (1992). Strategic-change research: An urgent need for usable rather than useful knowledged. *J. of Management Inquiry, 1*(2): 143–153.

Benedict, R. (1946). *The Chrysanthemum and the Sword*. Houghton Mifflin, Boston.

Berle, A. A., and Means, G. C. (1932). *The Modern Corporation and Private Property*. McMillan, New York.

Bigelow, J. (1992). Developing managerial wisdom. *J. of Management Inquiry, 1*(2): 143–153.

Business Week (1986). Oops: There are no excellent companies.

Connor, P.E., and Becker, B. W. (1977). Value biases in organizational research. *Academy of Management Review, 2*(3): pp. 421–430.

Dunnette, M. (1966). Fads, fashions and folderol in psychology. *American Psychologist, 21*(4): 343–352.

Dunnette, M. D., and Brown, Z. M. (1968). Behavioral science research and the conduct of business. *Academy of Management Journal, 11*(2): 177–189.

Durant, W. (1944). *The Story of Civilization, V. III: Ceasar and Christ*. Simon and Schuster, New York.

Ellis, R., and Wildavsky, A. (1989). *Dilemmas of Presidential Leadership*, Transaction, New Brunswick, N.J.

Fama, E. F., and Jensen, M. (1983). Separation of ownership and control. *J. of Law and Economics, 26*: 301–325.

Frankena, W. K. (1963). *Ethics*. Prentice-Hall, Englewood Cliffs, N.J.

Frost, P. J., Moore, L. F., Louis, M. R., Lundberg, C. C., and Martin, J. (1985). *Organizational Culture*. Sage, Beverly Hills, Calif.

Golembiewski, R. T. (1989). *Men, Management and Morality*. Transaction Publishers, New Brunswick, N.J. (Originally published by McGraw Hill in 1965).

Gouldner, A. W. (1973). Anti minotaur: The myth of a value free sociology. In *For Sociology* (A. W. Gouldner, ed.), Allen Lane, Harmondsworth.

Hirsch, P. (1987). *Pack Your Own Parachute*. Addison Wesley, Reading Mass.

Jensen, M., and Meckling, W. H. (1976). Theory of the firm: Management behaviour, agency costs, and ownership structure. *J. of Financial Economics, 3*: 305–360.

Kaplan, A. (1964). *The Conduct of Inquiry*. Chandler, San Francisco.

Kennedy, P. (1988). *The Rise and Fall of Great Powers: Economic Change and Military Conflict from 1500–2000*. Unwin Hyman, London.

Lorsch, J. W. (1979). Making behavioral science more useful. *Harvard Business Review, 57*(2): 171–180.

Machlup, F. (1961). Are the social sciences really inferior? *The Southern Economic Journal 27*: 178–183.

MacIntyre, A. (1981). *After Virtue*. University of Notre Dame Press, Notre Dame, Ind.

MacKenzie, K. D., and House, R. (1978). Paradigm development in the social sciences: A proposed research strategy. *Academy of Management Review, 3*: 7–23.

Maher, M. P. (1990). Business school research: Academics should be concerned. *Canadian Journal of Administrative Science*: 16–20.

March, J. G., and Olsen, J. P. (1976). *Ambiguity and Choice in Organizations*. Universitetsforlaget, Bergen, Norway.

Miner, J. B. (1984). The validity and usefulness of theories in an emerging organizational science. *Academy of Management Review, 9*(2): 296–306.

Nord, W. R., and Durand, D. E. (1978). What's wrong with the human resources approach to management? *Organizational Dynamics*: 13–19.

Partridge, E. (1966). *Origins: A Short Etymological Dictionary of Modern English*. Routledge & Kegan Paul, London.

Peck, M. S. (1978). *The Road Less Traveled*. Simon and Schuster, New York.

Peters, T., and Waterman, R. (1982). *In Search of Excellence*. Harper Row, New York.

Pfeffer, J. (1988). *Organizations and Organization Theory*. Pitman, Marshfield, Mass.

Phillips, D. C. (1976). *Holistic Thought in Social Science*. Stanford Univ. Press, Stanford, Calif.

Pinder, C. (1977). Concerning the application of human motivation theories in organizational settings. *Academy of Management Review, 42*: 384–397.

Porter, L. W., and McKibben, L. E. (1988). *Management Education and Development*. McGraw-Hill, New York.

Quine, W. V. (1960). *Word and Object*. MIT Press, Cambridge, Mass.

Quinn, R. E. (1988). *Beyond Rational Management*. Jossey Bass, San Francisco.

Rawls, J. (1971). *A Theory of Justice*. Harvard University Press, Cambridge, Mass.

Rimler, G. W. (1976). The death of management—A search for causes. *Academy of Management Review, 1*(2): 126–128.

Rokeach, M. (1973). *The Nature of Human Values*. Free Press, New York.

Rogers, C. R. (1956). Some issues regarding the control of human behavior. *Science, 124*: 1057–1066.

Russell, B. (1962). *Freedom Versus Organization: 1814–1914*. Norton, New York.

Strauss, G., and Sayles, L. R. (1972). *Personnel: The Human Problems of Management*. Prentice Hall, Englewood Cliffs, N.J.

Suzuki, S. (1975). *Zen Mind, Beginner's Mind*. Weatherhill, New York.

Thomas, K. W., and Tymon, W. G. Jr. (1982). Necessary properties of relevant research: Lessons from recent criticisms of the organizational sciences. *Academy of Management Review, 7*: 345–352.

Tosi, H. L., and Gomez-Mejia, L. R. (1989). The decoupling of CEO pay and performance: An agency theory perspective. *Administrative Science Quarterly, 34*(2): 169–189.

Walsh, J. P. (1990). Corporate control contests and the management of change: An agency theory perspective, paper delivered at the Academy of Mangement meetings, San Francisco.

Walter, G. A. (1984). Organizational development and individual rights. *J. of Applied Behavioral Science, 20*(4): 423–439.

Wildavsky, A. (1979). *Speaking Truth to Power: The Art and Craft of Policy Analysis*. Little Brown, Boston.

Whyte, W. H. (1957). *The Organization Man*. Doubleday, New York.

17
Behavioral Research in Auditing

Ronald A. Davidson

Simon Fraser University, Burnaby, British Columbia, Canada

I. INTRODUCTION

Research in accounting and auditing is a fairly recent development. Historically, accounting developed as a method of bookkeeping to measure results of business transactions. This function was viewed as no more than scorekeeping, and no research was considered necessary into ways in which to improve accounting. However, as business developed and increased in volume and significance, the importance of accounting for business activities became more apparent.

The history of auditing followed a similar pattern. Auditing was first developed to check the accuracy of bookkeeping numbers. As accounting became more complex, so did the work of auditors. With ever-increasing volumes of transactions, auditors could no longer check every transaction in detail. Their work changed from checkers of arithmetic to processors of complex information and sophisticated decision makers.

Interest in research in auditing is very recent and only became interesting as the role of the auditor became more complex. In a perfect world, auditors would be totally objective, allowing no personal characteristics or contextual factors to affect their decision making. However, auditors *are* affected by these factors, but our knowledge of how and why is limited.

The purpose of this chapter is to review the present status of auditing research that considers factors that may affect the decision making and other behavior of auditors. Relatively few auditing research studies have involved researchers from other disciplines such as behavioral scientists. By publicizing the current status of auditing research, other researchers should be able to see many opportunities for applying their research methods and findings to auditing and will come to appreciate the research opportunities in this applied discipline.

This chapter is intended to be comprehensive for the 1980s in the *leading* auditing and accounting research journals. All published studies that consider personal characteristics or contextual situations that may affect the auditor's decision making are included. The definition of *auditor* used is fairly broad, including external auditors, public accountants, and accounting students. Studies that involve internal auditors and other students are generally excluded. *All* studies published in the 1980s in the leading accounting research journals that appear to meet the above criteria are included. This review encompasses these seven leading accounting research journals: *Accounting, Organizations and Society, The Accounting Review, Auditing: A Journal of Practice & Theory, Behavioral Research in Accounting, Contemporary Accounting Re-*

search, Journal of Accounting Literature, and *Journal of Accounting Research*. A few studies from other journals are included where they are considered to be particularly relevant. Because of the large number of articles, only selected ones are described in detail. Limited critique or integration is made of individual studies; this chapter provides only a fairly complete survey of the area.

The basic purpose of this line of research is to enhance our understanding of how auditors make decisions, what affects their decisions, and eventually, how to improve their decision making. Studies involving accounting students are included, as accounting students generally enter the profession through auditing with a public accounting firm.

Several studies have surveyed the more general topic of behavioral accounting research (Birnberg and Shields, 1989; Burgstahler and Sundem, 1989; Dillard and Ferris, 1989); some have surveyed research in auditing generally (Felix and Kinney, 1982; Scott, 1984; Abdel-khalik and Solomon, 1988); and others reviewed certain aspects of behavioral auditing research, primarily decision making (Libby, 1981; Joyce and Libby, 1982; R. Ashton, 1982; 1983; Solomon, 1987; A. Wright, 1988b). To date, however, no study has attempted to survey the broad range of topics that might collectively be called behavioral auditing research. This chapter aims to fill this gap.

One of the main products of a survey or review paper is the framework used to categorize articles (Colville, 1981), and the approach used here is elemental. This chapter groups articles according to the *role* in which the auditor is considered, as a(n): (1) individual, (2) employee, (3) professional, or (4) decision maker. Research that considers the auditor as an individual considers his or her personal characteristics and background and whether or not these are unique to auditors. As an employee, the auditor is viewed as a member of a public accounting firm, subject to all the pressures and influences that any employee encounters on the job. As a professional, the auditor is seen as someone with special skills providing an important service to society. As a decision maker, the auditor is a processor of information who must form judgments about financial statements of client companies. These four categories are not mutually exclusive and are defined somewhat arbitrarily. Articles that fit into more than one category were included in the one that appeared to be dominant.

II. THE AUDITOR AS AN INDIVIDUAL

A. Introduction

As individuals, each auditor has a unique set of personal characteristics and background details. Auditing researchers believe that these unique features should affect how auditors work and make decisions, but the relationship is not clear. Most of the studies in this area are descriptive, and have not yet reached the point of generating hypotheses to be tested. The research commonly draws from other disciplines for methods and theories that may be applicable to auditors.

Three groups of factors are believed to affect individual behaviors: demographic/physiological, cognitive/psychological, and environmental/organizational (Dillard and Ferris, 1989). The studies included in this section concentrate on cognitive/psychological characteristics, such as education, experience, personality, personal needs, attitudes, and values, as very little research considers the other sets of factors.

B. Personality Studies of Auditors

Relatively little is known about common personality traits of auditors or if they are different from the general population. Most of the studies that use measures of personality attempt to find relationships between the personality scores and some other attribute, such as stress or commitment. This lack of descriptive attention is somewhat surprising, as accountants and auditors have a fairly strong historical stereotype that is not particularly flattering.

Aranya and Wheeler (1986) studied the degree of commitment of American Certified Public Accountants (CPAs) and Canadian Chartered Accountants (CAs) to both their employer organization and their profession (using a questionnaire adapted from the Porter organizational commitment instrument) and compared the resulting scores to measures of personality characteristics (measured by Holland's self-directed search). They received mail responses from 2016 accountants in California and Canada (with response rates of 43% and 46% for the U.S. and Canada, respectively) and found that the most common personality type was conventional (28.2%) followed by enterprising (22.4%). The conventional type is conforming, conscientious, orderly, persistent, practical, and self-controlled. The enterprising type is acquisitive, adventurous, ambitious, domineering, energetic, and self-confident. These personality types were also correlated most highly with the scores for both organizational and professional commitment.

Choo (1986) related personality characteristics with perceived job stress in a study of 172 mail questionnaires received from auditors (out of 315 sent out, for a 55% response rate). Auditors who tend to exhibit "type A" personality characteristics (competitive, intense, aggressive) experienced greater stress than auditors classified in three other types: "control" (characterized by a belief that the person can influence the course of events), "commitment" (tends to become involved in whatever he or she is doing or encountering), or "challenge" (more likely to seek change rather than stability). Although Choo states that these four groups are not mutually exclusive, he reports very low intercorrelations among the four types. In a second study of 167 responses from auditors (out of 433 mailed questionnaires, for a 39% response rate) reported in the same paper, he found that a moderate amount of perceived job stress resulted in better performance and excessive stress resulted in decreased performance.

Haskins, Baglioni, and Cooper (1990) also considered the relationship between stress and personality factors using audit seniors as subjects. They found that 61% of audit seniors had a type A personality and also found the relative amount of stress is associated with type A personality characteristics.

C. Other Personal Characteristics

There are many personal characteristics besides personality that may affect how auditors make decisions and behave, but, very few of them have been studied. Similar to the personality studies, the approach taken generally has been to attempt to relate a specific characteristic to a specific behavior or measure of success.

One study related personal characteristics to measures of success on the job. In a 2-year longitudinal study of 411 auditors, Harrell and Eickhoff (1988)—see also Harrell and Stahl (1984)—tested McClelland's theory that a persons needs for affiliation, power, and achievement affect work orientation. Their findings supported the theory as auditors with relatively large needs for power and small needs for affiliation (called "influence-oriented") expressed more job satisfaction, greater commitment to their organizations, and more positive career intention to remain in public accounting. Perhaps of most significance, these same auditors supported their expressions of intent by exhibiting less turnover than subjects with other patterns of needs. These findings are especially interesting as this was a longitudinal study.

The effect of education on the success of public accountants was examined by A. Wright (1988c) in a 9-year longitudinal study of 54 people with MBAs and 56 with BAs. Wright considered as measures of success the time required until they were promoted to a management position, turnover, and annual salary increases. He found the MBAs were promoted more quickly but received a slightly smaller percentage of salary increases. MBAs who graduated from highly rated schools advanced more rapidly and had lower turnover rates than MBA graduates from other schools and all BA graduates.

Dunn and Hall (1984) correlated 38 personal attributes with success on the CPA examination for 280 first-time writers. Of the 38 attributes, 12 were used in the final regression equation. Significant correlations were found for SAT scores, GPA, accounting hours completed, the university attended, hours of study, and completion of a CPA review course. No significant correlations were found for work experience, age, or completion of an audit course.

One study used the American Institute of Certified Public Accountants (AICPA) aptitude test to determine if it assisted in the prediction of the success rate of students in upper-level university courses (Ingram and Petersen, 1987). A total of 122 students were used as subjects, but little increase in the explanatory power of a regression model was found. The best predictor was the students' grades in the first 2 years of university studies.

One study considered differences in personal characteristics in public accountants in different countries (Ferris, Dillard, and Nethercott, 1980), but few differences were found.

Dillard (1981) related expected position utility and goal choice behavior with attained position level in a 4-year longitudinal study of 377 public accountants. His findings generally supported the goal-expectancy model that states that the expected utility of a position directly affects a person's choice of goals, goal-setting behavior, and eventual position attainment.

D. Studies Using Students as Subjects

Two studies have considered accounting students and the effects that universities can have on their selection and attitude toward accounting and auditing as a career. These studies each touch on an interesting area but do not appear to have been followed up.

Amernic and Beechy (1984) related the academic performance of 131 undergraduate accounting students with measures of tolerance for ambiguity and stated preference for complex and unstructured material. They used as performance measures the marks obtained for structured and unstructured questions on midterm examinations (questions asking for journal entries and those analyzing cases, respectively) for the performance measures. They found no differences in the structured questions, but students with higher levels of cognitive complexity did better on the unstructured questions. Amernic and Beechy state that an implication of their findings is that more unstructured educational materials should be used to attract students with higher abilities to handle complex materials.

Mayer-Sommer and Loeb (1981) suggest that universities can play a role in the development of a stronger professional identity among accounting students. They suggest this socialization process can be fostered by the accounting faculty having a strong "theory of practice" based on auditing experience and a professional identity, a collegial attitude toward the students, a cosmopolitan outlook that identifies more with the professional than with an organization, more clinical experience for the students such as internships, and a better "collective student experience" in which students can develop better interpersonal skills.

E. Summary

These relatively few studies that consider the auditor as an individual have just begun to describe auditors. No comprehensive picture of auditors can be made, and no conclusions are possible on the effects their sets of personal characteristics will have on their decisions.

III. THE AUDITOR AS AN EMPLOYEE

A. Introduction

The studies in this group are all characterized by their consideration of auditors as employees, especially considering problems that are encountered or may be encountered by auditors. The problems are the result of several factors, such as expectations held by employees, procedures used by the employees, and demands of the profession. A review of some of the studies of the effects on the behavior of accountants in professional accounting firms can be found in Dillard and Ferris (1989).

What is perhaps most surprising about this group of studies is the relatively low level of transfer of findings and methods from other disciplines. Many studies have considered problems faced by employees in diverse organizations, but few of them have been replicated in public accounting firms to determine if their findings also apply there.

B. Organizational Reality Shock and Career Choice

Little is known about how auditors first make their career choice and how they react when they first enter the profession. To become a qualified auditor (CPA), several steps must be taken. An almost universal prerequisite is a university degree, generally with a major in accounting. Then the national CPA examination is taken and students enter employment with a practicing CPA. Only after these steps and a period of training to gain experience will the person be considered a qualified auditor. However, how students make this career choice and what happens when they first enter into employment in this field are not well understood.

One longitudinal study examined the effects of unmet expectations of new employees upon joining an auditing firm (Dean, Ferris, and Konstans, 1988). They surveyed new accounting employees of a large industrial firm and new employees of an auditing firm, both on their first day of work and 1 year later. Of the original 53 and 162 new employees, respectively, they received complete responses from 50 (for a 90% response rate) and 122 employees (for a 75% response rate). They found that the new industrial employees had higher expectations in six of seven areas on entry that were generally repeated 1 year later. Both groups showed lower expectations after 1 year, with the auditing employees showing the larger decrease. These decreases in expectations during the first year of employment indicate that work experience does not meet expectations (the authors call this "organizational reality shock"). The auditing employees also scored lower on the commitment attitudes than the industrial employees. The authors suggest these factors may account for the high turnover recorded by auditing firms.

Paolillo and Estes (1982) surveyed members of four different professions (accountants, attorneys, mechanical engineers, and physicians) to ask what factors affected their choice of career. Of 625 questionnaires mailed to accountants who were mainly in public accounting, 219 were returned, for a response rate of 35%. For accountants, the most important factors were availability of employment, earnings potential, years of education required, aptitude for the subject, and teacher influence. Less significant factors were parental influence, cost, education, job satisfaction, and peer influence.

C. Commitment Conflicts

Several papers consider the possibility of a conflict of commitments between the organization and the profession. Since auditing includes membership in a professional association as well as an employing organization, the possibility of commitment conflicts exists. However, the degree of conflict does not appear to be high.

Norris and Niebuhr (1983) surveyed 62 employees of public accounting firms (for a response rate of 46%). They found that scores of professionalism and organizational commitment did not conflict, and both contributed to higher job satisfaction. In addition, they found that both scores increased for higher hierarchical levels.

Aranya and Ferris (1984; see also Aranya, Pollock and Amernic, 1981), in their survey of 2016 public accountants in Canada and the United States, asked questions about the amount of perceived conflict. They found that the amount of professional-organizational conflict was less for accountants in professional organizations such as public accounting firms than for accountants in other companies. For accountants in professional firms, the amount of conflict was inversely related to the person's position level.

A somewhat different approach was used by Senatra (1980). He used a questionnaire for 88 audit seniors (82% response rate) to consider the relationship between role conflict and role ambiguity as they impacted on job-related tension, low job satisfaction, and high propensity to leave the firm. He found a significant positive relationship between role conflict and tension, as well as a significant negative relationship between ambiguity and satisfaction.

Senatra's work was supported and extended by Bamber, Snowball, and Tubbs (1989) in a survey of 121 audit seniors from four firms (133 questionnaires were distributed). The latter authors found that audit seniors from audit firms that rely relatively more on professional judgment than on a more "structured" audit approach perceived higher amounts of role conflict and role ambiguity.

The findings in these studies appear to indicate that commitment to the profession and the organization is not straightforward. Many factors appear to complicate the relationship, but they are not yet well understood.

D. Dysfunctional Behavior: "Premature Sign-offs"

The accumulation of audit evidence is undertaken by following different audit steps that each includes; different sets of procedures that must be carefully undertaken to be effective. These steps are undertaken by audit staff who are under a written time budget that is expressed in hours allocated for the step and that is usually fairly tight. It is very difficult to ensure that each step is performed carefully and thoroughly. These pressures can lead to "premature sign-off," which occurs when an auditor does not complete a required audit step or misrepresents the amount of audit verification undertaken (Buchman and Tracy, 1982). It is important for senior auditors to know if this is happening and why.

Alderman and Deitrick (1982) found that such behavior did occur, mainly as a result of time budget pressure. Lightner, Adams, and Lightner (1982) also found that this behavior occurred in their mailed questionnaire sent to 1500 CPA firm employees. Of the 1016 responses (for a response rate of 68%), 63% reported this behavior. Reasons given were related to time budget pressure, the auditor's accepting attitude about such behavior, and the request from a supervisor.

Margheim and Pany (1986) used a case method to analyze some of the variables that may affect this behavior. They found that larger/smaller CPA firm size and higher/lower perceived necessity of the audit step affected the behavior more than time pressure or the materiality of the budget overrun. The existence of quality control standards had no effect. Relatedly, Kelley and Margheim (1990) found that time budget pressure and personality types were related to the occurrence of dysfunctional behaviors such as premature sign-offs.

E. Turnover

Turnover of auditor employees has been considered in many studies, since turnover has been found to be very high in public accounting firms, especially in the third and fifth years of employment. This high turnover appears to have several causes, such as dissatisfaction with the work, meeting the minimum length of service required for professional membership, and limited opportunities for advancement.

Gul (1984) attempted to quantify the costs of turnover by using an accounting model that included several factors that were affected by turnover. Using a case method and 57 auditors as subjects, he concluded that it would be useful to quantify turnover costs.

Waller (1985) also considered the problem of unforeseen turnover. He suggested that new auditors could be differentiated according to their intentions of staying with or leaving the firm after several years by offering a choice of several different contracts. The contracts differed in their schedule of salary payments over the first 3 years. Although Waller found this scheme would work from his laboratory study, no firm has adopted it in practice.

One study, a mailed questionnaire with 311 responses (Gregson, 1990), found a direct negative link between the intention to leave an accounting firm and job satisfaction. Communication satisfaction affected job satisfaction. Firm size and tenure were also directly related to communication satisfaction. An intervening variable that affected turnover intentions was work-related stress (Rasch and Harrell, 1990).

F. Job Satisfaction

Job satisfaction has also been studied frequently in many different types of organizations. As job satisfaction directly affects performance and turnover, it is a very important factor. However, it has not been the subject of many studies in public accounting firms.

Job satisfaction was studied by Aranya, Lachman, and Amernic (1982) in a survey of 1174 responses received from 2626 CAs (for a response rate of 47%). They found that both professional and organizational commitment were related to the intention to leave their employment and to job satisfaction. However, job satisfaction was not directly related to turnover intent. In contrast, Bullen and Flambholtz (1985) did find that job satisfaction was related to turnover intentions in their study of 125 auditors from one large CPA firm (representing a 76% response rate).

Benke and Rhode (1980) received mail responses from 255 CPAs and management consultants (which represented a 39% response rate) relating job satisfaction, personal characteristics, and job features. Their survey instrument consisted of three parts. The first asked questions about the job and personal variables, the second measured job satisfaction using the job descriptive index, and the third measured personality variables using two tests, the Gordon personality inventory and the Gordon personality profile. They tested for nonresponse bias by comparing the first responses with the last received and found no significant differences. They found that consultants were somewhat different from the tax and audit respondents and that the level of job satisfaction could be predicted to some extent for the audit and tax respondents.

One factor that can affect job satisfaction—role stress—was considered by Rebele and Michaels (1990) in a study of 155 auditors (a 73.5% response rate). They found that perceived environmental uncertainty is a critical factor affecting both the role stress perceived by auditors as well as job satisfaction.

G. Performance Evaluation

The nature of auditing work leads to staff scheduling problems, as audits are conducted shortly after the clients' years end, which occur unevenly throughout the year. The work typically has busy times and slack times. The organization structure is very bureaucratic, with partners at the top. Each partner will have one to four audit managers reporting directly to him or her. Managers are responsible for organizing each audit each year. The audit work is actually undertaken by staff who are either CPAs or accounting students. To increase the flexibility of staffing the scheduling of audits, public accounting firms generally organize their staff in one of two ways: either managers have a number of staff assigned to them, or they draw from a common pool.

If managers have certain staff assigned to them, performance evaluation is no problem as each manager has time to get to know those staff members. However, if they draw from a common pool of staff, they do not get to know the individual staff members well as they will report to them only as long as the specific jobs last. In this case, no one manager can be assigned the annual performance evaluation. Usually the approach used is to complete evaluations for all staff assigned to the manager after every job. Thus staff members receive a number of mini-evaluations every year. Under either method, performance evaluations are a key factor in the partners' decisions on annual increments and promotions. Not surprisingly, this area has been considered in a number of research studies (Christensen, 1982; Ferris, 1982; Kida, 1984a).

Murray and Frazier (1986) asked audit seniors to rate the importance of nine evaluation criteria and to state the amount of time spent on each. They found that time allocation was affected by the importance of the ratings. This finding was corroborated by A. Wright (1982), who found fairly high consensus among audit seniors in their rating of the importance of various evaluation criteria. In an additional test, Jiambalvo (1982) found that the relative importance of five of the nine ratings of evaluation criteria made by the audit seniors were significantly different from the rankings made by audit partners. Jiambalvo, Watson, and Baumler (1983) also found that the criteria used for staff evaluations within an auditing firm differed depending on the area (auditing, tax, and consulting).

Kaplan and Reckers (1985) used a series of case scenarios that described examples of poor performance by a staff member. Subject were audit managers and audit seniors who were asked to rate the importance of various possible causes for the poor performance. The possible causes included both external (uncontrollable) and internal or personal factors. As predicted by attribution theory, internal causes were found to be rated as most important when the staff person was described as having a poor work history and external causes when the external factors were described negatively. No differences in causal attributions were found between the rank of the subjects.

Ferris and Larcker (1983; see also Ferris, 1981; Hassell and Arrington, 1989) considered the variables that affect performance and found that performance is primarily a function of motivation and organizational commitment. To improve the usefulness of performance evaluation, A. Wright (1986) recommends that appraisals be made by using rating scales that are developed specifically for auditors.

H. Leadership

Although auditors are considered to be professionals, their work takes place in bureaucratically organized public accounting firms. The day-to-day work of gathering audit evidence is supervised by audit seniors while they report to audit managers. Audit managers have overall responsibility for planning and organizing each audit and ensuring that the work is performed properly.

Wolf (1981) undertook a descriptive study of the work of audit managers using interviews to determine and analyze critical incidents reported. He found that audit managers reported incidents that could be classified into the three general types of managerial roles proposed by Mintzberg: 26% interpersonal, 12% informational, and 62% decisional.

The effect of the group leader on auditor behaviors was studied by Pratt and Jiambalvo (1981; 1982) in a field study (see also Jiambalvo and Pratt, 1982). They found that audit staff behaviors were directly affected by the behaviors and style of the audit senior who was the supervisor on the job. Audit teams who were judged to be high performers had leaders who allowed staff innovation, were considerate to the staff's personal needs, administered frequent positive reinforcement, relied heavily on time budgets, assigned a small number of tasks per staff member, and administered negative reinforcement infrequently.

I. Control

Due to the nature of auditing, where most of the day-to-day work involves the gathering of audit evidence, it is very difficult to devise methods that will ensure that auditors are performing their work properly. Bureaucratic forms of control are not particularly effective, as a very important consideration is the thoroughness of the work done. Thus most firms rely heavily on informal control methods such as selection, training, and socialization to develop professional attitudes toward the work.

One study considered several informal control methods used in public accounting firms. Dirsmith and Covaleski (1985) examined the role of informal communication and found that it was used to inform organization members of politics and power relationships. Mentoring was also found to be used for communicating relationships and socializing firm members.

J. Summary

From the many different categories in this section, it is obvious that there are many different topics that should be included when considering the role of the auditors as an employee. However, no study has attempted to summarize what has been found in the studies that have been undertaken. There still appear to be many topics from related disciplines that have not been applied to auditing and public accounting firms.

IV. THE AUDITOR AS A PROFESSIONAL

A. Introduction

In addition to being an individual, an employee, and a decision maker, the auditor is especially seen as a professional. As professionals, auditors are expected to have specialized knowledge and skill to provide an independent assessment of financial statements issued by businesses. This professional role has many aspects and complications that must be considered if auditors are to maintain their credibility. Auditors are especially vulnerable to threats to their credibility as their fees are paid by the companies whose financial statements they are examining. Auditors are expected to be independent of the companies, and yet to provide services other than auditing to them. This potential conflict has been considered by a number of studies.

B. Studies of Auditor Independence

A fairly large group of 14 papers (see Table 1) examined the perceptions and attitudes of users and auditors about the independence of auditors who provide nonaudit services to their audit clients. The importance of nonaudit services to public accounting firms was indicated by Scheiner and Kiger (1982). A review of some of these paper can be found in Briloff (1987).

These perception studies vary with respect to method of selecting subjects, gathering the data, types and mix of subjects, and ranges of nonaudit services. Not surprisingly, the results also show substantial differences.

However, the studies do have a number of similarities. They generally: (1) select subjects from both auditing and user groups; (2) use either a case method or ask for opinions from the subjects; (3) find differences in the responses for the different types of nonaudit services; and (4) find substantial differences between the perceptions of auditors and users.

Perhaps the most significant general findings are that: (1) auditor subjects believe that the provision of nonaudit services by auditors has a less detrimental effect on the independence of the auditors than is believed by other subject groups tested; and (2) users appear to believe that the provision of nonaudit services can lessen an auditor's independence. Several of these papers attempted to find reasons for the differences in perceptions. Gul (1987) used the assessed cognitive style of the subjects. He found that cognitive style was related to the perceptions of independence for the cases used in his study. Farmer, Rittenberg, and Trompeter (1987) examined the effect of "acculturation" (experience) on the decisions made by subjects. They found that responses by subjects at similar organizational levels did show some similarities.

Two papers report results that used a different approach (McKinley, Pany, and Reckers, 1985; Pany and Reckers, 1988). Rather than asking for perceptions of independence, subjects responded to a loan application package that included audited financial statements and indications that the auditor provided management advisory services in varying amounts. McKinley, Pany, and Reckers (1985) report that they received 261 usable replies from 900 mailed instruments to bank loan officers, for a response rate of 29%. The instrument included two levels of management advisory services, either nil or 30% of audit fees for each of the last 3 years. No significant differences were noted in the loan decisions made, perceptions of financial statement reliability, or perceptions of auditor independence.

Pany and Reckers (1988) extended this study by including both loan officers (192) and financial analysts (104) as subjects. Four versions of a case were used, with the cases differing in the stated amount of management advisory services provided by the auditor. The value of the additional services was set at 25%, 60%, or 90% of the annual audit fees. Each subject received only one version of the case. Loan officers' decisions were affected by the level of nonaudit services as they recommended the loan be approved significantly more often with the 25% case than with the cases with higher levels of management advisory services. The financial analysts were asked to rate the companies for the relative safety of a 12-month investment. Their decisions were affected only by the 90% case as they rated the company in this case to be significantly more risky than the other versions. Pany and Reckers (1987; 1988) conclude that

Table 1 Papers on Perceptions of Auditors' Independence

Paper	Subjects				Method		Contact		
	Auditors	Users	Mgt.	Total	Case	Beliefs	Mail	Personal	Not Stated
Dykxhoorn and Sinning, 1981	X			108	X		X		
Dykxhoorn and Sinning, 1982		X		86	X		X		
Farmer, Rittenberg, and Trompeter, 1987	X			75	X			X	
Firth, 1980	X	X		389	X		X		
Firth, 1981		X		1252	X		X		
Gul, 1987	X			22	X			X	
Knapp, 1985		X		43	X				X
Pany and Reckers, 1980		X		107	X		X		
Pany and Reckers, 1983			X	92	X		X		
Pany and Reckers, 1984		X		113		X	X		
Pany and Reckers, 1987		X		333	X		X		
Pearson and Ryans, 1981–1982	X	X		259		X	X		
Reckers and Stagliano, 1981	X	X		100	X				X
Shockley, 1981	X	X		176	X		X		

results reported in other studies were affected by the provision of more than one version of the case to subjects.

A conflict situation was considered by Knapp (1985), who asked bank loan officers to analyze cases that involved conflicts between auditors and clients. At issue was the auditor's perceived ability to resist management pressure. Variables other than professionalism and professional commitment were considered. Knapp found that the financial condition of the client, as well as the nature of the conflict directly affected management's perceived ability to obtain their preferred resolution of the conflict.

C. Professionalism

The literature is not clear on what is meant by professionalism, and different levels of analysis complicate interpretation. The degree of professionalism displayed by individual auditors may reflect the degree of professionalism of their employing firm. A firm's professionalism may reflect expectations received from their clients.

This line of research was followed by Shockley and Holt (1983). They asked 25 chief financial officers of large banks to rank the Big Eight public accounting firms along several criteria: (1) prestige, (2) professionalism, (3) cost, (4) competence, (5) aggressiveness, (6) conservatism, (7) independence, (8) reliability, (9) helpfulness, and (10) bureaucracy. Five of these criteria were found to be highly correlated: professionalism, competence, conservatism, independence, and reliability. They found that the firms were perceived to be different for the various attributes, but no firms' names were used in this article to identify how each firm was rated.

D. The Auditor as a Deterrent

One of the roles of auditors is to act as a deterrent to prevent acts by clients that may be considered "irregular." The effectiveness of the auditor in this role may be a function of the auditor's perceived reputation for aggressiveness in detecting such acts. However, Uecker, Brief, and Kinney (1981) found no such effects in their field experiment using 86 (of 143 mailed questionnaires) business managers as subjects.

E. Structure of the Audit Firm

Since auditors perform their work as members of a bureaucratic public accounting firm, the way the firm is structured may affect their work. It may be more difficult to maintain a professional attitude in a firm that is more highly bureaucratized because of conflicting demands. One study considered how public accounting firms organized their various divisions, such as audit, tax, and management advisory services. Ballew (1982) tested the theory that the degree of routineness of the work performed in each division would affect the degree of bureaucratization in the division. No significant differences were found in the relative amount of bureaucratization in these divisions.

F. Summary

Relatively few studies have considered the professionalism or professionalization of auditors or the resulting effects. The only question that has been considered to any extent is the effect of the provision of nonaudit services to audit clients. The results found in these studies have been consistent in that auditor subjects do not believe this practice affects their professional independence, although other subjects do. However, there are many other questions about professionalism that have been considered in other disciplines that could be applied to auditing.

V. THE AUDITOR AS A DECISION MAKER

A. Introduction

By far the largest amount of behavioral research in auditing and accounting considers the factors that affect auditors' decisions and professional judgment, which was defined by Gibbins and Mason (1988: 5) as "judgment exercised with due care, objectivity and integrity within the framework provided by applicable professional standards, by experienced and knowledgeable people." Reviews can be found in Libby (1981), Libby and Lewis (1982), R. Ashton (1982; 1983), Dillard (1984), R. Ashton et al. (1988). Gibbins and Mason (1988), Bedard (1989), Johnson, Jamal, and Berryman (1989), and King and O'Keefe (1989). Given the extensive and frequent review articles in this area, the present survey intends only to complement the above papers.

Research that relates to the auditor as a decision maker is divided here into three groups: (1) how auditors make decisions, (2) what affects their decisions, and (3) how their decisions might be improved.

B. How Auditors Make Decisions

The research that attempts to describe and explain how auditors make decisions may be categorized by either (1) the underlying theory or model of decision making or (2) the research method applied. For this review, each study is grouped in terms of the theory or model used in its research design.

1. Theories from Cognitive Psychology

Theories from cognitive psychology are used to describe how auditors use their experience when encountering a new situation or when making a decision. These theories are very difficult to test empirically but are intuitively appealing as being descriptive of how our memories appear to work. The theories have been advanced to model how auditors formulate audit opinions, with the expectation that an understanding of this process may generate insights as to what might lead to better decisions and what might lead to inappropriate ones. These theories have not been tested fully in cognitive psychology, so their application to an applied area such as auditing may be premature. Discussion of the theories can be found in Waller and Felix (1984 a, b), Birnberg and Shields (1984), Libby (1985), Frederick and Libby (1986), and Choo (1989). An example of how these basic theories may be used to speculate on possible resulting consequences on audit judgment may be found in Gibbins (1984).

Several studies have attempted to describe the decision-making process using verbal protocol analysis. For a review of the use of verbal protocol analysis studies in auditing, see Klersey and Mock (1989). At least two different decision strategies have been found, called "directed" and "comprehensive" search patterns (Biggs and Mock, 1983; Bamber, Bamber, and Bylinski, 1988). A directed search pattern is characterized by a subject's generating a hypothesis after having considered only a relatively small part of the evidence. The subject then seeks additional evidence that will either prove or disprove this hypothesis. Using a comprehensive search pattern, a subject tends not to generate hypotheses until after all or least a large part of the available evidence has been examined. Several hypotheses are formulated, then the evidence that has already been examined will be considered to decide which of the several hypotheses is the most likely.

Biggs, Messier, and Hansen (1987) used verbal protocol analysis in a case analysis to describe the reasoning processes used by three auditors who were considered to be "computer experts." The subjects were found to devote almost all (80% to 90%) of their analysis to four areas: (1) information search, (2) conjecture, (3) evaluation, and (4) query. The patterns of analysis of these subjects were quite similar. Decisions made by these three subjects were quite similar to those reached by the 15 other individuals and 22 groups who analyzed the same case.

Blocher and Cooper (1988) applied verbal protocol analysis to five audit seniors who were requested to perform analytical review procedures on 14 cases adapted from real situations. The cases all concentrated on inventory and were presented in pairs, with one case having received a material adjustment. The subjects were informed of this and were instructed to identify the case with the adjustment. Three distinct phases—acquisition of information, evaluation, and decision making—were found for all subjects.

Other studies that use cognitive structures to model decisions include Pratt (1982), Moeckel and Plumlee (1989), Campbell (1984), and Moeckel and Williams (1990). Pratt (1982) related decisions and the complexity of a subject's cognitive structure after making the decision to two variables: the complexity of the information presented and the complexity of the subjects' predecision-making cognitive structure. Moeckel and Plumlee (1989) related auditors' confidence of remembering information presented to them in a case study. They found that auditors were confident of their memories even when they confused case material with information from their prior experience. Moeckel and Williams (1990) compared decisions made by auditors who rely on information contained in written working papers with decisions made by others who relied on their memories alone. They found that decisions made by auditors who rely on their memories without the assistance of written documentation were more accurate. Moeckel and Plumlee believe that auditors who must rely on their memories process the information in more detail. Auditors who are aware the information is in written form do not process the details, as they are aware they have access to an external memory storage, but they later fail to refer back to the written records to confirm details.

2. Other Decision Models

Two models that have been used in auditing research were adopted from other disciplines: the Brunswik lens model and the Bayesian revision model. The lens model assumes that there is a rational relationship between the stimulus (the cues or information provided) and the response (the decisions made). Some of the studies that adapted the lens model include Kida (1980) and W. Wright (1982). Kida asked audit partners to make decisions on a case and related the decisions to the data provided in the case. Wright discusses the differences between the lens model and subjective probability studies.

The Bayesian model predicts how new information is combined with old information to revise decisions (B. Johnson, 1982; Crosby, 1985; Abdolmohammadi, 1986; Trader and Huss, 1987; Amershi, Demski, and Fellingham, 1985). Generally, these studies have been descriptive and have attempted to model auditors' decision making rather than testing hypotheses derived from these models, although some studies have found that decisions do not appear to conform to results that would be expected from application of a Bayesian model.

One study, by Solomon et al. (1982), considered whether or not auditors have the cognitive abilities that are needed to use the Bayesian model of decision making, such as the ability to quantify their beliefs into scalars or prior probability distributions. The resulting distributions should be affected by both sampling and nonsampling evidence. The researchers asked 26 auditor subjects to express certain beliefs about account balances into fractiles, using the case method. They found that auditors are able to specify fractiles, but there was a large amount of variability among the responses. The distributions were affected by the case-specific information provided. The researchers concluded that Bayesian methods could be useful to auditors.

Another study that considered decision models is R. Ashton (1981), who manipulated the predictability and feedback cues in a case and considered the effects on subjects' abilities to acquire and apply decision-model knowledge.

Decisions made by auditor subjects have been compared to those predicted by the audit risk model. Total audit risk is assumed to be a multiplicative function of the inherent risk of a material error occurring in the account in the absence of internal controls, the control risk of a material error not being prevented or detected by the internal controls, and the detection risk of the auditor not detecting a material error. Libby, Artman, and Willingham (1985) found that decisions made by 12 experienced auditor subjects analyzing eight cases were consistent with predictions developed by the audit risk model. Different versions of the case were produced by manipulating the strength of all three risk factors. Inherent risk was manipulated by describing a manual processing of input data compared to the running of a routine computer program. Control risk was manipulated by describing a stronger checking and comparison routine for accounts payable vouchers. Detection risk (the risk that audit procedures will fail to detect an error) was manipulated by changing the types of audit tests used in the different versions of the case. Each subject was asked to rate the reliability of the control. The subjects displayed a fairly high level of consensus in their responses.

Other studies that considered or developed models of auditor decision making include Uecker (1981; Danos and Imhoff (1982; 1983); Lewis, Shields, and Young (1983); Mutchler (1985); and Butt (1988). These studies all add to our knowledge of audit decision making, but a complete model has yet to be developed.

3. Other Studies

Other articles did not use formal models but merely described the decision-making process found in their studies (Gibbins, 1982; Larcker and Lessig, 1983; Lewis and Bell, 1985; Mutchler, 1986; Jennings, Kneer, and Reckers, 1987; Mayper, Doucet, and Warren, 1989; Anderson and Marchant, 1989; Knechel and Messier, 1990). Waller and Felix (1987) attempted to determine the rules used by auditors to make judgments in situations in which several variables interact. A decision in such a situation depends on three interrelated factors: heeded joint frequency data, rules for integrating the data, and prior expectations about the covariation of interest. Waller and Felix administered two different sets of cases to 61 and 45 experienced auditors. They found the subjects relied on the bivariate data provided and used verifiable data integration rules. However, subjects often understated and/or overstated the covariations and were not internally consistent.

Causal judgments made by auditors were examined by Waller and Felix (1989), who conducted two case experiments using 56 and 58 "senior auditors" from Big Eight firms. Waller and Felix hypothesized that auditors would place more significance on conditionality (the combining of cues to cause an effect) when making forward causal inferences from causes to effects. They believed that auditors would place more emphasis on multiplicity (the consideration of multiple possible causes) when making backward causal inferences from effects to causes. Their cases involved providing a variety of cues that involved both conditionality and multiplicity. They found that auditors place more weight on conditionality information when making forward causal inferences and more weight on multiplicity information when making backward causal inferences. Waller and Felix point out that context may have a strong effect on responses, so their study should be replicated in different contexts before any attempt to generalize is made.

Schneider (1984; 1985) attempted to model the decision process used by auditors in their evaluation of the reliability of internal auditors. In a set of three experiments, the 18 auditor subjects rated the work done by internal auditors as most important, followed by the competence of the internal auditors, with their objectivity rated as least important of the three factors. Evaluation of internal auditors was also considered by Brown (1983) and Margheim (1986).

Several studies have suggested that these findings may not be accurate, since the experimental process may interfere with normal decision making and this intrusion may affect behaviors. Experiments that attempt to model behavior assume their subjects are acting the same as they would in normal situations, and assume the experimental method has no effect. Boritz (1986; see also Boritz, Gaber, and Lemon, 1988) and W. Wright (1988) found that different response elicitation methods resulted in different responses from subjects.

C. What Affects Decisions?

1. Experience

The effects of professional experience on judgment and on subjects' ability to improve their decisions have been considered in a number of studies (Snowball, 1980; Nanni, 1984; Waller and Felix, 1984c; Choo, 1989; Colbert, 1989; Davis and Solomon, 1989; Peters, Lewis, and

Dhar, 1989; Kaplan and Reckers, 1989; Marchant, 1989; Bonner, 1990). A review of the effects of experience can be found in Colbert (1989) and Davis and Solomon (1989). Results have been mixed. Burgstahler and Jiambalvo (1986) found some experience effects in two of seven cases completed by 109 auditor subjects, but no consistency across subjects. The most experienced subjects (more than 6 years) were more likely to conform to the expected responses than subjects with less than 6 years of experience. The cases involved asking the subjects whether errors found during an audit should be projected over the whole population or whether they should be considered unique and not likely to recur.

Ashton and Brown (1980) found that both judgment insight and consensus increase with increased years of auditing experience. They used 160 cases involving internal control evaluations in payroll subsystems with 31 auditor subjects. They assessed judgment insight by asking the subjects to assess the relative importance they had placed on the eight cues in the cases. However, Hamilton and Wright (1982) found no association between years of experience and consensus in their study of 78 auditor subjects who evaluated 32 cases involving internal control judgments. They defined consensus as similarity in the assessment of strength of internal controls.

Meixner and Walker (1988) found that the effect of experience depends on the length of time with the same audit group. Their study involved 76 state government auditors who analyzed 32 cases involving the evaluation of internal controls. They found consensus increased with experience, but only for experience with the same audit staff and not for audit experience generally.

Messier (1983) and Abdolmohammadi and Wright (1987) found significant experience effects with complex tasks. Messier's study used 29 audit partners as subjects who evaluated 32 cases involving materiality. Abdolmohammadi and Wright used three levels of case complexity and two levels of subjects (96 and 50 undergraduate students and 63 and 65 auditor subjects) for two sets of cases divided into the least complex and the two more complex cases, respectively.

Haskins (1987) found that experience did have an effect on how auditors perceived the importance of attributes used to rate the control environments of audit clients. He used a questionnaire survey of 146 auditors (for a 64% response rate) from all Big Eight audit firms. The questionnaire asked subjects to evaluate the importance of 48 control attributes that should be considered in evaluating internal control. Haskins used the position level of the respondents to indicate experience and acknowledged that the increased amount of responsibility associated with higher ranks may have an effect on the way they evaluate controls.

2. The Effect of Other Personal Variables

Studies considered the effect of training in general (Dittman, Juris, and Revsine, 1980) and for the effect on perceptions of auditors when compared to people who are not auditors (Bailey, Bylinski, and Shields, 1983; Pratt, 1980). Bailey, Bylinski, and Shields used 27 newly qualified CPAs and 44 fourth-year accounting students as subjects who responded to either 10 currently used audit reports or to 10 proposed audit reports. No differences in perceptions between the two groups were found. They then provided all 20 audit reports to 24 CPAs and 38 students from the original group of subjects. This test found some differences between the perceptions of the two groups.

Burgstahler and Jiambalvo (1986) found that firm affiliation had an effect on the decisions made in three of their seven cases completed by 109 auditor subjects. Their cases involved asking the subjects if errors found during an audit should be projected over the whole population or not.

Gul (1986) analyzed 33 graduating Australian accounting majors in terms of the approach they tended to use to solve problems and make decisions using the Kirton adaptor-innovator inventory test. This test measures whether people tend to "do things better" (adaptors) or to "do things differently" (innovators). Studies have found that scores from this test correspond to several aspects of behavior such as choice of career. Gul found that students who stated they were more interested in financial accounting, auditing, and taxation were consistently higher adaptors than students who did not state a preference for financial accounting. Students who preferred management subjects were higher innovators than students who did not state this preference. The scores for students who preferred management accounting and financial management showed no consistent tendencies.

Several personal characteristics were considered by Estes and Reames (1988), who used a set of two cases involving materiality mailed to 1406 CPAs who worked for both public accounting and other firms. A total of 596 (42%) responded. A test for nonresponse bias did not reveal any significant differences in late responses compared to early responses. They found that the number of years of experience did not affect the decisions but did increase confidence in the decisions made. Education and frequency of materiality decisions had no effect on decisions or confidence. Working for a public accounting firm decreased confidence in the decisions. Gender of the respondent did not affect the decision but did affect confidence, with women being more confident in their decisions about receivables but less about inventory. Age had some effect on the decisions in that older subjects tended to use a lower materiality level, but the effect was not significant.

3.   The Effect of External and Contextual Variables

Studies classified into this group also consider what variables affect the decisions made by auditors, but the variables considered are external to the decision maker. The studies included here are quite diverse. No clear framework emerged summarizing these findings into a coherent pattern.

Two studies consider the general environment in which the auditor operates. Gibbins and Wolf (1982) undertook a descriptive study of how auditors perceive the audit environment as it develops during the audit. They received questionnaire responses on the perceptions of 80 audit partners and managers (for an 82% response rate) of the importance of various factors for making decisions during an audit. Generally, the respondents considered client factors, client service considerations, and factors specific to the audit such as materiality, the audit team, time and fee constraints, GAAP, GAAS, and the firm's standards.

Kaplan (1985a) found that the environment of the client did not affect the auditor's decision on planned audit hours but that a more specific variable, the internal control evaluation, did have an effect. He used a case evaluated by 84 practicing auditors from one large firm, manipulating the description of the client's environment, the strength of its internal control, and the method used to elicit responses from the subjects.

Planned audit hours were also used as the dependent variable by Bamber and Bylinski (1987). They considered the effect of a different external variable, the planning memorandum, and found that it had a significant effect on the judgments made on the number of planned audit hours of the 73 audit managers who served as subjects. This study also used cases that asked the subjects to establish the number of hours they believed should be planned for review of the audit work.

Several studies considered the effect on decisions from the way evidence is presented to the decision maker. These studies indicate that the auditors' decisions will be affected by this apparently simple change. For example, Ricchiute (1984) found that the mode of presentation (visual or auditory or a combination) affected the likelihood of requiring an audit adjustment perceived to be necessary by 60 auditor subjects in two cases presented to them. Boritz (1985) varied the presentation of information in a case given to 40 auditor subjects at various levels. The information regarding a set of planned audit procedures was presented to the subjects in a format that was either highly structured or less structured. Subjects were required to evaluate the plan, revise it as necessary, and indicate the difficulty they found in making their decisions. The structured audit procedures were presented with internal control considerations as headings or subheadings. The unstructured procedures were identical but the headings and subheadings were deleted. Boritz found that the unstructured set was criticized more and was judged to be less reliable than the structured set.

Ashton and Ashton (1988) varied the order of evidence presented to 211 auditors and found that this did have an effect on the decisions made about internal control reliability in a series of five cases. This finding was confirmed by Tubbs, Messier, and Knechel (1990). Butt and Campbell (1989) also considered the effect of order and found that the order in which information is presented makes a difference when auditors have low prior beliefs about the hypothesis being tested.

Chewning and Harrell (1990) considered the effect of information load on the quality of the decisions they made. They found evidence that information load had an inverted U-shaped effect on decision quality.

One study considered the sensitivity of auditors to the perceived reliability of the group members and found that auditors were quite sensitive to the reliability of the source (Bamber, 1983). Other studies that consider the effect of presentation mode include Blocher, Moffie, and Zmud (1986), Purvis (1989), Trotman and Sng (1989), and Butt and Campbell (1989), as well as Wong-On-Wing, Reneau, and West (1989).

Blocher, Esposito, and Willingham (1983) asked 44 auditor subjects to develop an audit program for the audit of payroll expenses and set the budgeted number of audit hours, based on a case that described the work that had been done in the previous year. They presented different subjects with different versions of a case that varied in two aspects: the amount of audit work done in the previous year and the inclusion of a predetermined checklist that described standard audit procedures for payroll. They found that decisions varied significantly, suggesting the subjects were influenced not only by the details of the company being audited, but also by the level of work performed in the previous year and the use of a memory aid (the checklist).

Rebele, Heintz, and Briden (1988) varied the apparent reliability of the evidence used by 70 auditor subjects and found that the subjects were sensitive to the source reliability. Using a case method with subjects required to estimate uncollectible accounts, they found subjects placed significantly more reliance on evidence obtained from a high-expertise source than from a low-expertise source.

The perceived inherent risk (that a material error might occur in the accounts if adequate controls are not present) of an audit engagement was the dependent variable considered by Colbert (1988), who manipulated several variables in describing situations to 65 auditor subjects. She found that these variables were considered by the subjects who were asked to assess inherent risk in 20 cases. This approach was also used by Cohen and Kida (1989).

Another external variable, the general audit approach used by the auditing firm, may have an effect on the decisions made by auditors. Bamber and Snowball (1988) found that the amount of "structure" in the audit methods used by firms is related to differences in sample size decisions made by 113 auditor subjects who analyzed cases that varied in the amount of uncertainty included in each version of the case.

Another aspect of the auditing firm that has been considered is the firm's size (A. Wright, 1983). Wright found some significant differences in disclosure preferences when auditors from large firms were compared to those from smaller ones.

4. Cognitive Biases and Heuristics

A substantial amount of research has focused on possible sources of bias and decision errors that might be made by auditors, following the work of Tversky and Kahneman (1974), Einhorn and Hogarth (1981), and Joyce and Libby (1981). The main types of biases and heuristics that have been studied are availability (Libby, 1985), representativeness (Joyce and Biddle, 1981b; Frederick and Libby, 1986; Johnson, 1983), and anchoring and adjustment (Joyce and Biddle, 1981a; Kinney and Uecker, 1982; Shields, Solomon, and Waller, 1988). Availability involves the tendency to remember the most recent event or occurrence. Representativeness involves the release of a memory that is superficially similar to or has some similarity with the stimulus. Anchoring and adjustment involves using a starting point in a decision and making adjustments from this starting point, rather than attempting to arrive at a response based solely on the evidence provided. Since a recent work has reviewed this area for behavioral auditing research (Shanteau, 1989), the present survey will be limited to some of the main points.

The results of the studies in this area using auditors as subjects appear to show that auditors may be as susceptible to the same threats to decision making as any other people (Shanteau, 1987), but the results have not always been consistent. If auditors are professionals whose role depends on making supposedly unbiased decisions, the finding that auditors may not be immune to normal decision errors could have serious implications. For example, in considering anchoring and adjustment, Biggs and Wild (1985) found that the use of unaudited book values tended to act as an anchor that resulted in biased decisions. However, A. Wright (1988a) did not find that information from prior working papers impeded audit effectiveness by causing an anchor that resulted in incorrect decisions. Butler (1986) found that experienced auditors use an anchor for assessment of risk based on their experience. Heintz and White (1989) found that auditors do consider unaudited figures, especially when the figures indicated a decrease or trend reversal.

Other possible sources of decision bias that have been considered include how the question is presented, which was called the "framing" of the information. The main question here is whether or not different decisions are made for the same question when the exposition differs slightly but with the same facts. Shields, Solomon, and Waller (1987) found no significant effects for framing in their empirical experiment. Holt (1987) found that framing may account for possible decision errors noted in previous experiments that considered anchoring and adjustment questions. Trotman and Sng (1989) found that framing had a weak effect on the search for information.

Another interesting question is whether or not auditors appear to violate expected utility theory in their decision making. This was examined by A. Ashton (1982), who found that auditors also appear to be susceptible to the "Allais paradox," but to a lesser degree than other groups. This paradox involves asking subjects to make choices about gambles that include different probabilities of gaining certain amounts or nothing. Subjects do not appear to calculate or use the net expected value of each choice.

Other sources of bias in auditors' decisions relate to auditors who are expected to audit a system they helped develop. Plumlee (1985) found both memory and attributional biases in a laboratory experiment using 39 practicing internal auditors. Subjects who reviewed systems they developed reported the strengths of the system while subjects who only had familiarity with the type of system reported the weaknesses. Although this study considered only internal auditors, the findings may also apply to external auditors when they recommend changes to systems for their clients. This finding is potentially very important as it may reveal a bias that would provide a strong argument against the provision of any service other than auditing to clients by the incumbent auditor.

Kida (1984b) attempted to determine whether or not auditors use certain information search strategies such as confirmatory, disconfirmatory, or a more unbiased search pattern. He found some evidence of confirmatory searches for evidence using 44 auditor subjects who analyzed a case that required them to make a going concern decision.

D. How to Improve Decisions

1. Decision Quality

Researchers have not been able to agree on what criteria should be used to assess the quality of decisions made by auditors. Normative rules do not always exist for audit decision making. As a result, surrogates for decision quality have been used, such as consensus. Gaumnitz et al. (1982) asked 35 auditor subjects to make judgments on 20 cases involving internal control strength and subsequent audit time budgets. They found consensus decreased as the cases became more subject to uncertainty; that is, as the internal control strength decreased. They also found that consensus was affected by office affiliation and level of experience. This research was extended by Tabor (1983), who used 109 auditor subjects from four firms. He also found some firm effects in the patterns of responses received from the subjects.

A. Ashton (1985) specifically compared the consensus of responses with objective measures of accuracy. She analyzed the data reported by Kida (1980) that used the going-concern question in a series of 40 cases presented to 27 audit partners and found that correlations of consensus and accuracy measures ranged from .530 to .895. She concludes that consensus and accuracy are related in this setting. The multicase method (32 cases) was also used by Abdel-khalik, Snowball, and Wragge (1983), who found consistent responses for each subject and moderate consensus among 59 auditor subjects.

Other studies that use consensus as a surrogate for accuracy include Lewis (1980), Mayper (1982), Uecker (1982), Kaplan (1985b), Keasey and Watson (1989), Harrison and Tomassini (1989), and Pincus (1990). Lewis used 70 auditor subjects from four firms and two different cases. Using consensus as a criterion, he found differences between firms and in the amount of consensus within the different firms. Lewis also found higher consensus for the case that had a higher materiality level and thus less subjectivity. Mayper used 38 auditor subjects and 12 cases. He found no significant differences in the level of consensus for experience, but found some effect for geographical location and firm. Generally, he found relatively low levels of consensus for the cases that involved evaluating internal control weaknesses, with differing levels for the different cases. Kaplan used consensus to consider the effect of a two-step judgment process compared to a single judgment in a series of 16 cases involving the estimate of audit hours required for the audit of accounts receivable. The second step for one-half of the 54 auditor subjects was first to evaluate the strength of the internal control before estimating the number of audit hours. Kaplan found no significant increase in the consensus shown between the responses for the two different tasks.

Reckers and Schultz (1982) used cases that involved the level of probability needed to require disclosure of contingent events. They compared the variability of decisions made by 128 individual student subjects with decisions made by groups. They found that the variability of group decisions was significantly smaller than the variability of decisions made by individual subjects. They conclude that consensus is increased by a group decision process.

Consensus was also considered by Jiambalvo and Wilner (1985) when they compared the consistency of decisions made by 80 auditors for contingent claims with the guidelines prescribed by the Financial Accounting Standards Board's statement number 5. They found that auditors did not agree on the meaning of words and did not always make decisions as expected for the cases presented to them.

Otley and Dias (1982) considered the effect of the amount of information on decision quality. They generally found that too little or too much information resulted in lower-quality decisions.

2. Methods of Improving Decisions

Decision quality refers to the outcome of the decision process. Studies have considered the process as a means of improving decision quality. A general discussion of some of the difficulties encountered in the use of normative models of decision making as prescriptions for the improvement of decisions can be found in Waller and Jiambalvo (1984).

Reviews of the research in the area of expertise in auditing can be found in Bedard (1989), Choo (1989), and Davis and Solomon (1989). Bedard concluded that experts do not behave differently from novices while making decisions but they do have knowledge differences that may account for their different decisions. Perhaps the most general approach is illustrated by Arrington, Hillison, and Jensen (1984) and Bouwman (1984). Both these studies attempted to model judgments made by experts and (in Bouwman) with novices, while analyzing decision problems.

Emby and Gibbins (1988) asked 69 auditors (for a 78% response rate) in five countries (Canada, the United States, Australia, the United Kingdom, and the Netherlands) about what they considered to be important to good judgment, as well as about the importance to the auditor of justification after the decision had been made. They found little consensus regarding the factors considered to be important to good judgment except that factors that helped justify the decision were rated highly. All respondents indicated a greater need for justification in unfamiliar situations compared to familiar ones.

Several methods have been proposed that could improve the decision process used by auditors, such as the use of several different methods to elicit information, encouragement of group decisions, the use of decision aids such as questionnaires, and the use of statistical rather than judgmental sampling. Ijiri and Leitch (1980) discuss several statistical methods that can be used to improve the taking of audit samples.

Crosby (1980; 1981) used several elicitation methods to generate prior probability distributions and compared the results to the Bayesian model. He found significant differences and suggested that auditors may not be Bayesian information processors. The different elicitation methods were compared by Abdolmohammadi (1985), as well as Abdolmohammadi and Berger (1986). They found that the various methods resulted in different levels of consensus among different auditor subjects. Additional studies that compare different elicitation methods for probability assessments include the extensive work of Chesley (1986) and articles such as that by Beck, Solomon, and Tomassini (1985).

Several studies have compared how well individuals and groups make decisions (Solomon, 1982; Schultz and Reckers, 1981). Solomon studied decisions made by 103 auditors who made decisions either individually or in two types of groups. He found the decisions reached were different, with the group decisions being slightly "better" than the decisions reached individually. Schultz and Reckers used 64 auditor subjects who analyzed a case involving a disclosure question. They found different decisions were reached, depending on whether subjects acted alone or in a group, and also that the type of interaction in the group affected the decisions. Two types of group interactions were used: nominal/interacting and interacting/nominal. These differed in that in the nominal/interacting group, individuals first arrived at probability distributions individually, then came together to reach a group consensus. In the interacting/nominal group, they first achieved a group consensus, then separately arrived at probability distributions.

This work was extended by Trotman and Yetton (1985), who considered the effect of the hierarchical position of people in two-person noninteracting groups with a review process such as is typically found in auditing. They found this type of group did result in a decrease in decision variance compared to individuals acting alone. Trotman (1985) extended this area of research by using a case that uses a simulation model-based measure of accuracy and that permits interaction during the review process. He found that judgment accuracy improved significantly after the review.

Srinidhi and Vasarhelyi (1986) found that the quality of decisions was affected by the *lack* of an aggregation rule, but with such a rule, the decisions made were quite consistent. They concluded that the use of decision aids such as decision rules may be highly desirable. This finding was supported by Butler (1985) for a decision such as the assessment of sampling risk. The usefulness of predetermined standardized audit questionnaires as decision aids to improve auditor decisions was considered by Pincus (1989) for assessing possible fraud. Using 137 auditor subjects, two cases were analyzed, one of which involved a fraud and one of which did not. Half the subjects used a questionnaire, the others did not. Subjects were required to assess the likelihood of fraud. For the case involving no fraud, no significantly different results were found. For the case involving fraud, the subjects who did not use the questionnaire had better assessments.

Other studies that consider the use of decision aids are Brown (1981), Nichols (1987), Simnett and Trotman (1989), Libby and Libby (1989), and Kachelmeier and Messier (1990).

E. Summary

When auditing is considered at a "micro" level, the unit of study is the individual auditor. As one of the key roles of the auditor is as a decision maker, this line of research will probably prove to be most valuable in the long run. As can be seen from the large number of studies that have been undertaken in this area, a great deal of effort has been devoted to this research. However, the research has not reached the stage at which general conclusions or specific recommendations can be made that will result in improved decision making. This line of research is characterized by many difficulties, including not having a standard or "correct" response against which decisions can be compared. Many additional studies need to be undertaken before real benefits result.

VI. CONCLUSION

The purpose of this chapter was to review the research in auditing that considers auditors as people in their several roles. Many diverse studies were published in the 1980s. This review lists more than 250 references and concentrates on just seven of the leading accounting and auditing research journals. The research has drawn from many different disciplines such as cognitive psychology, psychology, organizational behavior, and economics, but even a preliminary review of the auditing research indicates that there are still findings in other areas that could be applied to auditing and auditors. An assumption was made that any study that considers the behavior of auditors in any of their various roles should have, as an ultimate objective, the possibility of improving the performance of and decisions made by auditors. However, since behavior and cognitive processes are so complex, considerable care is needed before any definite conclusions or recommendations can be made.

Considering the auditor as an individual, not much is known about who is attracted to auditing, who should be attracted to auditing, or whether or not the changing needs of the profession are being met by today's recruits. There are very few recent studies of the personal characteristics of auditors and accounting students. These few studies have not related the personal characteristics with resulting behaviors. Auditors do have a stereotype, but we cannot determine if this stereotype is accurate or if it effects areas such as recruiting even if it is accurate. We do not know which students are being attracted to accounting and auditing or what factors affect a student's choice. There are indications that younger and more junior members of auditing firms are different from the older, more senior members, but we cannot determine the reasons for this. Is it a result of attrition, learning, behavior modification, socialization, or societal factors?

Auditors can also be employees with many of the same problems as any other employees, but relatively few studies have considered this perspective. Recruiting for new auditors from accounting majors appears to be an inexact science. This may be related to problems of the shock to new employees when their initial expectations are not met on the job. In turn, this might be related to a low level of job satisfaction, auditors' disenchantment with their jobs, and increased employee turnover. All these are costly to auditing firms, but they do not appear to be well understood. Also not well understood are the effects of leadership and performance evaluation on the behavior of auditors. That all these problems have an effect on the behavior of auditors does not appear to be disputed. What is not known is the nature of the effect and its significance. Since these problems have been studied in the management and organizational behavior disciplines, auditing may be able to benefit from the application of the findings in these other areas of specialization.

Auditors are professionals who appear to be well respected and who have definite professional reputations. Some activities may endanger this respected position—for example, the provision of nonaudit services to audit clients may risk losing the appearance of independence to outsiders. This question has been studied fairly frequently, but no overall conclusions have been advanced. These studies indicate that auditors tend to believe their independence is not reduced, while outsiders believe independence is lessened. As professionals, auditors may be underestimating the long-term effects of this practice.

Another area that may affect the behavior of auditors as professionals is membership in professional bodies. Professional membership has several implications, such as the related training and experience requirements, the necessity to maintain professional standards, and the development of professional attitudes through a process of socialization. These all affect behavior, but the process has not been researched thoroughly. Professional membership also creates a conflict of divided loyalties between the profession and the employer. This conflict will cause stress, which may have negative results both in the physical and mental health of the person and in his or her job performance.

Many studies have considered the auditors' decision making, but few definite conclusions can be stated other than the obvious one that professional auditing judgment is very complex. We are just beginning to consider the cognitive aspects of memory and judgment and the implications for auditing decisions. There are indications that internal personal factors may have an effect on judgment, but not enough detail is known to be able to predict what characteristics result in what types of decisions. It appears to be fairly well established that external and contextual factors do affect decisions, but no general theory or model has been proposed to enable us to relate specific factors to decisions. Auditors may use cognitive heuristics and may display cognitive biases, but we cannot determine if these result in inaccurate decisions or are merely the result of normal cognitive processes.

A further difficulty encountered in studying professional auditing decision making is the absence of indicators of decision quality. Auditors are usually in the unfortunate position of not being able to know for sure that the decision they make on types of audit opinion to be rendered are the correct ones until some time later. Only with the passing of time are problems discovered that may indicate that an incorrect audit opinion was given. In this situation, what does audit decision quality mean? Is a consensus of auditors sufficient to indicate quality? What does expertise in auditing mean? What effect will decision aids have?

A general criticism that may be made of virtually all the research studies included is that they do not appear to be very rigorous. Behavioral research can easily be criticized as being "soft," with the results having no real merit when compared to other "hard" sciences. Three comments on this line of criticism would be that, (1) by their nature, behavioral studies can never be as rigorous as other types of research; (2) more than one research approach is warranted for a field such as auditing (Tomkins and Groves, 1983); and (3) since auditing research is in its early stages of development, harsh criticism is unwarranted. It would be expected that future auditing research will improve and be less subject to such criticisms. Most of the auditing research is still at a quasi-experimental level, but the trend is toward more rigorous designs.

A final general conclusion is that the behavioral auditing research appears to be at a stage at which different parts of it should be carefully summarized and analyzed so syntheses and models of what has been learned can be proposed. Further research could benefit from what has been already been learned.

ACKNOWLEDGMENTS

The helpful comments of Haim Falk, Dan Thornton, Mike Gibbins, Stephen Asare, and participants of the Accounting Research Workshops at the University of Calgary and Simon Fraser University are gratefully acknowledged.

REFERENCES

Abdel-khalik, A. R., Snowball, D., and Wragge, J. H. (1983). The effects of certain internal audit variables on the planning of external audit programs. *The Accounting Rev.*, LVIII: 215–227.

Abdel-khalik, A. R., and Solomon, I., eds. (1988). *Research Opportunities in Auditing: The Second Decade*. American Accounting Association: Auditing Section, Sarasota, Fl.

Abdolmohammadi, M. (1985). Bayesian inference research in auditing: Some methodological suggestions. *Contemporary Accounting Res.*, 2: 76–94.

Abdolmohammadi, M. J. (1986). Efficiency of the Bayesian approach in compliance testing: Some empirical evidence. *Auditing: A J. of Practice & Theory*, 5: 1–16.

Abdolmohammadi, M., and Berger, P. D. (1986). A test of the accuracy of probability assessment techniques in auditing. *Contemporary Accounting Res.*, 3: 149–165.

Abdolmohammadi, M., and Wright, A. (1987). An examination of the effects of experience and task complexity on audit judgments. *The Accounting Rev.*, LXII: 1–13.

Alderman, C. W., and Deitrick, J. W. (1982). Auditors' perceptions of time budget pressures and premature sign-offs: A replication and extension. *Auditing: A J. of Practice & Theory*, 2: 54–68.

Amernic, J. H., and Beechy, T. H. (1984). Accounting students' performance and cognitive complexity: Some empirical evidence. *The Accounting Rev.*, LX: 330–313.

Amershi, A. H., Demski, J. S., and Fellingham, N. J. (1985). Sequential Bayesian analysis in accounting. *Contemporary Accounting Res.*, 1: 176–192.

Anderson, U., and Marchant, G. (1989). The auditor's assessment of the competence and integrity of auditee personnel. *Auditing: A J. of Practice & Theory*, 8(supp.): 1–16.

Aranya, N., and Ferris, K. R. (1984). A reexamination of accountants' organization-professional conflict. *The Accounting Rev.*, LIX: 1–15.

Aranya, N., Lachman, R., and Amernic, J. (1982). Accountants' job satisfaction: A path analysis. *Accounting, Org. and Soc.*, 7: 201–215.

Aranya, N., Pollock, J., and Amernic, J. (1981). An examination of professional commitment in public accounting. *Accounting, Org. and Soc.*, 6: 271–280.

Aranya, N., and Wheeler, J. T. (1986). Accountants' personality types and their commitment to organization and profession. *Contemporary Accounting Res.*, 3: 184–199.

Arrington, C. E., Hillison, W., and Jensen, R. E. (1984). An application of analytical hierarchy process to model expert judgments on analytical review procedures. *J. of Accounting Res.*, 22: 298–312.

Ashton, A. H. (1982). The descriptive validity of normative decision theory in auditing contexts. *J. of Accounting Res.*, 20: 415–428.

Ashton, A. H. (1985). Does consensus imply accuracy in accounting studies of decision making? *The Accounting Rev.*, LX: 173–185.

Ashton, A. H., and Ashton, R. H. (1988). Sequential belief revision in auditing. *The Accounting Rev.*, LXIII: 623–641.

Ashton, R. H. (1981). A descriptive study of information evaluation. *J. of Accounting Res.*, 19: 42–61.

Ashton, R. H. (1982). *Human Information Processing in Accounting*. Studies in Accounting Research #17, American Accounting Association, Sarasota, Fl.

Ashton, R. H. (1983). *Research in Audit Decision Making: Rationale, Evidence, and Implications*, Research monograph number 6. the Canadian Certified General Accountants' Research Foundation, Vancouver, B.C.

Ashton, R. H., and Brown, P. R. (1980). Descriptive modeling of auditors' internal control judgments: Replication and extension. *J. of Accounting Res.*, 18: 269–277.

Ashton, R. H., Kleinmuntz, D. N., Sullivan, J. B., and Tomassini, L. A. (1988). Audit decision making. In *Res. Opportunities in Auditing: The Second Decade* (A. R. Abdel-khalik and I. Solomon, eds.), American Accounting Association, Auditing Section, pp. 95–132, Sarasota, Fl.

Bailey, K. E., Bylinski, J. H., and Shields, M. D. (1983). Effects of audit report wording changes on the perceived message. *J. of Accounting Res.*, 21: 355–370.

Ballew, Van (1982). Technological routineness and intra-unit structure in CPA firms. *The Accounting Rev.*, LVII: 88–104.

Bamber, E. M., Bamber, L. S., and Bylinski, J. H. (1988). A descriptive study of audit managers' working paper review. *Auditing: A J. of Practice & Theory*, 7: 137–149.

Bamber, E. M., and Bylinski, J. H. (1987). The effects of the planning memorandum, time pressure and individual auditor characteristics on audit managers' review time judgments. *Contemporary Accounting Res.*, 4: 127–143.

Bamber, E. M., and Snowball, D. (1988). An experimental study of the effects of audit structure in uncertain task environments. *The Accounting Rev.*, LXIII: 490–504.

Bamber, E. M., Snowball, D., and Tubbs, R. M. (1989). Audit structure and its relation to role conflict and role ambiguity: An empirical investigation. *The Accounting Rev.*, LXIV: 285–299.

Beck, P. J., Solomon, I., and Tomassini, L. A. (1985). Subjective prior probability distributions and audit risk. *J. of Accounting Res.*, 23: 37–56.

Bedard, J. (1989). Expertise in auditing: Myth or reality. *Accounting, Org. and Soc.*, 14: 113–131.

Benke, R. L., and Rhode, J. G. (1980). The job satisfaction of higher level employees in large certified public accounting firms. *Accounting, Org. and Soc.*, 5: 187–201.

Biggs, S. F., Messier, W. F., and Hansen, J. V. (1987). A descriptive analysis of computer audit specialists' decision-making behavior in advanced computer environments. *Auditing: A J. of Practice & Theory*, 6: 1–21.

Biggs, S. F., and Mock, T. J. (1983). An investigation of auditor decision processes in the evaluation of internal controls and audit scope decisions. *J. of Accounting Res.*, 21: 234–255.

Biggs, S. F., and Wild, J. J. (1985). An investigation of auditor judgment in analytical review. *The Accounting Rev.*, *LX*: 607–633.

Birnberg, J. G., and Shields, M. D. (1984). The role of attention and memory in accounting decisions. *Accounting, Organizations and Society*, *9*: 365–382.

Birnberg, J. G., and Shields, J. F. (1989). Three decades of behavioral accounting performance: A search for order. *Behavioral Res in Accounting*, *1*: 23–75.

Blocher, E., and Cooper, J. C. (1988). A study of auditors' analytical review performance. *Auditing: A J. of Practice & Theory*, *7*: 1–28.

Blocher, E., Esposito, R. S., and Willingham, J. J. (1983). Auditors' analytical review judgments for payroll expense. *Auditing: A J. of Practice & Theory*, *3*: 75–91.

Blocher, E., Moffie, R. P., and Zmud, R. W. (1986). Report format and task complexity: Interaction in risk judgments. *Accounting, Org. and Soc.*, *11*: 457–470.

Bonner, S. E. (1990). Experience effects in auditing: The role of task-specific knowledge. *The Accounting Rev.*, *65*: 72–92.

Boritz, J. E. (1985). The effect of information presentation structures on audit planning and review judgments. *Contemporary Accounting Res.*, *1*: 193–218.

Boritz, J. E. (1986). The effect of research method on audit planning and review judgments. *J. of Accounting Res.*, *26*: 335–348.

Boritz, J. E., Gaber, B. G., and Lemon, W. M. (1988). An experimental study of the effects of elicitation methods on review of preliminary audit strategy by external auditors. *Contemporary Accounting Res.*, *4*: 392–411.

Bouwman, M. J. (1984). Expert vs. novice decision making in accounting: A summary. *Accounting, Org. and Soc.*, *9*: 325–327.

Briloff, A. J. (1987). Do management services endanger independence and objectivity? *CPA J.*, *57*(8): 22–29.

Brown, C. (1981). Human information processing for decisions to investigate cost variances. *J. of Accounting Res.*, *19*: 62–85.

Brown, P. R. (1983). Independent auditor judgment in the evaluation of internal audit functions. *J. of Accounting Res.*, *21*: 444–455.

Buchman, T. A., and Tracy, J. A. (1982). Obtaining responses to sensitive questionnaires: Conventional questionnaire versus randomized response technique. *J. of Accounting Res.*, *20*: 263–271.

Bullen, M. L., and Flamholtz, E. G. (1985). A theoretical and empirical investigation of job satisfaction and intended turnover in the large CPA firm. *Accounting, Org. and Soc.*, *10*: 287–302.

Burgstahler, D., and Jiambalvo, J. (1986). Sample error characteristics and projection of error to audit populations. *The Accounting Rev.*, *LXI*: 233–248.

Burgstahler, D., and Sundem, G. L. (1989). The evolution of behavioral accounting research in the United States, 1968–1987. *Behavioral Res. in Accounting*, *1*: 75–108.

Butler, S. A. (1985). Application of a decision aid in the judgmental evaluation of substantive test of details samples. *J. of Accounting Res.*, *23*: 513–526.

Butler, S. A. (1986). Anchoring in the judgmental evaluation of audit samples. *The Accounting Rev.*, *LXI*: 101–111.

Butt, J. L. (1988). Frequency judgments in an auditing related task. *J. of Accounting Res.*, *26*: 315–330.

Butt, J. L., and Campbell, T. L. (1989). The effects of information order and hypothesis-testing strategies on auditors' judgments. *Accounting, Org. and Soc.*, *14*: 471–480.

Campbell, J. E. (1984). An application of protocol analysis to the "Little GAAP" controversy. *Accounting, Org. and Soc.*, *9*: 329–342.

Chesley, G. R. (1986). Interpretation of uncertainty expressions. *Contemporary Accounting Res.*, *2*: 179–199.

Chewning, E. G., and Harrell, A. M. (1990). The effect of information load on decision makers' cue utilization levels and decision quality in a financial distress decision task. *Accounting Org. and Soc.*, *15*: 527–542.

Choo, F. (1986). Job stress, job performance, and auditor personality characteristics. *Auditing: A J. of Practice & Theory*, *5*: 17–34.

Choo, F. (1989). Expert-novice differences in judgment decision making research. *J. of Accounting Lit.*, *8*: 106–136.

Christensen, J. (1982). The determination of performance standards and participation. *J. of Accounting Res.*, *20*: 589–603.

Cohen, J. and Kida, T. (1989). The impact of analytical review results, internal control reliability, and experience on auditors' use of analytical review. *J. of Accounting Res.*, *27*: 263–276.

Colbert, J. L. (1988). Inherent risk: An investigation of auditors' judgments. *Accounting, Org. and Soc.,* *3*: 111–121.

Colbert, J. L. (1989). The effect of experience on auditors' judgments. *J. of Accounting Lit.,* *8*: 137–149.

Coiville, I. (1981). Reconstructing "behavioural accounting." *Accounting, Org. and Soc.,* *6*: 119–132.

Crosby, M. A. (1980). Implications of prior probability elicitation on auditor sample size decisions. *J. of Accounting Res.,* *18*: 585–593.

Crosby, M. A. (1981). Bayesian statistics in auditing: A comparison of probability elicitation techniques. *The Accounting Rev., LVI*: 355–365.

Crosby, M. A. (1985). The development of Bayesian decision-theoretic concepts in attribute sampling. *Auditing: A J. of Practice & Theory,* *4*: 118–132.

Danos, P., and Imhoff, E. A. (1982). Auditor review of financial forecasts: An analysis of factors affecting reasonableness judgments. *The Accounting Rev., LVII*: 39–54.

Danos, P., and Imhoff, E. A. (1983). Factors affecting auditors' evaluations of forecasts. *J. of Accounting Res.,* *21*: 473–494.

Davis, J. S., and Solomon, I. (1989). Experience, expertise, and expert-performance research in public accounting. *J. of Accounting Lit.,* *8*: 150–164.

Dean, R. A., Ferris, K. R., and Konstans, C. (1988). Occupational reality shock and organizational commitment: Evidence from the accounting profession. *Accounting, Org. and Soc.,* *13*(3): 235–250.

Dillard, J. F. (1981). A longitudinal evaluation of an occupational goal-expectancy model in professional accounting organizations. *Accounting, Org. and Soc.,* *6*: 17–26.

Dillard, J. F. (1984). Cognitive science and decision making research in accounting. *Accounting, Org. and Soc.,* *6*: 343–354.

Dillard, J. F., and Ferris, K. R. (1989). Individual behavior in professional accounting firms: A review and synthesis. *J. of Accounting Lit.,* *8*: 208–234.

Dirsmith, M. W., and Covaleski, M. A. (1985). Informal communications, nonformal communications and mentoring in public accounting firms. *Accounting, Org. and Soc.,* *10*: 149–169.

Dittman, D. A., Juris, H. A., and Revsine, L. (1980). Unrecorded human assets: A survey of accounting firms' training programs. *The Accounting Rev., LV*: 640–648.

Dunn, W. M., and Hall, T. W. (1984). An empirical analysis of the relationships between CPA examination candidate attributes and candidate performance. *The Accounting Rev., LIX*: 674–689.

Dykxhoorn, H. J., and Sinning, K. E. (1981). Wirtschaftsprufer perception of auditor independence. *The Accounting Rev., LVI*: 97–107.

Dykxhoorn, H. J., and Sinning, K. E. (1982). Perceptions of auditor independence: Its perceived effect on the loan and investment decisions of German financial statement users. *Accounting Org. and Soc.,* *7*: 337–347.

Einhorn, H. J., and Hogarth, R. M. (1981). Behavioral decision theory: Processes of judgment and choice. *J. of Accounting Res.,* *19*: 1–31.

Emby, C., and Gibbins, M. (1988). Good judgment in public accounting: Quality and justification. *Contemporary Accounting Res.,* *4*: 287–313.

Estes, R., and Reames, D. D. (1988). Effects of personal characteristics on materiality decisions: A multivariate analysis. *Accounting and Business Res.,* *18*: 291–296.

Farmer, T. A., Rittenberg, L. E., and Trompeter, G. M. (1987). An investigation of the impact of economic and organizational factors on auditor independence. *Auditing: A J. of Practice & Theory,* *7*: 1–14.

Felix, W. L., and Kinney, W. R. (1982). Research in the auditor's opinion formulation process: State of the art. *The Accounting Rev., LVII*: 245–271.

Ferris, K. R. (1981). Organizational commitment and performance in a professional accounting firm. *Accounting, Org. and Soc.,* *6*: 317–325.

Ferris, K. R. (1982). Educational predictors of professional pay and performance. *Accounting, Org. and Soc.,* *7*: 225–230.

Ferris, K. R., Dillard, J. F., and Nethercott, L. (1980). A comparison of V-I-E model predictions: A cross-national study in professional accounting firms. *Accounting, Org. and Soc.,* *5*: 361–368.

Ferris, K. R., and Larcker, D. F. (1983). Explanatory variables of auditor performance in a large public accounting firm. *Accounting, Org. and Soc.,* *8*: 1–11.

Firth, M. (1980). Perceptions of auditor independence and official ethical guidelines. *The Accounting Rev., LV*: 451–466.

Firth, M. (1981). Auditor-client relationships and their impact on bankers' perceived lending decisions. *Accounting and Business Res.,* *11*: 179–188.

Frederick, D., and Libby, R. (1986). Expertise and auditors' judgments of conjunctive events. *J. of Accounting Res.*, *24*: 270–290.

Gaumnitz, B. R., Nunamaker, T. R., Surdick, J. J., and Thomas, M. F. (1982). Auditor consensus in internal program planning. *J. of Accounting Res.*, *20*: 745–755.

Gibbins, M. (1982). Regression and other statistical implications for research on judgment using intercorrelated data sources. *J. of Accounting Res.*, *20*: 121–138.

Gibbins, M. (1984). Propositions about the psychology of professional judgment in public accounting. *J. of Accounting Res.*, *22*: 103–125.

Gibbins, M., and Mason, A. K. (1988). *Professional Judgment in Financial Reporting*. Canadian Institute of Chartered Accountants, Toronto.

Gibbins, M., and Wolf, F. M. (1982). Auditors' subjective decision environment—The case of a normal external audit. *The Accounting Rev.*, *LVII*: 105–124.

Gregson, T. (1990). Communication satisfaction: A path analytic study of accountants affiliated with CPA firms. *Beh. Res. in Accounting*, *2*: 32–49.

Gul, F. A. (1984). An empirical study of the usefulness of human resources turnover costs in Australian accounting firms. *Accounting, Org. and Soc.*, *9*: 233–239.

Gul, F. A. (1986). Adaption-innovation as a factor in Australian accounting undergraduates' subject interests and career preferences. *J. of Accounting Ed.*, *4*: 203–209.

Gul, F. A. (1987). Field dependence cognitive style as a moderating factor in subjects' perceptions of auditor independence. *Accounting and Fin.*, *27*: 37–48.

Hamilton, R. E., and Wright, W. F. (1982). Internal control judgments and effects of experience: Replications and extensions. *J. of Accounting Res.*, *20*: 756–765.

Harrell, A., and Eickhoff, R. (1988). Auditors' influence-orientation and their affective responses to the "Big Eight" work environment. *Auditing: A J. of Practice & Theory*, *7*: 105–118.

Harrell, A. M., and Stahl, M. J. (1984). McClelland's trichotomy of needs theory and the job satisfaction and work performance of CPA firm professionals. *Accounting, Org. and Soc.*, *9*: 241–252.

Harrison, K. E., and Tomassini, L. A. (1989). Judging the probability of a contingent loss: An empirical study. *Contemporary Accounting Res.*, *5*: 642–648.

Haskins, M. E. (1987). Client control environments: An examination of auditors' perceptions. *The Accounting Rev.*, *LXII*: 542–563.

Haskins, M. E., Baglioni, A. J., and Cooper, C. L. (1990). An investigation of the sources, moderators, and psychological symptoms of stress among audit seniors. *Contemporary Accounting Res.*, *6*: 361–385.

Hassell, J. M., and Arrington, C. E. (1989). A comparative analysis of the construct validity of coefficients in paramorphic models of accounting judgments: a replication and extension. *Accounting, Org. and Soc.*, *14*: 527–538.

Heintz, J. A., and White, G. B. (1989). Auditor judgment in analytical review—Some further evidence. *Auditing: A J. of Practice & Theory*, *8*: 22–39.

Holt, D. L. (1987). Auditors and base rates revisited. *Accounting, Org. and Soc.*, *12*: 571–578.

Ijiri, Y., and Leitch, R. A. (1980). Stein's paradox and audit sampling. *J. of Accounting Res.*, *18*: 91–108.

Ingram, R. W., and Petersen, R. J. (1987). An evaluation of AICPA tests for predicting the performance of accounting majors. *The Accounting Rev.*, *LXII*: 215–223.

Jennings, M., Kneer, D. C., and Reckers, P. M. J. (1987). A reexamination of the concept of materiality: Views of auditors, users and officers of the court. *Auditing: A J. of Practice & Theory*, *6*: 104–115.

Jiambalvo, J. (1982). Measures of accuracy and congruence in the performance evaluation of CPA personnel: Replication and extensions. *J. of Accounting Res.*, *20*: 152–161.

Jiambalvo, J., and Pratt, J. (1982). Task complexity and leadership effectiveness in CPA firms. *The Accounting Rev.*, *57*: 734–750.

Jiambalvo, J., Watson, D. J. H., and Baumler, J. V. (1983). An examination of performance evaluation decisions in CPA firm subunits. *Accounting, Org. and Soc.*, *8*: 13–29.

Jiambalvo, J., and Wilner, N. (1985). Auditor evaluation of contingent claims. *Auditing: A J. of Practice & Theory*, *5*: 1–11.

Johnson, B. (1982). The impact of confidence interval information on probability judgments. *Accounting, Org. and Soc.*, *7*: 349–367.

Johnson, P. E., Jamal, K., and Berryman, R. G. (1989). Audit judgment research. *Accounting, Org. and Soc.*, *14*: 83–99.

Johnson, W. B. (1983). "Representativeness" in judgmental predictions of corporate bankruptcy. *The Accounting Rev.*, *58*: 78–97.

Joyce, E., and Biddle, G. (1981a). Anchoring and adjustment in probabilistic inference in auditing. *J. of Accounting Res.*, *19*: 120–145.

Joyce, E., and Biddle, G. (1981b). Are auditors' judgments sufficiently regressive? *J. of Accounting Res.*, *19*: 323–349.

Joyce, E. J., and Libby, R. (1981). Some accounting implications of "Behavioral decision theory: Processes of judgment and choice." *J. of Accounting Res.*, *19*: 544–550.

Joyce, E. J., and Libby, R. (1982). Behavioral studies of audit decision making. *J. of Accounting Lit.*, *1*: 104–123.

Kachelmeier, S. J., and Messier, W. F. (1990). An investigation of the influence of a nonstatistical decision aid on auditor sample size decisions. *The Accounting Rev.*, 65: 209–226.

Kaplan, S. E. (1985a). An examination of the effects of environment and explicit internal control evaluation on planned audit hours. *Auditing: A J. of Practice & Theory*, 5: 12–25.

Kaplan, S. E. (1985b). The effect of combining compliance and substantive tasks on auditor consensus. *J. of Accounting Res.*, 23: 871–877.

Kaplan, S. E., and Reckers, P. M. J. (1985). An examination of auditor performance evaluation. *The Accounting Rev.*, LX: 477–487.

Kaplan, S. E., and Reckers, P. M. J. (1989). An examination of information search during initial audit planning. *Accounting, Org. and Soc.*, 14: 539–550.

Keasey, K., and Watson, R. (1989). Consensus and accuracy in accounting studies of decision-making: A note on a new measure of consensus. *Accounting, Org. and Soc.*, 14: 337–346.

Kelley, T., and Margheim, L. (1990). The impact of time budget pressure, personality, and leadership variables on dysfunctional auditor behavior. *Auditing: A J. of Practice & Theory*, 9: 21–42.

Kida, T. (1980). An investigation into auditors' continuity and related qualification judgments. *J. of Accounting Res.*, 18: 506–523.

Kida, T. (1984a). Performance evaluation and review meeting characteristics in public accounting firms. *Accounting, Org. and Soc.*, 9: 137–147.

Kida, T. (1984b). The impact of hypothesis-testing strategies on auditors' use of judgment data. *J. of Accounting Res.*, 22: 332–340.

King, R. D., and O'Keefe, T. B. (1989). Belief revision from hypothesis testing. *J. of Accounting Lit.*, 8: 1–24.

Kinney, W., and Uecker, W. (1982). Mitigating the consequences of anchoring in auditing judgments. *The Accounting Rev.*, LVII: 55–69.

Klersey, G. F., and Mock, T. J. (1989). Verbal protocol research in auditing. *Accounting, Org. and Soc.*, 14: 133–151.

Knapp, M. C. (1985). Audit conflict: An empirical study of the perceived ability of auditors to resist management pressure. *The Accounting Rev.*, LX: 202–211.

Knechel, W. R., and Messier, W. F. (1990). Sequential auditor decision making: Information search and evidence evaluation. *Contemporary Accounting Res.*, 6: 386–406.

Larcker, D. F., and Lessig, V. P. (1983). An examination of the linear and retrospective process tracing approaches to judgment modeling. *The Accounting Rev.*, 58: 58–77.

Lewis, B. L. (1980). Expert judgment in auditing: An expected utility approach. *J. of Accounting Res.*, 18: 594–602.

Lewis, B. L., and Bell, J. (1985). Decisions involving sequential events: Replications and extensions. *J. of Accounting Res.*, 23: 228–239.

Lewis, B., Shields, M. D., and Young, S. M. (1983). Evaluating human judgments and decision aids. *J. of Accounting Res.*, 21: 271–285.

Libby, R. (1981). *Accounting and Human Information Processing: Theory and Applications*. Prentice-Hall, Englewood Cliffs, NJ.

Libby, R. (1985). Availability and the generation of hypotheses in analytical review. *J. of Accounting Res.*, 23: 648–667.

Libby, R., Artman, J. T., and Willingham, J. J. (1985). Process susceptibility, control risk, and audit planning. *The Accounting Rev.*, LX: 212–230.

Libby, R., and Lewis, B. L. (1982). Human information processing research in accounting: The state of the art in 1982. *Accounting, Org. and Soc.*, 7: 231–285.

Libby, R., and Libby, P. A. (1989). Expert measurement and mechanical combination in control reliance decisions. *The Accounting Rev.*, LXIV: 729–747.

Lightner, S. M., Adams, S. J., and Lightner, K. M. (1982). The influence of situational, ethical, and expectancy theory variables on accountants' underreporting behavior. *Auditing: A J. of Practice & Theory*, 2: 1–12.

Marchant, G. (1989). Analogical reasoning and hypothesis generation in auditing. *The Accounting Rev.*, *LXIV*: 500–513.

Margheim, L. (1986). Further evidence on external auditors' reliance on internal auditors. *J. of Accounting Res.*, *24*: 194–205.

Margheim, L., and Pany, K. (1986). Quality control, premature signoff, and underreporting of time: Some empirical findings. *Auditing: A J. of Practice & Theory*, *5*: 50–63.

Mayer-Sommer, A. P., and Loeb, S. E. (1981). Fostering more successful professional socialization among accounting students. *The Accounting Rev.*, *LVI*: 125–136.

Mayper, A. G. (1982). Consensus of auditors' materiality judgments of internal accounting control weaknesses. *J. of Accounting Res.*, *20*: 773–783.

Mayper, A. G., Doucet, M. S., and Warren, C. S. (1989). Auditors' materiality judgments of internal accounting control weaknesses. *Auditing: A J. of Practice & Theory*, *9*: 72–87.

McKinley, S., Pany, K., and Reckers, P. M. J. (1985). An examination of the influence of CPA firm type, size, and MAS provision on loan officer decisions and perceptions. *J. of Accounting Res.*, *23*: 887–896.

Meixner, W. F., and Welker, R. B. (1988). Judgment consensus and auditor experience: An examination of organizational relations. *The Accounting Rev.*, *LXII*: 505–513.

Messier, W. F. (1983). The effect of experience and firm type on materiality/disclosure judgments. *J. of Accounting Res.*, *21*: 611–618.

Moeckel, C. L., and Plumlee, R. D. (1989). Auditors' confidence in recognition of audit evidence. *The Accounting Rev.*, *LXIV*: 653–666.

Moeckel, C. L., and Williams, J. D. (1990). The role of source availability in inference verification. *Contemporary Accounting Res.*, *6*: 850–858.

Murray, D., and Frazier, K. B. (1986). A within-subjects test of expectancy theory in a public accounting environment. *J. of Accounting Res.*, *24*: 400–404.

Mutchler, J. F. (1985). A multivariate analysis of the auditor's going-concern opinion decision. *J. of Accounting Res.*, *23*: 668–682.

Mutchler, J. F. (1986). Empirical evidence regarding the auditor's going-concern opinion decision. *Auditing: A J. of Practice & Theory*, *6*: 148–163.

Nanni, A. J. (1984). An exploration of the mediating effects of auditor experience and position in internal accounting control evaluation. *Accounting, Org. and Soc.*, *9*: 149–163.

Nichols, D. R. (1987). A model of auditors' preliminary evaluations of internal control from audit data. *The Accounting Rev.*, *LXII*: 183–190.

Norris, D. R., and Niebuhr, R. E. (1983). Professionalism, organizational commitment and job satisfaction in an accounting organization. *Accounting, Org. and Soc.*, *9*: 49–59.

Otley, D. T., and Dias, F. J. B. (1982). Accounting aggregation and decision-making performance: An experimental investigation. *J. of Accounting Res.*, *20*: 171–188.

Pany, K., and Reckers, P. M. J. (1980). The effect of gifts, discounts, and client size on perceived auditor independence. *The Accounting Rev.*, *LV*: 50–61.

Pany, K., and Reckers, P. M. J. (1983). Auditor independence and nonaudit services. *J. of Accounting and Public Policy*, *2*: 43–62.

Pany, K., and Reckers, P. M. J. (1984). Non-audit services and auditor independence—A continuing problem. *Auditing: A J. of Practice & Theory*, *3*: 89–97.

Pany, K., and Reckers, P. M. J. (1987). Within- vs. between-subjects experimental designs: A study of demand effects. *Auditing: A J. of Practice & Theory*, *7*: 39–53.

Pany, K., and Reckers, P. M. J. (1988). Auditor performance of MAS: A study of its effects on decisions and perceptions. *Accounting Horizons*, *2*: 31–38.

Paolillo, J. G. P., and Estes, R. W. (1982). An empirical analysis of career choice factors among accountants, attorneys, engineers, and physicians. *The Accounting Rev.*, *LVII*: 785–793.

Pearson, M. A., and Ryans, J. K. (1981–1982). Perceptions of an auditor-management conflict. *Rev. of Business and Eco. Res.*, *XVII*: 1–10.

Peters, J. M., Lewis, B. L., and Dhar, V. (1989). Assessing inherent risk during audit planning: The development of a knowledge based model. *Accounting, Org. and Soc.*, *14*: 359–378.

Pincus, K. V. (1989). The efficacy of a red flags questionnaire for assessing the possibility of fraud. *Accounting, Org. and Soc.*, *14*: 153–163.

Pincus, K. V. (1990). Audit judgment consensus: A model for dichotomous decisions. *Auditing: A J. of Practice & Theory*, *9*: 1–20.

Plumlee, R. D. (1985). The standard of objectivity for internal auditors: Memory and bias effects. *J. of Accounting Res.*, *23*: 683–699.

Pratt, J. (1980). The effects of personality on a subject's information processing: A comment. *The Accounting Rev., LV:* 501–506.

Pratt, J. (1982). Post-cognitive structure: Its determinants and relationship to perceived information use and predictive accuracy. *J. of Accounting Res.,* 20: 189–209.

Pratt, J., and Jiambalvo, J. (1981). Relationships between leader behaviors and audit team performance. *Accounting, Org. and Soc.,* 6: 133–142.

Pratt, J., and Jiambalvo, J. (1982). Determinants of leader behavior in an audit environment. *Accounting, Org. and Soc.,* 7: 369–379.

Purvis, S. E. C. (1989). The effect of audit documentation format on data collection. *Accounting, Org. and Soc.,* 14: 551–564.

Rasch, R. H., and Harrell, A. (1990). The impact of personal characteristics on the turnover behavior of accounting professionals. *Auditing: A J. of Practice & Theory,* 9: 90–102.

Rebele, J. E., Heintz, J. A., and Briden, G. E. (1988). Independent auditor sensitivity to evidence reliability. *Auditing: A J. of Practice & Theory,* 8: 43–52.

Rebele, J. E., and Michaels, R. E. (1990). Independent auditors' role stress: Antecedent, outcome, and moderating variables. *Beh. Res. in Accounting,* 2: 124–153.

Reckers, P. M. J., and Schultz, J. J. (1982). Individual versus group assisted audit evaluations. *Auditing: A J. of Practice & Theory,* 2: 64–74.

Reckers, P. M. J., and Stagliano, A. J. (1981). Non-audit services and perceived independence: Some new evidence. *Auditing: A J. of Practice & Theory,* 1: 23–37.

Ricchiute, D. N. (1984). An empirical assessment of the impact of alternative task presentation modes on decision-making research in auditing. *J. of Accounting Res.,* 22: 341–350.

Scheiner, J. H., and Kiger, J. E. (1982). An empirical investigation of auditor involvement in non-audit services. *J. of Accounting Res.,* 20: 482–496.

Schneider, A. (1984). Modeling external auditors' evaluations of internal auditing. *J. of Accounting Res.,* 22: 657–678.

Schneider, A. (1985). The reliance of external auditors on the internal audit function. *J. of Accounting Res.,* 23: 911–919.

Schultz, J. J., and Reckers, P. M. J. (1981). The impact of group processing on selected audit disclosure decisions. *J. of Accounting Res.,* 19: 482–501.

Scott, W. R. (1984). The state of the art of academic research in auditing. *J. of Accounting Lit.,* 3: 153–200.

Senatra, P. T. (1980). Role conflict, role ambiguity, and organizational climate in a public accounting firm. *The Accounting Rev., LV:* 594–603.

Shanteau, J. (1987). Cognitive illusions, heuristics and biases in behavioral auditing, paper presented at University of Southern California/Deloitte Haskins & Sells, Audit Judgment Symposium.

Shanteau, J. (1989). Cognitive heuristics and biases in behavioral auditing: Review, comments and observations. *Accounting, Org. and Soc.,* 14: 165–177.

Shields, M. D., Solomon, I., and Waller, W. S. (1987). Effects of alternative sample space representations on the accuracy of auditors' uncertainty judgments. *Accounting, Org. and Soc.,* 12: 375–385.

Shields, M. D., Solomon, I., and Waller, W. S. (1988). Auditors' usage of unaudited book values when making presampling audit value estimates. *Contemporary Accounting Res.,* 5: 1–8.

Shockley, R. A. (1981). Perceptions of auditors' independence: An empirical analysis. *The Accounting Rev., LVI:* 785–800.

Shockley, R. A., and Holt, R. N. (1983). A behavioral investigation of supplier differentiation in the market for audit services. *J. of Accounting Res.,* 21: 545–564.

Simnett, R., and Trotman, K. (1989). Auditor versus model: Information choice and information processing. *The Accounting Rev., LXIV:* 514–528.

Snowball, D. (1980). Some effects of accounting expertise and information load: An empirical study. *Accounting, Org. and Soc.,* 5: 323–338.

Solomon, I. (1982). Probability assessment of individual auditors and audit teams: An empirical investigation. *J. of Accounting Res.,* 20: 689–710.

Solomon, I. (1987). Multi-auditor judgment/decision making research. *J. of Accounting Lit.,* 6: 1–25.

Solomon, I., Krogstad, J. L., Romney, M. B., and Tomassini, L. A. (1982). Auditors' prior probability distributions for account balances. *Accounting, Org. and Soc.,* 7: 27–41.

Srinidhi, B. N., and Vasarhelyi, M. A. (1986). Auditor judgment concerning establishment of substantive tests based on internal control reliability. *Auditing: A J. of Practice & Theory,* 5: 64–76.

Tabor, R. H. (1983). Internal control evaluations and audit program revisions: Some additional evidence. *J. of Accounting Res.,* 21: 348–354.

Tomkins, C., and Groves, R. (1983). The everyday accountant and researching his reality. *Accounting, Org. and Soc.*, 8: 363–374.

Trader, R. L., and Huss, H. F. (1987). An investigation of the possible effects of nonsampling error on inference in auditing: A Bayesian analysis. *Contemporary Accounting Res.*, 4: 227–239.

Trotman, K. T. (1985). The review process and the accuracy of auditor judgments. *J. of Accounting Res.*, 23: 740–752.

Trotman, K. T., and Sng, J. (1989). The effect of hypothesis framing, prior expectations and cue diagnosticity on auditors' information choice. *Accounting, Org. and Soc.*, 14: 565–576.

Trotman, K. T., and Yetton, P. W. (1985). The effect of the review process on auditor judgments. *J. of Accounting Res.*, 23: 256–267.

Tubbs, R. M., Messier, W. F., and Knechel, W. R. (1990). Recency effects in the auditor's belief-revision process. *The Accounting Rev.*, 65: 452–460.

Tversky, A., and Kahneman, D. (1974). Judgment under uncertainty: Heuristics and biases. *Science*, 185: 1124–1131.

Uecker, W. C. (1981). Behavioral accounting research as a source for experiential teaching aids: An example. *The Accounting Rev.*, LVI: 366–382.

Uecker, W. C. (1982). The quality of group performance in simplified information evaluation. *J. of Accounting Res.*, 20: 388–402.

Uecker, W. C., Brief, A. P., and Kinney, W. R. (1981). Perception of the internal and external auditor as a deterrent to corporate irregularities. *The Accounting Rev.*, LVI: 465–478.

Waller, W. S. (1985). Self-selection and the probability of quitting: A contracting approach to employee turnover in public accounting. *J. of Accounting Res.*, 23: 817–828.

Waller, W. S., and Felix, W. L. (1984a). The auditor and learning from experience: Some conjectures. *Accounting, Org. and Soc.*, 9: 383–406.

Waller, W. S., and Felix, W. L. (1984b). Cognition and the auditor's opinion formulation process: A schematic model of interactions between memory and current audit evidence. *Decision Making and Accounting: Current Research*, (S. Moriarity and E. Joyce, eds.), University of Oklahoma, pp. 27–48, Norman, Ok.

Waller, W. S., and Felix, W. L. (1984c). The effects of incomplete outcome feedback on auditors' self-perceptions of judgment ability. *The Accounting Rev.*, LIX: 637–646.

Waller, W. S., and Felix, W. L. (1987). Auditors' covariation judgments. *The Accounting Rev.*, LXII: 275–292.

Waller, W. S., and Felix, W. L. (1989). Auditors' causal judgments: Effects of forward vs. backward inference on information processing. *Accounting, Org. and Soc.*, 14: 179–200.

Waller, W., and Jiambalvo, J. (1984). The use of normative models in human information processing research in accounting. *J. of Accounting Lit.*, 3: 201–226.

Wolf, F. M. (1981). The nature of managerial work: An investigation of the work of the audit manager. *The Accounting Rev.*, LVI: 861–881.

Wong-on-Wing, B., Reneau, J. H., and West, S. G. (1989). Auditors' perceptions of management determinants and consequences. *Accounting, Org. and Soc.*, 14: 577–590.

Wright, A. (1982). An investigation of the engagement evaluation process for staff auditors. *J. of Accounting Res.*, 20: 227–239.

Wright, A. (1983). The impact of CPA firm size on auditor disclosure preferences. *The Accounting Rev.*, LVIII: 621–632.

Wright, A. (1986). Performance evaluation of staff auditors: A behaviorally anchored rating scale. *Auditing: A J. of Practice & Theory*, 5: 95–108.

Wright, A. (1988a). The impact of prior working papers on auditor evidential planning judgments. *Accounting, Org. and Soc.*, 13: 595–605.

Wright, A. (1988b). Behavioral research in auditing: The state-of-the-art. *The Auditor's Report*, 11(2): 1–5.

Wright, A. (1988c). The comparative performance of MBAs vs. undergraduate accounting majors in public accounting. *The Accounting Rev.*, LXIII: 123–136.

Wright, W. F. (1982). Comparison of the lens and subjective probability paradigms for financial research purposes. *Accounting, Org. and Soc.*, 7: 65–75.

Wright, W. F. (1988). Empirical comparison of subjective probability elicitation methods. *Contemporary Accounting Res.*, 5: 47–57.

18
The Role of Schema in Organizational Change
Change Agent and Change Target Perspectives

Achilles A. Armenakis and Hubert S. Feild

Auburn University, Auburn, Alabama

I. SCHEMA AND ORGANIZATIONAL CHANGE

The steps taken in introducing organizational change typically involve the action research process of organizational diagnosis, action planning, implementation, and evaluation. The basis for the change effort is preferably derived from an organizational diagnosis, that is, a formal ontological procedure involving collecting and manipulating data, reasoning, testing hypotheses, and drawing conclusions. From the diagnosis, objectives for the change effort are established; these are typically stated in outcome (e.g., increased productivity), behavioral (e.g., improved managerial practices), affective (e.g., more favorable job attitudes), and cognitive terms (e.g., enhanced job knowledge). Next, decisions are made regarding the selection and timing of the most suitable interventions for accomplishing these objectives. Interventions intended to bring about change range from training and development programs to redesigning jobs and restructuring organizations. An evaluation procedure determines whether or not the objectives established for the change effort have been accomplished.

As will be described later in this chapter, some interventions attempt to change behavior initially and cognitions subsequently. Others focus first on cognitions and then on behavior. Regardless of whether an intervention focuses on cognitions or behavior initially, for change to be successful and permanent, the change target must experience cognitive change (Benne, 1976).

The cognitive element is made up of what cognitive scientists call *schema*. A schema is the interpretive framework used by individuals to give meaning to observed objects, actions, and behaviors. Thus, a schema is used for processing information, and this includes *scanning* the environment, *selecting* stimuli (e.g., events, acts, and variables), *measuring* observed stimuli quantitatively (e.g., large or small) or qualitatively (e.g., good or bad), and either *making decisions* or *storing* information for later retrieval (Taylor and Crocker, 1981).

When processing information, individuals are exposed to a multitude of stimuli—too many to select, measure, and decide about or store. The schema determines those stimuli that will be mentally processed. Each individual develops numerous schemata that are refined and reinforced with experience. For example, an individual will have schemata used in performing one's job, interacting with superiors, peers, and subordinates, and other work-related activities. Thus, job performance is influenced by one's schemata.

Because of the dynamic environment in which most organizations function, changes in operations may be initiated. Although the need for change may arise from any number of factors, such as increased competition, tighter governmental regulations, or a succession in organizational leadership, the intended result is an improvement in the criteria used to judge organizational effectiveness. To achieve changes in these criteria, related changes are required in the behavior and schemata of organizational members.

The importance of schema in organizational change should be understood from the perspective of the change agent as well as the change target. Because diagnosis is an information-processing procedure, the change agent's schemata determine what and how problems will be diagnosed; that is, the data collection methods (e.g., interview, observation, questionnaire), the specific variables selected for analysis (e.g., management practices, financial data), and the inferences drawn. The schema, in turn, is a product of the change agent's training, education, and experience.

From the change target's perspective, organizations develop cultures—that is, the shared beliefs, attitudes, and values—from the collective schemata of organizational members. These schemata then influence the processing of information relevant to the change process. For example, creating readiness for change (unfreezing) and institutionalizing change (freezing) are stages of the change process that are influenced by how the change target processes information. Thus, a change target may resist a change if the effort is interpreted negatively, or a change may not be institutionalized because of a failure to reinforce properly the changes made.

Organizational change objectives may be stated in schema terms; that is, while some change programs intend to increase productivity and improve job satisfaction, there must also be an accompanying cognitive change, perhaps in the increase in job knowledge and improvement of job skills or in the organizational practices from an authoritative to a participative style of management. Furthermore, an organizational change that has an objective of increasing productivity through minor improvements in production methods would require less modification to one's schema than major interventions involving autonomous workgroups. These two examples represent extremes of a continuum—the former being labeled incremental change and the latter being labeled fundamental change. While any change represents a serious undertaking, incremental change would be less complex than fundamental change. Thus, the effort expended in the unfreezing, moving, and freezing stages would be commensurate with the ambitiousness of the objectives.

Organizational change is evaluated using criteria that are representative of the objectives. These criteria may be productivity or an outcome criterion that would indicate that the target's schema had undergone change. However, when workgroup outcomes cannot be easily measured, a change effort may be evaluated in terms of the target's schema; that is, such criteria as job satisfaction and perceptions of leader behavior and communication processes would be used.

Therefore, an understanding of schema from change agent and change target perspectives can influence the effectiveness of organizational change efforts. This chapter integrates relevant theory, research, and practice in describing how organizational change is diagnosed, planned, implemented, institutionalized, and evaluated. The specific information presented is:

1. The research on the role of schema in organizational diagnosis is summarized from empirical investigations conducted in the fields of consulting, economics, finance, management, medicine, and psychology. The findings explain why diagnostic bias exists and how it can be minimized.
2. The objectives of organizational change efforts are explained in terms of the change typology: alpha, beta, and gamma change. The development of plural change is traced back to early work published in the late 1950s (see Lindblom, 1959) and in a variety of disciplines, including psychoanalysis (see Watzlawick, Weakland, and Fisch, 1974). Thus, the concept of plural change has a sound foundation on which to build. Recent works, both methodological and conceptual, are cited to emphasize the growing interest change practitioners have in applying and advancing the typology. Several applications are summarized

that demonstrate the use of the typology in establishing objectives and in explaining the challenges facing organizational change efforts.

3. The reactions of individuals that make up the change target are a complex phenomenon influenced by numerous factors (e.g., the use of schemata in interpreting the legitimacy of change, the attributes of the change agent, the influence strategies used by change agents in communicating the need for change, the influence strategies used to institutionalize change, and the social dynamics existing in the change target). Research findings on the stages of change—unfreezing, moving, and freezing—are summarized in developing process models useful in designing change efforts. Then, actual organizational examples of creating readiness and institutionalizing change are described.

4. Finally, research on evaluating change is briefly reviewed. Cited research is categorized into quantitative and qualitative methodologies. No in-depth treatment of the methodological issues is presented. A more detailed treatment of methodological issues regarding the change typology can be found in an earlier synthesis by Armenakis (1988).

II. DIAGNOSIS: THE ROLE OF SCHEMA

When an organization's leadership begins thinking about whether or not planned organizational change is needed, a purpose must be established. In some instances, organizational change may follow a leadership succession in which the new leader pledges to accomplish some objective. Often, the need for change is obvious in such visible symptoms as losses in market share or decreases in profitability. In determining the causes of the unfavorable symptoms, the change agent (i.e., an organizational leader or a consultant) must perform a diagnosis, which involves the application of the change agent's schema.

For organizational change to be appropriate, the diagnosis must be accurate and free from bias. Armenakis, Mossholder, and Harris (1990) have described the role of the consultant's schema in conducting an organizational diagnosis. They have offered evidence for the existence of diagnostic bias, and ways to minimize bias were summarized from research conducted in consulting, economics, finance, management, medicine, and psychology.

To understand how diagnostic bias can influence the change process, the components of schema need to be understood. All schemata consist of two parts. One part is the frame of reference or diagnostic model comprising numerous variables and relationships. A second part consists of diagnostic heuristics.

A. Diagnostic Models

When individuals observe objects, actions, and behaviors, their frame of reference or diagnostic model controls what is interpreted. Thus, diagnosticians will likely correctly interpret an object, action, or behavior (i.e., a stimulus) if their diagnostic model includes that object, action, or behavior. Alternatively, diagnosticians will not correctly interpret a stimulus that is not included in their model. For example, a diagnostic specialist trained in behavioral science will *see* behavioral science issues and will have a greater likelihood of overlooking engineering problems because the diagnostic model emphasizes behavioral science variables. Conversely, an engineer will likely overlook a behavioral science problem for the same reason. Naturally, through training and experience a specialist in one discipline can develop the expertise necessary to accurately diagnose problems in other disciplines; that is, models used to observe stimuli are modified to include the relevant variables. A new schema may be added to those existing, thus expanding one's capabilities to accurately process information.

B. Diagnostic Heuristics

A second part of schema is used for reasoning and enables an individual to conduct analyses (a conscious activity) and exercise intuition (a subconscious activity). When intuition plays a major role in information processing, heuristics come into play. Behavioral decision theorists have provided a taxonomy of heuristics and labeled them as availability, representativeness, and anchoring (Tversky and Kahneman, 1974).

1.   Availability

When a change agent bases a diagnosis on the number of instances of an event that can be remembered, or the ease with which instances can be recalled, the availability heuristic has been evoked. For instance, if a behavioral scientist diagnoses a problem, his or her experience and training will likely cause him or her to diagnose the problem from a behavioral science perspective. Consultants who provide specialty advice on systems, compensation, technology, and finance may recognize that organization problems exist, but because of the availability heuristic, specialty issues may receive priority and other organizational problems may be addressed later (or never).

Anecdotal evidence that availability bias may influence organizational diagnoses can be found in an interview Tichy (1973) conducted with a consultant. Tichy was investigating the process the consultant followed in diagnosing organizations. The interviewee admitted that fads influenced his ways of exploring issues facing a client system

> at the moment, my great fad is concern about integration and differentiation of systems, using a model similar to that of Lawrence and Lorsch. So I go into the system and look for those things, because if I can find them then I can have an interesting experience and one that I'll learn from. I hope I don't do that to the point where I exclude strong signals about other issues (Tichy, 1973: 708).

An empirical study conducted by Tenkasi et al. (1991) investigated whether or not consultants who follow an action research paradigm have different expectations of their clients from consultants who follow an appreciative inquiry paradigm. According to Tenkasi et al., action researchers frame organizational issues as *problems* (e.g., is the glass half empty) while action inquirers frame organizational issues as the best of *what is* to provide an impetus for imagining *what might be* (e.g., is the glass half full). Fifteen students enrolled in an organizational development (OD) course at Case Western Reserve University diagnosed client organizations from an action research perspective and another 15 from the same class diagnosed client organizations from an action inquiry perspective. From the findings, Tenkasi et al. concluded that a consultant's diagnosis is impacted by schemata and that consultants should make conscious attempts to minimize diagnostic bias.

2.   Representativeness

When data are collected, organized, and analyzed in ways that do not accurately reflect the conditions being observed, the representativeness heuristic has been evoked. For example, bias may result if a complex problem is inferred erroneously to be analogous to previously experienced situations. In effect, the change agent has ruled out the possibility that the situation is unique and has ignored factors that are distinctive, thereby concluding that present circumstances resemble problems diagnosed elsewhere.

This phenomenon was found to contribute to noted failures in work redesign experiments in the United States, Canada, Great Britain, Norway, and Sweden (Walton, 1975). Walton concluded that in those instances in which diffusion of results failed, the experimental conditions (e.g., technology, age of plant, or union relationship with management) were mistakenly inferred as being representative of the rest of the organization.

3.   Anchoring

The anchoring heuristic is evoked when a decision maker resists changing a conclusion, even though information is presented to the contrary. For example, denying the need to abandon a tactic or strategy and committing additional resources to its execution evidences anchoring. Staw (1981) has investigated this tendency in decision makers, labeling the action as escalating commitment. Thus, the tendency to resist change is based in this heuristic. A diagnostician who draws conclusions from preliminary information and then resists changing the diagnosis despite disconfirming evidence is manifesting anchoring bias.

Arkes et al. (1981) conducted an experiment involving 75 practicing physicians to determine whether or not a previous diagnosis would bias physicians in diagnosing a current case. The findings revealed that previous diagnoses created biases for physicians in conducting their own diagnoses. Arkes et al. stressed that the subjects were quite knowledgeable ". . . about the likelihood of various diseases and about the relation between the given symptoms and diseases . . . Yet . . . the physicians are still susceptible to bias in their judgments" (Arkes et al., 1981: 254).

C. Control of Bias

A diagnosis involves collecting data, organizing the data into some framework or model, determining the causes of problems, and establishing the direction of the change effort. The data from the diagnosis represent the change agent's inference of the composite schema of organization members. Thus, the change agent may conclude that the strategic orientation of the organization needs to be changed. Naturally, this involves a change in the target's interpretive schema. If during the reasoning process the change agent makes errors and an incorrect diagnosis, the direction of change may not be appropriate and organizational resistance may be in the offing.

At least four options are available to consultants interested in minimizing diagnostic bias. First, simply be aware that the possibility exists. Labeled *metacognition* (see Flavell, 1979; Merluzzi, Rudy, and Glass, 1981), this concept refers to recognizing and monitoring one's own cognitive processing, which includes memory, comprehension, knowledge, goals, and cognitive resources.

Second, Levinson (1972) argues that availability bias can be reduced by using comprehensive diagnostic models that specify the data to be collected and analyzed. The models diagnosticians can use are numerous and vary in degree of specificity. One example, Fayol's (1949) management practices model, emphasizes the functions of planning, organizing, staffing, directing, and controlling. Diagnosticians would likely assess practices related to each function to identify needed changes that can be translated into improved performance. Limited or specialty models focus on a subset of issues, thereby restricting a diagnostician's attention to a simpler, more refined set of activities. One such model is SYMLOG as described by Polley (1985), which focuses on interpersonal relationships within intact workgroups. Any model provides a frame of reference for a diagnostician to use in analyzing data collected from organizational members during a diagnosis, and a diagnostician uses a model because of training and previous experience and, in general, acts on the philosophy that guides the diagnosis.

Third, the change agent can use diagnostic aids to reduce bias. The most effective bias reduction methods involve, among other things: generating conflict in thought processing, and using shadow consultants in unstructured and structured exercises like devil's advocacy, dialectical inquiry, or cognitive mapping (see Schweiger, Sandberg, and Rechner, 1989; Eden, Jones, and Sims, 1983).

A final way of minimizing diagnostic bias involves the use of quantitative methodology. McMillen (1991) described an empirical study of the causal schemata applied by upper-level managers of a *Fortune* 200 corporation in developing and implementing business strategy. This company was attempting to implement a change in strategic orientation from a cost advantage to a differentiation strategy. Thus, McMillen was explaining how to infer the composite schemata of the managers. Qualitative methods (e.g., critical incident interview methodology and content analysis) were used with 27 managers to infer two causal schemata, namely, commodity and value added. Quantitative methods (e.g., questionnaire responses statistically analyzed using multiple correlational procedures) were used with 66 managers to confirm and extend the patterns of causal beliefs identified in the interview, ". . . thus adding to the validity and potential replicability of the study" (McMillen, 1991: 20). The combination of the qualitative and quantitative methods served to minimize the potential for bias.

Naturally, a change agent can implement any or all four of the options in minimizing bias. At some point, objectives must be established that can be used to gauge the success of the change effort. These objectives can be stated in cognitive, affective, behavioral, and outcome terms.

III. MEASURABLE OBJECTIVES FOR ORGANIZATIONAL CHANGE

Measurable objectives for organizational change programs can be classified as *hard* and *soft*. Hard criteria have been acceptable for judging organizational effectiveness. To minimize the use of such externally influenced hard criteria as earnings-per-share or market share, change agents have relied on productivity or quality measures (i.e., outcome criteria). Often, however, objectives for change programs will be stated in terms of soft criteria, which can be further classified as affective (e.g., satisfaction and morale) and behavioral (e.g., leadership, communication, and decision making). Research supporting the link between soft and hard criteria can be attributed to Georgopoulos and Tannenbaum (1957), Likert (1967), and Hoffer (1987).

Prior to 1976, organizational change practitioners stated behavioral objectives quite simply; that is, change objectives were formulated as *more communication, more subordinate involvement in decision making*, and so on. However, Golembiewski, Billingsley, and Yeager (1976) conceptualized and operationalized a simple typology comprising three categories of change, namely, alpha change, beta change, and gamma change. Golembiewski, Billingsley, and Yeager's work was based on earlier work by Watzlawick, Weakland, and Fisch (1974) that categorized change into first-order and second-order change. Bartunek and her colleagues (see Bartunek, 1984; Bartunek and Franzak, 1988; Bartunek and Mock, 1987) and Poole, Gioia, and Gray (1989) provide excellent descriptions of change projects using the typology. Levy (1986) has given an explanation of the various change typologies proposed by change researchers beginning with the work of Lindblom (1959) and including the contributions of Golembiewski, Billingsley, and Yeager (1976) and Watzlawick, Weakland, and Fisch (1974).

A. Gamma Change

Gamma change—which may also be labeled second-order change, fundamental change, and concept redefinition—is the condition that exists when an individual changes the schema that governs the understanding and interpretation of concepts; that is, when one changes the interpretive model, gamma change has taken place. From an organizational perspective, this may be operationalized as a basic shift of an organization's strategy (Bartunek, 1984). For example, if an organization's strategy was one of expanding operations through acquiring companies that produced similar products or services, a basic redirection would result if the company began diversifying into different markets and products. Similarly, if an organization changes its productive technology from an assembly line to one involving work teams, a basic shift in the production process has occurred.

Bartunek and Mock (1987) describe a quality of work life (QWL) project in a food-processing plant in which the organization's culture was described as being paternalistic. The managers behaved paternalistically, and the workers expected a paternalistic relationship. For gamma change to take place, managers would have to change their management style from paternalistic to a participative style, typically advocated by QWL interventions. Similarly, workers would have to change their expectations to being managed participatively.

B. Beta Change

Beta change—also called scale recalibration—is a change in the standard used to measure stimuli within a single conceptualization. An individual establishes a standard that is used to determine whether a particular stimulus meets some quantitative or qualitative calibration. An example of beta change from a productivity perspective was reported in the classic resistance to change experiment reported by Coch and French (1948). Although the purpose of the experiment was to demonstrate the impact of participation in implementing change, one objective of the change was to get group members to recalibrate the standard used in productivity measurement. The change in this standard resulted in the amount of output considered acceptable, the cost of production, and ultimately the sales price of the product. Part of the design involved showing the experimental groups two identical garments produced in the factory. One garment was produced in 1946 and had sold for 100% more than the other produced in 1947. Group members were asked to identify the cheaper garment but were unable to do so. Coch and French pointed out that this demonstration effectively communicated the necessity of reducing cost. Obviously, the production standard was too low, relative to the competition. Then, through group decision making, the productivity standard was successfully raised, thereby increasing the standard of what was considered acceptable.

Another example of beta change can be described by using the concept of diagnostic norms. In this case, decisions to take action are based on a comparison of a quantitative or qualitative measure with an acceptable norm. Thus, norms are considered to be an acceptable standard used to judge whether or not a deviation exists in the measure. Diagnostic norms for self-report survey research questionnaires are often difficult to obtain, inappropriate for a specific situation, or nonexistent (see Armenakis and Feild, 1987). In an organization that has a long history of labor disputes, high absenteeism and employee turnover, and poor working conditions, employees will likely have lower acceptable standards of job satisfaction than in an organization that has much more favorable conditions. If this organization undertakes a successful large-scale change effort and begins to improve these conditions, the standard used to determine what is acceptable will likely increase with the improvement of organizational conditions. This is not a fundamental shift in the interpretive schema; rather it is a recalibration of the standard within an interpretive schema.

C. Alpha Change

Alpha change—which is also called first-order and incremental behavioral change—takes place when the feelings and behavior of the change target changes within a given interpretive schema. From an organizational perspective, this may be operationalized as an extension of an organization's strategy; that is, simply doing more of the same. In other words, if the strategy calls for expanding horizontally, then acquisitions of companies providing the same goods and services will be considered alpha change. Similarly, if the organizational culture is made up of a participative decision style, then improving the skill with which one executes this style will be classified as alpha change.

IV. THE STAGES OF CHANGE

Lewin (1951) proposed that successful change proceeds through three stages of change, namely, unfreezing, moving, and freezing. Unfreezing, synonymous with readiness, is the cognitive state comprising beliefs, attitudes, and intentions toward a change effort. Moving or changing is the adoption of the proposed change by the change target. Freezing is the same as institutionalizing the changes; that is, making the change permanent. Thus, institutionalization is the cognitive state in which the change target agrees that the change is acceptable.

Two issues are relevant at this point. The first is a subtle but significant point that should be stressed. The relationship between cognitive, affective, and behavioral variables has been demonstrated to be multidirectional rather than unidirectional (Bandura, 1982; Fishbein and Azjen, 1975); that is, the order of influence is not necessarily cognitive→affective→behavioral. Rather, each can be influenced by one or both of the other variables. In other words, cognitions are affected by behavior, as behavior is affected by cognitions. For instance, cognitive changes can be achieved through requiring individuals to change their behavior (e.g., through job rotation or assignment of special tasks). Bandura (1982) has demonstrated the success of this through enactive mastery. Furthermore, Beer, Eisenstat, and Spector (1990) argue that one of the fallacies of programmatic change is that changing the knowledge and attitudes of individuals changes their behavior. They argue, "the most effective way to change behavior . . . is to put people . . . in new roles, responsibilities, and relationships" (Beer, Eisenstat, and Spector, 1990: 159). This facilitates the development of new cognitions and behaviors.

The second issue is to understand the implications of the change typology in terms of the planning required to conceive, implement, and institutionalize change. Certainly, effecting any change cannot be taken lightly. However, gamma change may be expected to be more difficult to accomplish, because as operationalized, it requires individuals to redefine concepts and undergo fundamental change. Alpha change, on the other hand, may be expected to be less difficult to effect because, as operationalized, it is within an established interpretive schema; that is, it is incremental.

It is valuable to understand that change progresses through three phases. At the minimum, change agents will consciously plan for each phase. However, understanding that a hierarchy of difficulty exists contributes to an appreciation that people may react differently to some changes than others. Thus, the strategies and tactics employed to implement gamma change may be somewhat different from those for alpha change. Furthermore, the role of individual differences is important because some individuals may react to certain changes differently from other individuals.

V. UNFREEZING

The unfreezing stage consists of three steps—namely, knowledge, persuasion, and decision making (cf. Rogers, 1983). The purpose of the knowledge step is to make the target realize not only that there is a need for change, but also that change is possible. During persuasion, the target is encouraged to adopt the change. The decision-making stage is the point at which the target decides to either adopt or reject the change. The objective of the unfreezing stage is to create dissonance, a condition that the target will seek to avoid. Thus, dissonance is created if the target experiences a felt need and seeks a means in meeting the need (Rogers, 1983).

Unfreezing can be distinguished from resistance by considering readiness as a mental state and resistance as a set of behaviors. Thus, readiness, a cognitive element, is the precursor to resistance to or acceptance of change, the behavioral element. Schein (1979) has emphasized the importance of readiness by arguing that without it no change will occur regardless of the effort expended on rewarding, coaching, or punishing. Schein attributes resistance and outright failure of change programs to ineffective readiness programs. Therefore, in creating readiness, a change agent must first attempt to unfreeze the target by getting the target to decide that the new behavior is, in fact, beneficial to the target's interests.

Armenakis, Harris, and Mossholder (in press) have drawn on multiple literatures—individual-level cognitive change, collective behavior, social-information processing, mass communications, and organizational change literatures—in explaining how readiness for change can be created. Figure 1 depicts a model of the process of creating readiness.

A. Readiness Message

The process of creating readiness requires a message and strategies for transmitting the message (Armenakis, Harris, and Mossholder, in press). In general, the readiness message should incorporate two issues. One is *discrepancy* between the desired end state and the present state. The other is the individual and collective *efficacy* of the change target. Change practitioners have advocated creating intellectual pain (Nadler and Tushman, 1989) or diffusing dissatisfaction (Spector, 1989), which communicates that a discrepancy exists between some desired end state and the present state. However, to avoid defensive reactions (e.g., denial, flight, or withdrawal from negative information) the message should build the target's confidence that they can implement the change. This confidence is what Bandura (1982) refers to as efficacy.

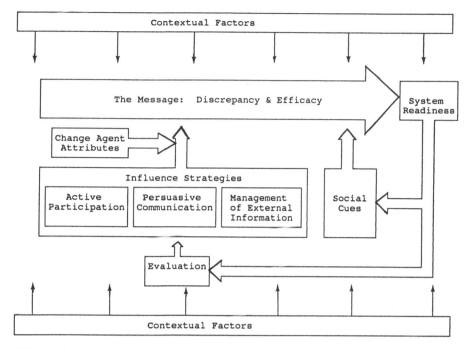

Figure 1 Creating readiness for change. (*Source*: Armenakis, Harris, and Mossholder, in press.)

B. Target Reaction

Drawing from research on mass communications (see DeFleur and Ball-Rokeach, 1989), theories of individual differences, social differentiation, and social relationships are helpful in explaining the reaction of organizational members to readiness interventions.

Research on individual differences has revealed that the cognitive structures of individuals are responsible for differing reactions to change programs. For example, early research on growth-need strength (see Hackman and Lawler, 1971) found that high-growth-need individuals would likely be more satisfied in enriched jobs than individuals who were low in growth-need strength. Although no specific research has been found on individual difference reactions to readiness interventions, other measures of individual differences could be used to infer possible reactions. For example, Kirton (1980) has developed an inventory to classify individuals into innovator or adaptor styles. Kirton's findings can be used to hypothesize that individuals who are innovators are likely to respond favorably to readiness programs designed to prepare a target for fundamental change. On the other hand, adaptors are likely to respond favorably to incremental change. As will be discussed below, Burkhardt (1991) found that Snyder's self-monitoring scale (Lennox and Wolfe, 1984) could be used to predict individual reactions to institutionalizing technological change. Thus, the implication of the individual differences theory is that reactions to readiness interventions may be explained by differing cognitive structures within the change target.

Social differentiation theory can be used to hypothesize that the cultures existing within a social group will influence the cognitive structures of its members. Thus, hierarchical differentiation (e.g., executives, managers, workers) and other differentiators (e.g., union/nonunion) may polarize the beliefs, attitudes, and intentions of group members (see Bushe, 1988). These psychological boundaries must be considered in planning readiness programs.

Social relationships theory argues that reactions to readiness interventions will be influenced by the relationships individuals have with specific individuals. Thus, individuals who are respected as opinion leaders can influence the cognitions of the target group. The implication of this is that effectiveness can be enhanced by initially succeeding in creating readiness in these opinion leaders. They then can act as change agents in disseminating the message to the other members of the target.

C. Strategies

The readiness strategies available to a change agent consist of persuasive communication (both oral and written), active participation (Bandura, 1982; Fishbein and Azjen, 1975), and management of external sources of information (Armenakis, Harris, and Mossholder, in press).

Oral persuasive communication consists of face-to-face speeches, either live (e.g., speaking in person or through teleconferencing technology) or recorded (e.g., audio- or videotape). Written communication consists of documents prepared by the organization (e.g., newsletters, annual reports, memos). Active participation consists of self-discovery experiences, including vicarious learning (i.e., observing others perform tasks) and enactive mastery (i.e., performing elementary tasks that can lead to mastering more complex tasks). Management of external information sources include cooperating with the news media in preparing features about the organization and inviting outside experts to critique the organization's operation.

D. Change Agent Attributes

The effectiveness of the strategies in transmitting the readiness message will be influenced by the perceived credibility, trustworthiness, sincerity, and the change agent's expertise. Readiness messages will be more effective when associated with reputable change agents than with unreputable ones (Gist, 1987). When opinion leaders are counted on to create readiness, they in effect become an extension of the change agent. Therefore, the desirable attributes apply to opinion leaders as well.

VI. CREATING READINESS: AN EXAMPLE

To demonstrate an application of the message issues and strategies in creating readiness, portions of an integrated program implemented by Whirlpool Corporation are summarized. The full explanation can be obtained from Armenakis, Harris, and Mossholder (in press).

A. The Message

Contextual factors are important to include in a readiness message. For example, increases in foreign competition, cyclical changes in the economy, and changes in consumer life-styles and tastes impact the profitability of consumer goods manufacturers. These contextual factors were affecting Whirlpool's operations. The discrepancy part of Whirlpool's message was that competitive pressures were mounting and that to remain competitive, the company would have to become more aggressive, more sensitive to the marketplace, more *lean and mean*, and a global player to remain competitive and even survive. To enhance efficacy, Whirlpool employees were sent to observe model manufacturing operations, were reminded of other companies that had successfully implemented changes resulting in classic turnaround examples, and were assured that the company would prosper in today's environment.

B. Readiness Strategies

A vicarious learning experience used by Whirlpool was the Global Awareness Program, which involved sending groups of employees drawn from various organizational levels to visit companies in Japan and Korea. Employees were to observe firsthand the nature of the competition they faced as well as build confidence that Whirlpool could implement the same processes.

In addition to offering an opportunity for active participation by a sample of employees, the company anticipated that the participants (i.e., the opinion leaders) would return and share their discoveries with their peers through persuasive communication. To facilitate this accomplishment, a 13-minute videotape (*Global Awareness Program*, 1986) summarizing the program and getting reactions from various participants was prepared, and all employees were encouraged to view it.

In 1982, the Whirlpool board of directors appointed a new CEO. With this change, the company made a concerted effort to increase its business magazine publicity. For example, the average number of magazine articles written about Whirlpool before the new CEO was fewer than two per year. After the appointment of the new CEO, the number of magazine articles increased to nearly five per year.

A prestigious consulting firm was contracted to analyze Whirlpool's structure. Several observations were offered about the structure's inadequacies, thus resulting in a recommended major reorganization. The information was released in one of two high-visibility speeches made by the CEO, who provided an important message regarding the need for change that was enhanced by the reputation of the consulting firm. Those two speeches—the New Vision Speech (1986) and the New Structure Speech (1988)—exemplify oral persuasive communication intended to create readiness for large-scale change at Whirlpool. The New Vision Speech was delivered 29 times in 13 different locations to approximately 5500 employees. A 52-minute videotape was also made and distributed to geographically dispersed locations for viewing. Simply stated, the focus of the message was the need for change with references to other successful large-scale change efforts. The message included such contextual factors as the increase in foreign competition, which in the appliance industry had increased 400% in 4 years, as well as the consolidation of appliance manufacturers resulting in four fierce competitors. The Chrysler Corporation example (in which individuals were reminded that in 1980 Chrysler was near bankruptcy but 5 years later it reported a $1.6 billion profit) was referred to in linking the change effort to efficacy. In addition, change was nothing new to Whirlpool. In its 75-year history, the company had experienced numerous changes in responding to its contextual factors.

In the New Structure Speech, the CEO explained that the old structure did not permit the company to be competitive. The speech justified the need for a new organizational arrangement built around the strategic business unit (SBU) concept. Two points were made to add credibility to this assertion. First, company performance had decreased, and second, a prestigious consulting firm had conducted a diagnosis of the company. After describing the benefits of the new structure, the CEO challenged Whirlpool people, saying the company needed their patience, support, and cooperation.

Whirlpool people were presented with information that was intended to initiate cognitive change, specifically gamma change. The market for appliances was changing. Visits to model manufacturers, attendance at speeches, reading about the company in the business media, and basing part of the new organization structure on a prestigious consulting firm's analysis were all intended to reconceptualize how these employees viewed the market and their company's performance. Their schemata were being changed—previously, foreign products were not considered a threat—and these employees were being exposed to information that should change the variables in the model used to judge their performance. This was not a matter of recalibration; it was reconceptualization. They needed to know their competitors, understand their culture, and anticipate their capabilities. It was difficult for the Whirlpool people to deny their competitors' impact on the future profitability and survival of the company. Thus, when an individual's availability heuristic is evoked and information accessed and processed, the legitimacy of foreign competition was established.

The information being presented by the readiness program may create intrapersonal conflict—an approach-avoidance situation in which both positive (efficacy) and negative (discrepancy) information are evaluated. The representativeness heuristic is evoked when an individual member of the change target focuses on potentially positive or negative outcomes, thus inferring that the planned change will result in some favorable or unfavorable set of circumstances. If an individual pays more attention to the negative outcomes than the positive, that individual will likely resist the change. If an individual pays more attention to the positive outcomes, that individual will likely embrace the change.

The readiness program likely creates cognitive dissonance for individuals in the target group. The natural tendency for an individual is to evoke the anchoring heuristic and restore balance by either discrediting the information that created the imbalance and resisting change or accepting the information as valid and reliable and changing cognitions and behavior.

Thus, the inference(s) made by an individual target member from the readiness program is (are) then relayed via social information processing to others comprising the change target. As the dynamics of social information processing develop, the change target formulates a collective opinion about the impending change. Therefore, the readiness program (i.e., the change agent), the message (discrepancy *and* efficacy aspects), the influence strategies, and the composition of the target must successfully unfreeze the target.

VII. MOVING: IMPLEMENTING CHANGE

During the moving stage, change is implemented and the appropriate behavior by the target becomes required. If the unfreezing stage is not successful, the change will be rejected, and the target will initiate negative behaviors (e.g., sabotage, absenteeism, output restriction). If the stage of readiness is successfully created, the target will embrace the change, and the adoption stage can begin.

Implementing change is attempted through some form of intervention focused on the change target. Numerous classifications of interventions can be found (see French and Bell, 1990). However, all interventions are intended to influence the target's cognitions, affect, and behavior. For example, management development programs are aimed at introducing improved ways of managing so participants can transfer the learning into job behavior. Training managers to be better decision makers or developing technically trained individuals to be general managers or functional specialists are examples of management and executive development programs. Organizational restructuring is intended to change how decision makers perform their designated duties as well as conceptualize the tasks necessary to perform their jobs. Thus, there is an attempt to change the cognitive element as well as the behavioral element of job performance.

These examples can be further described using the change typology. For example, job enlargement and producing more units of a product are representative of alpha change. Similarly, job enrichment and reorganizing an assembly line arrangement into an autonomous workgroup arrangement represent gamma change.

In the Whirlpool case, several interventions were coordinated. For example, the organization structure was changed from the functional form of organization to the SBU concept. This change in structure was consistent with the change in strategy to become a global appliance manufacturer. Shortly after this structure was in place, the company implemented three other interventions—namely, activity value analysis, reduction in force, and a modification of the compensation program. The activity value analysis was intended to eliminate all unnecessary activities—often those that made sense under the old structure—and to retain only those activities that added value under the new SBU structure. The reduction in force was intended to make appropriate adjustments in the number of employees required to perform the new jobs. The new compensation program was intended to reward employees on the basis of their job performance in their respective SBUs. Under the old structure, bonuses were awarded to managers according to the corporation's performance.

All of these changes are gamma changes in the managers' schemata. For example, by participating in the reorganization, the activity value analysis, and the reduction in force, managers were mandated to change their way of conceptualizing. They had to eliminate unnecessary activities, determine ways of accomplishing these activities with 10% fewer people, and then begin behaving accordingly. This involved not only a major shift in the way they conceptualized their jobs but also in standards of accomplishment (e.g., fewer people).

Furthermore, the previous functional organizational structure made managers think in terms of business functions for the multiple products the company manufactured. Reorganizing around the SBU concept made managers think in terms of the brand grouping for which they were responsible. In addition, the company's old reward system allocated a fixed percentage of its profitability as an annual bonus for designated manager classifications (e.g., officer, director, and manager). The new compensation system rewarded bonuses on the basis of the profitability of the SBU in which a manager worked. These changes required managers to be proactive (instead of passive), accountable (instead of unaccountable), risk taking (instead of risk averse), and change oriented (instead of status quo oriented). Thus, these organizational changes were fundamental (i.e., gamma change), requiring a new way of conceptualizing and behaving.

VIII. FREEZING: INSTITUTIONALIZING CHANGE

The freezing stage consists of confirmation and institutionalization (Rogers, 1983). This is the period in which the change becomes permanent. After a change has been successfully introduced and adopted by the target, however, the target may return to the prechange conditions. This is likely if information is received that contradicts the adoption decision. Isabella (1990) described the possibility of seeing double exposures; that is, perceptions of events, actions, and behaviors that are simultaneously judged from pre- and postframes of reference. Isabella proposes the use of symbols and ceremonials as ways to transmit intended messages, thereby minimizing the potential for conflicting information. According to Rogers (1983), this conflicting information creates dissonance, thereby reducing the commitment of those adopters to make the change permanent. Commitment, then, must be developed to continue the adopted changes.

A. Institutionalization Message

The message that must be transmitted to organizational members is essentially one of reinforcement. For a change to become permanent, the target must confirm that the adoption is appropriate and institutionalize the new behavior. Thus, the change agent is responsible for undertaking the steps necessary to confirm the appropriateness of the adoption decision resulting in change institutionalization. To make the changes permanent, potential dissonance must be anticipated and avoided. Dissonance will likely be highest for gamma change and lowest for alpha change.

The change agent must provide confirmation and reinforcement to the target by minimizing negative and maximizing positive results. In order to ensure the maximum positive impact on the organization the change agent should plan for the institutionalization phase. Figure 2 depicts the institutionalization process.

B. Target Reaction

As explained in the section on unfreezing, the theories of individual differences, social differentiation, and social relationships can be used to anticipate the extent to which the target institutionalizes the change.

The importance of the social element in individual behavior is often associated with the Hawthorne studies (see Roethlisberger and Dickson, 1939), which emphasize that the extent to which an individual institutionalizes change is influenced by others with whom he or she interacts. Individuals who are highly respected influence the willingness of individuals to change and to institutionalize the change. Thus, identifying opinion leaders and rallying their support is important to the institutionalization process. These opinion leaders in effect assume the role of change agents, because they serve as role models and provide social support (e.g., giving encouragement and positive feedback for adopting the change). Burkhardt (1991) found that individual differences, as measured with Snyder's self-monitoring scale (Lennox and Wolfe, 1984), accounted for institutionalizing technological change (i.e., the introduction of a local area network). High self-monitors were hypothesized in Burkhardt's study to be more likely to adjust their behaviors to be similar to significant others, because they are sensitive to social comparison information. Low self-monitors are less likely to be influenced by others because they are not sensitive (i.e., are inattentive) to social comparison information. Burkhardt's analyses revealed that high self-monitors were more influenced by influential co-workers and direct interaction partners (i.e., opinion leaders) than low self-monitors.

Appreciating the role of social differentiation and then developing plans to address the needs of the social differentiates can enhance the success of institutionalization. This is more than simply involvement of the change target. Rather, this is more akin to a partnership. Kochan (1987) reported on several change projects in which management, recognizing the importance of various groups, entered into contractual agreements with workers to adopt and institutionalize new production processes.

C. Strategies

The strategies that can be used to transmit the institutionalization message have been discussed by Goodman and his associates (Goodman, Bazerman, and Conlon, 1980; Goodman and Dean, 1982). As depicted in Figure 2, they include socialization, rewards, and diffusion.

Socialization encompasses the formal and informal organizational activities that encourage individuals to adapt to an organization's processes. These activities are quite comprehensive and include the same strategies and tactics useful in creating readiness—persuasive communication, active participation, and management of external information.

Burkhardt (1991) found that individuals serving as opinion leaders were effective in rallying others to institutionalize technological change. Through persuasive communication and serving as role models (as in vicarious learning), these opinion leaders were effective in institutionalizing change.

Rewards can be very effective in reinforcing change. Goodman and Dean (1982) in their analysis of nine QWL case studies, indicated that institutionalization was more likely when (1) extrinsic and intrinsic rewards were administered; (2) a clear contingency existed between behavior and rewards; (3) rewards were perceived as equitable; and (4) the attractiveness (i.e., novelty) of the rewards continued.

Kochan (1987) described a case in which Xerox and the Amalgamated Clothing and Textile

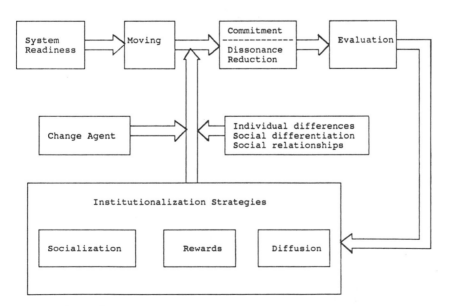

Figure 2 Institutionalizing change.

Workers Union agreed to implement several changes, including semiautonomous workgroups and other work and system changes. The agreements included employment security and gainsharing programs. Another case described by Kochan involved GM, Toyota, Budd, and the United Auto Workers (UAW). The principals agreed to employment security and adjustments in compensation to accommodate the new production system and protect the rights of employees affected by the changes. These examples are illustrative of the criteria—extrinsic rewards, behavioral contingencies, equity, and attractiveness—described by Goodman and Dean (1982).

Diffusion is the spread of an adoption to other target organizations. The individuals within a target will be reinforced to institutionalize change when they realize that other targets are adopting the change.

Research by Johnston and Leenders (1990) on the diffusion of minor technical improvements in operations revealed that diffusion was accomplished through an interpersonal exchange between the potential user and the originating unit. Thus, opinion leaders can visit other target sites to disseminate the value of the change, or opinion leaders from the new target organization can visit the site that has recently adopted the change, and from the vicarious experience diffuse the change throughout the new target system. Diffusing change to the new target will serve to reinforce the adoption decision of the old target.

D. Change Agent Attributes

Just as change agent attributes were significant in creating readiness, they are equally important in institutionalizing change. When opinion leaders contribute to institutionalizing change, they should possess favorable attributes, since they are, in effect, extensions of the change agent.

IX. INSTITUTIONALIZING CHANGE: AN EXAMPLE

Examples of unfreezing and moving were summarized earlier from Whirlpool Corporation's strategic change interventions. As part of the same change effort, examples of how the company attempted to institutionalize strategic change will be described. The strategies employed were socialization and rewards. The socialization strategy included persuasive communication, ceremonial announcements, and symbolic reinforcement.

A. Persuasive Communication

The large-scale change in Whirlpool began in February 1988. For the next 4 months, the top managers implemented the SBU reorganization, the activity value analysis, and the 10% reduction in force. In June 1988, the chairman and CEO addressed the 250 officers, directors, and managers (and spouses) in an 80-minute, after dinner speech.

The purposes of the speech were to justify retrospectively the need for change, summarize the procedures followed in implementing the change, communicate a sense of urgency and a feeling of empathy for Whirlpool employees, assure them that the change was permanent, and challenge the employees to make the change work.

Regarding urgency, the CEO reiterated that the changes were needed because of increased global competition and the accelerated rate of industry consolidation. In communicating his empathy for Whirlpool people, he expressed he understood how these changes affected them, and that they "have a right to feel annoyed, angered, and frightened" (*Confirmation Speech*, 1988). The confirmation part of the speech summarized the procedures followed and assured them that they could not return to the old Whirlpool. In summarizing the procedures followed in designing and implementing the changes, the CEO reminded them that the seven designated business unit heads were brought together in January and presented the design. Two alternatives were discussed. One was to put the structure together and decide who would fill the positions and then make announcements. The second and more thoughtful way was to get participation of those closest to the action. "The right and intelligent way to do it was to do it over time. We would do it the same way—even though it was painful" (*Confirmation Speech*, 1988). In communicating the permanency of the change at Whirlpool, the CEO assured them that "there is no turning back. Whirlpool of the past will be no more" (*Confirmation Speech*, 1988).

The final part of the speech was to address questions from the attendees. Each was given an opportunity to submit questions in advance. These were content-analyzed and grouped according to subject. Several were addressed after the prepared remarks. Those unanswered that night were deferred and addressed every Tuesday at 12:00 P.M. in the headquarter's auditorium until all questions, numbering more than 100, were answered.

B. Ceremonial Announcements

In August 1988, an unscheduled meeting was called for the officers, directors, and managers to announce formally the completion of a joint venture with N. V. Philips of the Netherlands. The atmosphere of the meeting was ceremonial; that is, the agreement was considered to be a major accomplishment. This joint venture made Whirlpool the world's largest home appliance manufacturer. Cards with *We're # 1* were distributed to all attendees. The audience was then briefed (for approximately 60 minutes) on the strategic logic employed in seeking the joint venture with Philips.

C. Symbolic Reinforcement

An innovative symbolic attempt to institutionalize large-scale change in the Whirlpool Corporation was the preparation (in 1990) of a 44-minute videotape of three top executives (the CEO, the chief financial officer, and the executive vice president) being interviewed by a French newscaster (*Business in Profile, 1995*, 1990). The setting for the interview was the year 1995, and the three executives were answering questions related to the reasons for Whirlpool's success during the last decade of the 20th century. In introducing the executives, the newscaster referred to Whirlpool as the *renaissance company of the 1990s*. The executives attributed the company's outstanding performance to the organizational changes implemented in the late 1980s. These changes were believed to have permitted the company to respond to changes in world markets much faster than the company's competitors. According to Bill Marohn (the executive vice president), "in the late 80s it took Whirlpool five years to bring a new dishwasher to production. However, in the last 18 months we brought a new range from concept into design and through production" (*Business in Profile, 1995*, 1990).

Other changes were in less tangible issues, such as trust, values, loyalty, and communication. For example, Dave Whitwam (the chairman and CEO) described loyalty at Whirlpool in the 1980s as paternalistic (i.e., "childlike"), based on blind trust that the company would take care of the people. The "new" loyalty, however, is based on intellectual maturity; that is, "the people create stability, success, and career security that they are looking for" (*Business in Profile, 1995*, 1990).

These actions at institutionalization are significant because they required time and effort in planning, reinforced the change effort, and were symbolic. For example, making arrangements for all directors, officers, and managers (and their spouses) for a formal dinner and preparing a videotape of the speech required much effort. The preparation of the *Business in Profile, 1995* (1990) required writing a script for all actors and allocating the time and other resources to practice and tape the session. The symbolism of these actions was equally strong. The confirmation speech was intended to do more than summarize the process and communicate urgency and empathy. By incorporating the spouses at the dinner, the intent was apparently to acknowledge the impact of the changes on the whole family and to enlist familial support. The meeting to announce the joint venture was to add credibility to the changes and to provide positive results after months of implementing the changes. Furthermore, *Business in Profile, 1995* (1990) was a creative production intended to acclaim the wisdom, foresight, and determination of Whirlpool people in responding to challenges presented to them by market forces. Finally, all of these actions were intended to communicate the expectations of Whirlpool leaders and to reinforce the changes made.

D. Rewards

In Whirlpool's change effort, the compensation program was changed to be consistent with the new SBU organization. Before the reorganization, Whirlpool's bonus system rewarded managers for the performance of the corporation. With the SBU reorganization, bonuses were based on the performance of the SBU. Thus, the extrinsic rewards that were administered were contingent on the performance of a manager's SBU. Equity issues should not have been of concern since all managers were treated equitably, based on the performance of their SBU.

X. EVALUATION

Evaluation of change can be viewed as a procedure to determine the extent to which change objectives for each stage (i.e., unfreezing, moving, and freezing) have been accomplished. Evaluation findings can be used in making decisions about proceeding to the next stage (see Figures 1 and 2). For example, an assessment can be made of the success regarding the efforts involved in creating readiness for large-scale change. If a new vision is planned—with an accompanying new strategy, structure, processes, etc.—an assessment can be conducted to determine whether or not the change target is ready for the moving stage. This assessment may require gathering information of a cognitive and affective nature. The results of the assessment can be used to determine whether the unfreezing stage should be continued with revised messages and/or different strategies. During the moving and freezing stages, affective and behavioral information may be required. If the objective of the change effort is to improve productivity, progress can be determined by gauging productivity, absenteeism, employee turnover, and the like. Affective information may add valuable insight to understanding the progress of the moving stage and in designing efforts during the freezing stage. Assessing these same criteria can be useful in determining whether or not to modify the institutionalization strategies. Thus, an understanding of the theory and methodology of evaluation is crucial to the success of organizational change. The research methods used to assess whether or not the objectives of a change effort have been accomplished can be categorized into qualitative and quantitative research methods.

A. Qualitative Research Examples

The methods used in qualitative research permit the investigator to decode, translate, and describe the meaning of phenomena in the organization under study (van Maanen, 1979). Data collection methods used in qualitative research include observation, interviews, and self-report written descriptions from the change target and review of organizational archival records (e.g., press releases, meeting minutes, speeches, and memoranda). Unless these data are somehow transformed into a coding scheme that can be used to quantify and statistically manipulate the data, the investigator will use anecdotes in describing the phenomena.

Bartunek (1984) and Poole, Gioia, and Gray (1989) provide examples of qualitative research used in interpreting the impact of planned organization change efforts. For example, Bartunek observed that a religious order (i.e., the change target) had become more participative because order members participated more in analyzing basic principles and in forming new provinces. In the study by Poole, Gioia, and Gray (1989), the researchers describe several behavioral incidents between top managers and subordinate managers. One incident was of a bank's (i.e., the change target's) chief operating officer (COO) and a branch manager engaged in a heated discussion about the excessive length of meetings. In another incident, the bank's CEO and COO berated an officer for disagreeing with the CEO. These descriptions are the ways in which qualitative researchers link observed behaviors to change objectives and infer changes in schema. They are used to determine the extent to which change has been detected.

B. Quantitative Research Examples

Quantitative research involves analyzing data (i.e., hard and soft criteria) that satisfy the requirements for nominal, ordinal, interval, and ratio levels of measurement using a variety of univariate and multivariate statistical techniques. Thus, quantitative research permits the investigator to detect the types of change using sophisticated techniques to manipulate data collected from the change target. Armenakis (1988) has summarized the quantitative research and categorized the approaches to detecting the change types into statistical and design approaches. Each procedure is intended to compare temporal data collected from the change target in order to determine the types of changes detected.

Statistical approaches include: (1) a Procrustean procedure (see Golembiewski, Billingsley, and Yeager, 1976; Randolph, 1982); (2) a correlation procedure (see Armenakis and Zmud, 1979; Bedeian, Armenakis, and Randolph, 1988); and (3) an analysis of covariance structures (see Schmitt, 1982; Bartunek and Franzak, 1988; Millsap and Hartog, 1988).

Design approaches consist of a variety of research designs employed to logically deduce which type of change has been detected. The four approaches include (1) the criterion approach (see Golembiewski, 1986; van de Vliert, Huismans, and Stock, 1985); (2) the ideal scale approach (see Armenakis and Zmud, 1979); (3) the typical scale approach (see Granier, Green, and Armenakis, 1991; Maurer and Alexander, 1991); and (4) the retrospective approach (Terborg, Howard, and Maxwell, 1980).

Gamma change has been detected statistically through multivariate procedures used to manipulate responses to survey research questionnaires. Schmitt (1982) described how LISREL can be used, while Golembiewski, Billingsley, and Yeager (1976) and Armenakis and Zmud (1979) compared factor structures. For example, the responses to an organizational survey administered before and after a change effort can be factor analyzed and the factor structures compared. If the before- and after-factor structures are not statistically equivalent, respondents have reconceptualized the dimensions being measured and gamma change has been detected.

Gamma change has also been assessed through design approaches (see Golembiewski, 1986; Terborg, Howard, and Maxwell 1980). Golembiewski, using burnout as an example, concluded that individuals can progress through eight burnout phases. By assessing the burnout phases over time, an individual's progress to successively higher or lower phases can be recorded and differences in state associated with different conceptualizations—thereby signaling gamma change. Terborg, Howard, and Maxwell (1980) propose computing correlation coefficients between pairs of pretest, posttest, and retrospective responses to a survey questionnaire. Gamma change can be deduced by analyzing the profile shapes and profile dispersions of the responses.

Beta change has been discussed and detected exclusively by survey research methods using statistical and design approaches. Examples of statistical approaches have been described by Bartunek and Franzak (1988) and Schmitt (1982) by using LISREL to analyze covariance structures. The design approaches have included the ideal scale approach (Armenakis and Zmud, 1979), the typical scale approach (Granier, Green, and Armenakis, 1991) the retrospective procedure (Terborg, Howard, and Maxwell, 1980), and the criterion approach (van de Vliert, Huismans, and Stok, 1985). In both approaches the standard of measurement is assessed over time. Beta change is detected when the standard used to articulate perceptions varies temporally.

Alpha change has been detected statistically through significance tests that determine whether or not the mean or variance of the criterion changes after a change effort is implemented (see Armenakis and Smith, 1978; Golembiewski, Billingsley, and Yeager, 1976). Thus, alpha change takes place within a single interpretive schema and with a consistent measuring standard.

XI. SUMMARY

The purpose of this chapter was to describe the importance of schema in organizational change from the perspective of the change agent as well as the change target. Schema was explained in information-processing terms as guiding the selection, measurement, and decision-making processes. Two aspects of schema were described as models and heuristics. From the change agent's perspective, diagnostic models represent the configuration of variables, including their relationships. Diagnosticians rely on models to determine what data to collect and how the data are to be organized. Heuristics are used in the reasoning process. Availability, representativeness, and anchoring heuristics assist in the reasoning process, but can result in biased diagnoses when misapplied. Examples were identified from the relevant literature and summarized to explain the role of models and heuristics in organizational diagnosis. Emphasis was placed on being aware of the possible misapplication and use of diagnostic aids in minimizing the possibility of bias.

From a diagnosis, change objectives are conceived. Objectives can be set using both hard criteria (e.g., productivity, quality) and soft criteria. Soft criteria were further subdivided into cognitive, affective, and behavioral criteria. Examples of cognitive criteria, those that deal with one's knowledge, were described as a manager's strategic orientation and managerial philosophy regarding leadership. Examples of affective criteria, those that deal with feelings, were described as satisfaction and morale. Examples of behavioral criteria, those that deal with individual behavior, were described as leadership, communication, and decision-making practices. Because organizational changes are intended to bring about changes in individuals, and hence, organizations, change objectives were presented in terms of the change typology: namely, alpha, beta, and gamma changes. Examples of each were taken from published research in the organizational change literature.

The change typology is a convenient way of conceptualizing change objectives and in evaluating the effectiveness of change interventions. From the standpoint of stating objectives, the change typology can be used to connote the ambitiousness of the change effort, hence, gamma change presents more challenges than alpha change. Thus, the activities implemented in the unfreezing, moving, and freezing stages must be commensurate with the change objectives. From the standpoint of evaluating change, numerous methodologies exist that can be used to detect the types of changes resulting from various interventions. Therefore, unintended as well as intended changes can be isolated. Change practitioners can then systematically defend and explain the results of change efforts. Furthermore, refinements in change practices can be made that advance the effectiveness with which change is diagnosed, planned, implemented, institutionalized, and evaluated.

Change involves a modification in cognitive, affective, and behavioral terms. Research was presented to support the argument that the change in these variables is multidirectional instead of unidirectional; that is, a cognitive change can be accomplished through requiring new behaviors. Conversely, new behaviors can be brought about through cognitive changes.

The stages of change through which individuals and organizations progress were described as unfreezing, moving, and freezing. Unfreezing, considered synonymous with readiness, is accomplished by transmitting a message through various strategies to the change target. The message consists of discrepancy and efficacy aspects. The strategies used in transmitting a message are persuasive communication, active participation, and management of external information sources. Moving is the stage in which the change target embraces the change effort and adopts the new behaviors in accomplishing job tasks. Freezing, the stage in which the change becomes permanent, was described as being accomplished by developing commitment, through various strategies, including socialization, rewards, and diffusion.

In a similar manner to change agents, individuals in the change target utilize frames of reference (models) and heuristics in formulating reactions to a change effort. For example, creating readiness is intended to initiate changes in one's frame of reference. In the Whirlpool case, an objective of the readiness program was to convince individuals of the real threat of foreign competition. The availability heuristic would then access this information in reacting to the change effort. Similarly, the representativeness heuristic would be evoked in making inferences from the negative and positive information presented to the target. Moreover, the anchoring heuristic would be relevant in resolving the cognitive dissonance generated from the readiness program. The individual responses would then be influenced by the social dynamics operating within the target, resulting in favorable or unfavorable reactions.

Evaluation was described in terms of each stage; that is, evaluation or assessment can be useful in determining whether or not the target is ready for the moving stage. Once moving has been initiated, evaluation can be used to monitor progress and to determine how to go about institutionalizing the changes adopted in the moving stage. Evaluation was also considered to be significant in determining whether or not the changes have been institutionalized.

XII. FUTURE CONSIDERATIONS

The information on schema and organization change presented in this chapter was intended to draw attention to selected issues. Some of these issues can be documented from the literature while others are more subtle and cannot be documented. In closing, several points seem worthy of further consideration.

A. Change Agent Perspective

There appears to be a lack of concern that change philosophies can be biased. Bias can manifest itself in numerous ways: for example, in the diagnostic models used, the diagnostic heuristics applied, the diagnostic strategies executed (i.e., action research vs. action inquiry), and the data collection methods employed (e.g., observation, interview, questionnaire). It should be emphasized that the examples described in this chapter were not contrived but drawn from published sources. They are evidence that bias can be a real threat. This phenomenon is not unique to organizational change practitioners, however; it is also congruent with other disciplines (see Balla, 1985). Thus, more research should be conducted on this issue and more training offered to practitioners.

From a research standpoint, an intriguing avenue may be to investigate whether or not individual differences contribute to bias. In other words, are some consultants more susceptible to bias than others? Slocum (1978) found a relationship between cognitive style (i.e., sensation thinker, intuitive thinker, sensation feeler, and intuitive feeler) and the focus of diagnostic information (i.e., task, structure, and people). Tichy and Nisberg (1976) found that consultant type (i.e., whether a consultant was an internal or external consultant) was related to the importance placed on organizational variables (e.g., leadership and culture). Other individual difference variables (e.g., cognitive complexity) may reveal additional useful findings.

From available knowledge, meaningful educational programs can be offered. Designing workshops to reveal the existence of bias through convincing pedagogy (e.g., experiential exercises, real case analyses) would be helpful in stimulating and initiating a concerted movement within the academic and practitioner communities.

B. Change Target Perspective

Applications of the change typology in the literature and hence, its popularity, need boosting. Sashkin and Burke (1987) have argued that too few research papers use the change typology in accounting for change unless the intent is to study how to measure one or more types of change. Sashkin and Burke argue that this finding "may be due to the difficulty in applying the concepts, in actually trying to identify and take into account the type of change" (p. 404).

Some work has been published to facilitate understanding and use of the typology. Armenakis (1988) summarized the methodological contributions of researchers regarding the detection of the typology. The work of Barktunek and her colleagues (Bartunek, 1984; Bartunek and Mock, 1987) and that of Poole, Gioia, and Gray (1989) provided needed conceptual explanations of the change typology.

This chapter has built on previous work in explaining how change agents can beneficially use the change typology in establishing change goals to be used as criteria in evaluating the extent to which the objectives have been accomplished. The use of the typology in goal setting and evaluation should be helpful to the change agent in anticipating the challenges of change and in planning for the interventions needed to accomplish the objectives. For example, gamma change, as described in the Whirlpool case, required extensive readiness interventions spanning over a long time frame. Researchers were able to advise the company regarding system readiness prior to proceeding to the moving stage. Currently, the company is in the process of institutionalizing the change and is planning on follow-up efforts to assess the extent of institutionalization.

In terms of evaluation, without testing for each type of change, the target may have experienced one or more types and the change agent not be aware of it. Thus, incorrect conclusions may be drawn, resulting in misguided efforts. Inappropriate interventions may be implemented, or appropriate interventions may be implemented at the wrong time.

The relationship of individual differences to organizational change has not been adequately researched. Burkhardt's (1991) research on self-monitoring and institutionalization should serve as an example for other researchers to imitate. Similarly, the use of Kirton's (1980) adaptor-innovator inventory poses some interesting possibilities for research ideas that could prove helpful in planning, implementing, and institutionalizing change.

REFERENCES

Arkes, H., Wortmann, R., Saville, P., and Harkness, A. (1981). Hindsight bias among physicians: Weighting the likelihood of diagnoses. *J of Applied Psychology*, 66(2): 252–254.

Armenakis, A. (1988). A review of research on the change typology. In *Research in Organizational Change and Development*, vol. 2 (W. Pasmore and R. Woodman, eds.), JAI Press, Greenwich, Conn., pp. 163–194.

Armenakis, A., and Feild, H. (1987). The development of organizational diagnostic norms: An application of client involvement. *Consultation: An International Journal*, 6: 20–31.

Armenakis, A., Harris, S., and Mossholder, K. (in press). Creating readiness for organizational change. *Human Relations*.

Armenakis, A., Mossholder, K., and Harris, S. (1990). Diagnostic bias in organizational consultation. *Omega*, 18(6): 563–572.

Armenakis, A., and Smith, L. (1978). A practical alternative to comparison group designs in OD evaluations: The abbreviated time series design. *Academy of Management Journal*, 21: 499–507.

Armenakis, A., and Zmud, R. (1979). Interpreting the measurement of change in organizational research. *Personnel Psychology*, 32: 709–723.

Balla, J. (1985). *The Diagnostic Process: A Model for Clinical Teachers*. Cambridge University Press, Cambridge, U.K.

Bandura, A. (1982). Self efficacy mechanism in human agency. *American Psychologist*, 37(2): 122–147.

Bartunek, J. (1984). Changing interpretive schemes and organizational restructuring: The example of a religious order. *Administrative Science Quarterly*, 29: 355–372.

Bartunek, J., and Franzak, F. (1988). The effects of organizational restructuring on frames of reference and cooperation. *J. of Management*, 14(4): 579–592.

Bartunek, J., and Mock, M. (1987). First-order, second-order, and third-order change and organization development interventions: A cognitive approach. *J. of Applied Behavioral Science*, 23(4): 483–500.

Bedeian, A., Armenakis, A., and Randolph, A. (1988). The significance of congruence coefficients.: A comment and statistical test. *J. of Management*, 14: 339–365.

Beer, M., Eisenstat, R., and Spector, B. (November–December 1990). Why change programs don't produce change. *Harvard Business Review*, 68: 158–166.

Benne, K. (1976). The processess of re-education: An assessment of Kurt Lewin's views. In *The Planning of Change* (W. Bennis, K. Benne, and R. Chin, eds.), Holt, Rinehart, and Winston, New York, pp. 272–283.

Burkhardt, M. (August 1991). Institutionalization following a technological change, paper presented at the Fifty-first Annual Academy of Management Meeting, Miami.

Bushe, G. (1988). Developing cooperative labor-management relations in unionized factories: A multiple case study of quality circles and parallel organizations within joint quality of work life projects. *J. of Applied Behavioral Science*, 24(2): 129–150.

Business in Profile, 1995 (videotape; 1990). Whirlpool Corporation, Benton Harbor, Mich.

Coch, L., and French, J. (1948). Overcoming resistance to change. *Human Relations*, 1(4): 512–532.

Confirmation Speech (videotape; 1988). Whirlpool Corporation, Benton Harbor, Mich.

DeFleur, M., and Ball-Rokeach, S. (1989). *Theories of Mass Communication*. Longman, Inc., New York.

Eden, C., Jones, S., and Sims, D. (1983). *Messing About in Problems: An Informal Structured Approach to Their Identification and Management*. Pergamon Press, Oxford, U.K.

Fayol, H. (1949). *General and Industrial Management* (C. Storrs, trans.). Pitman, London.

Fishbein, M., and Azjen, I. (1975). *Belief, Attitude, Intention, and Behavior: An Introduction to Theory and Research*. Addison-Wesley Publishing Company, Reading, Mass.

Flavell, J. (1979). Metacognition and cognitive monitoring: A new area of cognitive developmental inquiry. *American Psychologist, 34*: 906–911.

French, W., and Bell, C. (1990). *Organization Development: Behavioral Science Interventions for Organization Improvement*. Prentice-Hall, Englewood Cliffs, N.J.

Georgopoulos, B., and Tannenbaum, A. (1957). A study of organizational effectiveness. *American Sociological Review, 22*: 534–540.

Gist, M. (1987). Self-efficacy: Implications for organizational behavior and human resource management. *Academy of Management Review, 12*(3): 472–485.

Global Awareness Program (videotape; 1986). Whirlpool Corporation, Benton Harbor, Mich.

Golembiewski, R. (1986). Contours in social change: Elemental graphics and a surrogate for gamma change. *Academy of Management Review, 11*: 550–566.

Golembiewski, R., Billingsley, K., and Yeager, S. (1976). Measuring change and persistence in human affairs: Types of change generated by OD designs. *J. of Applied Behavioral Science, 12*: 133–157.

Goodman, P., Bazerman, M., and Conlon, E. (1980). Institutionalization of planned organizational change. In *Research in Organizational Behavior*, vol. 2 (L. Cummings and B. Staw, eds.), JAI Press, Greenwich, Conn., pp. 215–246.

Goodman, P., and Dean, J. (1982). Creating long-term organizational change. In *Change in Organizations: New Perspectives on Theory, Research, and Practice* (P. Goodman, ed.), Jossey-Bass Publishers, San Francisco, pp. 226–279.

Granier, M., Green, S., and Armenakis, A. (1991). An experimental approach to evaluate methods to detect scale recalibration. *Educational & Psychological Measurement, 51*: 597–607.

Hackman, J., and Lawler, E. (1971). Employee reactions to job characteristics. *J. of Applied Psychology, 55*(3): 259–286.

Hoffer, S. (1987). Behavior and organization performance: An empirical study. *Dissertation Abstracts International, 47*(9): 3368–3369A.

Isabella, L. (1990). Evolving interpretations as a change unfolds: How managers construe key organizational events. *Academy of Management Journal, 33*(1): 7–41.

Johnston, D., and Leenders, M. (1990). The diffusion of innovation within multi-unit firms. *International Journal of Operations and Production Management, 10*(5): 15–24.

Kirton, M. (1980). Adaptors and innovators in organizations. *Human Relations, 3*: 213–224.

Kochan, T. (1987). Strategies for sustaining innovations in U.S. industrial relations. *J. of State Government, 60*(1): 30–35.

Lawrence, P., and Lorsch, J. (1969). *Organization and Environment*. R. D. Irwin, Inc., Homewood, Ill.

Lennox, R., and Wolfe, R. (1984). Revision of the self-monitoring scale. *J. of Personality and Social Psychology, 46*(6): 1349–1364.

Levinson, H. (1972). *Organizational Diagnosis*. Harvard University Press, Cambridge, Mass.

Levy, A. (Summer 1986). Second-order planned change: Definition and conceptualization. *Organizational Dynamics, 15*: 4–20.

Lewin, K. (1951). *Field Theory in Social Science*. Harper and Row, New York.

Lindblom, C. (1959). The science of muddling through. *Public Administration Review, 21*: 78–88.

Likert, R. (1967). *The Human Organization*. McGraw-Hill Book Company, New York.

Maurer, T., and Alexander, R. (1991). Contrast effects in behavioral measurement: An investigation of alternative process evaluation. *J. of Applied Psychology, 76*(1): 3–10.

McMillen, M. (August 1991). Causal schemata of middle managers and the implementation of strategic change. Paper presented at the Fifty-first Academy of Management Meeting, Miami.

Merluzzi, T., Rudy, T., and Glass, C. (1981). The information-processing paradigm: Implications for clinical science. In *Cognitive Assessment* (T. Merluzzi, C. Glass, and M. Genest, eds.), Guilford Press, New York.

Millsap, R., and Hartog, S. (1988). Alpha, beta, and gamma change in evaluation research: A structural equation approach. *J. of Applied Psychology, 73*(3): 574–584.

Nadler, D., and Tushman, M. (1989). Organizational frame bending: Principles for managing reorientation. *Academy of Management Executive, 3*(3): 194–204.

New Structure Speech (videotape; 1988). Whirlpool Corporation, Benton Harbor, Mich.

New Vision Speech (videotape; 1986). Whirlpool Corporation, Benton Harbor, Mich.

Polley, R. (1985). Diagnosis of intact work groups. *Consultation: An International Journal*, *4*(4): 273–283.

Poole, P., Gioia, D., and Gray, B. (1989). Influence modes, schema change, and organizational transformation. *J. of Applied Behavioral Science*, *25*(3): 271–289.

Randolph, A. (1982). Planned organization change and its measurement. *Personnel Psychology*, *35*: 117–139.

Roethlisberger, F., and Dickson, W. (1939). *Management and the Worker*. Harvard University Press, Cambridge, Mass.

Rogers, E. (1983). *Diffusion of Innovations*. The Free Press, New York.

Sashkin, M., and Burke, W. (1987). Organization development in the 1980s. *J. of Management*, *13*(2): 393–417.

Schein, E. (1979). Personal change through interpersonal relationships. In *Essays in Interpersonal Dynamics* (W. Bennis, J. Van Maanen, E. Schein, and F. Steele, eds.), The Dorsey Press, Homewood, Ill., pp. 129–162.

Schmitt, N. (1982). The use of analysis of covariance structures to assess beta and gamma change. *Multivariate Behavioral Research*, *17*: 343–358.

Schweiger, D., Sandberg, W., and Rechner, P. (1989). Experiential effects of dialectical inquiry, devil's advocacy, and consensus approaches to strategic decision making. *Academy of Management Journal*, *32*: 745–772.

Slocum, J. (1978). Does cognitive style affect diagnosis and intervention strategies? *Group & Organization Studies*, *3*: 199–210.

Spector, B. (Summer 1989). From bogged down to fired up: Inspiring organizational change. *Sloan Management Review*: 29–34.

Staw, B. (1981). The escalating commitment to a course of action. *Academy of Management Review*, *6*: 577–587.

Taylor, S., and Crocker, J. (1981). Schematic bases of social information processing. In *Social Cognition: The Ontario Symposium* (E. Tory Higgins, C. Peter Herman, and Mark P. Zanna, eds.), Lawrence Erlbaum Associates, Hillsdale, N.J., pp. 89–134.

Tenkasi, R., Thachankary, T., Cooperider, D., Barrett, F., and Manning, M. (August 1991). The impact of schemas and inquiry frames on consultants constructions of expectations about the client system. Paper presented at the Fifty-first Academy of Management meeting, Miami.

Terborg, J., Howard, G., and Maxwell, S. (1980). Evaluating planned organizational change: A method for assessing alpha, beta, and gamma change. *Academy of Management Review*, *5*: 109–121.

Tichy, N. (1973). An interview with Roger Harrison. *J. of Applied Behavioral Science*, *9*(6): 701–726.

Tichy, N., and Nisberg, J. (1976). Change agent bias: What they view determines what they do. *Group & Organization Studies*, *1*: 286–301.

Tversky, A., and Kahneman, D. (1974). Judgment under uncertainty: Heuristics and biases. *Science*, *185*: 1124–1131.

van de Vliert, E., Huismans, S., and Stok, J. (1985). The criterion approach to unraveling beta and alpha change. *Academy of Management Review*, *10*: 269–274.

van Maanen, J. (1979). Reclaiming qualitative methods for organizational research: A preface. *Administrative Science Quarterly*, *24*(4): 520–526.

Walton, R. (1975). Explaining why success didn't take. *Organizational Dynamics*, *3*(4): 3–21.

Watzlawick, P., Weakland, J., and Fisch, R. (1974). *Change: Principles of Problem Formation and Change Resolution*. Norton, New York.

Weisbord, M. (1976). Organizational diagnosis: Six places to look for trouble with or without a theory. *Group & Organization Studies*, *1*(4): 430–447.

19

Compensation
Trends and Expanding Horizons

Elizabeth M. Doherty

University of Nevada, Reno, Reno, Nevada

Walter R. Nord

University of South Florida, Tampa, Florida

I. INTRODUCTION

Most students of compensation, and of modern organizations more generally, seem to emphasize one of two perspectives. Some, assuming that the future will be much like the past, focus on incremental improvements on present approaches. Others assume greater discontinuity with the past, and propose more sweeping changes.

This chapter attempts to advance the study of compensation by combining these perspectives; we propose that both continuity and discontinuity need to be assumed simultaneously. On the one hand, many problems and solutions from the past are still relevant to compensation today. On the other hand, substantial discontinuities may require major changes in some aspects of compensation philosophy and practice. Consequently, students of compensation must distinguish between the continuous and the discontinuous in order to determine what problems may be best addressed by fine-tuning traditional compensation practices and what others require more radical changes. As a first step, compensation theories and practices need to be considered in the context in which they emerged. Further, consideration of how the past is preserved in assumptions and institutions of the present will be helpful. Accordingly, in this chapter we attempt to integrate assumptions and knowledge about compensation designs and practices, the contexts in which knowledge developed, and the ways in which previous understandings constrain those of the present.

A. Compensation Underpinnings: Assumptions and Theories

The theory and practice of compensation rest on a number of assumptions. Among the most fundamental are beliefs about individuals—specifically, assumptions about why people work provide the foundation for conceptualizing and theorizing how to motivate human behavior. In addition, social/organizational-level assumptions have pronounced effects. Many of these assumptions are usually left implicit in the compensation literature. They are, however, so central to our understanding of compensation that we begin by making them explicit. We also present several of our own assumptions that provide a basis for what follows.

1. Assumptions About Individuals

Perhaps the most pervasive assumption is that human activity is initiated and directed by physiological and psychological needs. This needs-based view posits that human actions are directed toward keeping particular needs at optimal levels of arousal, a process referred to as need satisfaction. Further, it presumes that a wide variety of resources—among them material items, information, and social stimuli (e.g., social approval)—can help satisfy needs. While "normative-affective" outcomes (Etzioni, 1988), including moral and emotional development and symbolic gestures, also satisfy needs, students of compensation generally pay little attention to them.

The needs-based view directs attention to psychological matters, especially to tensions that individuals experience and the ways they attempt to reach and sustain optimal levels of need satisfaction. (See also Chapter 2 in this book.) Often, individuals are treated *as if* much (although not necessarily all) of their behavior is primarily self-interested. Although serious challenges to this position exist (e.g., Etzioni, 1988), most students of compensation appear to assume that self-interest explains much of why people do what they do, including why they work. Specific explanations about why people work can be summarized under two headings: financial gain and other valued outcomes.

a. Reason to Work: Financial Gain. Beginning with early students of management such as Charles Babbage, financial remuneration has been assumed to be the key reason why people work. Although other forms of compensation are possible, money is almost a synonym for compensation in modern industrialized societies.

Money is an especially useful form of compensation because it adds considerable flexibility to exchanges in two ways. First, as B. F. Skinner (1953) explained, money is a generalized reinforcer par excellence: "although 'money won't buy everything,' it can be exchanged for primary reinforcers of great variety" (p. 79). Second, money facilitates "tit-for-tat" reciprocity (Gouldner, 1960) by serving to compensate a wide variety of deeds. Tit-for-tat exchanges are far more flexible than those in which valued items must be paid for in the same form as given; that is, "tat for tat."

Although money is valued by essentially everyone, it is not valued equally by all. Economists warn us that the same absolute amount of money can have quite different utilities for different people, or even for the same person at different times. In addition, people from different professional backgrounds vary in the symbolic value they attach to money (Wernimont and Fitzpatrick, 1972). Further, Tang (1992) revealed how the experiences people have with money affect the meanings they assign it. Thus, although money is widely valued, the psychological meaning and level of satisfaction associated with a given quantity of it cannot be assumed to be uniform.

Additional information about the role of financial compensation can be derived from studies of employee satisfaction. Considerable attention (see, e.g., Lawler, 1971; Dyer and Theriault, 1976; H. Heneman, 1985; Berkowitz et al., 1987; R. Heneman, Greenberger, and Strausser, 1988) has been devoted to understanding, promoting, measuring, and predicting pay satisfaction and its consequences. Nevertheless, even with all this research, individual differences concerning the importance of economic outcomes is an underresearched topic (Brief and Aldag, 1989).

b. Reason to Work: Other Valued Outcomes. The human relations theorists who conducted the Hawthorne studies in the 1930s are usually given credit for showing that workers seek more than just monetary remuneration from their work. As Roethlisberger (1941) observed, the "economic man" view of the meaning people assign to their work experiences was "screwy" (p. 19); workers were motivated by more than just economic objectives. Viewing humans as "social animals," Roethlisberger focused on employees' feelings and sentiments toward one another as well as to their "routine patterns of interactions" (p. 59), both of which bind them "together in collaborative effort" (p. 49). Consequently, Roethlisberger was not surprised to find workers every bit as interested in comparisons of their wages to those of others, as in the absolute amount of their earnings. He observed that "the job and all those factors connected with it serve to define the position of the person performing that job in the social organization of the company of which he is a member" (p. 33).

The Hawthorne studies did not challenge the needs-based view as much as point to other needs. Since then, countless researchers, most guided by the needs-based view, set out to develop more complete accounts for why people worked. Many drew on the work of the psychologist Abraham Maslow (1943; 1954), who indicated that people seek to fulfill their basic needs (e.g., physiological, safety, love, esteem, and self-actualization) according to a "hierarchy of prepotency" (1943:395). In a similar vein, Herzberg, Mausner, and Snyderman (1959) found that workers were only satisfied with jobs that contained "motivators"—for example, opportunities for personal growth, responsibility, recognition, and achievement. This line of research produced the intriguing (although highly controversial) view that "hygiene" factors, including pay, were not "motivators"; their major function was preventing job dissatisfaction. Over time, numerous theorists (e.g., Maslow, 1970; Bandura, 1977; deCharms, 1968; Deci, 1975) have pointed to a number of additional needs that people meet through work.

2. Theories

Many important assumptions are associated with commonly accepted theories. Now, two theoretical perspectives, the behavioral and the cognitive, dominate our understanding of what motivates people to work. Both schools of thought recognize the role of rewards in motivating job behavior, but differ markedly in the nature of their accounts.

a. Behavioral Perspective. The behavioral perspective assumes that much behavior is a function of its consequences (Skinner, 1953); that is, reinforcement contingencies control behavior. In other words, the likelihood that people perform or do not perform a particular behavior depends on the consequences that follow. Through the use of various contingencies (e.g., positive and negative reinforcement, punishment, extinction) applied on various schedules of reinforcement (e.g., fixed or variable ratio, fixed or variable interval), behavior can be shaped and governed.

Although the behavioral view has been applied to organizations with considerable success (see Frederiksen, 1982; O'Brien, Dickinson, and Rosow, 1982) and seems to account for much of what managers and theorists actually do and advocate to motivate people (Nord, 1969), its specialized vocabulary and its connotations that humans are "controlled" rather than "free" seem to have reduced its attractiveness relative to its major rival, cognitive theory.

b. Cognitive Perspective. Two cognitive perspectives are most prominent in the study of compensation. Expectancy theory (Vroom, 1964; Porter and Lawler, 1968), the more general of the two, assumes that forces in the individual and the environment interact to determine behavior. Motivation to perform is presumed to be a function of needs and perceptions of three variables: effort-performance probability (the individual's perception that expenditure of effort will lead to successful performance of a task), performance-outcome expectancy (the perceived probability that performance of the task will yield a particular outcome or reward), and the valence (perceived value) of the reward.

The second major cognitive approach to rewards stems from the work of Deci (1972; 1975) on intrinsic and extrinsic motivation. According to Deci (1975), when people behave so as to receive a reward such as money, and are dependent on some external source for their satisfaction, they are "extrinsically motivated." When people engage in behaviors that satisfy their needs for competence and self-determination, no external contingency is required. In such instances, people may be described as "intrinsically motivated"; they are rewarded by the feelings they get from performing the task itself.

A most interesting facet of this theory is that often extrinsic rewards undermine intrinsic motivation. Deci (1972) proposed that when one perceives choice and feels competent in performing a task, then that activity is likely to provide internal satisfaction. Extrinsic rewards often reduce intrinsic motivation by reducing feelings of choice and self-determination.

Often known as cognitive evaluation theory, Deci's work suggests that effective rewards provide at least an illusion of choice, and focus attention on task performance and not just the acquisition of the reward. As Deci and Ryan (1980) noted, rewards that provide information are more likely to meet this objective than rewards that control.

3. Social/Organizational Assumptions

We assume, as we believe most students of compensation do, that compensation systems seek to advance organizational goals by making individuals' need satisfaction contingent on their cooperating with others. When we speak of cooperation we refer to individual *behavior*—to actions of one person that contribute, either intentionally or unintentionally, to the need satisfaction of other individuals. Viewing cooperation in this way enables us to proceed without making inferences about jointly held goals (cooperative spirits, etc.), although it does not deny that they may exist.

There are many ends to which cooperation (i.e., cooperative behavior) may lead. For the present purposes, we are primarily concerned with behavior associated with achieving one or more goals of an organization. We adopt this commonly held stance with considerable trepidation, in view of the problems in assuming that organizations and people have clear goals that guide and direct their behavior (see, e.g., Cyert and March, 1963; Gross, 1968; Weick, 1979). Nevertheless, for reasons primarily of convention and convenience, cooperative behavior is viewed as actions directed toward organizational goals.

a. Compensation Systems as Tools for Cooperation. Beliefs about human motivation interact with social structures and ideologies. In the United States, the individualistic entailments of the needs-based account of motivation have both supported and been supported by social Darwinism and a dominant economic paradigm that emphasizes how economic welfare benefits from the pursuit of self-interest.

In such a context, the quest for cooperation becomes defined in a particular way. Following Hobbes, if people are self-interested, motivating them to cooperate is problematic. Possible sources of cooperation such as altruism, moral principles (e.g., "Do unto others . . ."), and communal bonds ("From each according to his or her abilities . . .") appear utopian. In contrast, consciously designed and closely monitored social arrangements (e.g., rules and contracts)—enforceable by law and coercion if need be—seem far more practical. Among other things, this latter view is conducive to mechanistic and short-run approaches to gain cooperation. Certainly this emphasis is reflected in many contemporary approaches to compensation.

The perception that cooperation needs to be "coerced" and the emphasis on short-term relationships sometimes obscure two additional ways that incentive systems can support cooperation. First, they provide information. Even when motivated to cooperate, people still need signals about what to do and when to do it. Second, incentives, and compensation systems more generally, can motivate and send signals to individuals about the competencies needed for future cooperation. Thus, in addition to serving as tools for motivating short-term behavior, compensation systems promote cooperation by providing information to guide current performance and prepare to meet future requirements.

As we will show, compensation systems are extremely useful tools for gaining cooperation. However, they are far from perfect; designing and using incentives entail a number of problems, many of which stem from the complex and often contradictory nature of what organizations want people to do. Sometimes, for instance, incentive systems encourage people to act in ways that advance some important organizational goals, while simultaneously promoting the neglect or even hindering the accomplishment of others. Such contradictions are common when managers' compensation is contingent on their performance, and performance is measured in ways that motivate managers to emphasize parochial interests (e.g., their departments). Moreover, it is often difficult to change compensation systems rapidly enough to meet changing demands. They are sources of rigidity that interfere with people redirecting their effort and attention when needed. Also, mechanistic compensation systems can be very expensive tools for achieving cooperation because of high enforcement and monitoring costs. For example, self-interested individuals generally realize that they can satisfy their needs most easily by underworking (e.g., soldiering: Taylor, 1967), free-riding, shirking, or being opportunistic with guile (Williamson, 1981). Therefore, incentive systems need to detect and respond to such actions. Under many conditions, doing so is extremely costly.

b. Evaluating Cooperative Behavior. Our view of compensation's role in promoting cooperation has been influenced by Williamson's (1981) discussion of transaction costs. Williamson defined a transaction as an event involving the transfer of "a good or service . . . across a technologically separable interface" (p. 552). Transaction costs are those resources that must be expended on the *process* of conducting the transfers, as opposed to the market prices of the goods or services themselves. Although Williamson was primarily concerned with exchanges between two social units, exchanges between an individual and an organization can be viewed in much the same way. From this perspective, compensation costs are of two types: direct expenditures on wages and benefits, and the costs associated with regulating the exchange itself (i.e., transaction costs). Often students of compensation ignore the latter.

The importance of including transaction costs when evaluating compensation systems is highlighted by viewing compensation as a tool for achieving cooperation. Judging the effectiveness of compensation systems must include the amount and quality of the cooperative behavior achieved, and three types of costs: resources exchanged as compensation, resources devoted to administering the system, and the costs of obtaining future cooperation.

The amount and quality of cooperation can be assessed, at least in part, by using the elements of cooperative behavior noted earlier—motivation, signaling, and laying the groundwork for future cooperation. Therefore, in addition to indicators of the time and energy people give to their present work (e.g., productivity, profits, and other outcome measures), evaluation of compensation systems should ask: How effective is a given system for increasing the willingness of people to cooperate both now and also in the future?

We must also ask: How costly is it to achieve a given level of cooperation, both now and in the future, and are there less costly ways to do so? Monitoring costs provides a useful way to illustrate what we have in mind.

As we have noted, monitoring performance is often one step toward obtaining cooperation. Assuming that if equally effective ways to achieve cooperation exist, *ceteris paribus*, the least expensive means should be employed. Consequently, the costs of approaches that involve monitoring must be compared with those of alternative ways of gaining the desired level of cooperation. Although seldom discussed in recent work on compensation, this issue has been central to the development of modern organizations and systems of compensation.

Karl Marx (1967), for one, observed in 1867 that employers really want to buy an employee's effort and diligent application of skill, but often rely on a poor surrogate—the employee's time—to calculate worker's pay. Employers settle for this surrogate when the costs of monitoring effort and diligence precisely (other things, such as technology, being equal), are high, in comparison to the incremental gains in levels of cooperation. Also, the poor surrogate may be supplemented by other ways of gaining cooperation (e.g., supervision). Of course, supervision entails costs too. Thus, other things being equal, the optimal way of attaining a desired level of cooperation must be determined by comparing the costs and benefits of hourly pay plus close supervision with the costs and benefits of alternatives (e.g., a piece-rate system). These comparisons must include the full costs and benefits of a particular compensation system as well as those of alternative approaches.

The fact that supervision can be at least a partial substitute for a component of a compensation system is extremely important. It implies, among other things, that evaluating the costs of alternative compensation systems must include variables that to date have seldom been discussed in the compensation literature. In deciding which of two machines to purchase, for example, the differential administrative and other transaction costs associated with compensating employees need to be included.

On the benefit side, the typical criterion of "worker productivity"—measured in terms of output per hour or output per dollar spent on direct compensation and benefits—is also only a partial indicator of effectiveness. Other outcomes, such as the ease of attaining cooperation in the future, must be factored in. Suppose, for example, that two compensation systems have different effects on some of the dimensions Axelrod (1984) noted as influencing the probability of cooperative behavior: the amount of envy they foster among members, the willingness of employees to sacrifice their interests for the organization's, the willingness to reciprocate, the length of time employees use in evaluating their exchanges within the organization, and the levels of trust. The system that has the most favorable effects on these dimensions—even if it yields less short-term productivity, and even if it is substantially more expensive in the short run—may be the better course. Among other things, such a system is far less likely to contribute to antagonistic relationships (e.g., hostile unions and embittered management) that make it increasingly costly to agree about terms. Further, it is less prone to stimulate a positively accelerating cycle of distrust and its entailments: more lawyers, monitoring devices, inefficient work rules, and work stoppages.

In short, the "externalities" of compensation systems must become part of the calculus. Unfortunately, long-term outcomes of this sort are difficult to measure and predict. Our search of the compensation literature revealed, with the exception of equity, little attention to this type of outcome. We propose that viewing compensation explicitly as one of a number of tools to achieve cooperation and evaluating these alternatives in cost/benefit terms may help draw attention to them.

B. Compensation Defined and Protocol for Review

Viewed broadly, compensation is a process through which something is given as an equivalent to make amends for loss or damage *(Webster's New World Dictionary)*. More specifically, Belcher and Atchison (1976) defined compensation as a two-party game in which each party participating in a "double input-output system" (p. 569) contributes and receives something. Both of these definitions are generic in the sense that neither one limits the content of what is gained, lost, or exchanged. As noted earlier, however, in the organization literature "compensation" typically refers to payment (particularly money) for work of some sort.

In organizations, structured routines guide the exchanges of service and rewards between the employee and the firm. We call these "compensation systems." While theoretically these routines could take many forms, in practice only a few of them are widespread. We suggest that the prevalent forms reflect the context of their creators, including the problems and the ideologies of their times.

It is generally assumed that compensation systems must be congruent with several dimensions of the context in which they exist. For one thing, they need to mesh with the organization whose ends they are intended to support. As Lawler (1991) noted, reward systems "must fit with the overall management style of the organization and must reinforce and support the kind of behavior and culture that is desired" (p. 593). Moreover, the process is dynamic. Since the specific circumstances within an organization or its subunits may vary dramatically over space and time, compensation systems must continually change to maintain "fit." Further, the major components of these systems must mesh with the cultural milieu and political economy in which organizations exist. Since these aspects of context are also dynamic, they provide additional pressures for compensation systems to change over time.

Many, if not most, contemporary compensation systems reflect the special circumstances of the first part of the early twentieth century, especially the development of bureaucratic structures. We call these "traditional" pay systems. Although many aspects of traditional systems are still visible, some significant changes have accompanied shifts in organization structures and goals. In some cases, the changes have been substantial enough to deserve the label "nontraditional."

Nontraditional compensation strategies developed and became aligned with fluid, adapting organizations. Although these organizations are often not true adhocracies in Mintzberg's (1979) sense, we call them adhocracies to highlight their dynamic properties. These nontraditional systems are also products of a particular time. They reflect the problems of gaining cooperation efficiently in dynamic environments. However, they developed at a time in which many of the tenets of bureaucratic thinking were still prevalent. Thus, many of the innovations complement traditional systems, rather than substitute for them.

We view bureaucratic and adhocratic structures as "ideal" types. No organization is purely bureaucratic or adhocratic. The same is true of traditional or nontraditional compensation systems. However, these concepts help to highlight developments in compensation systems and reveal the evolution in the ways rewards are used to motivate and signal and to promote cooperation.

II. TRADITIONAL COMPENSATION SYSTEMS AND BUREAUCRATIC STRUCTURES

The primary components of traditional compensation systems began to emerge with the Industrial Revolution, and became more clearly defined during the rapid growth of the manufacturing sector in the late 1800s and early 1900s. At this time, efficiency and related economic objectives (e.g., profitability and low-cost production) were the primary goals (Jacoby, 1985).

Owners and management viewed controlling the workflow and workers as critical for achieving efficiency and making profits. This interest in control was intensified by beliefs that the workforce was recalcitrant; the term *labor problem* serving as a euphemism for the fear of a working class revolt. Control was gained through standardizing work and dividing it into discrete, routine tasks. The special emphasis given to creating simple and repetitive tasks was fostered by a poorly educated workforce, many members of which were immigrants who knew little English (Jacoby, 1985).

Key components of bureaucratic structures took root in this period. In retrospect, organization hierarchy, militaristic metaphors (Clancy, 1989), centralized decision making, and formalization addressed what managers of the day saw as critical: controlling and motivating the workers to perform increasingly specified tasks. Similarly, compensation systems founded upon individual financial incentives, such as those made famous by F. W. Taylor and his followers, fit the times well. Although some firms did attempt to introduce profit sharing and more "modern" compensation systems (see Rodgers, 1974), they were in the minority. Further, since the employment relationship was temporary (Jacoby, 1985), pay for immediate performance with little concern for the longer term made sense. In short, an individual-based compensation system with a short-term focus was consistent with the spirit and realities of the times.

This picture, including the central role of Taylorism, is consistent with much of the historical record, but it oversimplifies the history of the compensation process considerably. First, since it is based almost totally on information about production activities, the picture misses white collar employees. For the most part, employers trusted their white collar workers and viewed them as committed to the firm's objectives. Consequently, employment of these individuals, in contrast to that of production workers, was governed by "gentlemen's agreements" with their employers (Jacoby, 1985). Second, Taylor saw his system as part of a "great mental revolution" (Wren, 1972) leading to employers and workers cooperating in their common interests. This fact is obscured in many discussions of his work. Third, and closely related, Taylor was far less influential on actual practice than many assume (Nelson, 1975).

In short, "bureaucratic structure" is an ideal type. Moreover, our picture of the origins of bureaucratic structures and the pay systems associated with them is but a sketch. However, we take it to be an adequate basis for highlighting components of traditional views of organizations, people, and compensation.

A. Dimensions of Traditional Compensation Designs

Compensation systems can be summarized according to their positions on four dimensions: (1) the basis upon which pay is determined, (2) the level and mix of the compensation package, (3) how compensation is administered, and (4) key compensation practices. Table 1 presents the

Table 1 Characteristics of Traditional and Nontraditional
Compensation Systems

	Traditional (bureaucratic)	Nontraditional (adhocratic)
Basis of pay	Job	Performance
	Time worked	Person-skills
Level		
Equity	Internal	External
Criteria	Market	Performance
Mix		
Emphasis	Salary	Incentives
Risk taking	Low	High
Reward	Seniority	Performance
Benefit choice	Low–fixed	High–variable
Administration		
Decision making	Centralized	Decentralized
Communications	Closed	Open
Employee input	Low	High
Pay status	Secret	Open
Policies	Nonflexible	Flexible
Common practices	Individual incentives	Gain-sharing
	Merit pay	Skill-based
	Profit-sharing	pay

position of traditional and nontraditional systems on these dimensions. In this section we focus
on the former.

1. Basis of Pay: The Job

Traditional compensation systems rely heavily on *job-based* pay. Job-based arrangements link
an individual's rate of pay to a classification of his or her job, and determine the amount of pay
by multiplying the rate by the time worked. Such systems reward holders of precisely defined,
specialized jobs for performing tasks specified by their job descriptions (Mahoney, 1989).

A key advantage of job-based compensation is that decisions about salary are easily
structured and standardized. Moreover, to the degree that bureaucratic structures benefit from
long-term tenure and commitments, job-based compensation reinforces the significance of
hierarchical position. If, as has often been the case in bureaucratic organizations, seniority is
important for advancement to higher-paying jobs, job-based compensation provides incentives
to stay on.

Typically, in a job-based system, jobs are classified through job evaluation (Mahoney,
1989; Lawler, 1990). Although many dimensions are used, Wolfe (1991) noted, all job
evaluation systems "are based on three things: what you know, what you do, and, to a degree,
what you have to put up with" (p. 44). These three elements are generally measured as skill,
effort and responsibility, and working conditions (Kanin-Lovers, 1991; Wolfe, 1991).

While the Hay system is the best-known approach, a variety of job evaluation methodologies are available (Lawler, 1990; Kanin-Lovers, 1991; Rock and Berger, 1991). Many of these
methods are based on point-factor systems in which points are assigned on the basis of how
many predetermined factors constitute each job description. Then, adjustments are made to
reflect the relative weight of each factor, and the points are totaled. Salary survey data are used
to determine the monetary value of the points given to each job. [See Kanin-Lovers (1991) for a
comprehensive description of point-factor methods.]

2. Level and Mix

Compensation systems must maintain a delicate balance between individual and organizational interests (Belcher and Atchison, 1976), with this balance depending on the level and mix of compensation (Lawler, 1990). Using Lawler's terms, compensation *level* is the total amount of material rewards the organization offers the employee; and *mix* is the makeup of the total package. Both the substance of these decisions about level and mix, and the process used to make them, affect the employees' motivation and behavior, as well as ultimately the effectiveness of the organization.

a. Level: Equity and Market Considerations. Students of management, at least since Emerson (1911) and Fayol in 1926 (1949), have recognized the importance of equity and fairness. Over time, however, an important change has taken place. Early treatments tended to see these issues as resolvable through the judgment of management, but recent treatments center on complex social psychological and perceptual processes.

Adams (1965) provided the cornerstone for conceptualizing the social psychology of perceived fairness. He suggested that employees assess pay equity by comparing the ratio of their "inputs" and "outputs" to those of other people. According to Adams, perceived inequity causes psychological tension. When individuals feel underrewarded, they attempt to reduce the tension by lowering their productivity or withdrawing mentally and/or physically from the job. On the other hand, when they feel overrewarded, they may react by increasing their efforts.

More recently, another trend emerged as research indicated that in addition to these reactive responses people deal with possible inequity proactively—by attempting to create payments and procedures that they perceive as fair (Greenberg, 1987). This research makes us aware that perceptions of equity and justice are a function of process as well as substance.

Of course, compensation managers have long recognized, at least implicitly, the importance of employees' perceptions of *how* pay is determined. Their emphasis on the process of job evaluation is witness to this concern. *The Compensation Handbook* (edited by Rock and Berger, 1991) demonstrates how much attention has been devoted to such topics as conducting job analyses (Lange, 1991), using survey strategies for examining external pay levels (Lichty, 1991), designing salary structures (Roy, 1991), and developing budgeting, auditing, and control systems (Ingster, 1991) to oversee the whole process. While all of these actions can contribute to rational decisions, by making the process *appear* rational, they also contribute to perceptions of justice and equity.

Besides employers, other organizations—especially unions and governments—have helped define equity, both substantively and procedurally. Among other things, as a result of the efforts of these groups, compensation practices have become increasingly embroiled in legal controversies. Although the exact consequences are far from clear, many people sense that these controversies have produced more just rewards. Also, there can be little doubt that they have made the compensation process more mechanistic, legally driven, and procedurally specific.

b. Defining Mix. An organization's goals influence the mix of compensation; that is, the relative role of cash, benefits, and perquisites that make up an employee's compensation package. Consistent with the emphasis bureaucracies place on stability, traditional compensation systems emphasize low-risk packages (e.g., fixed benefits and fixed—as opposed to performance-based—compensation; Lawler, 1990). Other factors affecting the mix include: government regulations (e.g., tax laws, insurance requirements, or minimum wage laws), practices of other organizations, and social norms.

Benefits and perquisites have become an increasingly important aspect of the compensation package. In traditional systems the mix (and level) of benefits depends heavily on position and hierarchical status. For example, part-time and temporary employees often receive no benefits. Further, hourly workers are seldom eligible for vacation time or retirement benefits comparable to those of executives and many salaried employees. Similarly, lower- and higher-level managers often do not have equivalent perquisites (e.g., dining rooms, parking privileges, or office settings). In fact, wide variations in perquisites seem to blend in with the emphasis on hierarchy.

Fanning (1990) revealed how extreme the benefits of hierarchy can get. For example, a J. Walter Thompson executive had a uniformed butler deliver a peeled orange to him daily at the cost of $300 per day ($80,000 a year). Hopefully such situations are rare; but the fact that they exist at all reveals much about the distribution of compensation in at least some hierarchical organizations.

3. Administration

Administration of traditional compensation systems reflects bureaucratic norms. Although level and mix differ according to position, highly similar rules and guidelines are used throughout the organization. Often, decision making is centralized and top-down; there is little employee input (except if forced by unions or some other pressure).

Although the consistency this approach can achieve offers important advantages, it has disadvantages as well. First, corporatewide performance and uniformity may be over-emphasized at the expense of divisional or business unit objectives (Lawler, 1987). Moreover, bureaucratic approaches to administering compensation are "closed" in important ways. For example, often pay decisions are kept secret (Lawler, 1987). Consequently, possible benefits of employee involvement—feelings of control, commitment, and information (Lawler, 1975)—are lost.

4. Compensation Practices

Although sometimes contemporary promoters of "pay-for-performance" make it appear other-wise, traditional compensation systems have long employed monetary incentives, merit pay, and profit sharing. In traditional systems these methods emphasize production goals, corporate-wide profitability objectives, and mechanistic processes.

a. Monetary Incentives. Mechanistic perspectives are conducive to viewing the performance of entire organizations as the sum of individual performances. Consequently, attempts to improve overall performance often consist of supervisors and/or staff specialists setting produc-tion targets for individual jobs. Employees who meet these standards are rewarded through a predetermined set of rules. Individual piece rates are the best-known form of such incentive systems.

Traditional incentive systems have both advantages and disadvantages. Marriott (1957) noted that piece-rate systems are easy and relatively cheap to install. [Lawler (1987; 1990) disputed this point, noting that the need to monitor and change rates makes maintenance costs high.] Moreover, workers are rewarded in direct proportion to their output, and the relationship between effort and reward is clear.

Other forms of incentives have a long (and controversial) history, too. For example, in the 1830s, Charles Babbage proposed offering bonuses to workers for cost-saving suggestions (Wren, 1972). Historically, however, most bonus plans were based on measured output per unit of time (Marriott, 1957). According to Marriott, two types of bonus plans were typically used: (1) task bonuses, through which a worker was paid for the amount of time saved over the standard time set for performing an operation, and (2) point systems (e.g., Bedaux), through which a worker was rewarded for exceeding some production standard. These approaches reflect our earlier discussion about the economic assumptions made by students of compensa-tion.

A major difficulty with piece-rate systems, as Whyte (1955) pointed out, is that human behavior is more complicated than reward and punishment systems of this sort allow for. People respond to the social environment in which incentives are offered. Consequently, even if workers operate only in their own self-interest, they may restrict productivity to avoid disrupting social relationships. Of course, workers are not alone in this regard.

Managers often devise ways to gain resources for their departments and themselves (even $300 peeled oranges!) with little regard for the organization's profitability. Thus, it is no surprise to find problems with managerial incentives as well (Patton, 1972; Rich and Larson, 1984). Perhaps most noteworthy are the findings by Jensen and Murphy (1990) that, despite the fact that the CEOs they studied received about 50% of their base pay in the form of bonuses, there was only a very small relationship between increases in CEO compensation and changes in their firm's performance.

Some problems stem from difficulties in measuring performance (Whyte, 1955). Additional complications stem from workers trying to beat the system, the emergence of a divided workforce on the basis of incentive pay eligibility, and employees focusing only on those behaviors for which they are rewarded (Lawler 1987; 1990). It is worth noting that many of these difficulties exist even under conditions in which traditional pay systems should be most effective; that is, in situations in which work is repetitive, stable, and simple, the task can be easily measured, and employees can pace their own performance (Lawler, 1990). It is to be expected that at managerial levels, where the conditions are less favorable on these dimensions, a number of problems would occur. Rich and Larson's (1984) findings support this expectation. Their study of managers in 46 companies revealed that incorrect performance measures and improperly set performance targets reduced the value of incentive pay.

Despite difficulties, traditional incentive systems do achieve important objectives. Although individual-based incentives have begun to fade in some areas (e.g., production), they continue to be an effective motivator for some employees (e.g., sales representatives); bonuses for managers and other professionals also work well (O'Dell and McAdams, 1987). In addition, there is some evidence that incentive systems have more far-reaching effects, including increasing the willingness of employees to accept the basic social structure in which they work. For one thing, if rates appear to have been set equitably, incentive systems contribute to a perception that individuals are getting what they deserve. Second, as Burawoy (1979) reported, piece-rate systems induce workers to define success in terms of "making out" (i.e., meeting certain production standards) *within* their local work setting. This preoccupation, according to Burawoy, fosters social stability by blinding workers to the exploitative nature of the political economic system. Whether this is a benefit or a cost depends on one's point of view, of course.

b. Merit Pay. Merit pay systems have been defined by R. Heneman (1990) as "individual pay increases based on the rated performance of individual employees in a previous time period" (p. 205). Mahoney (1989) noted that although merit pay is often used as a salary supplement, it is linked to the job and its defined base pay.

R. Heneman (1990) summarized a number of other important variations in merit pay systems. For one, a wide variety of formulas is used to relate merit pay to performance. Some plans base pay only on measured performance; others take into account such factors as the cost of living. Additionally, the ratio of the pay based on merit to that consisting of fixed salary and benefits varies considerably. Further, while merit pay is often distributed on a yearly basis, sometimes payment is made more frequently. Finally, merit pay either may be permanent and incorporated into the person's base pay, or may be limited to a designated period of time.

Research has shown that merit pay can elevate performance levels but even when it does not, investigators note other desirable outcomes (R. Heneman, 1990). For example, Schay (1988) reported that merit pay may improve work attitudes. Similarly, R. Heneman (1990) and Miceli et al. (1991) found merit pay was positively associated with job and/or pay satisfaction.

A number of factors are known to affect the success of merit plans. First, such plans require clearly defined, measurable, and accepted standards for performance, and specific criteria for pay increases (Hills, 1979; Perry and Petrakis, 1988). Second, performance appraisal systems must be closely linked to the determination of merit increases (Perry and Pearce, 1983; Miceli et al., 1991). Further, employees must perceive merit rewards to be worth the effort (Gaertner and Gaertner, 1985); small pay increases may not be perceived as meaningful or motivating (Hills, 1979). Fourth, employees who mistrust the performance appraisal process (Perry and Pearce, 1983) or who perceive reward distribution as inconsistent with policy or not as fruitful as other systems (Miceli et al., 1991) tend to view merit pay unfavorably. Finally, ability to perform must be considered. Merit pay often centers almost exclusively on eliciting effort; however, as expectancy theorists (e.g., Porter and Lawler, 1968) suggest, deficits in capability impair performance too.

Often, the success of merit plans depends on how managers implement them. Unfortunately, assessment and evaluation problems are inherent in performance appraisal and pay determination (Meyer, 1975; Hills, 1979). Then too, politics can distort the process. Longenecker, Sims, and Gioia (1987) reported that the appraisal process itself is a highly political one. Moreover, even the best of managers can be stymied if the wage structure does not permit pay for performance (Hills, 1979) or if the merit budget is underfunded (Silverman, 1983; Schay, 1988; Miceli et al., 1991). Further, merit pay is supposed to ensure equity and reward high performance, but these are not necessarily compatible objectives if, in making sure parity exists, pay turns out to be insufficient or not dispensed in a way that reflects performance distinctions (Hills, 1979; Perry and Pearce, 1983).

Actually, some difficulties with merit pay stem from faulty assumptions. Echoing Whyte's (1955) critique of piece rates, Perry and Petrakis (1988) noted that many merit pay systems may be too simplistic for complex organizations. Most notably, when merit pay centers on individual performance, it may fail to foster necessary cooperation or team performance (Perry and Petrakis, 1988; Wisdom, 1989). Also, the motivational value of merit pay is often less than assumed. For example, high performers are unlikely to be motivated without substantial merit awards. In fact, it is questionable that they need monetary incentives in the first place (Hills, 1979).

If administered poorly, merit plans can actually be dysfunctional. For example, without well-defined performance criteria and clear ties to the business unit's or organization's goals, employees may expend high levels of energy but direct it in ways that are counterproductive. The federal government's merit pay plan (Perry and Pearce, 1983; Silverman, 1983; Gaertner and Gaertner, 1985) is a good example of how a complicated or cumbersome system, based on ill-defined policies and inconsistent practices, can generate highly undesirable effects.

Other dysfunctional results occur when the rewards employees receive do not match their own beliefs concerning their performance. When people are evaluated less favorably than they evaluate themselves, their self-esteem, performance, and perseverance may decrease (Meyer, 1975; Taylor and Brown, 1988). Finally, employees may actually become demotivated if too much attention is paid to extrinsic rewards (Deci, 1972) or to the task itself (Wisdom, 1989).

In sum, a great deal is known about merit pay plans. However, their success is determined by the interplay of many factors. Accordingly, R. Heneman (1990) concluded, far more research is needed to understand merit pay and its outcomes.

c. Profit Sharing.   Profit-sharing systems compensate employees according to the organization's financial performance. Kendrick (1987) indicated that three forms of profit sharing are common: a predetermined percentage of profits is put into a pool, and (1) distributed as cash to eligible employees, (2) deferred and deposited into a retirement program in which case the money is tax-free until withdrawn, or (3) allocated as a combination of cash and deferment.

In the 1830s, Charles Babbage advanced profit sharing based on a system that was widely used in the Cornish mines (Hyman, 1982). His belief that profit-sharing plans were desirable because they gave employees interest in the prosperity of the whole enterprise has been enduring.

Well over a century later, Metzger (1966) observed that profit sharing aims to link the employees' self-interest directly with the firm's objectives by giving them a stake in the company's profitability. In addition to the benefits from this sense of partnership, profit sharing works by helping to attract and retain employees, increasing their job security, and giving them "suprawage benefits" without requiring a fixed commitment by the organization (Metzger, 1966).

Metzger's point about the absence of fixed organizational commitments is noteworthy. As Stiglitz (1987) suggested, profit sharing instills partnership while building sufficient flexibility to permit effective responses to unforeseen circumstances. In a similar vein, Kendrick (1987) noted that profit-sharing plans are useful because they are coupled to the firm's ability to pay. This type of flexibility is especially important during economic downturns. By putting some compensation at risk, layoffs and other disruptive cutbacks may be less necessary.

A final set of advantages of profit-sharing plans stems from the ways they calculate compensation. Kendrick (1987) stated that profit sharing is advantageous because the formula is consistent with standard accounting practices. Further, the plans can be applied even in industries in which measuring output and productivity precisely is so difficult that many other pay-for-performance programs are infeasible.

The major criticism of profit sharing is the lack of perceived contingency between effort and reward. For example, in large organizations it is hard to see a direct relationship between an individual's actions and the firm's profits (Metzger, 1966; Kendrick, 1987; Stiglitz, 1987). In these cases, the motivational value of profit sharing is apt to be small. Nevertheless, after reviewing a variety of research investigations (e.g., econometric, attitude surveys), Weitzman and Kruse (1990) expressed cautious optimism in suggesting that profit-sharing plans enhance productivity.

B. Overview

Traditional compensation's wide use and long track record speaks to its success, at least in bureaucratic settings. It is hard to deny its positive contribution to the development of modern organizations in the American context. Even though they could have been designed and implemented better, traditional compensation systems fostered high levels of cooperation during a century that began with intense industrial conflict and witnessed monumental social change and economic growth.

Centrally administered job-based pay was congruent with the emphasis on organizational stability and hierarchy of the times. Compensation systems based on job evaluation contributed to specification of requirements for structured tasks, uniformity through standardization, and at least the appearance of objectivity and equity in employee treatment. Moreover, while the heavy reliance on hourly wages and annual salaries associated with job-based pay did not make rewards as directly contingent on performance as students of motivation would advocate, many of the supplementary incentive systems alleviated this deficiency. Although it is fashionable to criticize the traditional approach, many organizations continue to benefit from it. Indeed, even adhocratic organizations employ many aspects of the traditional approach.

Still, bureaucratic systems became dominant in a particular social and political economic era. In the next section, we suggest that there is good reason to expect that in some (but not all) important respects, they are not well-suited to compete in the complex, dynamic environments of today. New forms of organization will arise, and they will encourage (if not require) new compensation approaches.

It is important to note, however, that the new forms will resemble their predecessors in important ways. Thus, with respect to compensation, we can expect both dramatic innovations as well as a number of constancies and incremental changes. Parts of the older forms will live on in a new context.

III. NONTRADITIONAL COMPENSATION SYSTEMS AND ADHOCRATIC STRUCTURES

Although managers have probably always experienced uncertainty, in recent decades they have expressed concern about environmental turbulence and the need for transforming organizations. While dating the origins of these trends is speculative, since about 1960, such trends as technological advancements, economic fluctuations, global competition, corporate restructuring, and changing demographics have called forth new organization designs and ways to manage human resources (Schein, 1986; Schuler, 1990; Berger, 1991). While efficiency is still emphasized, so are other things: greater flexibility, customer satisfaction, product variety and quality, and faster delivery (Mahoney, 1989).

Burns and Stalker (1961) warned that bureaucratic organization structures are ill-suited for rapidly changing environments. Formalization and standardization become liabilities for promoting new ideas or the quick responses demanded in more dynamic, less predictable settings. Accordingly, many organizations have redesigned themselves, becoming less hierarchical, centralized, formalized, and rule-bound. In some cases we see boundaryless organizations (Hirschorn and Gilmore, 1992) and network forms (Charan, 1991) emerging. Increasingly, many organizations come closer to being adhocracies (Mintzberg, 1979).

The nature of work has also changed. Although documenting the extent of change is difficult, many experts believe that jobs increasingly call upon workers to use a wide variety of skills, to make more decisions, and to coordinate, communicate, and cooperate with others in unprogrammed ways. (This is not to say that all or even most jobs have changed in these ways; it is only to suggest that many have, and more will.)

Also, organizations have come to relate to individuals in new ways. The "drive system," so dominant in the early part of the century, had already been modified by the human relations model. That view, in turn, became challenged by the human resources model (Miles, 1975), calling on managers to nurture workers' personal and professional growth, and give them opportunities to exercise their talents.

In the 1960s and 1970s, job enlargement/enrichment, management-by-objectives (MBO; Kondrasuk, 1981), autonomous work groups (Cummings and Molloy, 1977; Kelly, 1982), matrix structures, and team building were among the most widely discussed and practiced ways of putting the spirit of the human resources view into practice. More recent interventions along this line include: quality circles (Munchus, 1983; Meyer and Stott, 1985), self-managed work groups, and "strong" cultures. Unfortunately, these efforts often failed to provide the desired flexibility because traditional ideas and practices were so well ingrained. For example, the bureaucratic mentality of control often made MBO systems appear to be more concerned with following MBO procedures than with the work itself (Nord and Durand, 1975).

Nevertheless, attempts to interject greater flexibility, in combination with revised assumptions about worker motives, altered managerial thinking and practice. Nontraditional compensation designs are components of these changes.

A. Dimensions of Nontraditional Compensation Designs

To reiterate, in no way does the emergence of nontraditional compensation schemes mean that traditional systems have vanished. As Table 1 shows, the basic dimensions of traditional and nontraditional compensation systems are the same. Further, nontraditional schemes generally supplement or modify traditional practices. Still, the newer approaches do entail important changes on a number of dimensions.

Nontraditional systems give high priority to increasing worker productivity while reducing fixed labor costs (Kanter, 1987). As some have put it, nontraditional compensation schemes seek to entice workers to work smarter, not just harder.

1. Basis of Pay: Performance and Skills

Although job-based compensation continues to exist in many adhocratic organizations, additional methods of pay are often evident. Mahoney (1989) used the terms *performance-based* and *person-based* to highlight salient features of these newer approaches.

Performance-based compensation links rewards with outputs. It relies on establishing performance goals to: communicate the organization's priorities, provide needed direction, and help employees formulate objectives so that their achievements can be easily and reliably measured. If done properly, not only is compensation tied to performance, but employees' control over their work is enhanced and the organization has greater control over labor costs.

Many features of performance-based pay are the same in adhocratic and bureaucratic settings, however, there are also important differences. First, performance is defined in a more comprehensive fashion in adhocracies, where "qualitative" aspects (e.g., customer satisfaction and knowledge) receive greater attention. (The degree of emphasis given to quantifying these "qualitative" dimensions varies widely.) Second, in adhocracies performance-based compensation is more likely to extend beyond the traditional factory to staff, service, and even managerial personnel. Third, in addition, to emphasizing the need for high productivity, these systems are intended to enhance employee involvement and provide workers with information they need to adjust their performance.

Person-based compensation links rewards to employees' knowledge and skills (Mahoney, 1989). Person-based compensation is not new; it has long been evident in teaching, research, and other occupations in which career ladders are present. Now, however, it is used by more organizations and applied to more jobs within them. As we will see, person-based pay is well suited for adhocratic organizations.

2. Level and Mix

a. Equity Issues.   Like their predecessors, designers of nontraditional compensation systems are concerned with equity, but what constitutes fairness has shifted. Kanter (1987) noted that employees compare their compensation, both externally to people performing similar work in other organizations, as well as internally, to people within their own organization and to organization profits.

Internal comparisons may become more important for at least two reasons. First, if reliance on internal labor markets grows, jobs will be more idiosyncratic to particular organizations. Consequently, external comparisons are less meaningful to both employers and employees. Second, internal equity issues may become more salient when organizations attempt to create egalitarian, cooperation-based cultures.

When internal equity becomes more salient, concern with procedural justice may grow. This is likely because as the external market becomes less of a factor, an important source of apparent objectivity is lost and judgments of equity will center more on internal comparisons. Moreover, to the degree that the "objective" market provides a less useful source of data to justify allocations, perceptions of the internal procedures may become even more crucial.

b. Pay Level Characteristics.   In attempting to link a greater percentage of employee rewards to performance, nontraditional approaches put more compensation "at risk." In so doing, they augment flexibility. In good economic times, the link between organization performance and pay can stimulate the increased employee effort that is needed to meet the strong demand, thereby reducing the need to expend additional resources on hiring and training new employees. In bad times when output decreases, the organization's compensation costs drop automatically, thereby minimizing the need for layoffs or cuts in wage rates. In short, the firm's compensation bill adjusts "spontaneously" to economic conditions. This process generally benefits the organization unless, as Lawler (1990) noted, the drop in compensation during a downturn becomes so great that the high-performing employees leave.

The newer systems also place greater emphasis on group relative to individual rewards. Group incentives are well suited to adhocracies, in which complex and interdependent jobs make it difficult to measure individual contributions. Accordingly, interest in group-level pay has grown.

c. Compensation Mix.   Under nontraditional approaches, benefits and perquisites continue to be important components of compensation. Here too, however, the trend is toward greater flexibility. Stonebraker (1985) predicted that even though benefit programs will increasingly be mandated to provide certain basic coverage (e.g., medical, retirement), they will also become more flexible, featuring more individually selected components and greater use of benefits as incentives. Little has changed that would alter the validity of Stonebraker's predictions.

Lawler (1990) noted that making benefit plans flexible has become a key mechanism for supporting involvement-oriented organizations. Pressures for flexible benefits also come from the heterogeneous preferences stemming from an increasingly diverse workforce, greater demands by workers for enriching work, and heightened concern about the roots of benefits (Siegel, 1989).

A major advantage of flexible offerings stems from the choices they provide. Economists assert that as the opportunity for individual consumers to choose among alternatives increases, so does the total utility achieved from a given pool of resources. It follows that a shift to flexible plans, even if total benefits do not increase, can make employees better off. Of course, firms are apt to benefit as well, since they can provide their employees with higher levels of satisfaction at no additional cost. In fact, costs may even decrease; Siegel (1989) observed that organizations typically accrue, or at least anticipate, cost savings from installing flexible plans.

On the other hand, flexible programs may experience higher costs due to start-up expenditures and a loss of large-group savings. Still, these costs are generally considered relatively minor in comparison to the positive returns flexibility provides both employees and employer (Lawler, 1990).

3. Administration

The administration of nontraditional compensation plans reflects the teachings of the human resources (Miles, 1975) and organizational development (OD; Beer, 1980) perspectives. Greater employee involvement in the design and implementation of compensation plans (Lawler, 1981; Graham-Moore and Ross, 1990) is the clearest example.

There is good reason to expect that decentralized decision making and employee involvement will yield greater employee understanding and acceptance of a given compensation package (Lawler, 1990). For one thing, information sharing and open feedback channels contribute to the success of compensation systems (O'Dell and McAdams, 1987; Lawler, 1990) in several ways. First, information about the compensation plans themselves helps employees use them more effectively. In addition, although not all agree (e.g., Cook, 1991), open reward decisions may have several positive consequences. Lawler (1981; 1990), long an advocate of making reward decisions public, argued: "Rewards in the public domain have much more status value than do rewards that are secret. It is hard for people to receive acknowledgment from others if their good performance and rewards are secret" (1990:17). Information provided as a result of open pay policies will often increase the credibility of the compensation system, minimize the distortions inevitable with secrecy, and reduce the chances for corrupt pay systems. We suspect that some of these benefits may stem from the fact that openness pressures decision makers to do a better job.

4. Compensation Practices

Nontraditional reward strategies appear to be growing in popularity. In a survey of 1598 organizations (some of which were parts of larger organizations), O'Dell and McAdams (1987) found that 75% of their respondents used at least one type of nontraditional reward system.

While these findings are noteworthy, care must be taken to avoid overstating the degree of change. These nontraditional systems combine substantial innovations with many traditional strategies and techniques. In fact, some of the practices (e.g., nondeferred profit sharing and small group incentives) have a long history. Others, such as an all-salaried workforce, simply expand the application of a well-established system. Only a few, such as the two-tier plan, which aims to reduce overall compensation costs and slow pay rate increases by bringing new hires into the organization at a lower wage rate then prior salary scales would permit (O'Dell and McAdams, 1987), seem more novel. (Of course, even this is not totally new; undoubtedly job reclassification has often been used to achieve similar results.)

There is also considerable continuity in the types of rewards, although some nontraditional compensation practices do involve changes in the rewards themselves. For example, as O'Dell and McAdams (1987) and McAdams (1991) noted, nonmonetary awards (e.g., travel, home appliances) have become increasingly popular. These tangible rewards have certain advantages over cash because they have "trophy value," are easier to promote, provide more flexibility (the programs are "add ons" that can be promoted as temporary and terminated if desired), and are less expensive. While the rationale for such programs reflects growing sophistication, such rewards are far from new; they have been employed in sales departments for decades.

The more novel practices and benefits include flextime, flexplace, job sharing, child care, and sabbaticals. (Of course, sabbaticals have been common in universities for a long time.)

These changes emerged primarily in response to changing demographics, greater diversity in the workforce, and the special needs of adhocracies.

Two of the most widely discussed programs that make up nontraditional compensation— gain sharing and skill-based pay—also reflect an interesting pattern of new and old. Gain sharing is primarily a performance-based form of compensation; skill-based pay systems are person-based.

a. Gain Sharing. Gain sharing is a generic term for unitwide bonus systems that reward productivity improvements (Hauck, 1987; Miller and Schuster, 1987). They revolve around organizations committed to share a percentage of the financial gain with employees whose performance exceeds designated goals. The Scanlon plan, introduced in the 1930s, serves as the model or starting point for many gain-sharing programs (Frost, Wakeley, and Ruh, 1974). Improshare (Fein, 1976) and the Rucker plan are more recent. In addition, many organizations now custom design their own gain-sharing plans (O'Dell and McAdams, 1987; Graham-Moore and Ross, 1990).

Central to all gain-sharing plans is a formula for measuring and rewarding improvements in productivity. Often, for example, the amount of labor required to produce a specified quantity of goods is measured and used as a standard in calculating a bonus. In effect, then, the bonus is a function of labor cost savings that result from comparing actual labor costs to standard production costs.

While gain sharing is best noted for improving productivity and return on investment (ROI; Graham-Moore and Ross, 1990), it often reduces costs and increases quality (O'Dell and McAdams, 1987). Other positive results commonly reported are: improved coordination, greater teamwork among employees, better labor relations, higher employee involvement, enhanced communications, and more positive attitudes (O'Dell and McAdams, 1987; Lawler, 1988; 1990).

Doherty and McAdams (1993) explored the factors that contribute to gain sharing's effectiveness. Gain sharing is effective because it incorporates sound principles about rewards and motivation. Most plans make rewards contingent upon desired behavior—a key tenet of behavior modification and expectancy theories. Moreover, some forms of gain sharing increase the salience of rewards by separating rewards from basic compensation (e.g., through providing lump-sum or noncash payments), thereby making them extraordinary. Success also depends on employees perceiving that their share of the "gain-sharing pie" is fair (Cooper, Dyck, and Frolich, 1992) and significant. Most organizations respond by establishing a 50/50 split between employees and the firm (O'Dell and McAdams, 1987). In the current context, such a distribution is apt to be viewed as fair by employees.

Success is also a function of the process used to introduce and implement gain sharing (Hatcher and Ross, 1985; Doherty, Nord, and McAdams, 1989; Graham-Moore and Ross, 1990). Communication of the rules, procedures, and program objectives heads the list of critical components (O'Dell and McAdams, 1987; Doherty, Nord, and McAdams, 1989). Information about the goals and status (including financial) of the organization and what specific actions are required to achieve the desired goals is also vital. Employee involvement in the design and implementation of gain sharing can help to foster fuller acceptance and participation of the plan, increase the level of trust between workers and management, and overcome the problems of social dilemmas (e.g., free-riding) that seem to plague cooperation among people (Cooper, Dyck, and Frohlich, 1992). Finally, management support and commitment to gain sharing (White, 1979; Preiwisch, 1981; Doherty, Nord, and McAdams, 1989), assurances of employee job security (O'Dell and McAdams, 1987), and adequate training, continued inspiration, follow-up, and frequent assessments (Wallace, 1991) all help increase the likelihood that gain sharing will be effective.

Despite its potential, a host of contextual and process-related variables can limit gain sharing's success. Several reviewers (White, 1979; Lawler, 1981; Preiwisch, 1981; Goodman and Dean, 1983; Ross, 1983) noted the effects of structural (e.g., size, technology) and situational (e.g., market and labor force conditions) factors on gain sharing's success. Further, when gain sharing fails (few failures are reported in the literature) or is marred by problems, shortcomings in the plan's construction and/or implementation are often responsible. Reported difficulties include: faulty designs (e.g., problems in construction of the pay formula), lack of support or commitment by management, distrust by employers, poor communications, competing priorities within the organization, and objectives that workers either feel they cannot control or are not contingent on performance (Preiwisch, 1981; Ross, 1983; Doherty, Nord, and McAdams, 1989; Cooper, Dyck, and Frohlich, 1992). Unquestionably, process factors are crucial in the success or failure of gain sharing.

b. Skill-Based Pay. As noted earlier, skill-based or pay-for-knowledge systems tie a person's base wage or salary to his or her repertoire of skills. Employees are paid for the knowledge and skills they have, many of which they acquire while employed by the organization, not the actual job they perform at a given time.

Although little published information and few guidelines exist, several researchers (Lawler and Ledford, 1985; Tosi and Tosi, 1986; Lawler, 1990) have commented on the advantages of skill-based pay. First, skill-based pay provides incentives to be able (and willing) to do more than one job. Consequently, it facilitates reassignment of personnel to solve problems or fill in for others. The organization benefits from leaner staffing, greater flexibility, and fewer problems from absenteeism and turnover.

When embedded within a participative culture, skill-based pay often fosters innovativeness, problem solving, and communication among employees (Lawler and Ledford, 1985). Further, in such contexts, these systems may enhance employees' experiences of control over their pay levels (because of opportunities to affect their pay by increasing their repertoire of skills) and growth (from the variety of skills they have and use). The little evidence available suggests that skill-based pay is associated with increased satisfaction with pay and the job, and fewer feelings that pay is inequitable. The likelihood that workers will be committed to the organization and become self-managing appears to increase as well.

Of course, matters of context and process are important here too. Both Tosi and Tosi (1986) and Lawler (1990) noted that skill-based pay has the best chance of being effective if it is introduced into cultures in which participative management and worker input in decision making are accepted. Finally, skill-based pay is usually not sufficient by itself. However, when it is used in conjunction with other human resource strategies (e.g., job enrichment, autonomous work groups) it enhances the cooperation among workers that is so important for highly interdependent tasks.

On the other hand, skill-based pay has limitations. First, it does not necessarily make rewards contingent on actual performance; therefore, it may be best to supplement it with gain sharing or other performance-based incentive programs. Second, Lawler (1990) noted that it is less valuable when it it difficult to pinpoint and assess skills (e.g., staff support work). Third, large investments in training are necessary and direct pay costs are generally higher. Further, market comparisons are less useful in pricing skills. Finally, as people learn all the relevant skills ("top out"), they may become less motivated (Lawler, 1990).

Other difficulties are encountered in making trade-offs between production and skill acquisition, managing added administrative complexity, and dealing with technological or organizational changes (Lawler and Ledford, 1985; Lawler, 1990). Finally, not all workers respond well to skill-based pay. Tosi and Tosi (1986) indicated that workers with low self-esteem, ability, and/or tolerance for work ambiguity are less likely to be satisfied.

B. Overview

As organizations and society change, so must the ways people are managed. The growth of nontraditional compensation systems is one result. As with most social changes, the present arrangements are stimulated by current events, but they also reflect previous patterns and understandings. Accordingly, many of their components represent extensions or new applications of existing approaches. Then too, many of the problems they encounter may stem from their incompatibilities with thoughts and structures that linger on from the past.

The nontraditional systems we have reviewed foster a particular combination of accountability, flexibility, and innovativeness that fits many of today's more adhocratic organizations. Moreover, nontraditional compensation practices respond to the changing demographics of the workplace and are consistent with the human resources model described by Miles (1975).

As organizations continue to evolve, further changes in compensation systems are likely. Charan's (1991) description of network organizations (i.e., "small companies" inside "larger companies") and the revised compensation systems needed to support them is instructive. According to Charan, the managers in these "small companies" are selected from across the organization's departments and represent several hierarchial levels. To accomplish their mission of shaping and implementing key components of corporate strategy, the networks attempt "to empower managers to talk openly, candidly, and emotionally . . . to evaluate problems from the perspective of what is right for the customer and the company rather than from narrow functional or department interests" (p. 105). Key attributes of performance include sharing information openly, asking for and offering help, and providing emotional commitment to the business. New compensation arrangements are vital to support this work. At the Royal Bank of Canada, for example, network managers are evaluated on such criteria as: business-profit orientation, evidence of making qualitative shifts (e.g., vision, willingness to experiment and change things), intellectual curiosity, and global orientation. Novel approaches to rewards are required. Interestingly, at the Royal Bank, subordinates and peers play important roles in the evaluation process.

In sum, in all probability, organizations will continue to change. As they do, the traditional and the nontraditional arrangements we have reviewed will continue to change as well.

IV. A SYSTEMS VIEW OF COMPENSATION

While students of compensation have long sought to improve organizational performance, until recently they have worked almost exclusively at micro levels—the job or perhaps the workgroup. Traditional and even nontraditional compensation systems have often been advanced as generic solutions, without careful consideration of how well they fit a particular organization's type of business, management style, culture, or strategic objectives. With few exceptions, only in the past few years has compensation been viewed explicitly from a strategic perspective.

The remainder of this section is divided into two parts. The first considers the relationship of compensation and organization strategy—the role compensation systems play as tools for helping organizations achieve strategic goals. In the second part, the use of compensation for purposes of targeted change (and maintenance) is explored.

A. Fit of Compensation to Organization Strategy

Recently, the importance of fitting compensation schemes to organizational and environmental conditions has been noted (Balkin and Gomez-Mejia, 1987; Milkovich, 1988; Balkin and Gomez-Mejia, 1990). Still, for the most part, arguing that effective performance depends on fitting compensation with strategy must depend primarily on intuition and logic. Few empirical findings exist. As Milkovich (1988) noted: "Research on compensation strategy is so recent that little work has been reported on its effects on organization performance or employee behavior" (pp. 283–284). The findings that do exist, however, support intuition and logic.

In an investigation of 20 large industrial firms, Kerr (1985) found that strategic objectives of effective organizations often coincided with features of their reward systems. For example, organizations that adopted a steady-state approach to diversification and focused on existing products and markets typically utilized reward systems that evaluated performance subjectively and based rewards on position. In contrast, performance-based compensation was associated with evolutionary diversification strategies and emphasis on growth through mergers and acquisitions.

Similarly, Balkin and Gomez-Mejia (1987) investigated the relationship between compensation and organizational strategy in high-tech and non-high-tech firms. In profiling the mix of salary, incentives, and benefits offered as a function of the firm's stage in its product life cycle (e.g., growth or mature) and size (e.g., small or large), they found the ratio of incentive pay to total compensation was highest in small, high-tech firms at the growth stage of the product life cycle. The more closely the organizations fit this profile, the greater their effectiveness.

In a later study, Balkin and Gomez-Mejia (1990) considered relationships of the design of pay packages, marketing position, and pay policies with corporate and business unit strategy. The labels they used to describe their findings, "mechanistic" and "organic," closely parallel the bureaucratic/traditional versus adhocratic/nontraditional distinctions used in this chapter. Mechanistic firms (ones at the maintenance stage that emphasized related products diversification) typically relied on traditional salary and benefits, and paid above market levels. Their pay policies were job-based, short-term oriented, and characterized by pay secrecy, seniority, and low employee input. In contrast, organic firms (those at growth stages, relying on single-product diversification) emphasized incentives, paid below the market, and featured open communication about pay and pay-for-performance. They also were likely to feature skill-based systems, employee participation, and a long-term orientation.

In a related study, Gerhart and Milkovich (1990) concluded that individual, job, and environmental factors were necessary, but not sufficient for explaining compensation practices. Based on a survey of 14,000 managers in 200 firms, they suggested that organizational strategy is critical for understanding the use and success of different pay systems.

While the evidence is sparse, what does exist suggests some answers to a question of considerable theoretical and practical importance: What compensation systems are best for advancing various organization strategies? Some time ago, Salter (1973) attempted to answer this question regarding incentives for executives. He concluded that compensation systems reflect four policy choices: (1) maintaining a short- versus long-run perspective, (2) assuming a risk-aversion versus risk-taking position, (3) supporting interdivisional relationships, and (4) supporting necessary company-division relationships. Six specific decisions operationalize the policy choices: (1) specific financial instruments to gain motivation and cost-effectiveness, (2) appropriate performance measures for allocating incentives, (3) degree of reliance on management or formula-based methods in determining rewards, (4) size and frequency of incentive awards, (5) degree of uniformity in performance measures and rewards among levels and divisions, and (6) method for funding the compensation plan.

Hufnagel's (1987) examination of the fit among three compensation systems and strategic planning provided a more finely tuned perspective. Hufnagel observed that "output-oriented" systems: reward outcomes rather than behavior, leave little opportunity for management discretion, and reward goal achievement over the long term. She concluded that they are best suited to firms with "linear" strategies (rational, long-range planning approaches) and organizations that are relatively insulated from the environment. Such firms are able to anticipate or predict changes, and are thus able to benefit by integrating their decisions, actions, and plans and managing their current capabilities.

"Flexible" compensation systems are concerned with both outcomes and behavior. Hufnagel indicated that they use performance goals to match business needs and strategic issues. Flexible systems are best suited to organizations having "adaptive" orientations—planning based on constant monitoring of the environment. These organizations adjust their businesses and change resource allocations to match perceived opportunities.

"Process-oriented" compensation, Hufnagel's third type, encourages organizational learning, teamwork, and innovation. Challenging performance standards are set and risk taking is not penalized. This orientation, according to Hufnagel, is best suited to an "interpretative" strategy—one based on optimizing social exchange, negotiating objectives, and fitting the organization's values to its strategic mission.

While the literature we have reviewed reflects considerable diversity, Milkovich (1988) was able to distill the variables concerning the fit of compensation systems to strategic objectives into two dimensions: (1) defining the critical employee groups (e.g., executives, R&D, sales), and (2) making appropriate policy choices (competitiveness, internal structure, mix of compensation types, basis for increases, role in overall human resources strategy, and administrative style). Factors that might affect these decisions concern the organization's business strategy (corporate, business unit, human resources), internal environment (e.g., organization type, use of internal labor market, size, profitability, costs), and external environment (e.g., legislative changes, labor unions, and product and labor market pressures).

Compensation systems provide organizations with effective tools to translate the general and long-term dimensions of strategy to the specific and day-to-day actions of employees. As Lei, Slocum, and Slater (1990) noted, fitting an organization's reward system with its culture and strategic objectives is critical for securing a competitive advantage.

B. Compensation as an Agent of Change

Just as they can serve to translate general strategic aims into concrete terms, compensation systems can also guide changes in an organization's overall development and culture.

Lawler (1981) noted that to change successfully, organizations often need to alter many components (e.g., human resources, accounting). Since changing multiple subsystems simultaneously is difficult (to say the least), Lawler observed that often "one or more systems become lead systems in the change effort and others become lag systems" (p. 197). Reward systems can play both roles; they may either lead or lag in an initiative.

Whether reward systems should lead or lag depends in part on the degree of fit among the strategy, culture, and reward system that currently exists (Doherty and McAdams, 1993). In some organizations this fit is strong. The highly publicized Lincoln Electric Company is a prime example. For decades, its reward system has contributed to an organizational culture that is well suited to the company's low-cost strategy, and the existing subsystems generally support each other. In such organizations, Doherty and McAdams (1993) argued that rewards may best play "supportive" (or lag) roles, reinforcing incremental changes and highlighting underattended areas.

When reward, strategic, and cultural subsystems do not support each other, Doherty and McAdams argued that organizations are generally in trouble and experience frequent and major changes. Reward systems in these contexts can be excellent means for stimulating or leading change efforts. By calling attention to the need for a different protocol in rewarding performance, new reward systems can signal that maintaining the status quo is no longer sufficient and that different ways of behaving are required. Introduction of gain sharing may be very useful in such situations.

In short, compensation systems can do more than merely reinforce existing patterns; they may be used to instigate or catalyze desired change. Once the strategic role that reward systems can play is recognized, it is clear that most organizations have failed to tap the full potential of compensation for reaching their goals.

V. EXPANDING THE STUDY OF COMPENSATION

We have argued that a compensation system is influenced by and must be responsive to an organization's changing environment. Further, we have suggested that macro political/economic environments help to shape compensation systems in many ways, including by influencing the assumptions managers (and researchers) hold about organizations and their employees. However, our review of the compensation literature revealed little attention to these macro level factors. Unfortunately, this omission tends to characterize much of the work on rewards in the field of organization behavior.

As Baron and Cook (1992:196), the editors of the *Administrative Science Quarterly*'s special issue on rewards, lamented the papers submitted to this special issue seem characteristic of the literature as a whole, in that the strongest contributions generally paid limited attention to the larger milieu within which organizational reward systems are embedded. As recent events in Eastern Europe and the former Soviet Union so vividly demonstrate, the political, social, and economic context can have profound organizational implications. There appears to be a shortage of scholarship aimed at understanding how macro-level concerns (including societal-level inequalities) shape allocative processes within organizations and, conversely, how inequalities and injustices within organizations influence the broader society.

Baron and Cook's last point is extremely important; compensation systems are dialectically related to the structure of societies. Compensation systems reflect, introduce, institutionalize, and otherwise perpetuate social values and norms. They also affect the distribution of wealth and life chances (Dahrendorf, 1979) among members of society. Recognition of these facts is critical for understanding the dynamics of our own political economy and those of nations with whom we are becoming increasingly interdependent. In this light, we urge students of compensation to expand their work to encompass political, economic, and sociological dimensions more fully.

Such inquiry demands historical grounding. Braudel's (1982) analysis of the complex social evolution associated with the movement from feudal and agrarian society to urbanization and wage labor is a good place to embark. Starting there positions us to see the interplay of continuity and discontinuity in fostering cooperation. We become more aware of how systems of compensation coevolve with the larger networks of social and economic exchanges and how compensation systems help to construct social realities and vice versa. We come to see how any given compensation system and the ideologies that surround it are special cases of the general process through which humans satisfy their needs individually and collectively.

Such a perspective should make understanding compensation less parochial and less tied to traditional beliefs. It should help us to come to terms with the growing diversity organizations face because of changing life-styles at home and with participation in a global economy. For example, recognition that today's compensation system is a special case—a product of a particular social context—should increase receptivity to consideration of the "strange" forms compensation takes in other nations. It also reveals that new forms of fringe benefits (e.g., day care) to serve single-parent and dual-career families are parts of the broad spectrum of social evolution, not some special concession. They are simply another move in the changing relationship between employers and employees (Jacoby, 1985). Finally, the contextual view calls attention to "externalities" of compensation, including social stratification. Although we leave detailed treatment of these externalities for another time, we view them as extremely important.

In sum, the study of compensation needs to be expanded for both intellectual and practical reasons. As our understanding becomes less constrained by traditional, parochial beliefs, we will find it easier to come to terms with the diversity of life-styles at home and the contrasting social patterns in other nations. As a result, we will be better prepared to design compensation systems that gain high levels of cooperation in diverse settings at low cost—all the while contributing to human welfare.

ACKNOWLEDGMENT

The help of Norma Walker and Angie Lane is preparing this chapter is gratefully acknowledged.

REFERENCES

Adams, J. S. (1965). Injustice in social exchange. In *Advances in Experimental Social Psychology* (L. Berkowitz, ed.), Academic Press, New York, pp. 267–299.
Axelrod, R. (1984). *The Evolution of Cooperation*. Basic Books, New York.

Balkin, D. B., and Gomez-Mejia, L. R. (1987). Toward a contingency theory of compensation strategy. *Strategic Management Journal, 8*(2): 169–182.

Balkin, D. B., and Gomez-Mejia, L. R. (1990). Matching compensation and organizational strategies. *Strategic Management Journal, 11*(2): 153–169.

Bandura, A. (1977). *Social Learning Theory.* Prentice Hall, Englewood Cliffs, N.J.

Baron, J. N., and Cook, K. S. (1992). Process and outcome: Perspectives on the distribution of rewards in organizations. *Administrative Science Quarterly, 37*(2): 191–197.

Beer, M. (1980). *Organizational Change and Development: A Systems View.* Goodyear, Santa Monica, Calif.

Belcher, D. W., and Atchison, T. J. (1976). Compensation for work. In *Handbook of Work, Organization, and Society* (R. Dubin, ed.), Rand McNally, Chicago, pp. 567–611.

Berger, L. A. (1991). Trends and issues for the 1990s: Creating a viable framework for compensation design. In *The Compensation Handbook* (M. L. Rock and L. A. Berger, eds.), McGraw-Hill, New York, pp. 12–23.

Berkowitz, L., Fraser, C., Treasure, F. P., and Cochran, S. (1987). Pay, equity, job gratifications, and comparisons in pay satisfaction. *Journal of Applied Psychology, 72*(4): 544–551.

Braudel, F. (1982). *The Wheels of Commerce* (vol. 2 of Civilization & Capitalism 15th–18th century). Harper & Row, New York.

Brief, A. P., and Aldag, R. J. (1989). The economic functions of work. *Research in Personnel and Human Resources Management, 7:* 1–23.

Brief, A. P., and Nord, W. R. (1990). *Meanings of Occupational Work.* Lexington Books, Lexington, Mass.

Burawoy, M. (1979). *Manufacturing Consent: Changes in the Labor Process Under Monopoly Capitalism.* University of Chicago Press, Chicago.

Burns, T., and Stalker, G. M. (1961). *The Management of Innovation.* Tavistock, London, U.K.

Charan, R. (1991). How networks reshape organizations—for results. *Harvard Business Review, 69*(5): 104–115.

Clancy, J. J. (1989). *The Invisible Powers.* Lexington Books, Lexington, Mass.

Cook, F. W. (1991). Merit pay and performance appraisal. In *The Compensation Handbook* (M. L. Rock and L. A. Berger, eds.), McGraw-Hill, New York, pp. 542–566.

Cooper, C., Dyck, B., Frohlich, N. (1992). Improving the effectiveness of gainsharing: The role of fairness and participation. *Administrative Science Quarterly, 37:* 471–490.

Cummings, T. G., and Molloy, E. S. (1977). *Improving Productivity and the Quality of Work Life.* Praeger, New York.

Cyert, R. M., and March, J. G. (1963). *A Behavioral Theory of the Firm.* Prentice Hall, Englewood Cliffs, N.J.

Dahrendorf, R. (1979). *Life Chances.* University of Chicago Press, Chicago.

deCharms, R. (1968). *Personal Causation: The Internal Affective Determinants of Behavior.* Academic Press, New York.

Deci, E. L. (1972). The effects of contingent and noncontingent rewards and controls on intrinsic motivation. *Organizational Behavior and Human Performance, 8:* 217–229.

Deci, E. L. (1975). *Intrinsic Motivation.* Plenum, New York.

Deci, E. L., and Ryan, R. M. (1980). The empirical exploration of intrinsic motivational processes. In *Advances in Experimental Social Psychology,* vol. 13 (L. Berkowitz, ed.), Academic Press, New York, pp. 39–80.

Doherty, E. M., Nord, W. R., and McAdams, J. L. (1989). Gainsharing and organizational development: A productive synergy. *Journal of Applied Behavioral Science, 25*(3): 209–229.

Doherty, E. M., and McAdams, J. L. (1993). Micro and macro perspectives on gain sharing: Achieving organizational change with alternative reward strategies. In *Handbook of Organizational Consultation* (R. T. Golembiewski, ed.), Marcel Dekker, New York, pp. 161–171.

Dyer, L., and Theriault, R. (1976). The determinants of pay satisfaction. *Journal of Applied Psychology, 61*(5): 596–604.

Emerson, H. (1911). *Efficiency as a Basis for Operation and Wages.* Engineering Magazine Co., New York.

Etzioni, A. (1988). *The Moral Dimension: Toward a New Economics.* The Free Press, New York.

Fanning, D. (Feb. 4, 1990). Butlers and crystal, as well as a view. *New York Times,* sec. 3, pt. 2, p. 29.

Fayol, H. (1949). *General and Industrial Management* (trans. by, C. Storrs), Pitman Publishing, London, U.K.

Fein, M. (1976). Motivation for work. In *Handbook of Work, Organization, and Society* (R. Dubin, ed.), Rand McNally, Chicago.

Frederiksen, L. W. (1982). *Handbook of Organizational Behavior Management*. John Wiley, New York.

Frost, C. F., Wakeley, J. H., and Ruh, R. A. (1974). *The Scanlon Plan for Organization Development: Identity, Participation, and Equity*. Michigan State University Press, East Lansing.

Gaertner, K. N., and Gaertner, G. H. (1985). Performance–contingent pay for federal managers. *Administration & Society, 17*(1): 7–20.

Gerhart, B., and Milkovich, G. T. (1990). Organizational differences in managerial compensation and financial performance. *Academy of Management Journal, 33*(4): 663–691.

Goodman, P. S., and Dean, J. W. Jr. (1983). Making productivity programs last. In *Productivity Gain Sharing* (B. E. Graham-Moore and T. L. Ross, eds.), Prentice–Hall, Englewood Cliffs, N. J., pp. 122–140.

Gouldner, A. W. (1960). The norm of reciprocity: A preliminary statement. *American Sociological Review, 25*(2): 161–179.

Graham-Moore, B., and Ross, T. L. (1990). *Gainsharing: Plans for Improving Performance*. The Bureau of National Affairs, Inc., Washington, D.C.

Greenberg, J. (1987). A taxonomy of organizational justice theories. *Academy of Management Review, 12*(1): 9–37.

Gross, B. M. (1968). *Organizations and Their Managing*. Free Press, New York.

Hatcher, L. L., and Ross, T. L. (1985). Organization development through productivity gain sharing. *Personnel, 62*(10): 42–50.

Hauck, W. C. (1987). Productivity improvement at branch banks. *National Productivity Review, 6*(3): 243–249.

Heneman, H. G. III (1985). Pay satisfaction. In *Research in Personnel and Human Resources Management*, vol. 3 (K. M. Rowland and G. R. Ferris, eds.), JAI Press, Greenwich, Conn., pp. 115–139.

Heneman, R. L. (1990). Merit pay research. *Research in Personnel and Human Resources Management*, vol. 8 (G. R. Rowland & K. M. Ferris, ed.), JAI Press. Greenwich, Conn., pp. 203–263.

Heneman, R. L., Greenberger, D. B., and Strasser, S. (1988). The relationship between pay-for-performance perceptions and pay satisfaction. *Personnel Psychology, 41*(4): 745–759.

Herzberg, F., Mausner, B., and Snyderman, B. B. (1959). *The Motivation to Work*. John Wiley, New York.

Hills, F. S. (1979). The pay-for-performance dilemma. *Personnel, 56:* 23–31.

Hirschorn, C., and Gilmore, T. (1992). The new boundaries of the "boundaryless" company. *Harvard Business Review, 70*(3): 104–115.

Hufnagel, E. M. (1987). Developing strategic compensation plans. *Human Resource Management, 26*(1): 93–108.

Hyman, A. (1982). *Charles Babbage: Pioneer of the Computer*. Princeton University Press, Princeton, N. J.

Ingster, B. (1991). Budgeting, auditing, and control systems for salary administration. In *The Compensation Handbook* (M. L. Rock and L. A. Berger, eds.), McGraw-Hill, New York, pp. 113–121.

Jacoby, S. M. (1985). *Employing Bureaucracy*. Columbia University Press, New York.

Jensen, M. C., and Murphy, K. J. (1990). CEO incentives: It's not how much you pay, but how. *Harvard Business Review, 68:* 138–153.

Kanin-Lovers, J. (1991). Job-evaluation technology. In *The Compensation Handbook* (M. L. Rock and L. A. Berger, eds.), McGraw-Hill, New York, pp. 72–86.

Kanter, R. M. (1987). The attack on pay. *Harvard Business Review, 65:* 60–67.

Kelly, J. E. (1982). *Scientific Management, Job Redesign and Work Performance*. Academic Press, London, U.K.

Kendrick, J. W. (1987). Group financial incentives: An evaluation. *Incentives, Cooperation, and Risk Sharing* (H. R. Nalbantian, ed.), Rowman & Littlefield, Totowa, N. J., pp. 120–136.

Kerr, J. L. (1985). Diversification strategies and managerial rewards: An empirical study. *Academy of Management Journal, 28*(1): 155–179.

Kerr, J. L., and Slocum, J. W. Jr. (1987). Managing corporate culture through reward systems. *Academy of Management Executive, 1*(2): 99–108.

Kondrasuk, J. N. (1981). Studies in MBO effectiveness. *Academy of Management Review, 6*(3): 419–430.

Lange, N. R. (1991). Job analysis and documentation. *The Compensation Handbook* (M. L. Rock and L. A. Berger, eds.), McGraw-Hill, New York, pp. 49–71.

Lawler, E. E. III. (1971). *Pay and Organizational Effectiveness: A Psychological View*. McGraw-Hill, New York.

Lawler, E. E. (1975). Pay participation and organization change. In *Man and Society* (E. L. Cass and F. G. Zimmer, eds.), Van Nostrand Reinhold, New York, pp. 137–149.

Lawler, E. E. III (1981). *Pay and Organization Development*. Addison-Wesley, Reading, Mass.

Lawler, E. E. III (1987). Pay for performance: A motivational analysis. In *Incentives, Cooperation, and Risk Sharing* (H. R. Nalbantian, ed.), Rowman & Littlefield, Totowa. N. J., pp. 69–86.

Lawler, E. E. III (1988). Gainsharing theory and research: Findings and future directions. In *Research in Organizational Change and Development*, vol. 2 (W. A. Pasmore and R. Woodman, eds.), JAI Press, Greenwich, Conn., pp. 323–344.

Lawler, E. E. III (1990). *Strategic Pay*. Jossey-Bass, San Francisco, Calif.

Lawler, E. E. III (1991). Employee involvement and pay system design. In *The Compensation Handbook* (M. L. Rock and L. A. Berger, eds.), McGraw-Hill, New York, pp. 592–603.

Lawler, E. E. III, and Ledford, G. E. Jr. (1985). Skill-based pay: A concept that's catching on. *Personnel, 62*(9): 30–37.

Lei, D., Slocum, J. W. Jr., and Slater, R. W. (1990). Global strategy and reward systems: The key roles of management development and corporate culture. *Organizational Dynamics, 19*(2): 27–41.

Lichty, D. T. (1991). Compensation surveys. In *The Compensation Handbook* (M. L. Rock and L. A. Berger, eds.), McGraw-Hill, New York, pp. 87–103.

Longenecker, C. O., Sims, H. P. Jr., and Gioia, D. A. (1987). Behind the mask: The politics of employee appraisal. *The Academy of Management Executive, 1*(3): 183–193.

Mahoney, T. A. (1989). Multiple pay contingencies: Strategic design of compensation. *Human Resource Management, 28*(3): 337–347.

Marriott, R. (1957). *Incentive Payment Systems: A Review of Research and Opinion*. Staples Press, London, U.K.

Marx, K. (1967). *Capital: A Critique of Political Economy*, vol. 1. International Publishers, New York.

Maslow, A. H. (1943). A theory of human motivation. *Psychological Review, 50:* 370–396.

Maslow, A. H. (1954). *Motivation and Personality*. Harper and Brothers, New York.

Maslow, A. H. (1970). *Motivation and Personality*. 2nd ed., Harper and Row, New York.

McAdams, J. L. (1991). Nonmonetary awards. In *The Compensation Handbook* (M. L. Rock and L. A. Berger, eds.), McGraw–Hill, New York, pp. 218–235.

Metzger, B. L. (1966). *Profit Sharing in Perspective*, 2nd ed., Profit Sharing Research Foundation, Evanston, Ill.

Meyer, H. H. (1975). The pay-for-performance dilemma. *Organizational Dynamics, 3:* 39–50.

Meyer, G. W., and Stott, R. G. (1985). Quality circles: Panacea or Pandora's box? *Organizational Dynamics, 13:* 34–50.

Miceli, M. P., Jung, I., Near, J. P., and Greenberger, D. B. (1991). Predictors and outcomes of reactions to pay-for-performance plans. *Journal of Applied Psychology, 76*(4): 508–521.

Miles, R. E. (1975). *Theories of Management: Implications for Organizational Behavior and Development*. McGraw–Hill, New York.

Milkovich, G. T. (1988). A strategic perspective on compensation management. In *Research in Personnel and Human Resources Management*, vol. 6 (G. R. Ferris and K. M. Rowland, eds.), JAI Press, Greenwich, Conn., pp. 263–288.

Miller, C. Z., and Schuster, M. H. (1987). Gain sharing plans: A comparative analysis. *Organizational Dynamics, 16*(1): 44–67.

Mintzberg, H. (1979). *The Structuring of Organizations*. Prentice Hall, Englewood Cliffs, N.J.

Munchus, G. III (1983). Employer-employee based quality circles in Japan: Human resource policy implications for American firms. *Academy of Management Review, 8*(2): 255–261.

Nelson, D. (1975). *Managers and Workers: Origins of the New Factory System in the United States, 1880–1920*. University of Wisconsin Press, Madison.

Nord, W. R. (1969). Beyond the teaching machine: The neglected area of operant conditioning in the theory and practice of management. *Organizational Behavior and Human Performance, 4:* 375–401.

Nord, W. R., and Durand, D. E. (1975). Beyond resistance to change: Behavioral science on the firing line. *Organizational Dynamics, 4*(2): 2–19.

O'Brien, R. M., Dickinson, A. M., and Rosow, M. P. (1982). *Industrial Behavior Modification: A Management Handbook*. Pergamon Press, Elmsford, N.Y.

O'Dell, C., and McAdams, J. L. (1987). *People, Performance, and Pay*. American Productivity Center, Houston, Tex.

Patton, A. (1972). Why incentive plans fail. *Harvard Business Review, 50*(3): 58–66.

Perry, J. L., and Pearce, J. L. (1983). Initial reactions to federal merit pay. *Personnel Journal, 62*(3): 230–237.

Perry, J. L., and Petrakis, B. A. (1988). Can pay for performance succeed in government? *Public Personnel Management, 17*(4): 359–367.

Porter, L. W., and Lawler, E. E. III (1968). *Managerial Attitudes and Performance*. Irwin, Homewood, Ill.

Preiwisch, C. F. (1981). GAO study on productivity-sharing programs. In *Productivity Improvement: Case Studies of Proven Practice* (V. M. Buehler and Y. K. Shetty, eds.), AMACOM, pp. 177–200.

Rich, J. T., and Larson, J. A. (1984). Why some long-term incentives fail. In *Incentives, Cooperation, and Risk Sharing* (H. R. Nalbantian, ed.), Rowman & Littlefield, Totowa, N.J., pp. 151–162.

Rock, M. L., and Berger, L. A. (1991). *The Compensation Handbook*. McGraw-Hill, New York.

Rodgers, D. T. (1974). *The Work Ethic in Industrial America: 1850–1920*. University of Chicago, Chicago.

Roethlisberger, F. J. (1941). *Management and Morale*. Harvard University Press, Cambridge, Mass.

Ross, T. L. (1983). Why PG fails in some firms. In *Productivity Gain Sharing* (B. E. Graham-Moore and T. L. Ross, eds.), Prentice-Hall, Englewood Cliffs, N.J., pp. 141–156.

Roy, T. S. Jr. (1991). Pricing and the development of salary structures. In *The Compensation Handbook* (M. L. Rock and L. A. Berger, eds.), McGraw-Hill, New York, pp. 104–112.

Salter, M. S. (1973). Tailor incentive compensation to strategy. *Harvard Business Review, 51*(2): 94–102.

Schay, B. W. (1988). Effects of performance-contingent pay on employee attitudes. *Public Personnel Management, 17*(2): 237–250.

Schein, E. H. (1986). International human resource management: New directions, perpetual issues, and missing themes. *Human Resource Management, 25*(1): 169–176.

Schuler, R. S. (1990). Repositioning the human resource function: Transformation or demise? *Academy of Management Executive, 4*(3): 49–60.

Siegel, G. B. (1989). Compensation, benefits and work schedules. *Public Personnel Management, 18*(2): 176–192.

Silverman, B. R. S. (1983). Why the merit pay system failed in the federal government. *Personnel Journal, 62*(4): 294–302.

Skinner, B. F. (1953). *Science and Human Behavior*. MacMillan, New York.

Stiglitz, J. E. (1987). The design of labor contracts: The economics of incentives and risk sharing. *Incentives, Cooperation, and Risk Sharing* (H. R. Nalbantian, ed.), Rowman & Littlefield, Totowa, N.J., pp. 47–68.

Stonebraker, P. W. (1985). Flexible and incentive benefits: A guide to program development. *Compensation Review, 17*(2): 40–53.

Tang, T. L. (1992). The meaning of money revisited. *Journal of Organizational Behavior, 13*(2): 197–202.

Taylor, F. W. (1967). *The Principles of Scientific Management*. The Norton Library, New York.

Taylor, S. E., and Brown, J. D. (1988). Illusion and well-being: A social psychological perspective on mental health. *Psychological Bulletin, 103:* 193–210.

Tosi, H., and Tosi, L. (1986). What managers need to know about knowledge-based pay. *Organizational Dynamics, 14*(3): 52–64.

Vroom, V. H. (1964). *Work and Motivation*. Wiley, New York.

Wallace, M. J. Jr. (1991). Sustaining success with alternative rewards. In *The Compensation Handbook* (M. L. Rock and L. A. Berger, eds.), McGraw-Hill, New York, pp. 147–157.

Weick, K. E. (1979). *The Social Psychology of Organizing*. Addison-Wesley, Reading, Mass.

Weitzman, M. L., and Kruse, D. L. (1990). Profit sharing and productivity. In *Paying for Productivity* (A. S. Blinder, ed.), The Brookings Institution, Washington, D.C., pp. 95–140.

Wernimont, P. F., and Fitzpatrick, S. (1972). The meaning of money. *Journal of Applied Psychology, 56*(3): 218–226.

White, J. K. (1979). The Scanlon plan: Causes and correlates of success. *Academy of Management Journal, 22:* 292–312.

Whyte, W. F. (1955). *Money and Motivation*. Harper & Brothers, New York.

Williamson, O. E. (1981). The economics of organization: The transaction cost approach. *American Journal of Sociology, 87:* 548–577.

Wisdom, B. L. (1989). Before implementing a merit system: Know the environments and situations that demand caution. *Personnel Administrator, 34*(10): 46–49.

Wolfe, M. G. (1991). Theories, approaches, and practices of salary administration: An overview. In *The Compensation Handbook* (M. L. Rock and L. A. Berger, eds.), McGraw–Hill, New York, pp. 48–48.

Wren, D. A. (1972). *The Evolution of Management Thought*. Ronald Press Company, New York.

20

Technological Competence, Ethics, and the Global Village
Cross-National Comparisons for Organization Research

Urs E. Gattiker

The University of Lethbridge, Lethbridge, Alberta, Canada

Kelvin Willoughby

University of Western Australia, Perth, Western Australia, Australia

International trade is thriving, while the diversity of people within countries and firms is increasing (e.g., guest workers, immigrants, refugees, and illegal aliens). In light of such developments, demand grows for sociological, psychological, and organizational behavior research and theory applicable beyond one firm, country, or continent. In addition, the growing importance of technology for remaining competitive in the market is leading to rapid changes affecting workers and society alike.

A response by researchers to the above developments has resulted in a rise in cross-national studies assessing and comparing attitudes toward technology and how they relate to its effective use (e.g., Gattiker and Nelligan, 1988; Early and Stubblebine, 1989). Others have appraised and compared the efforts of countries in keeping their workers abreast of new technology-related developments, thereby assuring that workers' competence levels match the requirements of the workplace (e.g., Muszynski and Wolfe, 1989). While some research grounded in ideological beliefs suggests deskilling of workers through increased technology applications in the United States (e.g., Braverman, 1974), labor market developments in Germany suggest instead that upskilling accelerates with increased use of technology (Littek and Heisig, 1991).

Politicians, too, have responded to the changing times by placing a high priority upon technology-related training of citizens. All this flurry of activity is intended to improve the workforce's technological competence (e.g., technological skills and knowledge), ultimately allowing countries to remain competitive in the international marketplace.

However, without an appropriate theoretical framework, researchers encounter great difficulty in interpreting why one country's workforce may have the necessary technological

An earlier version of this paper was presented at the Seventh Annual Conference of the Society for Industrial and Organizational Psychology, Inc. held in Montreal in 1992. Portions were also presented at the 1993 Annual Convention of the American Psychological Association held in Toronto and at one of the "Rip-Off" research seminars at The University of Lethbridge. We thank seminar and conference participants for their useful comments and encouragement on earlier drafts.

457

competence to succeed, while another's may not. Differences between nations and firms may suggest, for instance, why technology sometimes leads to deskilling of jobs in the United States while it may lead to upskilling in Germany. However, researchers are required to explain the "why" of such differences (cf. Hoff, Lappe, and Lempert, 1983, Part 1) in order to allow managers and politicians to use this information for the benefit of both workers and citizens. A visible example is that of politicians making public policy decisions about continuous education programs and expenditures.

This chapter attempts to inject some order into the cross-national debate about how technological change may affect worker skills and competence. In Section I, the authors selectively review and evaluate the current status of research dealing with cross-national issues, and develop a new framework integrating cross-cultural psychological, anthropological, and sociological thought. Section II outlines how internationalization affects an individual's or region's efforts to develop technological competence and skills. Section III discusses the cultural and ethical challenges for society in an environment in which competitiveness and technology have been heralded as the solution to most, if not all, economic woes. Finally, Section IV outlines conclusions and implications for managers as well as the most promising directions for future research.

I. CROSS-NATIONAL ISSUES

Existing cross-national comparisons indicate numerous differences in the definition of work (England and Harpaz, 1990), in self-rating of performance compared with supervisory ratings by Taiwanese and U.S. workers (Farh, Dobbins, and Cheng, 1991), and in organizational commitment levels in Japan and the United States (e.g., Luthans, McCaul, and Dodd, 1985; Near, 1989), as well as between the United States and Canada (Cohen and Gattiker, 1992). Conceptual models concerning how cross-national issues affect technology transfer (e.g., Kedia and Bhagat, 1988) and training effectiveness (e.g., Black and Mendenhall, 1990) have also been offered.

Although such research and theoretical work are important, they often fail to explain or account for the behavioral differences between groups of workers. In part this difficulty is perpetuated by the concept of culture, which can be defined in various ways. Even if the researcher were to choose an appropriate concept of culture, its successful application in the field would be constrained by the scarcity of financing, time, and human resources (cf. Adler, 1982). In this section, a framework is developed that integrates cultural contributions from the fields of management, psychology, anthropology, and sociology. The objective is to develop a model for cross-national research that takes into consideration budgetary and time constraints. This model allows for a thorough understanding of the differences and similarities reported between samples.

A. The Meaning of Culture

Any society may be thought of as having a variety of cultural "themes," rather than a single culture. These themes are composed of various interpretations and heterodoxies of the core culture, in addition to any incursions that may have developed around the core, as by ethnic groups. Cultural diversity in countries has been increasing due to the internationalization of business via, for example, subsidiaries in foreign countries, while the workforce has become more varied because of the entry of guest workers, immigrants, and refugees[1]. Cross-national studies about individual and organizational phenomena are concerned with the systematic study of the behavior and experience of organizational participants in different cultures. A brief discussion of the most pertinent cultural issues is given below. For an extensive review see also Triandis (1977).

1. Anthropology and Sociology

Most anthropological studies contain one or more of the following cultural derivatives: *symbol* (including language, architecture, and artifacts), *myth, ideational systems* (including ideology), and *ritual*. While anthropologists and sociologists continue to debate the correct usages and meanings of these concepts, most studies treat them only as motivational factors for individuals and groups (Silverman, 1970).

Another important dimension of cross-cultural research has been cultural stability, of which the common view is that less stability encourages cultural diversity and change. Goldstone (1987) suggested that cultural diversity and ferment favor innovation. In contrast, enforcement of a state of orthodoxy, which perpetuates old models, is likely to result in society's hostility toward innovation and risk taking. A tolerance of pluralism, therefore, enhances openness toward these two elements. For organizations this means that cultural instability encourages innovation and adaptation, while orthodoxy reduces the tolerance for new ideas and therefore hinders innovation (Perry and Sandholtz, 1988).

Organizational theory using a sociological framework has formed the basis for the "culture-free hypothesis" (see Hickson et al., 1974; and Hickson and McMillan, 1981). This hypothesis suggests that cultural differences, or contextual variables, may have little, if any, effect on such organizational structure variables as size, specialization, and formalization (e.g., Miller, 1987). However, as Meyer and Scott (1983: 14) emphasized, the role of institutional environments, defined as "including the rules and belief systems as well as the relational networks that arise in the broader societal context," will influence organizational structure and behavior. For instance, Maurice, Sorge, and Warner (1980) show that organizational processes develop within an institutional logic that is unique to a society. Therefore, while structure, specialization, and technology may appear similar across countries, their interpretation and application may differ according to the national context (e.g., Hofstede, 1984).

Research indicates that concern about transferability of concepts, models, theories, and frameworks across national boundaries is growing. Cross-national studies on technological issues allow for the transcending of limits in one society while establishing the generality (or the limitations) of a theory and/or model (Kohn, 1989). Researchers try to use inductive logic for understanding the similarities and dissimilarities between populations in order to explain different results.

2. Psychology

Like the sociologists, psychologists have recently questioned the ability of theories and concepts to enable researchers to generalize beyond one context, whether firm or country. Specifically, most organizational theories and research have originated in North America (i.e., the United States and to a very small extent, Canada). Cultural issues are addressed from a North American point of view, and for better or worse, the approaches propagated there predominate (e.g., Moghaddam, 1987). As a result, this North American dominance has been rejected by Europeans who have tried to move toward a European type of social psychology. This separate development is partly due to European social psychology's greater emphasis on cooperation and conflict, conformity, philosophy of science, criticisms of science, and racial and ethnic issues than is found in its North American equivalent (Fisch and Daniel, 1982)l.

A dominant North American framework, especially in cross-cultural psychology and management, is that proposed by Triandis and Vassiliou (1972). These authors posed the distinction between *subjective* and *objective culture*, and although researchers have made considerable efforts in applying these concepts in various studies (e.g., Pepitone and Triandis, 1987), wide applicability has been difficult. Subjective culture is defined as a group's characteristic way of perceiving its social environment. For example, office workers could differ in their attitudes toward computers based on demographic characteristics such as gender (e.g., Gattiker, Gutek, and Berger, 1988).

Triandis (1977: 144) suggested several sets of variables that should help in classifying subjective culture (see Table 1). A subjective culture study can be classified into five groups of variables, and as Table 1 outlines, objective culture can be measured using two groups of variables.

Often cultural moderators are used to interpret findings about the subjective culture, such as data from studies assessing attitudes, for example, about the political system and market (Farh, Dobbins, and Cheng, 1991), or formal and/or legal/political support structures for worker participation in firms (Heller et al., 1988: 224). Unfortunately, what Triandis calls objective culture is not directly measurable, so its relationship and possible moderating effect on subjective culture cannot be assessed (e.g., formal and/or legal structures for worker participation and their effects upon satisfaction; Heller et al., 1988, chap. 5). Thus, the reader can either accept the interpretation given by the authors or use his or her own, while in either case a comprehensive understanding of "why" and "how" these differences occurred is not possible.

This problem is not only prevalent for researchers. Many students attending universities away from home write papers dealing with technological and cross-national issues based primarily on U.S.-grounded models and studies. Thus, North American ethnocentrism (i.e., the tendency by scholars to overlook the applicability of their concepts and theories beyond their own country and/or culture) will extend into the training of future managers by those learning about technology and cross-national issues through North American "tinted glasses."

B. Defining Culture: An Interdisciplinary Approach

In summary, the currently utilized frameworks for studying cross-national issues tend to operationalize culture by either (1) determining its degrees of stability and orthodoxy or (2) using a temporal continuum to assess subjective culture. In the context of this chapter the authors assume that *culture represents both a stability and an individual/environmental dimension* (objective/subjective continuum using Triandis' terminology).

As Figure 1 reflects

1. The x-axis (horizontal) is a continuum that ranges from the micro focus (i.e., the individual) to the macro perspective (i.e., the environment) of a culture.
2. The y-axis (vertical) represents the level of stability of the culture ranging from low stability [e.g., approximate subjective (opinions)] to high stability [e.g., innate subjective (cognitive style)].

The left rectangle represents the individual dimension of Figure 1, hence its location is to the left (x-axis = micro focus), and the stability of these factors decreases from heredity down to opinions (y-axis). For instance, public opinion polls show that the electorate changes support for a government rapidly and frequently depending upon the latter's most recent decision. In contrast, people's beliefs are relatively stable and resistant to change (e.g., Rokeach, 1985). This example shows that when we try to comprehend culture from a micro perspective, we must accept that an individual's opinions are less stable than his or her beliefs. Moreover, while we

Table 1   Classifying Cultural Variables: Objective and Subjective Culture

---

SUBJECTIVE CULTURE
1. Subsistence system (methods of exploitation of the ecology to survive, such as industrial work)
2. Cultural system (human-made environment)
3. Social system (patterns of interaction, such as roles)
4. Interindividual system (e.g., social behaviors)
5. Individual system (e.g., perceptions, attitudes, and beliefs)

OBJECTIVE CULTURE
1. Ecology (e.g., the physical environment, resources, geography, climate, fauna, and flora)
2. Objective portion of the cultural system or infrastructure (e.g., roads, tools and factories)

Note: This list of variables is adapted from Triandis (1977: 144).

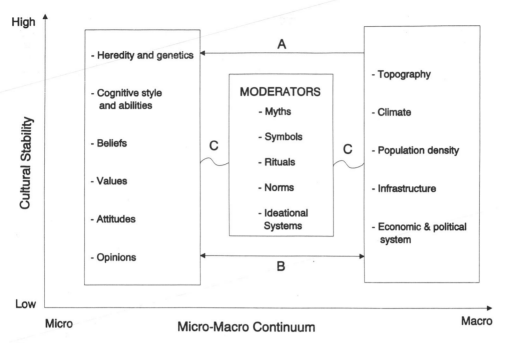

Figure 1   Relationship between the micro–macro continuum and the degree of cultural stability. The micro dimension is represented by the individual whose attitudes and opinions are likely to change frequently during his or her lifetime (low cultural stability); that is, what is "cool and in" today may be "out" tomorrow. The macro side represents the natural and human-made environment. While topography may remain stable over thousands of years, a political system can change several times within a century (e.g., Germany and Yugoslavia).

Arrow A symbolizes the influence of the natural environment upon the individual. For instance, a change in climate may lead to the survival of only those individuals whose genetic makeup, as the result of favorable mutations over generations, has adapted them for survival.

Arrow B symbolizes the *bi-directional* relationship between the approximate factors, such as the individual's beliefs, values, attitudes, and opinions, and the human-made environment, as represented by the infrastructure and the economic, legal, and political systems of a country.

Wave C illustrates the intermediary effect of cultural moderators upon the approximate individual factors and the human-made environment. For instance, myths and symbols about fertility and manhood may influence how a society values offspring. A positive societal view of fertility will result in an increase in population density if the children survive and become adults. High population density and a political system that provides negative reinforcement for childbearing may help to establish a norm of small families. The People's Republic of China under Communist leadership has followed this path, thereby making small families (even those without male offspring) more acceptable than in the past. The literature does not support the view that cultural moderators and the natural environment affect innate individual factors. However, this does not mean that a certain topography and climate may not foster certain myths and symbols. For instance, the Inuit language contains various labels for snow, and Inuit fairy tales likewise reflect the importance of snow and ice.

can measure genetic factors such as eyesight and reproductive behavior, it is far more difficult to assess opinions comprehensively. It follows that while opinions are approximate, heredity and genetic factors are innate, whereby changes occur as a result of genetic mutations over generations (Plomin and Rende, 1991).

The right rectangle in Figure 1 illustrates the environment, which is natural at the top and human-made at the bottom. Similarly, while the natural parts of the environment, such as topography and climate, are stable over generations and centuries until the next natural disaster, population density and infrastructure, including roads and cities, are the results of human actions and policies. To illustrate, the Italian summer climate (especially south of Rome) invites spending the evening outdoors in street cafes, socializing and enjoying the warm air and cooling breezes. Although the summer climate in Canada's far north might permit such behavior, low population density and brief summers would result in an acute scarcity of cafes, while black flies and mosquitoes would make sitting outdoors in the evening a less-than-pleasant experience.

Arrow A symbolizes the unidirectional influence of the natural environment upon innate individual factors. For instance, a change in climate may alter a society's degree of pigmentation over generations, while a hunting and gathering society's diet is such that their wisdom teeth are better developed than are those of the average person in an industrialized society. Again, these hereditary changes and mutations occur over generations.

Arrow B is bidirectional so approximate factors, such as people's beliefs or attitudes, will influence the human-made environment, and vice versa. For instance, when the steam train was first used in England many people believed it to be evil, and consequently resisted its further development and use. Hence, the development of the infrastructure necessary to make better use of this new technology was obstructed by societal beliefs. Medical technology has made it possible for a 12-week-old fetus to develop further in the body of its brain-dead mother until its life may be maintained in an incubator. In autumn 1992, such a case occurred at the Nuremberg-Erlangen university hospital in Germany, resulting in vivid discussions between politicians, doctors, churches, and the public about the ethics of such medical action. The doctors defended their procedure in part by referring to a precedent case which occurred in 1987 in the United States, whereby a brain-dead pregnant mother had been attached to a respirator for 94 days, sufficiently long for her fetus to grow enough to be able to survive. It may be inferred that people's values and beliefs ultimately decide if the medical infrastructure can be used for such medical procedures.

Arrow B also indicates that the economic, legal, and political systems or the human-made environment can influence people's beliefs and opinions. In the above German medical case, for instance, economic constraints may force the government to exclude such procedures from the health insurance scheme, and thereby limit their use to those who can finance them privately. In turn, this initiates discussion about fairness and discrimination against the poor, whereby public opinion can pressure the government into various restrictive courses of action. Similarly, while in some countries abortions are legal and paid for by health insurance, they are illegal or at least not covered by national health plans in others, depending upon the values and attitudes held by their peoples. Modern medicine has provided the technology to perform abortions relatively safely; nevertheless, the electorate may, on the basis of ethical and moral constraints, require the government to prohibit such procedures. To illustrate, Irish voters have rejected a proposed change in the abortion law that would have permitted women to abort in Ireland if certain medical conditions were met, such as the endangering of the mother's life. If the new law had passed in the national referendum in November 1992, Irish women would have been allowed to travel abroad to get an abortion.

Figure 1 also illustrates the moderating effects of rituals, symbols, myths, and norms, which derive from economic, political, and ideational systems. For instance, in the former East Germany, at the age of about 16, teenagers experienced the Jugendweihe (youth dedication, administered and financially supported by a ministry of the central government), a ritual that symbolized becoming an adult and comrade within the Communist system. In contrast, at about the same age West German Protestants perform a church ritual called Konfirmation (confirmation), which symbolizes their entrance into the church as consenting members. Apparently, Jugendweihe was an "equivalent" to Konfirmation created by East German leaders for their citizens. After reunification, the public's appreciation and value of Jugendweihe diminished rapidly, and increasing numbers of adolescents attended Konfirmation ceremonies throughout the former East Germany. This example illustrates how changes in the political system can manifest themselves by altering or replacing former rituals, while also suggesting a shift in individual cognition.

In conclusion, researchers as well as professionals, dealing with cross-national issues must be aware that (1) various methodological and measurement approaches for assessing culture (national and/or firmwide) make comparisons across studies difficult; (2) the unidisciplinary approach to measuring culture (in which psychologists ignore sociologists, and vice versa) impedes understanding of cross-national issues and phenomena; and (3) ethnocentrism exacerbates the issues raised under points 1 and 2. The use of an interdisciplinary approach such as that outlined in Figure 1 is a small but important step in the right direction.

II. DEVELOPING TECHNOLOGICAL COMPETENCE

Increased internationalization of trade and business [e.g., Common Market liberalization in 1992; the process ultimately leading to free trade between the Common Market and the European-Free-Trade Association (EFTA) was started in 1993[2]; Mexico and Chile ratified a free-trade agreement in October 1991; ASEAN countries are in the process of implementing such a program] has made the replicating of research across national boundaries a more paramount issue than ever. For instance, free movement of labor augments workforce diversity. Free movement of capital encourages firms to locate in various countries to increase the efficient allocation of resources (e.g., labor costs in Greece are lower than those in Germany). Even though farmers enjoy trade protection in most countries, the changes outlined above have further increased competition for farmers within the Common Market and EFTA[3]. Without high-quality products (i.e., good value for a decent price), neither capital nor marketing savvy will enable a firm to triumph. Indeed, all three components may be required, while a *skilled workforce* with the necessary *technological competence* is the framework of such a venture. To remain competitive, therefore, a firm must manage a diverse, versatile, and technologically competent workforce while successfully exporting its products and/or services to foreign markets.

A. Distinctive Competence

Selznick (1957) first used the words *distinctive competence* to describe the character of an organization. The term refers to those things that a firm does especially well when compared with others within a similar environment (Andrews, 1971; Snow and Hrebiniak, 1980). In one research project, competence was measured by having managers rate each of 10 broad functions on a three-point scale that indicated areas of strong, weak, and average competence. The functions used were: (1) general management; (2) financial management; (3) marketing/selling; (4) market research; (5) product research and development; (6) engineering, basic and applied; (7) production; (8) distribution; (9) legal affairs; and (10) personnel. The authors reported that most managers indicated strong competence for their companies in *all* functions (Snow and Hrebiniak, 1980), confirming the results of Stevenson's (1976) study, which found that managers at the top level of their firms perceived more strengths than weaknesses in their organizations.

Most successful companies will have strengths in more areas than those mentioned above. These strengths might be in communications systems, organization of work, organizational culture (Morgan, 1986, chaps. 4 & 5), technology and innovation (Gattiker, 1990a, chap. 1), and strategic management (Teece, Pisano, and Shuen, 1990). Basically, technological competence will, therefore, build upon the firm's distinctive capabilities and draw upon its strengths in various areas (cf. Blakley and Willoughby, 1991).

B. Defining Technological Competence

For economic analysis, a particularly important kind of competence is *technological competence*, which may be defined as the competence to *receive* and *use* information for solving technology and economic-related problems and opportunities and for making appropriate decisions. Technological competence refers to what is often called "optimizationabilities" or "rationality." Three of these properties should be noted and are thus outlined in Table 2. Technological competence has a micro and macro dimension. As each worker has a certain degree of technological competence (micro), the firm's challenge is to secure the most appropriate levels of technological competence in its workforce (macro) to promote success in the marketplace. In turn, a region's technological competence comprises its people, firms, associations, and universities.

Table 2 defines technological competence and provides definitions for the three properties of technological competence: learning process, determination of technology behavior, and degree of scarcity. Technological competence provides part of the person's frame of reference when making decisions about technology-related aspects of work. Technological competence is an unusual type of information and is not comparable to economic types of information generally used, such as data about prices, quantities, goods, and markets, that can usually be communicated at a cost to another agent (Pelikan, 1989). In contrast, technological competence is a type of information and know-how capital that is inseparably tied to each agent, whereby the agent's direct ability to communicate and use other information exists, but cannot be communicated directly. It is, therefore, *tacit* (Polanyi, 1962). The difficulty in measuring technological competence is illustrated by its frequent overestimation or underestimation by agents. Nevertheless, as Table 2 suggests, a person or firm may increase one's technological competence or capital by learning.

Determination of technology behavior means that technological competence is embedded in the very ways in which technology decisions are made in organizations. Consequently, two individuals with the same job function and work situation may make systematically different decisions if endowed with different technological competence, and a firm may incur financial and social losses if an inappropriate decision is made.

An analogy with computer software may help to illustrate this concept. The software permits the use of hardware for the execution of tasks. Similarly, technological competence permits the firm or workgroup to use technological information and make technology-related decisions (e.g., R&D efforts and technology acquisition). Moreover, in the same way that program codes for software are written as precisely and concisely as possible in the appropriate sequence, the firm's or workgroup's technological competence must be produced by situating employees with various levels of individual technological competence in the most appropriate positions and functions. The ever-changing environment (e.g., trade and safety laws, competitor-launched "better" products, difficulty in hiring qualified labor) makes continuous improvement of technological competence a necessity for a firm and its workers. Moreover, culturally diverse workforces (within a country or between plants in two countries) make the presence of workers with different levels of technological competence inevitable.

Table 2 The Three Properties of Technological Competence

First property of technological competence:
Learning process used to increase technological competence is dependent upon tacit skills and intelligence held at any point in time.
Second property of technological competence:
Determinance of technology behavior. This means that technological competence is embedded in the very ways in which technology decisions are made in organizations or countries by individuals or groups.
Third property of technological competence:
Degree of scarcity, which requires an efficient allocation of this resource for the economic success of a firm and/or geographic region.

Note: The three properties of technological competence are interlinked in determining its level for an individual, firm, and/or geographical region. Similar to Tables 5 and 6, it is implied that each technological competence property has both a *micro* (i.e., individual worker) and a *macro* level of measurement (e.g., workgroup, firm, and region).

C. Technological Competence Capital and the Firm's Governance Structure

In this section our focus is on the learning process of technological competence and the strategies available to the firm. We concentrate on R&D in particular for two reasons: (1) R&D includes product- and service-related activities and is, therefore, not limited to the laboratory, and (2) the increased level of global competitiveness requires every firm to do some degree of R&D, if only library research. Table 3 provides a general definition of the R&D term using the above two points as guidelines.

Industrial economics indicates that innovation is affected by market concentration and levels of competition. The literature indicates that an acceleration of innovation increases the decentralization of market structures (Geroski and Pomroy, 1990) and that organizations actively pursuing export markets invest more in R&D efforts (Braga and Wilmore, 1991). This

Table 3 Integration, Outsourcing, and Adaptation of R&D Efforts and Outcomes: Fostering the Learning Process for Increasing the Firm's Technological Competence

---

R&D could be defined as: a firm's defensive or innovative efforts undertaken to perform basic or applied research in various settings, whose magnitude and focus depend upon the product or service life cycle and the degree of market concentration in which the firm finds itself.

Integration of R&D

1. Development of internal supply of specific technology-related knowledge by providing and/or encouraging on-the-job and off-the-job continuous education
2. Continuous organizational and/or plantwide change efforts to increase the effective use of technology (e.g., quality control and change in the work process and/or use of information technology as suggested by employees)
3. Vertical integration of R&D with other in-house activities within the firm's organizational structure
4. Strategic alliance with a firm such as purchasing a sizable amount of stock (e.g., Ford purchasing 25% of Mazda's shares in 1979; Delta Airlines, Swissair, and Singapore Airlines acquiring 10% of each other's stock in 1989)
5. Acquisition of innovative firms or business units

Outsourcing of R&D

6. Use of long-term joint ventures (e.g., with university laboratory, including interfirm R&D cooperation in general; see Tapon, 1989) for R&D projects/efforts
7. Provision of part of the capital (venture capital and/or funds with first choice clause for subsequent licensing) for a specific R&D project with an independent laboratory (e.g., private or university) or small/medium-sized research-intensive firm
8. Technology purchasing/imports (e.g., contract R&D; licensing in)
9. Technology scanning (including legal and illegal forms of acquiring technological knowledge from outside without any direct purchasing from the original source, cf. Pelikan, 1989)

Implementation, Adaptation, and Institutionalization of R&D Outcomes from In-House and External Efforts

10. The management application and adaptation of R&D outcomes with the help of lead users
11. Implementation into the firm's transformation process to produce new, or enhance current, products and/or services
12. Continuous training of employees for skill-upgrading to secure the necessary know-how to satisfactorily perform job-related tasks
13. Adaptation and modification of products and/or services based on information gathered with the help of steps 1 and 12
14. The selling/exporting of the firm's capital in the technological competence domain, such as consulting for others and providing licenses and franchise contracts

---

Note: Integration or disintegration of R&D efforts is intended to reduce the firm's transaction costs. The strategies and steps are chosen to apply and adapt R&D outcomes to the firm's transformation processes such as production and marketing. Once a firm arrives at any of the stages between 10 and 14, the cycle may start all over again (i.e., fostering the learning process for improving the capital held by the firm, with respect to technological competence, is a continuous and evolutionary process).

suggests that imperfect competition will have a positive effect upon innovation because firms can limit imitations and are more likely to reap R&D benefits in situations in which the market has a high degree of concentration (Kraft, 1989). Extensive discussions of these issues are, however, beyond the scope and focus of this chapter and the reader is referred to the appropriate literature in the field of industrial economics (Willoughby, 1992; Willoughby and Blakeley, 1990). Today's accelerated growth in international trade increases international competition, necessitating continuous R&D efforts and the development of a firm's technological competence within a workforce that includes diversity in skill levels and ethnic and cultural backgrounds.

1.   Transaction Costs

In the context of this chapter, R&D efforts require contracts and agreements between parties, and therefore the firm will incur transaction costs. Coase (1937) is credited with having coined the term *transaction costs* while interpreting the emergence of the firm (the organization) in light of the costs of determining market prices (transaction costs). Coase, however, (1988: chap. 1) credited George Stigler (1972) with coining the economic term transaction costs. Williamson (1981; 1544) followed this economic definition by stating that "the transaction is made the basic unit of analysis." However, the literature proposes that this concept is not unified and interpreted in such a way. For instance, one could suggest that the previously negotiated exchange of property rights, using the contract to facilitate this process, represents the transaction itself.

Dow (1987: 15) pointed out that the first step in using transaction cost analysis is to define precisely the "transaction," thus allowing comparison of costs across alternative governance structures. Economists have proposed two types of transaction costs, namely *technological*, which are those costs having transportation character, and *strategic*, the implicit expenses of monitoring and enforcing budget-balance and contracts (Ostroy, 1987: 516). Consequently, transaction costs are simply the costs incurred to run a system (cf. Arrow, 1969) or the slack/friction in physical systems, to be distinguished from production costs. This context refers to strategic transaction costs as they pertain to the development and retention of technological competence for individuals and/or firms.

In Table 3 the authors have differentiated between three major types of governance classifications: (1) integration of R&D (see points 1–5), (2) outsourcing of R&D (see points 6–9), and (3) implementation, adaptation, and institutionalization of R&D outcomes from in-house and/or external efforts. The unit of analysis or transaction is the learning effort undertaken by a firm to improve its technological competence (see points 1–14 in Table 3). Firms will likely use a combination of integration and outsourcing, depending upon certain factors. For instance, if a competitor has a new product, licensing may become a viable option.

The last section is probably the most difficult one and illustrates the evolutionary nature of technological competence. Even if a firm chooses to sell its capital in the domain of technological competence in the form of a nonexclusive licence, it will continue its R&D efforts to sustain its lead using integration and/or outsourcing mechanisms while trying to keep its strategic transaction costs as low as possible. Technological competence is the evolutionary process undertaken by a company to attain or sustain a competitive edge in the technological domain of which R&D efforts are an integral part. By studying the firm as a governance structure rather than as a neoclassical production function, and by stressing internal organization rather than market structure, researchers are better able to understand the firm's alternatives for advancing its technological competence. To illustrate, when General Electric sold its Sylvania division to Osram (Siemens, Germany—the Canadian/U.S. operations) and a group of investors (worldwide activities), this represented Osram's acquisition of R&D capital (point 5 in Table 3) and the strengthening of its market position in North America. Since General Electric did not feel that the Sylvania division would become the market leader, management was reluctant to provide financial resources to develop its technological competence. Hence, its divesture of Sylvania appeared to be the best decision for General Electric's long-term strategy.

2. Properties of Technological Competence and Governance of R&D Efforts

From a phenomenological viewpoint, researchers can speak of technological competence learning (i.e., 1st property of technological competence = learning process) as being relative to the frame of reference and tacit skills currently available to the individual and/or the firm's employees; that is, the firm's aggregate technological competence. This technological competence frame of reference affects the firm's decision-making processes that involve its choice of and preference for any one of the fourteen options outlined in Table 3, or combinations thereof (i.e., 2nd property of technological competence = technology behavior).

It is hypothesized that the firm will try to choose the strategy (or strategies) outlined above based on their transaction costs. Thus, negotiations for improving technological competence may reduce R&D efforts and accelerate learning. For instance, while Ford benefits from Mazda's engineering and manufacturing knowledge, the latter benefits from the former's marketing and financial savvy. Both partners have used this learning opportunity to produce better cars (e.g., the 1992 Ford Escort combined improved Mazda engineering with a highly competitive price).

A firm may also choose a different governance structure of R&D and technology-related projects. For instance, Arora and Gambardella (1990) report that large chemical and pharmaceutical producers in the United States, Europe, and Japan increase their technological competence by entering into various relationships with universities and small to medium-sized research-intensive firms. Their data suggest that such linkages in the form of long-term joint ventures for R&D with a university laboratory (see point 6 in Table 3) or other joint ventures (see point 7) are complementary and thus increase large firms' technological competence. Transaction costs are reduced by some pharmaceutical and chemical firms with the help of outsourcing of R&D activities (see point 6 in Table 3). These firms regard market failures related to the organization of their R&D activities as less significant than the organizational failures incurred in carrying out in-house R&D. Consequently, long-term R&D between pharmaceutical and chemical firms and university laboratories is used to improve the efficient allocation of technology (Tapon, 1989).

In today's international business world, a firm may have to consider cross-national factors when deciding which options to select and how to undertake them (i.e., 3rd property of technological competence = efficient allocation of scarce resources). For instance, if an American firm intends to engage in a joint venture for R&D efforts with a Japanese firm, careful management of cross-national differences between the two countries and firms must be assured from the beginning [e.g., setting up the legal agreement, locating the facility, and deciding the composition of the workforce (Osborn, Strickstein, and Olson, 1988)].

The authors are primarily interested in the first property of technological competence, namely the acquisition and learning of additional skills in order to improve an employee's level of technological competence (micro dimension) as well as the firm's human capital in this domain (macro dimension). The focus is on the activities and strategies undertaken by the firm to increase the technological competence of its workforce (i.e. individual employees, workgroups, divisions, and the overall organization).

3. Skills

The firm's primary objective is to increase technological competence capital for the firm by such means as facilitating technological competence learning of its workforce and/or hiring individuals to complement the technological competence mix already present in the firm. An employee's technological competence capital will be affected by his or her current skills, such as being functionally literate or knowing how to do calculus. If current job demands allow regular, if not extensive, use of one's skills and technological competence on the job (e.g., writing or doing calculus problems using computer technology), the individual's current technological competence capital and frame of reference is thereby positively influenced. However, if current job demands fail to take advantage of the employee's technological

Table 4 Defining Skills

Skills are *learned behaviors* required for the achievement of desirable performance levels when doing
job-related tasks necessitating the use of technology, while the content and type of skill required for
doing a job is in part a *relational phenomenon* (i.e., how many and what type of people have or do not
have the necessary skills; cf. Gattiker, 1991; 1992).

Note: Similar to Tables 2 and 6, it is implied that the skills have both a *micro* (i.e., individual worker) and a *macro* (i.e.,
workgroup, firm, and region) level of measurement.

competence know-how, the individual will lose the skill and require a refresher course or its
equivalent to become reacquainted with it.

A working definition of *skills* was provided by Adams (1987) in a recent review of human
motor skills research. He proposed three defining characteristics: "(1) skills are a wide behavioral domain in which behaviors are assumed to be complex; (2) skills are gradually learned
through training; and (3) attaining a goal is dependent upon motor behavior and processes"
(Adams, 1987: 42).

Table 4 provides a definition of skill, while Table 5 presents a categorization of skills listed
in descending order of transferability (see also Gattiker 1990a, chap. 12; 1990b). In this
context, tacit skills represent the knowledge of the individual attained through formal and
informal education, experience, and life in general. Although knowing and understanding one's
need to adjust when working in a different culture is important, the successful adaptation to such
an environment, while applying and interpreting verbal and written communication signals
appropriately in this new cultural context, is a result of one's tacit skills (cf. Berry et al., 1989).
A narrower definition suggests that tacit skills consist of officially and actually required skills
for the job and actually used skills for doing job-related tasks, as well as skills acquired through
preliminary training (e.g., Leplat, 1990). The definition given in Table 5 builds upon Polanyi's
work (1962).

4.   Technological Competence, Human Abilities, Work Structures, and Processes

The importance of certain skills (e.g., reading and writing) to the acquisition of technological
competence know-how remains to be explored. The relational approach to skills would suggest
that training during childhood and adolescence (e.g., primary and high school) as well as a

Table 5 Five Skill Categories Listed in Descending Order of Transferability

---

Transferability of skills decreases from
Tacit skills are acquired through practice and experience and cannot be articulated explicitly; they include
    the person's knowledge about how to avoid errors and overcome inperfections in the work system, and
    are tied inseparably to the individual; they cannot be communicated directly to somebody else and are
    difficult to observe and measure.
To *basic* (reading, writing, and arithmetic).
To *social* (e.g., interpersonal skills and the person's ability to organize his or her own efforts and task
    performance, and possibly that of his or her peers and subordinates).
To *conceptual* (including planning, assessing, decision making about task- and people-related issues, and
    judging or assessing tasks done by self or others).
To *technology* (encompasses appropriate use of technology, such as a computer, thereby preventing
    breakdowns/accidents).
To *technical* (physical ability to transform an object or item of information into something different).
To a person's *task skills* (usually job-specific, such as doing the weekly petty cash report).

Note: The above is adopted from Gattiker (1990a, chap. 12; 1990b). In each position the individual acquires additional
skills through formal and informal ways. Tacit skills will change as one's experience and practice of the various skills
increases during his or her working life.

continuous education largely determine the skill base available to the individual and have a substantial effect upon the worker's frame of reference about technology. Consequently, basic skills provide the foundation for a satisfactory level of technological competence capital for the firm.

Table 6 outlines in more detail the six factors that can hinder the success of learning efforts undertaken by an individual seeking to attain a higher level of technological competence. Points 1 and 2 in Table 6 focus on the micro dimension, namely the employee. In both cases, an assessment or inventory may be undertaken to determine an individual's current abilities and skills. Points 3 and 4 integrate sociological thought, which focuses attention on the firm's work processes and job structure. Sociological literature indicates that skills are multidimensional (Spenner, 1983; 1990); specifically, substantive complexity refers to the level, scope, and integration of mental, manipulative, and interpersonal tasks in a job. Autonomy-control alludes to the discretion of leeway available in a job to control the content, manner, and speed with which tasks are done (Spenner, 1983).

Points 5 and 6 have micro and macro foci. Future learning efforts initiated by the individual and/or the firm in the technological competence domain are influenced by the individual's technological competence history (e.g., past learning efforts) and the current technological competence situation (e.g., level attained by the worker and/or workforce to date).

Table 6 assumes that technological competence (points 4 and 5) is built upon points 1 through 3; thus, limitations in ability, skills, knowledge, and substantive complexity/autonomy in one's job will hinder future efforts to upgrade technological competence. Whatever a person's other abilities may be, competency in writing and reading skills will facilitate the acquisition of new technological competence, even in enabling one to fully utilize training and instruction manuals.

III. TECHNOLOGICAL COMPETENCE AND ORGANIZATIONAL COMPETITIVENESS: CULTURAL AND ETHICAL CHALLENGES

Several questions arise from our previous discussions, namely

1. How can the technological competence level and frame of reference by improved for a firm's international workforce (e.g., a California plant with African- and Mexican-American workers vs. a plant in Germany employing Turks, Spaniards, and Germans)?

Table 6 Achieving a Satisfactory Level of Technological Competence Capital

Factors influencing the technological competence learning process undertaken for improving an employee's technological competence level listed in descending order of importance
1. The worker's individual abilities (motor and cognitive process capabilities, e.g., information processing), which are, to a significant degree, innate and genetically determined
2. The mix of declarative knowledge (i.e., knowledge about something) and procedural knowledge (i.e., knowledge of how to do something) possessed by the employee in basic, social, conceptual, technology, technical, and task skills (cf. Table 4)
3. The degree of substantive complexity and autonomy-control for performing well offered or required by the current job
4. The level of technological competence currently dictated by one's job (cf. Table 2)
5. The employee's current technological competence frame of reference
6. The employee's past and current record for the efficient allocation of technology as a scarce resource

Note: The above describes the six variables that may affect a person's current technological competence level, as well as the additional training and upgrading necessary to meet those work-related technological competence demands that require additional and/or new skills. As in Table 2, it is implied that each of the six factors outlined here has both a *micro* (i.e., individual worker) and a *macro* (i.e., workgroup, firm, and region) level of measurement.

2. What opportunities and ethical challenges are faced by managers and employees in a global business environment when it comes to technological competence?
3. What can researchers do to improve our understanding of technological competence and its development, particularly in the international contexts, of business and trade?

The above issues and their possible answers are discussed below and research propositions are derived.

A.   Developing Technological Competence

Previous formal education (e.g., graduating from high school and being functionally literate) as well as continuous education undertaken by the worker (e.g., participating in a skill upgrading course for tradespeople) will influence the level of mastery of the five skills outlined in Table 4. Moreover, technological competence and the frame of reference held by the employee are influenced by such past work experience factors as autonomy and complexity in previous jobs. In other words, an employee brings a certain frame of reference and level of technological competence to each new job. This pretechnological competence capital is the culmination of one's education and work experiences.

Table 7 presents proposition 1 for the testing of individual and organizational factors influencing the current level of technological competence and the frame of reference of each employee. The term *average* used in proposition 1 is assumed to mean relative to the external labor market. If skills are below average, the employee needs additional training to achieve a satisfactory level of technological competence. A worker's inability to read (basic skill) will hinder any training toward technological competence. In addition, an employee's familiarity with an outdated version of a computer program (e.g., for Lotus and MaxThink), provides part of his or her current frame of reference. The more thorough the person's understanding of the previous version (i.e., one portion of one's technological competence capital), the more helpful this frame of reference will be for reducing the time required for learning the upgraded program.

Table 7   Developing Technological Competence: Research Propositions 1 and 2

Proposition 1: Improving an individual's current technological competence through learning will be positively moderated by
Individual factors
1. A high level of mastery of various skills (i.e., basic, social, conceptual, technological, technical, and task skills) and an above-average level of technological competence[a].
2. The perceptual speed and psychomotor abilities held by the individual are above average.
Organizational factors
1. The autonomy and complexity levels in one's current or past job(s) require regular application of the skill outlined in Table 5, including the individual's current and previously acquired technological competence.
2. The level of technological competence required in one's current job is comparable to, or greater than, that of similar jobs within the firm.
Proposition 2: The firm's workflow and the complexity and autonomy of each job must be adjusted according to recently acquired skills. This adjustment will positively boost the potential and actual transfer of newly acquired skills from training to work, and will therefore enhance the determinance of technological competence behavior and the efficient allocation of technological competence resources (second and third properties of technological competence, see Table 2).

Note: It is implied that each proposition outlined here has both a *micro* (i.e., individual worker) and a *macro* (e.g., workgroup, firm, and region) level of measurement. Accordingly, both propositions must be assessed and tested at the individual and, possibly, the workgroup levels and beyond.
[a]The term *average* used in proposition 1 assumes a comparison to the external labor market. If skills are below average, the employee requires additional training to achieve a satisfactory level. Equally important, if a worker is unable to read (basic skill), any additional training in the technological competence learning process will be impeded.

An organization's structure of work and processes will affect the autonomy and complexity levels required to perform well in one's job (cf. organizational factors listed in Table 7 and point 3 in Table 6). Individual and organizational factors interrelate and may influence an employee's current technological competence level. Accordingly, if an individual with a high level of technological competence and planning skills was hired to do a job requiring limited use of these skills, he or she is likely to lose some of these skills. For example, an individual may excel at writing essays and reports during high school, yet experience writing difficulties 20 years later. A plausible explanation for this loss of skill may be that she or he may not have written an essay or report since high school!

As is illustrated in Figure 2, researchers assume that individuals first acquire what is called a *pretechnological competence* capital and frame of reference, which is based on personal experience and tacit skills; that is, skills that are acquired through practice and that cannot be articulated explicitly (see also Table 5). In some cases this pretechnological competence capital and frame of reference may be inadequate or outdated. Also, the performance of tasks without making mistakes is a result of tacit skills that include learning how to avoid errors and overcome systematic imperfections. Intermediaries of tacit skills include books, research reports, theoretical study, and training. Finally, the experiences of friends and co-workers may help to form general impressions, and thereby influence the pretechnological competence capital level and frame of reference possessed by an individual.

Figure 2 outlines how a person's pretechnological competence capital level and frame of reference are formed. These two components are the basis of technology-related decisions involving the efficient allocation of scarce resources. Every individual may augment his or her frame of reference and level of technological competence capital by obtaining additional training, learning new skills, or drawing upon the technological competence capital of others, as indicated in Figure 2. Thus, the model illustrates that *the acquisition of additional technological competence capital and skills is a continuous learning process.*

The complexity of a particular job depends upon the design and structure of the current workflow in the firm (cf. Van Houten, 1989; Sorge and Warner, 1986). Using longitudinal self-report data, Kohn and Schooler (1983) reported that intellectual flexibility of workers declined over time due in part to poor job design and to the repetitiveness of the workflow. It may be inferred that enhancing one's technological competence capital may require changes in work design and structure, workflow, and complexity to adequately utilize newly acquired skills and knowledge. The technological competence capital base of the firm's workforce is enhanced by this positive transfer of skill from training to work ((cf. Baldwin and Ford, 1988; Gattiker, 1990 b, c). Accordingly, proposition 2, as presented in Table 7, might be tested.

B. Multicultural Workforce

When Volkswagen took over the Trabant plant facilities in the former East Germany, subsequent learning initiated by Volkswagen for its new workforce was not limited to technological competence. Cultural concerns had to be addressed before Volkswagen could implement training programs. For instance, the demands of the new capitalistic economy included higher output by former Trabant employees. Additionally, employees had to remain on the job during working hours (i.e., walking off the job to do private business during the day was no longer possible), and unsatisfactory performance could lead to involuntary turnover. Thus, careless work attitudes developed during the Communist regime were now detrimental to one's success in the new profit-maximizing firm.

The learning process for technological competence is also affected by cultural moderators, such as economic and political systems (see also Figure 1). Accordingly, public policy encouraging continuous education by offering additional certification, tax incentives, and training opportunities to both individuals and firms is an important step toward improving the workforce's technological competence capital. This is a pivotal issue for older employees who may be most vulnerable to skill obsolescence (Fossum et al., 1986; Gattiker, 1990c; Gattiker,

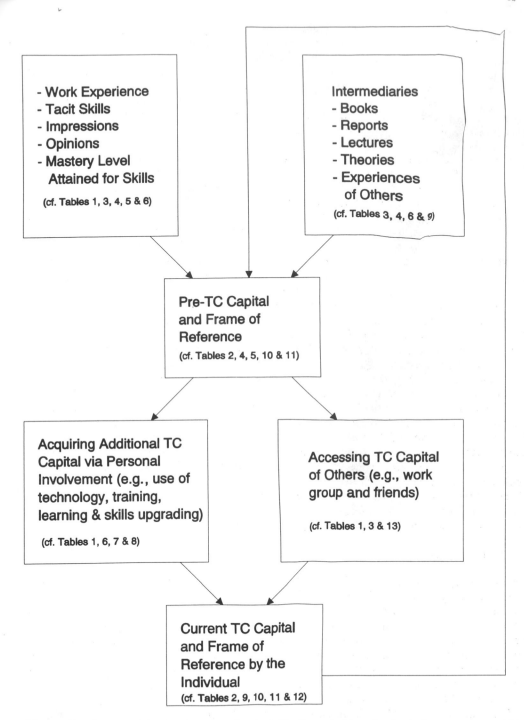

Figure 2 Sources of the development of an individual's capital in technological competence and his or her frame of reference. The assumption is that the improvement and/or the upgrading of one's technological competence is an evolutionary, continuous, and lifelong process. References to tables within each box are made to facilitate the reader's efforts in referring to previous material, while assessing its relationship to this illustration.

1992a). Of cardinal importance is the need for individuals with positive attitudes toward continuous education efforts (cf. Gattiker and Hlavka, 1992), and who take advantage of such opportunities even on their own time. In Switzerland, for example, this "positive" attitude is quite common (see also BIGA, 1988), while Canadian employees generally undertake only limited efforts to upgrade their skills beyond 40 years of age (e.g., Statistics Canada, 1988).

Reports of Canadian firms spending less money on recurrent education than do their American counterparts are alarming (e.g., Muszynski and Wolfe, 1989), and are therefore spotlighted in the media. Such reports are misleading until one considers that about one-third of such expenditures by American firms are spent on remedial programs to help improve the literacy levels of their workforces. Thus, the focus should be not only on expenditures, adjusted for price levels between countries, but the *type of training* attended as well. Interestingly, German and Japanese firms not only spend much more for training than do their American or Canadian counterparts (Employment and Immigration Canada, 1992), but more important, only a minimal percentage of such resources is spent on remedial training. The higher the organizational tenure of the average worker, the more likely it is that a firm will recover its training investment. In contrast, lower organizational tenure by the average Canadian and American worker, compared to their German/Japanese counterparts, puts a greater responsibility on the individual employee to invest in continuous education, since such efforts are less likely to be forthcoming from the firm.

It is also very likely that international differences in vocational training will result in discrepancies in workers' pretechnological competence knowledge. For instance, federal policy in Germany assures universal training regardless of the location and type of firm, while in Canada, regional considerations and policies affect the content of vocational training in British Columbia and Newfoundland (Gattiker, in press-a).

Research must expand beyond the unicultural domain so that concepts about technological competence learning and strategies may be applicable beyond one country. The dual phenomenon of global integration (e.g., international trade) and regionalism (e.g., free trade between Australia and New Zealand) indicated the need for further work in this area (see Table 8).

Propositions 3.1 and 3.2 in Table 8 imply that the way a society, and therefore a firm, apply a particular technology depends upon culture (see Figure 1). For instance, using computerized technology to reduce labor costs may be a necessity in the United States, while in Nepal, the combination of low labor costs and high unemployment suggests that the computer is not the appropriate technology. Moreover, maintenance, service and software programs in the local languages may be unavailable. Proposition 3.2 also implies that it is possible to measure cultural moderators and objective factors as well as subjective factors such as opinions and attitudes toward technology. A study comparing American and Nepalese workers may be of limited use (see Figure 1). For instance, Nepalese workers may have less positive attitudes about a particular technology simply because service is difficult to obtain while program instructions are available in English only! Consequently, reports that Nepalese workers have more negative attitudes toward a certain computer technology than do Americans are interesting but incomplete and uninformative.

Table 8 Developing Technological Competence in the Global Village: Research Proposition 3

Proposition 3: Improving technological competence in the workforce in order to increase a firm's/region's competitiveness requires careful assessment of global and regional issues, in particular
1. The appropriate use/application of technology will be significantly affected by the objective/subjective culture of society as well as its history and state of economic development.
2. The testing of propositions 1 and 2 in different organizational and geographical settings, and the understanding of the differences and similarities to be found in such data, will be significantly facilitated if cultural factors (individual, environmental, and other moderators influencing culture, see Figure 4) are measured and assessed in a comprehensive manner (i.e., the simple reporting of differences is complemented by addressing the *why* of these findings).

Table 9 Defining Competitiveness

Competitiveness is a continuous process that involves division and repossession of goods, materials, and wealth (e.g., capital) between parties (e.g., individuals, firms, and countries).

Note: The above is adapted from Gattiker (in press-b, chap. 4, Table 7.1)

C. Ethics and Morality in an Increasingly Competitive Environment

If a firm or region can develop technological competence and manage the multicultural workforce successfully, and thereby improve its competitive advantage in global markets, it will ultimately succeed in securing more resources and wealth. This raises once again the question asked earlier in this section: What ethical and moral challenges must be considered? As Table 9 suggests, competition results in the continuous transfer of capital, goods, and wealth from one party to others and back again. In a perfect market, the fittest competitor will survive and the weaker participants will not (see also Table 9), therefore, the establishment and growth of new firms will ultimately help to compensate for job losses resulting from mergers and bankruptcies of larger firms (Baldwin and Georcki, 1990). Upon observing developments in countries or geographical regions, is it possible to conclude that the weak become even weaker and that the power of rich and strong countries or regions becomes overbearing?

No complete answer can be given without addressing various ethical and .moral issues. Ethics are essentially the values that permit one to judge right from wrong (e.g., Stead and Stead, 1991: 18). Therefore, if a firm or geographical region raises its technological competence and competitiveness, it will ultimately garner for itself additional resources and wealth, and remove the same from other market participants.

A definition of the term ethics is given in Table 10. It is imperative that the observer be in a position to understand an individual's ethical framework, because only then will he or she be able to deduce the reasons for the person's action(s). Of course, in an emergency the individual might act "appropriately" out of character without using any deductive reasoning. An individual's innate sense of right and wrong may lead to a behavioral response (e.g., helping somebody in dire need), which may even endanger his or her own life. A further limitation exists even if the observer has an idea about the person's ethical framework, in that he or she may still be unable to follow exactly those thought and deductive processes that enable the subject to justify a particular action or behavior.

The word *moral* derives from *mores*, a Latin term that means customs. Morals are grounded in ethics and then moral capacities are developed toward those individuals and things in whom one takes a special interest (e.g., Goldman, 1980: 40). Accordingly, moral behavior extends from intimate relations within the family to one's friends and then toward strangers, within acceptable social limits. Goldman (1980: 5) suggests that without human intimacy or interest in other individuals, one may be unable to develop moral behavior at all.

Gauthier (1986: 59) maintains that although an individual's values (e.g., freedom to use a particular technology) are subjective and relative, they are proper because they are preferred.

Social morality provides the opportunity to confront the principal/agent, employer/worker and government/firm relationships in such a way as to reduce opportunism, cheating, free-riding

Table 10 Defining Ethics

Ethics is a system of goals, ideals, interests, and values that, in its completeness, guides personal behavior in one's daily life. Therefore, reason given to an action by the individual and/or observer is grounded in
1. An understanding of the ethical framework adhered to by the individual.
2. The fact that the individual utilized his or her ethical framework to deduce the reason(s) causing the subsequent action(s) or behavior(s).

Note: The above is adapted from Gattiker (in press-b, chap. 4, Table 4.4).

and other such means of placing one party at a disadvantage (see also Gattiker, in press-b, chap. 5). Morals by agreement ensure that a rationally acceptable distribution of goods can be realized in the exchange activity. A definition of social morality is provided in Table 11.

In the management literature, social morality in the organization is usally indicated by customs such as rituals. In other words, the multiplicity of cultures possible within a large firm affects the pervasiveness of organizational culture (e.g., how far down in the hierarchy) and the consistency/homogeneity of the shared meanings among individuals. Such customs may be as simple as the dress code, or as complex as the negotiating strategies used by managers or politicians. Consequently, the ethical framework (i.e., what is valued in a society) sets the basis for selecting and executing one's actions and activities.

D. Technological Competence and Cross-National Issues

What are the ethical and moral challenges faced by the employees, managers, firms, public policy decision makers, and union representatives in the global village? If the individual is successful in improving his or her technological competence, employment opportunities are likely to increase. To illustrate, research indicates that without certain basic computer skills whole groups of employees may be excluded from the labor market, and therefore require government support to acquire these skills and secure employment (Jantzen, 1989).

Higher labor costs per employee are partly negated by increasing technological competence held by the workforce, thereby permitting better use of technology. In turn, this results in the firm providing goods and/or services at a competitive price in the world market. Nevertheless, the ethical and moral point arises

> If a country is continuously increasing its economy's competitiveness, could this be pernicious or even harmful to the environment and the existence of other peoples' (firms' and countries') economic well-being?

For instance, if a country such as Germany, Korea, or Japan maintains a trade surplus (i.e., exports exceed imports) as well as a current account surplus [including trade balance, capital balance (import/export of capital and interest payments paid and received), as well as services (e.g., payments made or received for insurance policies)] over a length of time, its currency will appreciate (e.g., the value of the U.S. dollar decreased relative to the German mark and the Japanese yen in the 1970s through 1990s). To offset the continuous upward pressure on the currency that increases the prices of one's product for importers (e.g., American consumers purchasing Japanese computers), Korea, Germany, and Japan continue to improve their competitiveness by making better and more extensive use of technology. In turn, this helps to retain their market share abroad and strengthen each country's efforts to maintain its employment and salary levels.

This behavior is driven by an ethical framework that places an individual's interest in better living conditions at the core. Hence, the continuous demand for higher wages and profits successively drives this tournament, whereby wealthy countries continue to increase their competitiveness in order to raise or maintain current standards of living. Nonindustrialized

Table 11 Defining Social Morality

Social morality is concerned with actors and individuals who execute, choose, and are implicated in the consequences of their deeds and choices. Morality is traditionally understood to involve an impartial constraint on the pursuit of individual interests.

Moral constraints are generally accepted since they allow interaction between parties within an orderly and stable framework. *Agreed mutual constraint* is the rational response to certain structures of interaction between individuals pursuing their own interests.

Note: The above is adapted from Gattiker (in press-b, chap. 4, Table 4.5).

countries continue to struggle for improved economic conditions that will expedite growth in the jobs that offer decent remuneration packages. For example, El Salvador and Honduras are trying to entice U.S. firms to locate some of their operations in their economies by pointing out the availability of a nonunionized labor force earning between U.S.$0.50–0.70/hour, which is far lower than wages paid to American workers doing a similar job.

1. Skills and Employment

Some of the issues that must be addressed are listed in Table 12. Proposition 4 suggests that we have some choices to make not only as individuals, managers, and decision makers, but also as researchers. If technology as a leitmotif is grounded in an ethical framework based on competition to foster wealth and productivity, this framework will determine the focus and direction of technological applications. Moreover, certain skills may become requirements for entering the labor market. For instance, in Canada a high school graduate is assumed to be computer-literate, while college and university graduates should be well-versed in using such technology (e.g., Gattiker and Paulson, 1987). Hence, the pretechnological competence capital of computer technology and knowledge in the workplace is rising. The worker who does not possess these skills may therefore face increasing difficulty with competition in the labor market (Gattiker, in press-a).

2. International Issues

Proposition 5 in Table 12 suggests that although a country involved in a conflict may justifiably refuse to compromise if it is likely to win, a *legitimate* agreement between the parties involved may depend on what can be reasonably asked of the other. For instance, it may seem obvious that the grain subsidy war between the United States, the Common Market, Australia, and Canada cannot be won by any one of the countries involved. Instead, the ever-escalating "farm subsidies war" can be stopped only if a compromise leading to a modus vivendi can be reached.

Table 13 outlines the three types of reasons for trying to find a fair means of resolving these potential conflicts. Equality and partiality must be striven for, however recent developments indicate that these are not being achieved, partly because firms and individuals overemphasize point 2: national/individual economic interests. This may be illustrated by a controversy regarding the genetic material deoxyribonucleic acid (DNA). In 1991, Craig Venter and his supervisor, Bernadette Healy (director of the National Institute of Health), applied for patents for nearly 2,500 DNA sections which are of substantial importance to the human nervous system. As the full biological meaning of these DNA sections is not yet known, this entailed a request for proprietorship of parts of an important foreign language that the applicants can read but not understand! Some scientists argue that these findings are technically a discovery and *not* an invention. One may also question, on moral grounds, the right to patent human DNA, which has evolved through mutations over generations, especially as this could lead to the patenting of any plant or insect, every new chemical or physical formula simply because it might provide

Table 12 Competitive, Ethical, and Moral Challenges: Research Propositions 4 and 5

Proposition 4: If industrialized countries continue to stress an ethical framework that has the individual's continuous betterment in economic wealth as the ultimate value
1. The appropriate use or application of technology will be driven to serve this maxim.
2. Efforts to improve technological competence will continue to benefit an ever-smaller portion of the overall population, thereby increasing inequality and partiality.

Proposition 5: To ensure a morally acceptable use of technology in various cultural settings it is required that countries
1. Agree to a gradual development of international sovereignty as a consequence rather than as a precondition of the development of a common sense of technological *benefits/rights* and *costs/wrongdoing*.
2. Are willing to accept, adhere to, and enforce a *modus vivendi*.

Table 13 Equality and Partiality

Each party or country is subject to three types of reason
1. Equality and partiality[a]
2. Personal/national interests and commitments
3. Consideration of what can be asked reasonably of others

[a]The impersonal standpoint in us produces a demand for impartiality and equality, whereas our personal standpoint gives rise to individualistic motives and requirements. This contrast represents an obstacle to the pursuit and realization of equality and partiality in political and economic systems (cf. Nagel, 1991, chap. 2).

some utility and commercial benefit in the future. Following this incident, the Medical Research Council in Britain also demanded patents for about 200 DNA sections. In 1992 Alan Bromley (scientific advisor to President George Bush) raised doubts about such procedures, and as a result, the British council is willing to drop this absurd behavior if the United States will do the same.

The above conflict indicates that personal/national interests may be dominant in determining how technology may be used. The primary issue is how much can be asked reasonably of others when one possesses a patent. To illustrate, patenting human genes can lead to monopolies (e.g., Hoffmann-La Roche's polymerase chain reaction, or PCR, technology) that hinder subsequent research. For instance, Yale University felt unable to meet La Roche's demands for payments on the PCR patent for research on genetically transmitted health problems in the early 1990s. In essence, the development of this technology in a manner satisfying principles of equality and partiality was impeded by a firm's economic interests. Morality questions both the acceptability of such behavior on the part of Hoffmann-La Roche and what can reasonably be asked of others (i.e., how much should Yale University pay without making it economically infeasible?)

Although the United States has pushed "forward" in allowing patents on DNA structures and genetically altered animals, the international ramifications have not been resolved. For instance, the patent for the "Harvard cancer mouse" with human genes was given by the European patent agency in 1992, only to be challenged by a Swiss interest group based on ethical and moral foundations.

The accelerating development of technology and its use requires international agreements guiding these efforts in a satisfactory and beneficial manner for all parties concerned. Moreover, the inequality of pretechnological competence capital between a Canadian worker, say, and her Mexican counterpart may be substantial. Accordingly, proposition 5.1 must be addressed in order to prevent a morally unacceptable yet widening gap between countries in pretechnological competence workforce and industry capital. Second, the practical limit on the leverage of any legal system that is not based on true legitimacy must be determined (e.g., the United States pushing its patent laws and interests in science and technology upon others). Unfortunately, the limited capacity of people to place their regard for humanity ahead of their particular ethnic identities and self-interests, and to use this regard as a principle of political motivation creates some difficulty. In summary, a kind of technological world order must be secured, within which the natural pursuit of national and personal interests forms part of a universally acceptable pattern of international business relations.

IV. SUMMARY AND CONCLUSIONS, OR IS THERE LIGHT AT THE END OF THE TUNNEL?

The extensive study of technological competence in a cross-national research framework dealing with ethical and moral issues is too new, and the systematic investigation of its application to organizational settings is too limited, for a theory about its applicability in firms (i.e., effective allocation of technology) and its effects to have evolved and received general acceptance. As a result, the propositions set forth here were not derived from a generally accepted theory. Instead, they were pieced together from educational, sociological, psychological, and industrial economics research dealing with skill acquisition and technological competence, extrapolating only when it seemed reasonable.

A theory may be defined as a set of related propositions that specify relationships among variables (cf. Blalock, 1984, chap.1). The propositions in this chapter relate to one another through possession of a common independent variable or culture (subjective/objective; high and low stability), and therefore pass this defining test of a theory. Even so, more should be expected from a theory, such as a framework that integrates the propositions.

These propositions serve as building blocks for the development of a less atomistic, more conceptual theory dealing with technological competence learning and the interrelationship between culture and competitiveness within a firm and/or region. Moreover, the framework presented must be subjected to review, critique, and discussion over an extended period of time before gaining general acceptance.

Although human reason cannot tell us where to go, it can probably facilitate our getting there. Reason is instrumental, while values provide a suitable set of premises for whatever is valuable, acceptable, and legitimate (Simon, 1983: 5–12). In a legitimate system, those people living under the legal umbrella have no grounds for complaints against its basic structure, nor should they have any reason to withhold cooperation. Unfortunately, some people or nations may reasonably feel that their interests and viewpoints have not been adequately accommodated when it comes to technology. The current "world order" may be stable because it is illegitimate; that is, the poor have little power to subvert. Hence, they find and accept a *modus vivendi* instead of risking conflict and possible defeat (e.g., Taiwan changed its patent laws to accommodate U.S. interests and prevent the latter from imposing stiff trade sanctions).

Business, public decision makers, and researchers have examined cross-cultural issues, technological competence, and competitiveness in isolation without addressing their interrelationship. Although cross-national research is important, organizational research must surpass ordinary boundaries to understand the phenomena investigated. Simply researching the technological competence and competitiveness of firms without addressing ethical and moral concerns will likely be unjust and will not result in a legitimate system satisfying individual and communal values across nations!

A. Implications for Researchers

An important conclusion drawn from the research on technological competence, learning skills, and competitiveness of firms is that limited cross-feeding and integration is occurring between research in industrial economics, personnel psychology, industrial sociology, and organizational behavior. A special "Theory Development Forum" in the April 1991 issue of the *Academy of Management Review* addresses these future directions and theoretical concerns from a North American perspective. Thus, while purporting to support internationalization of research, a narrow ethnocentric approach is reflected by the inclusion of only North American authors, and more important, by citing U.S.-developed theories and models in over 90% of the contributions and citations. Below is a list of some of the more pertinent issues that must be tackled to improve the interdisciplinary nature of future cross-national research dealing with the technological competence of a firm or nation.

1. Past findings dealing with technology, firms, work design, and processes must be advanced by determining whether or not models and theories can be confirmed across situations and cultures. Only then can researchers thoroughly assess the viability of the propositions. A narrow focus can lead to reinvention of the wheel, rather than the advancement of our knowledge in an important area of scientific endeavor.
2. Cross-national research dealing with technological competence should use the framework presented in Figure 1. Measuring objective and subjective dimensions of culture as well as moderators will permit a greater understanding of why differences in attitudes and be-

haviors (e.g., continuous education efforts by firms and employees) may exist (cf. Tables 1 and 6).

3. The unresolved problem of technological competence is the need to reconcile the standpoints of the collectivity (country and world) with the standpoint of the individual. Accordingly, technology behavior (2nd property of technological competence) and its efficient allocation (3rd property of technological competence; cf. Table 2) must be carefully balanced between the individual (or firm or country) and the collective (region or world). Research has to address this problem of designing institutions that do justice to the equal importance of the individual (micro) and collective (macro) perspectives of technology (cf. Tables 7 and 8).

4. Solving the three issues suggested above requires less specialized training of doctoral students and more research by junior and established scholars. The primary determinant of research, rather than large numbers of publications per period, should be its impact upon the thinking and research of others. Doing research within the framework of Figure 1 while testing technological competence and the propositions outlined here requires more time, patience, and resources than is currently rewarded by the publish-or-perish game. The "quick-fix" approach will drive research into further oblivion and result in esoteric topics of little interest and help to society at large.

B. Practical Implications

The most important implications of these issues for managers, politicians, interested citizens, and other decision makers may be stated as follows:

1. Unless we minimize the inequalities in economic well-being and technology around the world, conflicts between individual and community interests will continue, so that acceptable frameworks and international agreements will be even more difficult to ratify, implement, and enforce.

2. Developing technological competence is a continuous process that requires effort and investment of time and other resources by employees, firms, and governments, while market concentration, competition, R&D strategies, and cultural factors will influence how technological competence is further developed. Two major challenges for reducing inequality while increasing partiality (see also Table 13) are the widening gaps of technological competence between skilled and unskilled workers within an economy and between industrialized and developing countries (cf. Tables 2–5). The wider these gaps, the less likely it becomes that we accomplish a fair and morally justifiable economic system for the benefit of many.

3. The increasing complexity of technological competence, other technology-related issues, and their effects upon society requires better communication between people and their elected representatives as well as between countries. Employees and voters must understand the interrelationships between their demand for higher wages, lower-priced and higher-quality products, and the increasing use of technology. Unfortunately, instead of facilitating understanding of these issues, current political systems support, if not encourage, ignorance, apathy, and political abstinence.

4. The escalating demand for greater competitiveness between countries thwarts any efforts to achieve equality (cf. Table 9). Personal and national interests and commitments must be balanced in consideration of what can reasonably be asked of others (cf. Table 13). Therefore, applying technology in a certain context or country requires the understanding and appreciation of local peculiarities and moral issues.

The above suggestions and strategies focus on greater voter participation in the political decision-making process. Direct democracy (e.g., Switzerland) does not solve the problem. However, it ensures that a greater proportion of people recognizes and understands the issues faced by a society in today's technological world. Within such a system, it is nearly impossible to demonstrate the pluralism that exists within a nation (e.g., ethnic, religious, and linguistic diversity), despite the enforcement of individual rights, toleration, and freedom of voluntary association. Additionally, one must look beyond one's own boundaries, interests, and needs. For instance, France's nuclear energy policy will affect its neighbors (e.g., availability of electricity and economic/environmental costs). Striving for legitimacy and acceptance of technology-related public policy decisions will ultimately slow the decision-making process about technology and the development of technological competence in a nation, while increasing the partiality of any solution reached. Morality by agreement is based on such a process and widespread cooperation hinges on acceptance of the final policy.

V. ISSUES FOR THE 21ST CENTURY

The following represents an incomplete catalogue of some issues and questions dealing with technological competence to facilitate an ethical and morally acceptable use of technology in this increasingly dynamic world and workplace. If we fail to address these issues within the next decade, further conflicts between various interest groups and parties may arise and harm society to the detriment of all. Some of these challenges are

1. If fundamental technology interests and values are too diametrically opposed among countries, it may be impossible to find a conflict-resolving framework on which all parties agree. Accordingly, we should encourage the gradual development of international sovereignty as a consequence rather than as a precondition of the development of a common sense of what is just and morally acceptable about technology (cf. Table 13).
2. A practical limit on the leverage of the framework/system outlined above is not based on true legitimacy; instead, the international protection of individuals, the environment, and health will inevitably remain rather weak and dependent on informal pressure. The affirmation of human rights and needs when assessing technology and developing technological competence by international agreements is an important investment in the long term, as today there may be constraints on the exertion of pressure.
3. A more just social order will evolve only if the natural pursuit of national technological interests forms part of a universally acceptable pattern of international relations.
4. Cross-cultural and -national issues with an increasingly diverse workforce (see Figure 2) must be discussed within the ethical and moral framework discussed here (cf. Tables 2, 10, and 11). Of greater importance is the need for formal and continuous education for technological competence to integrate these issues into their curricula. Unless voters, students, and workers understand how ethical and moral choices interrelate with the equality and partiality of our system (Table 13) and its technology, we cannot manage its unavoidable limitations (economic, environmental, and social) in a fair and just manner.
5. Today's progressively individualistic society, whereby one chooses and makes decisions guided by self-interest, will make it increasingly more difficult to further the development of technological competence while striving for partiality and equality. Individuals, interest groups, and employers must share in the responsibility and costs incurred to acquire, improve, and modify technological competence, while accepting the reality that continuous education is here to stay. Moreover, efforts must be undertaken to facilitate the growth of technological competence for those less fortunate people, such as the homeless, who have been excluded from sharing in these benefits.

Organizational research dealing with technological issues, regardless of the methodology used by scientists, must address cross-national comparisons as outlined in this chapter. Moreover, international political, ethical, and moral issues must be investigated to achieve morals by agreement within the limits of morality. Therefore, researchers, political decision makers, employees, and managers are required to promote the good, necessitating a change in our beliefs, actions, and interests in the application of technology, the development of technological competence, and the achievement of competitiveness. In addition, a leitmotif for technology, whose pursuit is in accordance with the promotion of the good, must be developed. Failure in this endeavor will occur only if we have been willing to sacrifice those interests and overcome our biases in favor of them (e.g., patenting DNA structures to pursue the economic interests of a small minority of individuals and firms primarily located in North America and Europe).

Only additional research and a greater understanding of the issues outlined here will produce the data needed to assure adequate skill levels and technological competence for an increasingly heterogenous workforce, and more important, to meet ethical and moral standards for the betterment of all of us regardless of where we live in this global village.

NOTES

1. In some countries the economy would not develop as fast as it does without the presence of foreign workers (e.g., Koreans working in Kuwait and Saudi Arabia). In the case of the Common Market, workers from member states move freely across national boundaries, availing themselves of better economic opportunities (e.g., British bricklayers commuting weekly to German construction sites). Additionally, an increasing number of refugees are fleeing their homelands because of political oppression and the lure of economic freedom. Some have argued that the Hungarian (1956) and Czechoslovakian (1968) refugees to Switzerland fled their homelands not only because of the Russian crackdown, but because of insecurity about their future economic well-being in a totalitarian Communist state (Cattani, 1991). Similarly, today's Guatemalan refugees to Canada or the United States may have fled their homeland for economic as well as political reasons. In most industrialized countries immigration laws make political reasons the decisive factors for granting an individual refugee status. However, economic factors are becoming paramount for many refugees, while political instability may be partly responsible for this economic hardship in their home country. Political realities often lead to ethically unacceptable outcomes. Specifically, while Cubans are accepted as refugees in the United States, Haitians, as seen in 1992, are repatriated. But in either case, political reasons for fleeing the homeland are generally secondary to the economic ones.

2. Since 1992, the Common Market permits the free movement of goods, services, capital, and labor between member countries. In 1993, this system will be expanded to include EFTA countries [i.e., Austria, Finland, Fürstentum Liechtenstein (Principality of Liechtenstein), Iceland, Norway, and Sweden], permitting the free movements of goods (except for agricultural and fishing products), services, capital (EFTA countries will not be linked to the Common Market's currency system), and labor to form the European Economic Area (EEA). Nonetheless, EFTA countries will maintain their own currencies, be able to negotiate trade agreements with other countries, and retain their respective customs, laws, and services. These additional 26 million people (average annual income U.S.$26,485) will be added to the 345 million (average income of U.S.$18,324) in the Common Market (cf. NZZ, 1991). Implementation of the EEA will occur gradually over several years and require, in some cases, the approval of the populace via national referendums.

3. Even though the trade of agrarian products is restricted to within the Common Market countries and EFTA (e.g., Switzerland), some researchers estimate that in border regions about 10% of Swiss dairy product purchases have occurred across the border. Accordingly, some Swiss mountain farmers in the Grison are producing "biological" milk products, including a variety of cheeses. By supplying a product to fill this market niche, price sensitivity becomes less of an issue. This proactive strategy toward future change allows mountain farmers to establish their enterprises under more competitive conditions.

4. Bounded rationality is a concept that assumes than an individual has basically three cognitive limitations that affect the decision-making process: (1) the human brain has a limited capacity to process information; (2) information is processed sequentially by the human brain; and (3) as a result of the previous two points, optimizing is replaced by satisfying—not all

available information can be taken into consideration—thus the individual concentrates on information relating to some important criterion variables, such as costs.

ACKNOWLEDGMENTS

The authors would like to thank John Baldwin, Aaron Cohen, Robert Golembiewski, Paul Goodman, Katherine Klein, George Lermer, and Toby Wall for their insightful comments made on an earlier draft of this chapter, as well as Valerie Sherwood, Brenda Baptista, and Michelle Seeman for their editorial assistance. Special thanks to UEG's students in various sections of his seminar on technological change and competitiveness whose insightful questions, reflections, and suggestions helped him in further clarifying his own thoughts and hopefully his writing. Thanks also to Tony Lowe and his colleagues at the University of the South Pacific, Fiji, as well as Robert Wood and his colleagues at the University of Western Australia, who enabled the first author to find office space and intellectual nurturing at their respective institutions where portions of this paper were written. The usual disclaimers apply.

Financial support for this research project was provided in part by the Labour Market Evaluation Branch–Alberta Career Development and Employment under Contract No. 497-77-89, Social Sciences and Humanities Research Council of Canada under Contract #494-85-1022, the Economic and Science Council of Canada under Contract No. 316, Statistics Canada and Industry, Science & Technology under Contract No. 48107-2-0021/01-ZG, the University of Lethbridge Research Fund under Contract No. 86-1934-405, and by the Burns Endowment Fund, Faculty of Management, the University of Lethbridge, as well as the Stanford Center for Organizations Research (SCOR), Stanford University, to the first author. The analysis and conclusions of this paper represent those of the authors and do not necessarily reflect the views of the sponsoring agencies.

REFERENCES

Adams, J. A. (1987). Historical review and appraisal of research on the learning, retention, and transfer of human motor skills. *Psychological Bulletin, 101*: 41–74.

Adler, L. L., (ed.) (1982). *Cross-Cultural Research at Issue.* Academic Press, New York.

Andrews, K. R. (1971). *The Concept of Corporate Strategy.* Irwin, Homewood, Ill.

Arora, A., and Gambardella A. (1990). Complementarity and external linkages: The strategies of the large firms in biotechnology. *Journal of Industrial Economics, 38*: 361–379.

Arrow, K. J. (1969). The organization of economic activity: Issues pertinent to the choice of market versus non-market allocation. In *The Analysis of Evaluation of Public Expenditure: The PPB System*, vol. 1. U.S. Joint Economic Committee, 91st Congress, lst Session, Washington, D.C., U.S. Government Printing Office, pp. 59–73.

Baldwin, J. R., and Gorecki, P. K. (1990). *Structural Change and the Adjustment Process.* Minister of Supply and Services, Ottawa, Canada.

Baldwin, T. T., and Ford, J. K. (1988). Transfer of training: A review and directions for future research. *Personal Psychology, 41*: 63–105.

Berry, J. W., Kim, U., Power, S., Young, M., and Bujaki, M. (1989). Acculturation attitudes in plural societies. *Applied Psychology: An International Review, 38*: 185–206.

BIGA (Bundesamt für Industrie, Gewerbe und Arbeit—Swiss Federal Office for Industry, Trades and Work; 1988). *Weiterbildung in der Schweiz—Auswertung einer Umfrage* (Continuous education in Switzerland—Evaluation of a Poll.) Bern: Author.

Black, J. S., and Mendenhall, M. (1990). Cross-cultural training effectiveness: A review and a theoretical framework for future research. *Academy of Management Review, 15*: 113–136.

Blakely, E. J., and Willoughby, K. W. (1991). Transfer or generation? Biotechnology and local industry development. *Journal of Technology Transfer, 15*(4): 31–38.

Blalock, H. M. (1984). *Basic Dilemmas in the Social Sciences.* Sage Publications, Beverly Hills, Calif.

Braga, H., and Willmore, L. (1991). Technological imports and technological effort: An analysis of their determinants in Brazilian firms. *Journal of Industrial Economics, 39*: 421–432.

Braverman, H. (1974). *Labor and Monopoly Capital*. Monthly Review Press, New York.

Cattani, A. (August 1991). Erwünschte Flüchtlinge (Desired Refugees). *Neue Zürcher Zeitung—Folio*, *1*(1): 12–19.

Coase, R. H. (1937). The nature of the firm. *Economica*, *4*: 386–405.

Coase, R. H. (1988). *The Firm, the Market and the Law*. University of Chicago Press, Chicago.

Cohen, A., and Gattiker, U. E. (1992). Assessing organizational commitment among employees in Canada and the USA. *Relations Industrielles*, *47*: 439–461.

Dow, G. D. (1987). The function of authority in transaction cost economics. *Journal of Economic Behavior & Organization*, *8*: 13–38.

Earley, P. C., and Stubblebine, P. (1989). Intercultural assessment of performance feedback. *Group & Organization Studies*, *14*: 161–181.

England, G. W., and Harpz, I. (1990). How working is defined: National contexts and demographic and organizational role influences. *Journal of Organizational Behavior*, *11*: 253–266.

Farh, J. L., Dobbins, G. H., and Cheng, B. S. (1991). Cultural relativity in action: A comparison of self-ratings made by Chinese and U.S. workers. *Personnel Psychology*, *44*: 129–147.

Fisch, R., and Daniel, H. D. (1982). Research and publication trends in experimental social psychology: 1971–1980. A thematic analysis of the Journal of Experimental Social Psychology, the European Journal of Social Psychology, and the Zeitschrift für Sozialpsychologie. *European Journal of Social Psychology*, *12*: 395–412.

Fossum, J. A., Arvey, R. D., Paradise, C. A., and Robbins, N. E. (1986). Modelling the skills obsolescence process: A psychological/economic integration. *Academy of Management Review*, *11*: 362–374.

Gattiker, U. E. (1990a). *Technology Management in Organizations*. Sage Publications, Newbury Park, Calif.

Gattiker, U. E. (1990b). Individual differences and acquiring computer literacy: Are women more efficient than men? In *Studies in Technological Innovation and Human Resources*, vol. 2 —End-User Training (U. E. Gattiker, ed.). Berlin and New York, Walter de Gruyter, pp. 141–179.

Gattiker, U. E. (1990c). Technological adaptation and human resource management in the high technology firm: Developing a model for training. In *Organizational Issues in High Technology Management* (L. R. Gomez-Mejia and M. W. Lawless, eds.), JAI Press, Greenwich, Conn., pp. 265–296.

Gattiker, U. E. (1991). Technologie informatique et formation de l'utilisateur final: Intégration du traitement de l'information et des perspectives d'interface homme-machine (Computer technology and end-user training: An integration of information processing and man-machine interface perspectives). *TIS (Technologies de l'Information et Société)*, *3*: 197–229.

Gattiker, U. E. (1992a). Computer skill acquisition: Implications for end-user computing. *Journal of Management*, *18*: 547–574.

Gattiker, U. E. (1992b). Where do we go from here? Directions for future research and managers. In *Studies in Technological Innovation and Human Resources*, vol. 3—*Technology-Mediated Communication* (U. E. Gattiker, ed), Walter de Gruyter, Berlin and New York, pp. 289–311.

Gattiker, U. E. (in press-a). New technology, vocational training and recurrent education in Canada and Germany. In *Managing the High Technology Firm*, *Global Management of High Technology* (L. R. Gomez-Mejia and M. W. Lawless, eds.), JAI Press, Greenwich, Conn.

Gattiker, U. E. (in press-b). *Productive Versus Destructive Technology: Competitive Challenges and Opportunities*.

Gattiker, U. E., and Hlavka, A. (1992). Computer attitudes and learning performance: Issues for management education and training. *Journal of Organizational Behavior*, *13*: 89–101.

Gattiker, U. E., and Nelligan, T. (1988). Computerized offices in Canada and the United States: Investigating dispositional similarities and differences. *Journal of Organizational Behavior*, *9*: 77–96.

Gattiker, U. E., and Paulson, D. (1987). The quest for effective teaching methods: Achieving computer literacy for end-users? *INFOR (Information Systems and Operational Research)*, *25*: 256–272.

Gattiker, U. E., Gutek, B. A., and Berger, D. E. (1988). Office technology and employees attitudes. *Social Science Computer Review*, *6*: 327–340.

Gauthier, D. (1986). *Morals by Agreement*. Clarendon Press, Oxford, U.K.

Geroski, P. A., and Pomeroy, R. (1990). Innovation and the evolution of market structure. *Journal of Industrial Economics*, *38*: 299–314.

Goldman, A. H. (1980). *The Moral Foundations of Professional Ethics*. Rowman and Littlefield, Totowa, N.J.

Goldstone, J. A. (1987). Cultural orthodoxy, risk, and innovations: The divergence of east and west in the early modern world. *Sociological Theory*, 5: 119–135.

Heller, F., Drenth P., Koopman, P., and Rus, V. (1988). *Decisions in Organizations: A Three-Country Comparative Study*. Sage Publications, London, U.K.

Hickson, D. J., and McMillan, C. J., eds. (1981). *Organizations and Nation: The Aston Program IV*. Gower, Westmead, U.K.

Hickson, D. J., Hinings, C. R., McMillan, C. J., and Schwitter, J. P. (1974). The culture-free context of organization structure: A trinational comparison. *Sociology*, 8: 59–80.

Hofstede, G. (1984). *Culture's Consequences: International Differences in Work-Related Values*. Sage Publications, Beverly Hills, Calif.

Hoff, E., Lappe, L., and Lempert, W. (1983). *Methoden zur Untersuchung der Sozialisation junger Facharbeiter* (Methods for investigating the socialization of young journeymen), *Materialien aus der Bildungsforschung* (Materials from educational research), Nr. 24. Max-Planck-Institut für Bildungsforschung, Berlin, Germany.

Jantzen, R. H. (1987). Adult CETA training in Boston: Impact on earnings, hours worked, and wages. *Journal of Economics and Business*, 39: 1–17.

Kedia, B. L., and Bhagat, R. S. (1988). Cultural constraints on transfer of technology across nations: Implications for research in international and comparative management. *Academy of Management Review*, 13: 559–571.

Kohn, M. L. (1989). Cross-national research as an analytic strategy. In *Cross-National Research in Sociology* (M. L. Kohn, ed.), Sage Publications, Newbury Park, Calif., pp. 77–102.

Kohn, M. L., and Schooler, C., in collaboration with Miller, J., Miller, K. A., Schoenbach, C., and Schoenberg, R. (1983). *Work and Personality: An Inquiry into the Impact of Social Stratification*. Ablex, Norwood, N.J.

Kraft, K. (1989). Market structure, firm characteristics and innovative activity. *Journal of Industrial Economics*, 37: 329–336.

Leplat, J. (1990). Skills and tacit skills: A psychological perspective. *Applied Psychology: An International Review*, 39: 143–154.

Littek, W., and Heisig, U. (1991). Competence, control and work redesign. Die Angestellte (the employee) in the Federal Republic of Germany. *Work and Occupations*, 18: 4–28.

Luthans, F., McCaul, H. S., and Dodd, N. G. (1985). Organizational commitment: A comparison of American, Japanese, and Korean employees. *Academy of Management Journal*, 28: 213–219.

Maurice, M., Sorge, A., and Warner, M. (1980). Societal differences in organizing manufacturing units: A comparison of France, West Germany, and Great Britain. *Organization Studies*, 1: 59–86.

Meyer, J. W., and Scott, W. R. (1983). *Organizational Environment: Ritual and Rationality*. Sage Publications, Newbury Park, Calif.

Miller, G. A. (1987). Meta-analysis and the culture-free hypothesis. *Organization Studies*, 8: 309–325.

Moghaddam, F. M. (1987). Psychology in the three worlds: As reflected by the crisis in social psychology and the move toward indigenous Third-World psychology. *American Psychologist*, 42: 912–920.

Morgan, G. (1986). *Images of Organization*. Sage Publications, Beverly Hills, Calif.

Muszynski, L., and Wolfe, D. A. (1989). New technology and training: Lessons from abroad. *Canadian Public Policy*, 15: 245–264.

Nagel, T. (1991). *Equality and Partiality*. Oxford University Press, New York.

National Academy of Sciences (1991). *In the mind's eye*. Washington, DC: The author.

Near, J. P. (1989). Organizational commitment among Japanese and U.S. workers. *Organization Studies*, 10: 281–300.

NZZ (October 27/28, 1991). Binnenmarktähnliche Verhältnisse vom Nordkap bis Sizilien (Domestic market situation from the North Cape to Sicily). *Neue Zürcher Zeitung*, Fernausgabe Nr. 249, pp. 13–14.

Osborn, R. N., Strickstein, A., and Olson, J. (1988). Cooperative multinational R&D ventures: Interpretation and negotiation in emerging systems. In *Studies in Technological Innovation and Human Resources*, vol. 1—*Managing Technological Development: Strategic and Human Resources Issues* (U. E. Gattiker and L. Larwood, eds.), Walter de Gruyter, Berlin and New York, pp. 33–54.

Ostroy, J. M. (1987). Money and general equilibrium theory. *The New Palgrave: A Dictionary of Economics*, vol. 3. Macmillan Press, London, U.K., pp. 515–518.

Pelikan, P. (1989). Evolution, economic competence, and the market for corporate control. *Journal of Economic Behavior & Organization*, 12: 279–303.

Pepitone, A., and Triandis, H. C. (1987). On the universality of social psychological theories. *Journal of Cross-Cultural Psychology*, 18: 471–498.

Perry, L. T., and Sandholtz, K. W. (1988). A "liberating form" for radical product innovation. In *Studies in Technological Innovation and Human Resources*, vol. 1—*Managing Technological Development* (U. E. Gattiker and L. Larwood, eds.), De Gruyter, Berlin and Hawthorne, N.Y., pp. 9–31.

Polanyi, M. (1962). *Personal Knowledge: Towards a Post-Critical Philosophy*. Harper Torchbooks, New York.

Rokeach, M. (1980). *Beliefs, Attitudes, and Values*. Jossey-Bass, San Francisco.

Selznick, P. (1957). *Leadership in Administration*. Harper & Row, New York.

Silverman, D. (1970). *The Theory of Organizations*. Heinemann, London, U.K.

Simon, H. A. (1983). *Reason in Human Affairs*. Stanford University Press, Stanford, Calif.

Snow, C. C., and Hrebiniak, L. C. (1980). Strategy, distinctive competence and organizational performance. *Administrative Science Quarterly*, 25: 317–336.

Sorge, A., and Warner, M. (1986). *Comparative Factory Organisation: An Anglo-German Comparison of Management and Manpower in Manufacturing*. Gower, Aldershot, U.K.

Spenner, K. I. (1983). Deciphering Prometheus: Temporal change in the skill level of work. *American Sociological Review*, 48: 824–837.

Spenner, K. I. (1990). Skill: Meanings, methods, and measures. *Work and Occupations*, 17: 399–421.

Statistics Canada (1988). *Education in Canada*. Minister of Supply and Services, Ottawa.

Stead, W. E., and Stead, J. G. (1992). *Management for a Small Planet*. Sage Publications, Newbury Park, Calif.

Stevenson, H. H. (1976). Defining corporate strengths and weaknesses. *Sloan Management Review*, 17: 51–68.

Stigler, G. J. (1972). The law of economics of public policy: A plea to the scholars. *Journal of Legal Studies*, 1: 12.

Tapon, F. (1989). A transaction costs analysis of innovations in the organization of pharmaceutical R&D. *Journal of Economic Behavior and Organization*, 12: 197–213.

Teece, D. J., Pisano, G., and Shuen, A. (1990). *Firm Capabilities, Resources and the Concept of the Strategy: Four Paradigms of Strategic Management* (CCC Working Paper #90-8). Center for Research in Management, Haas School of Business, University of California at Berkeley.

Triandis, H. C. (1977). Cross-cultural social and personality psychology. *Personality and Social Psychology Bulletin*, 56: 143–158.

Triandis, H. C., and Vassiliou, V. (1972). Interpersonal influence and employee selection in two cultures. *Journal of Applied Psychology*, 56: 140–145.

Van Houten, D. R. (1987). The political economy and technical control of work humanization in Sweden during the 1970s and 1980s. *Work and Occupations*, 14: 483–513.

Williamson, O. E. (1981). The modern corporation: Origins, evolution, attributes. *Journal of Economic Literature*, 19: 1537–1568.

Willoughby, K. W. (1990). *Technology Choice*. Westview Press, Boulder, Colo.

Willoughby, K. W. (1992). *Biotechnology in New York: A Global Industry in a Global Community*. Center for Biotechnology, State University of Stony Brook, Stony Brook, N.Y.

Willoughby, K. W., and Blakeley, E. J. (1990). *The Economic Geography of Biotechnology in California* (working paper no. 90-176). Center for Real Estate and Urban Economics, Institute for Business and Economic Research, University of California at Berkeley.

Author Index

Subject Index